CITY
OF
NEW YORK

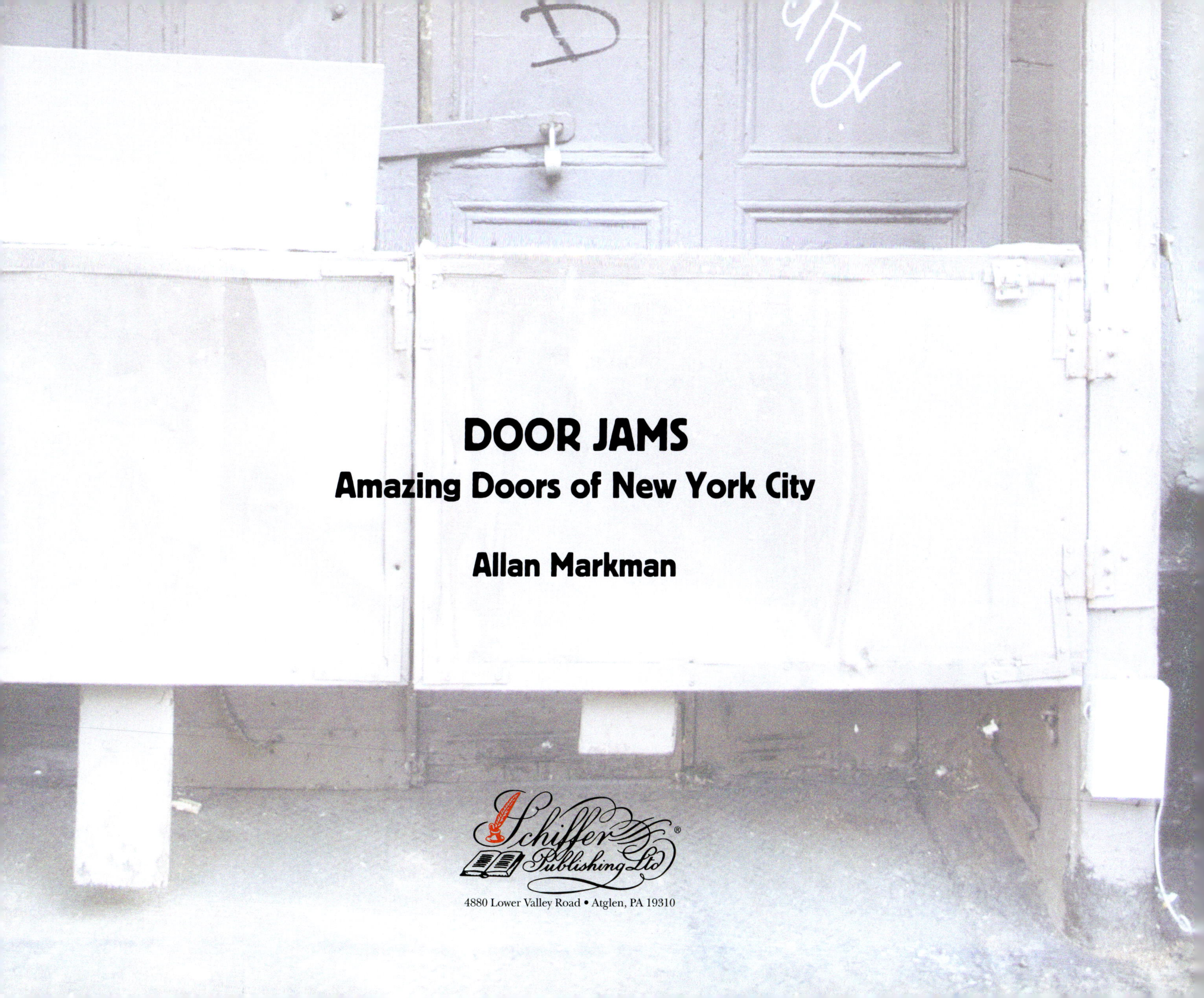

DOOR JAMS

Amazing Doors of New York City

Allan Markman

Schiffer Publishing Ltd

4880 Lower Valley Road • Atglen, PA 19310

Library of Congress Control Number: 2013940244

Type set in Frutiger LT Std

ISBN: 978-0-7643-4491-6
Printed in China

Published by Schiffer Publishing, Ltd.
4880 Lower Valley Road
Atglen, PA 19310
Phone: (610) 593-1777; Fax: (610) 593-2002
E-mail: Info@schifferbooks.com

For our complete selection of fine books on this and related subjects, please visit our website at **www.schifferbooks.com**.
You may also write for a free catalog.

This book may be purchased from the publisher. Please try your bookstore first.

We are always looking for people to write books on new and related subjects.
If you have an idea for a book, please contact us at proposals@schifferbooks.com.

Schiffer Publishing's titles are available at special discounts for bulk purchases for sales promotions or premiums. Special editions, including personalized covers, corporate imprints, and excerpts can be created in large quantities for special needs. For more information, contact the publisher.

In Europe, Schiffer books are distributed by:
Bushwood Books
6 Marksbury Ave.
Kew Gardens
Surrey TW9 4JF England
Phone: 44 (0) 20 8392 8585; Fax: 44 (0) 20 8392 9876
E-mail: info@bushwoodbooks.co.uk
Website: www.bushwoodbooks.co.uk

ACKNOWLEDGEMENTS

For Atar and Nirata, whose constant encouragement, implicit belief in me, and helpful critique of my work enabled this project to reach fruition. Thanks to Douglas Florian, poet, artist, and friend, for the perfect title. A shout out to Ziad and my friends and colleagues at the United Nations Graphic Design Unit (past and present) where this whole project started. Thanks to my brother Irwin and his best friend Herbie Teicher, who helped me to discover the doors of Staten Island, the one borough I had never explored. Thanks to Pete Schiffer and the team at Schiffer Publishing for giving *Door Jams* a chance to see the light and to all my friends and family who have encouraged me over the years, in both large and small ways.

Lastly, with profound gratitude to my Guru, Sri Chinmoy, who advised me a few months before he passed, not to take a job in management but to occupy my time with projects that contribute joy to my own life and the lives of others. This advice set me on the path that ultimately led to the improbable publication of this book.

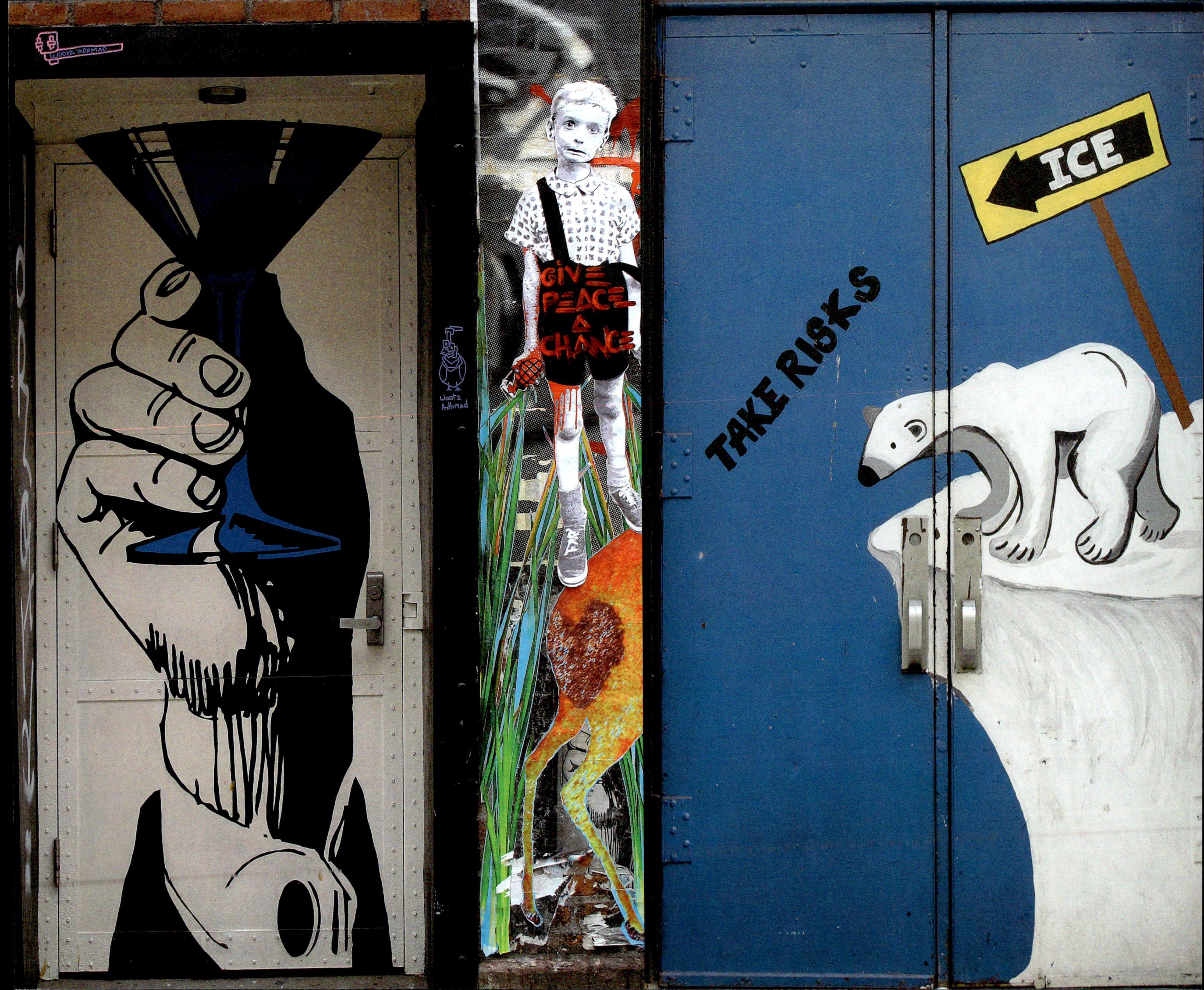
GIVE PEACE A CHANCE
TAKE RISKS
ICE

INTRODUCTION

IN THE SPRING OF 2006, I WAS APPOINTED SENIOR GRAPHIC DESIGNER FOR THE United Nations. The first high profile job assigned to me was to create an in-house poster announcing the newly formed UN Ethics Office. In a huge international organization with offices all over the world, it is very difficult to define ethical behavior for the staff. What is acceptable in one culture can be quite scandalous in another. The poster had to be both beautiful and convey this difficult concept graphically.

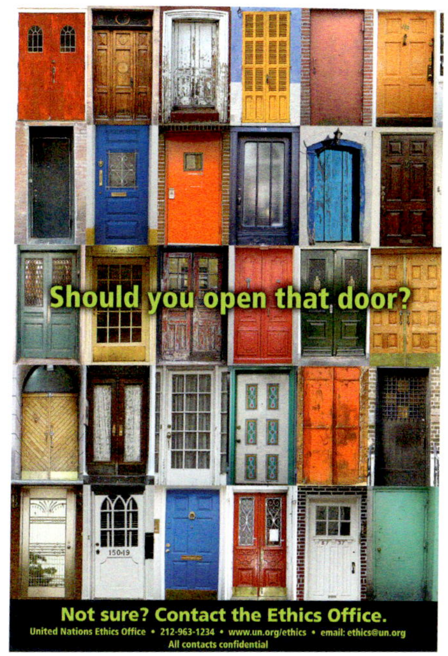

Alas, this poster was rejected, but it did ignite my interest in the beauty and mystery of doors.

The idea I came up with was a grid of interesting, diverse, and beautiful doors with the following copy: "Not sure if you should open that door? Contact the Ethics Office." But where to find the doors? The UN had no budget to purchase stock photos and I could not find enough high quality public domain images. My boss suggested I take my camera and photograph doors in and around Manhattan. That was the beginning of *Door Jams* — seven years in the making.

It took me four days to find enough doors for the poster (which the Ethics Office loved, but upper management rejected). The poster was never printed, but I was hooked. I've been obsessively taking photos of doors in Manhattan and the other boroughs ever since.

The whole beautiful, multifaceted, ever-changing nature of New York can be seen in its doors. When artists move into a neighborhood (Williamsburg, Long Island City, Bushwick, the Lower East Side) doors often become a major target for expression. The collision of the old working class industrial culture with the new artistic aesthetic creates a unique urban landscape. A door in Hell's Kitchen is covered in post-it notes creating the shape of the Buddha and two weeks later the image is gone — replaced by a warning - Caution: Hard Hats Only. Astonishing doors turn up in places you'd least expect to see them — graveyards, quiet neighborhoods in Queens, or small retail establishments in Manhattan.

Doors speak of class, culture, wealth, poverty, change, neglect, revolution, and even death. Some boast, while others are humble and self-effacing. Some invite you in with their beauty and individuality, while others make it clear that you had better keep your distance. Many provide a small glimpse of a forgotten past, while others reflect the sad dysfunction of our present.

In New York City, where construction and change are a constant racing presence, the temporal nature of our existence is quite stark. Often, time is the artist; peeling paint, layers of stickers, or rust and decay can turn an otherwise ordinary door into an urban time capsule. Unique architectural wonders are demolished to make way for luxury hi-rises. Small mom and pop stores struggle to keep up with the ever rising rents and the brutal competition of the corporate chains. Even old venerable institutions, like schools and neighborhood hospitals, disappear. This dynamic is poignantly reflected in the doors that can be found throughout the city and its boroughs.

The exterior of a car wash in Queens is completely decorated with a grand circus motif, including a tiger whose open mouth becomes the entrance (see page 27). In 1988, this car wash found its way into Eddie Murphy's movie *Coming to America*. I took a photo of the car wash in 2003, and, in 2011, returned to find the circus motif replaced by a flat, dull khaki surface.

I consciously omitted narrative from these layouts in order to keep the focus visual. All the doors are grouped thematically to complement and enhance each other. The photographs run across a two page spread, creating what I hope becomes an eye-catching "Jam Session." I have to confess that all the photographs herein are not, strictly speaking, always doors, (I've included some gates and tromp l'oeil doors) but they are each, in their own way, compelling and tell the New York story.

New York is one of the most frenetic cities in the world. Often its residents and visitors don't notice the visual feast that exists on almost every block. It is my hope that this collection of photographs awakens an awareness of the dazzling urban beauty that can be seen in each and every neighborhood, through the amazing doors of New York.

ALLAN MARKMAN

NOTE: There is an index starting on page 167 which gives the location and, when possible, some information about the doors.

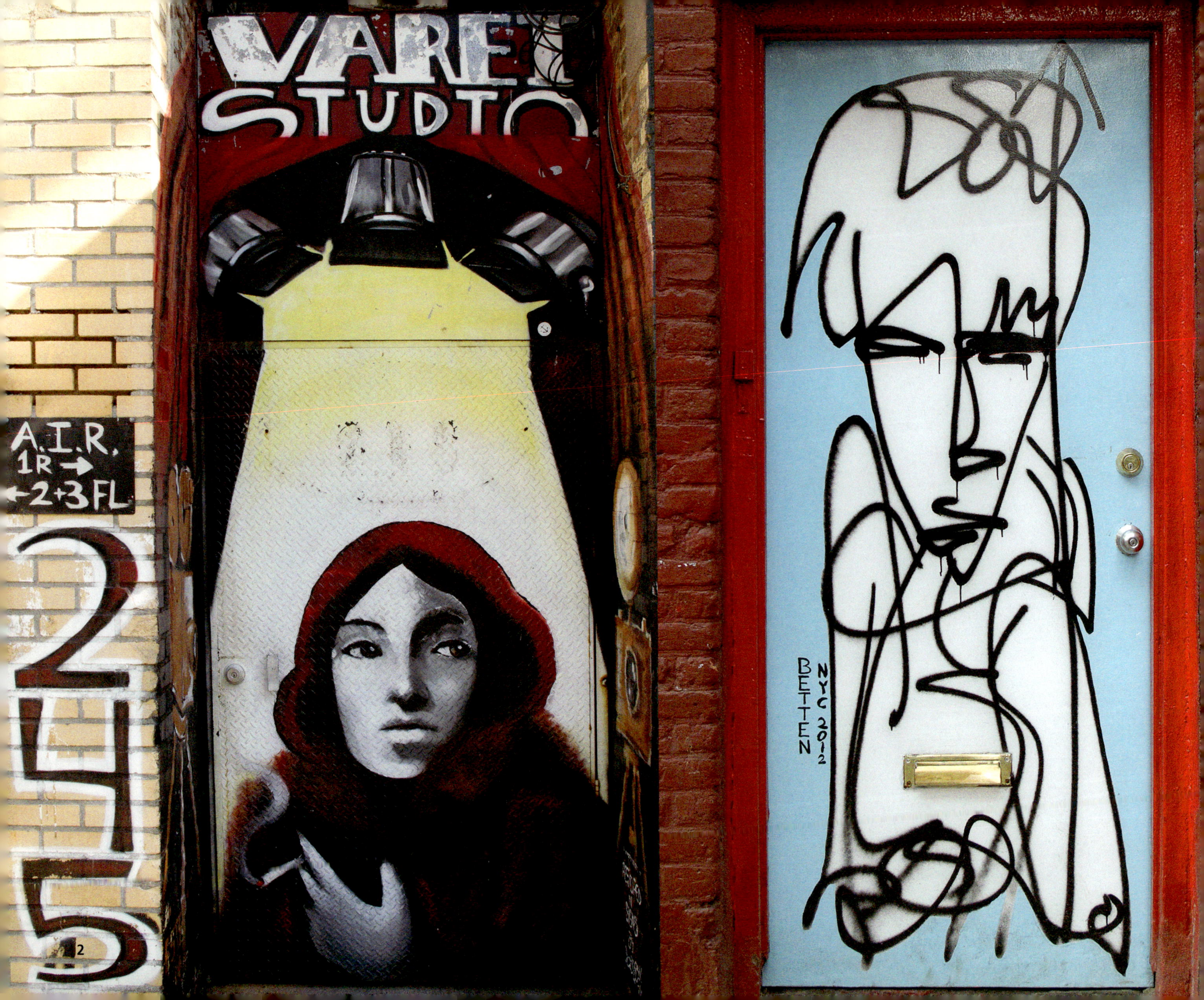
VARE
A.I.R.
1R →
←2+3FL
245
BETTEN
NYC 2012

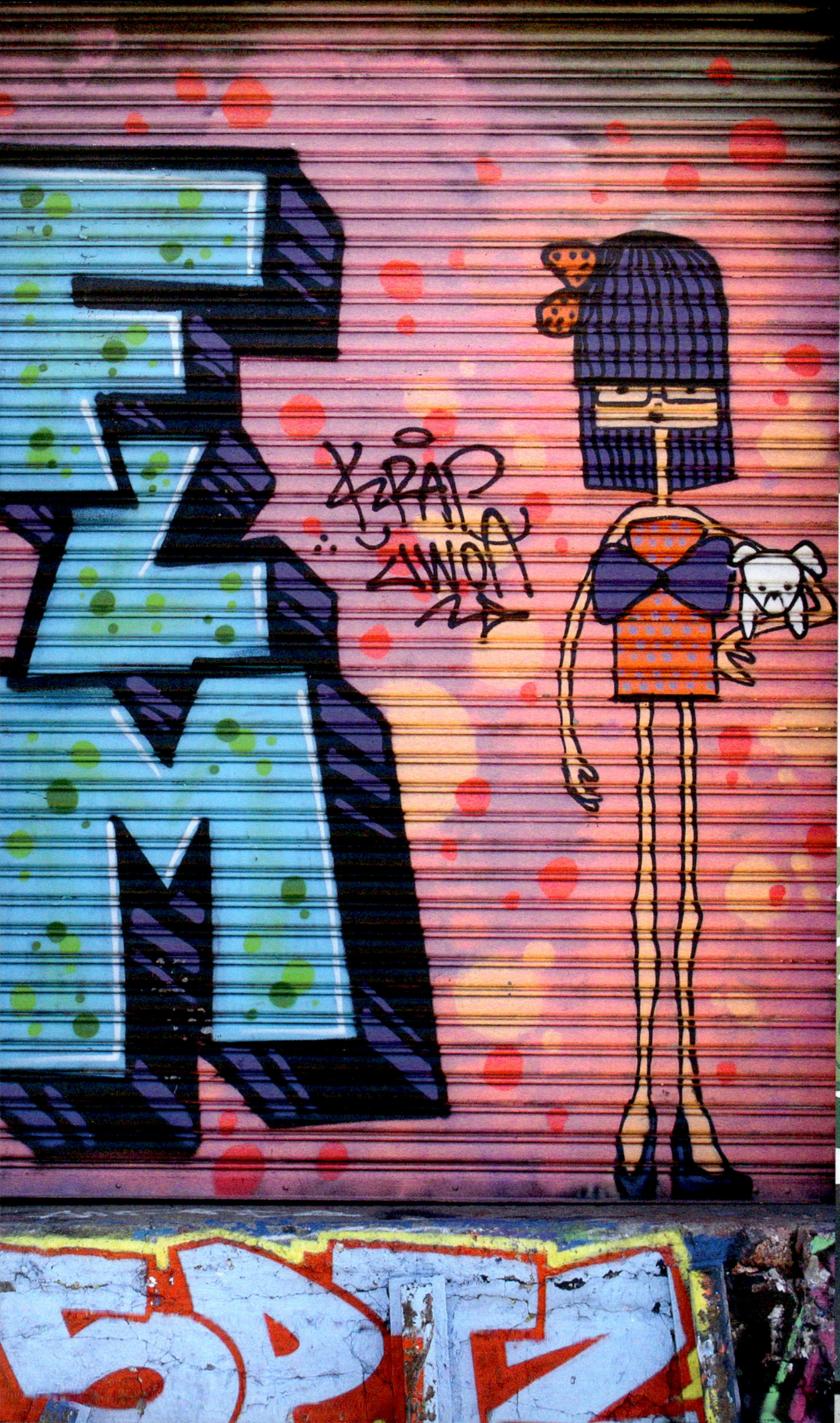

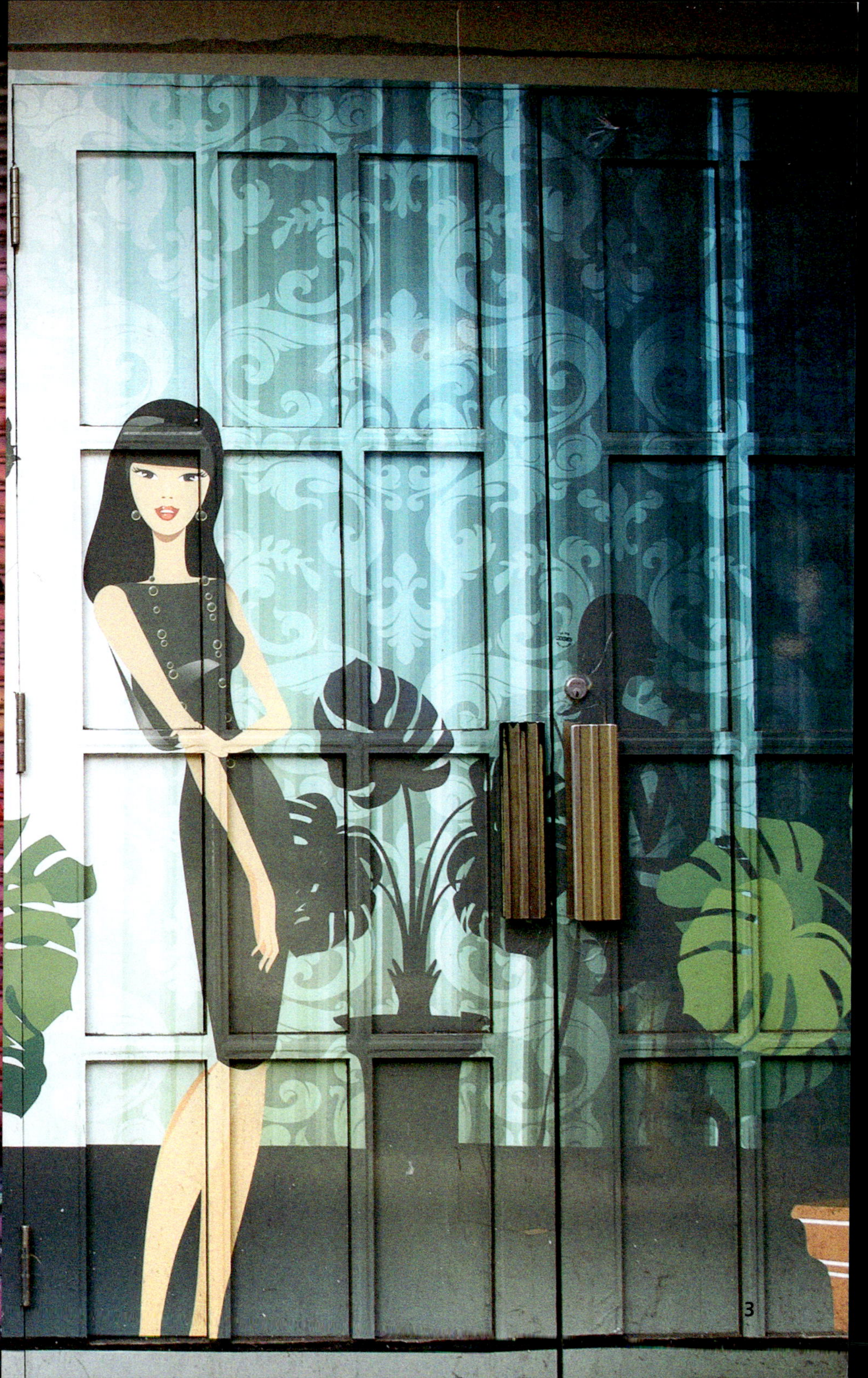

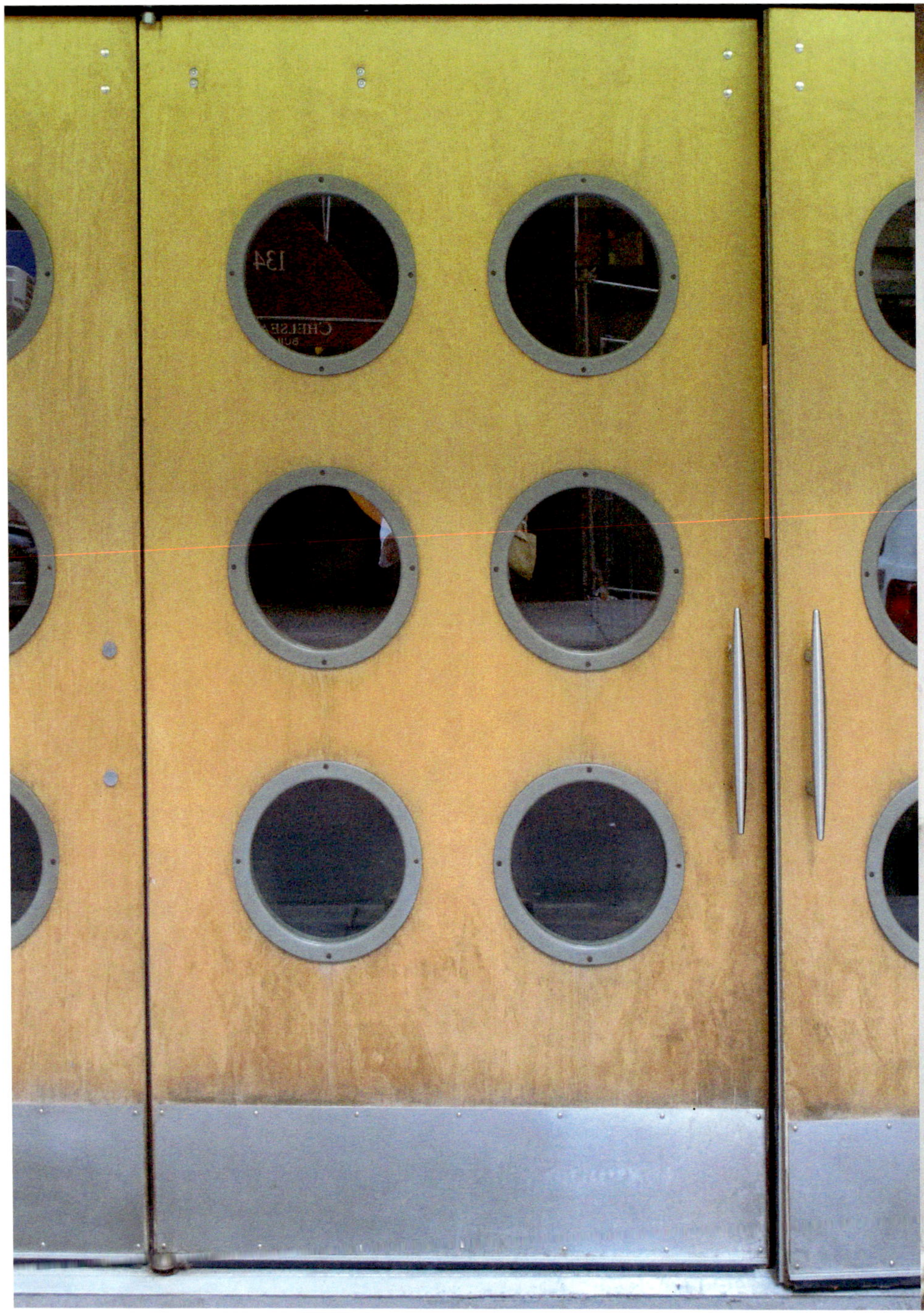

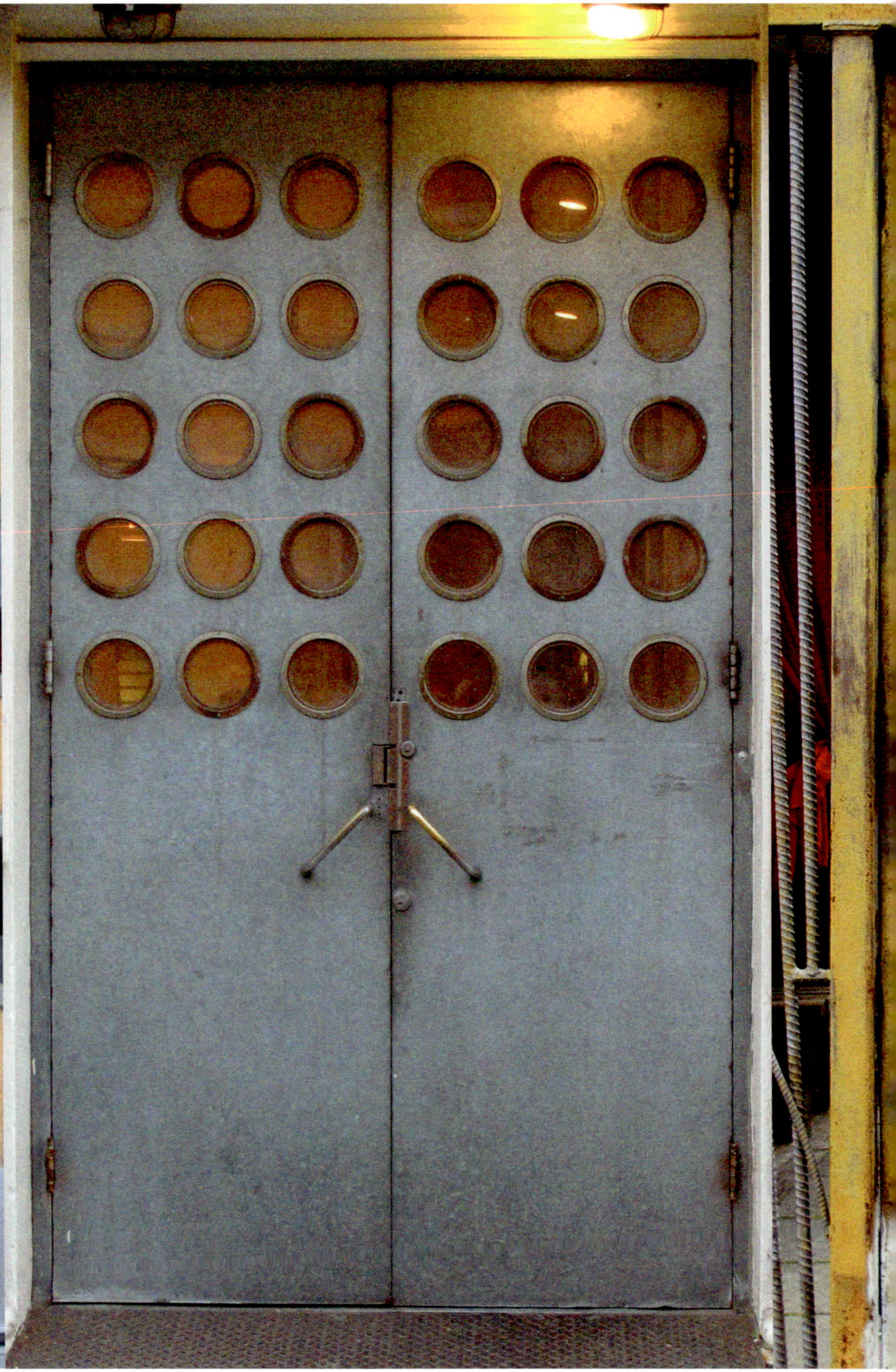

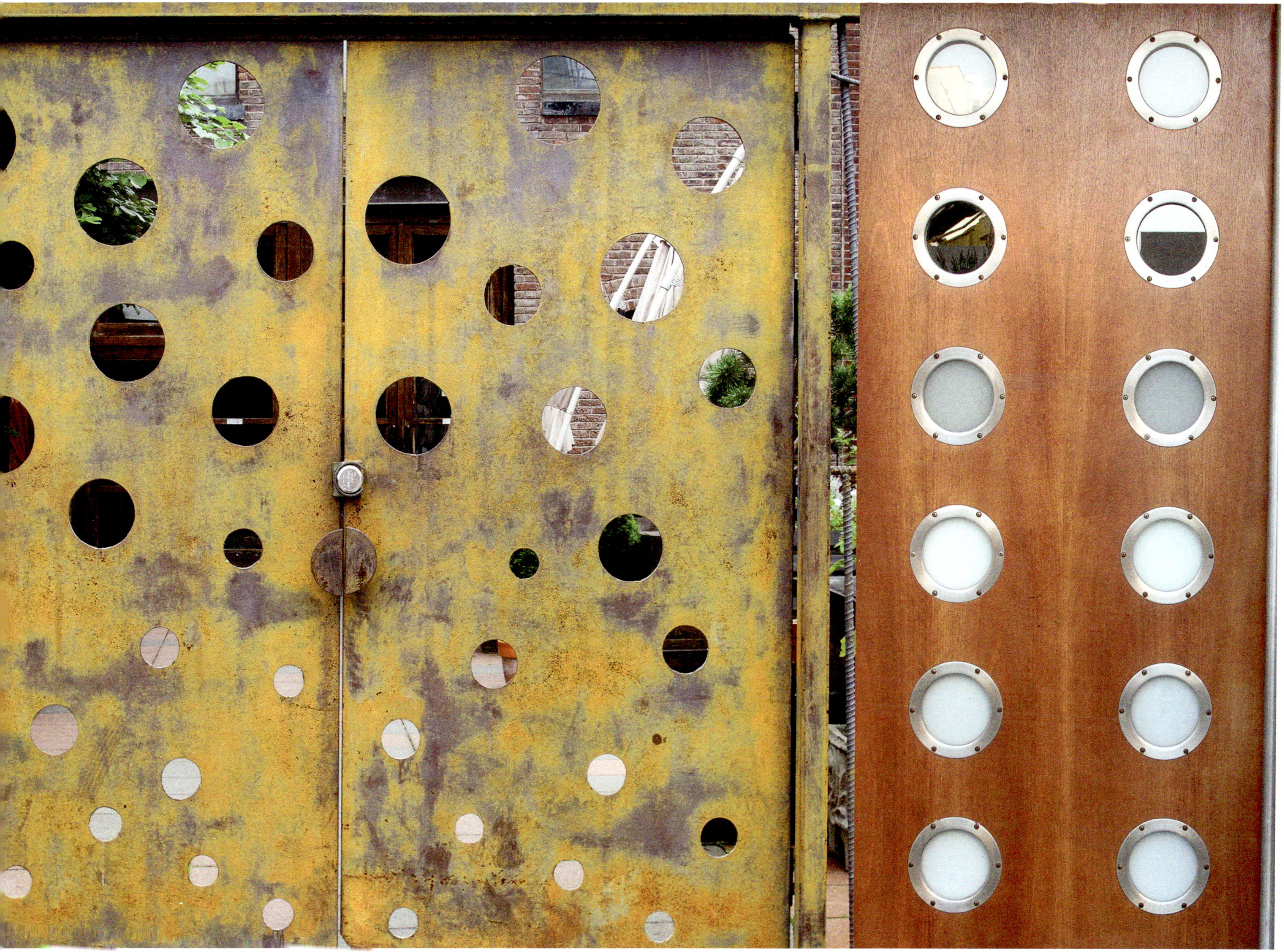

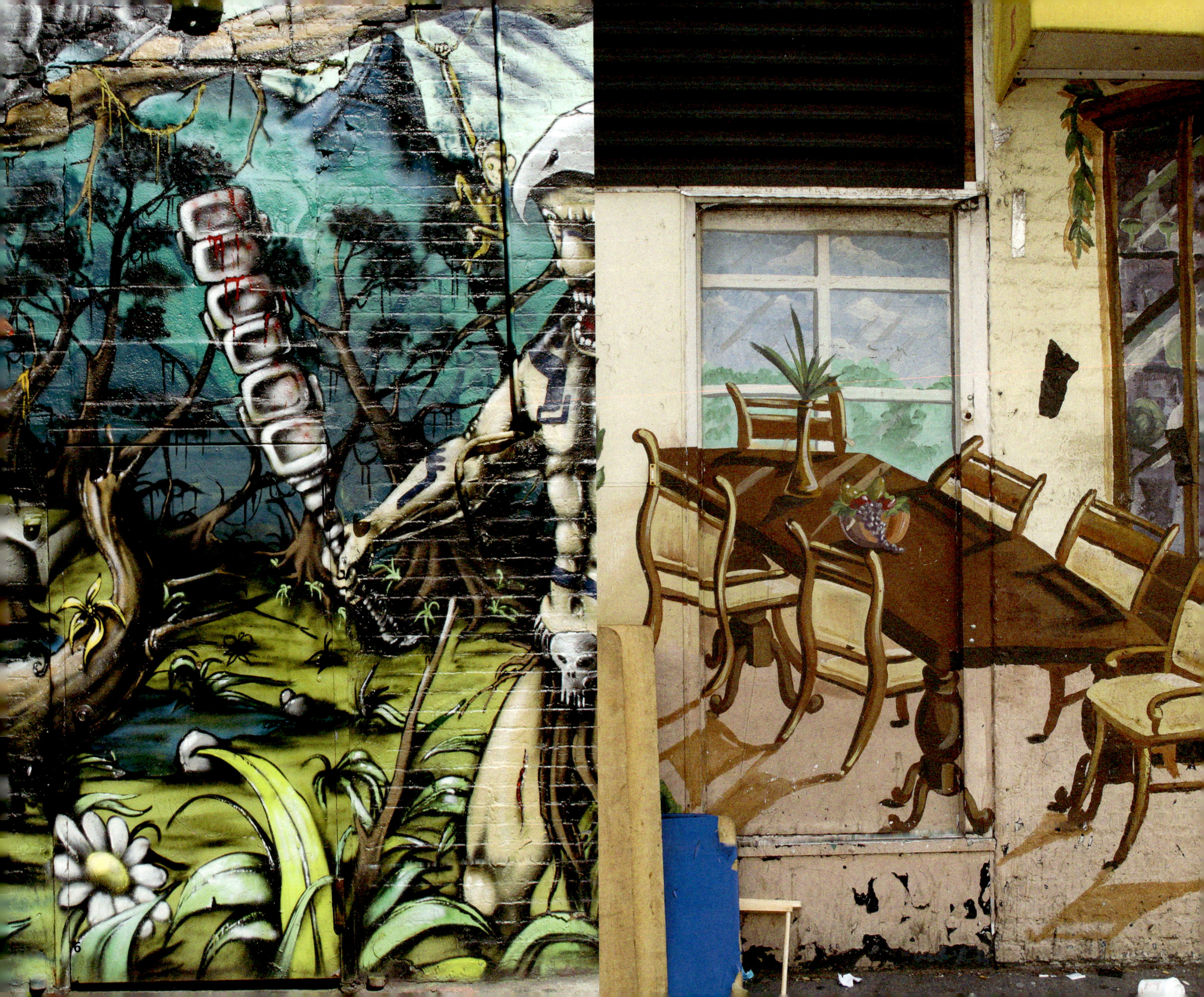

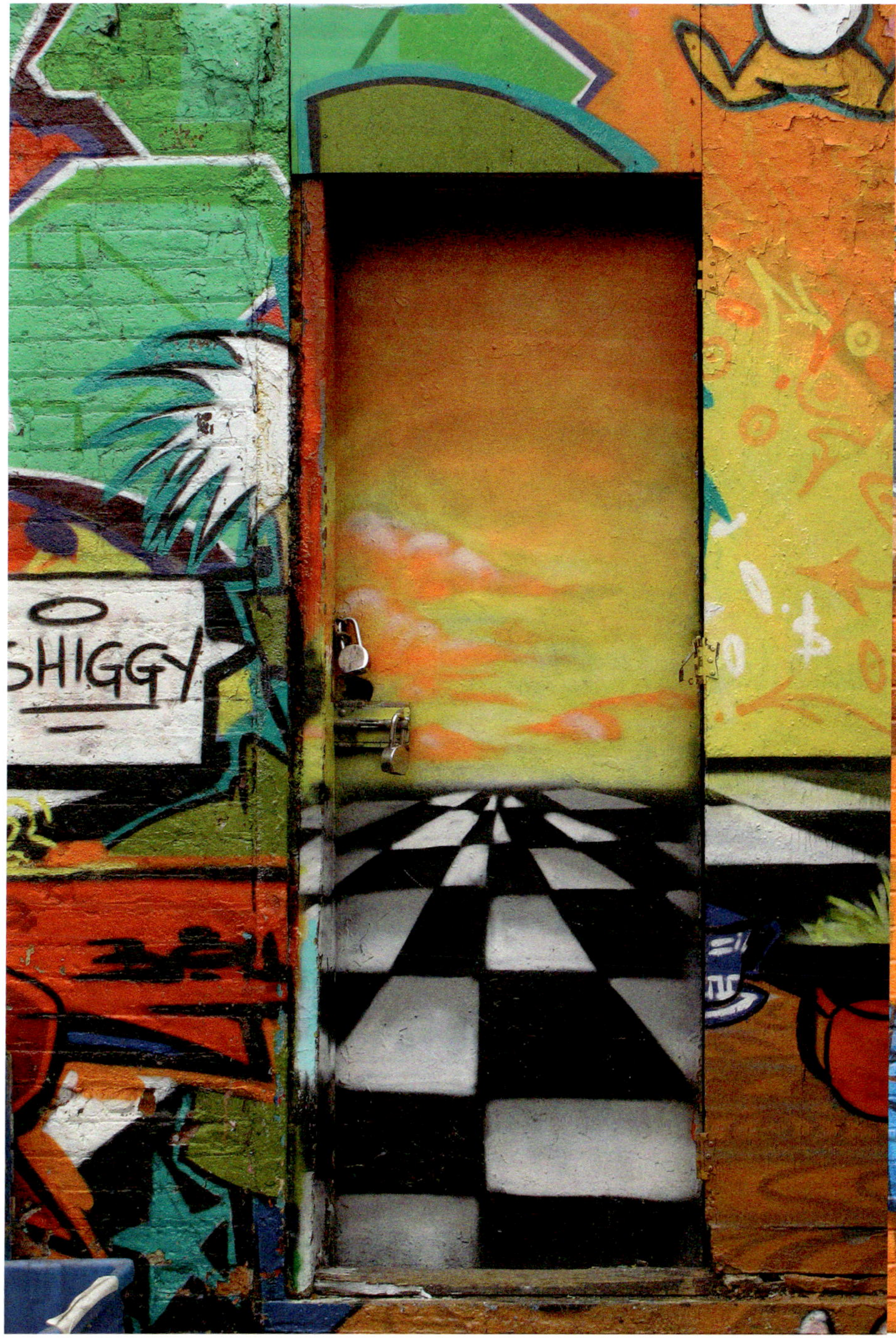
SHIGGY
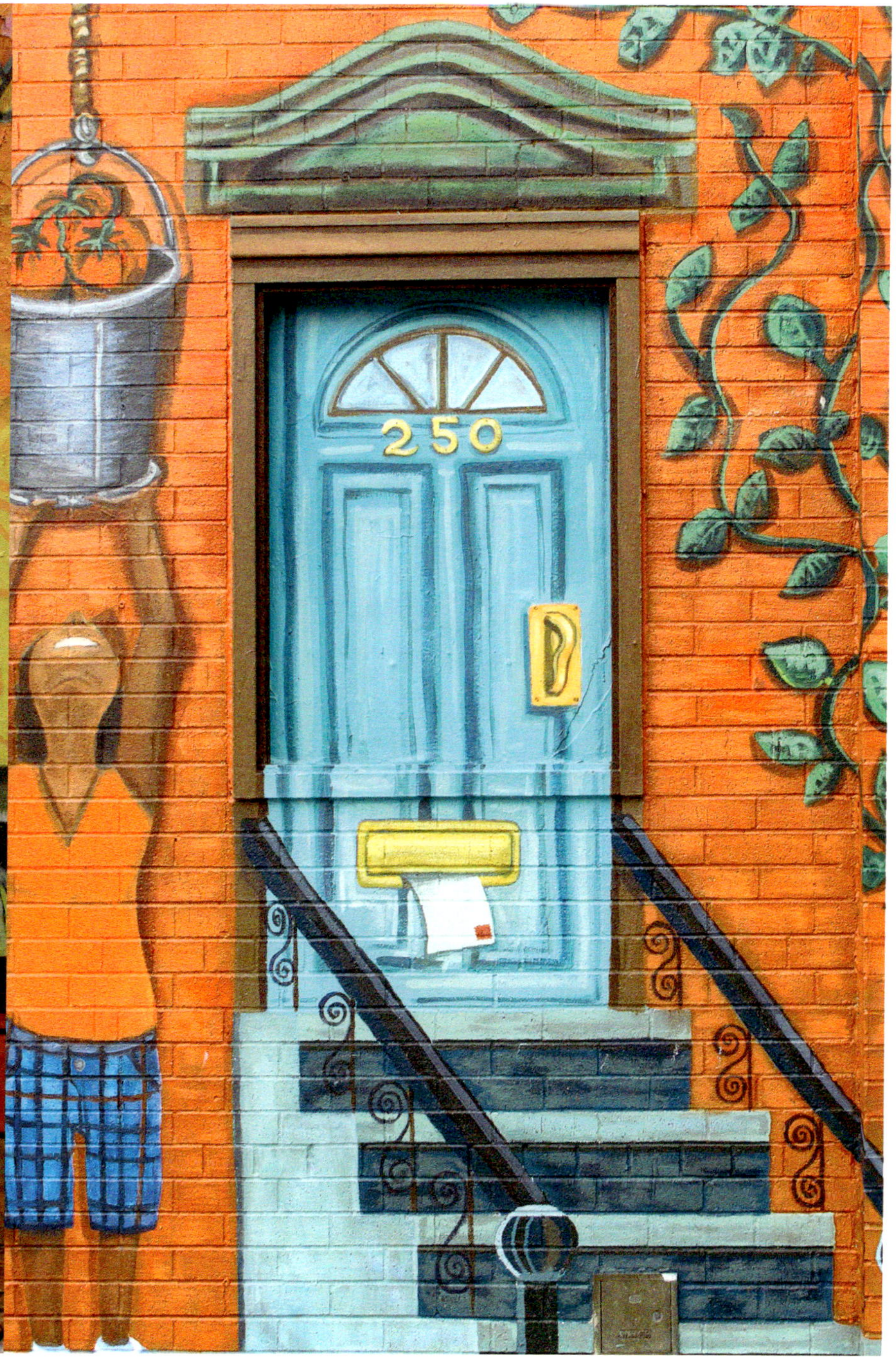
250

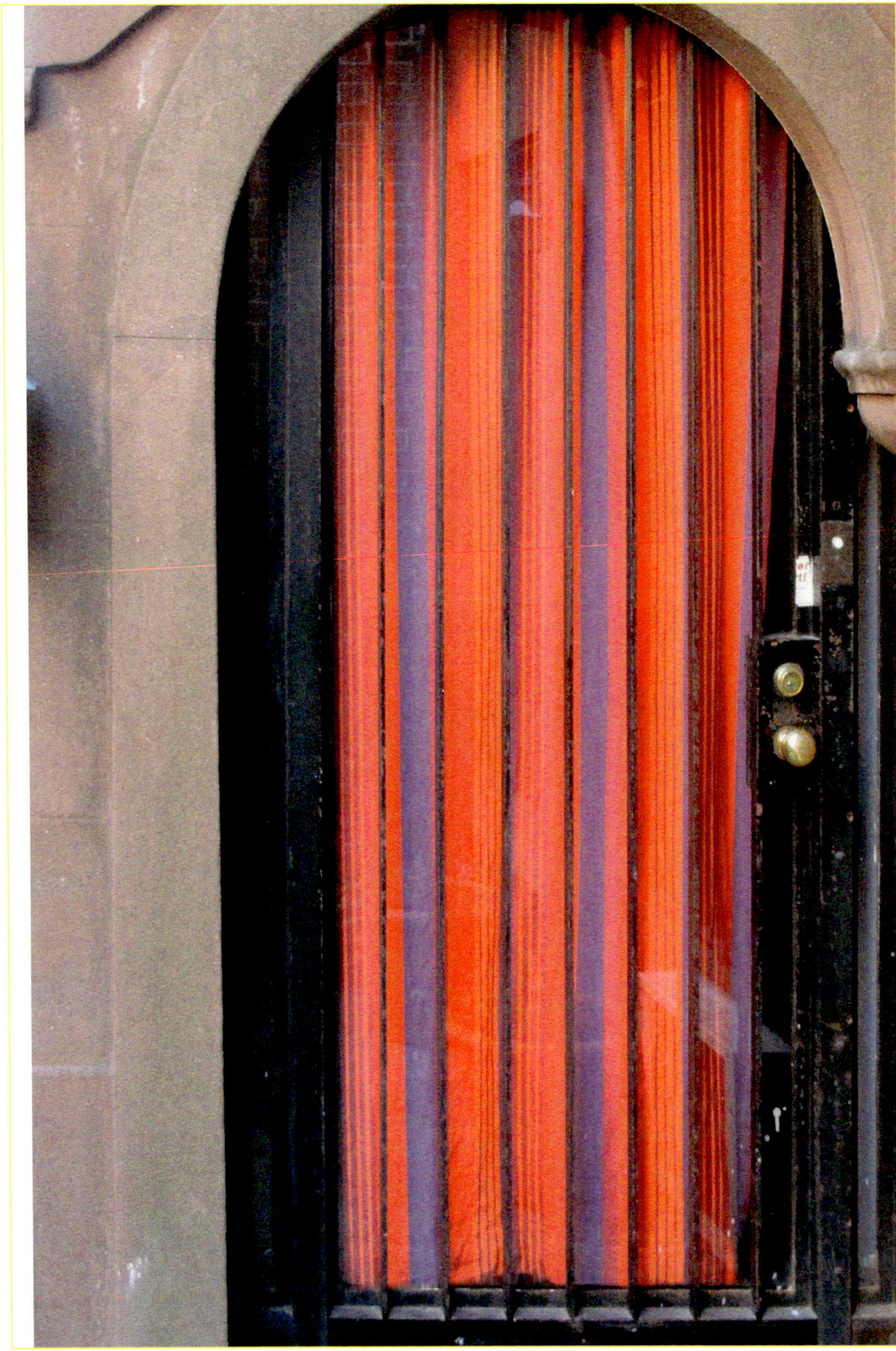

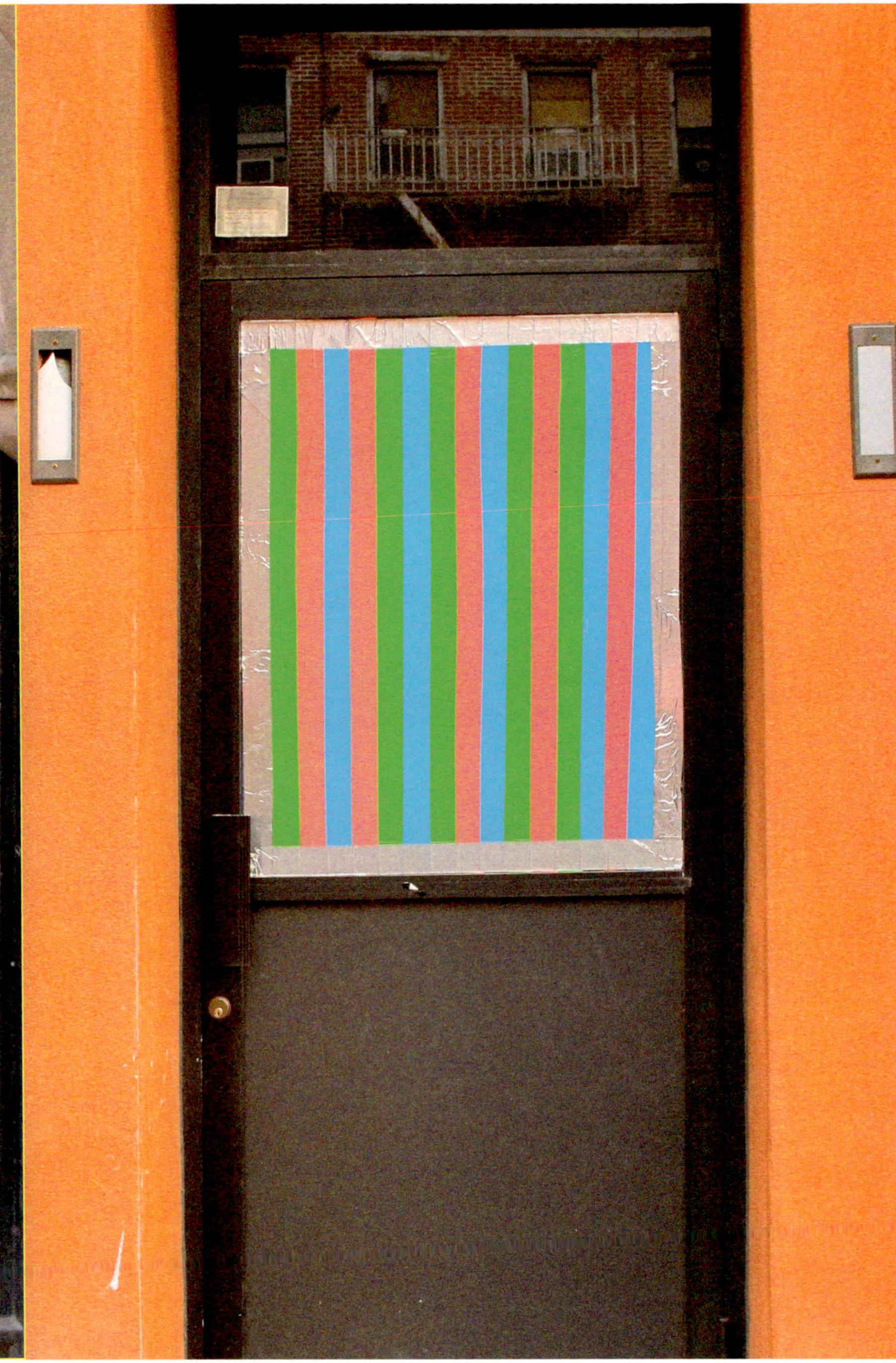

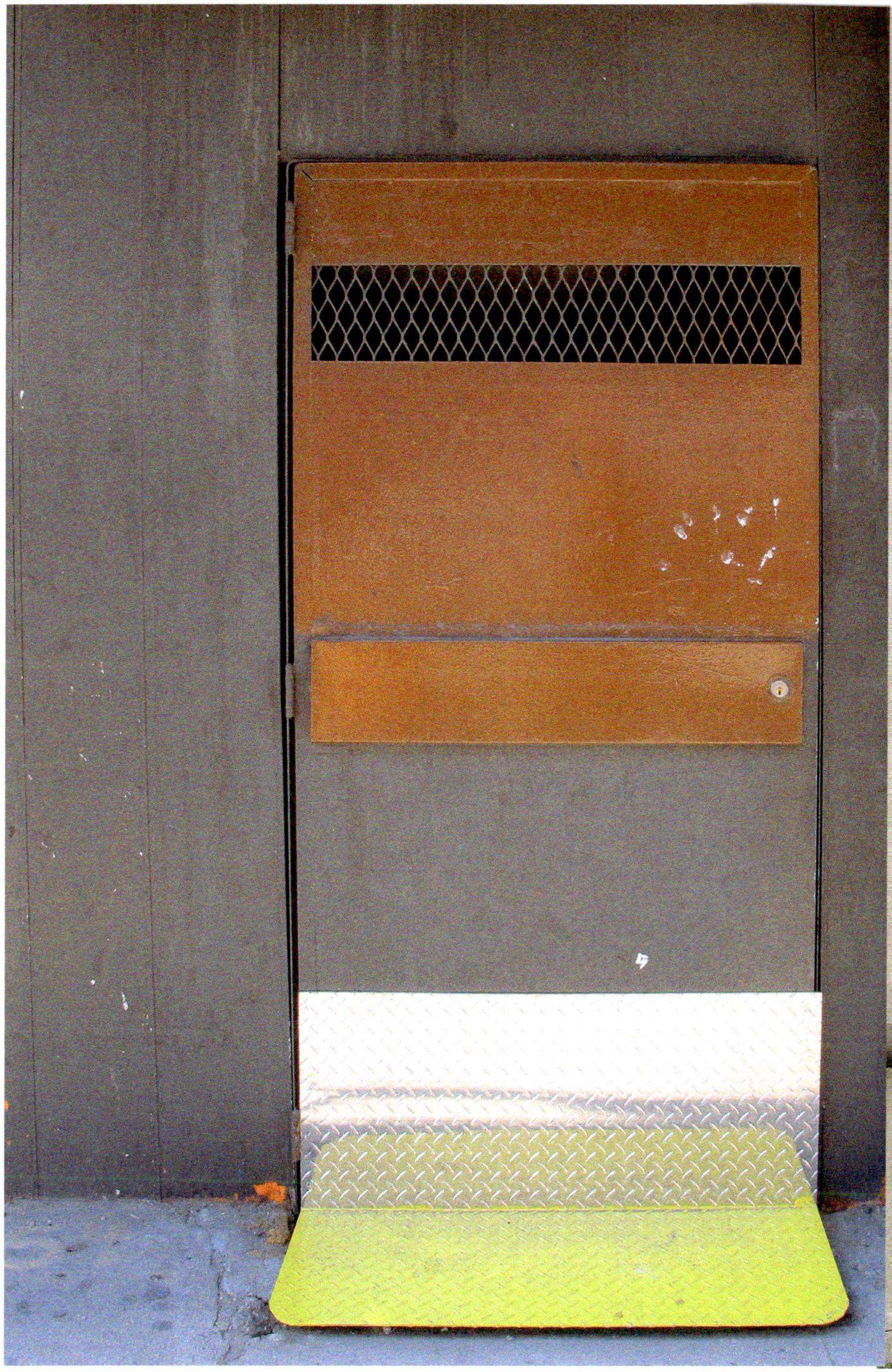
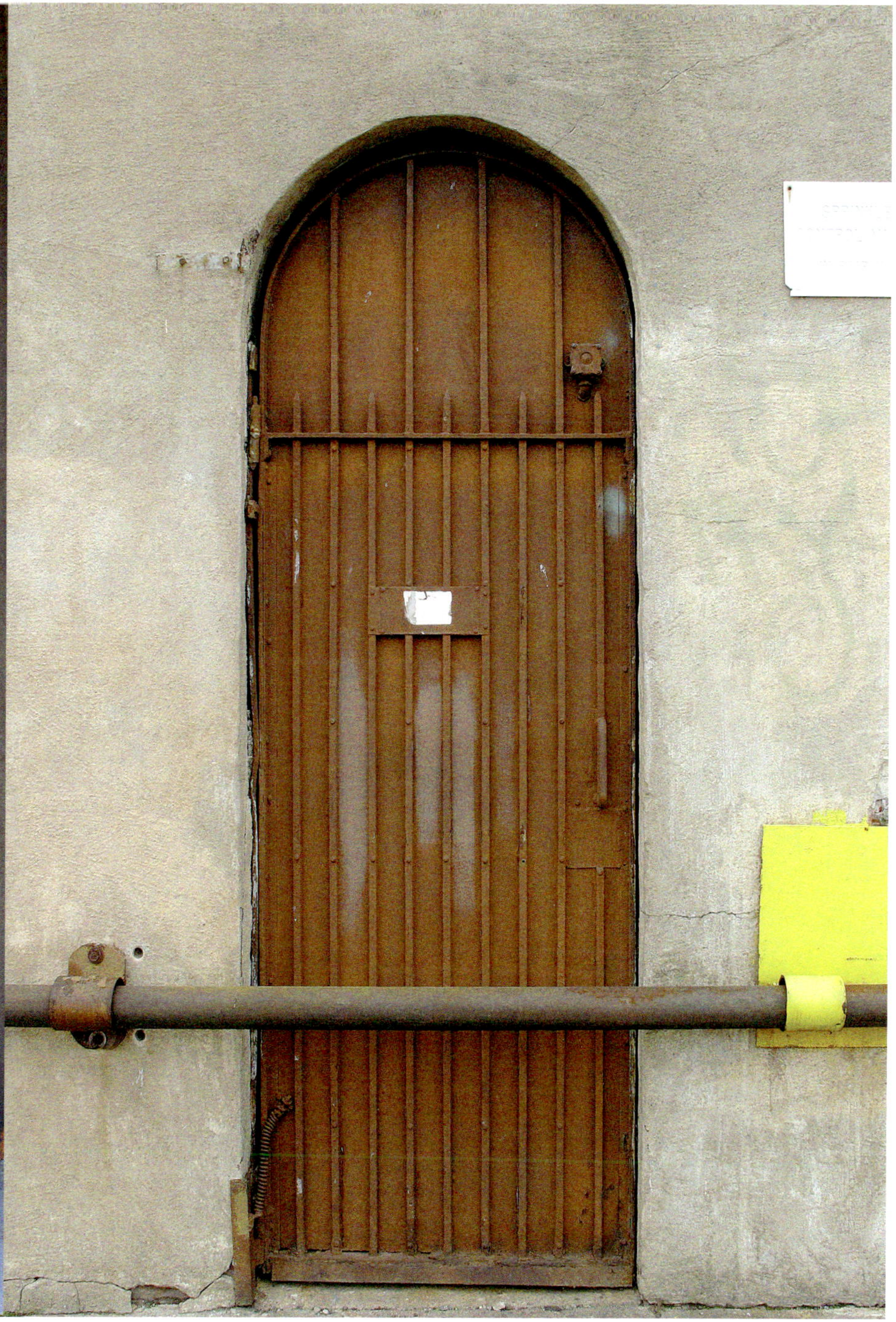

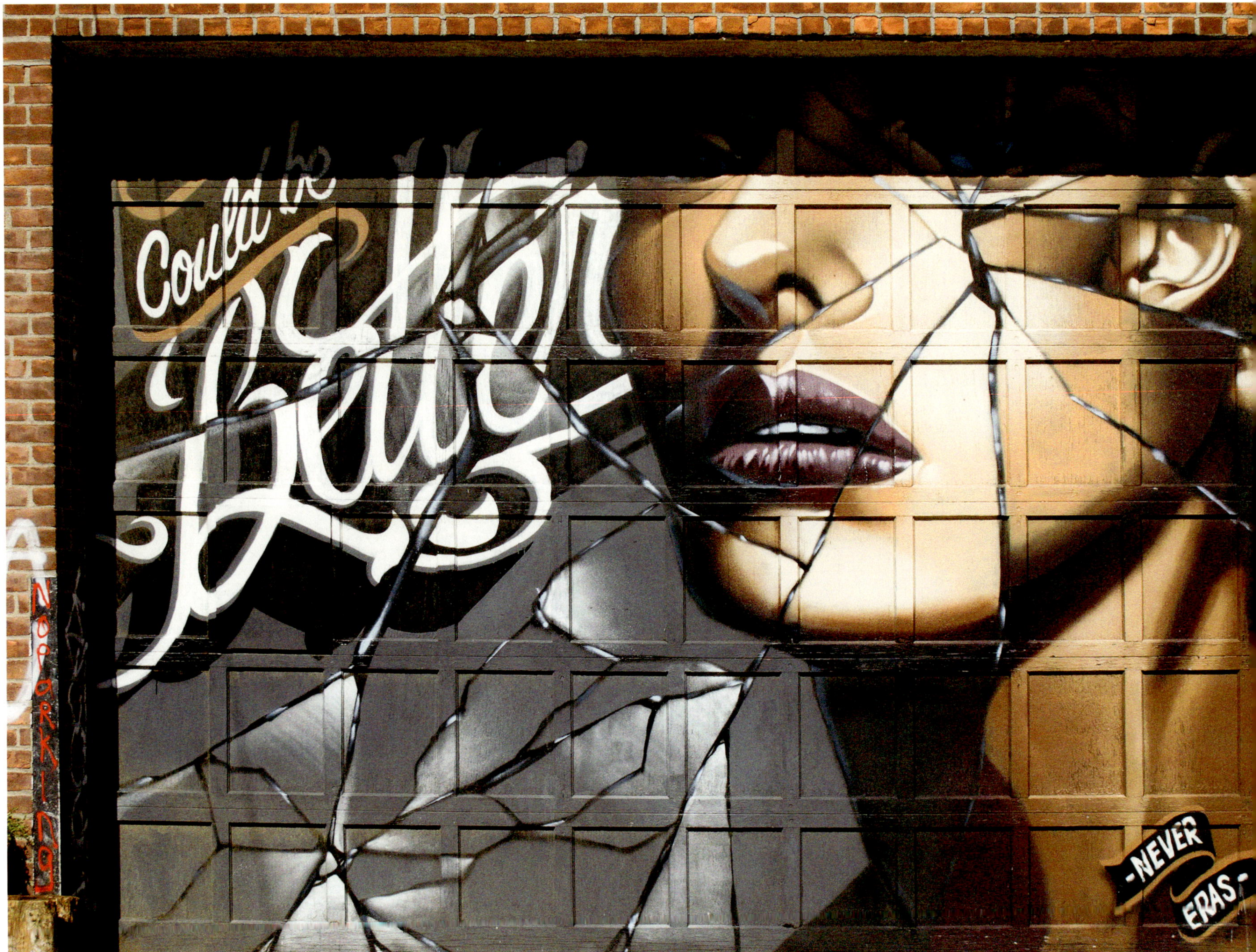
Could be
Better
-NEVER
ERAS-

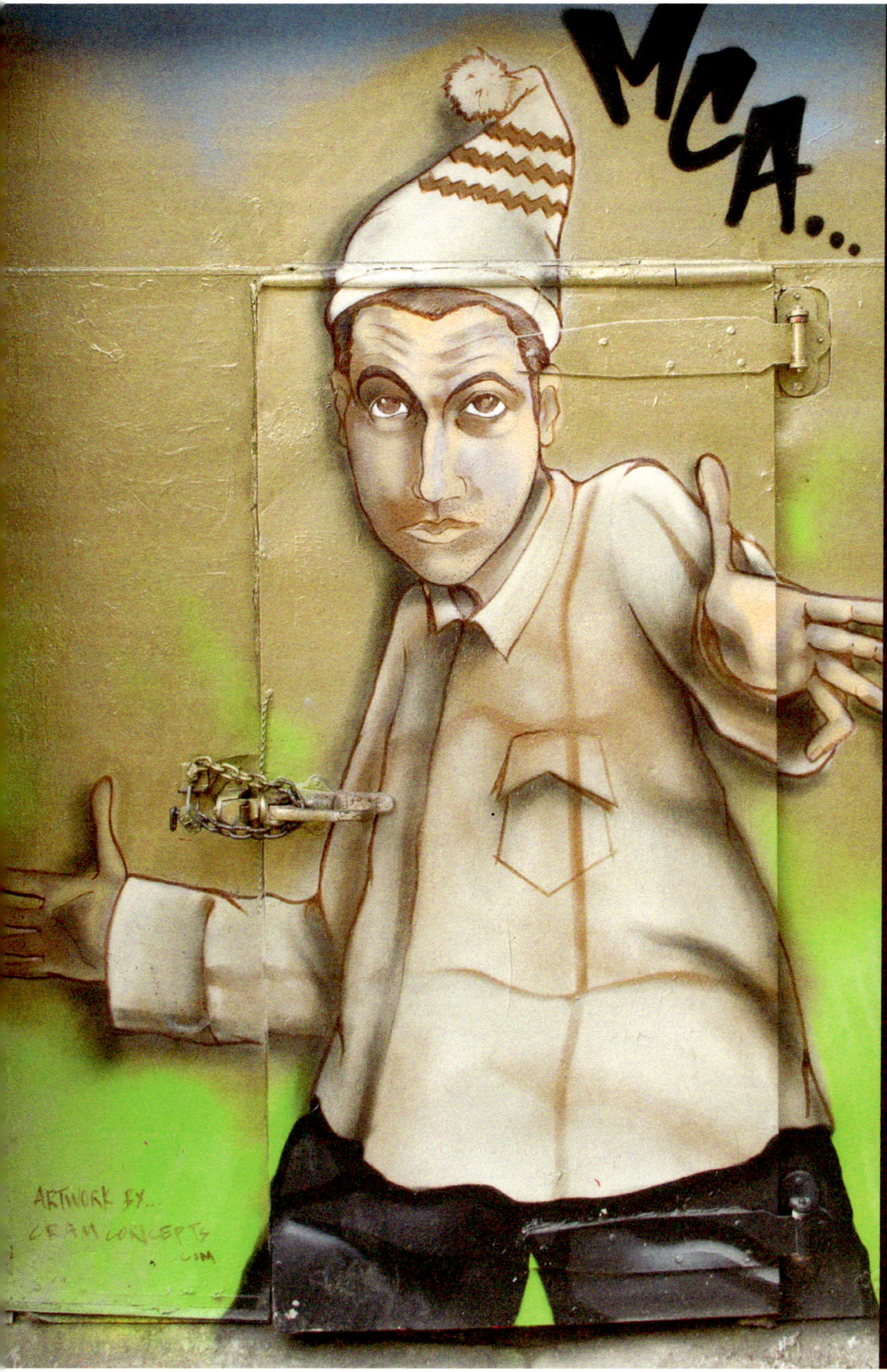
MCA...
ARTWORK BY...

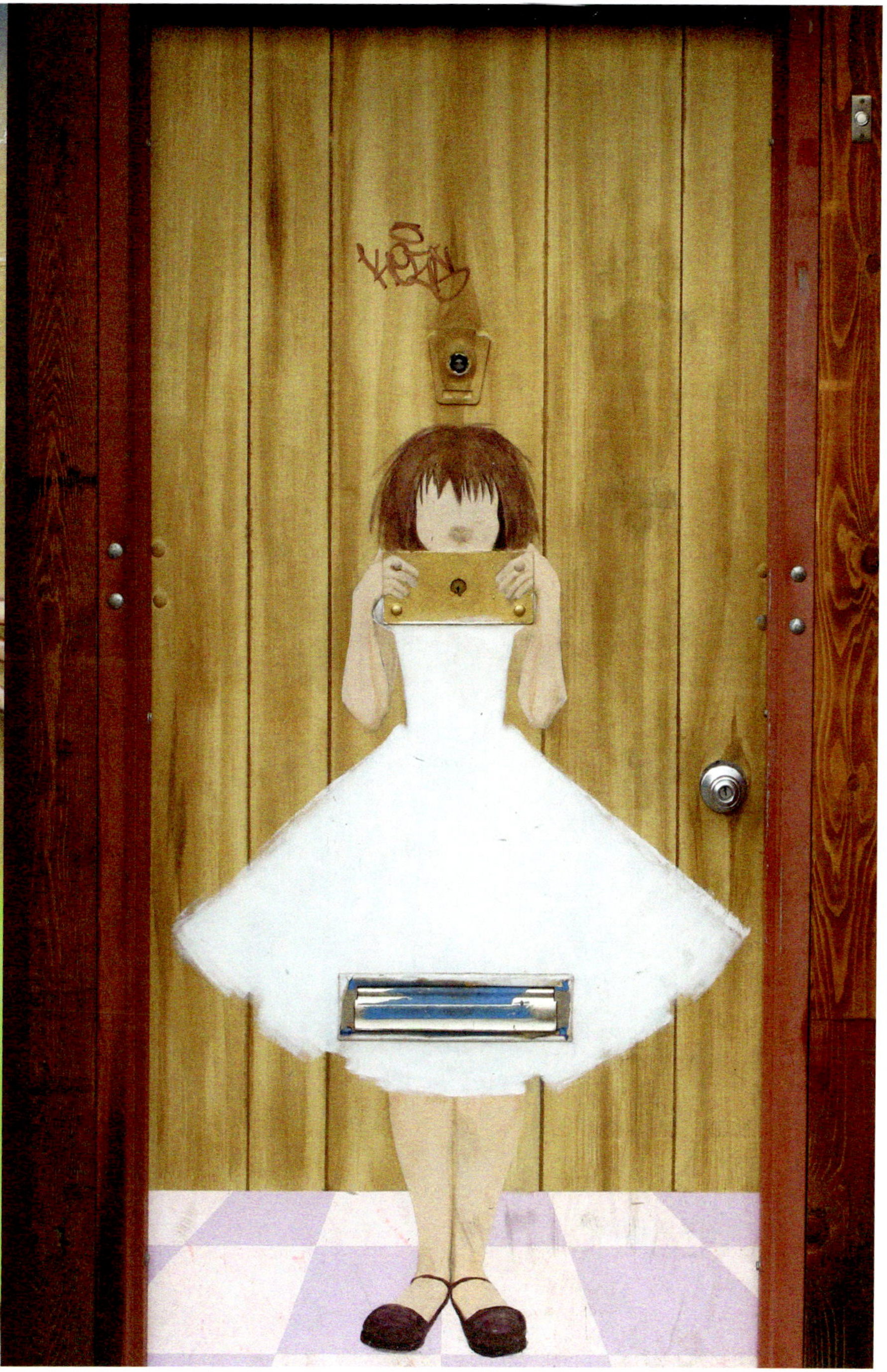

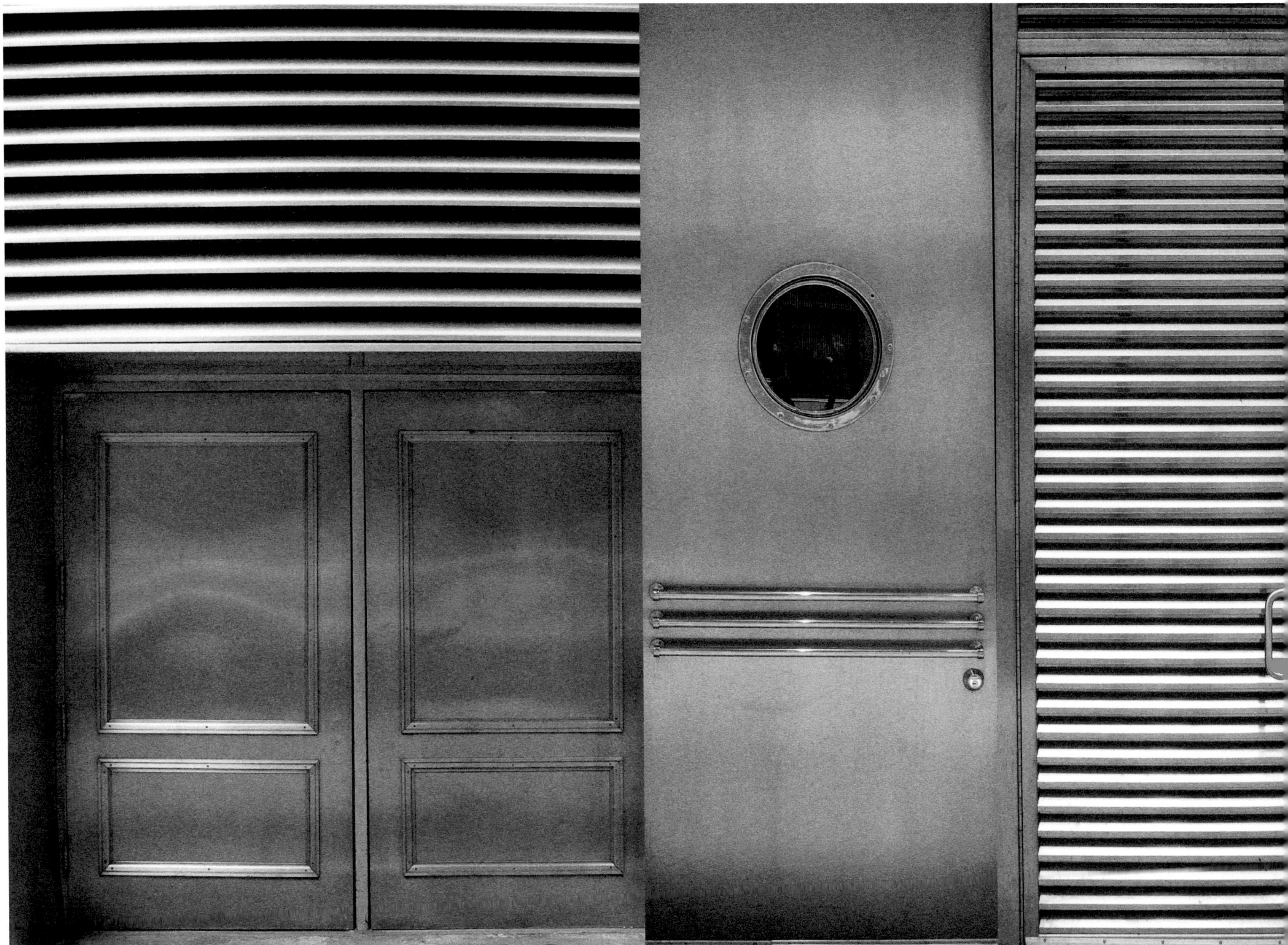

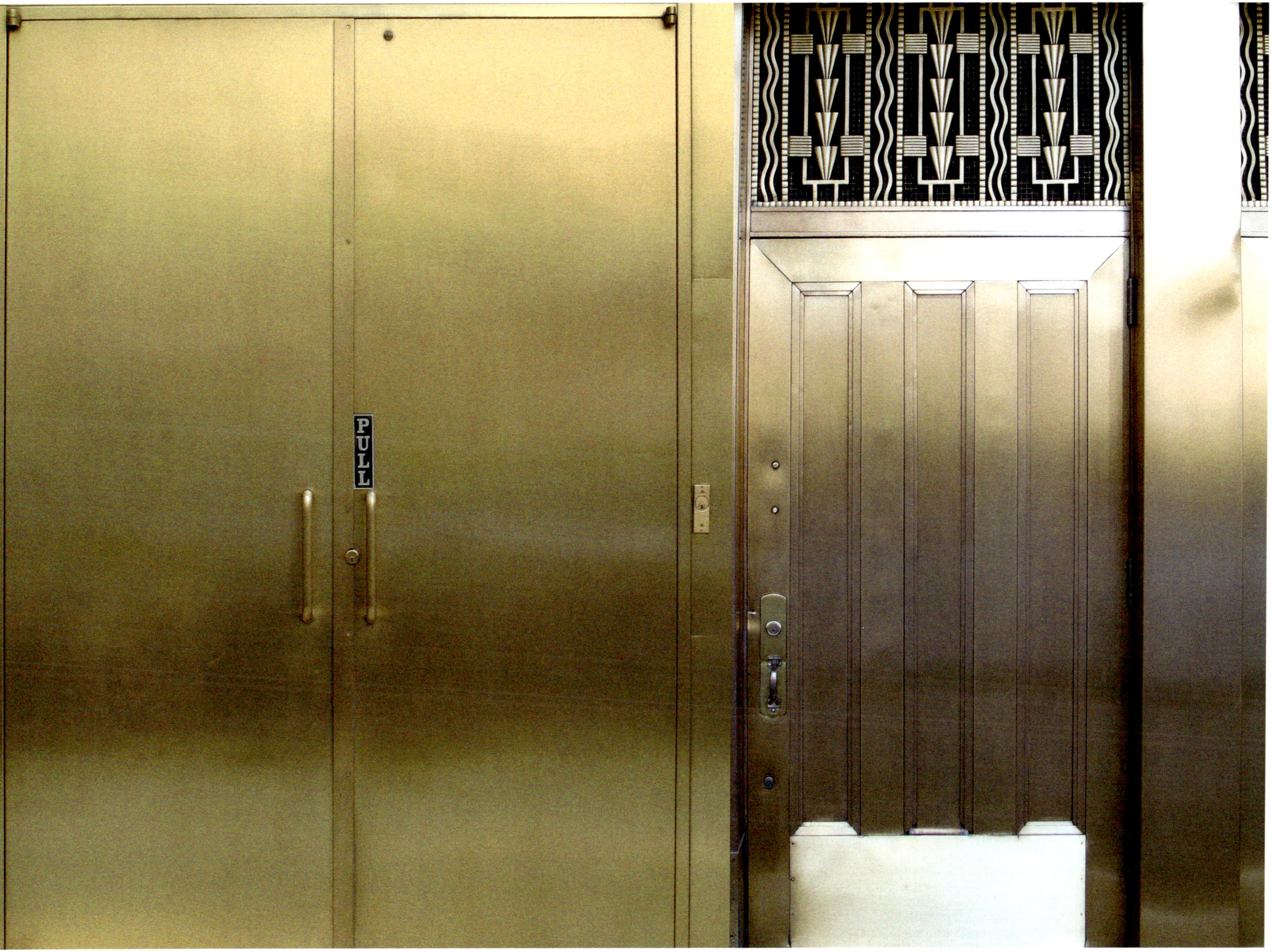
PULL

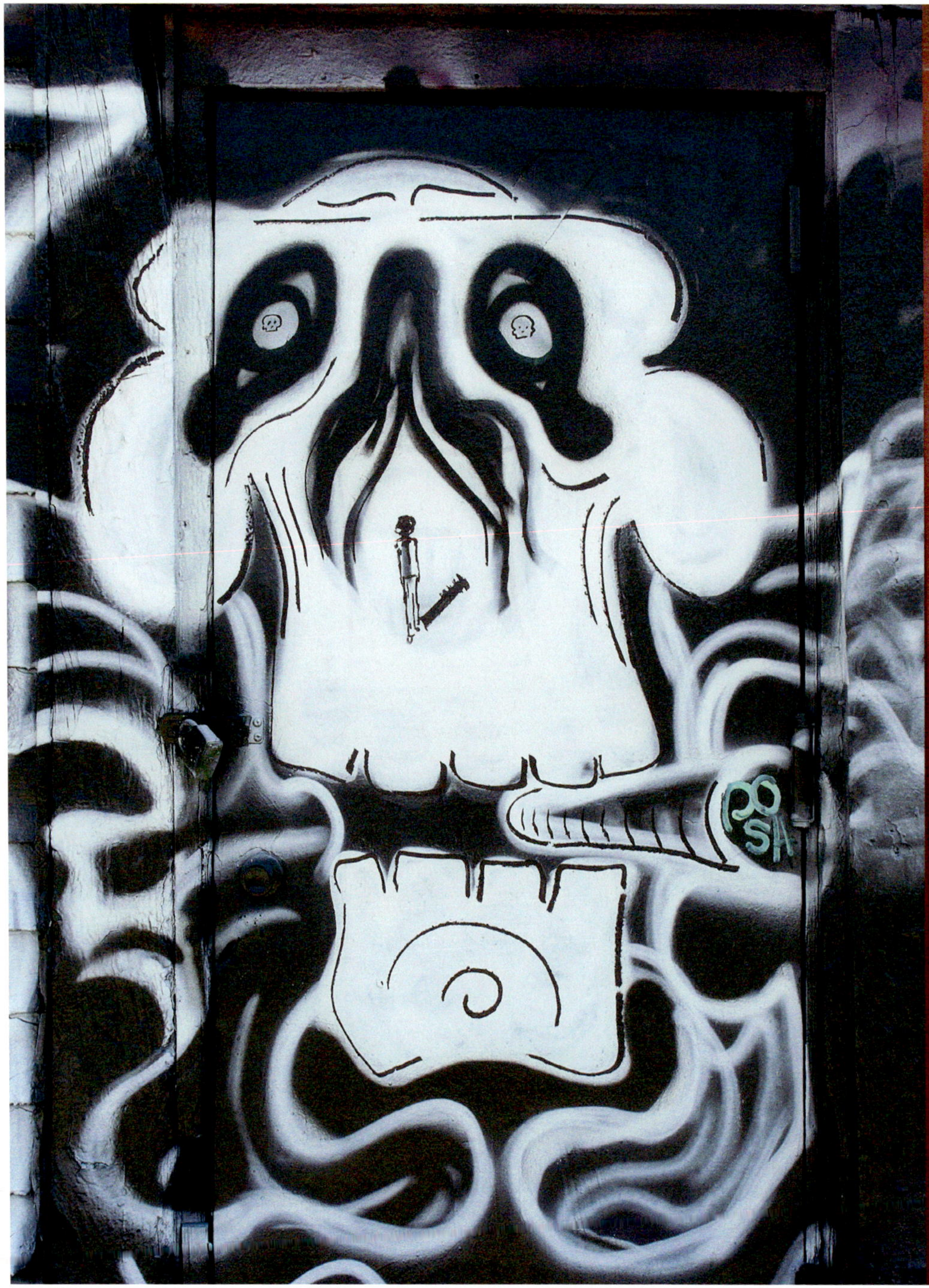

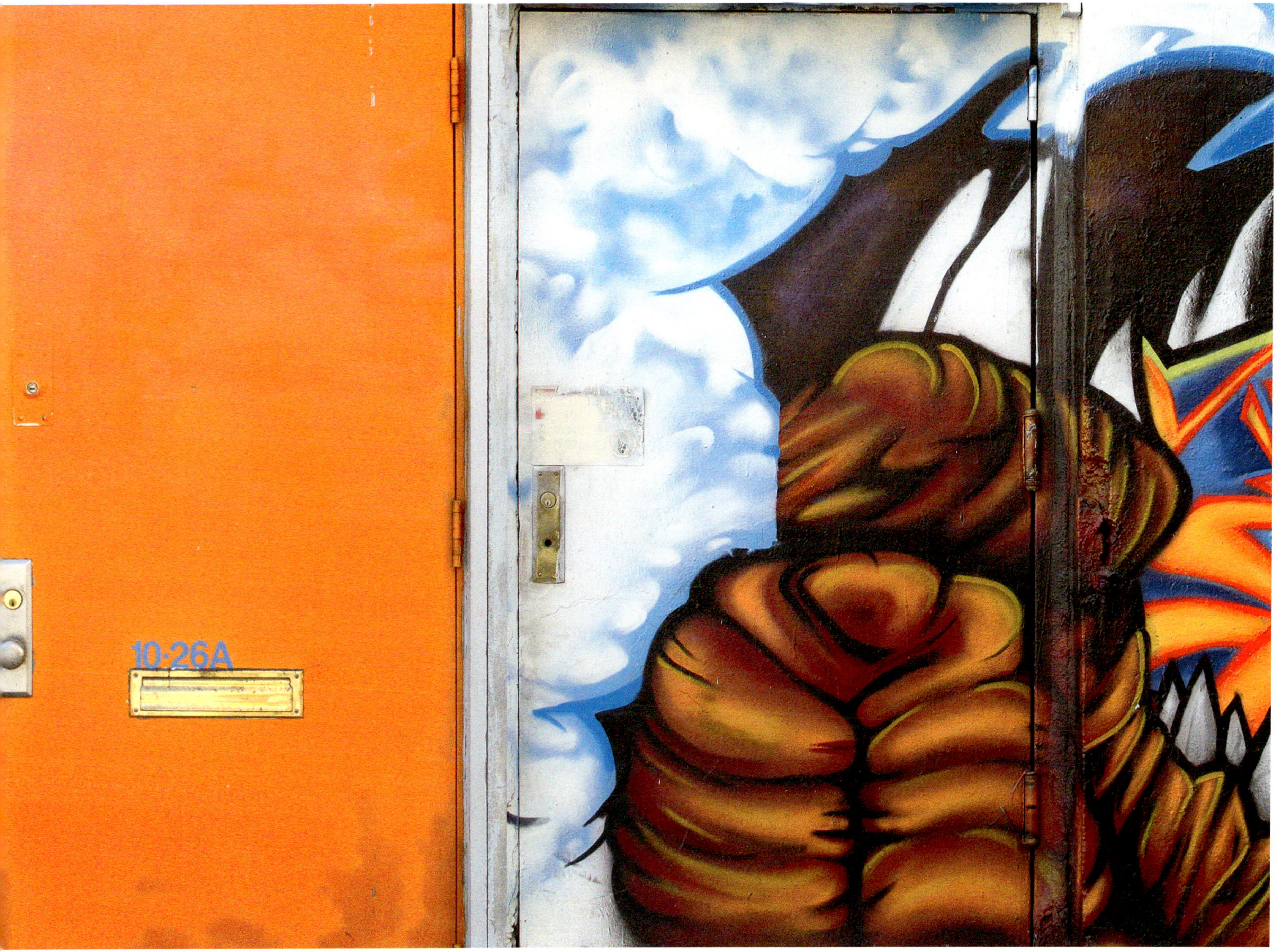
10-26A

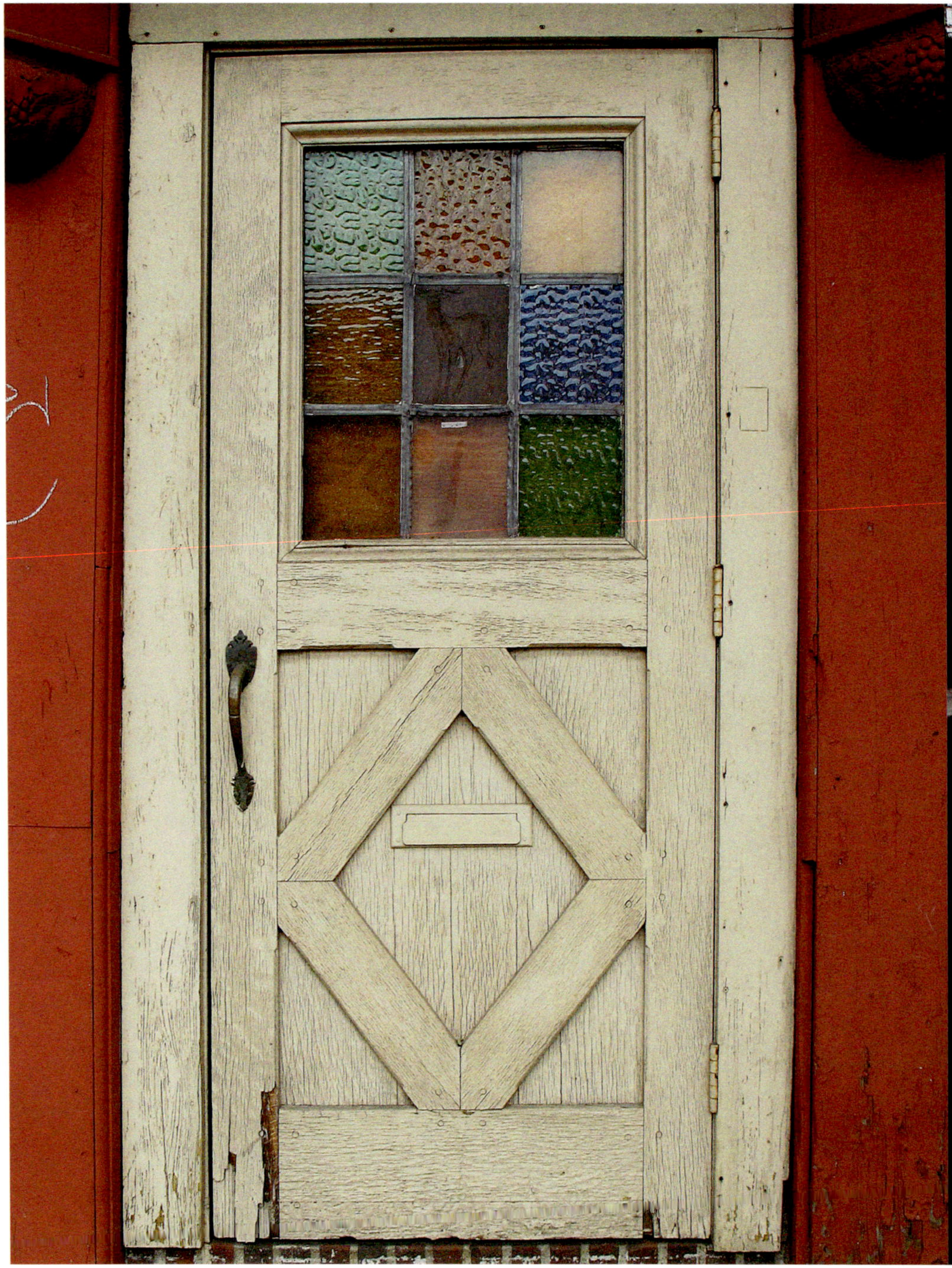

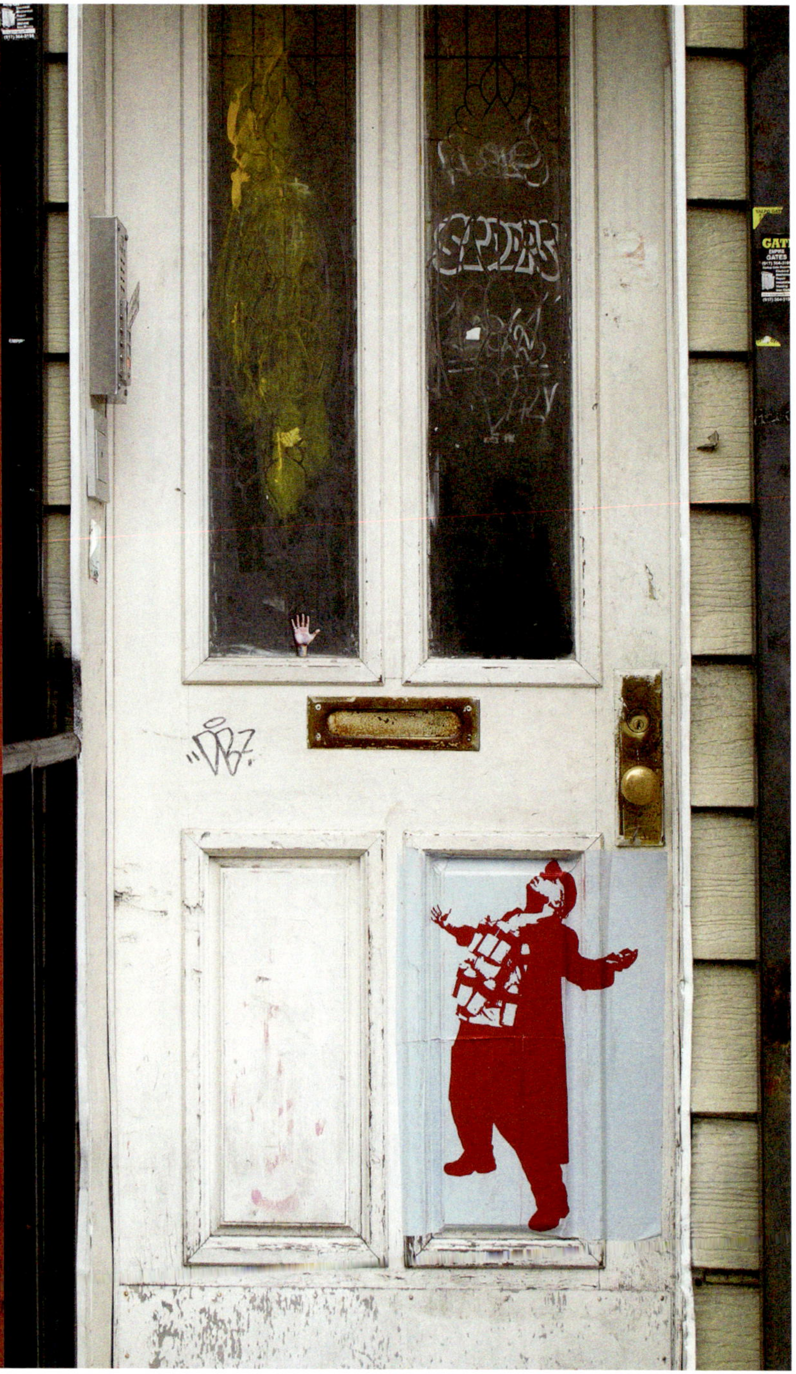

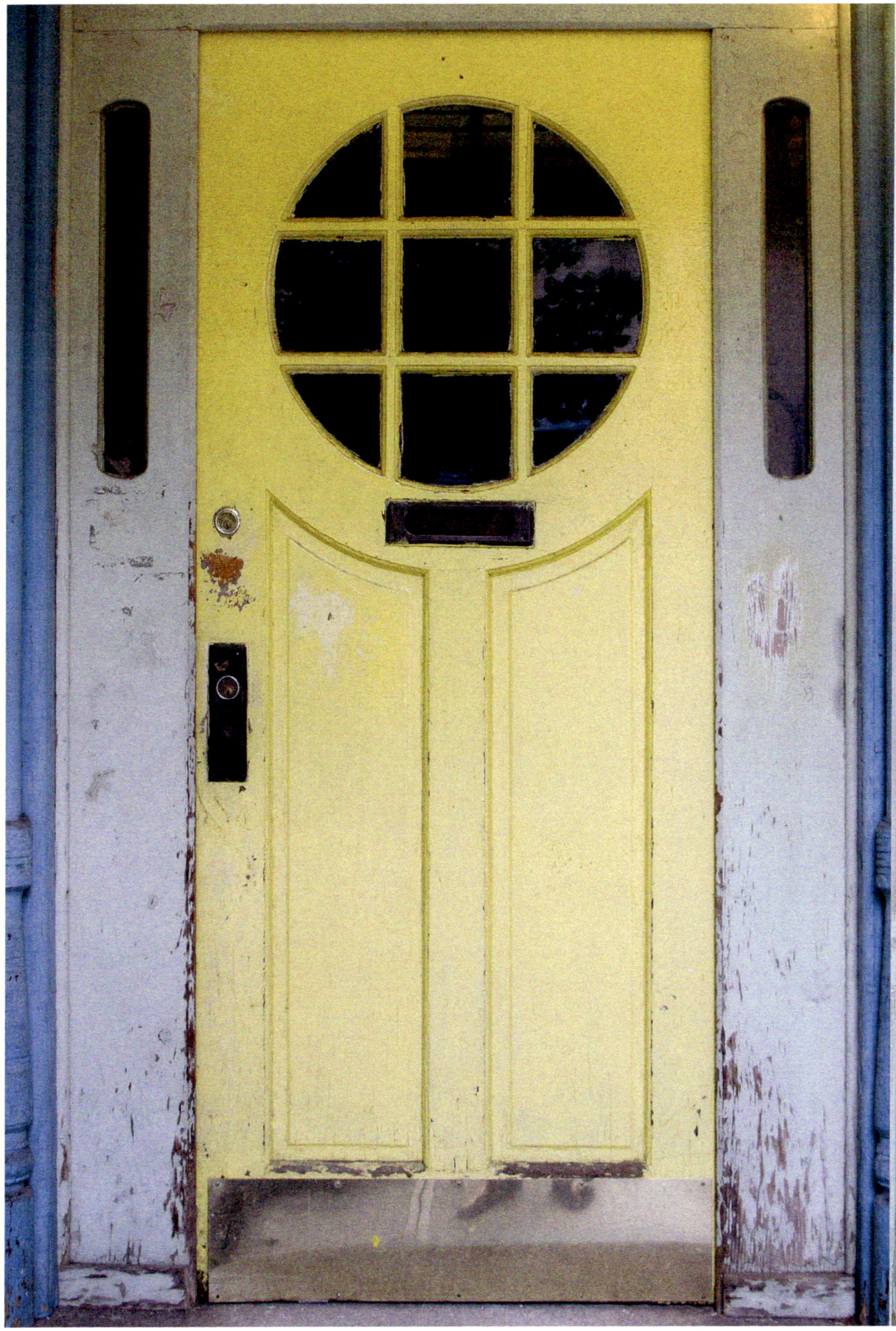

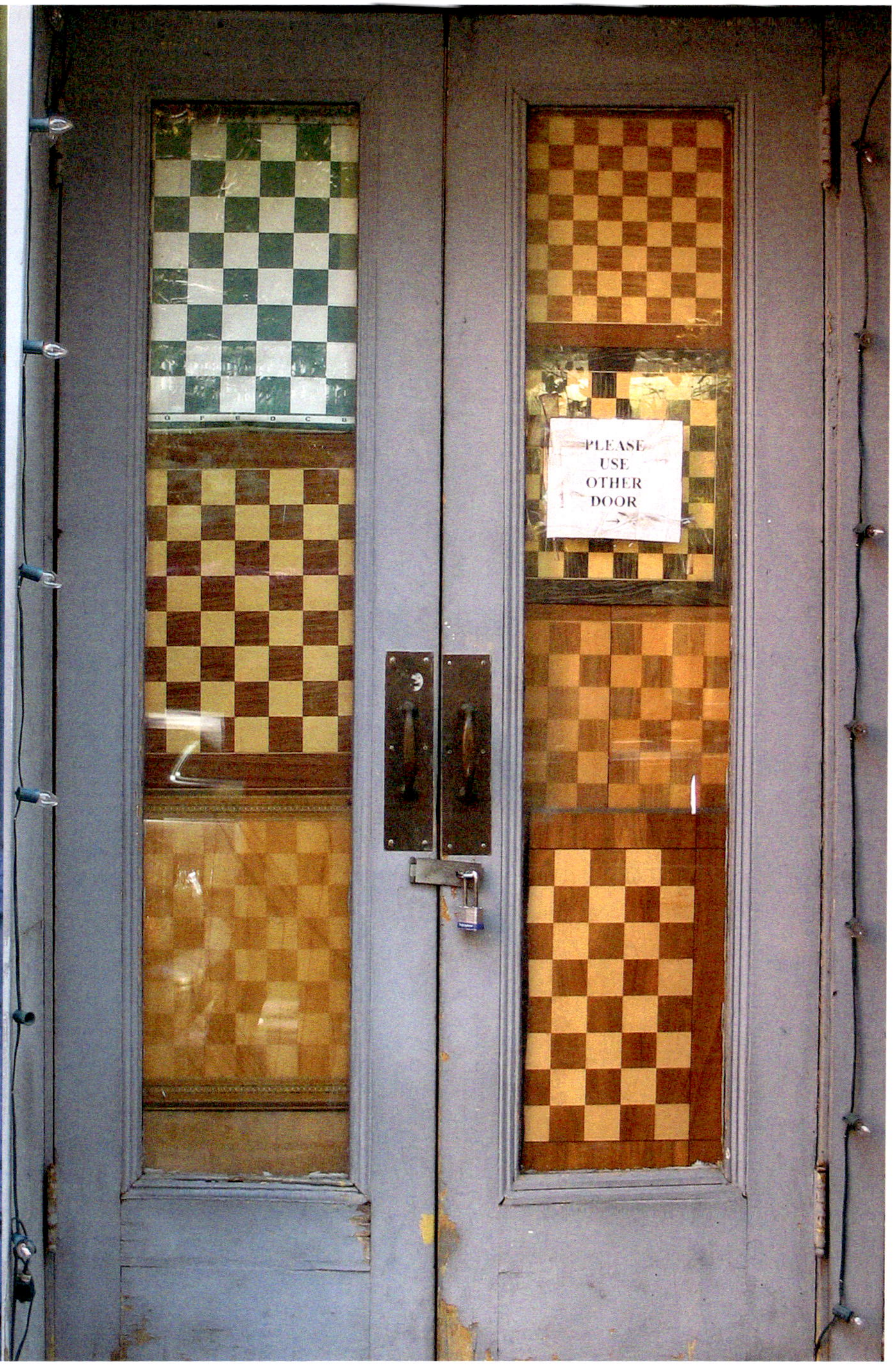
PLEASE
USE
OTHER
DOOR

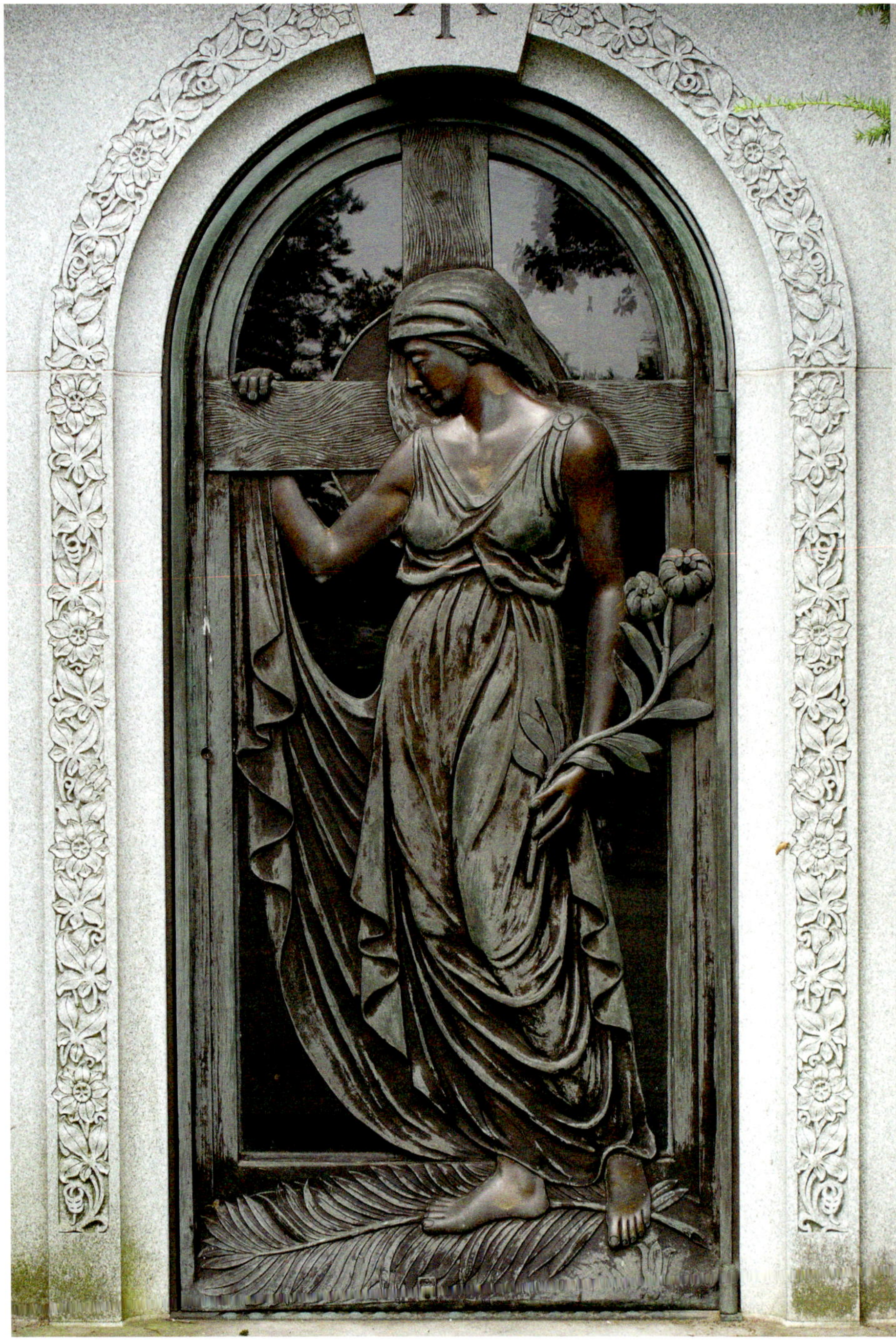

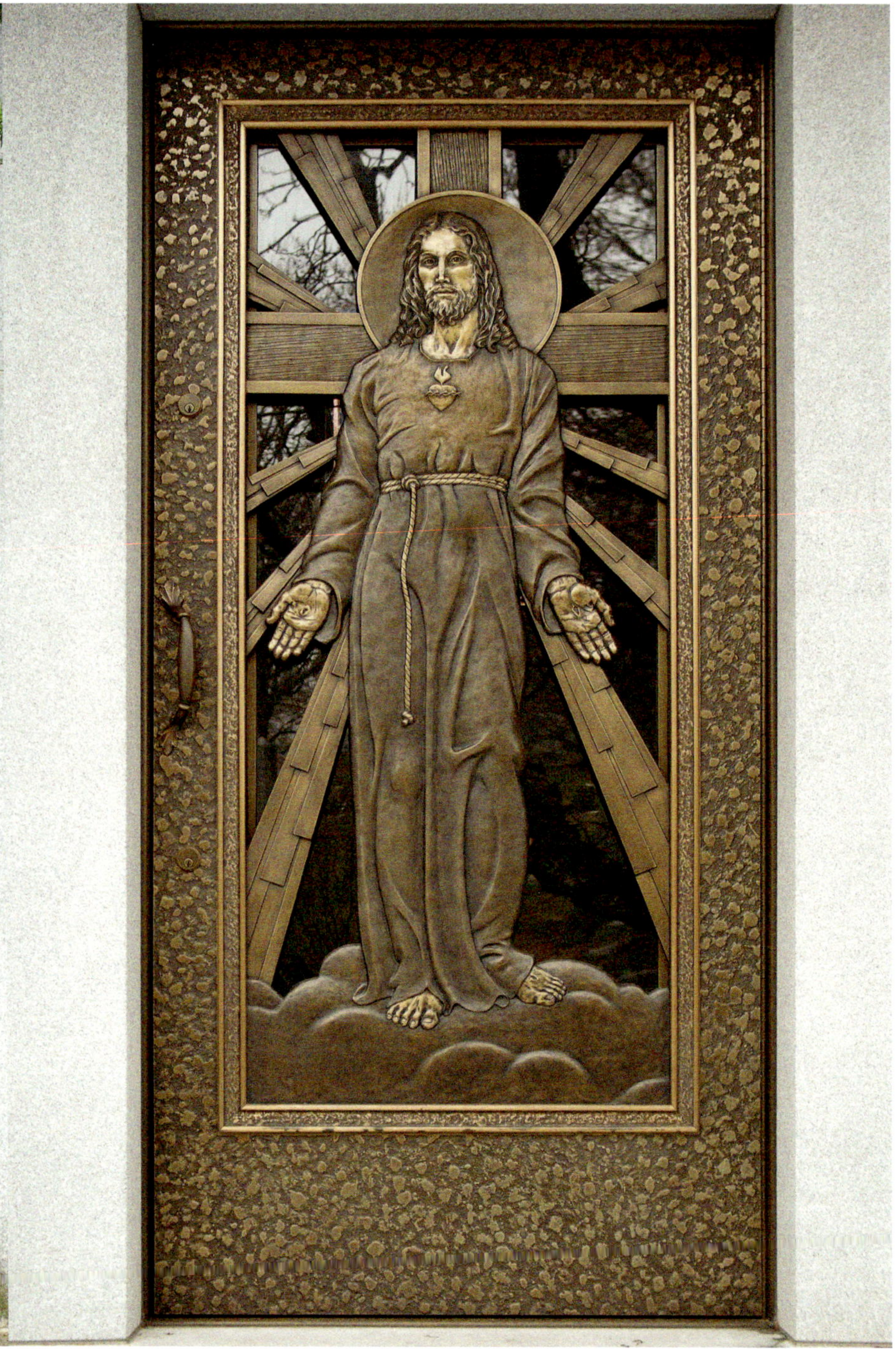

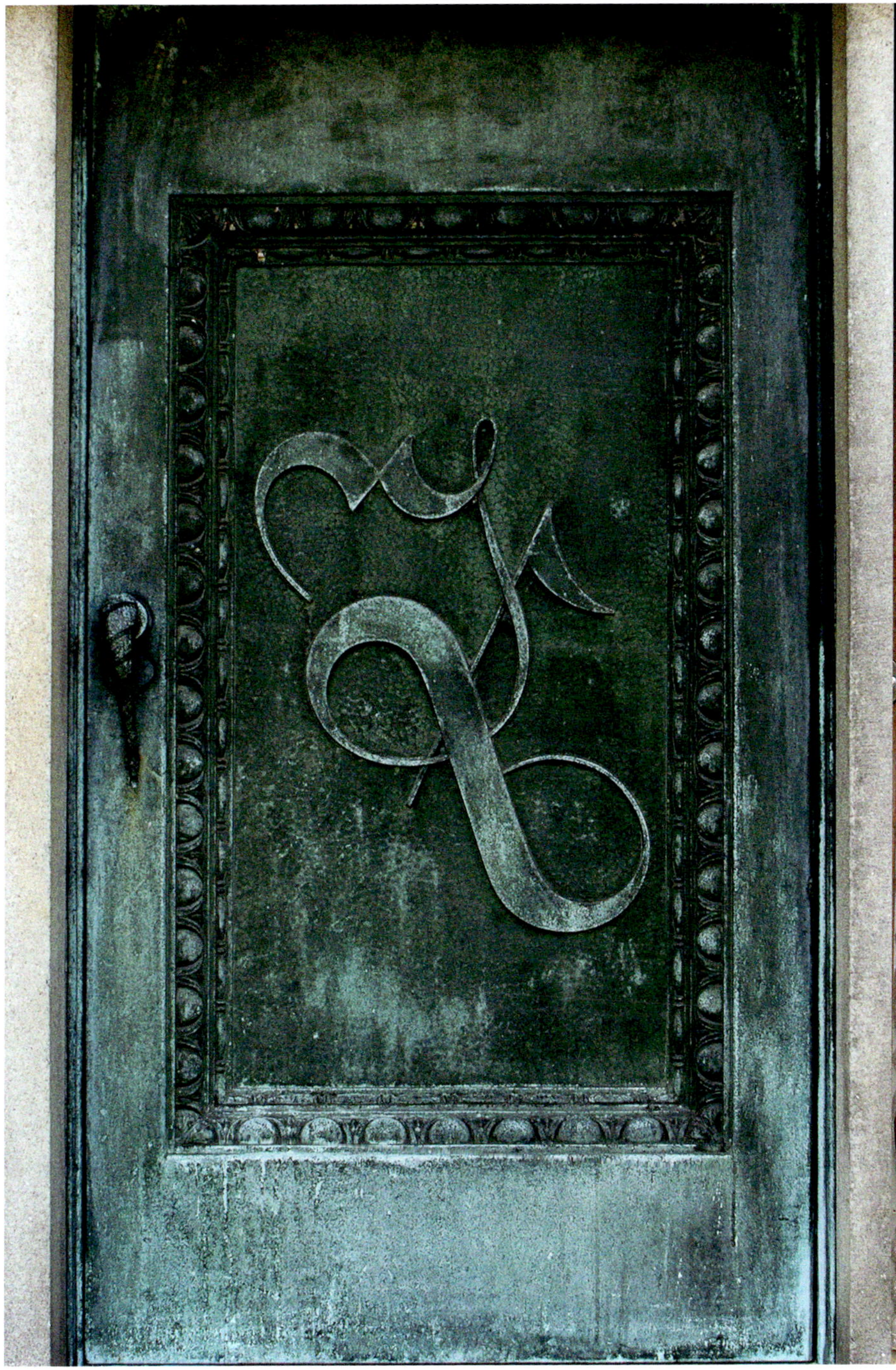
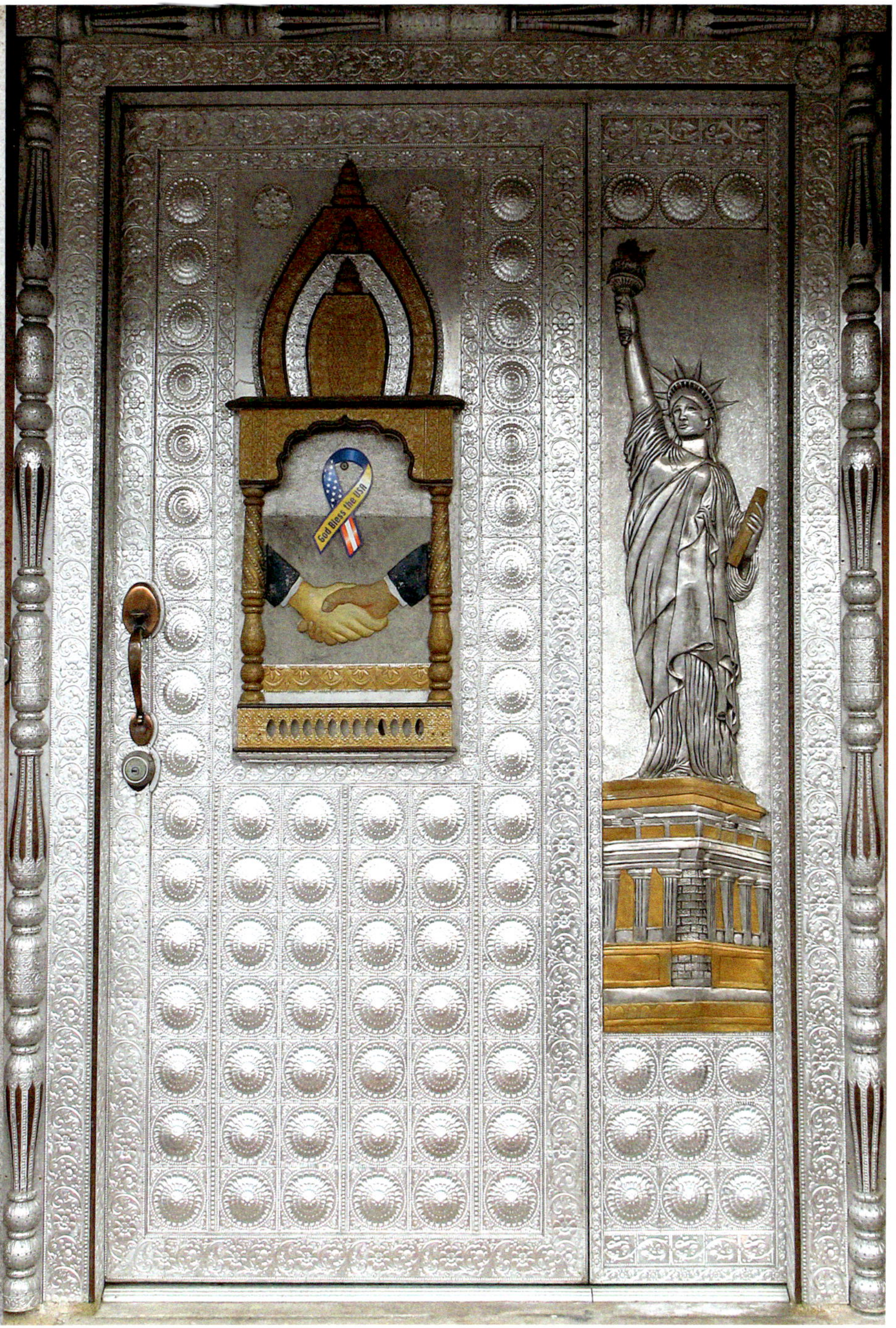

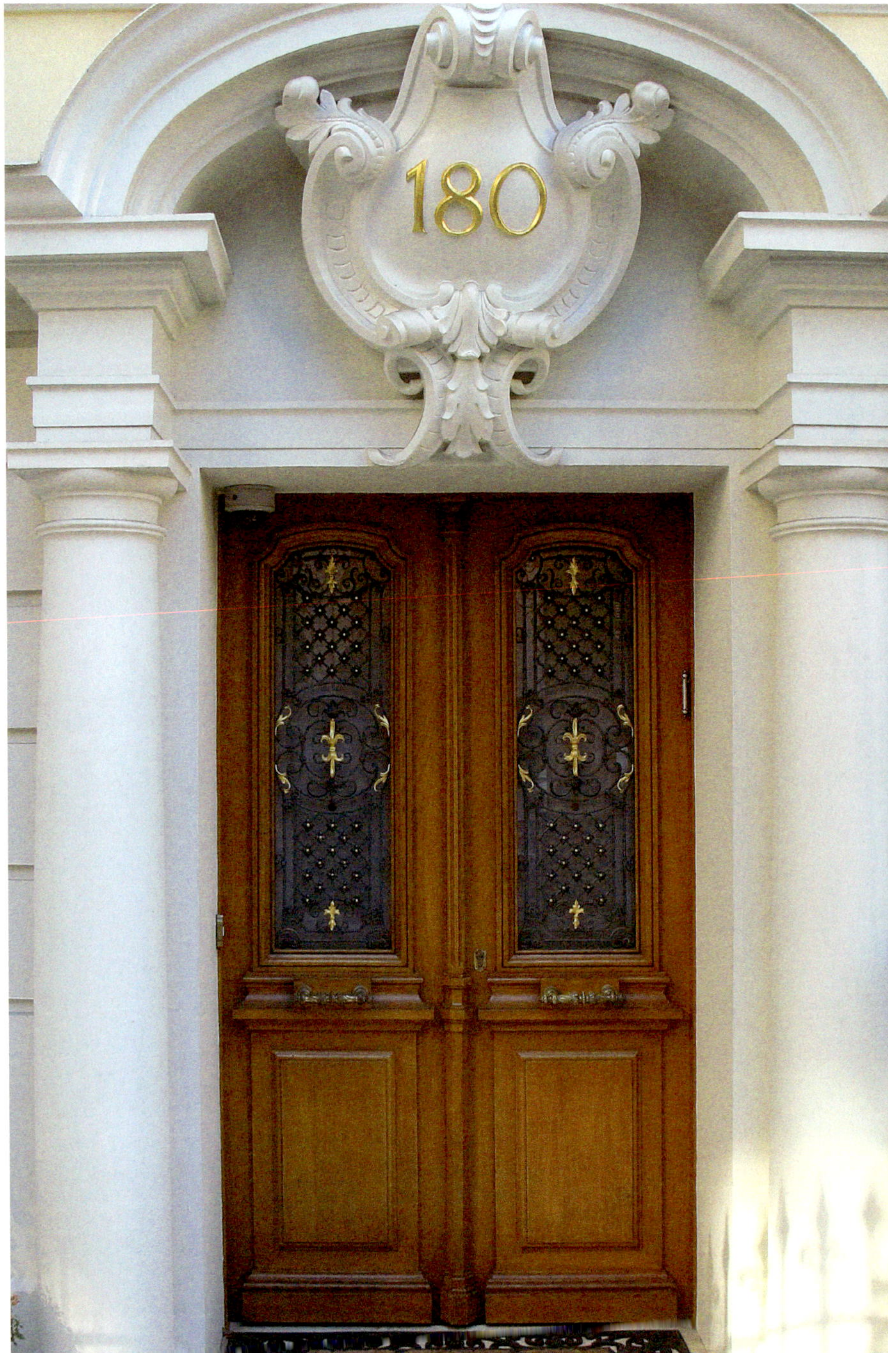
180
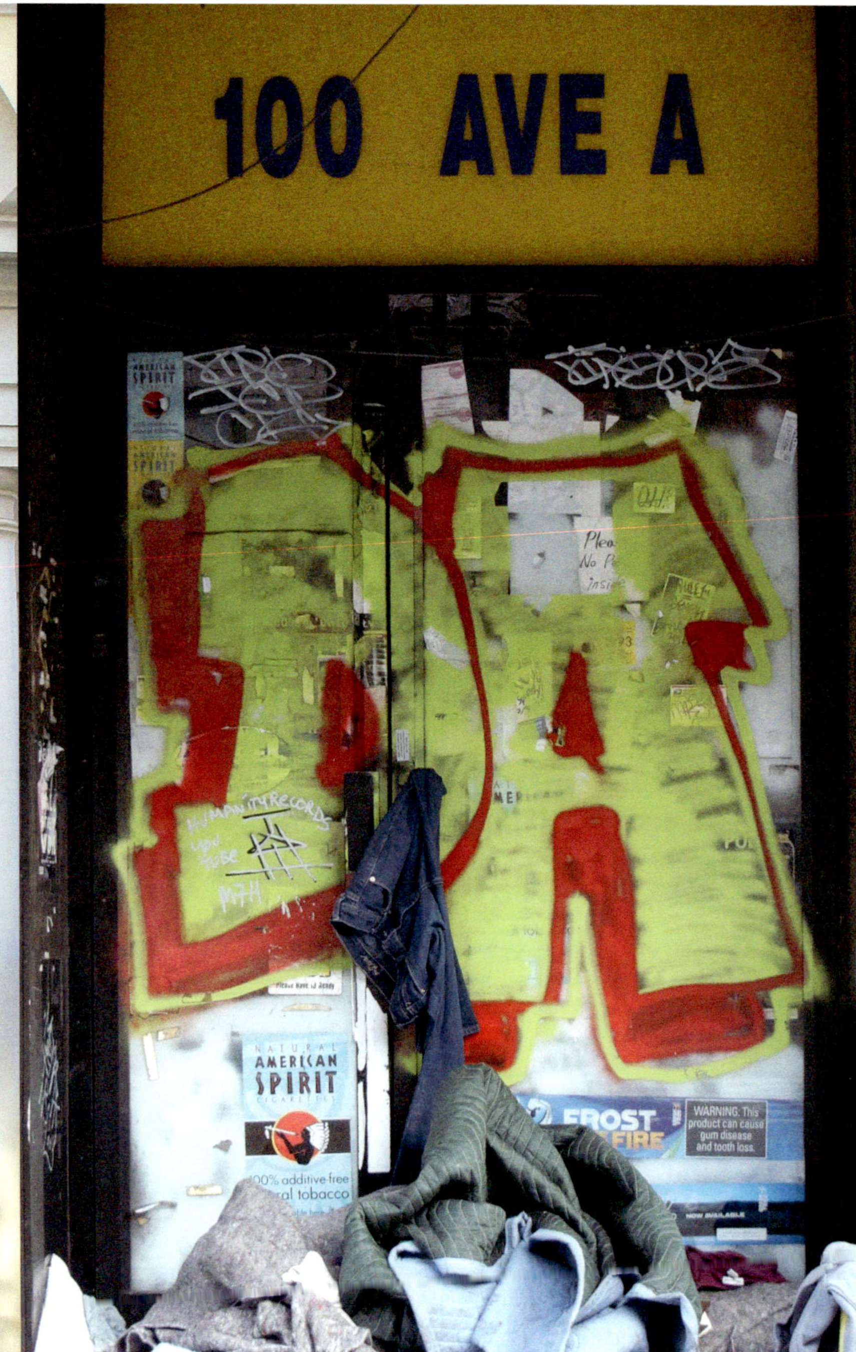
100 AVE A
NATURAL AMERICAN SPIRIT
100% additive-free
FROST
FIRE
WARNING: This product can cause gum disease and tooth loss.

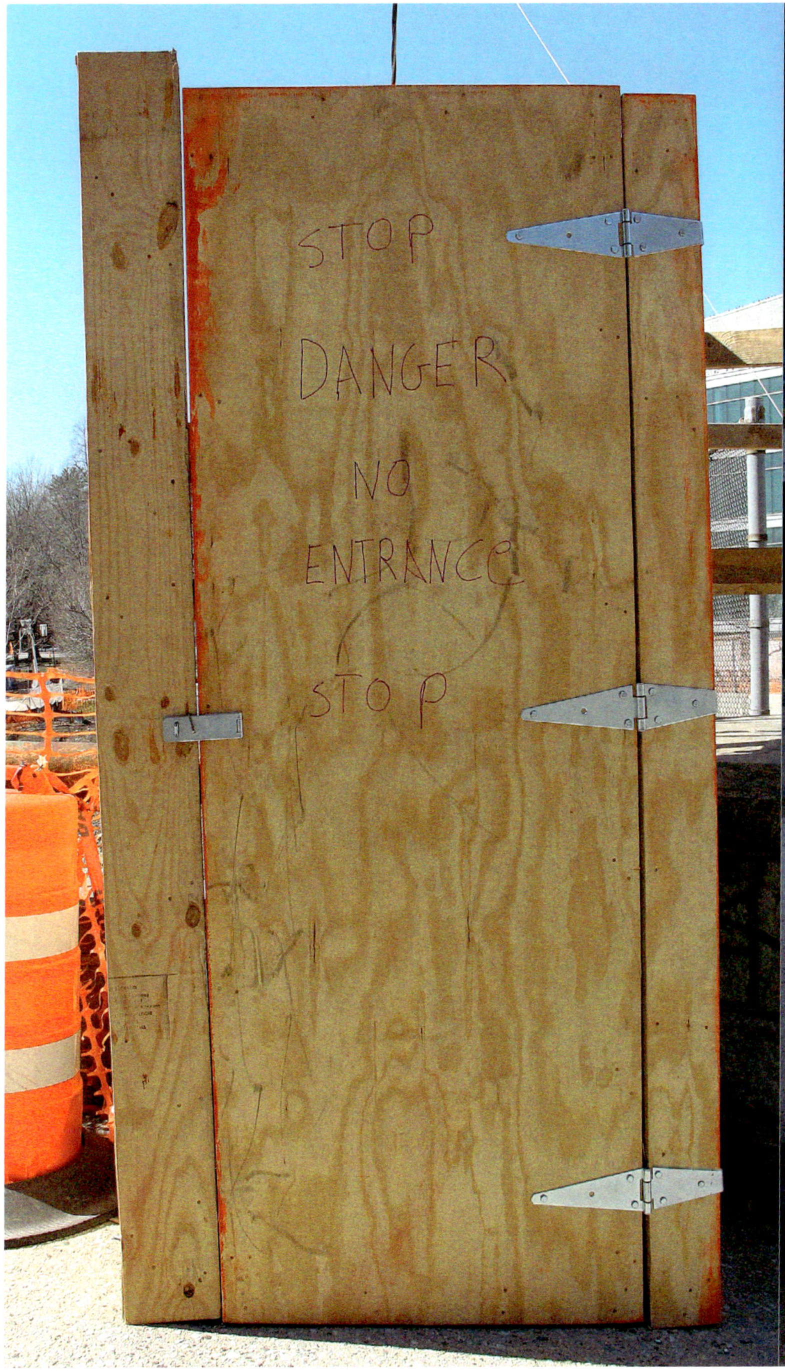
STOP
DANGER
NO
ENTRANCE
STOP

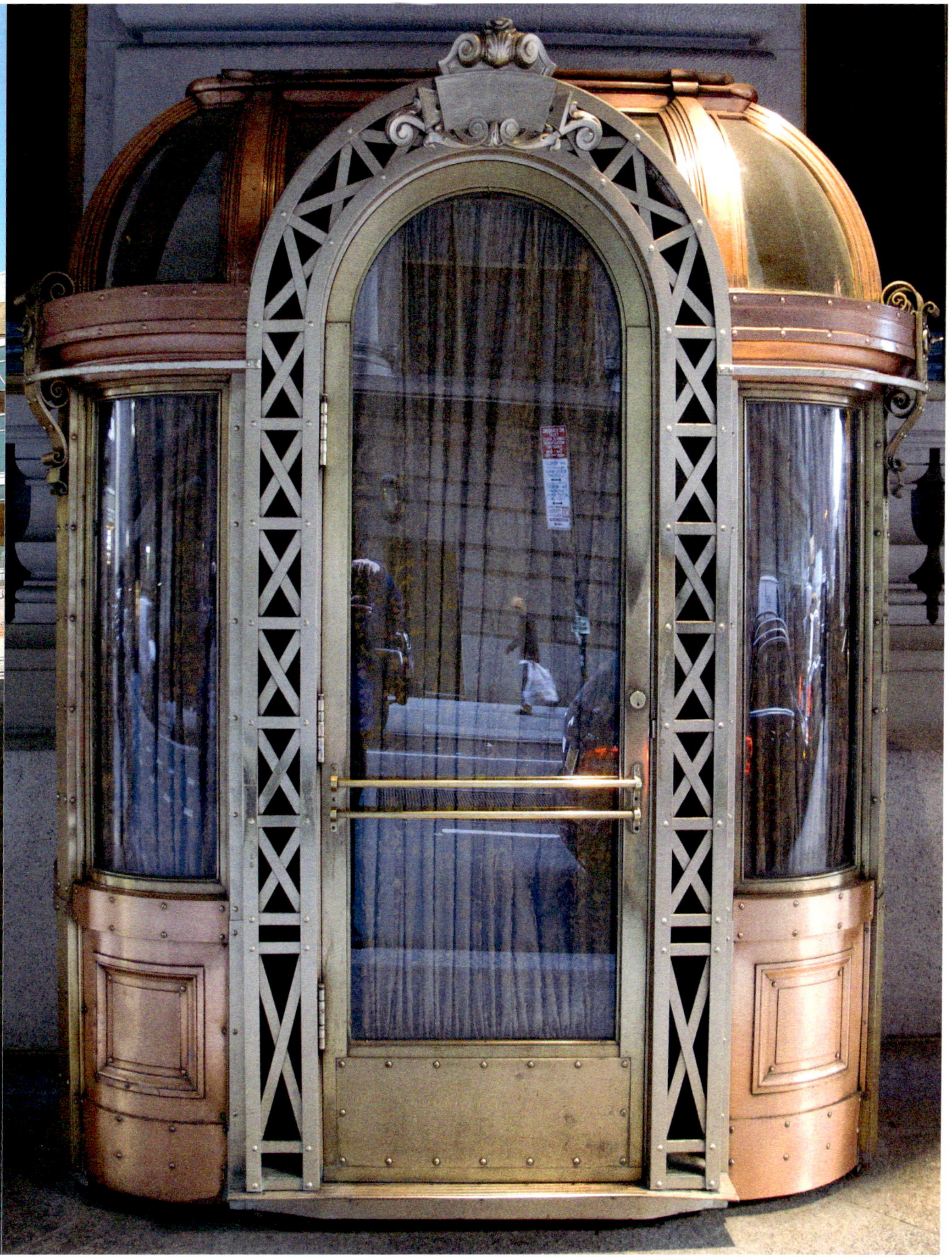

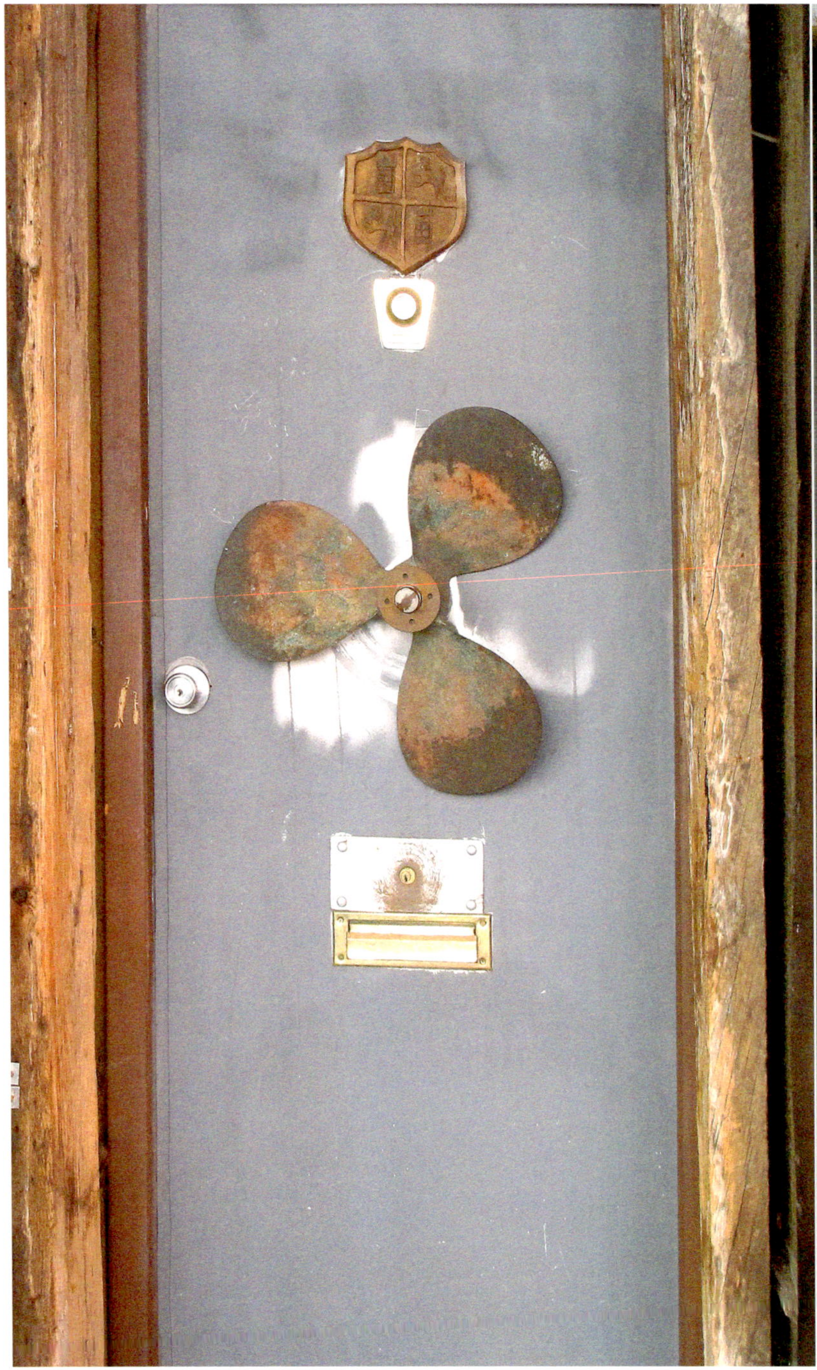

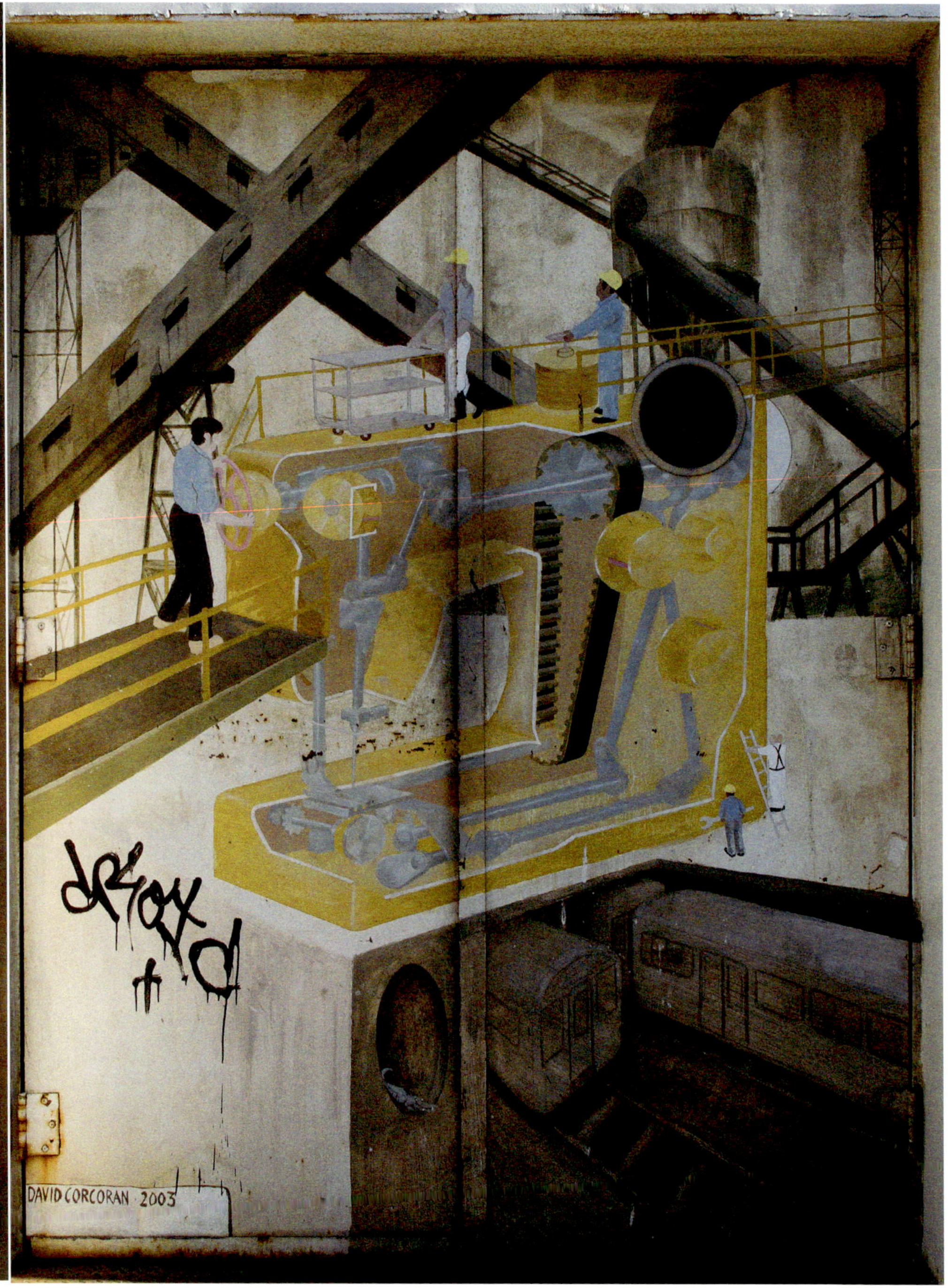
DAVID CORCORAN 2003

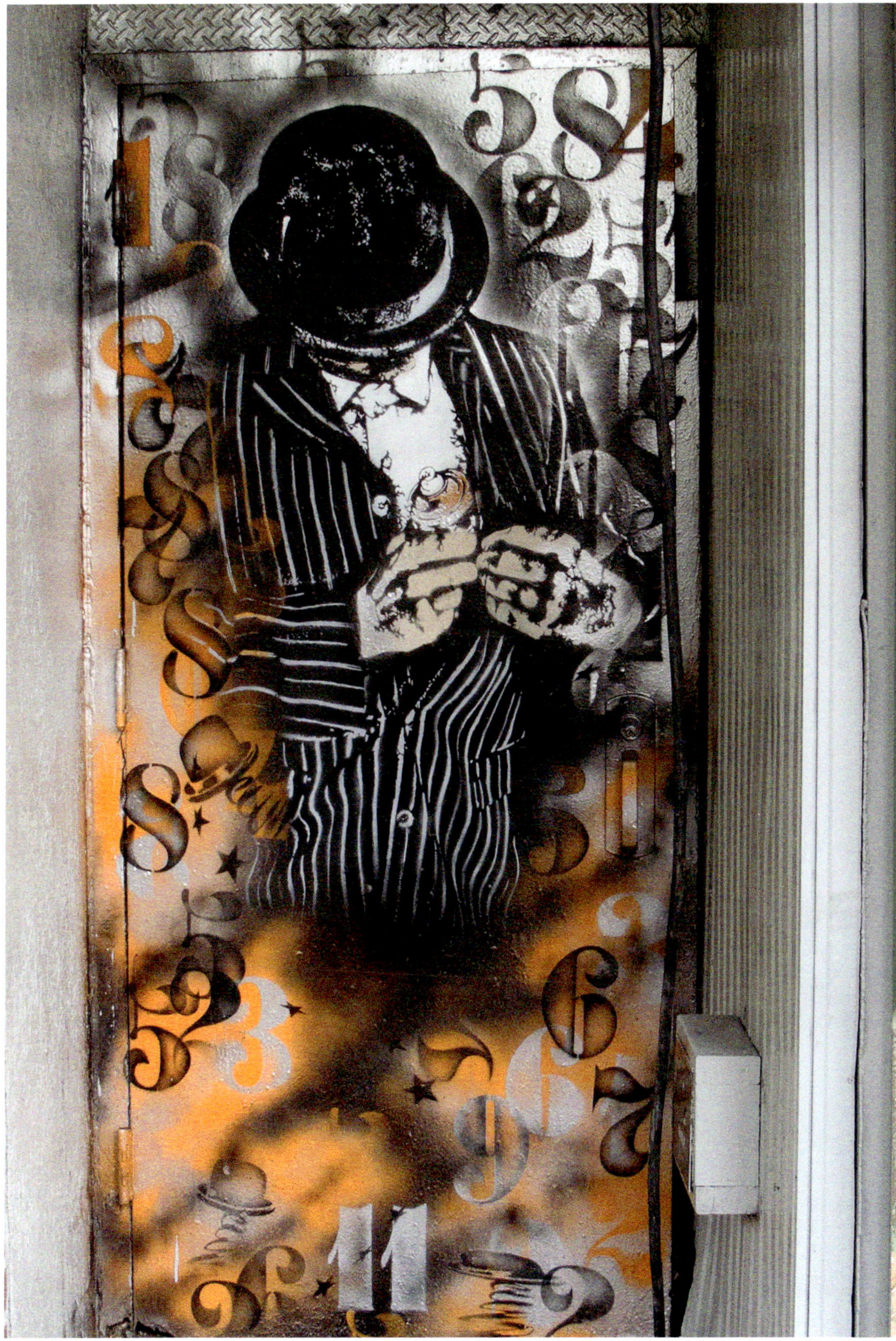

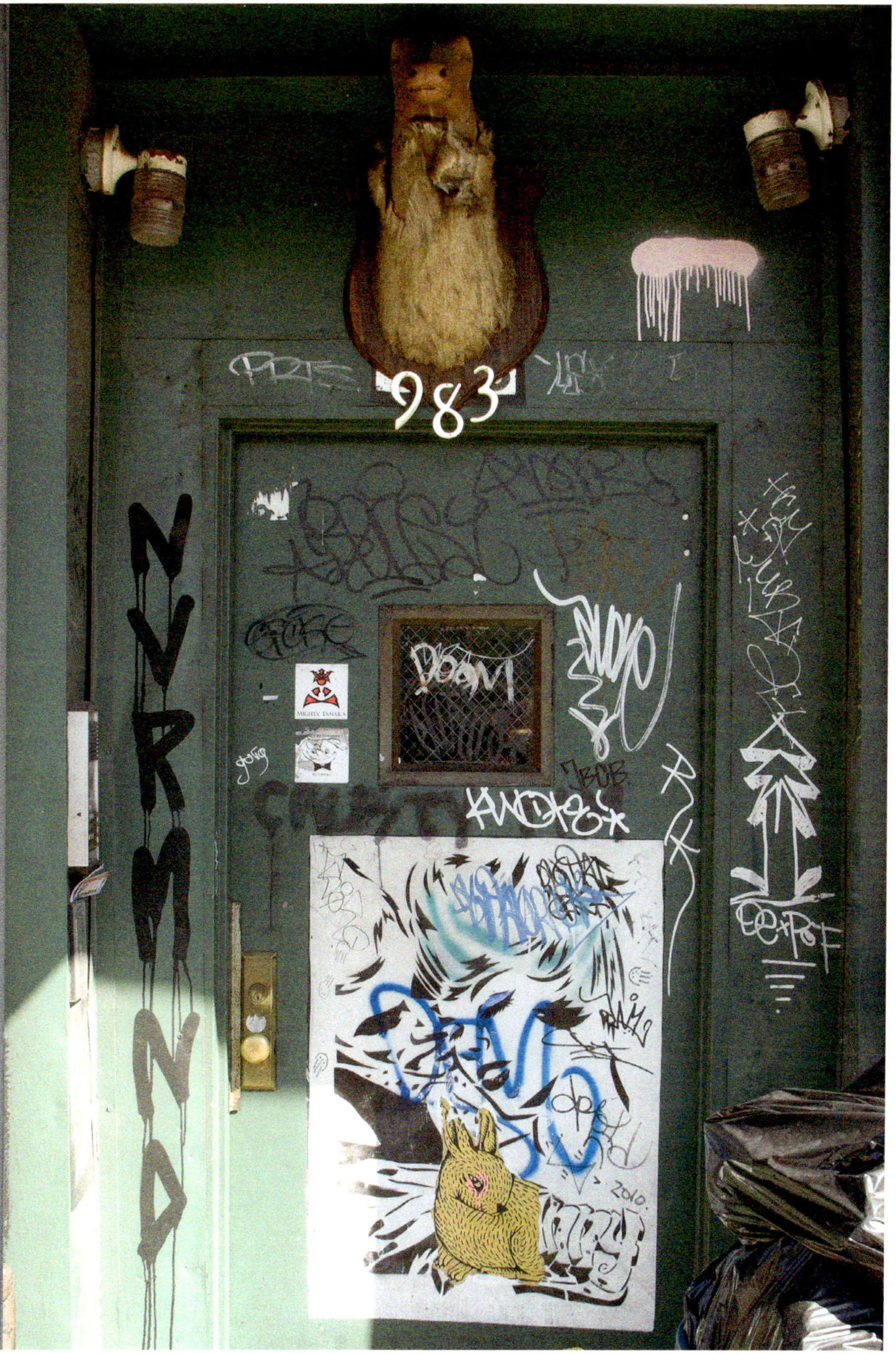
983

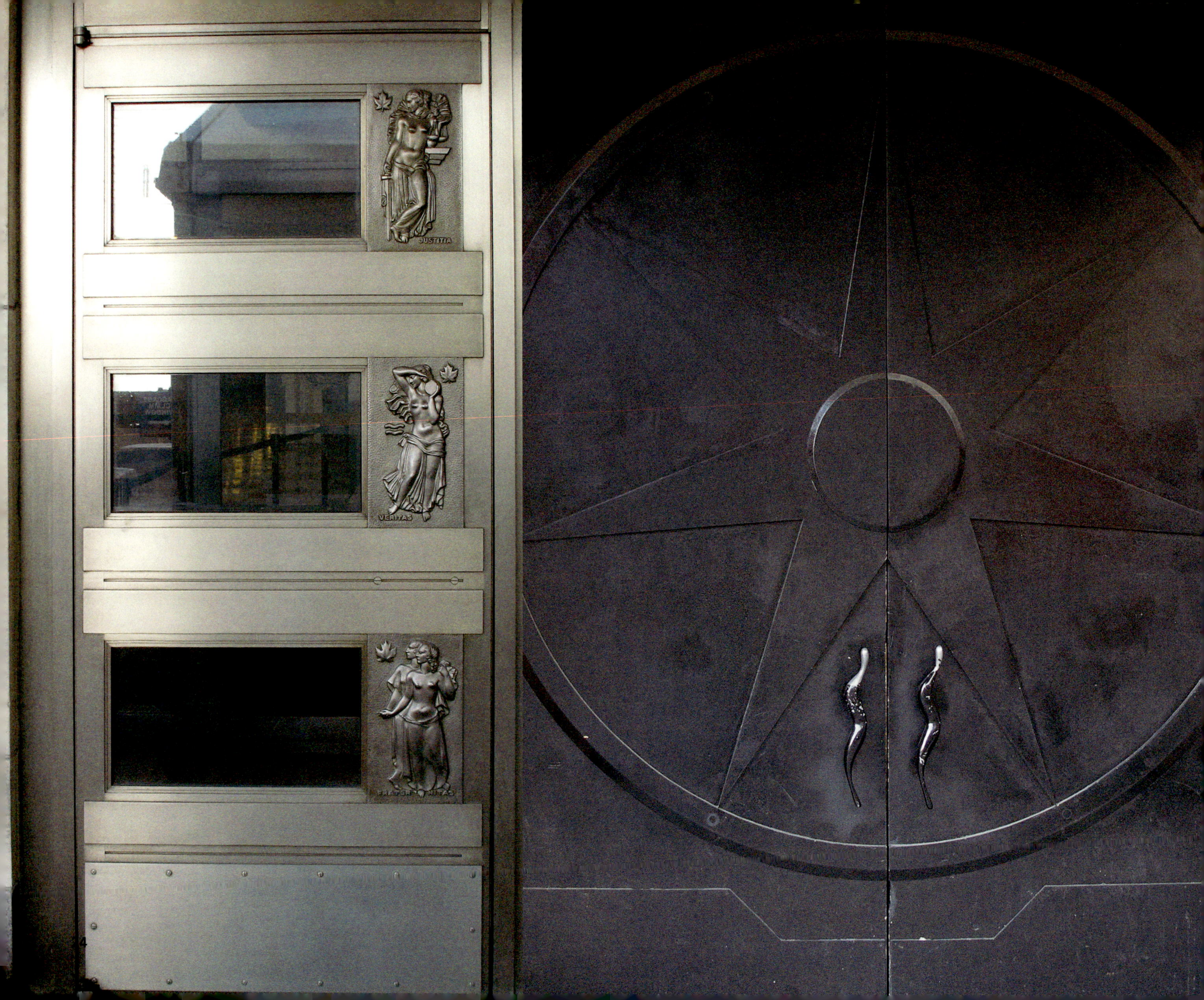
JUSTITIA
VERITAS

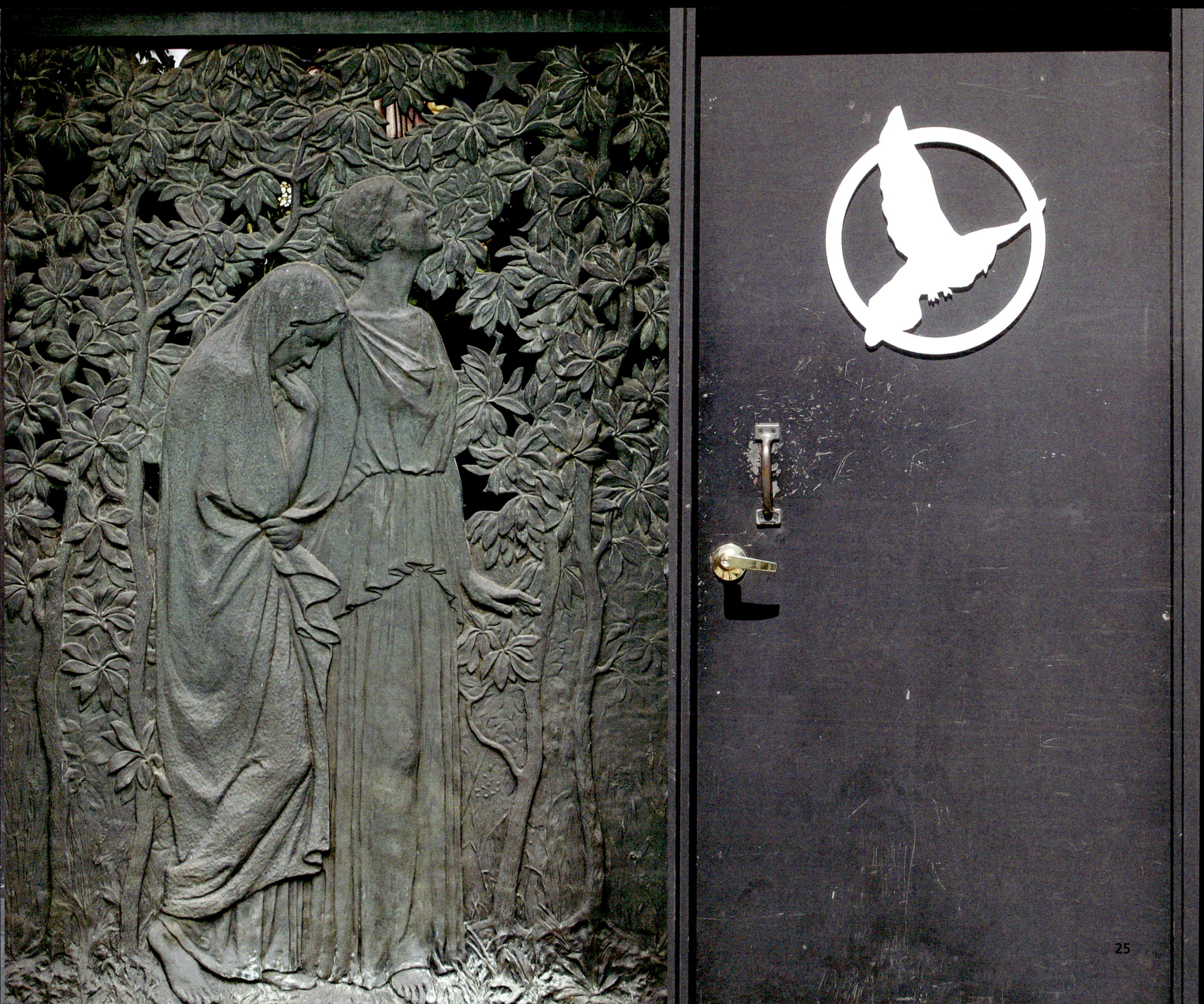

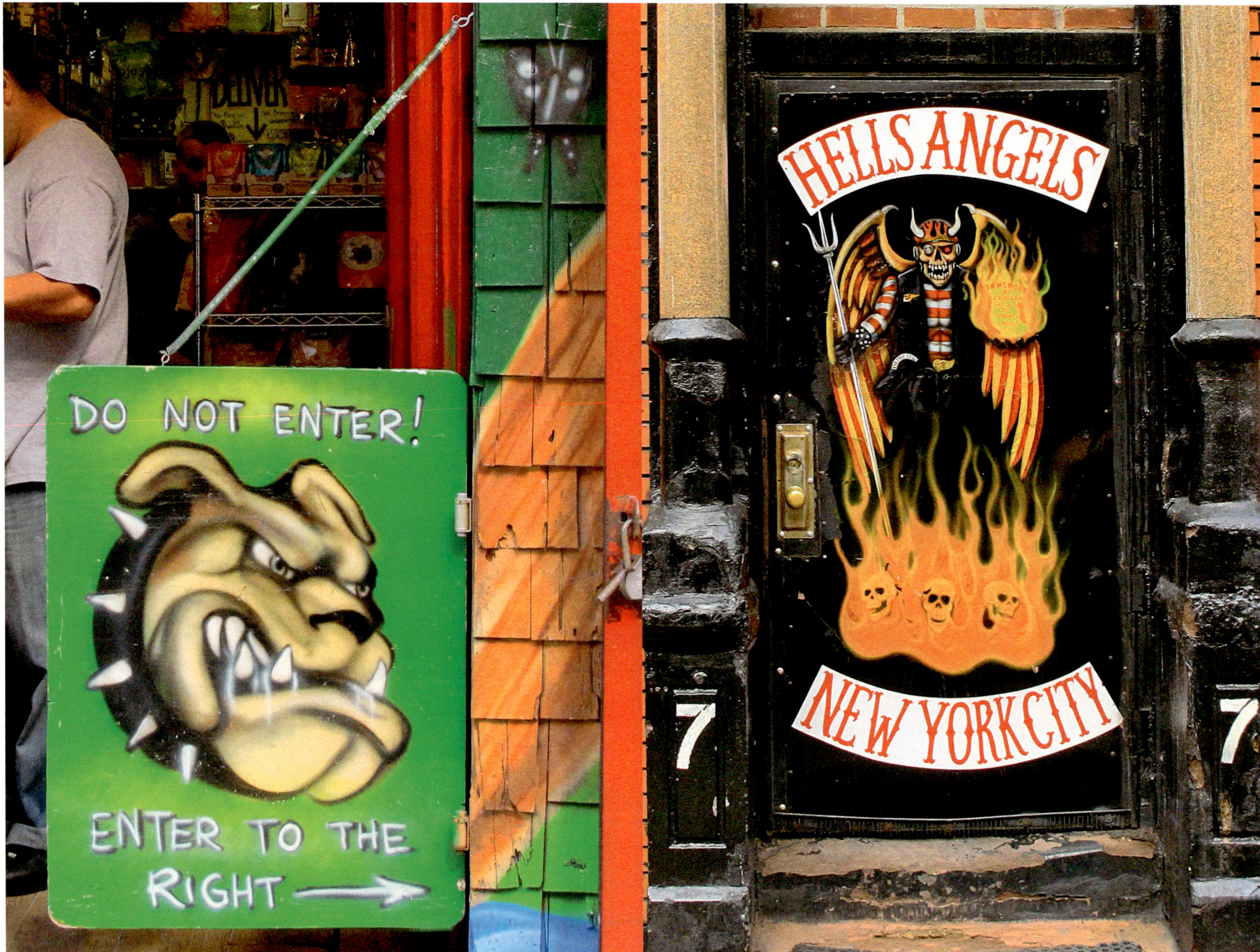
DO NOT ENTER!
ENTER TO THE RIGHT
HELLS ANGELS
NEW YORK CITY
7
7

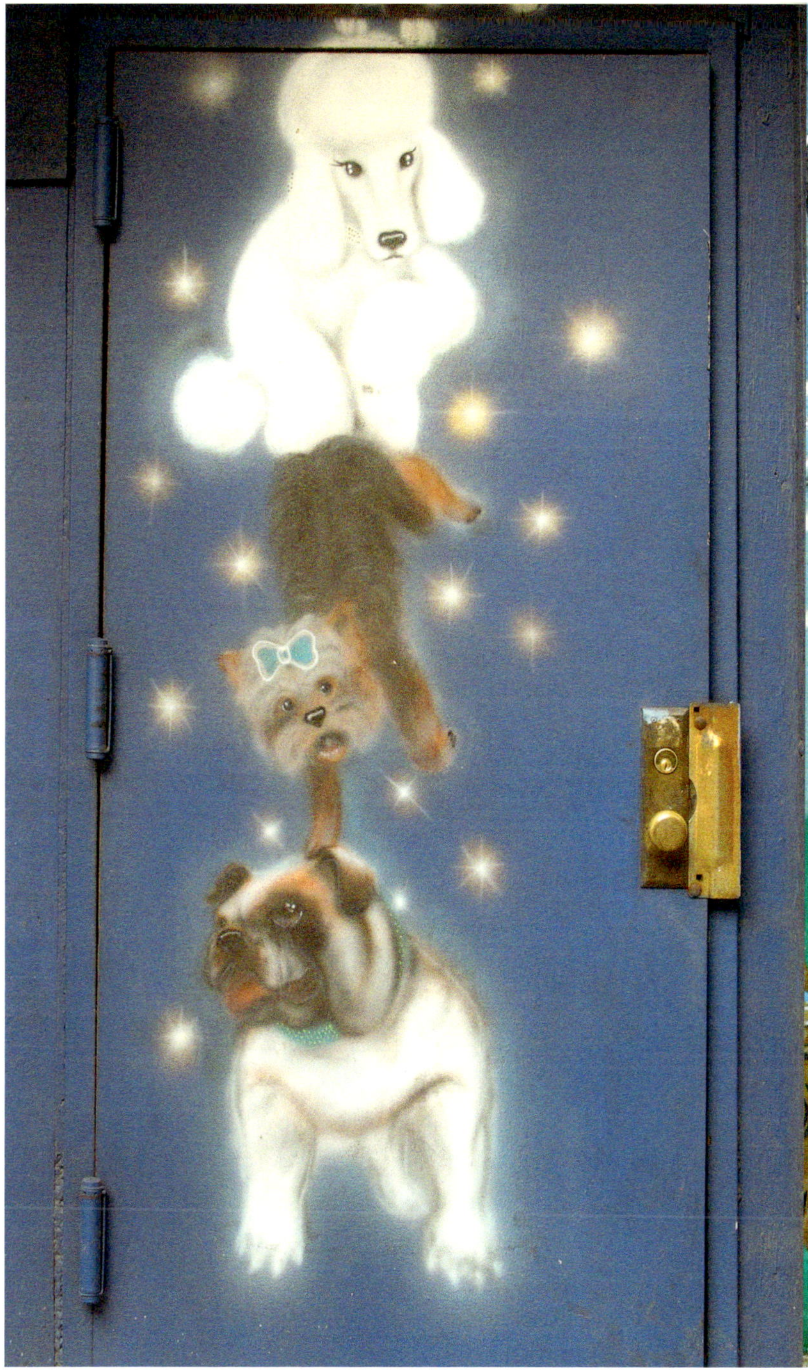

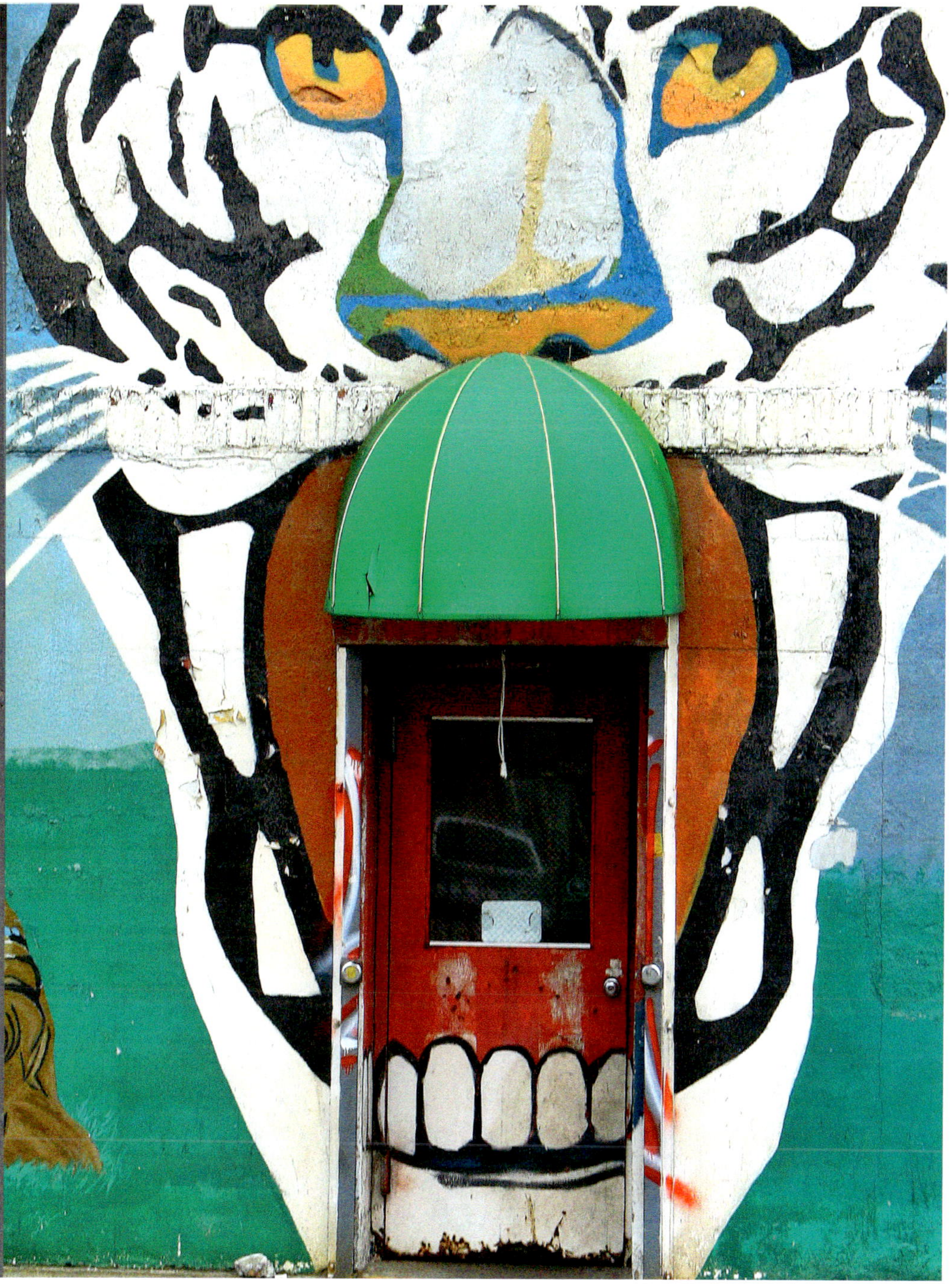

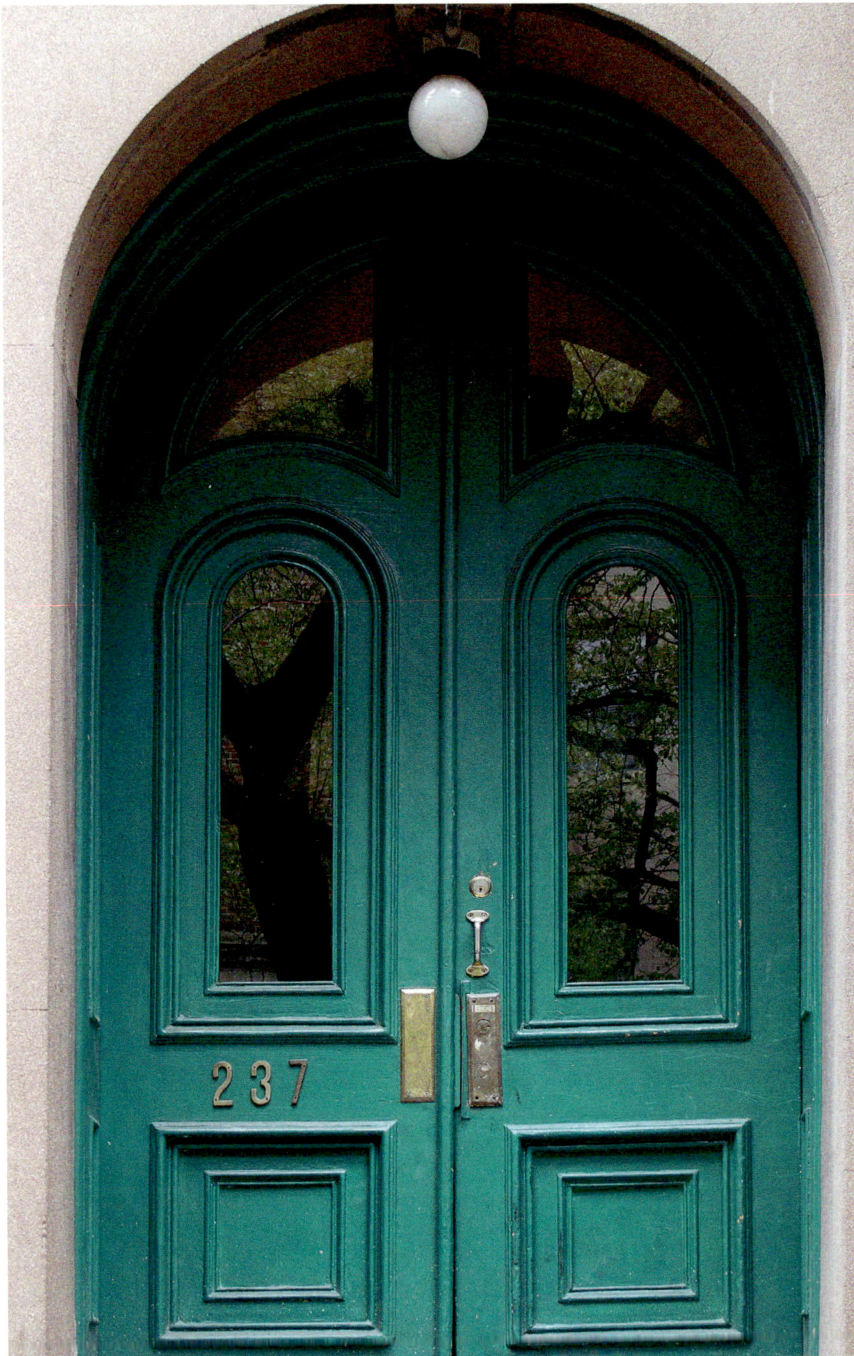
237
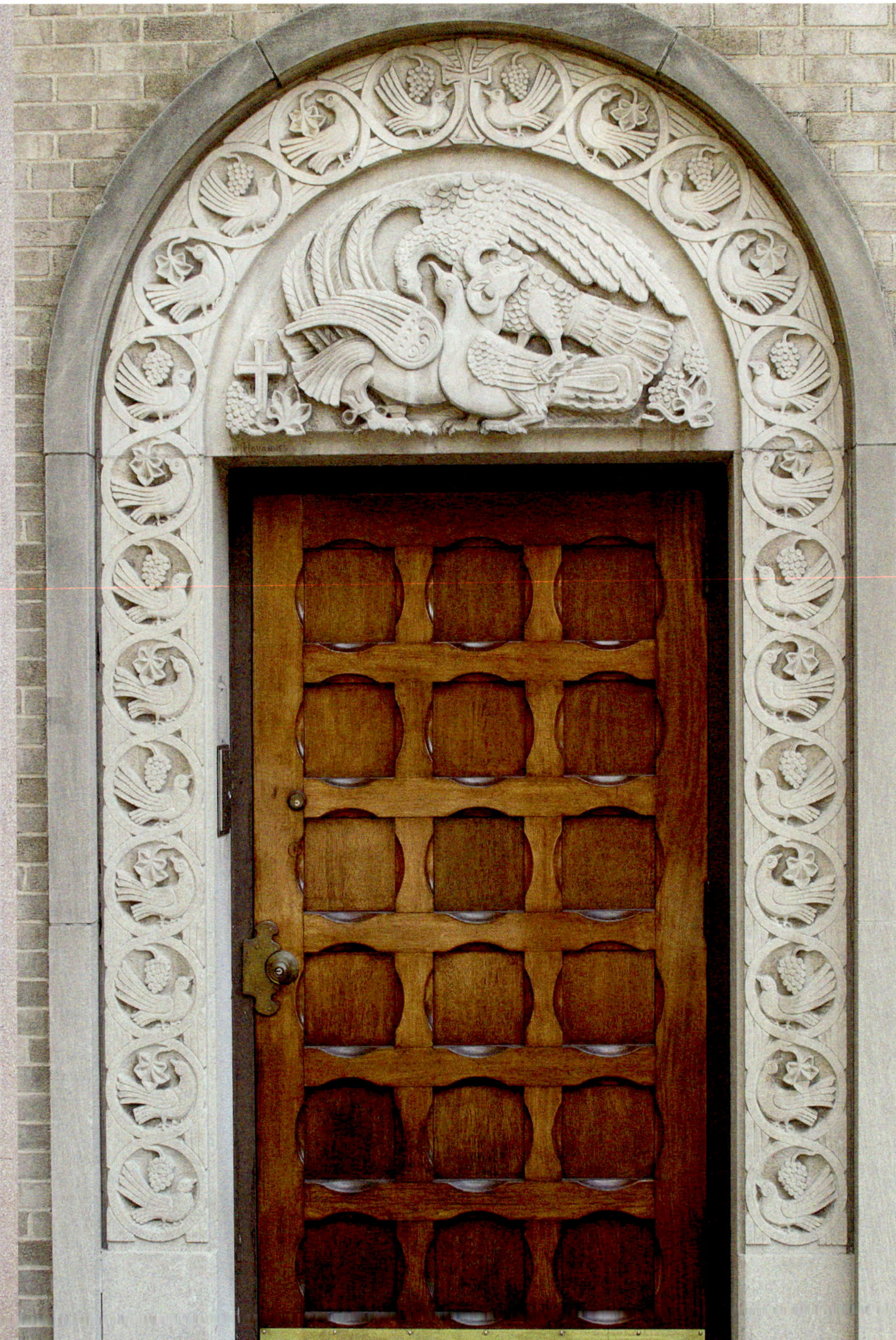

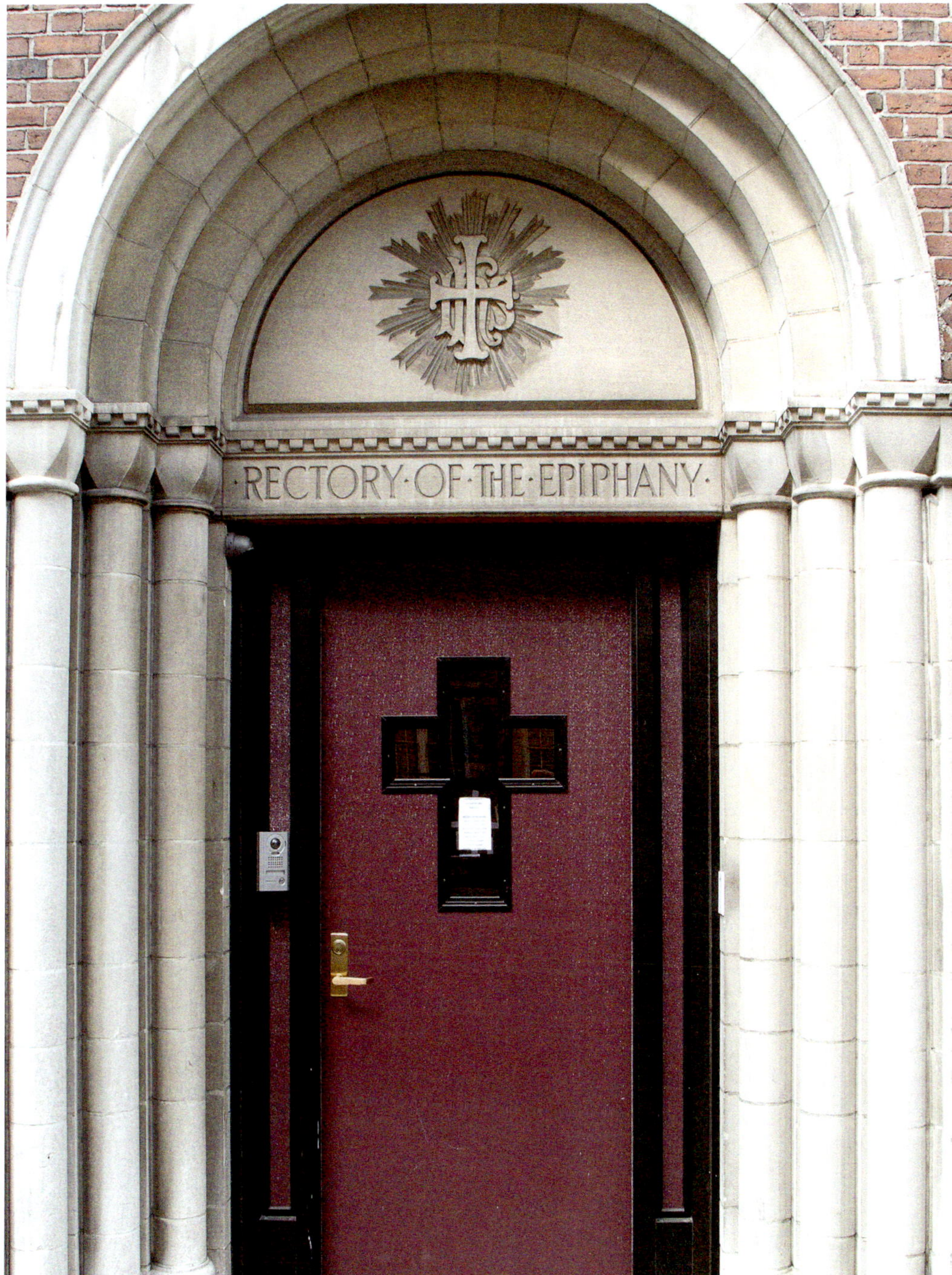
·RECTORY·OF·THE·EPIPHANY·

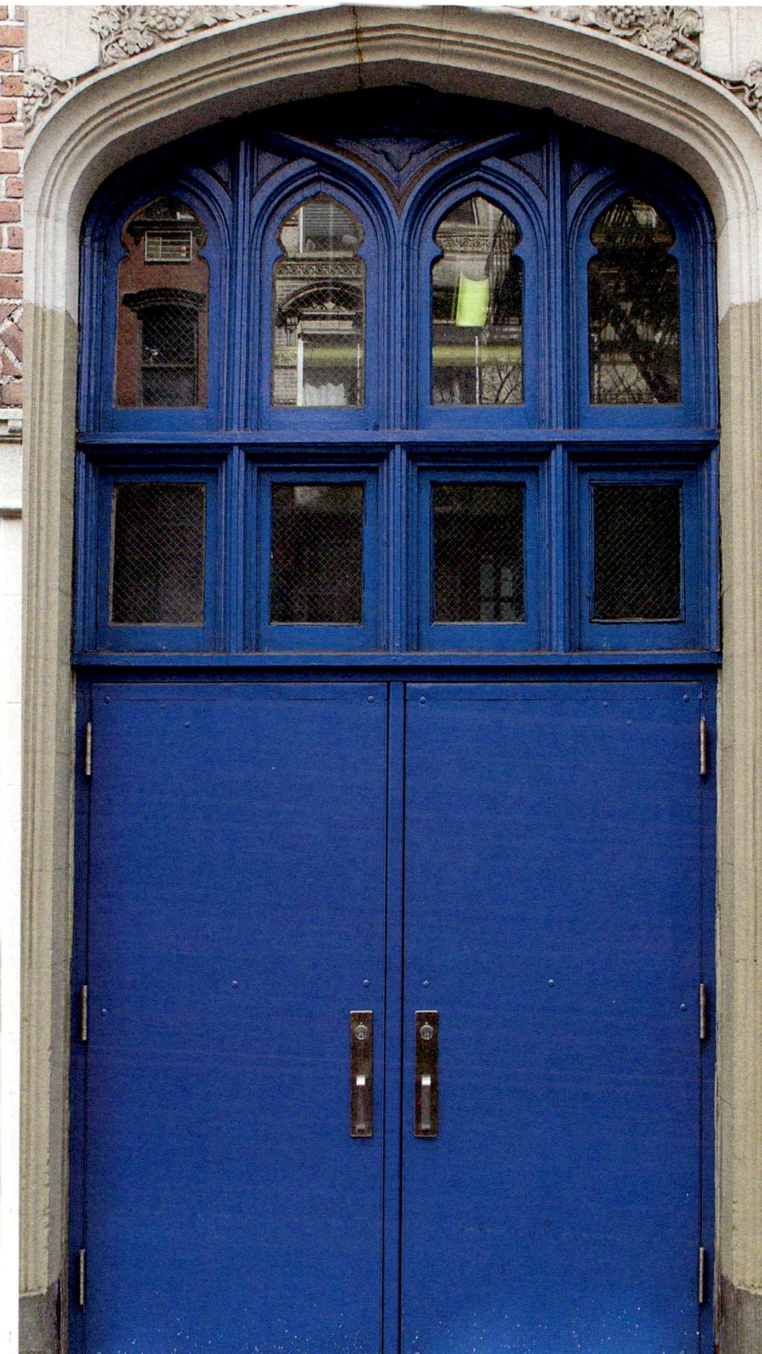

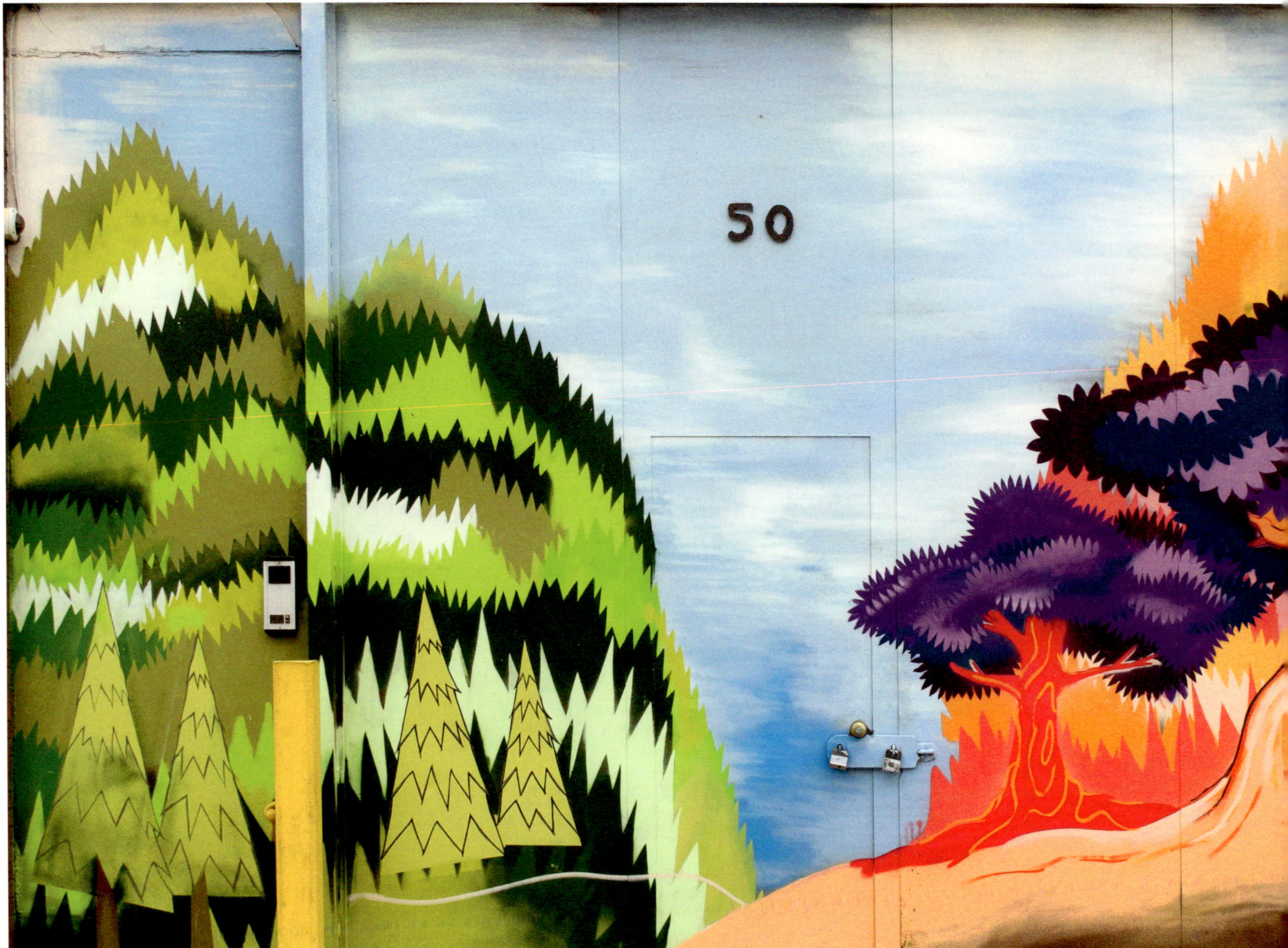
50

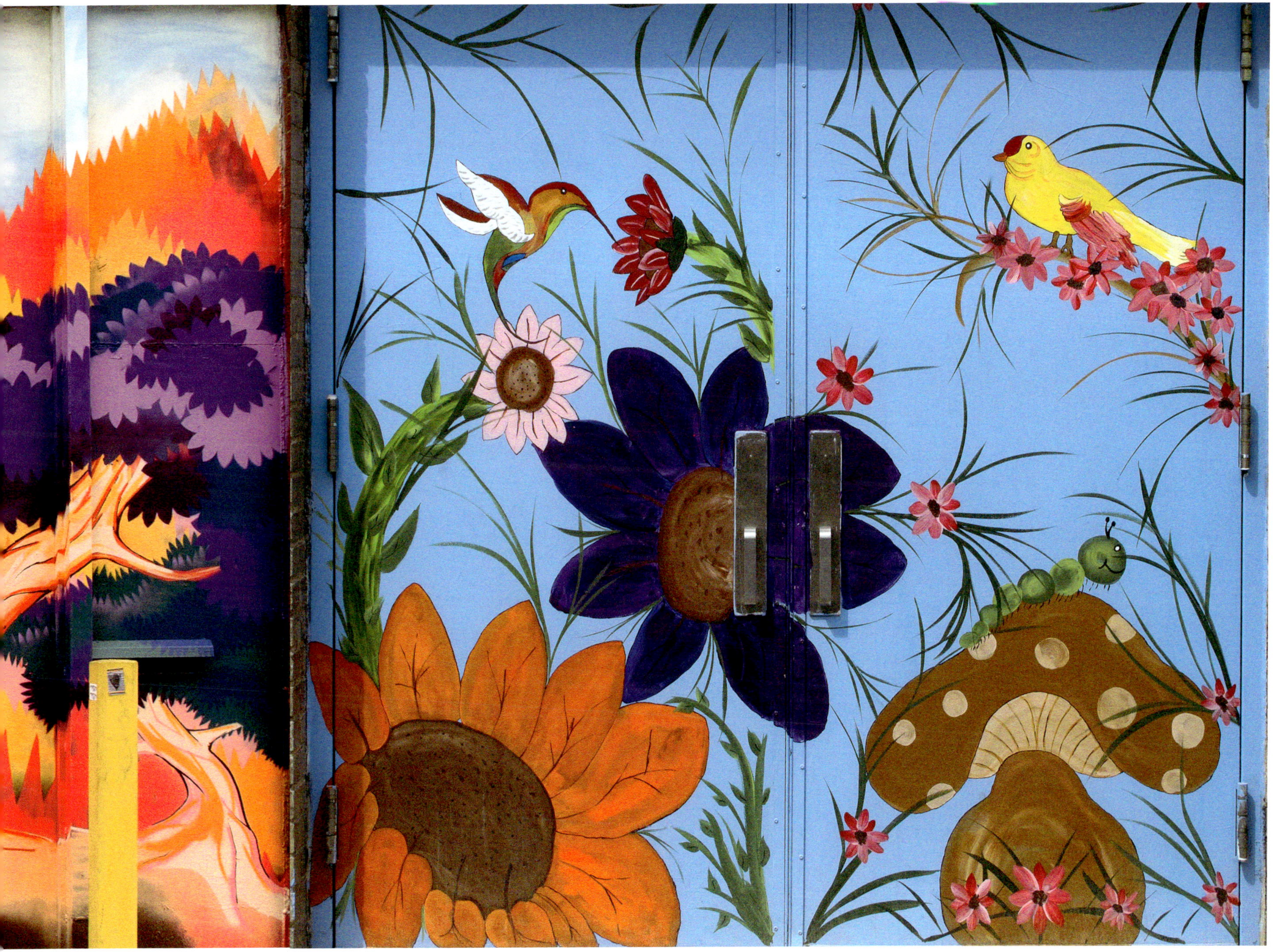

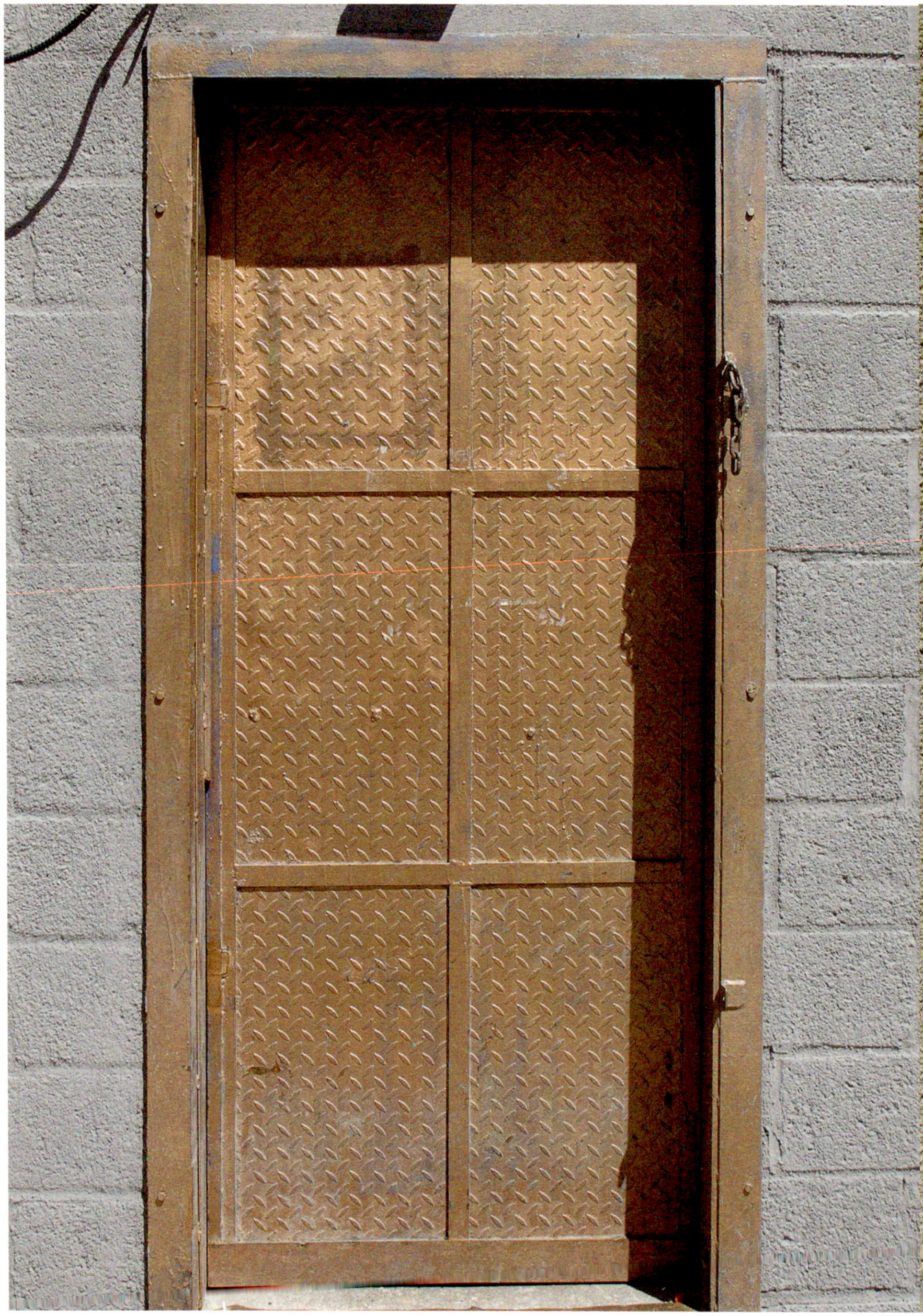

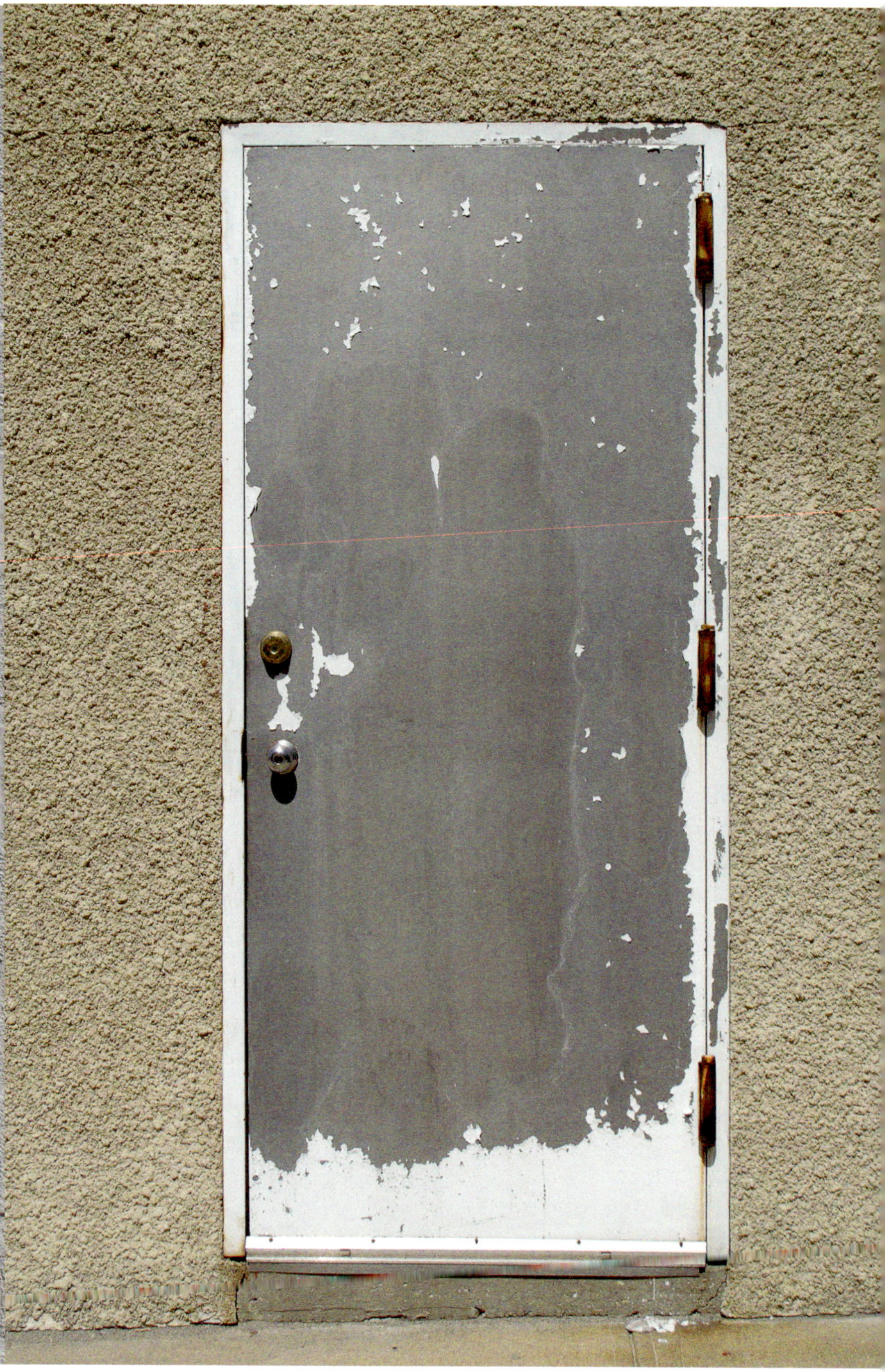

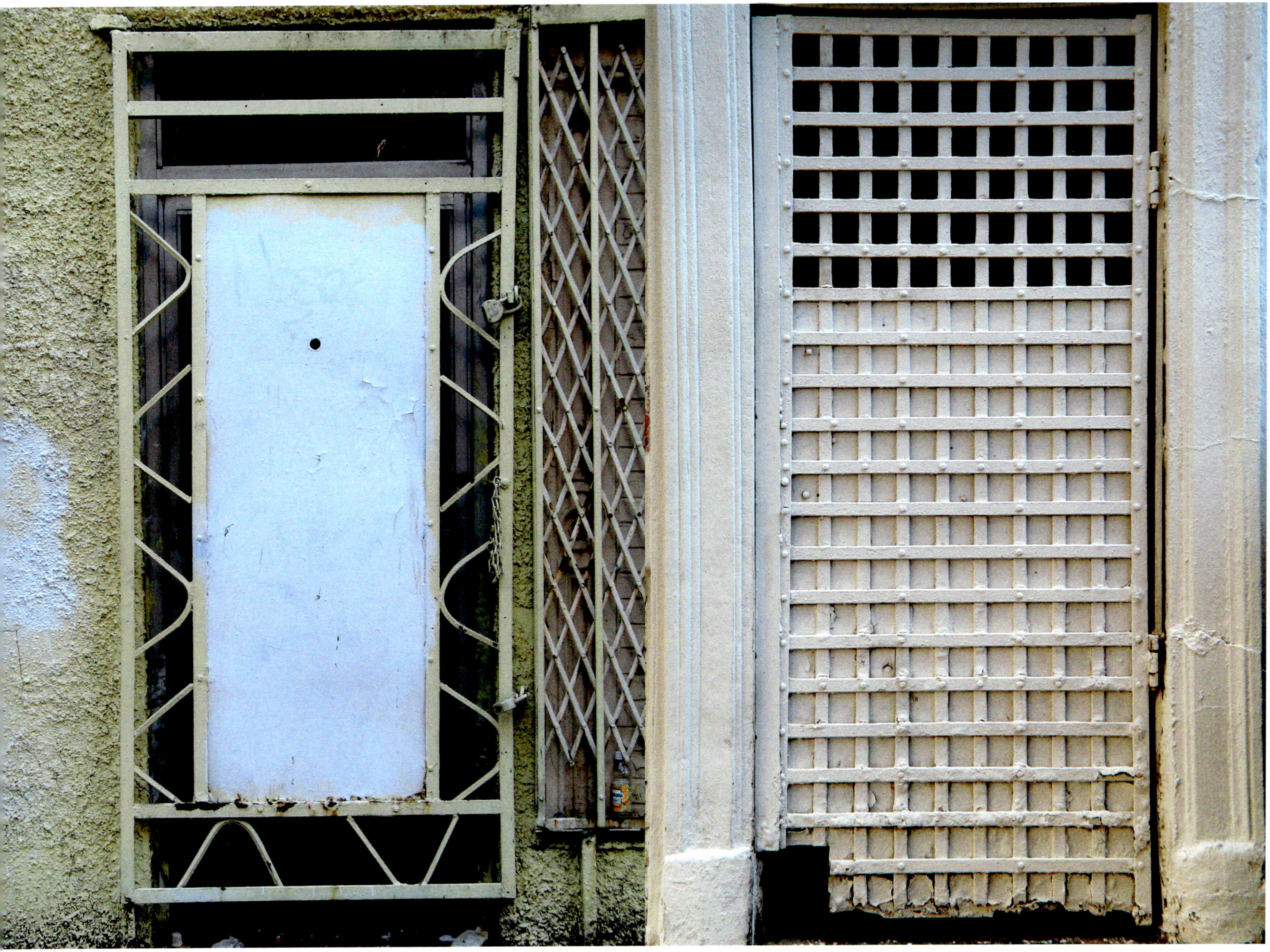

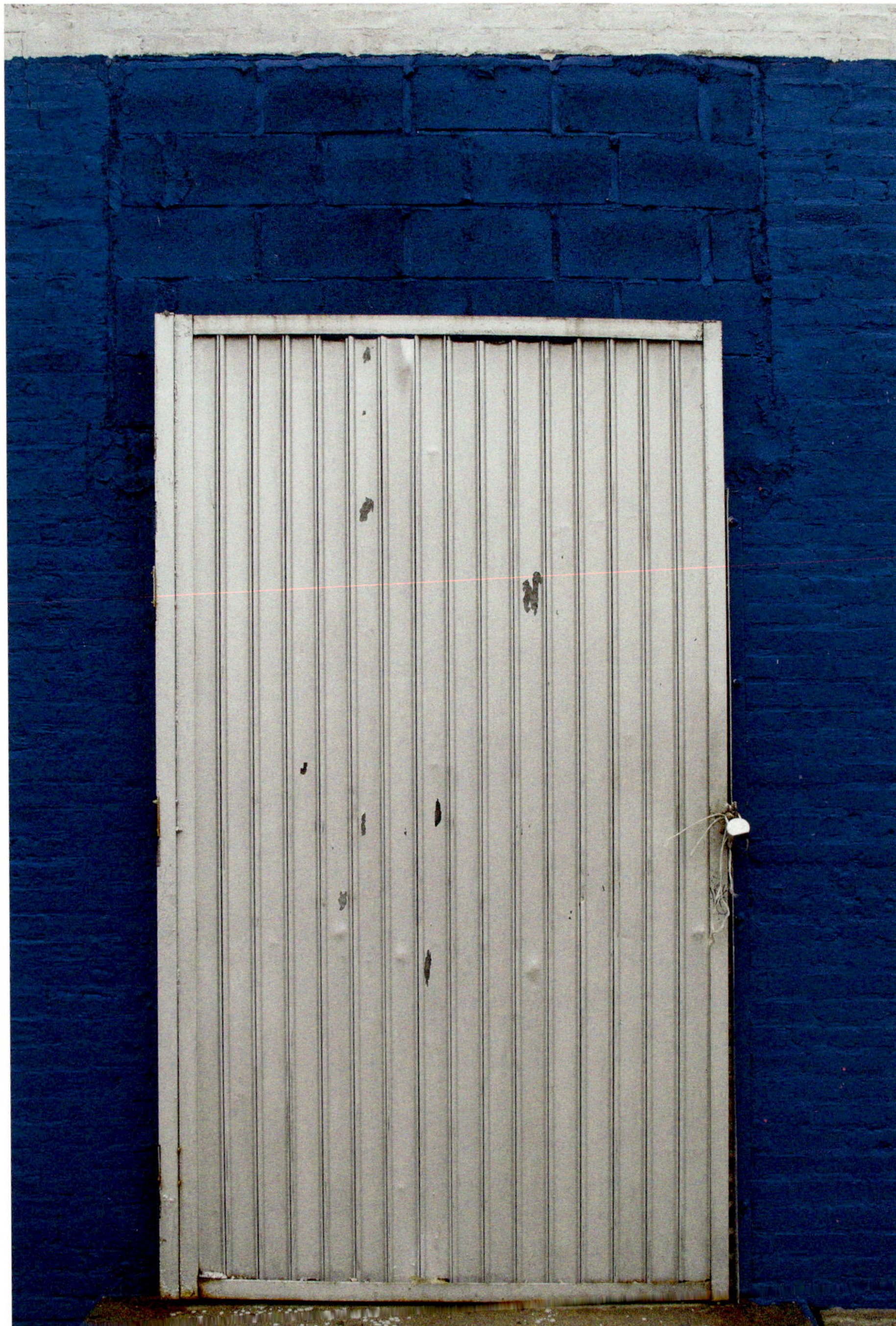

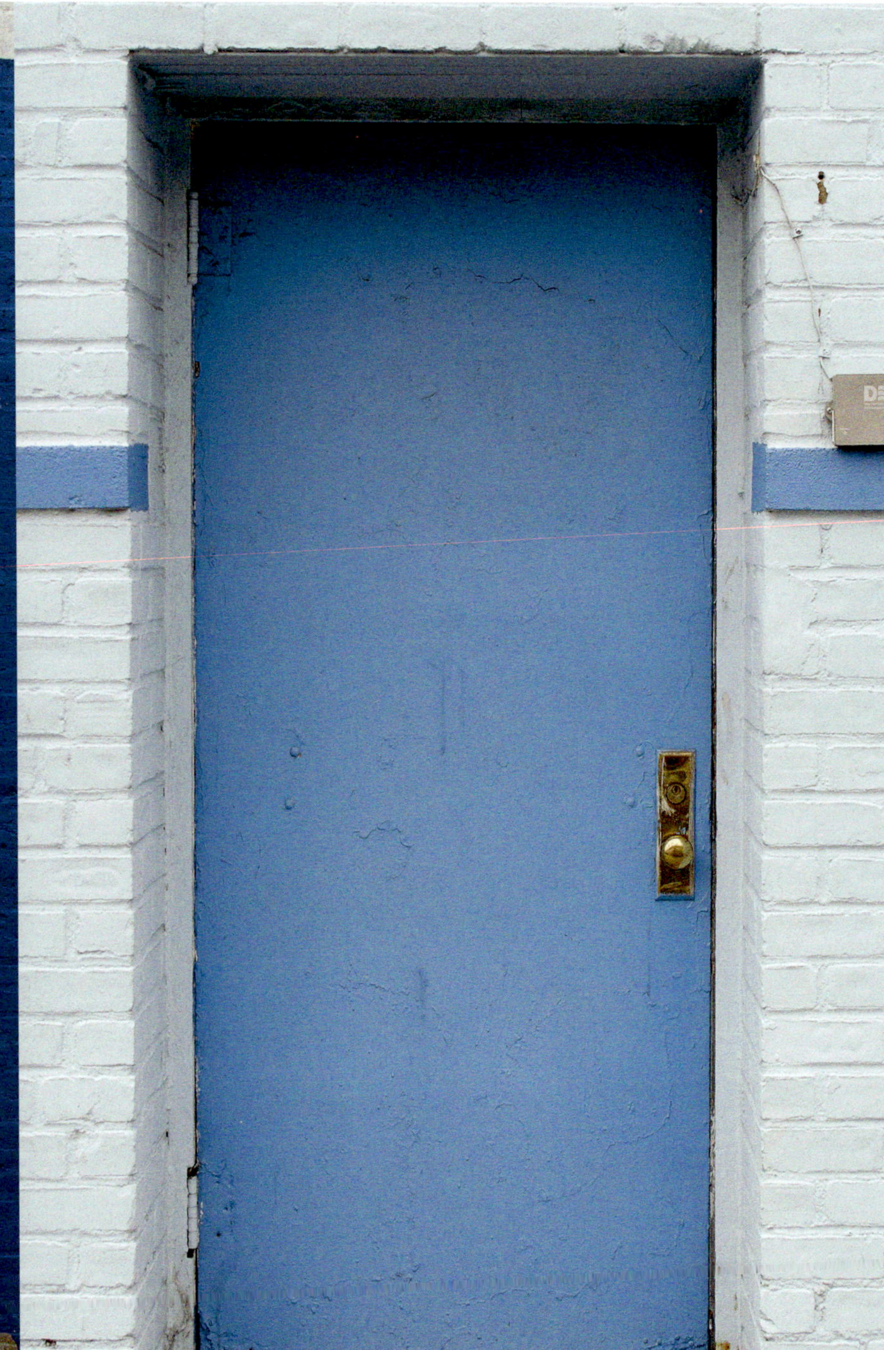

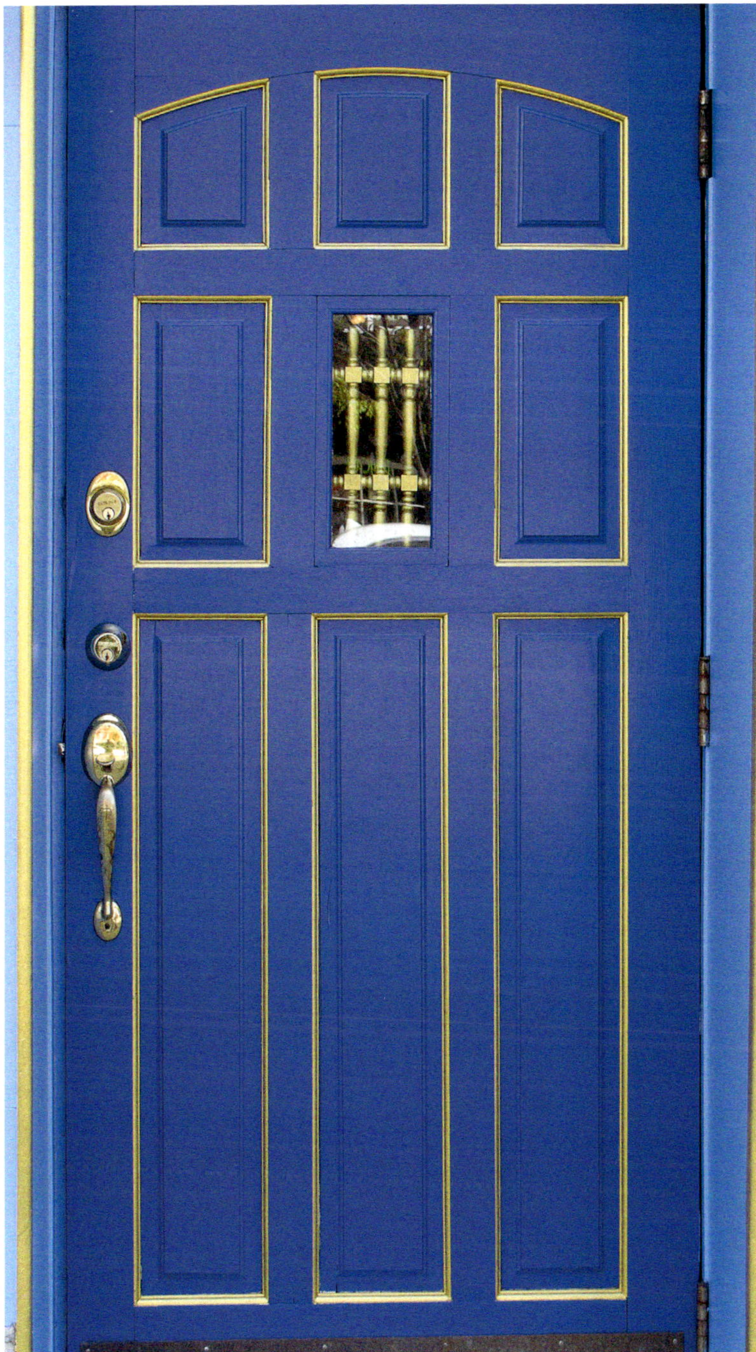

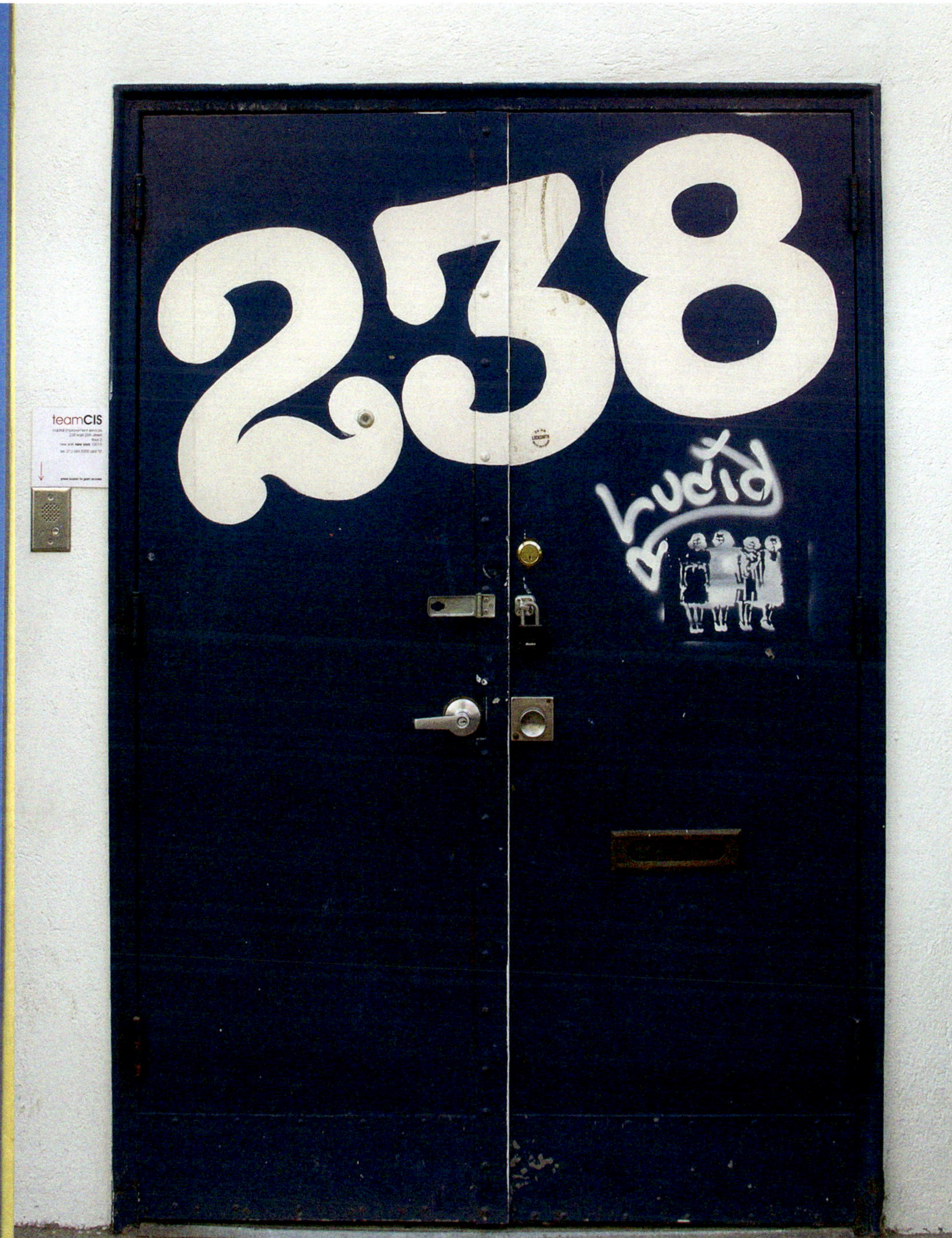
teamCIS
238

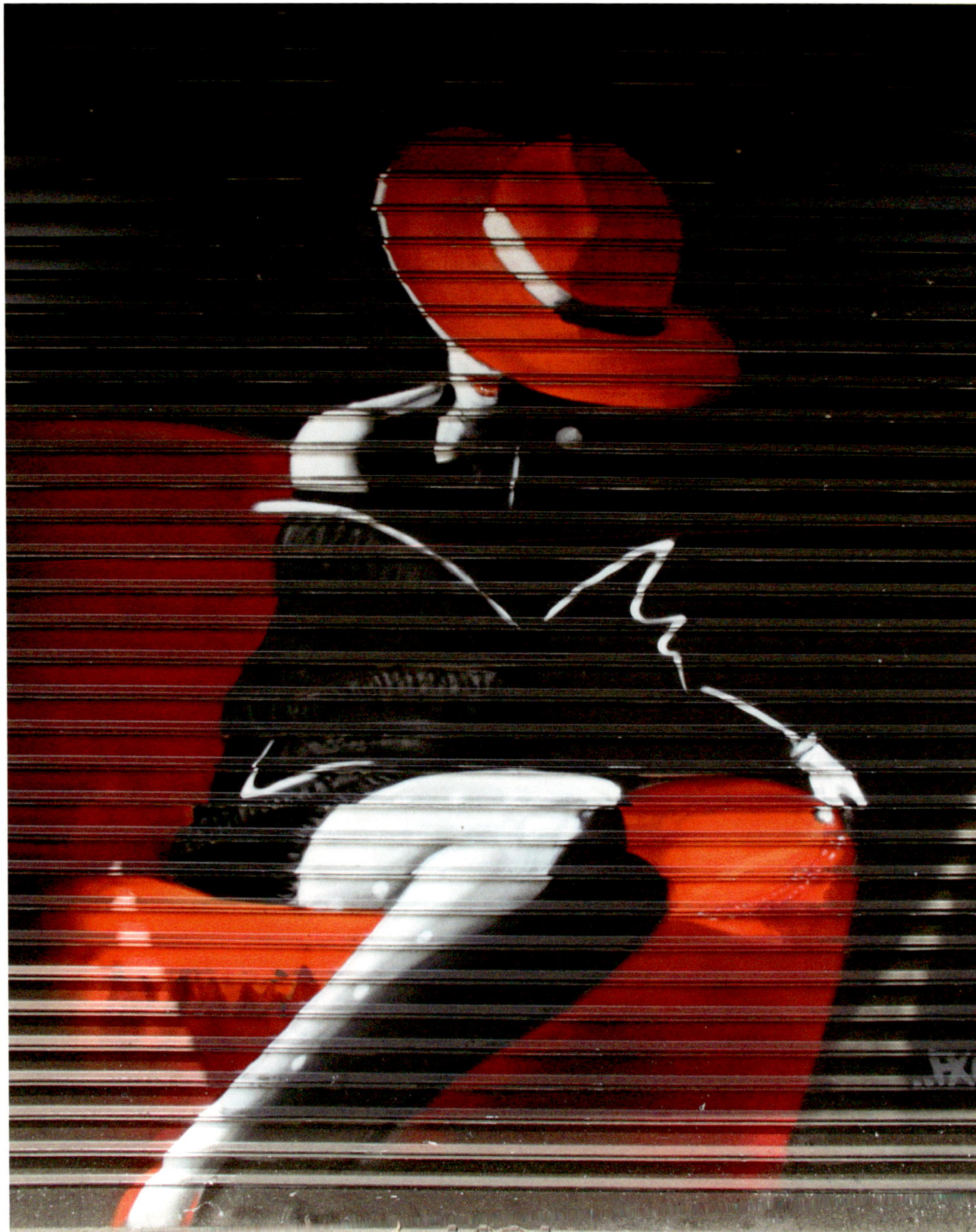

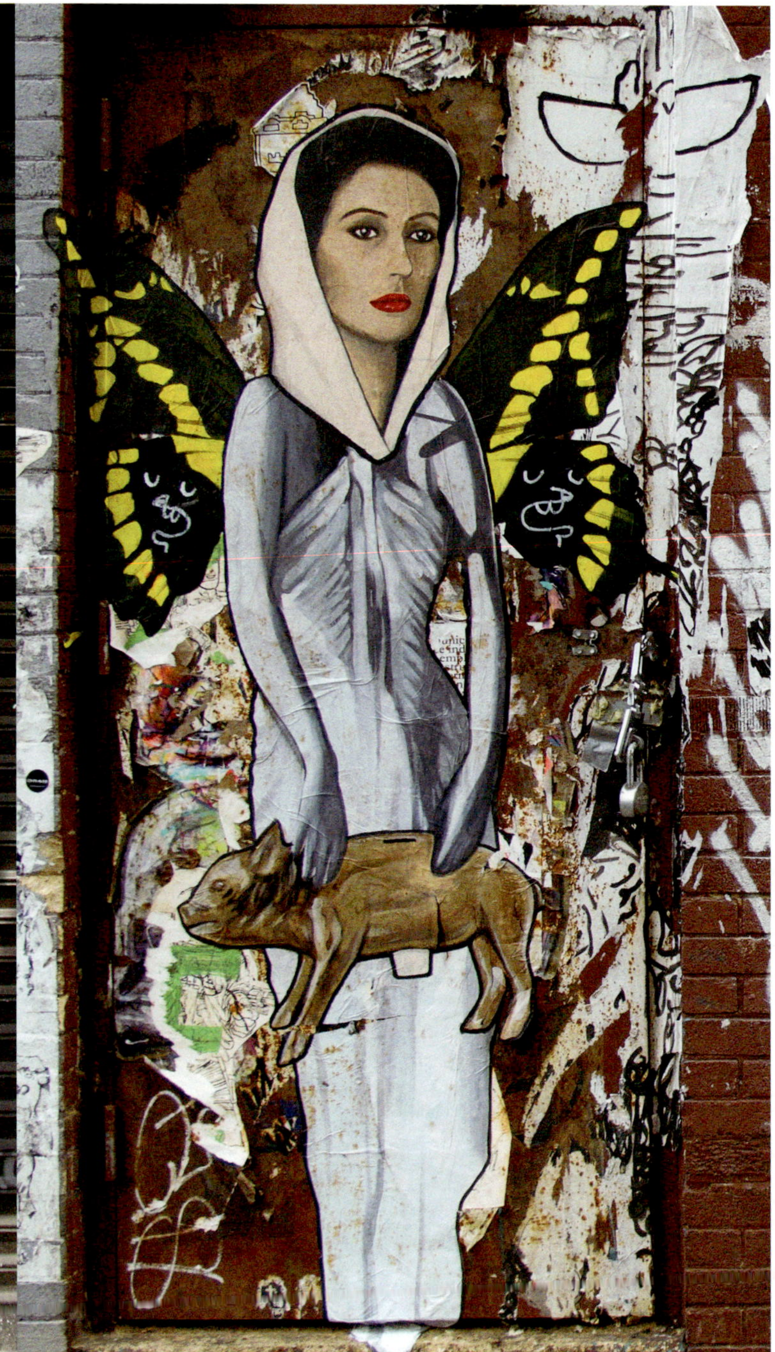

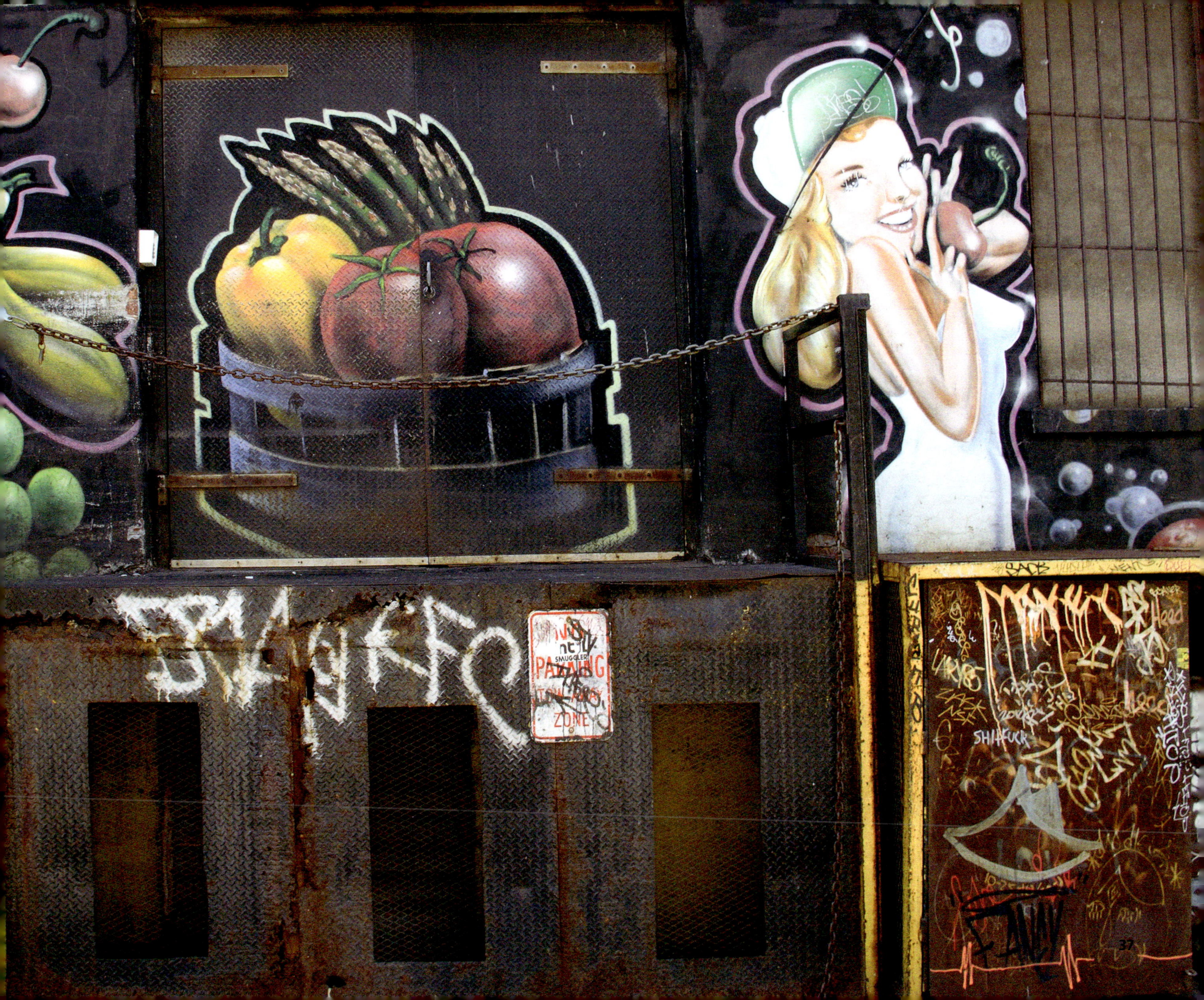
PARKING
ZONE

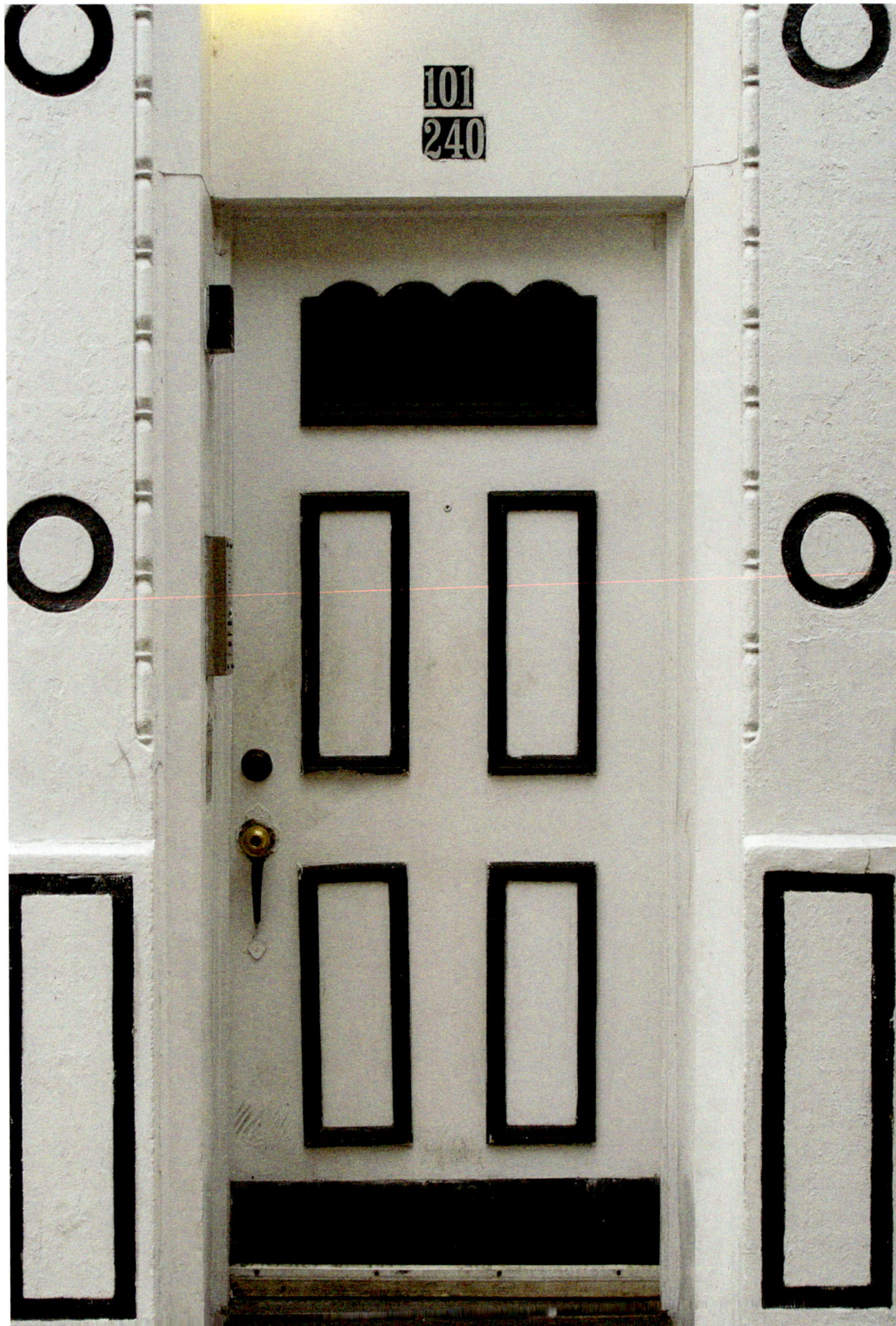
101
240

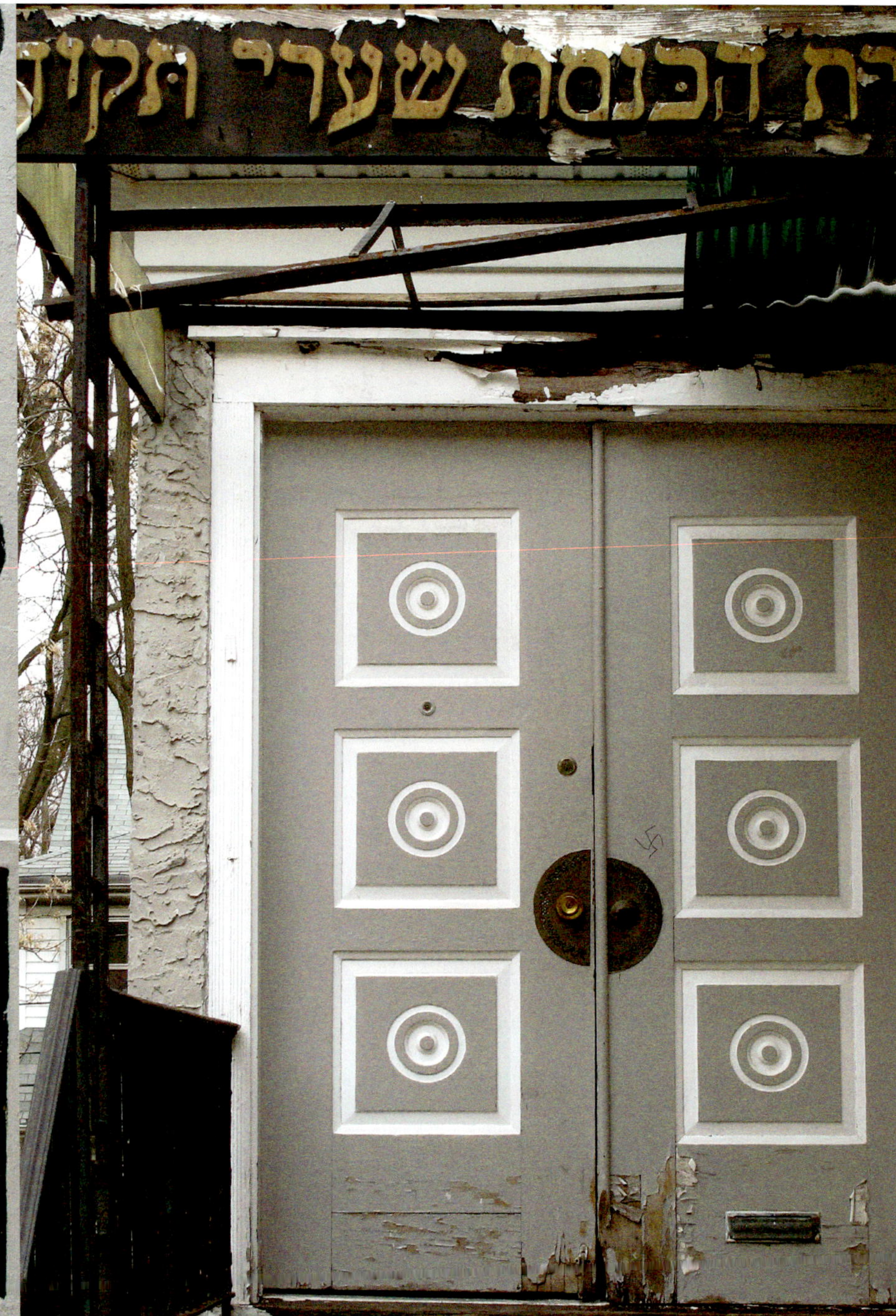
הכנסת שערי

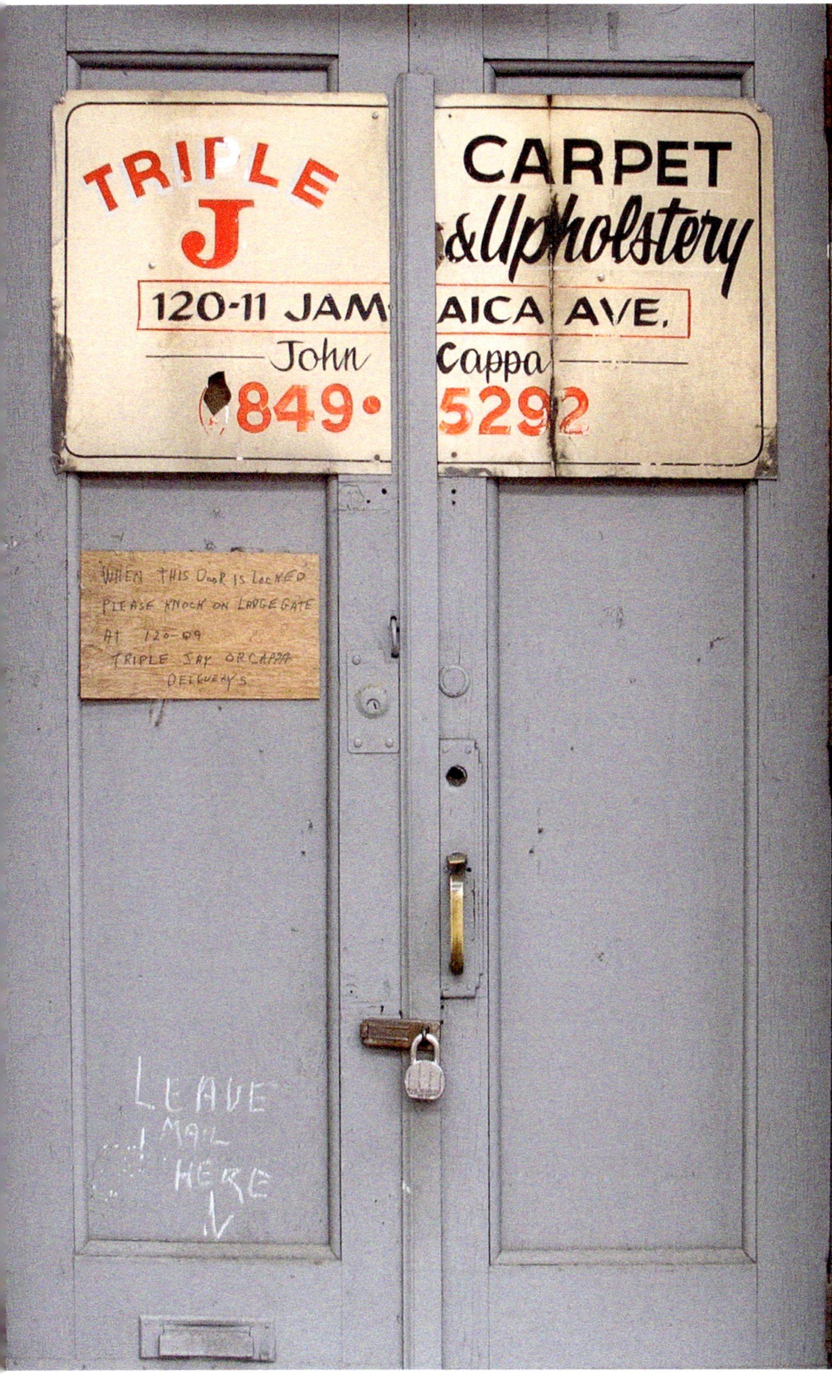
TRIPLE
J
CARPET
&Upholstery
120-11 JAMAICA AVE.
John Cappa
849-5292
WHEN THIS DOOR IS LOCKED
PLEASE KNOCK ON LARGE GATE
AT 120-09
TRIPLE JAY OR CAPPA
DELIVERYS
LEAVE
MAIL
HERE

UPHOLSTERY
OF
FURNITURE
tel. 441-1818

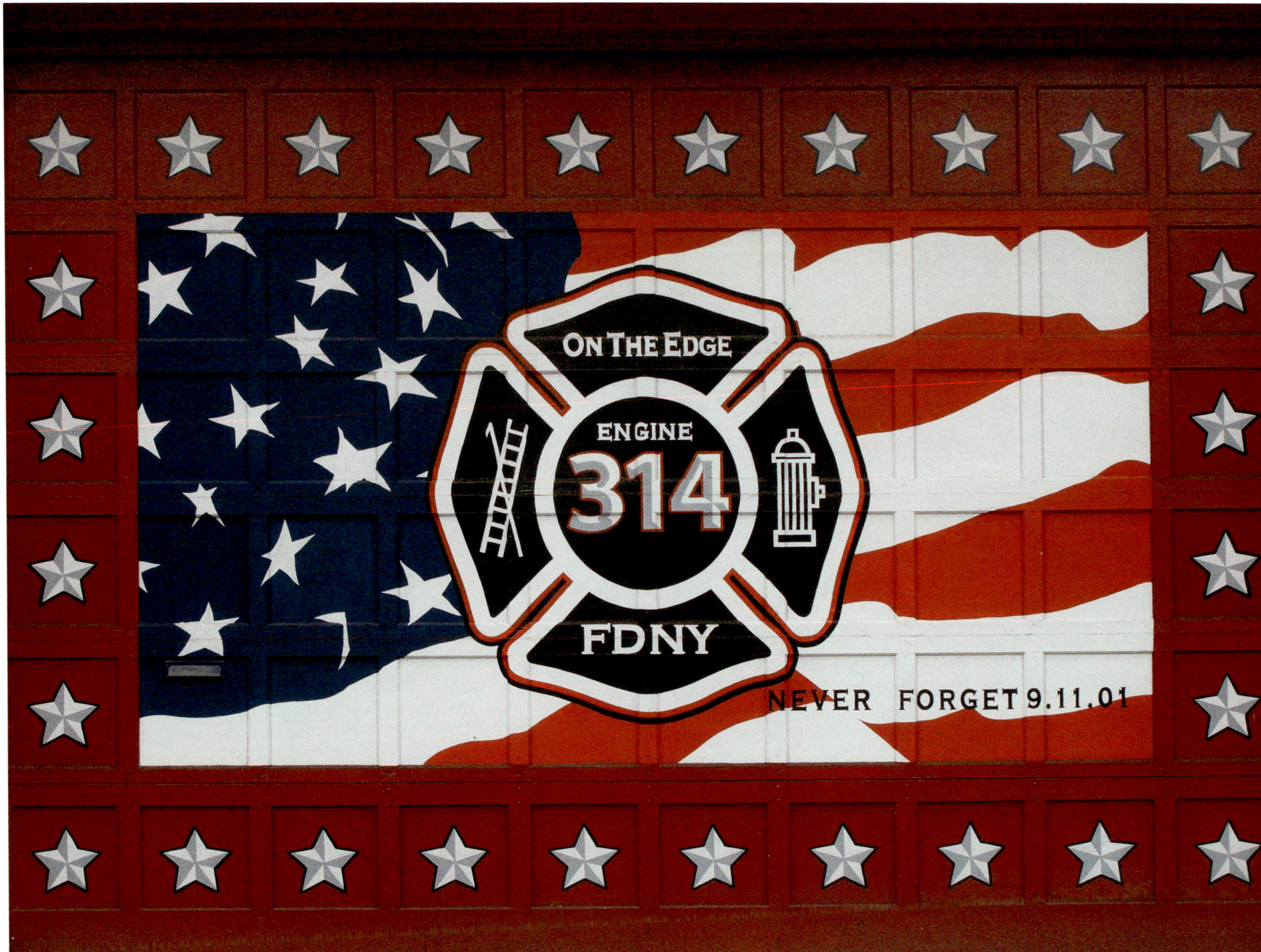
ON THE EDGE
ENGINE
314
FDNY
NEVER FORGET 9.11.01

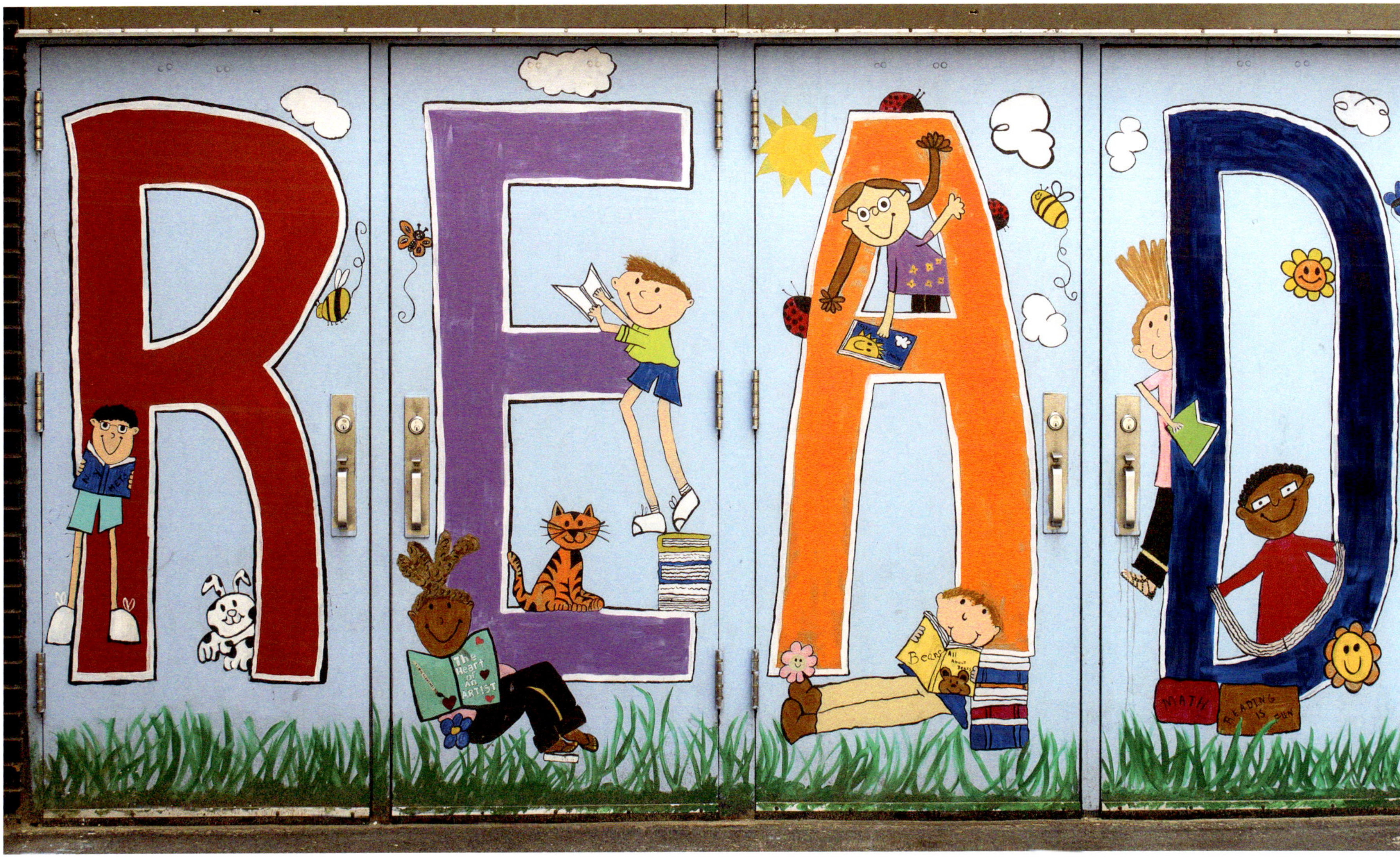
READ
The Heart of an ARTIST
Bears
All About Bears
MATH
READING IS FUN

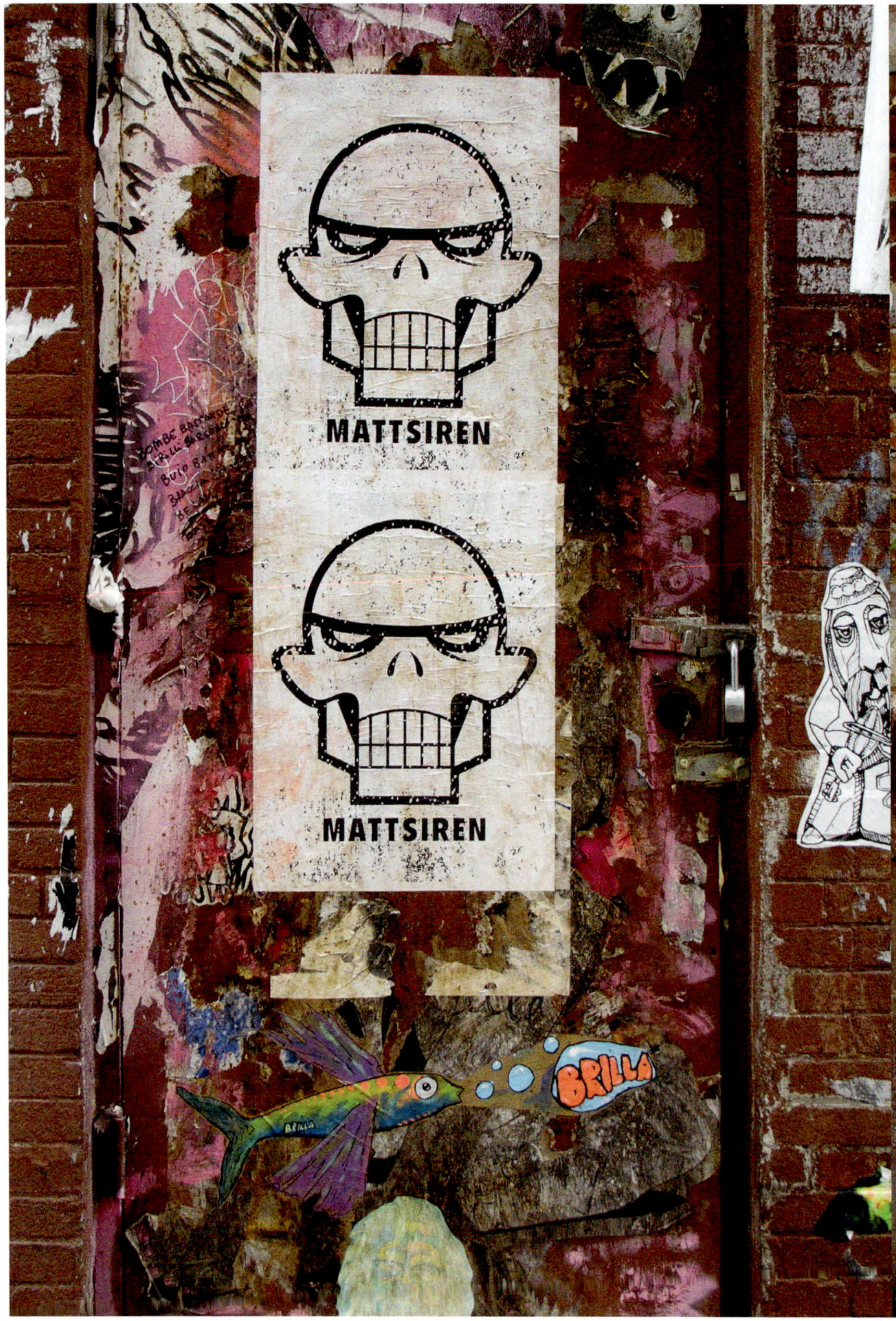
MATTSIREN
MATTSIREN
BRILLA

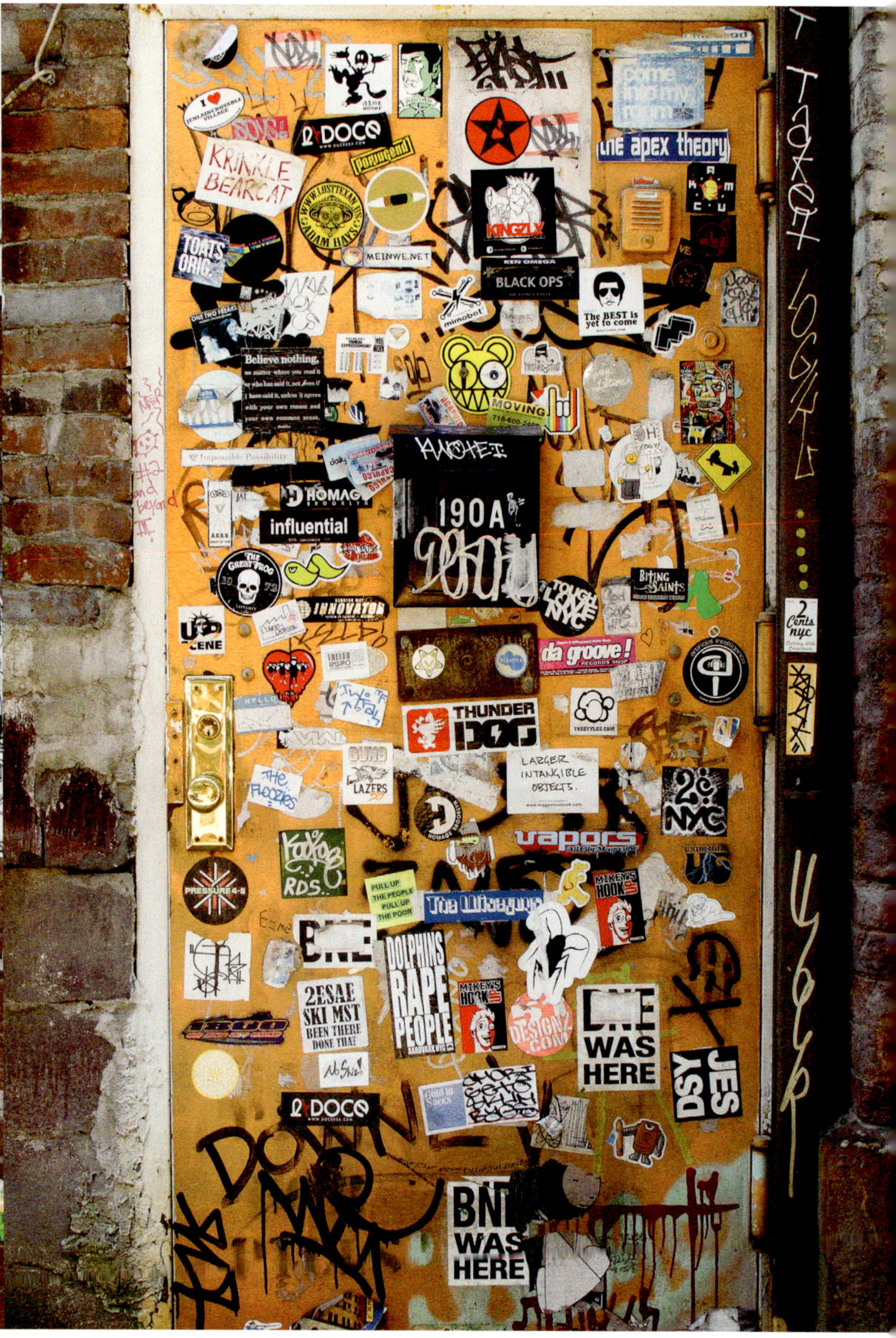
KRINKLE BEARCAT
the apex theory
MEINWE.NET
BLACK OPS
The BEST is yet to come
influential
190A
INNOVATOR
da groove!
THUNDER DOG
LARGER INTANGIBLE OBJECTS.
vapors
2¢ NYC
PULL UP THE PEOPLE PULL UP THE POOR
DOLPHINS RAPE PEOPLE
2ESAE SKI MST BEEN THERE DONE THAT
WAS HERE
BNE WAS HERE

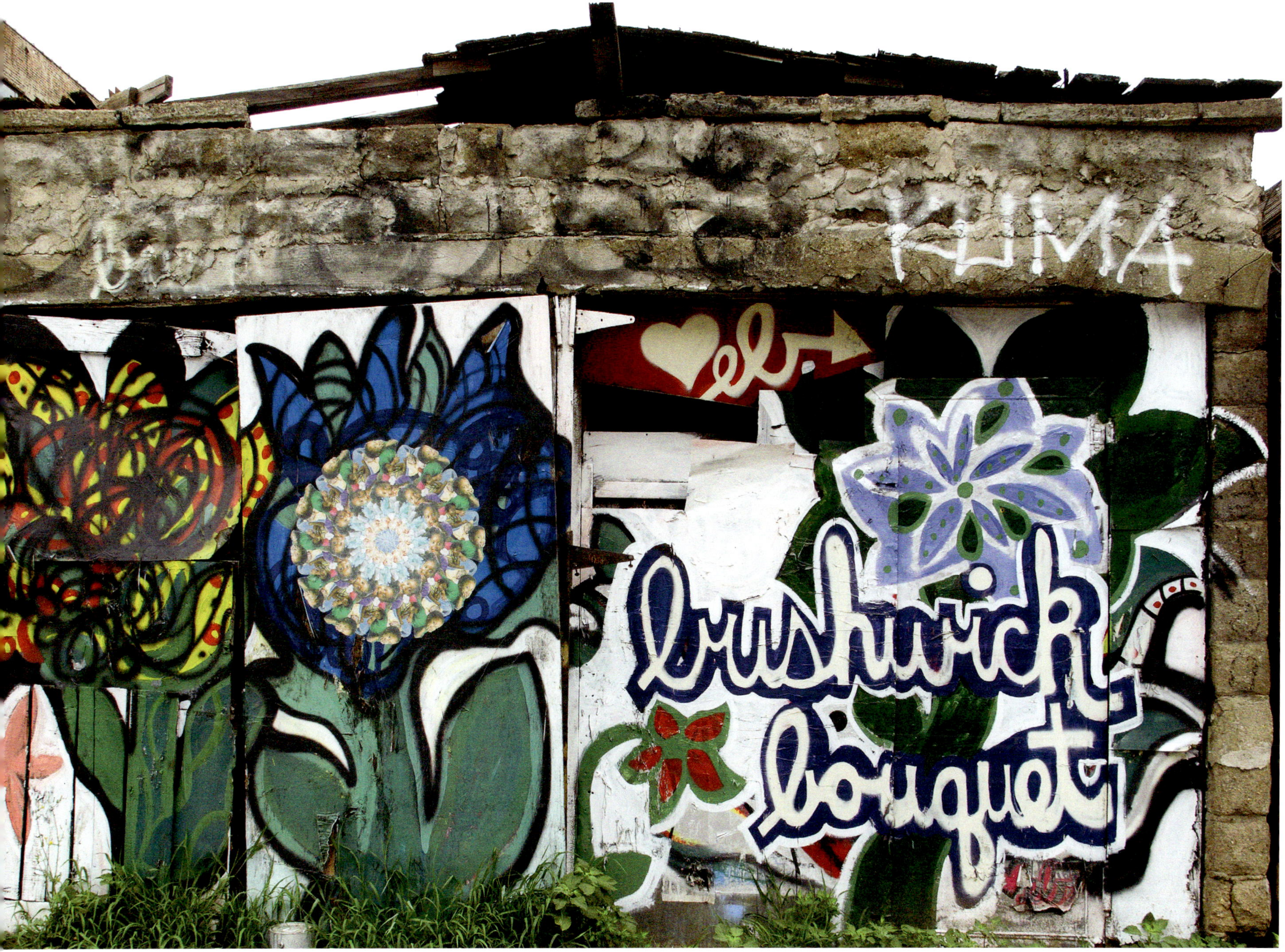
KUMA
bushwick
bouquet

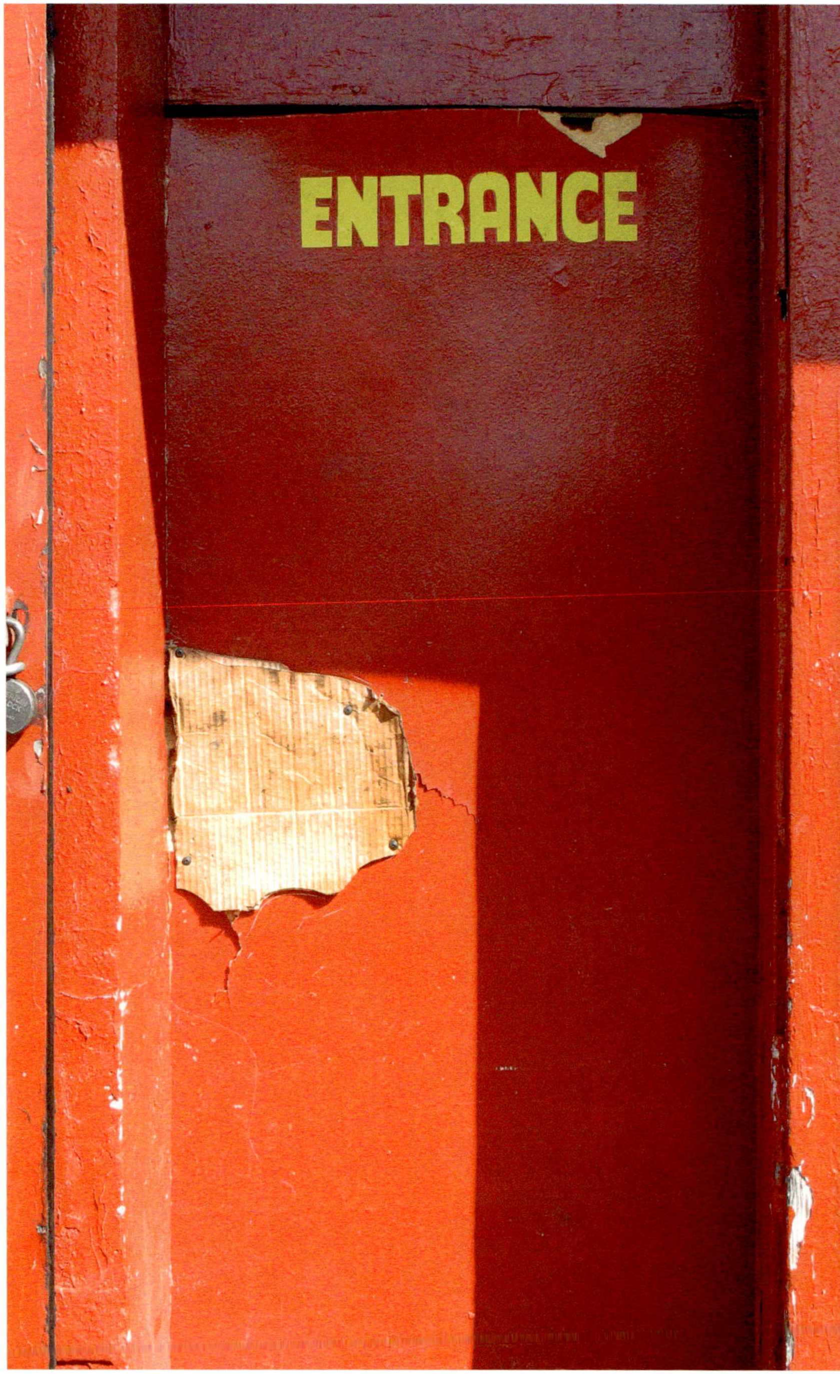
ENTRANCE

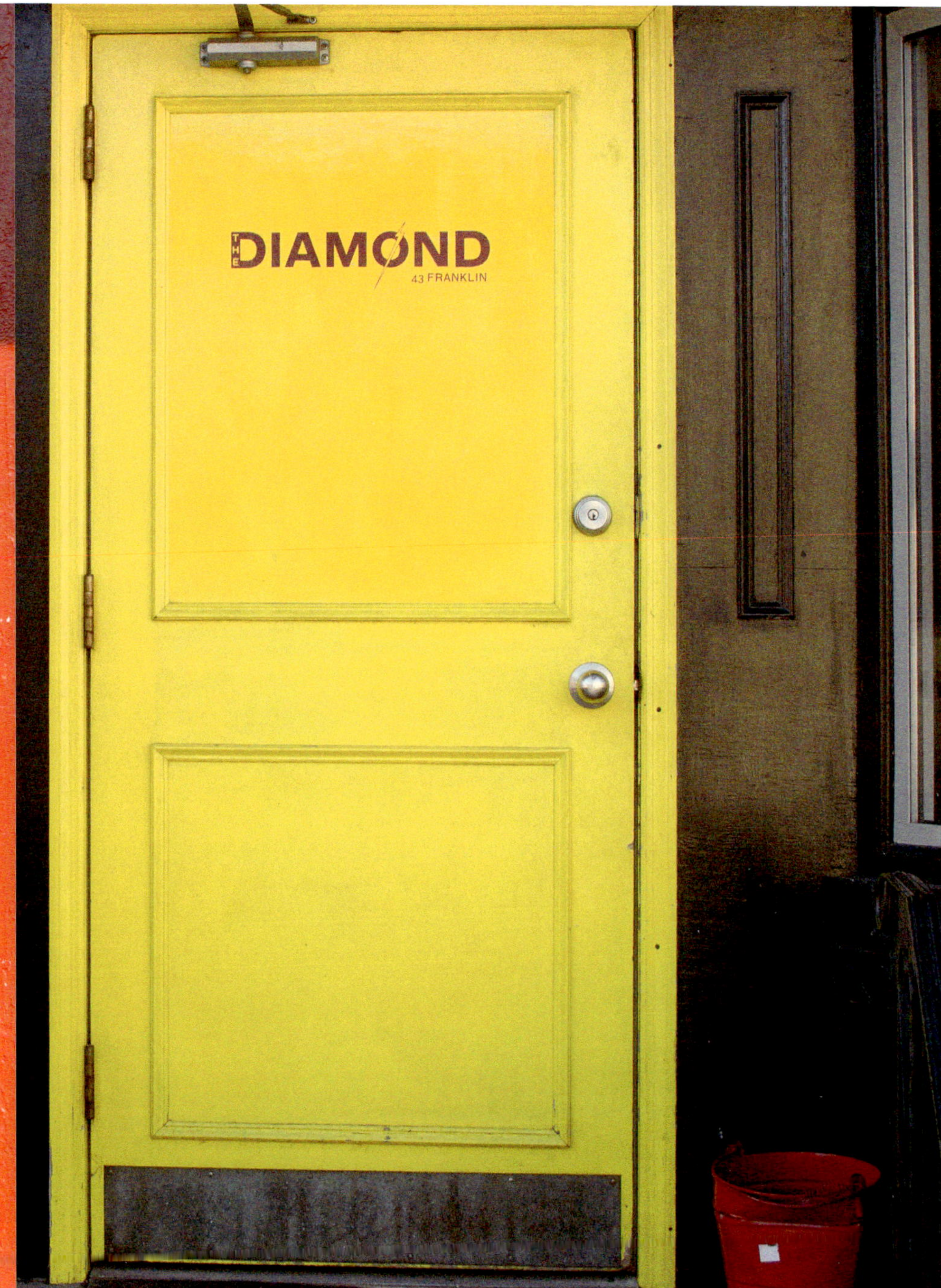
THE
DIAMOND
43 FRANKLIN

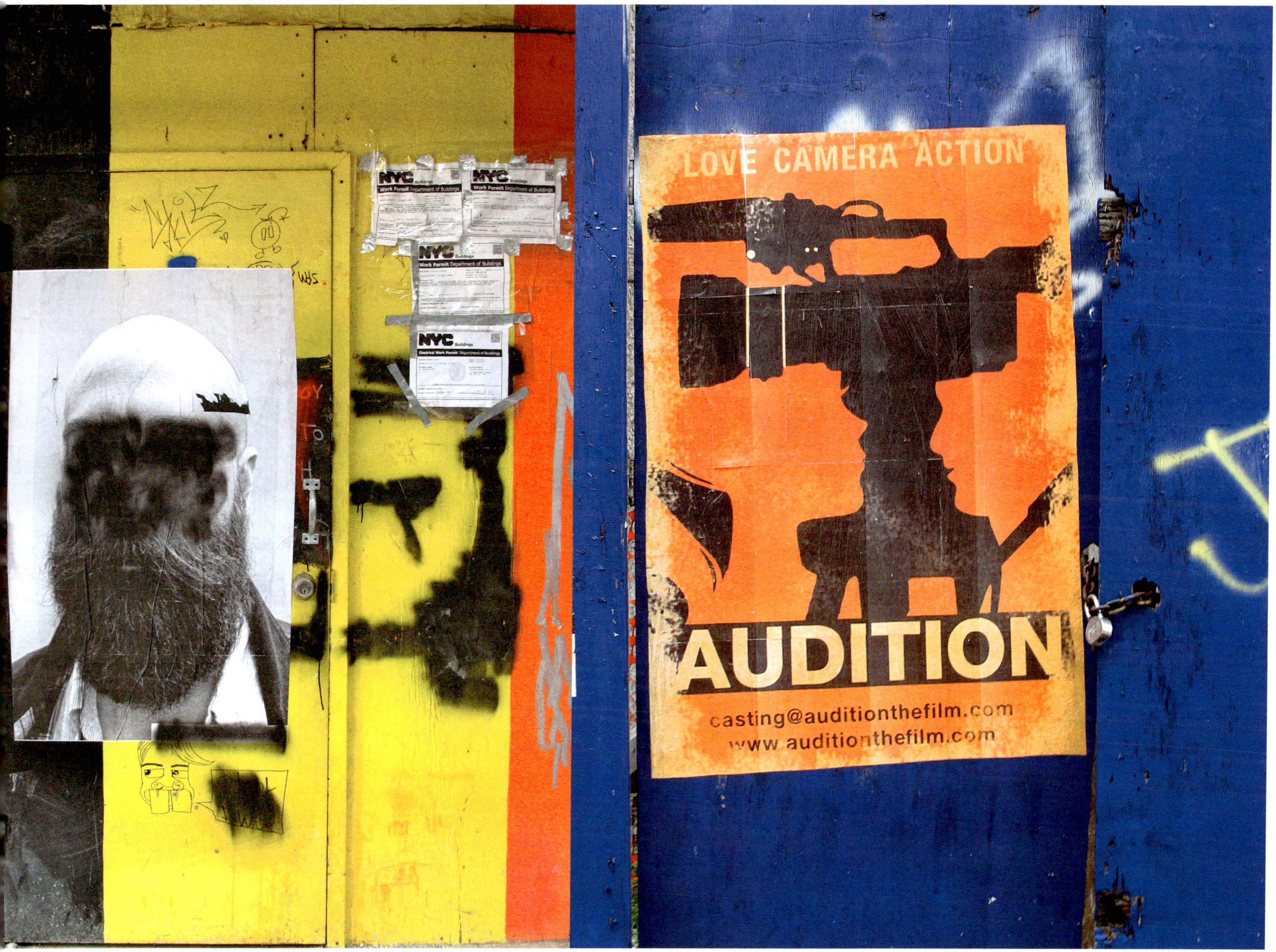
LOVE CAMERA ACTION
AUDITION
casting@auditionthefilm.com
www.auditionthefilm.com

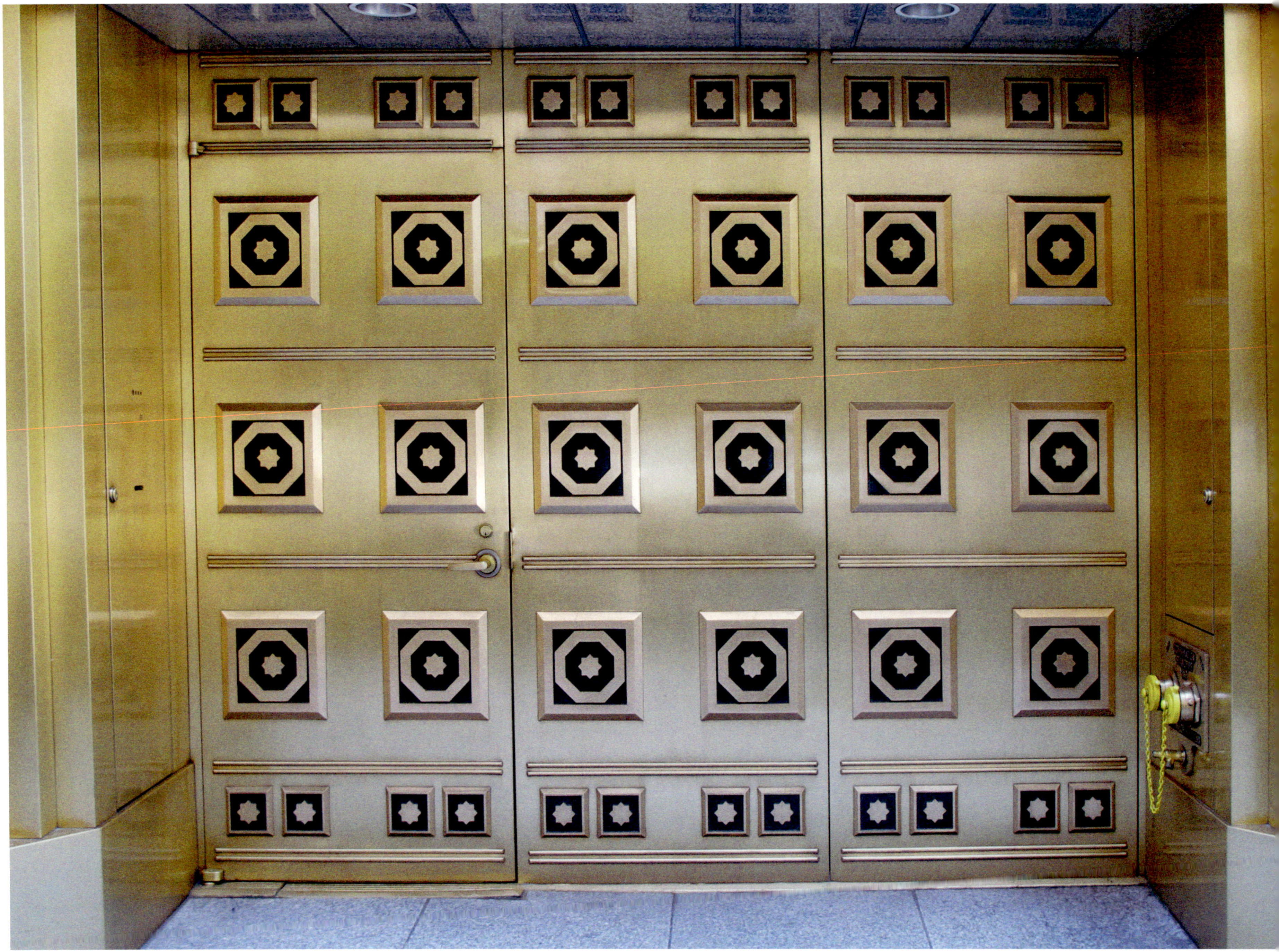

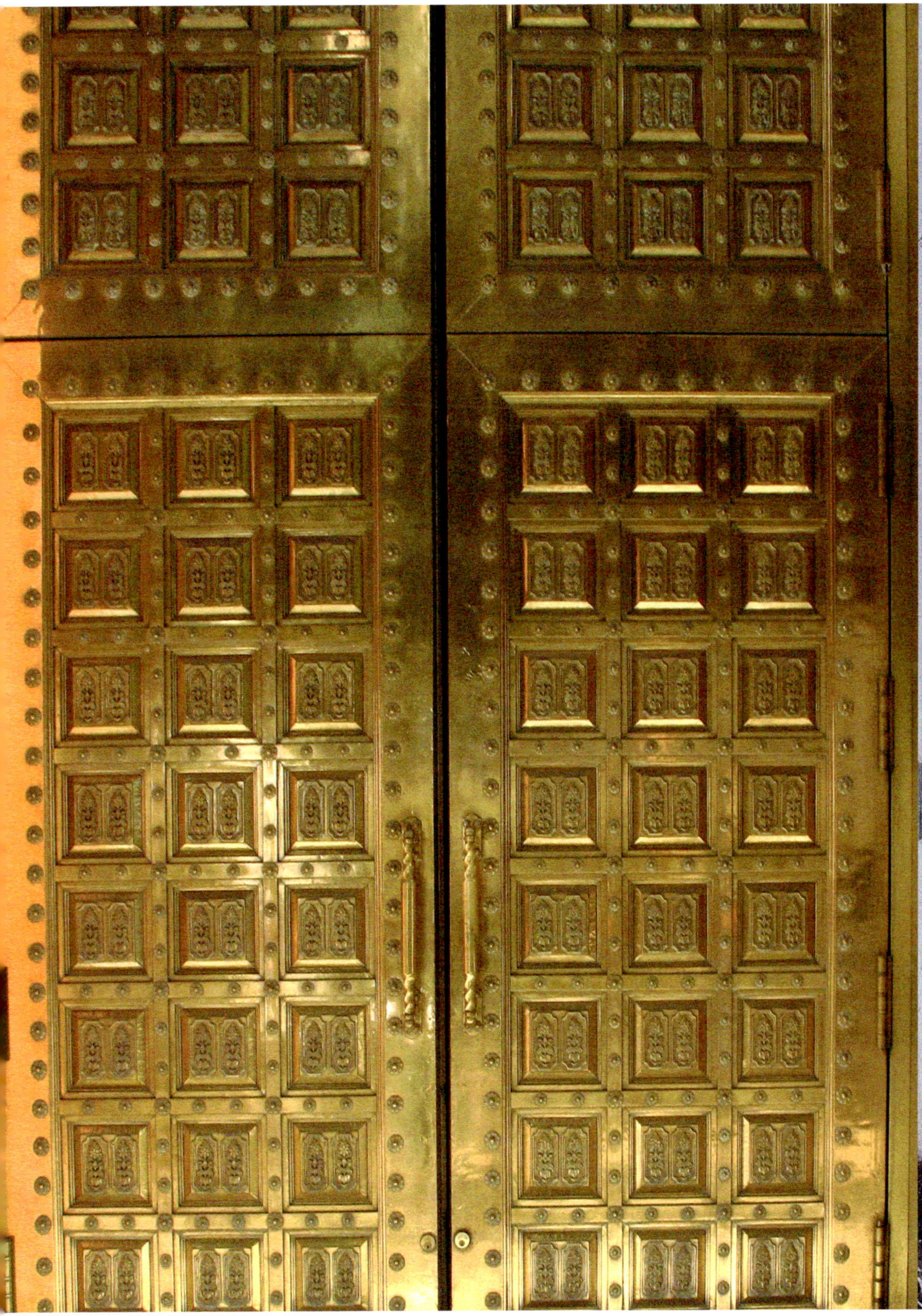

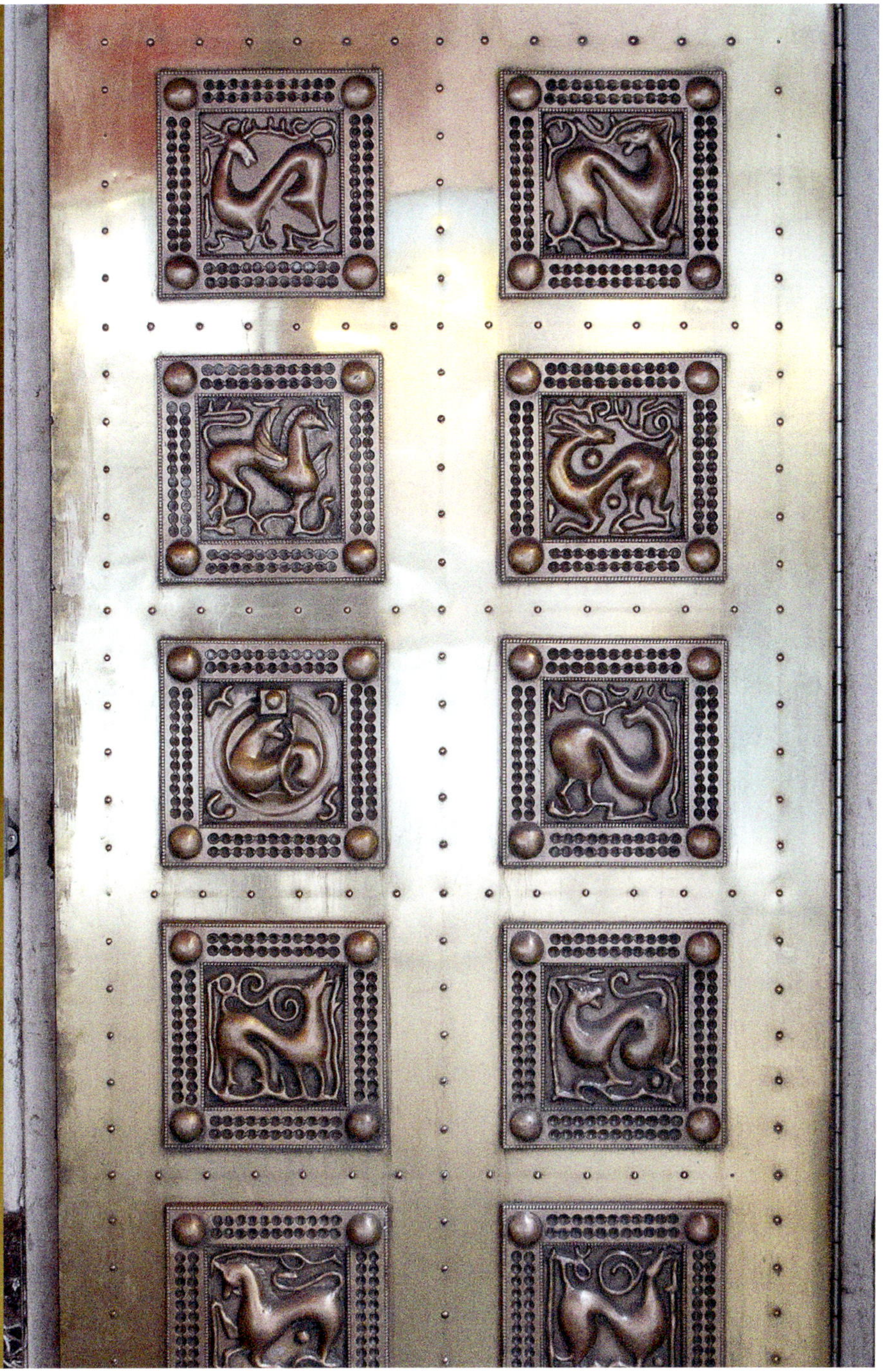

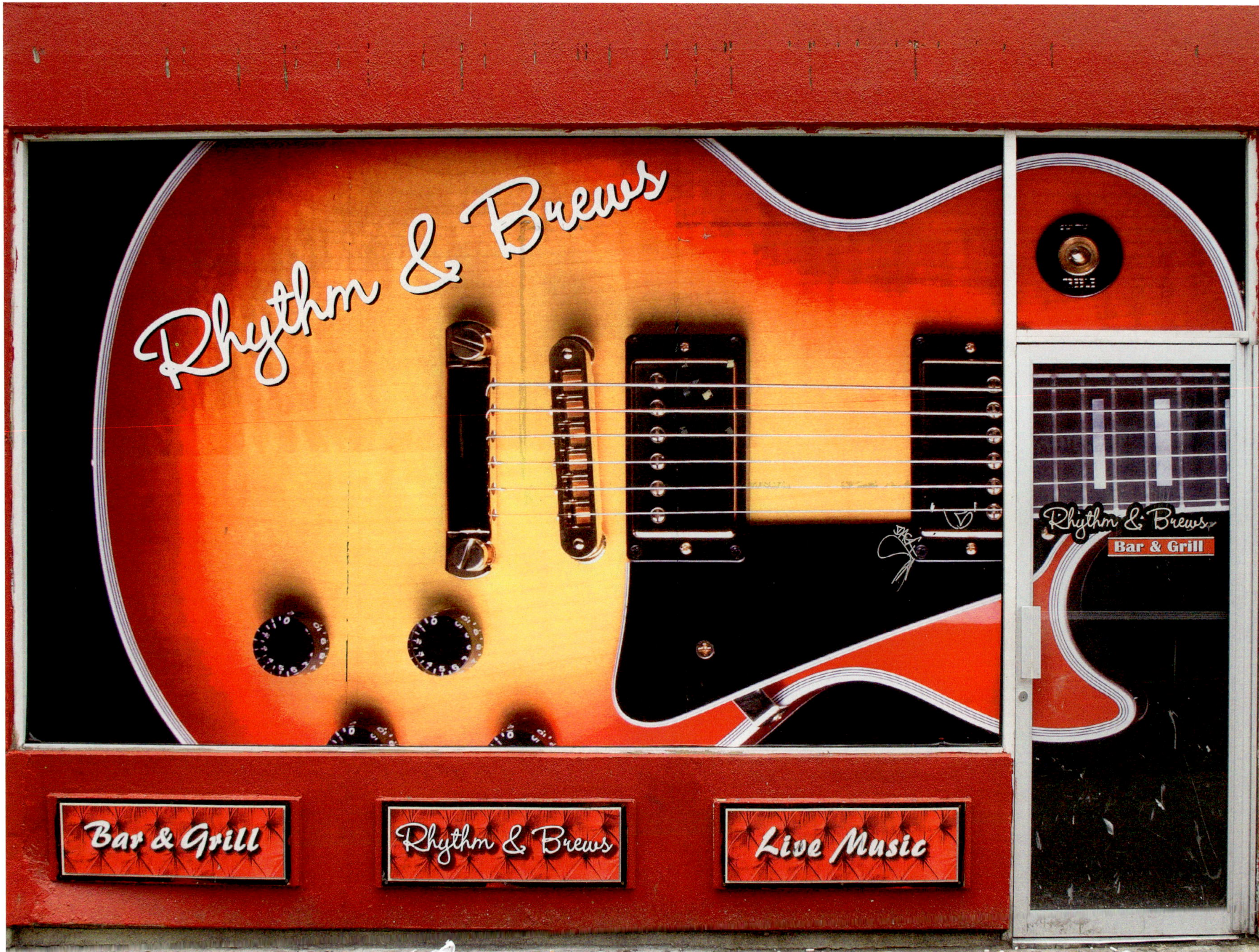
Rhythm & Brews
Rhythm & Brews
Bar & Grill
Bar & Grill
Rhythm & Brews
Live Music

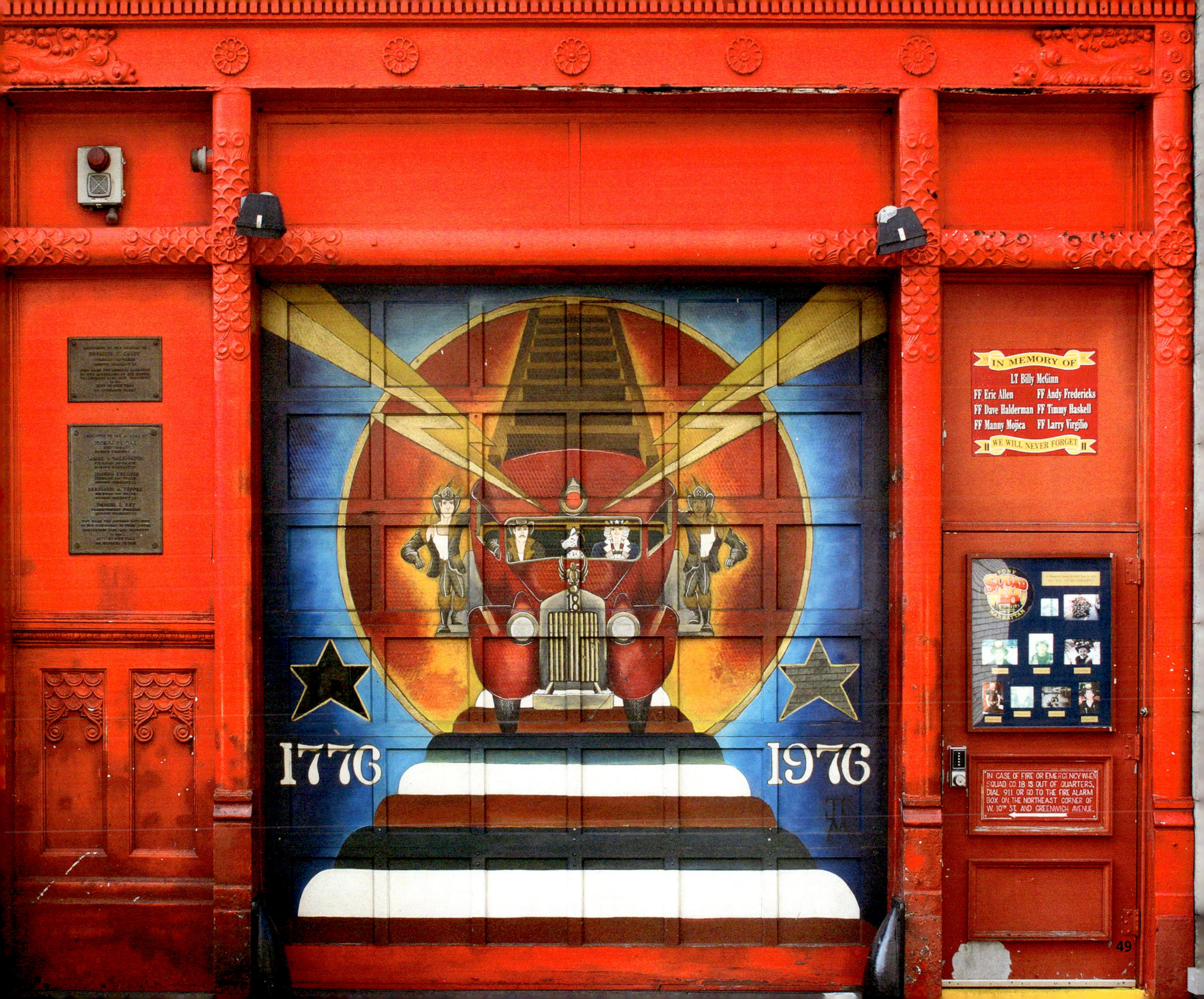
IN MEMORY OF
LT Billy McGinn
FF Eric Allen
FF Andy Fredericks
FF Dave Halderman
FF Timmy Haskell
FF Manny Mojica
FF Larry Virgilio
WE WILL NEVER FORGET
1776
1976
IN CASE OF FIRE OR EMERGENCY WHEN SQUAD CO. 18 IS OUT OF QUARTERS, DIAL 911 OR GO TO THE FIRE ALARM BOX ON THE NORTHEAST CORNER OF W. 10TH ST. AND GREENWICH AVENUE.

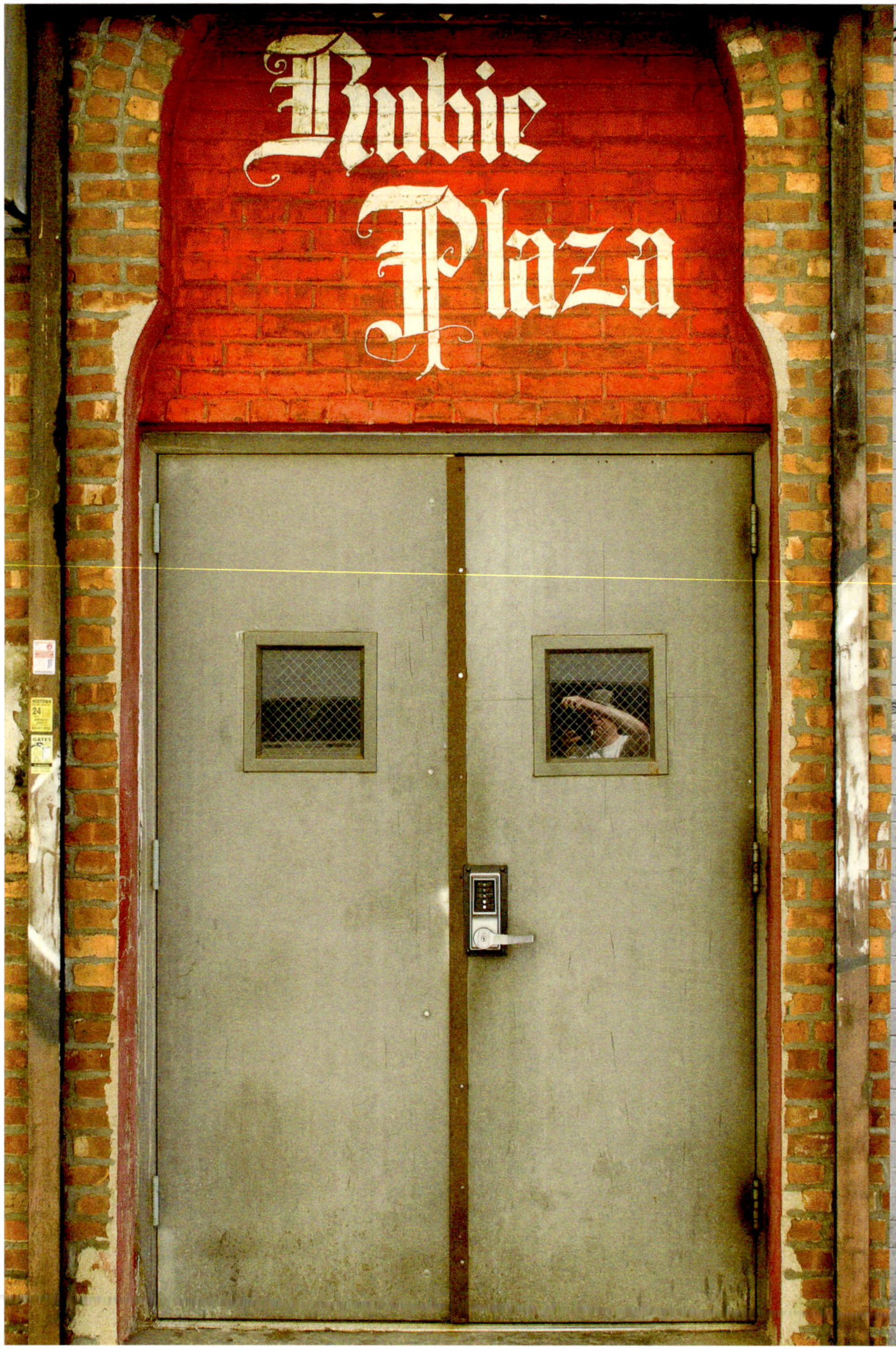
Rubie
Plaza

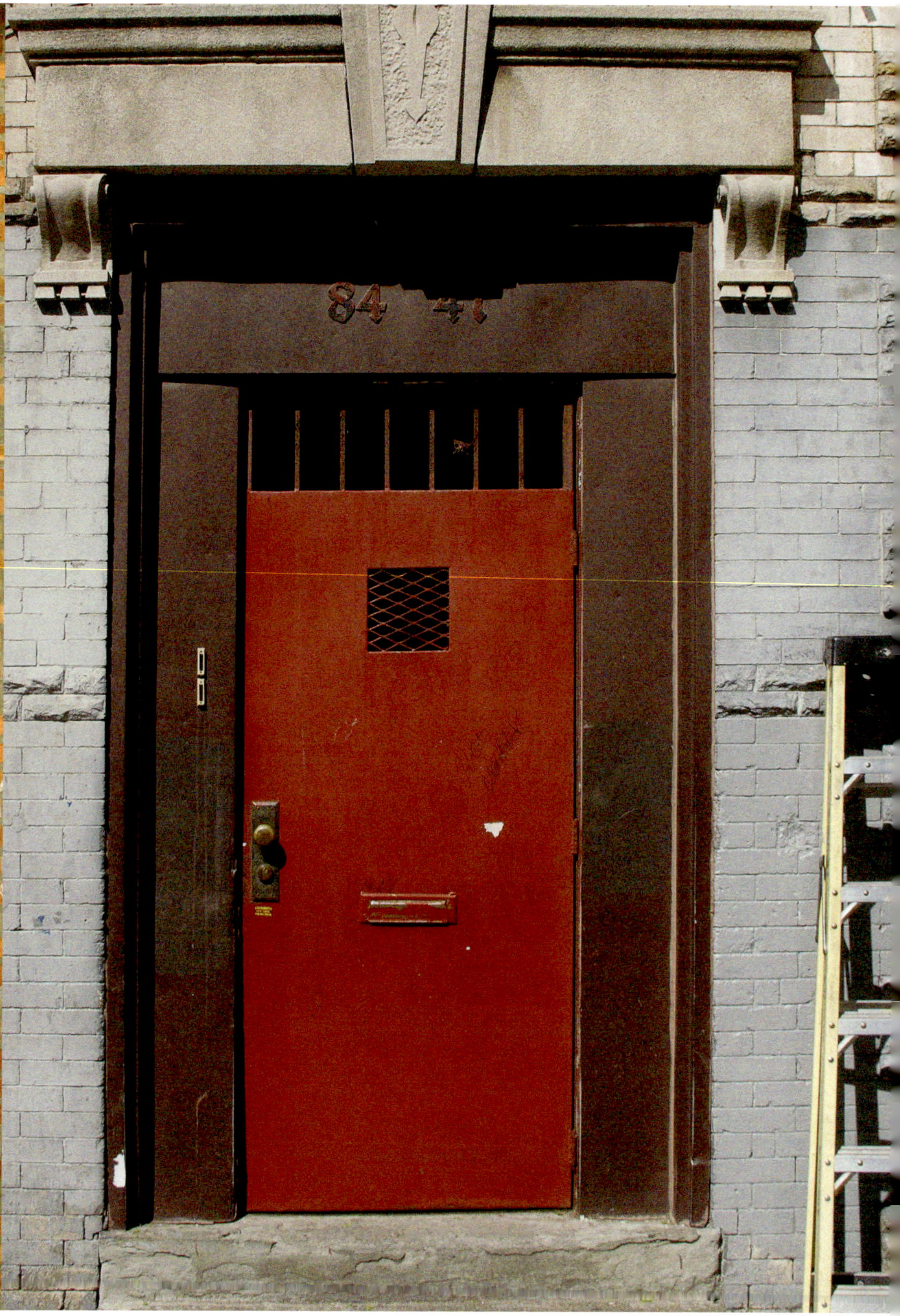
84

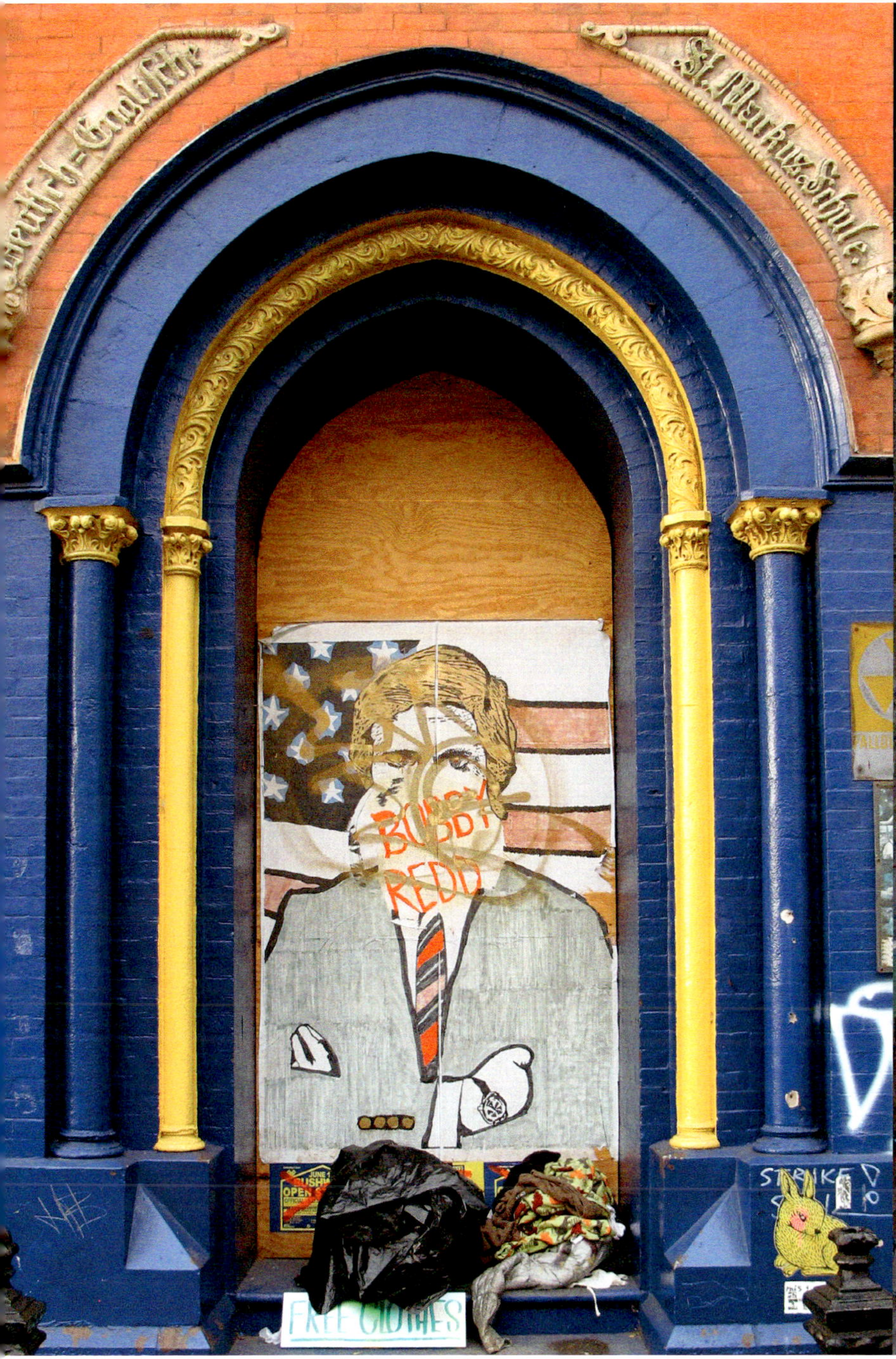
St. Markus Schule
BOBBY REDD
FREE CLOTHES

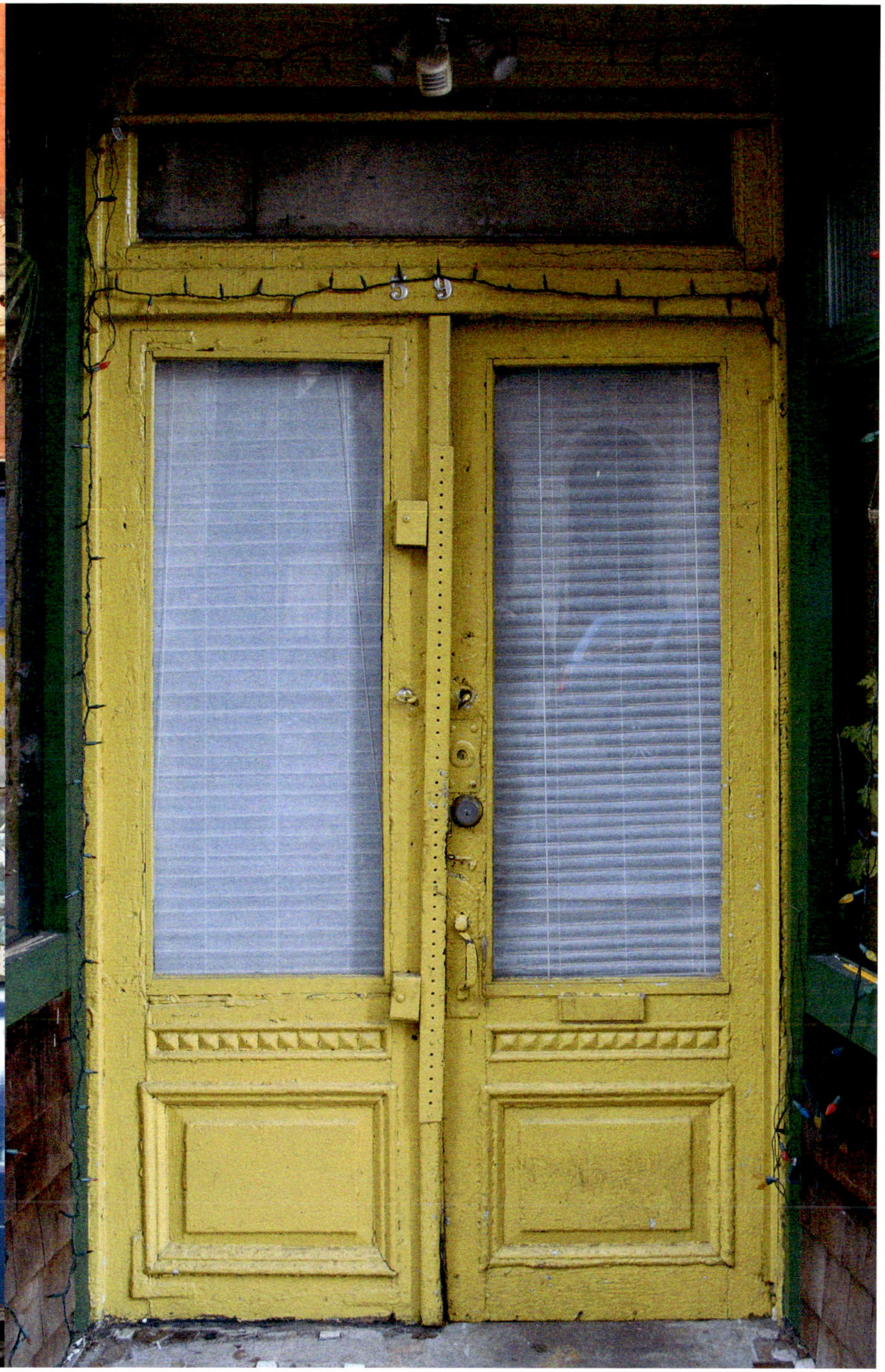
59

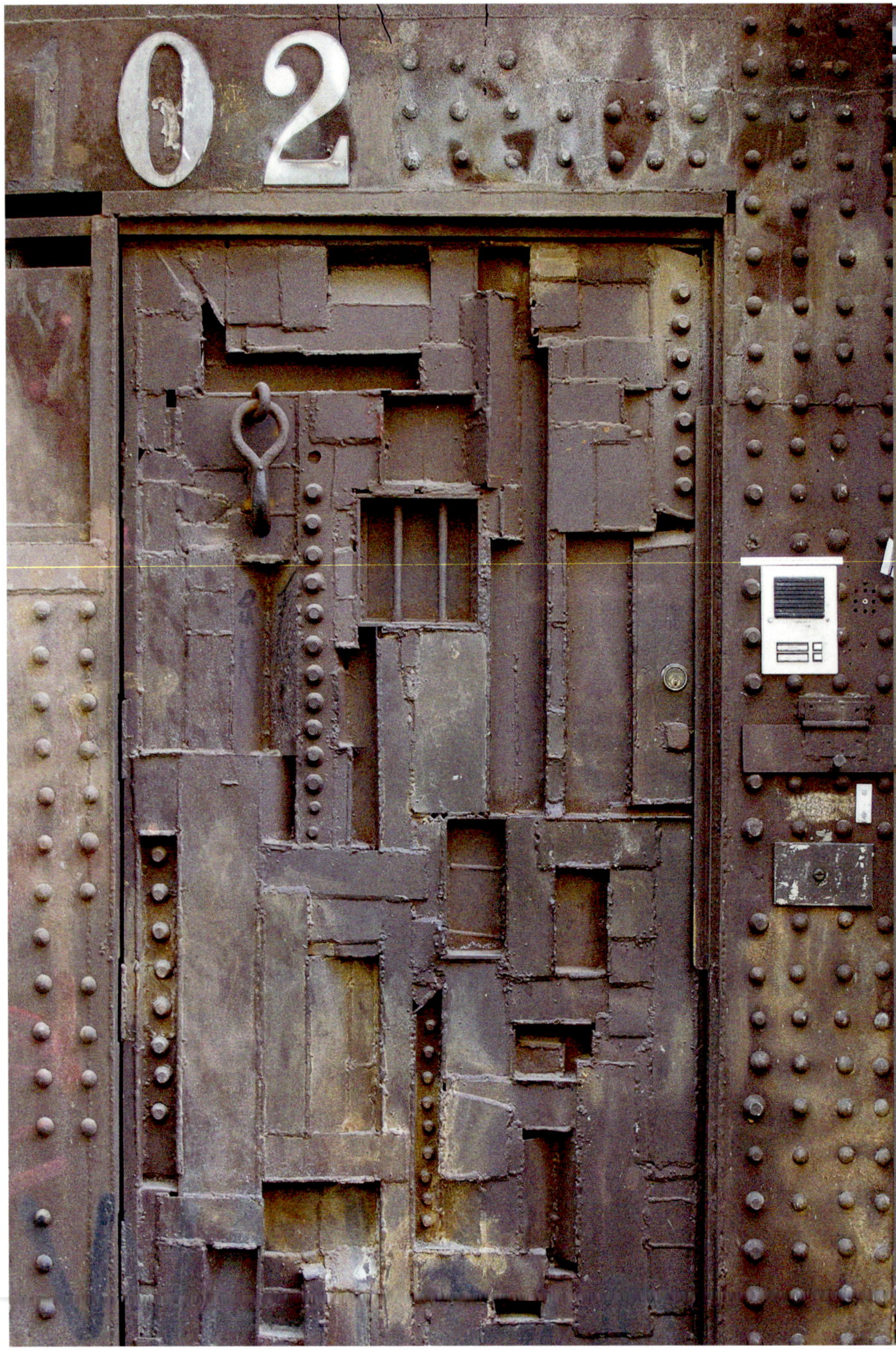
102
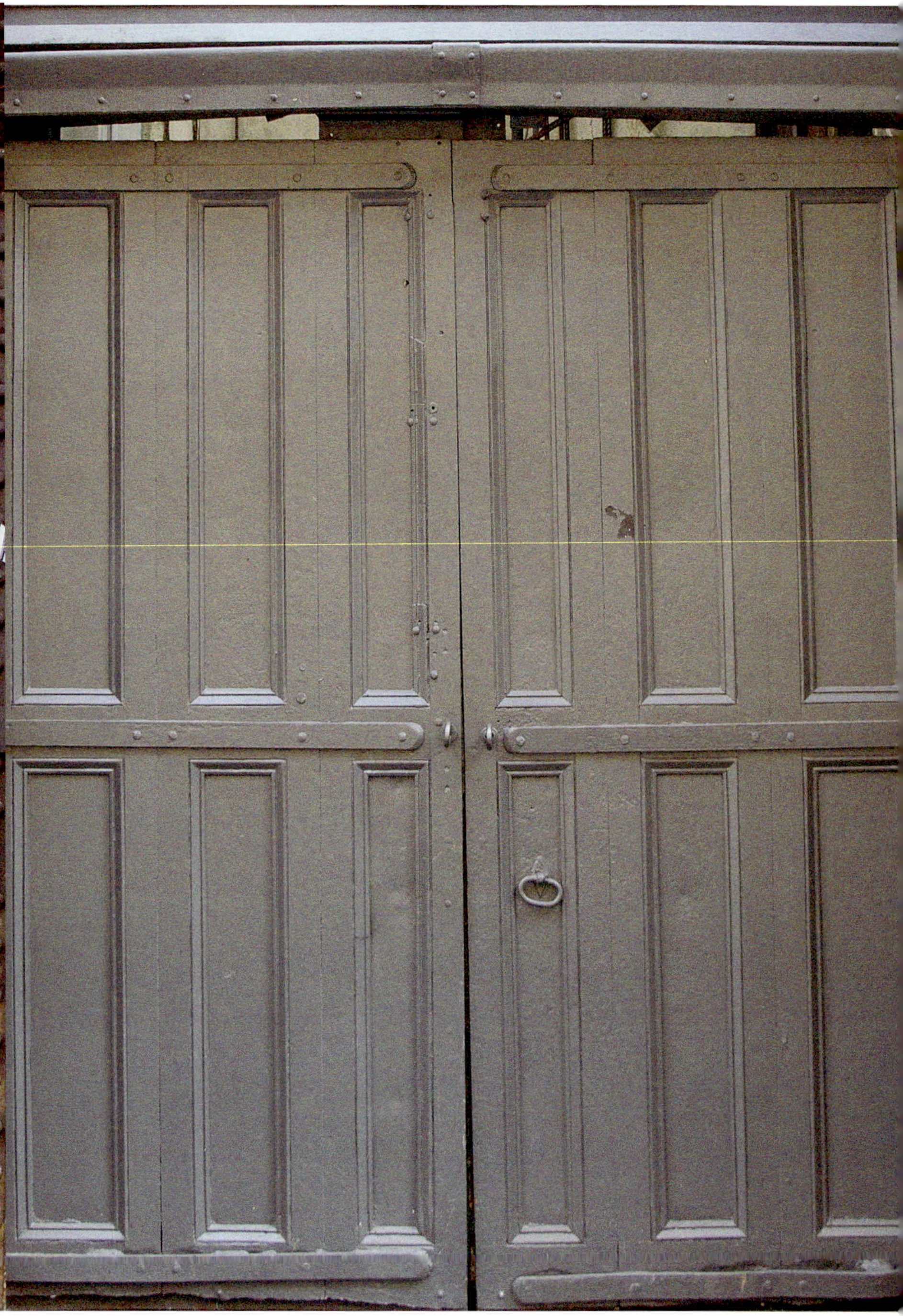

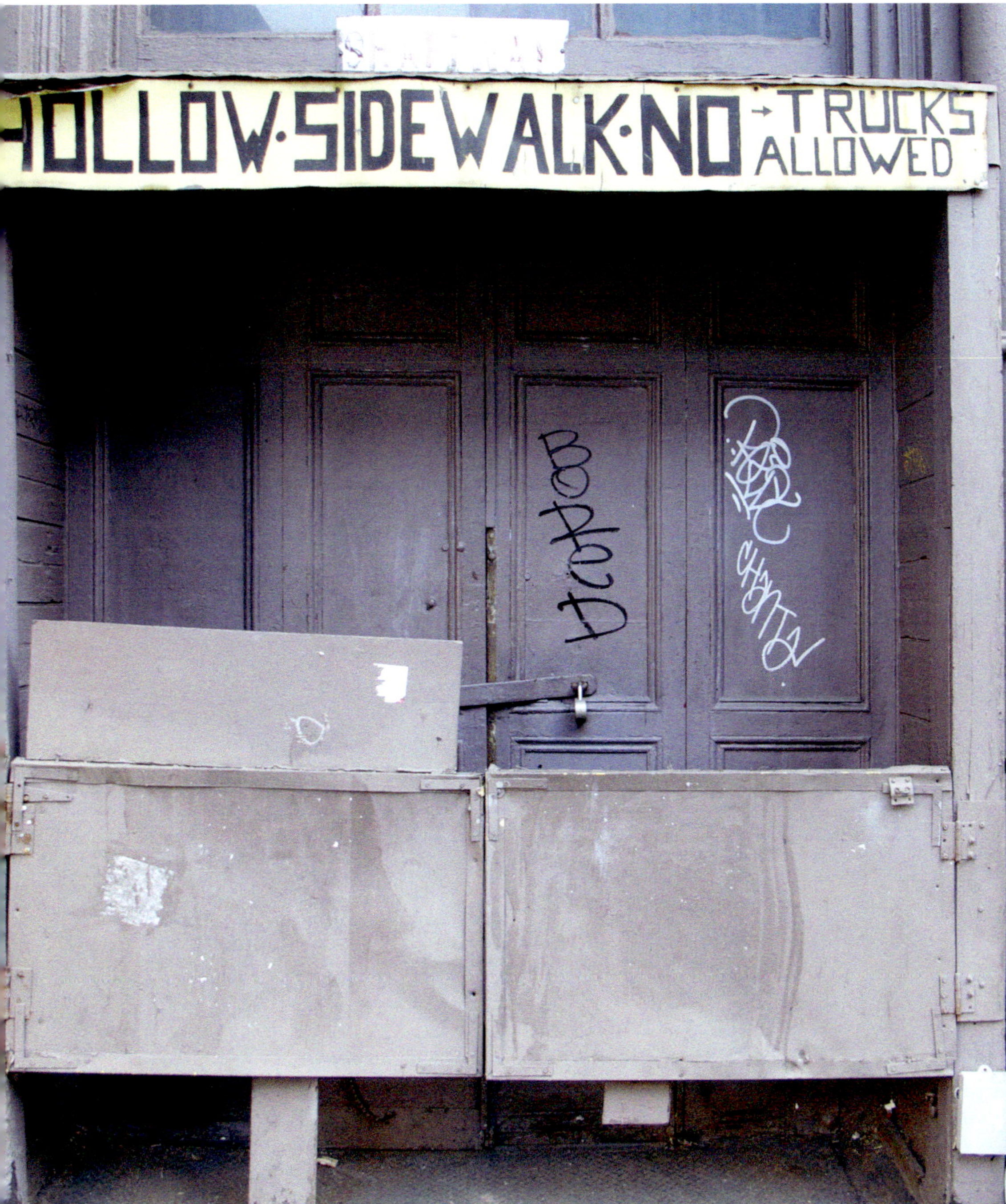
OLLOW·SIDEWALK·NO
→TRUCKS
ALLOWED
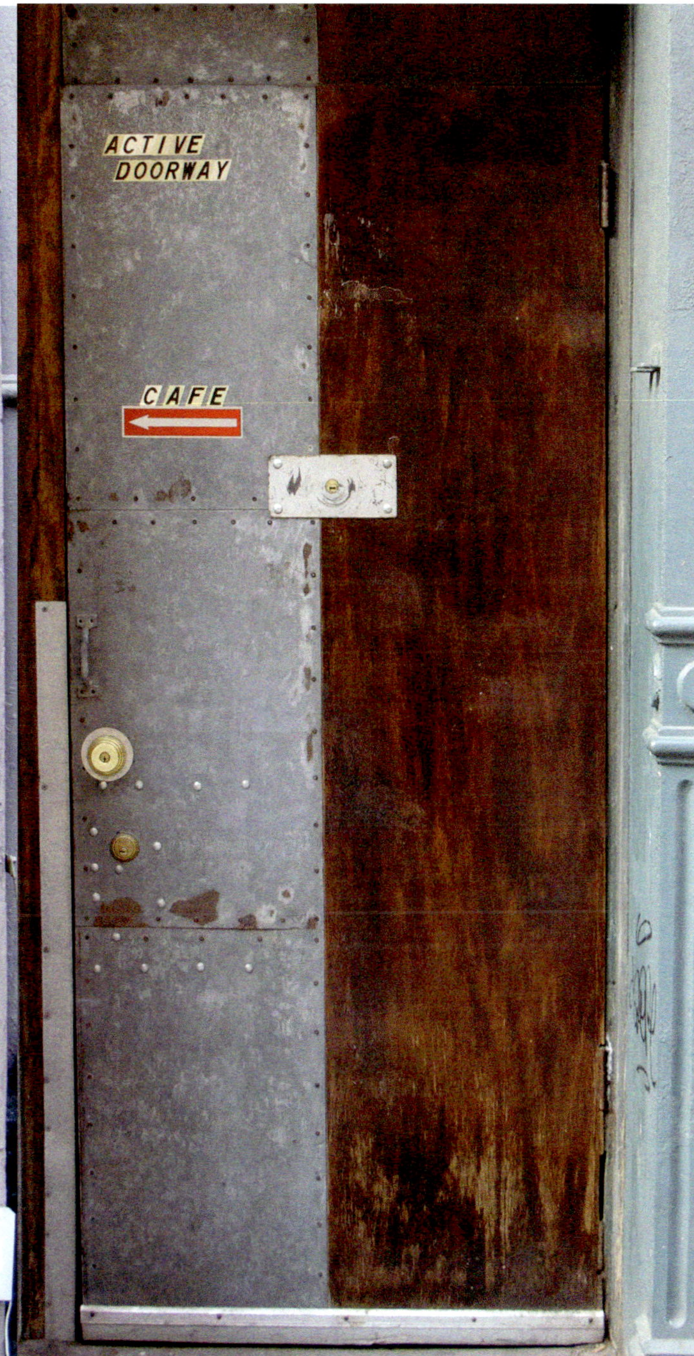
ACTIVE
DOORWAY
CAFE

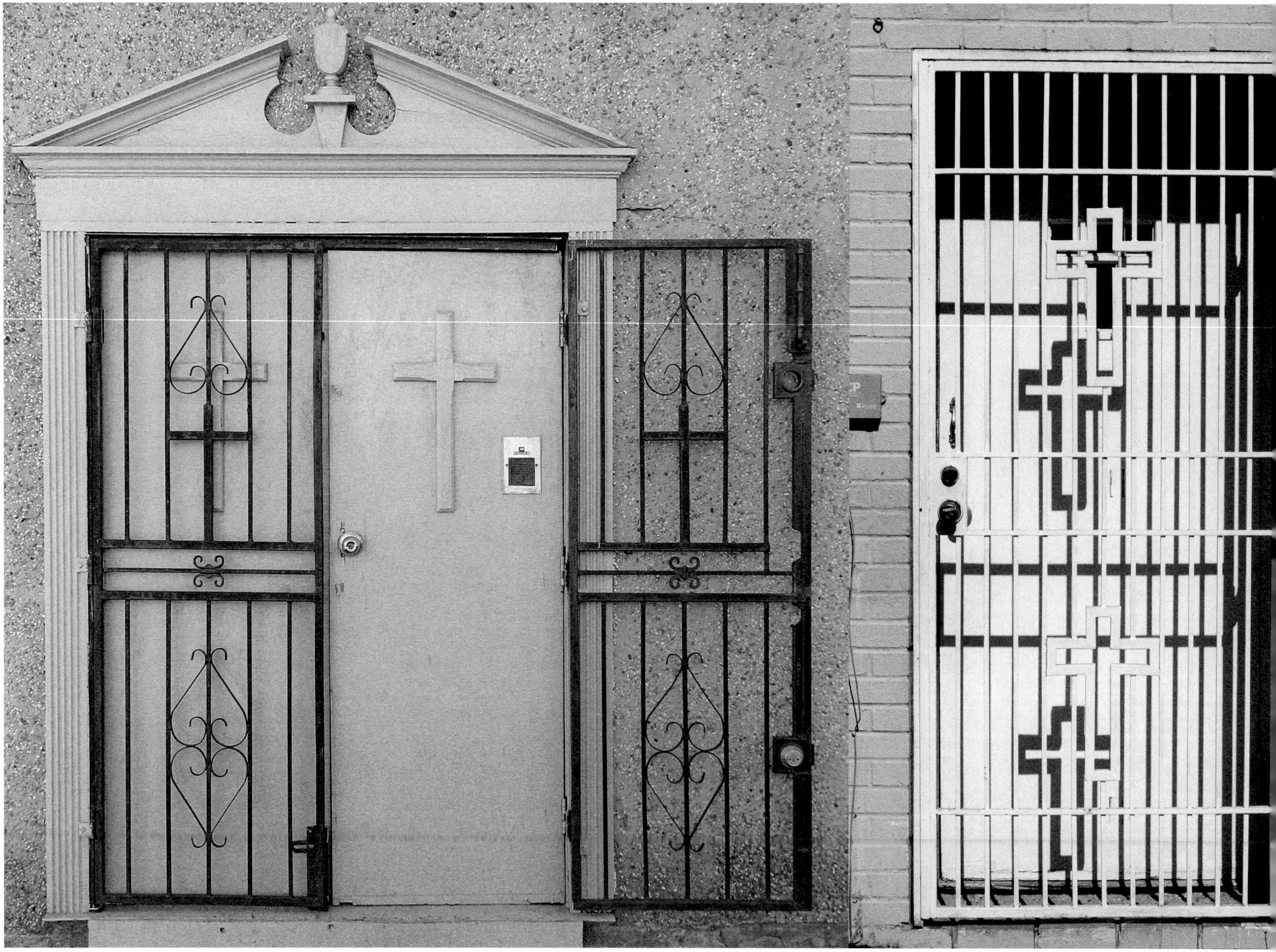

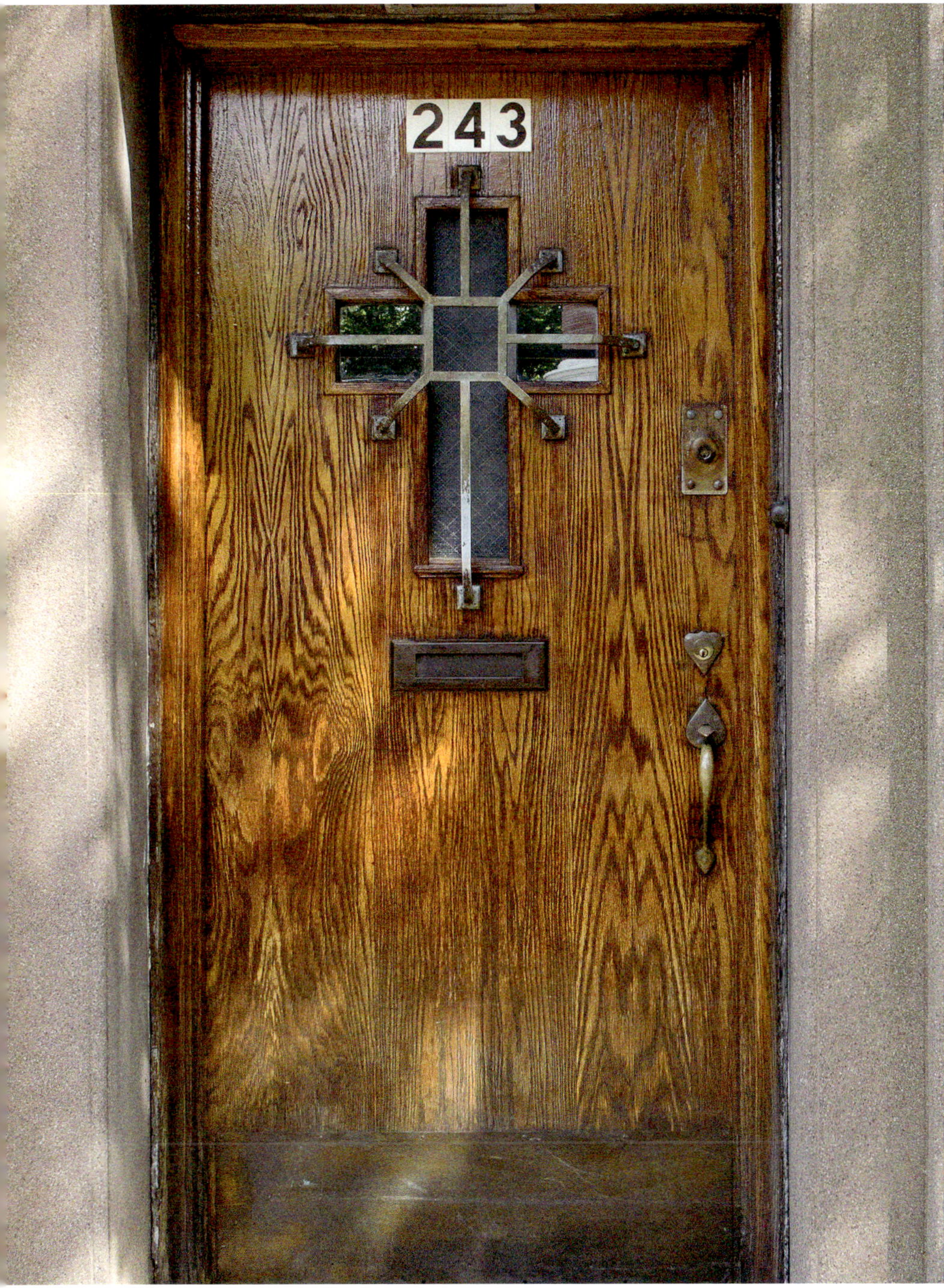
243
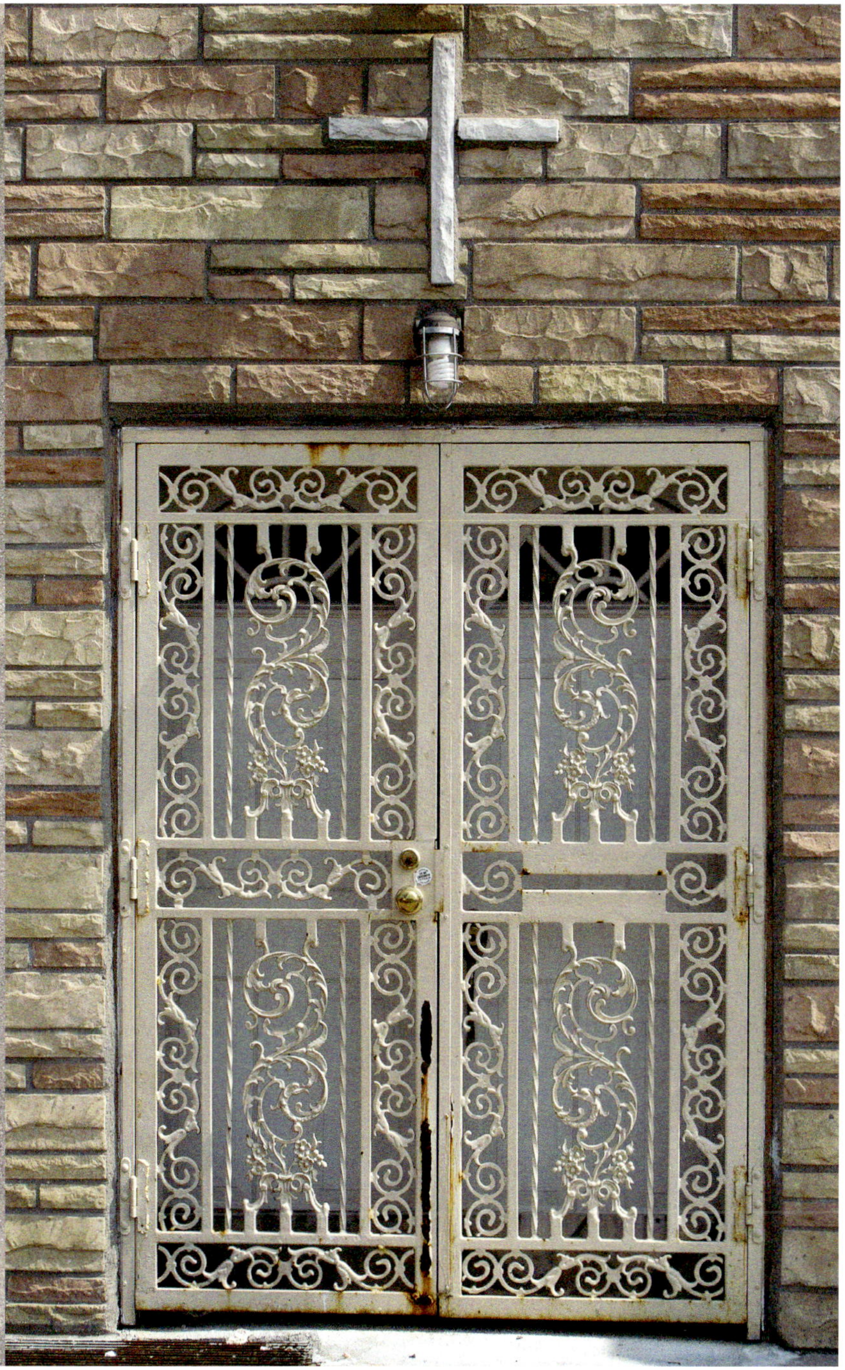

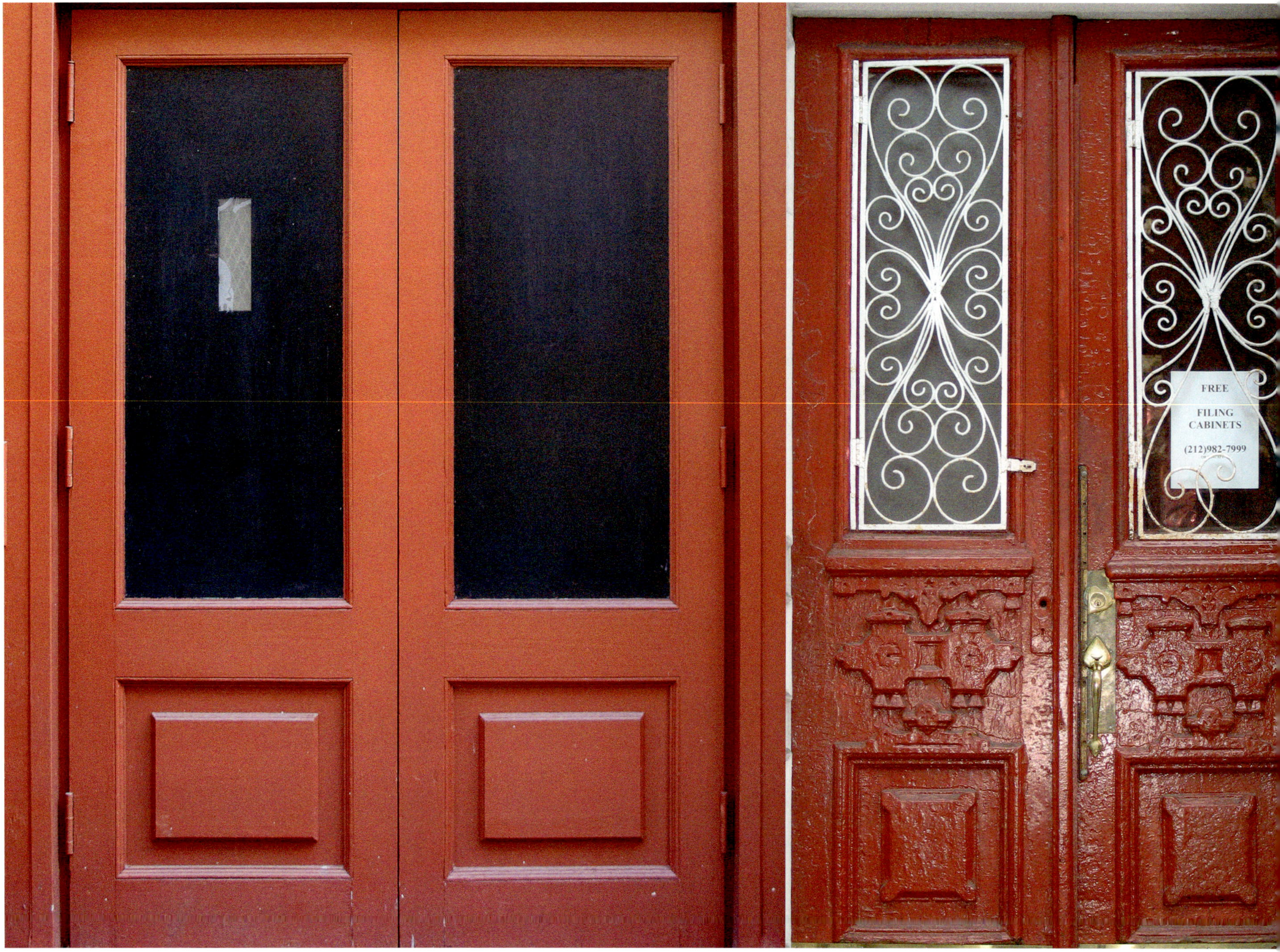
FREE
FILING
CABINETS
(212)982-7999

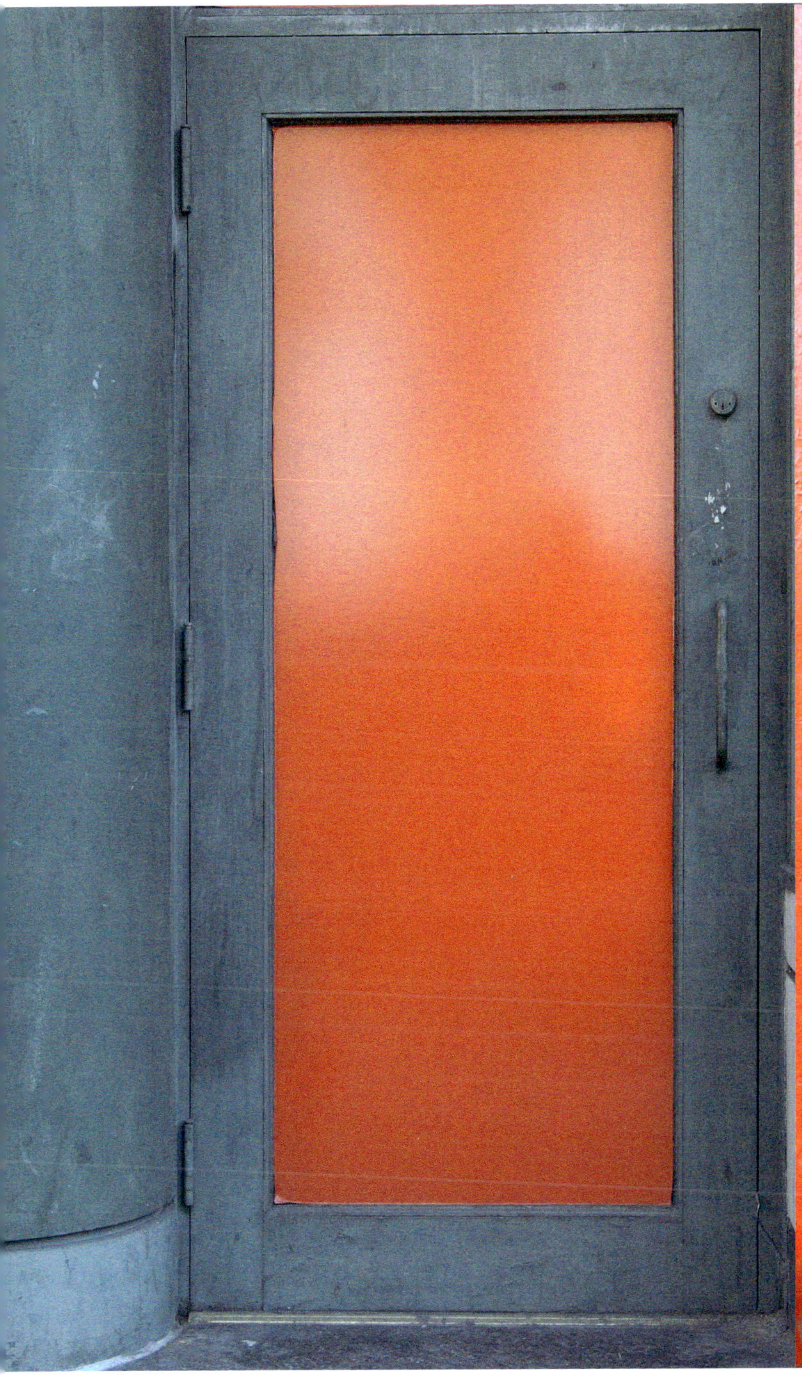

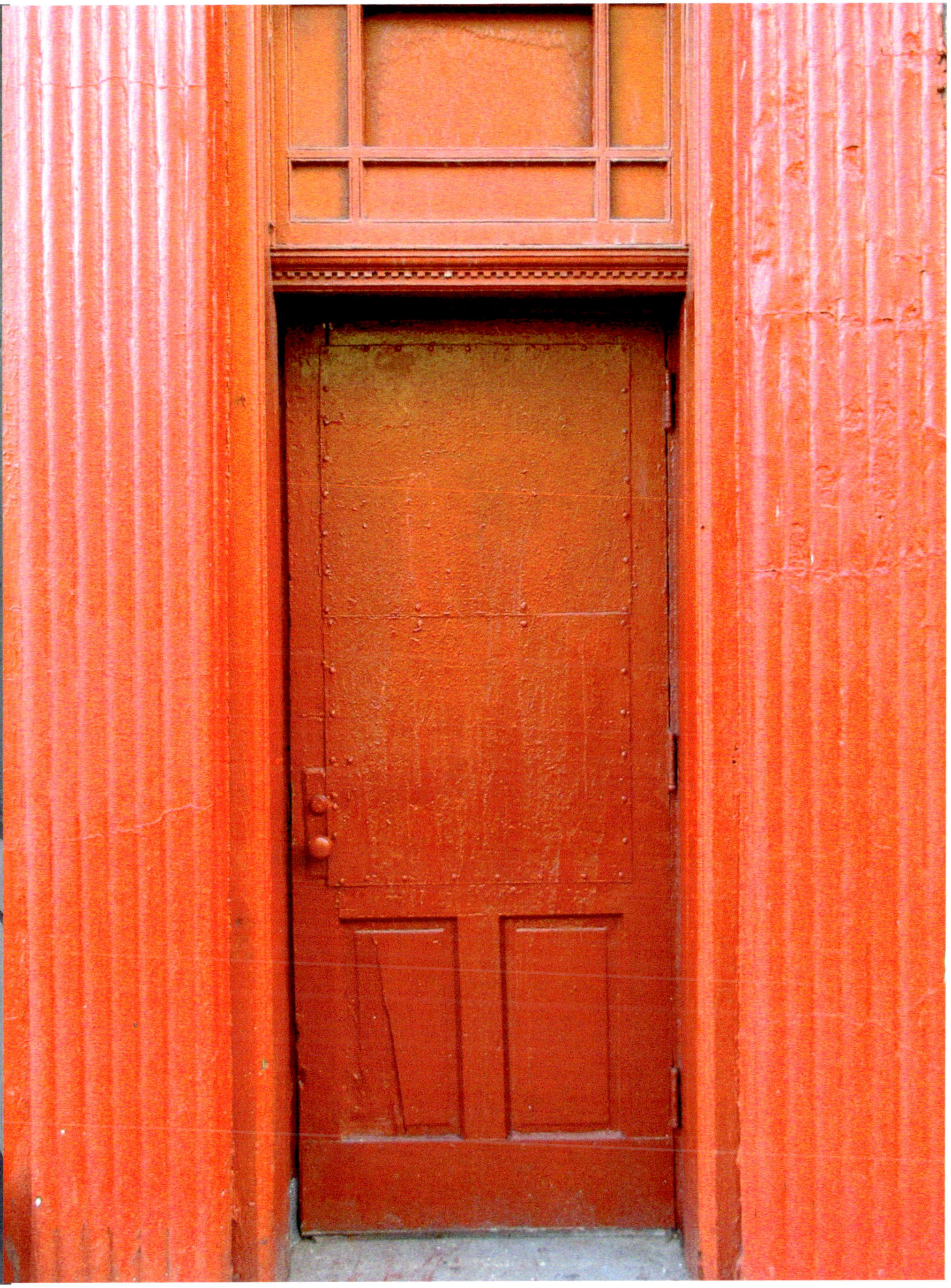

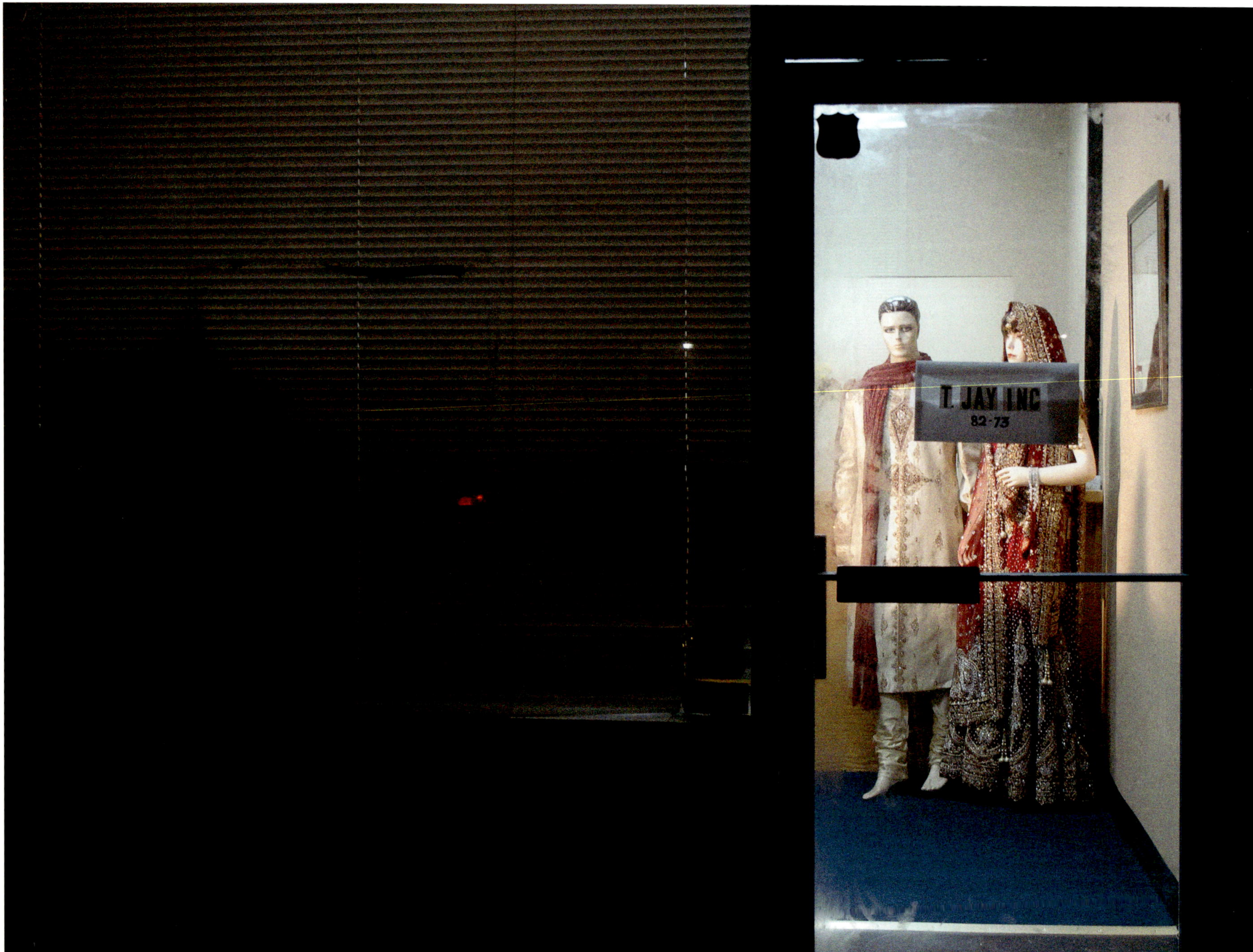
T. JAY INC
82-73

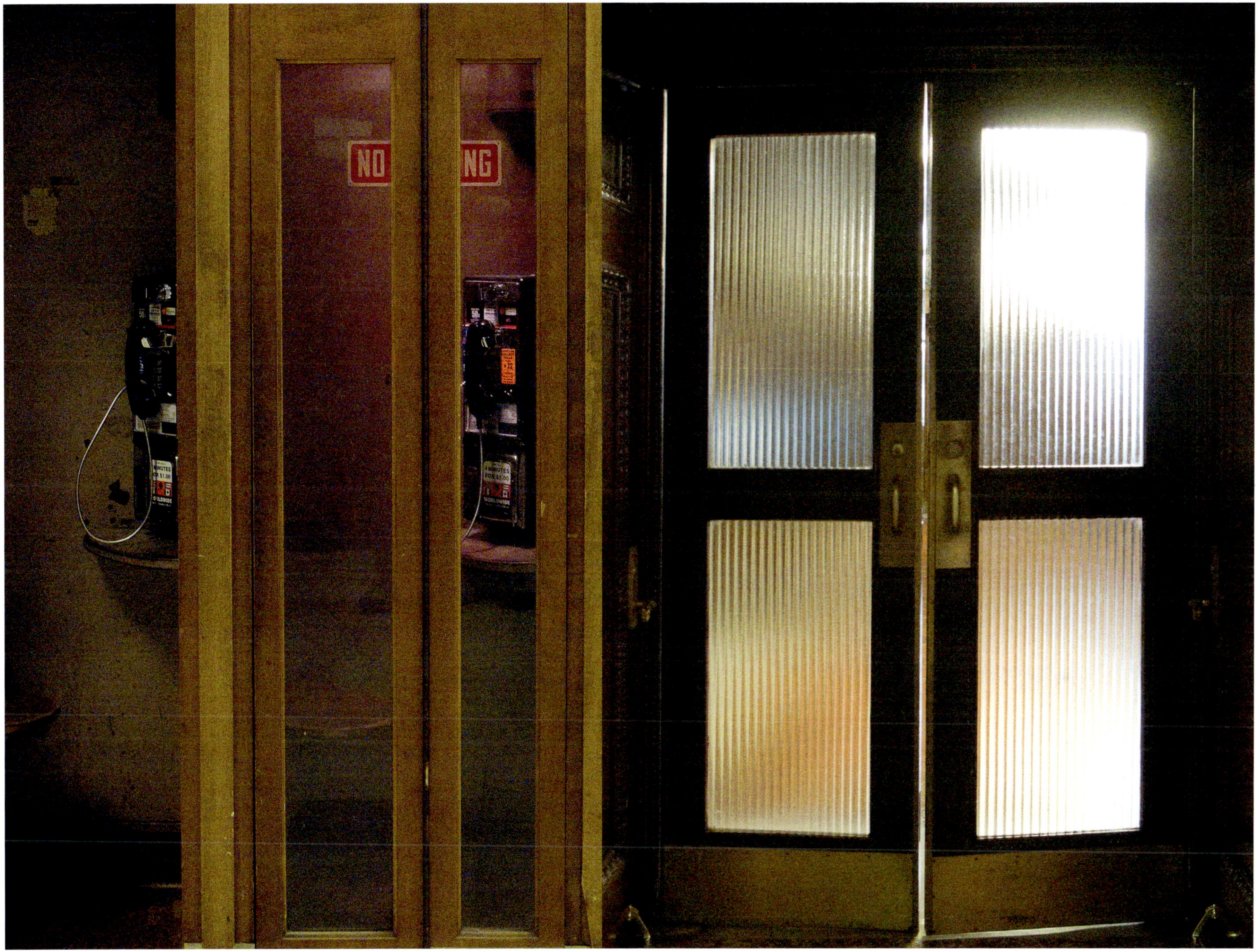
NO

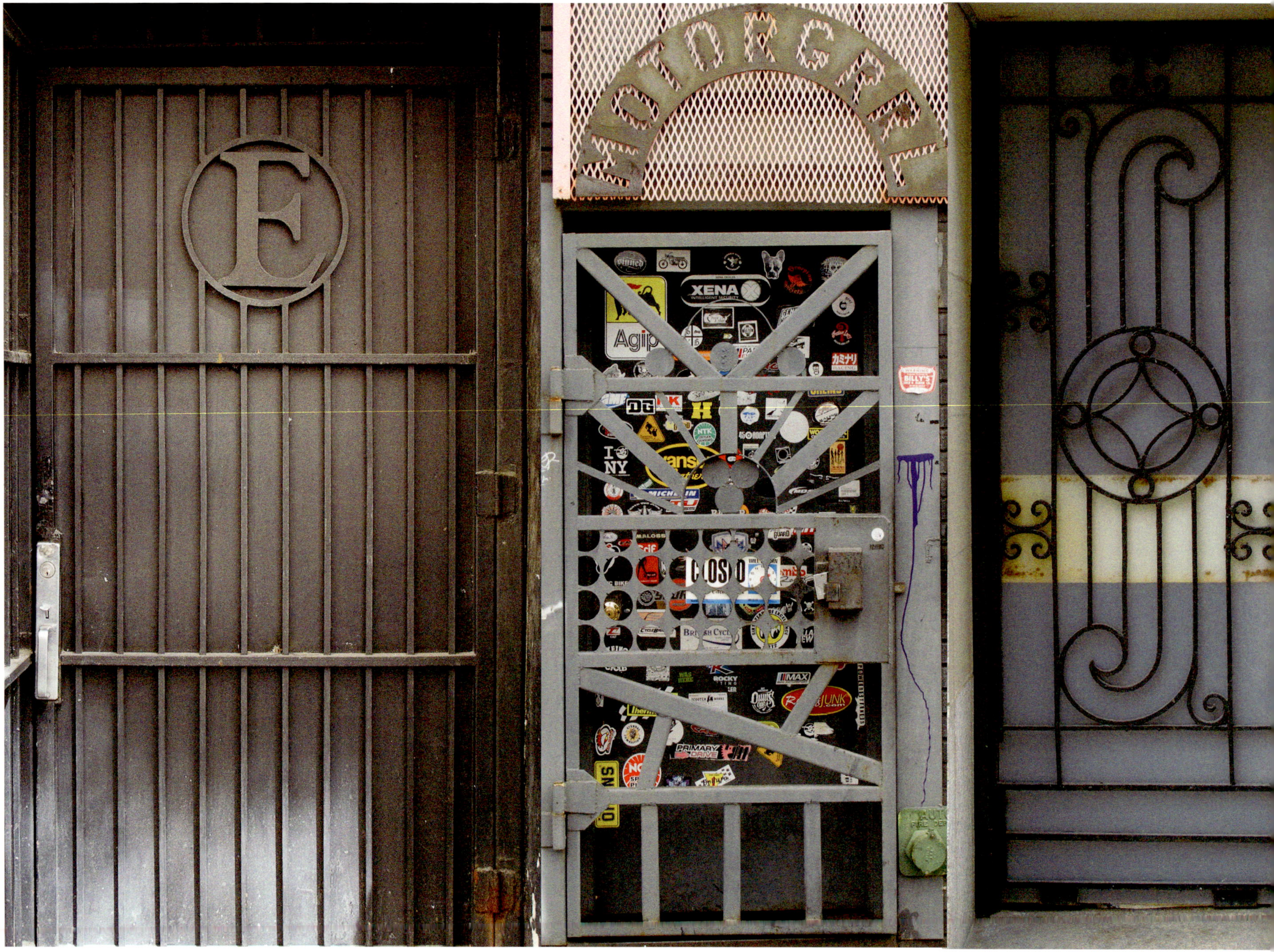
E
XENA
Agip
PRIMARY DRIVE

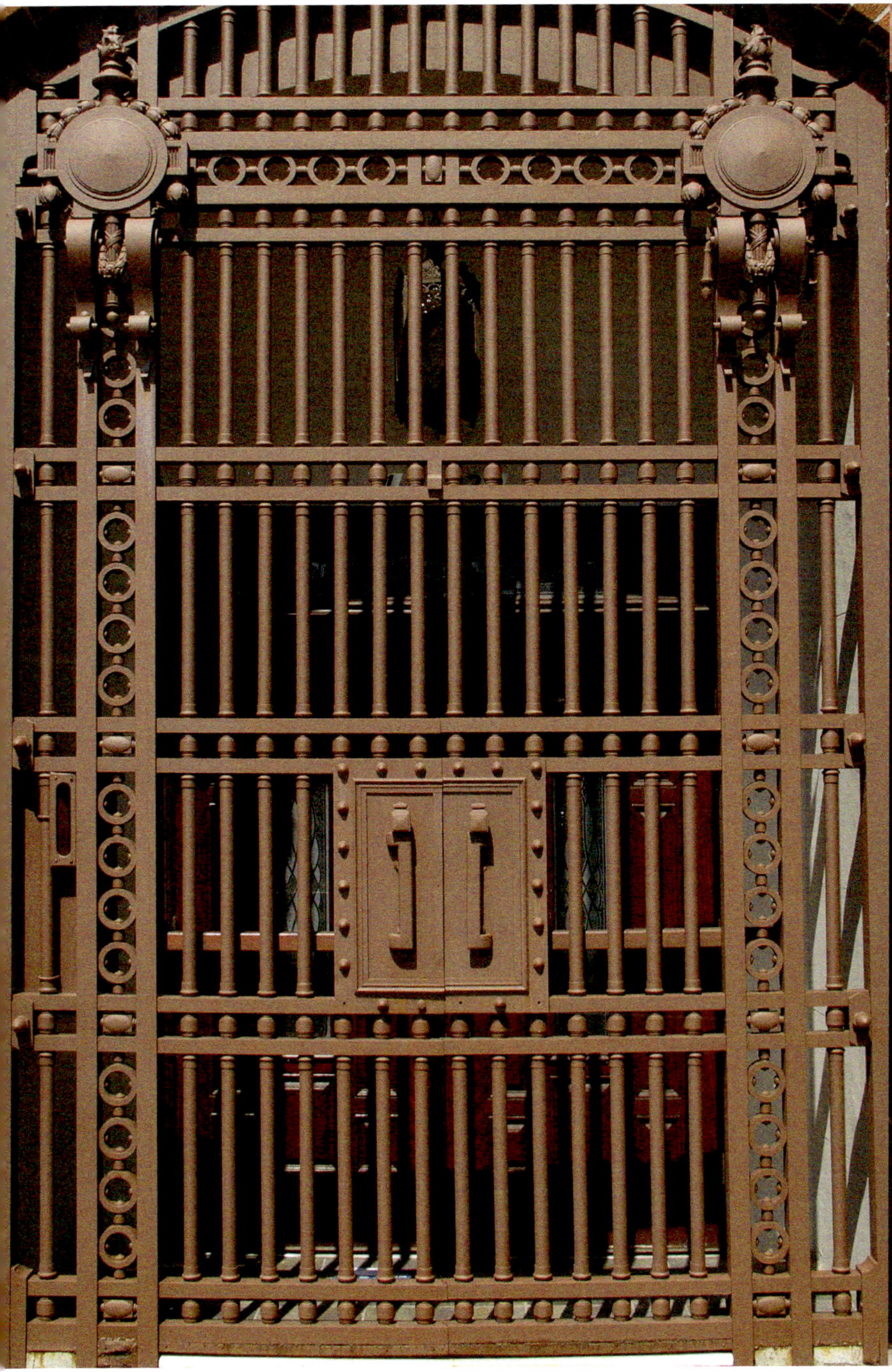

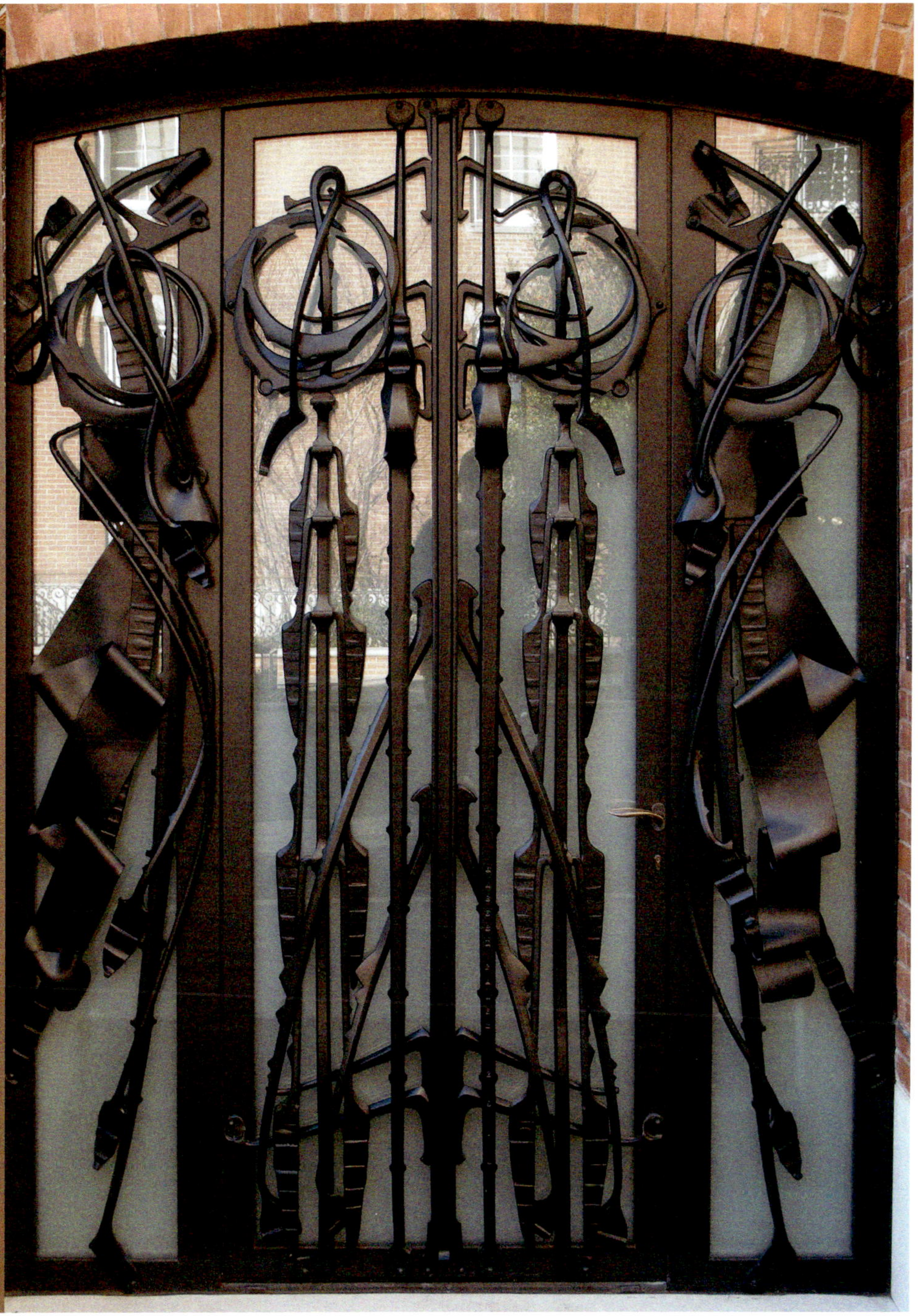

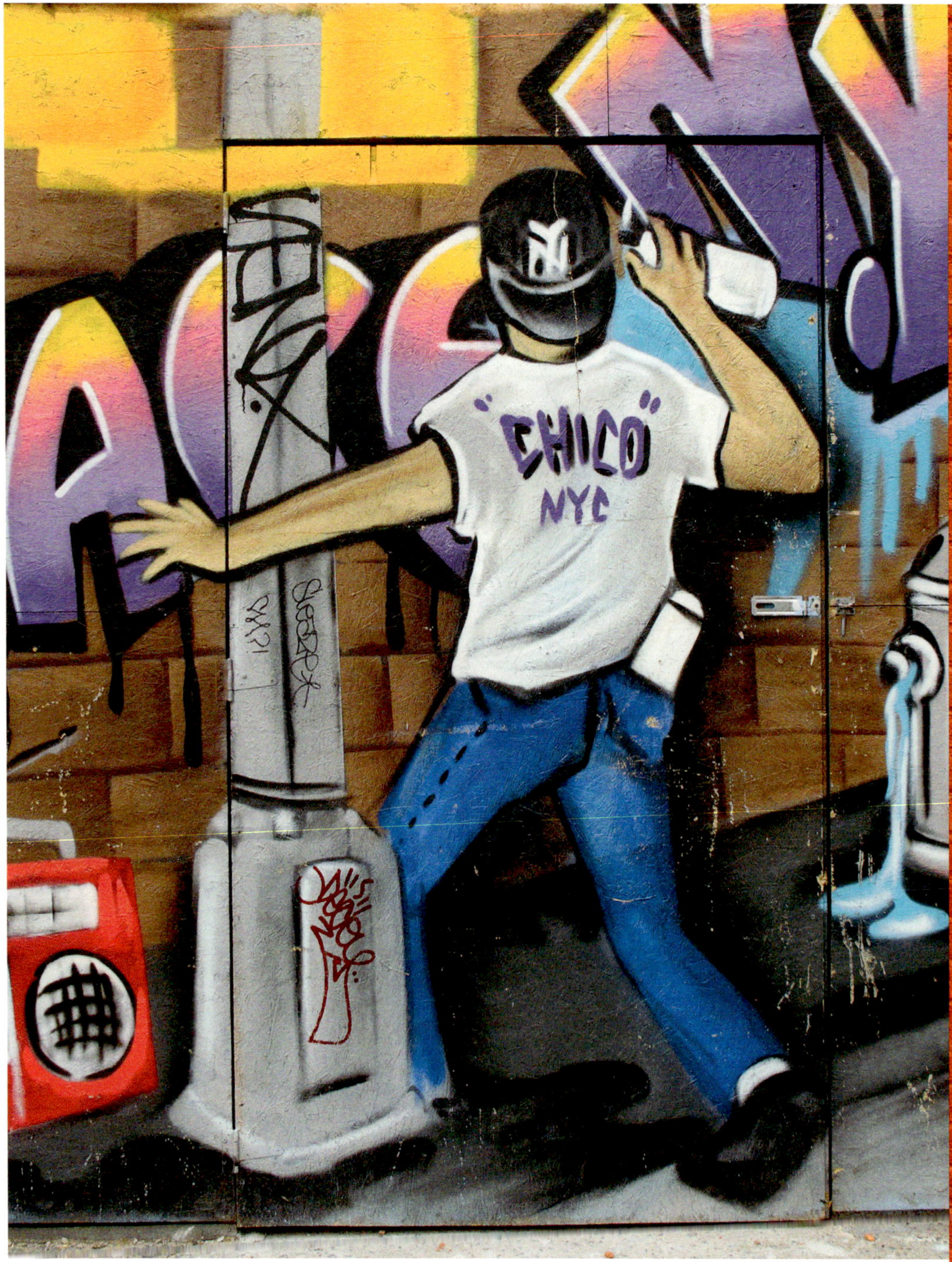
"CHICO"
NYC
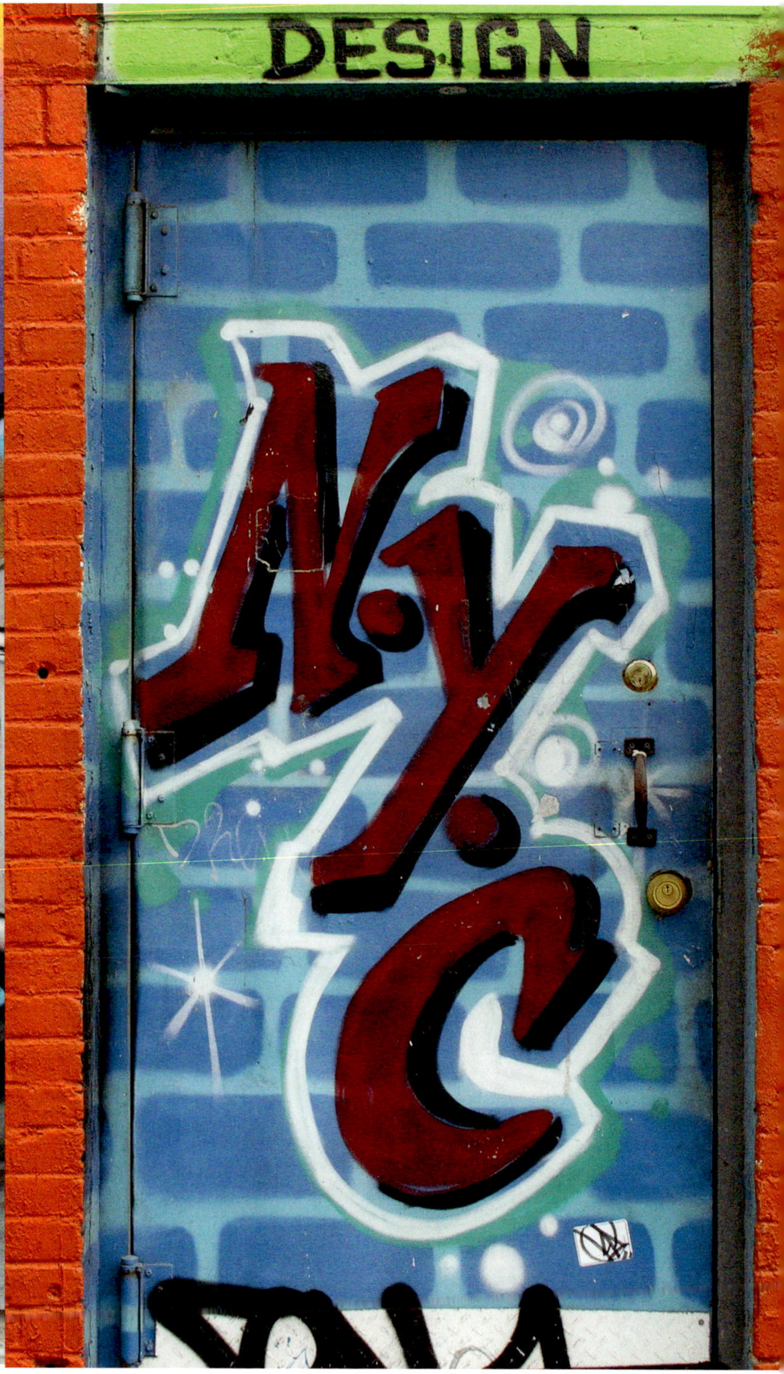
DESIGN
N.Y.C

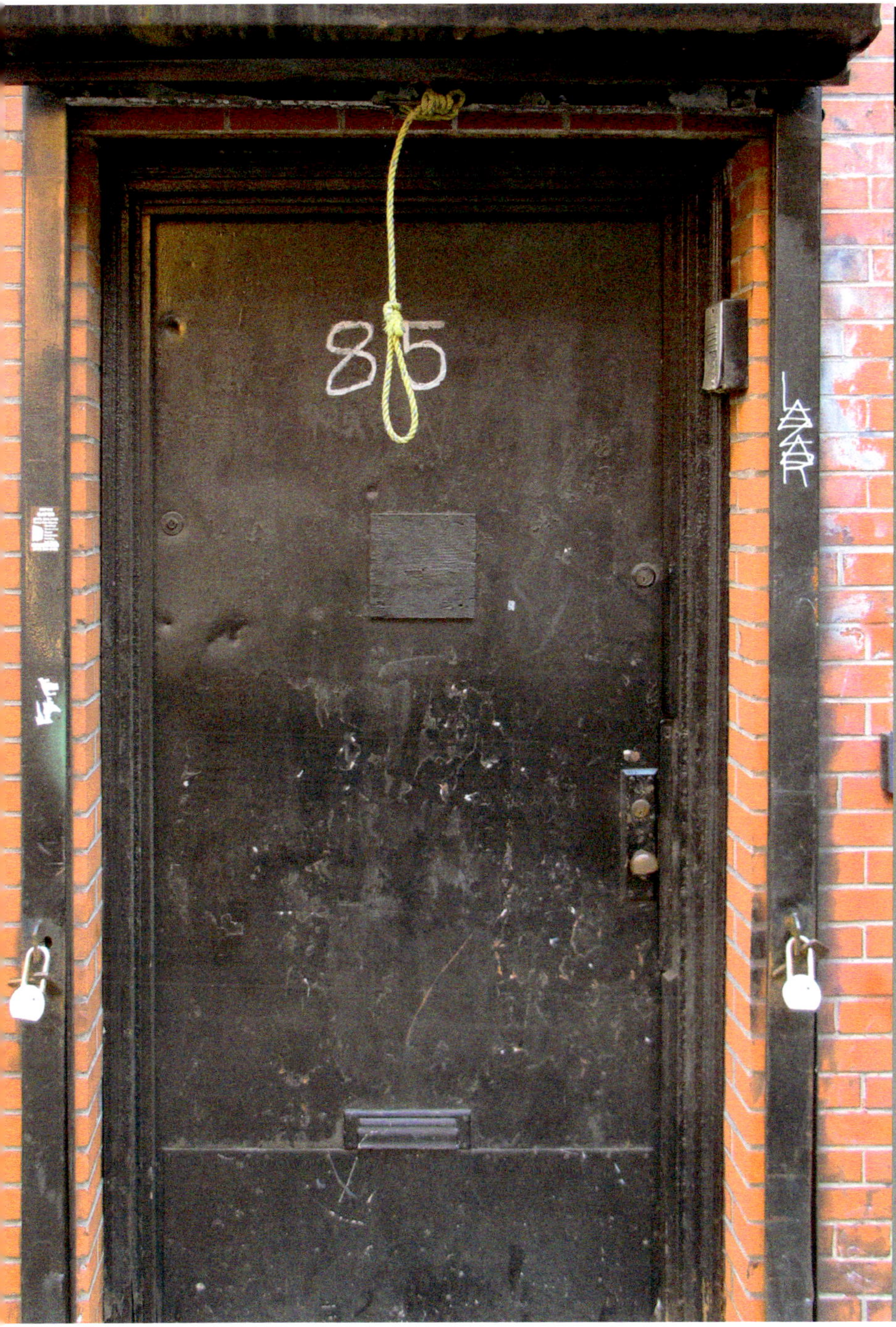
85
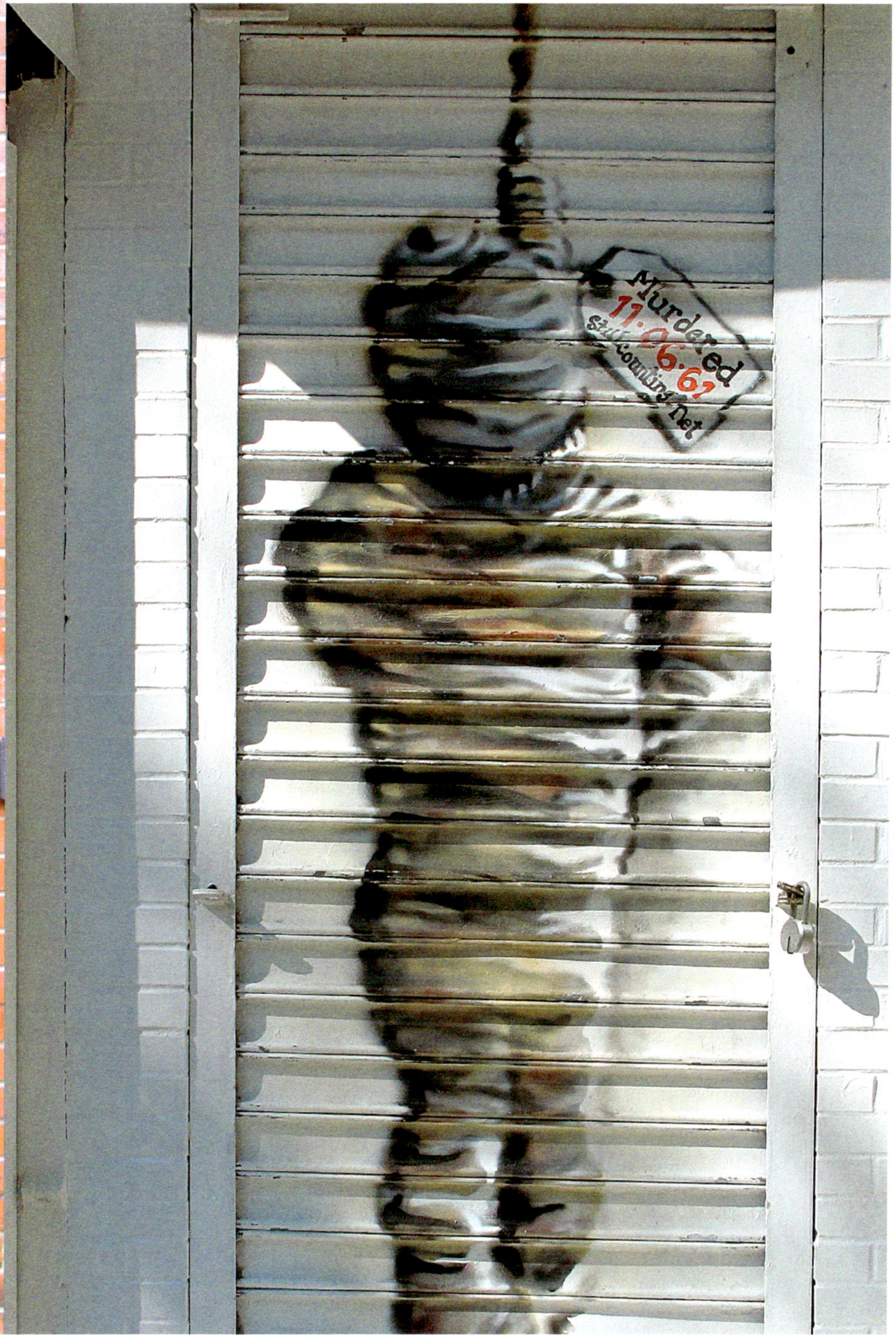
Murdered
11·06·67

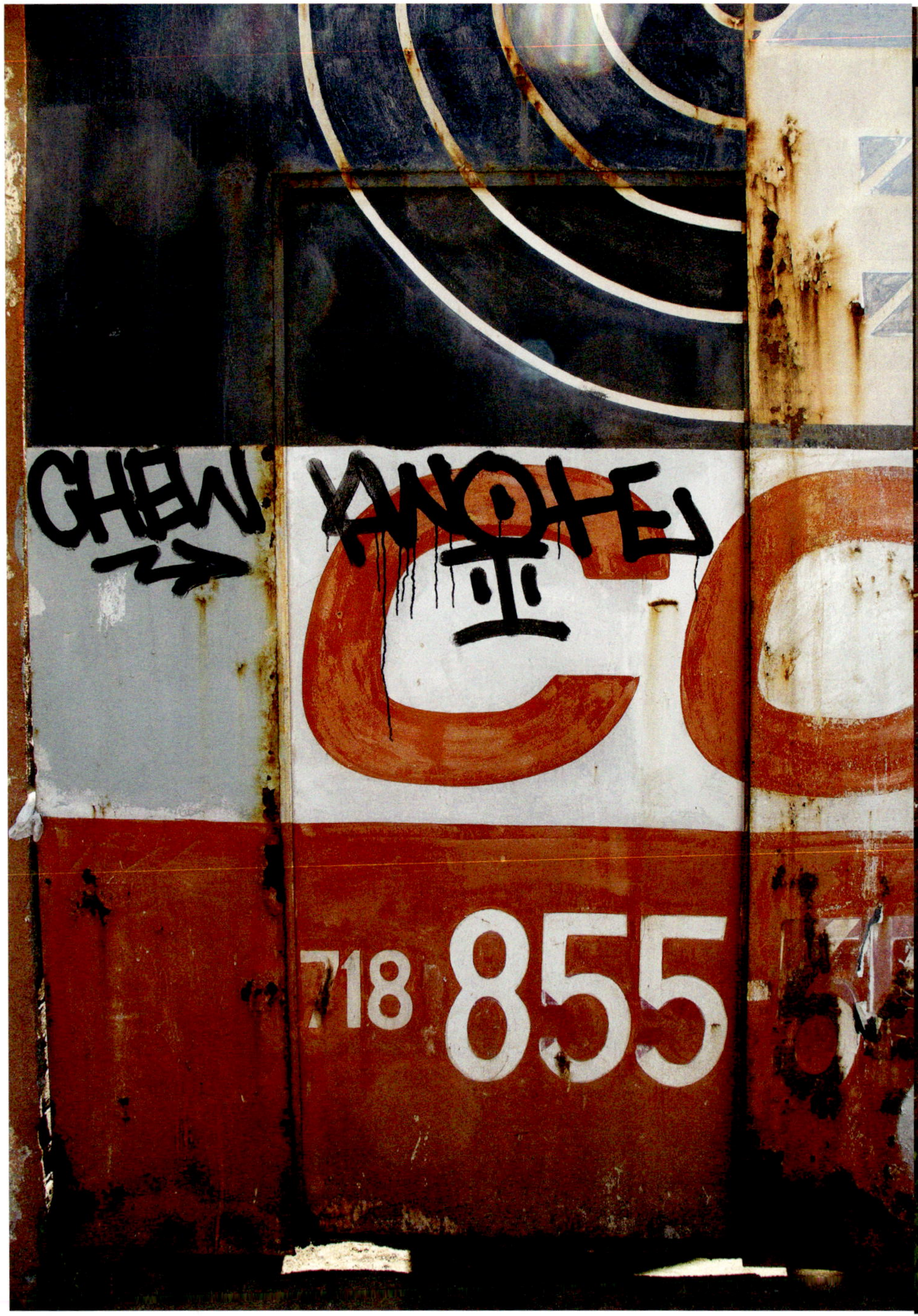
CHEW
718 855

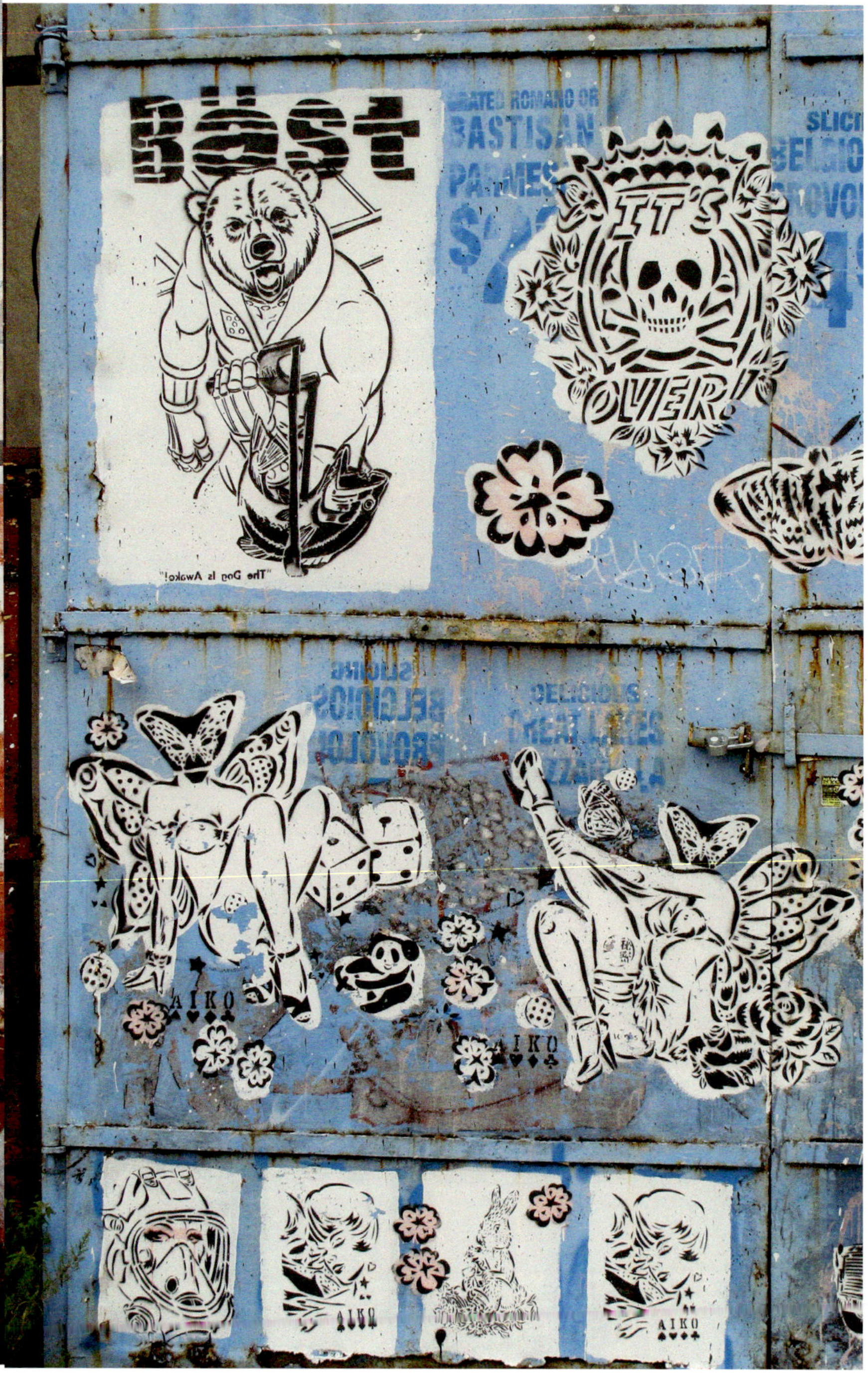
Bäst
IT'S
OVER
AIKO

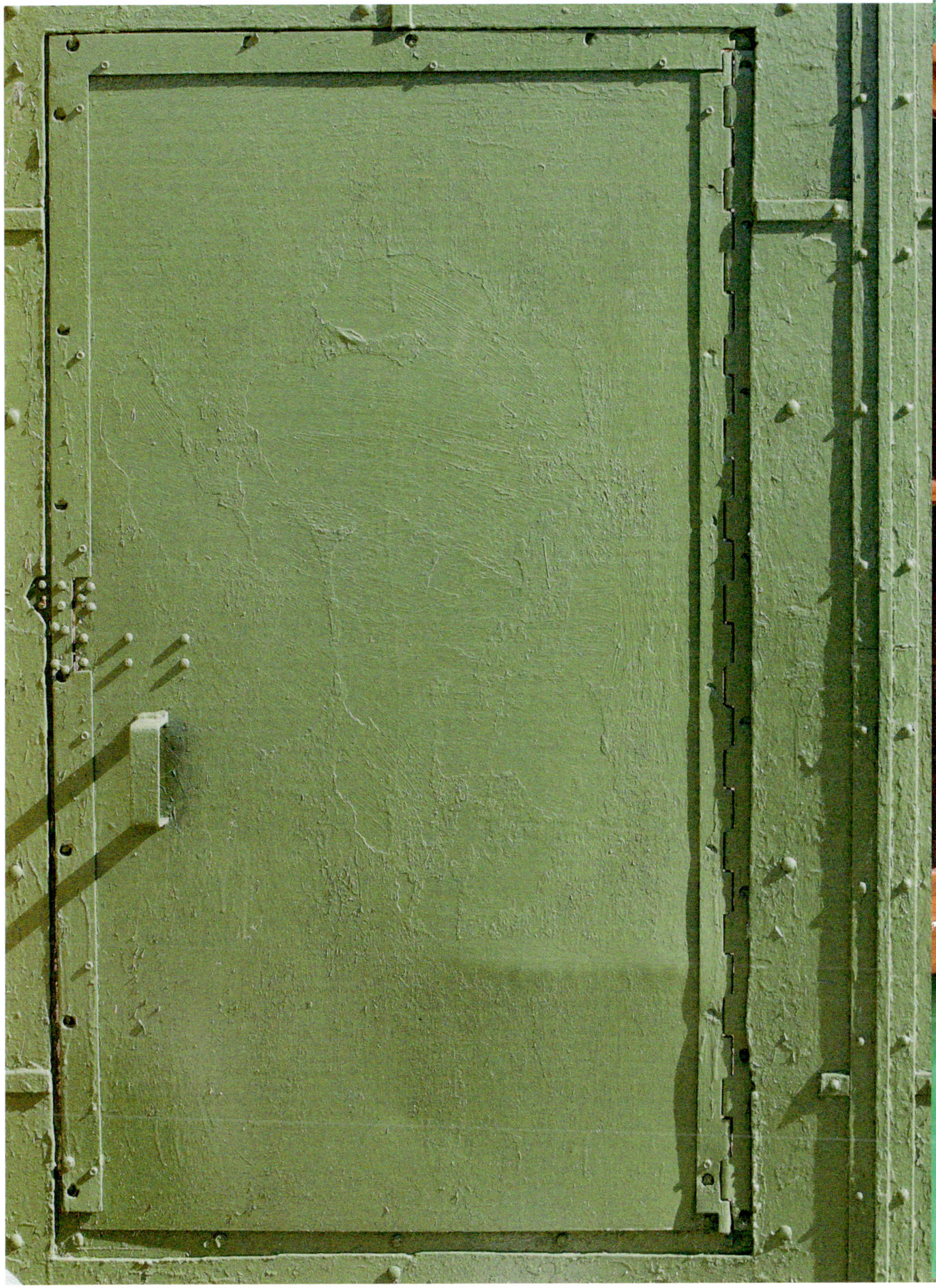
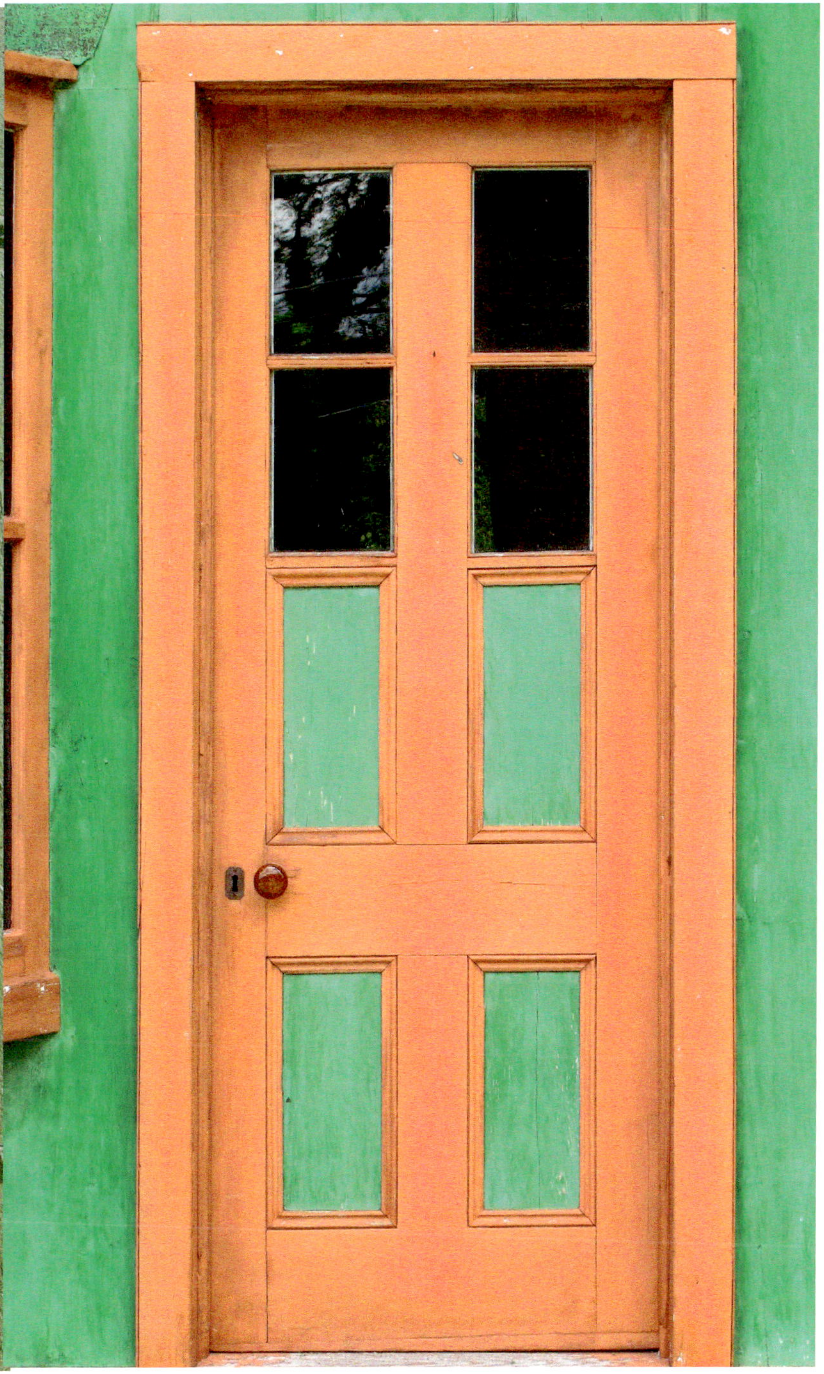

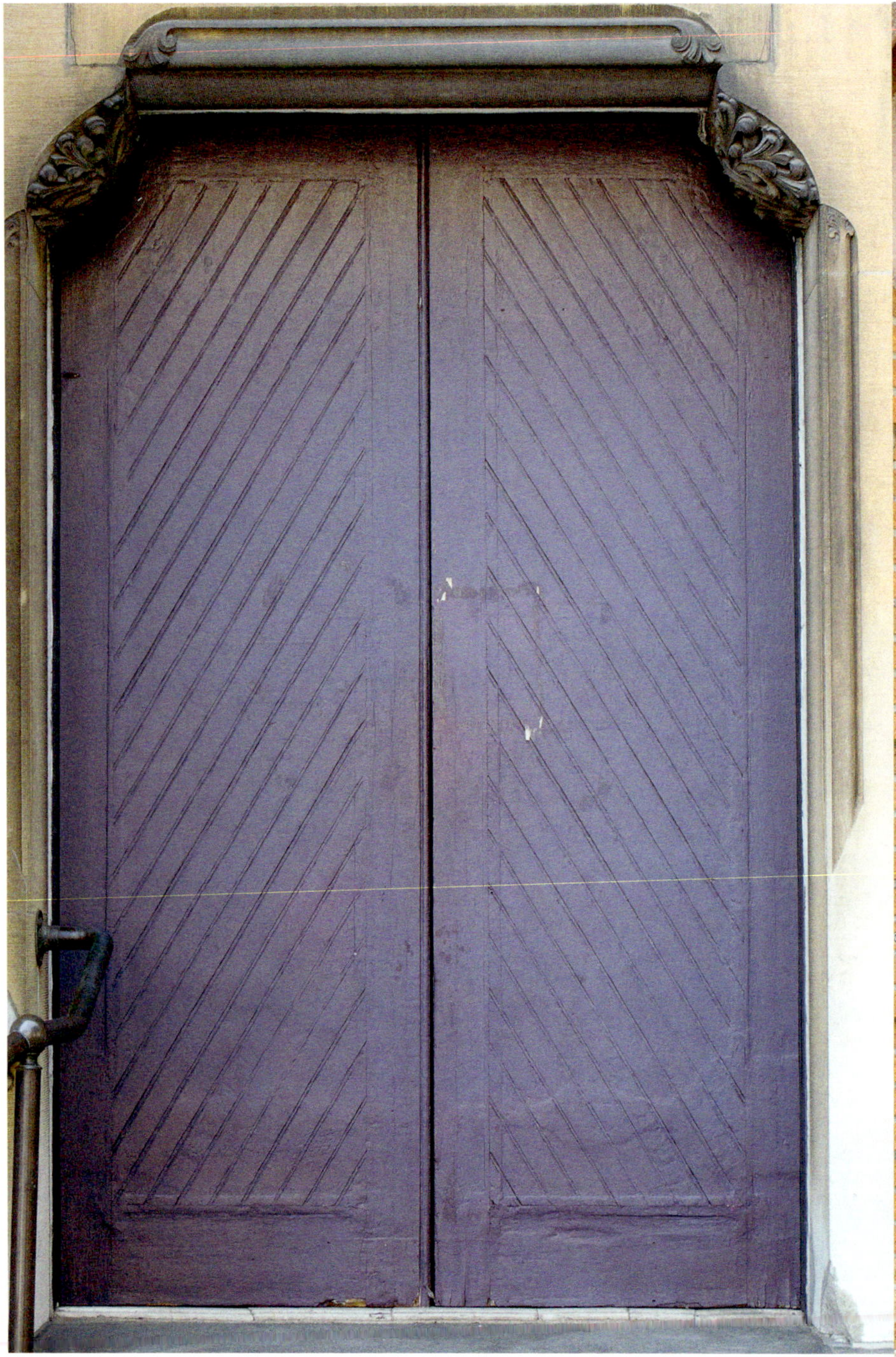

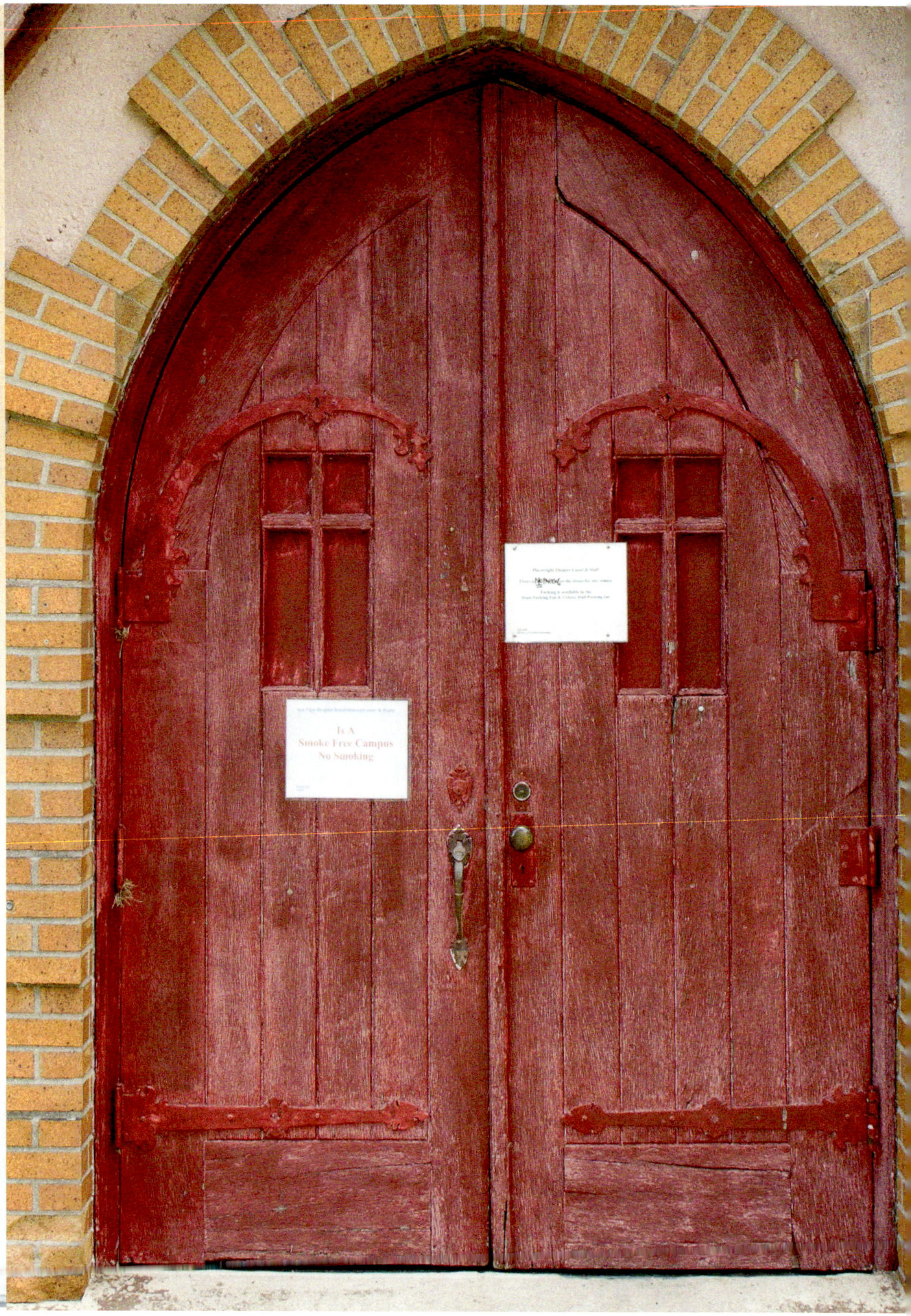
Is A
Smoke Free Campus
No Smoking

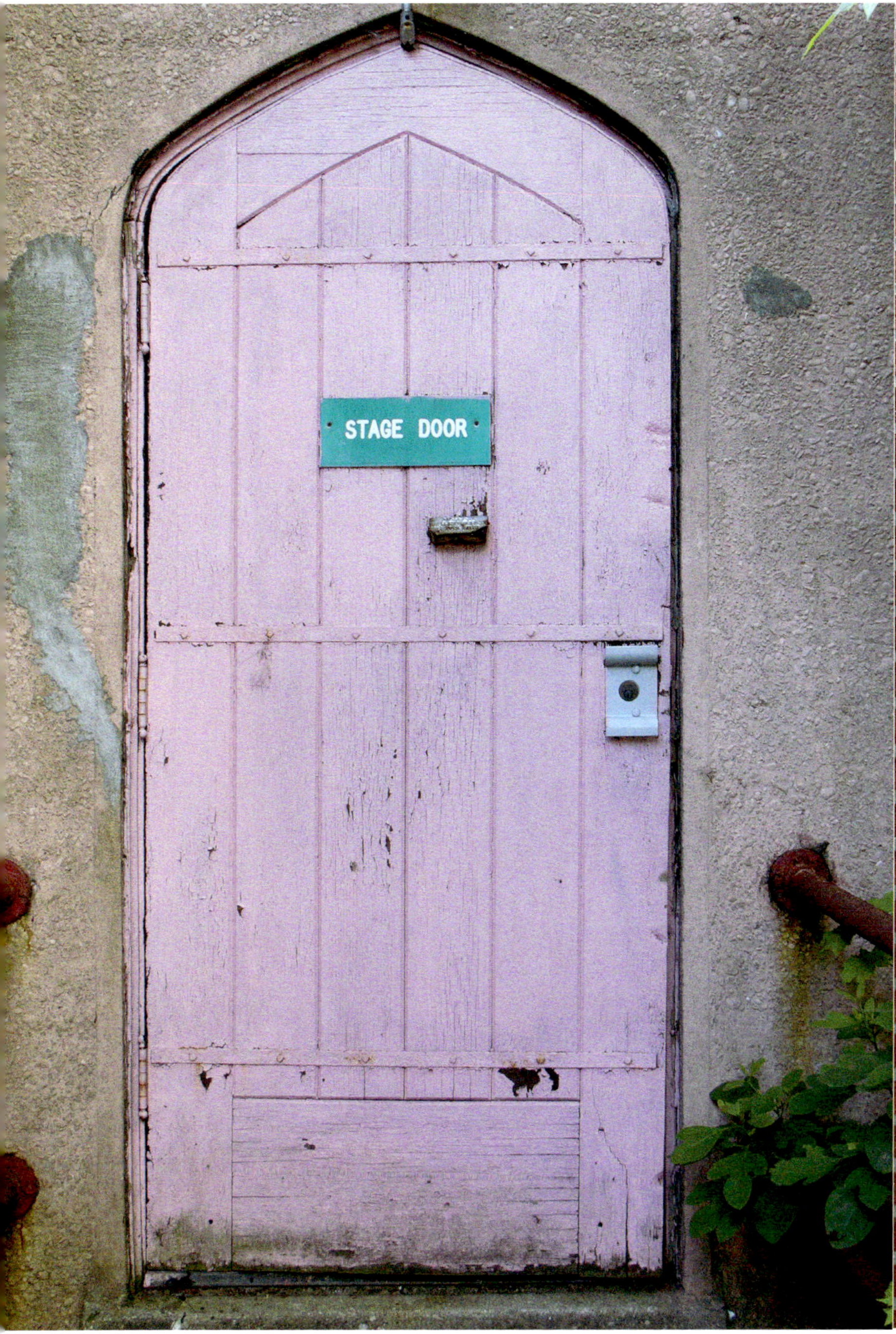
STAGE DOOR

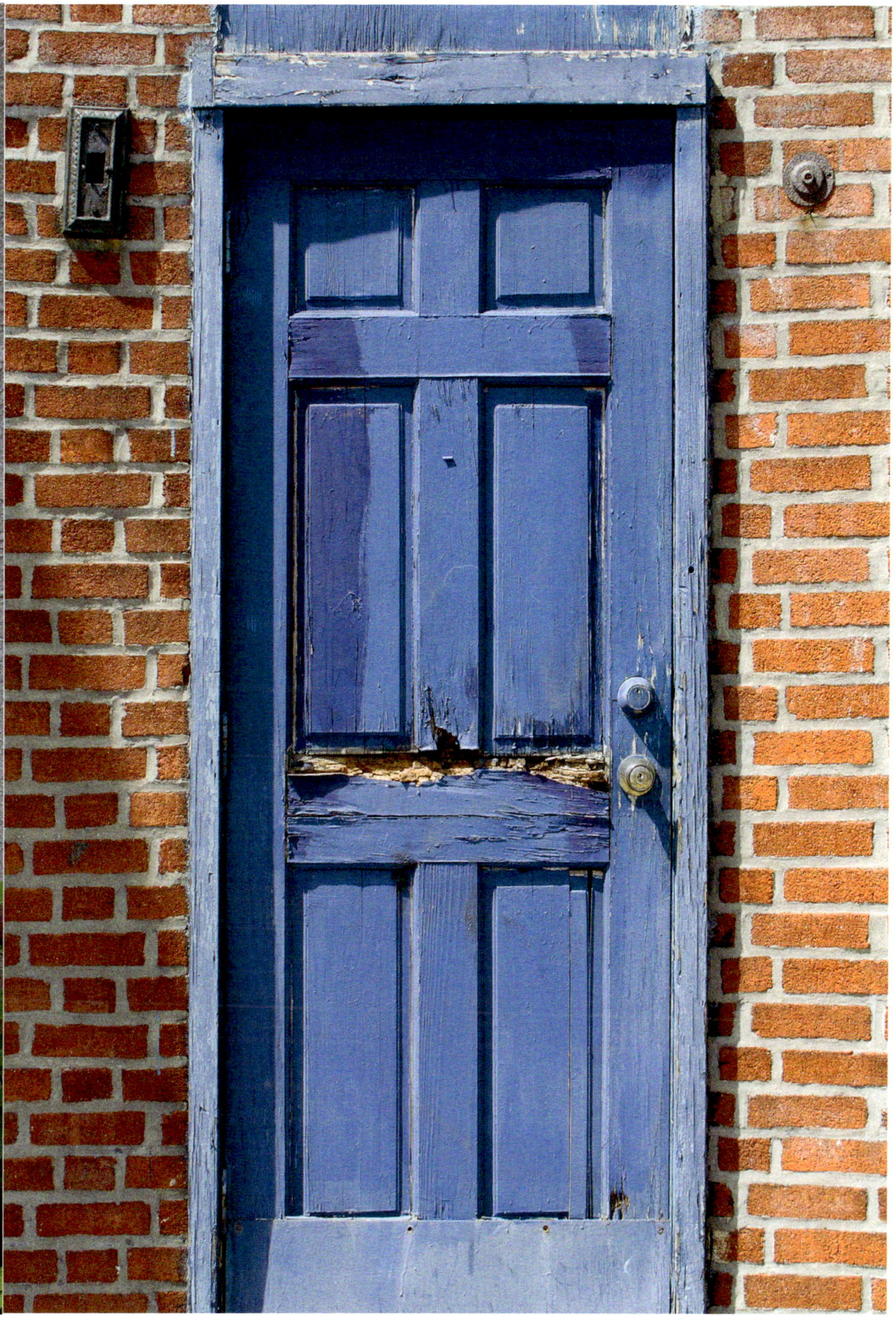

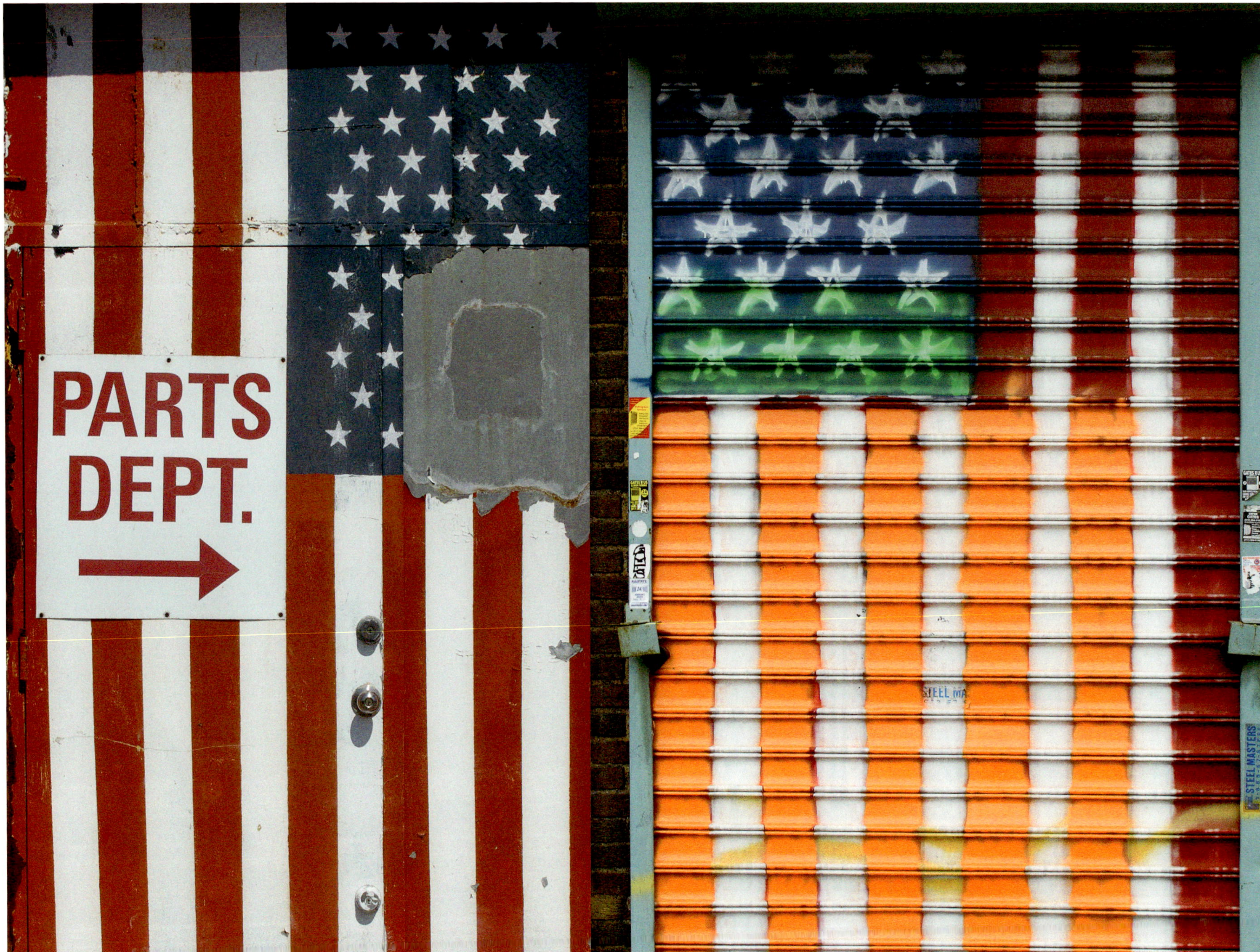
PARTS
DEPT.

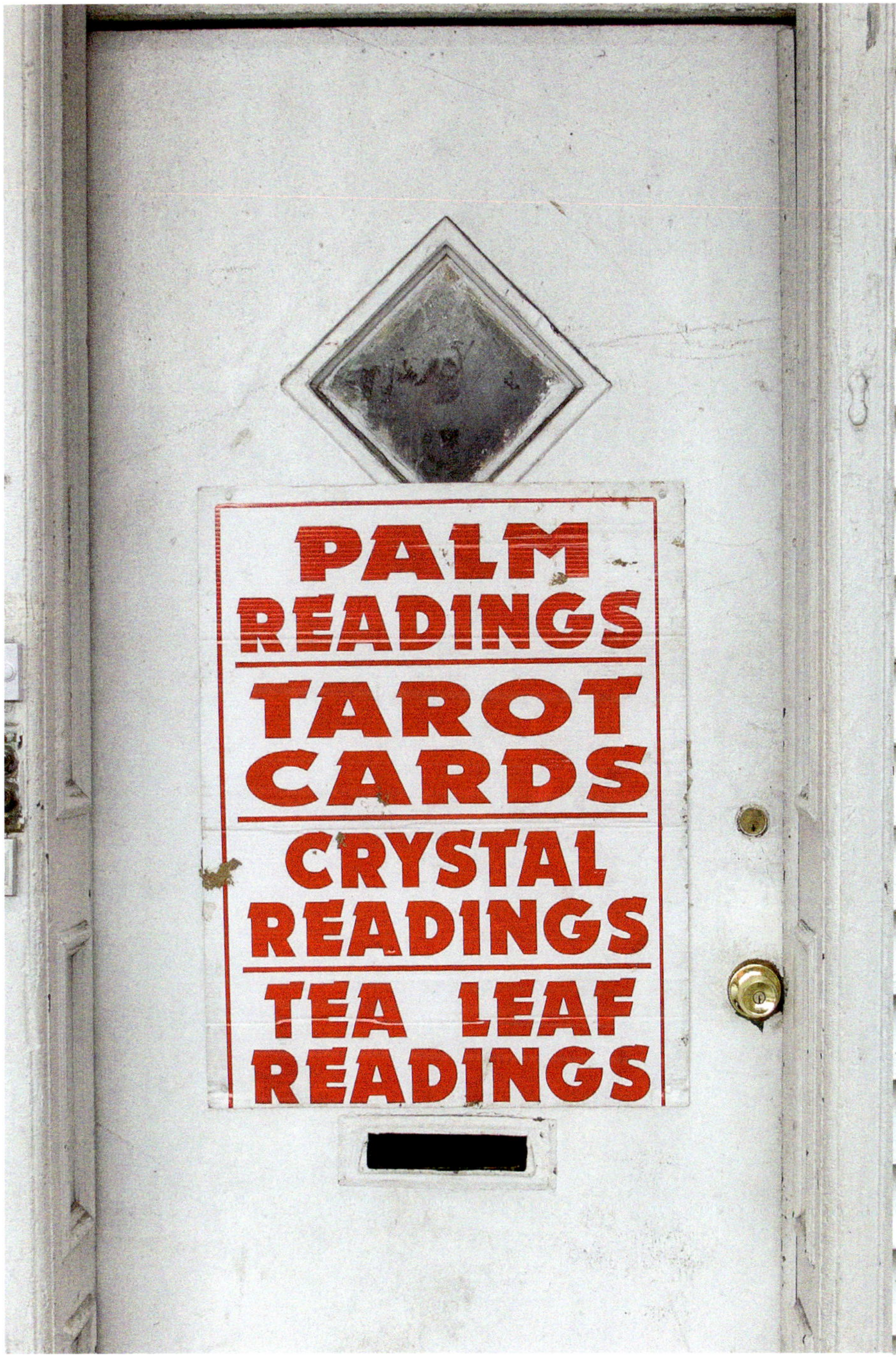
PALM
READINGS
TAROT
CARDS
CRYSTAL
READINGS
TEA LEAF
READINGS

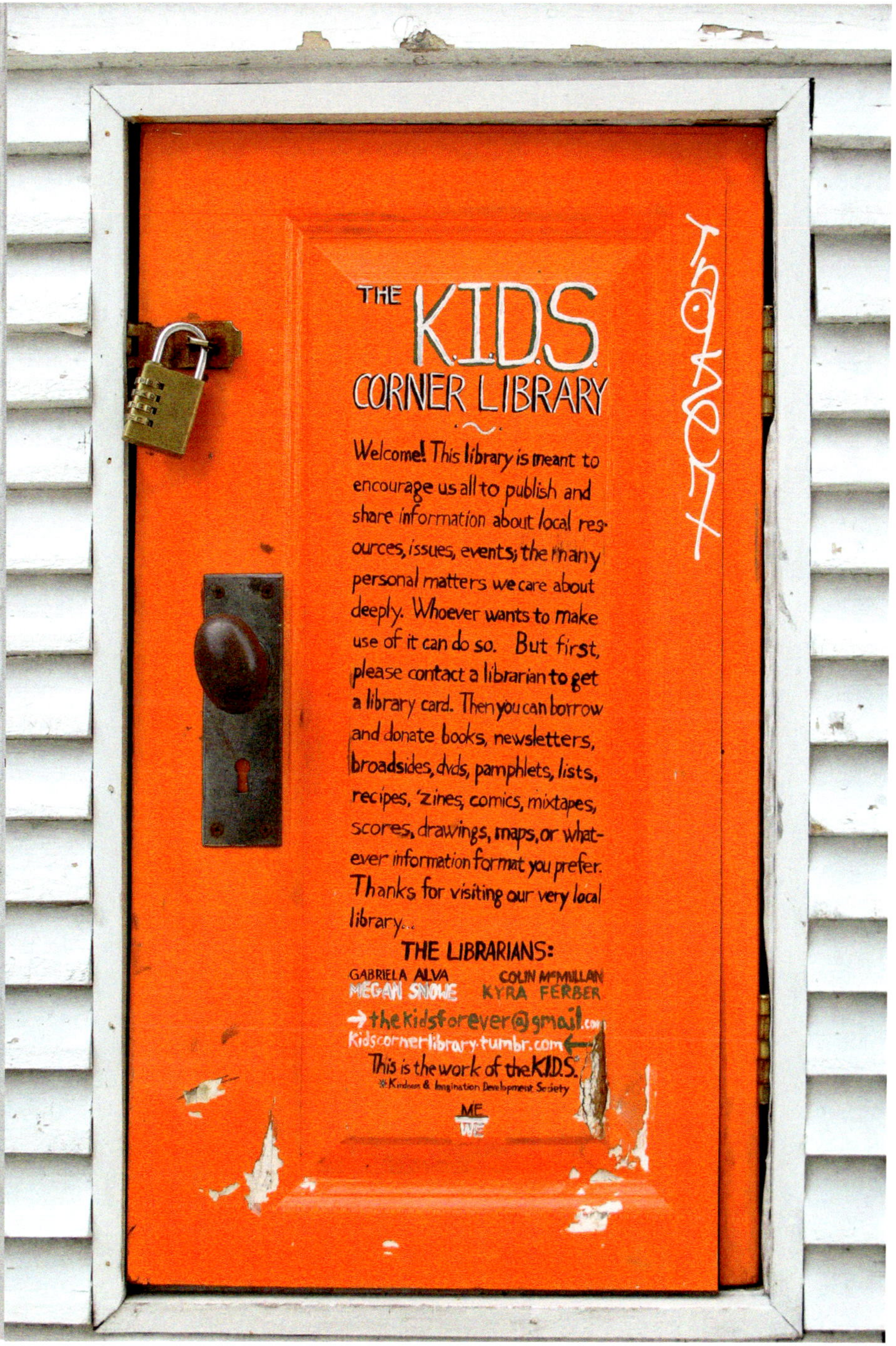
THE K.I.D.S.
CORNER LIBRARY
Welcome! This library is meant to encourage us all to publish and share information about local resources, issues, events; the many personal matters we care about deeply. Whoever wants to make use of it can do so. But first, please contact a librarian to get a library card. Then you can borrow and donate books, newsletters, broadsides, dvds, pamphlets, lists, recipes, 'zines, comics, mixtapes, scores, drawings, maps, or whatever information format you prefer. Thanks for visiting our very local library...
THE LIBRARIANS:
GABRIELA ALVA
COLIN McMILLAN
MEGAN SNOWE
KYRA FERBER
→ thekidsforever@gmail.com
Kidscornerlibrary.tumblr.com ←
This is the work of the K.I.D.S.*
*Kindness & Imagination Development Society
ME
WE

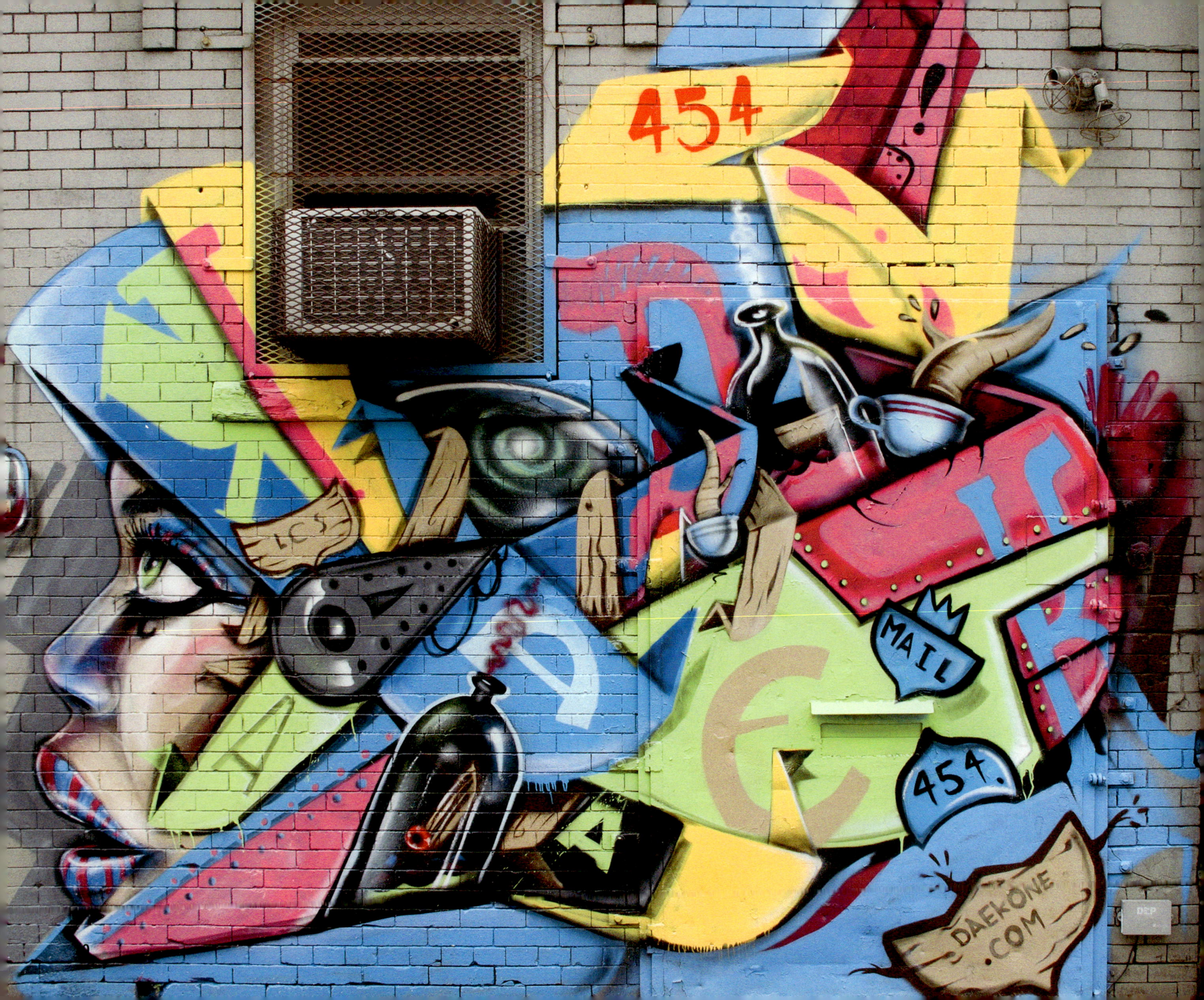
454
MAIL
454.
DAEKONE
.COM

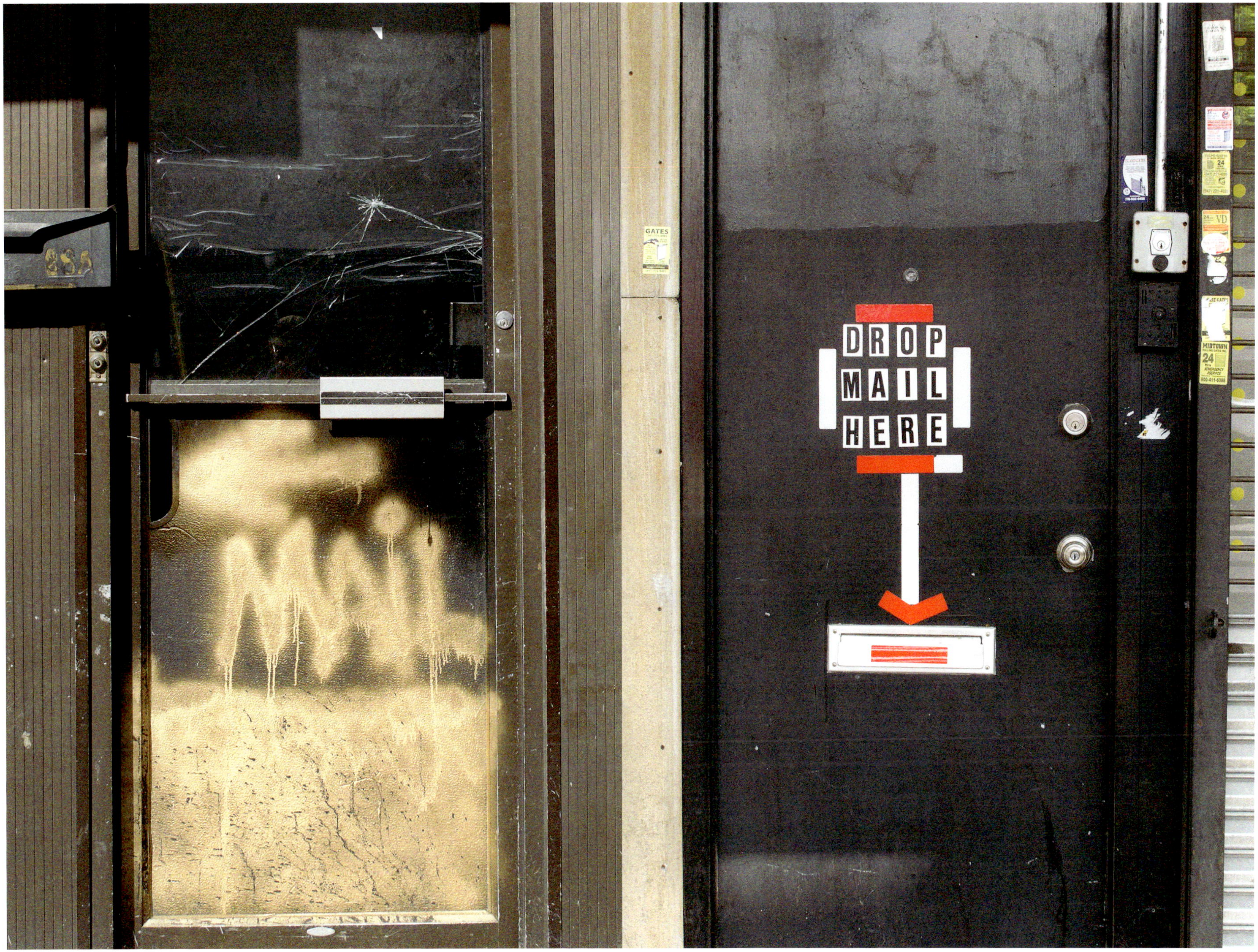
MAIL
GATES
DROP
MAIL
HERE
MIDTOWN

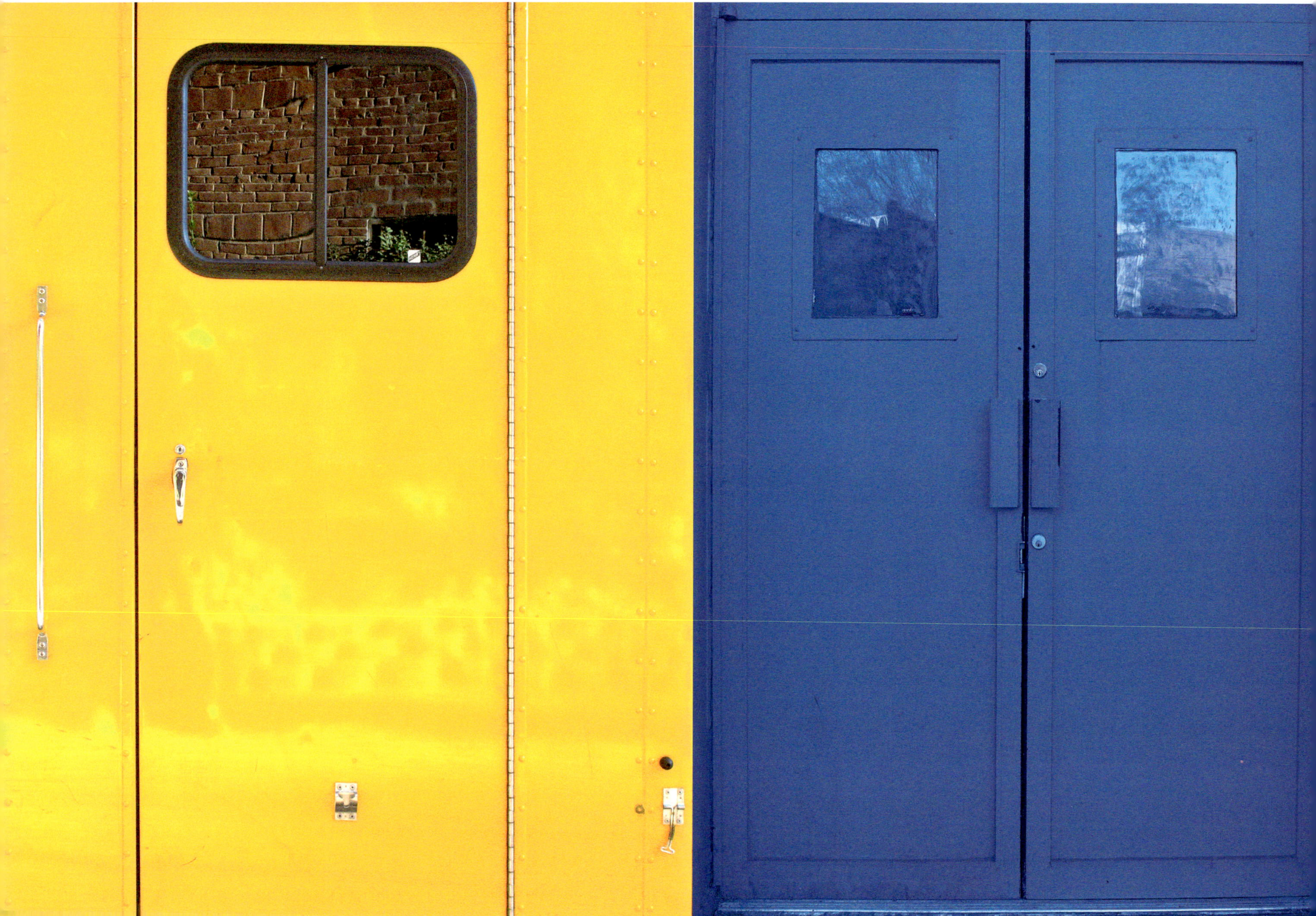

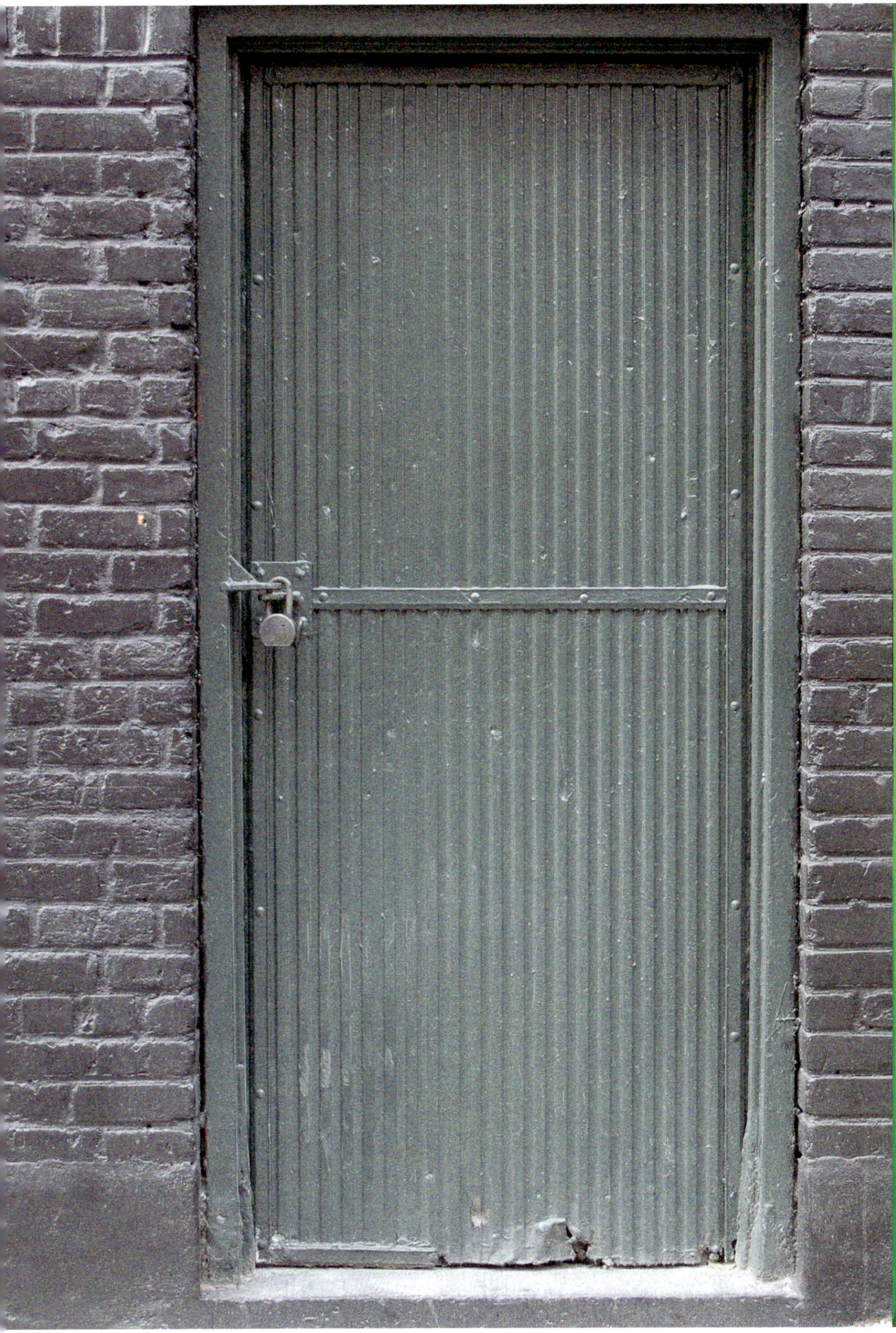

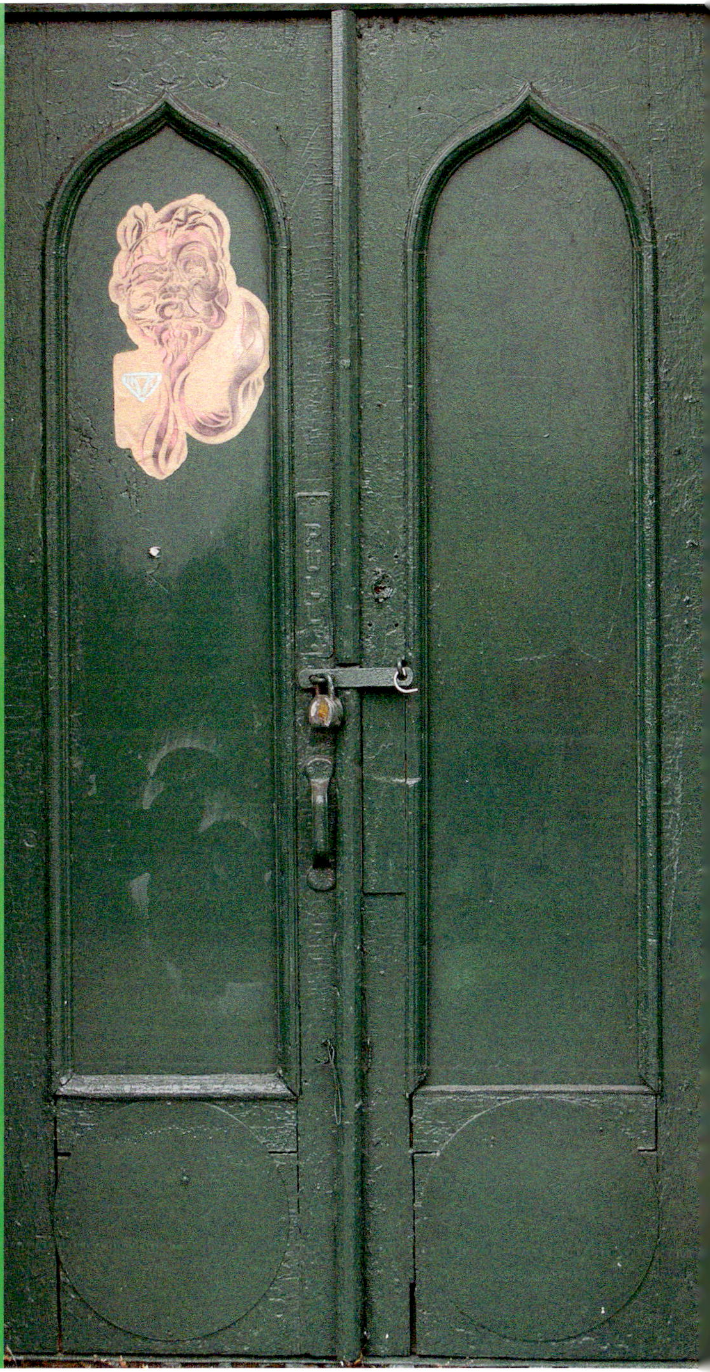

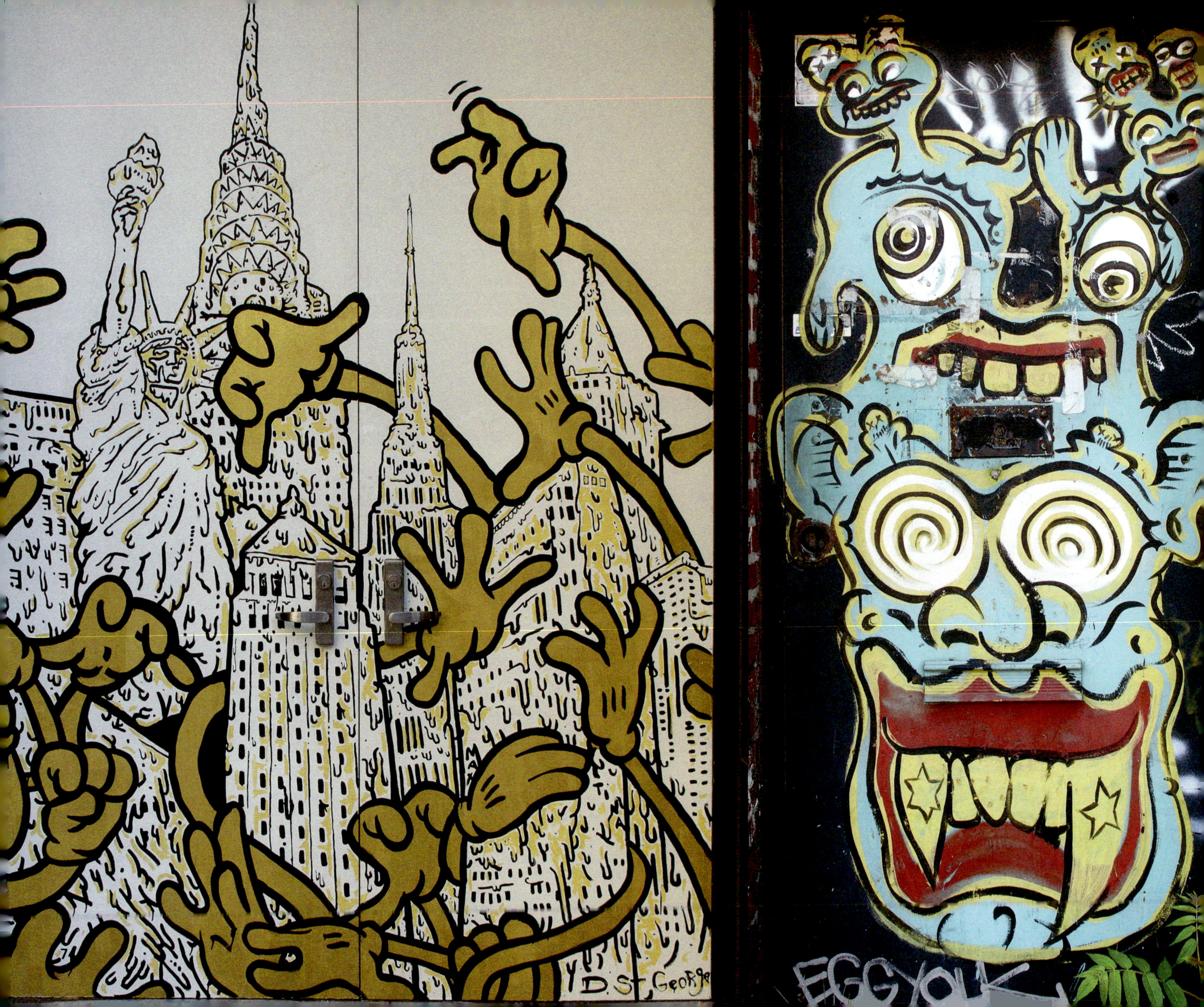
D. St. George
EGGYOLK

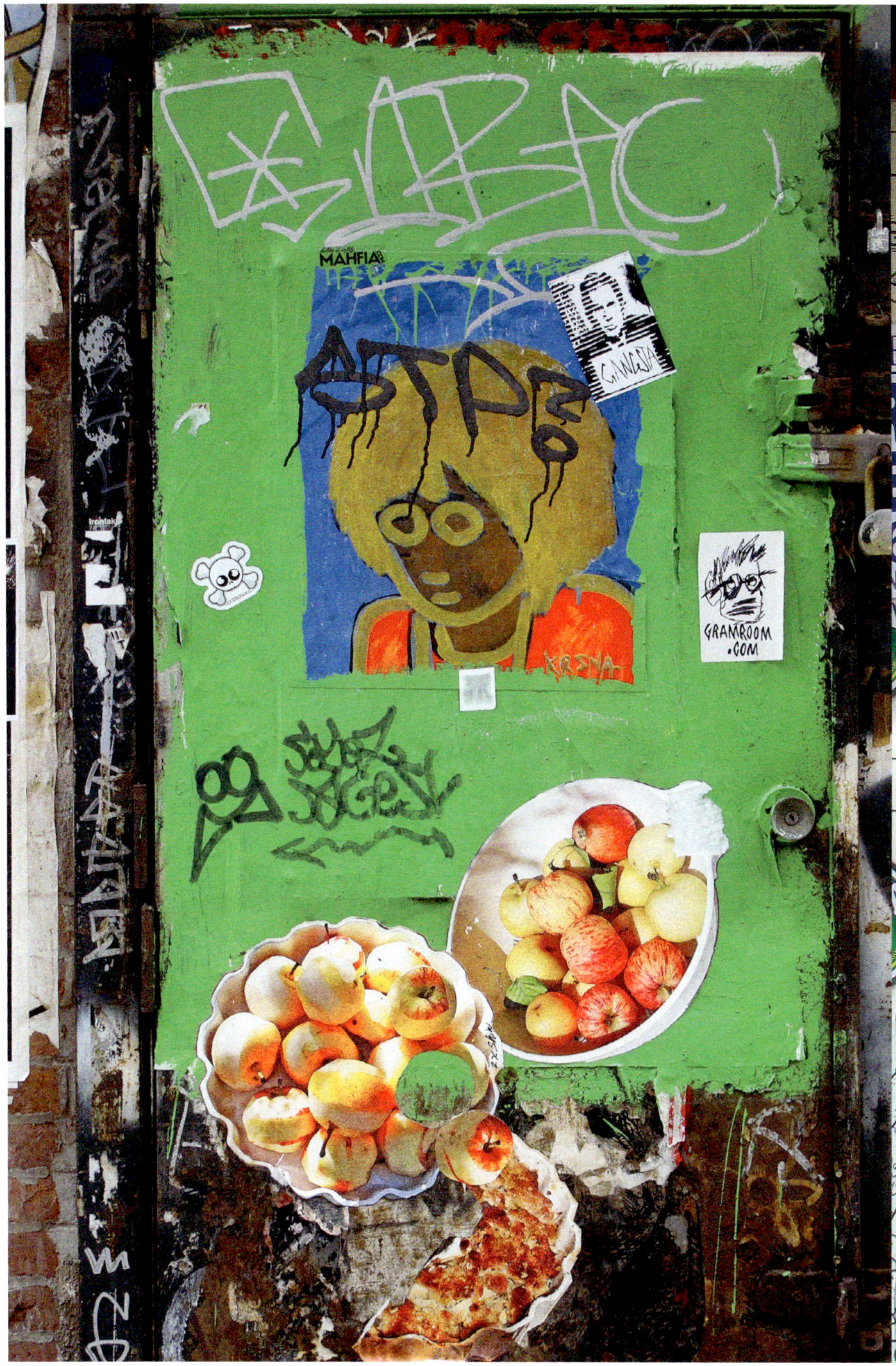
MAHFIA
GRAMROOM
.COM
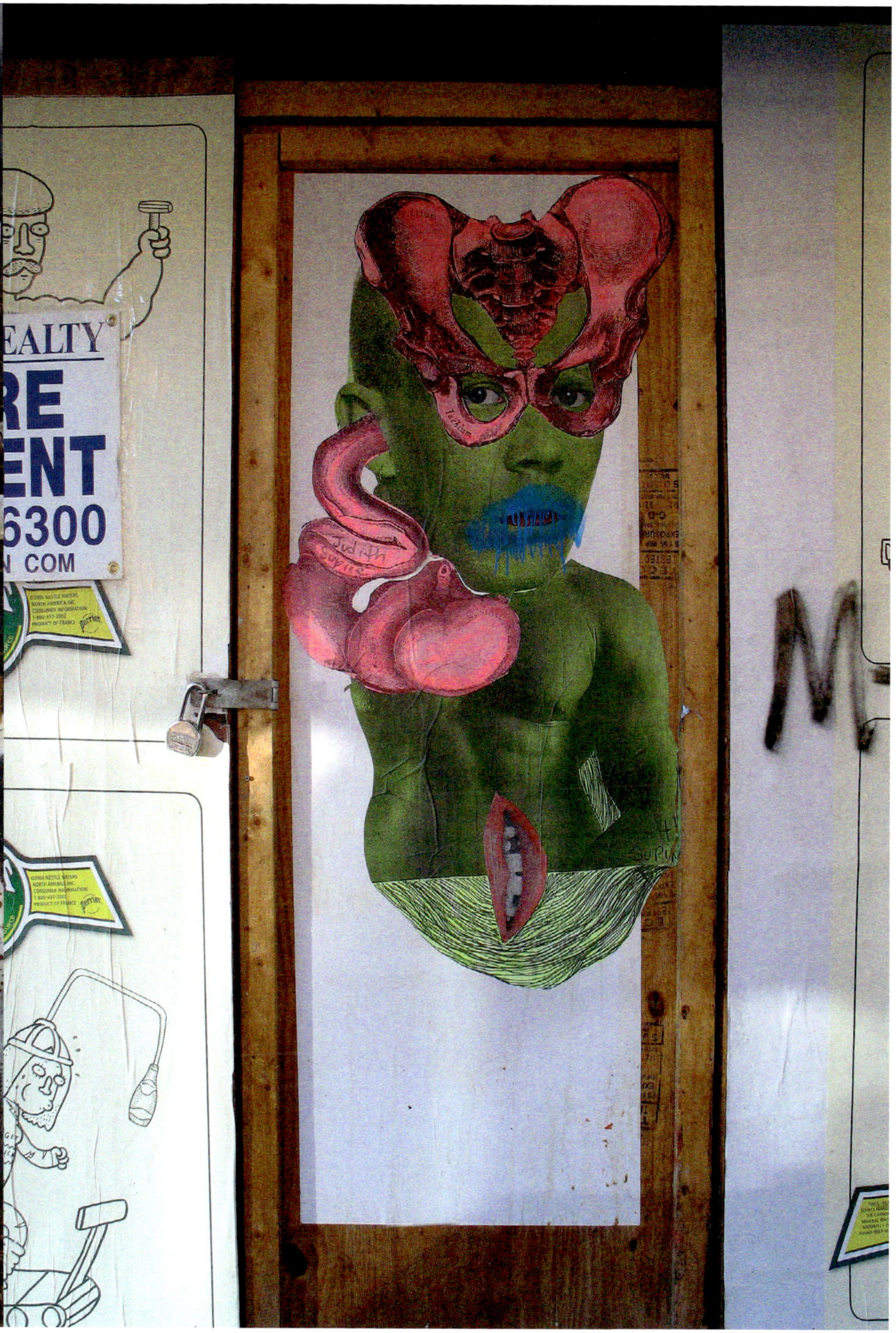
EALTY
RE
ENT
6300
N COM

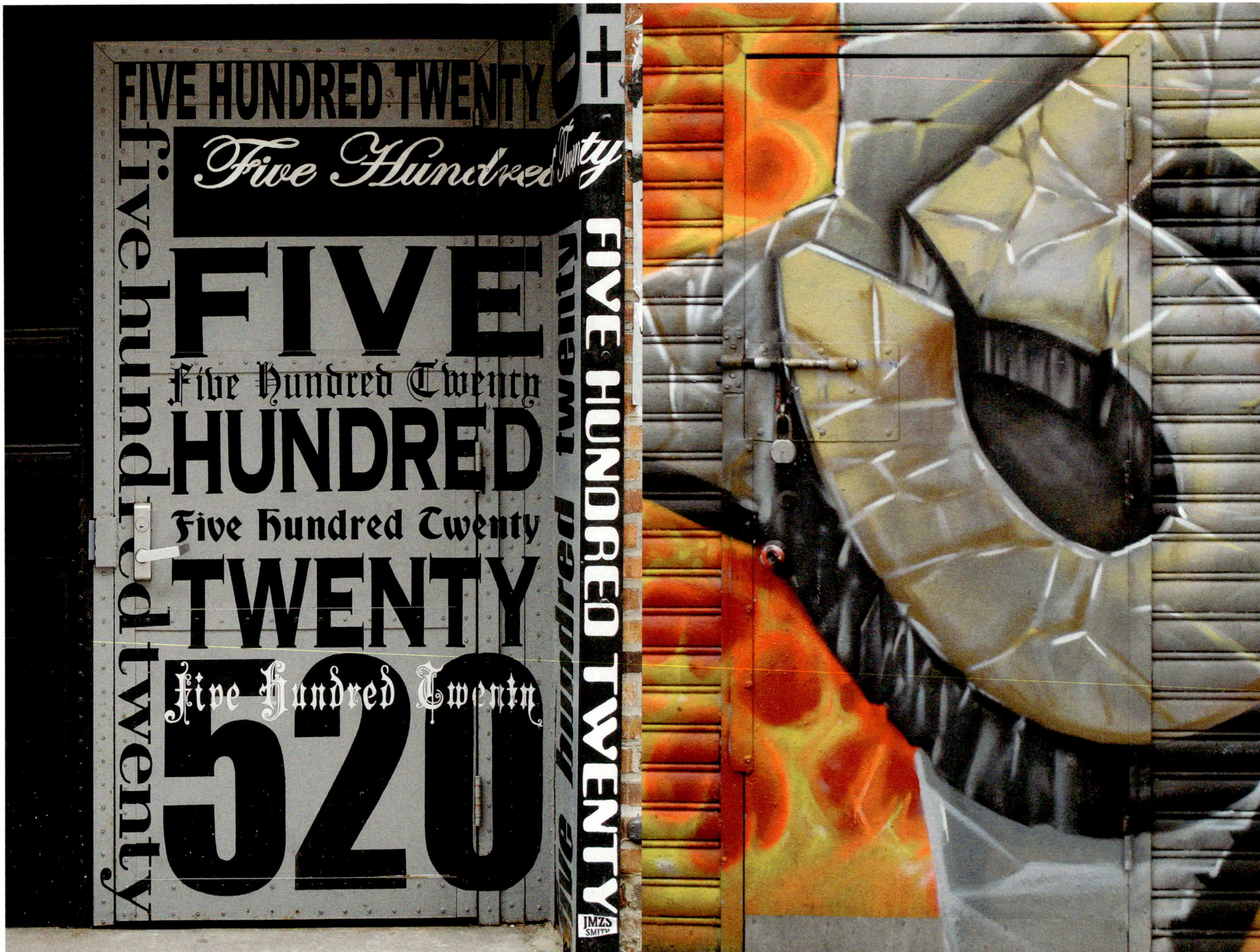
FIVE HUNDRED TWENTY
Five Hundred Twenty
five hundred twenty
FIVE
Five Hundred Twenty
HUNDRED
Five Hundred Twenty
TWENTY
520
FIVE HUNDRED TWENTY
JMZS SMITH

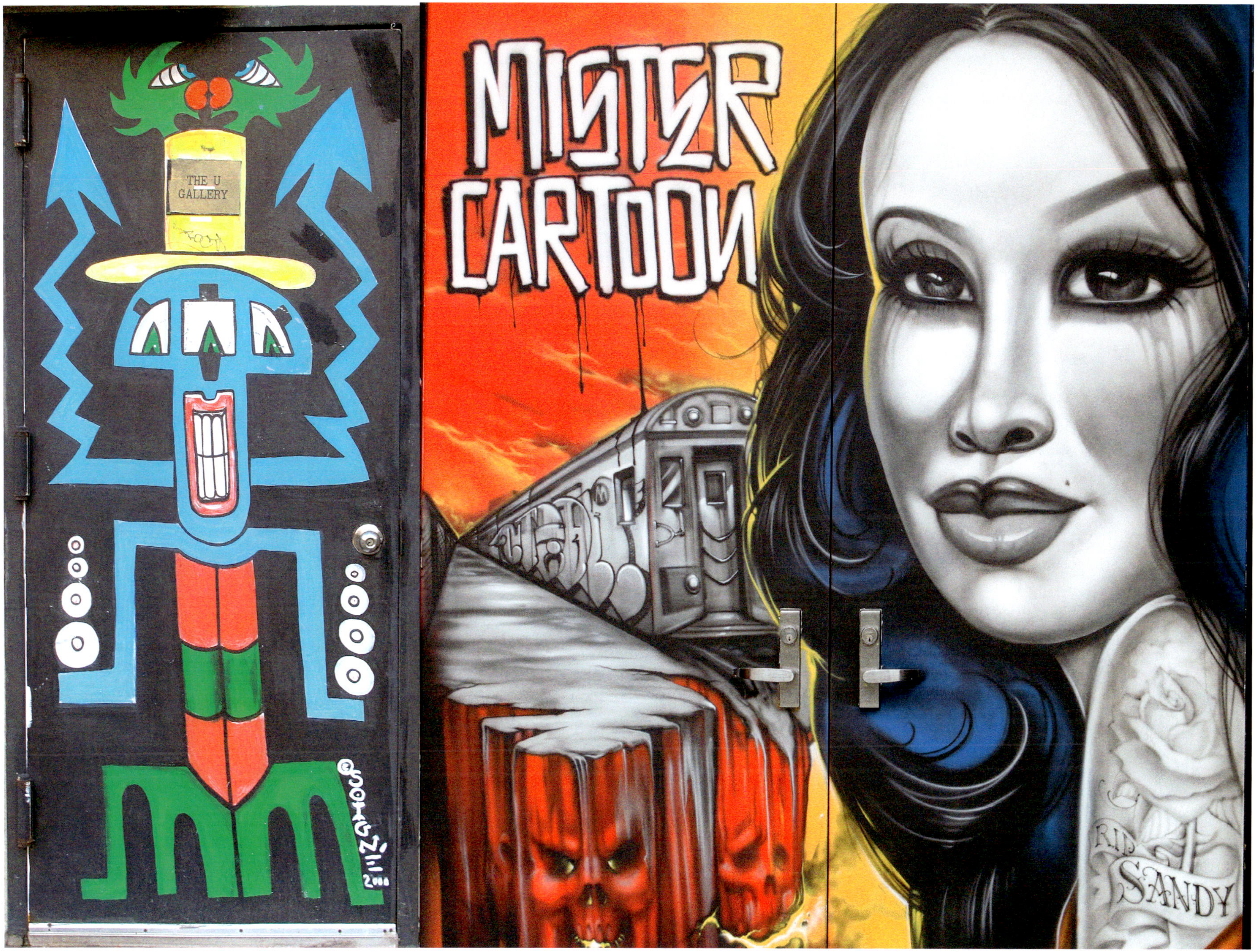
THE U
GALLERY
MISTER
CARTOON
RIP
SANDY

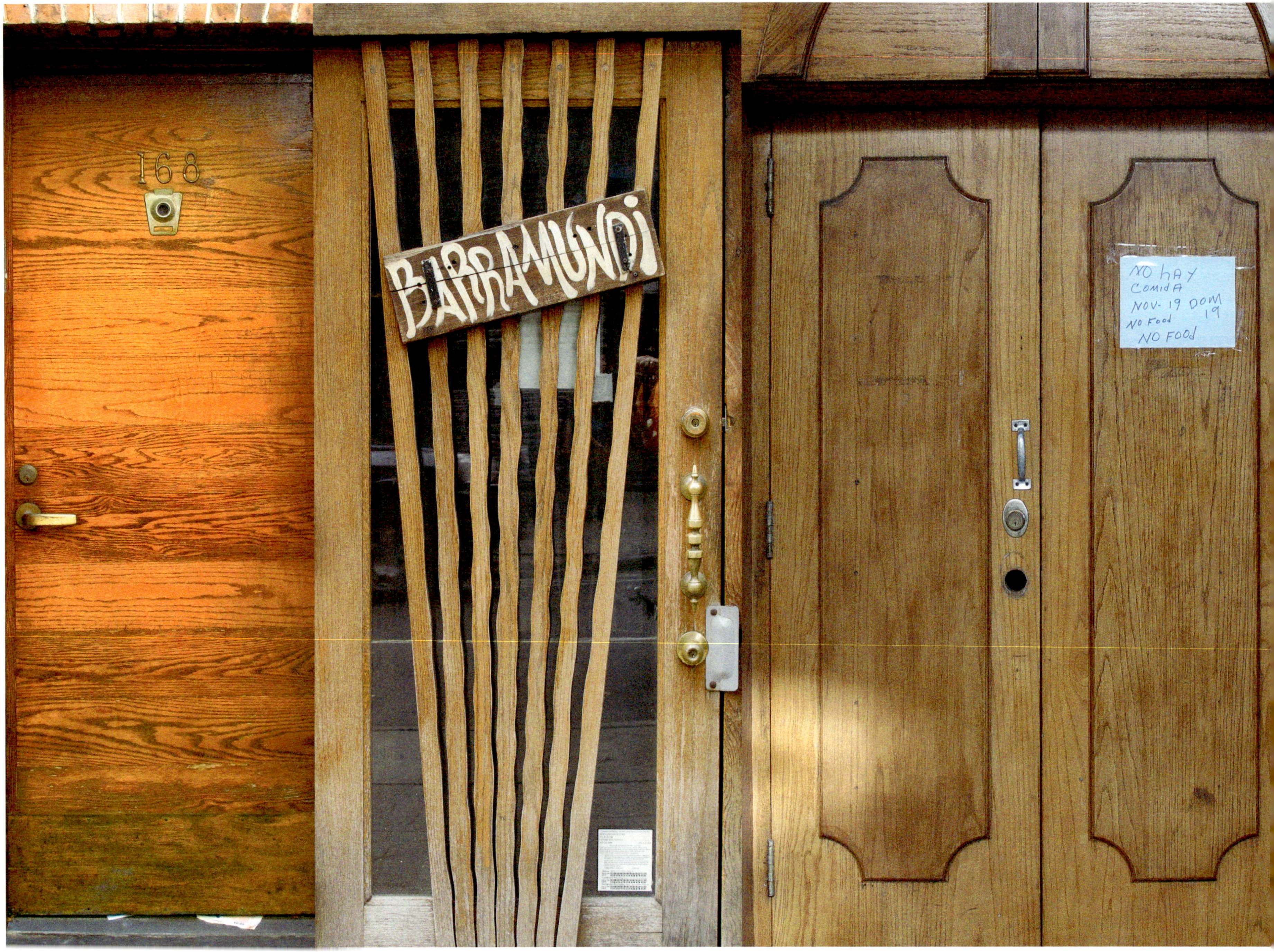
168
BARRAMUNDI
NO hAY
COMidA
NOV. 19 DOM
19
NO Food
NO FOOd

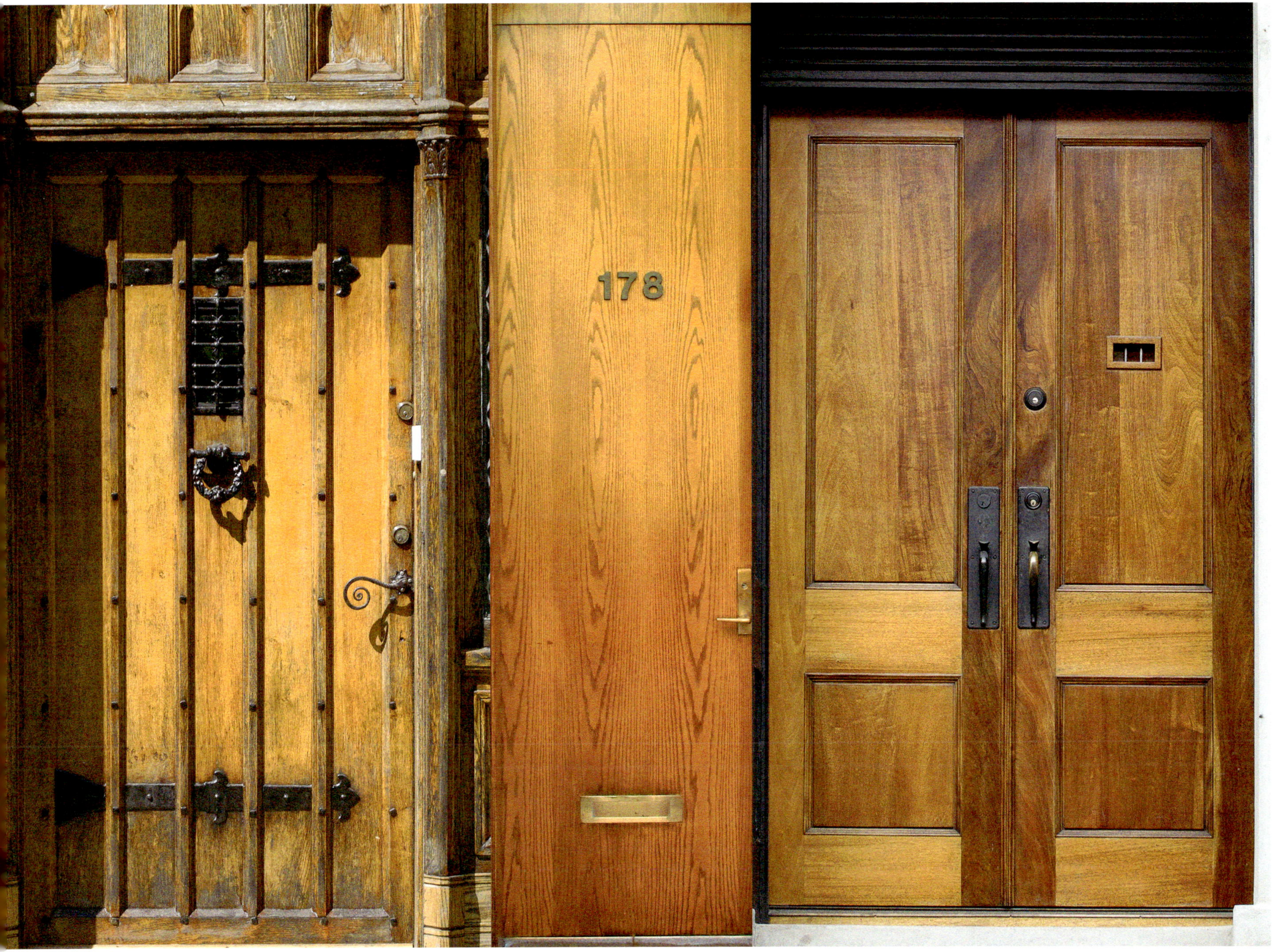
178

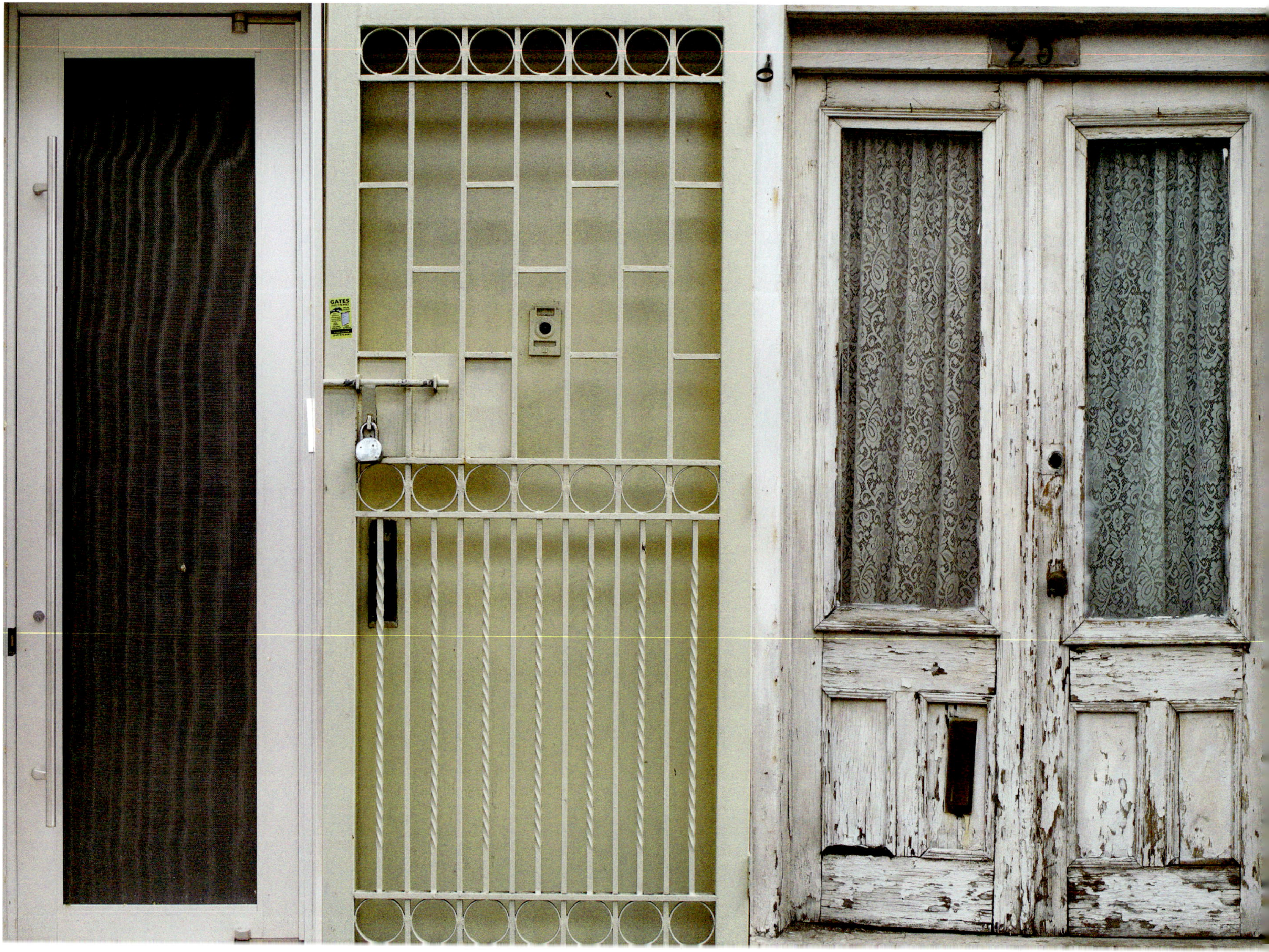
GATES

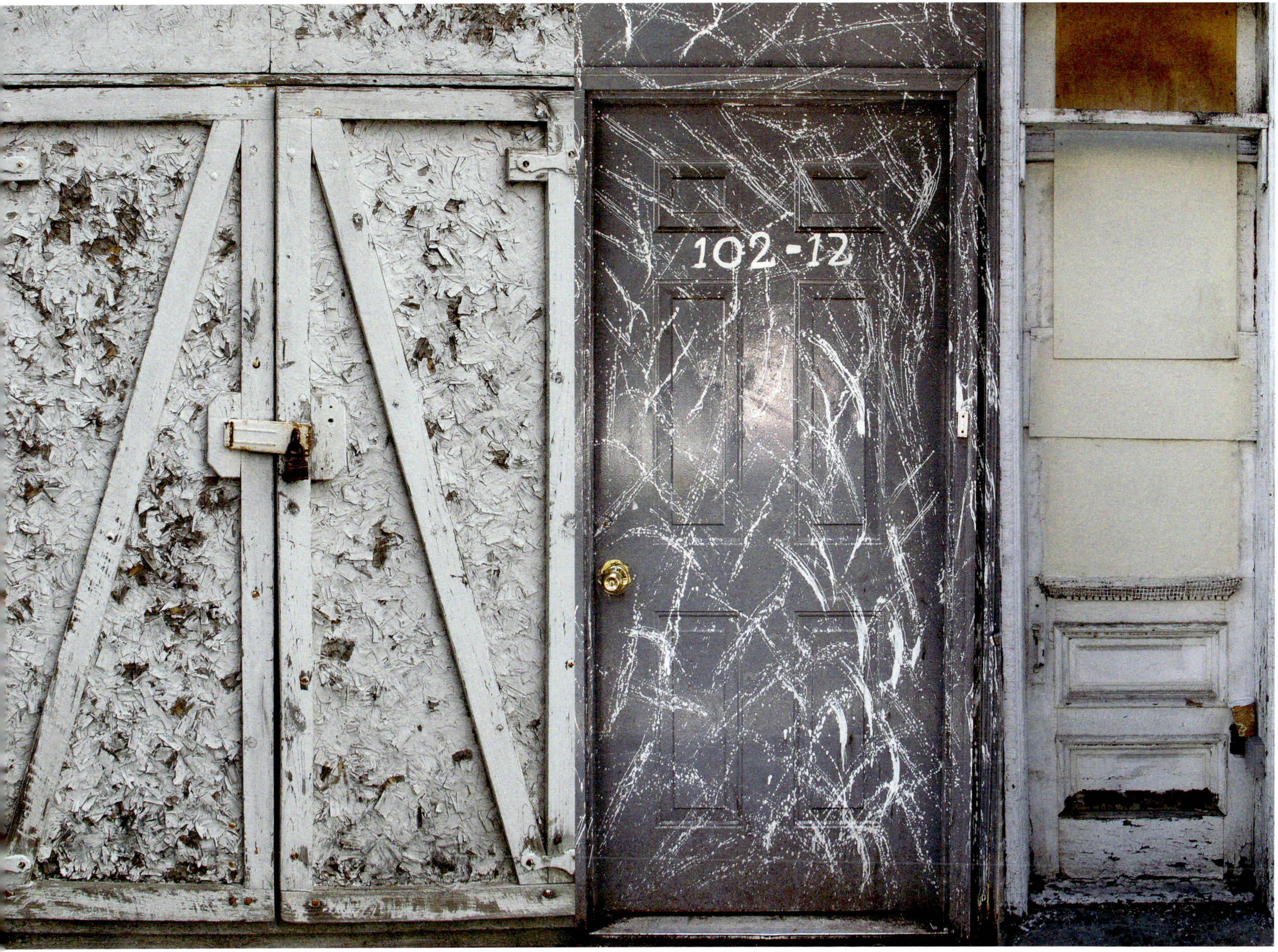
102-12

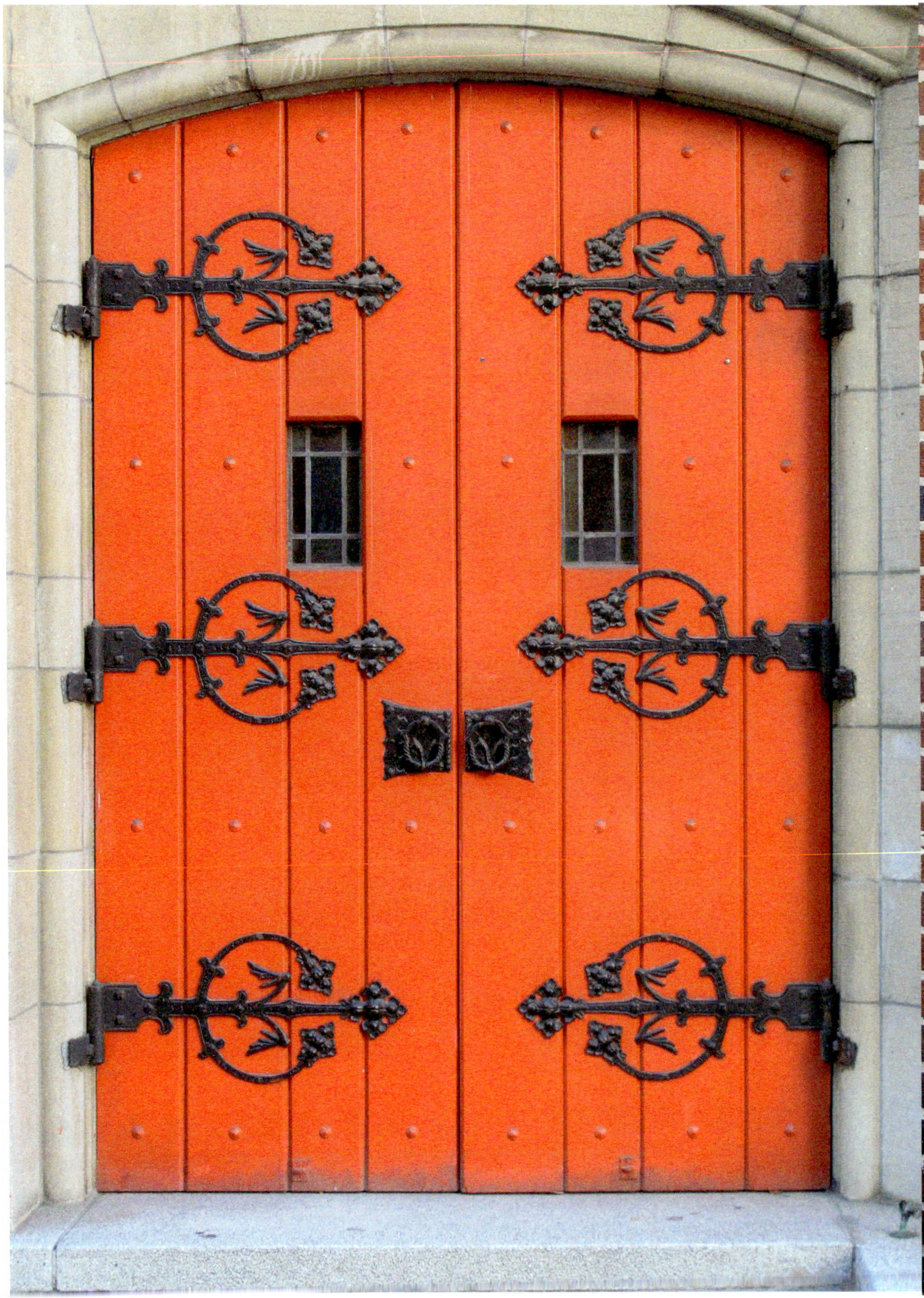

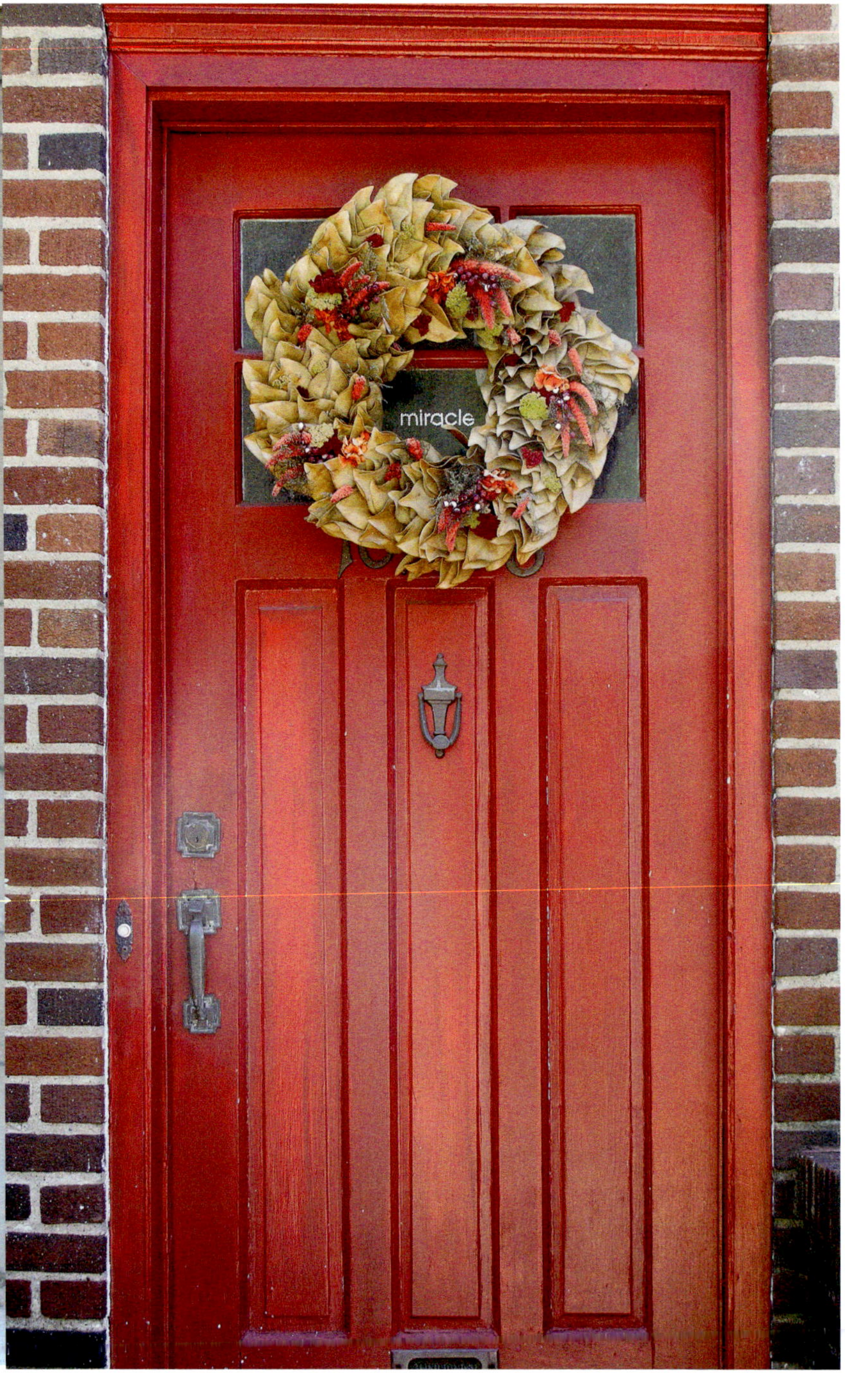
miracle

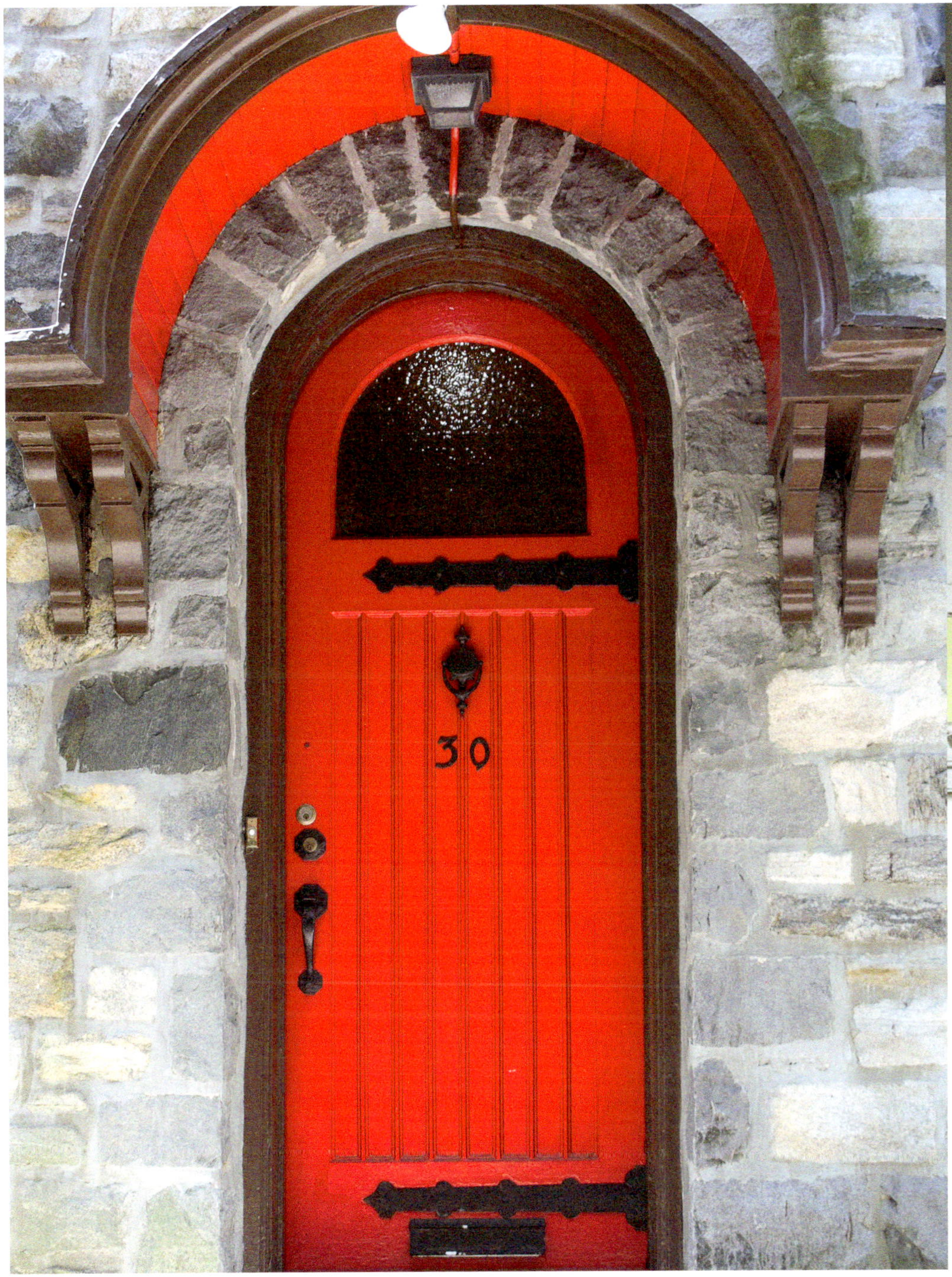
30

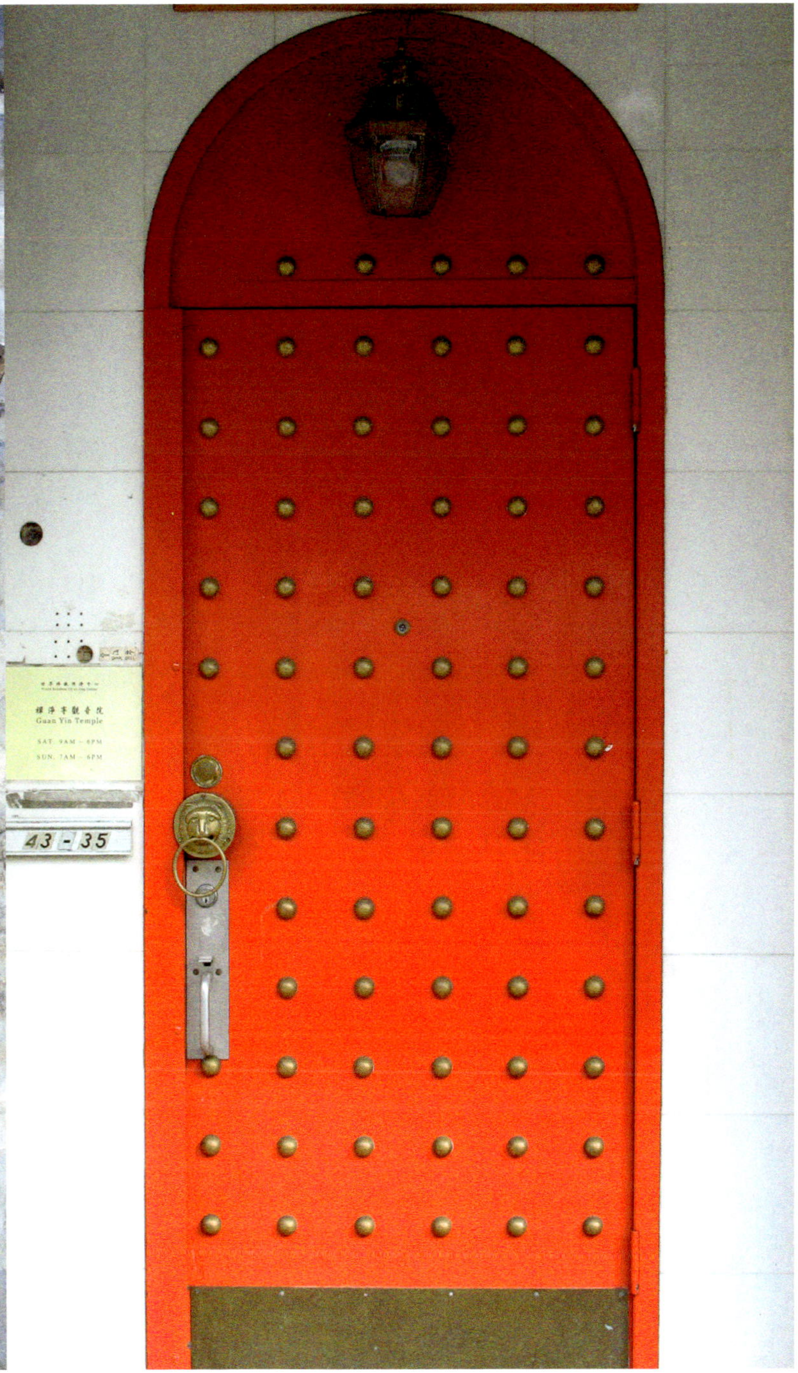
Guan Yin Temple
43 - 35

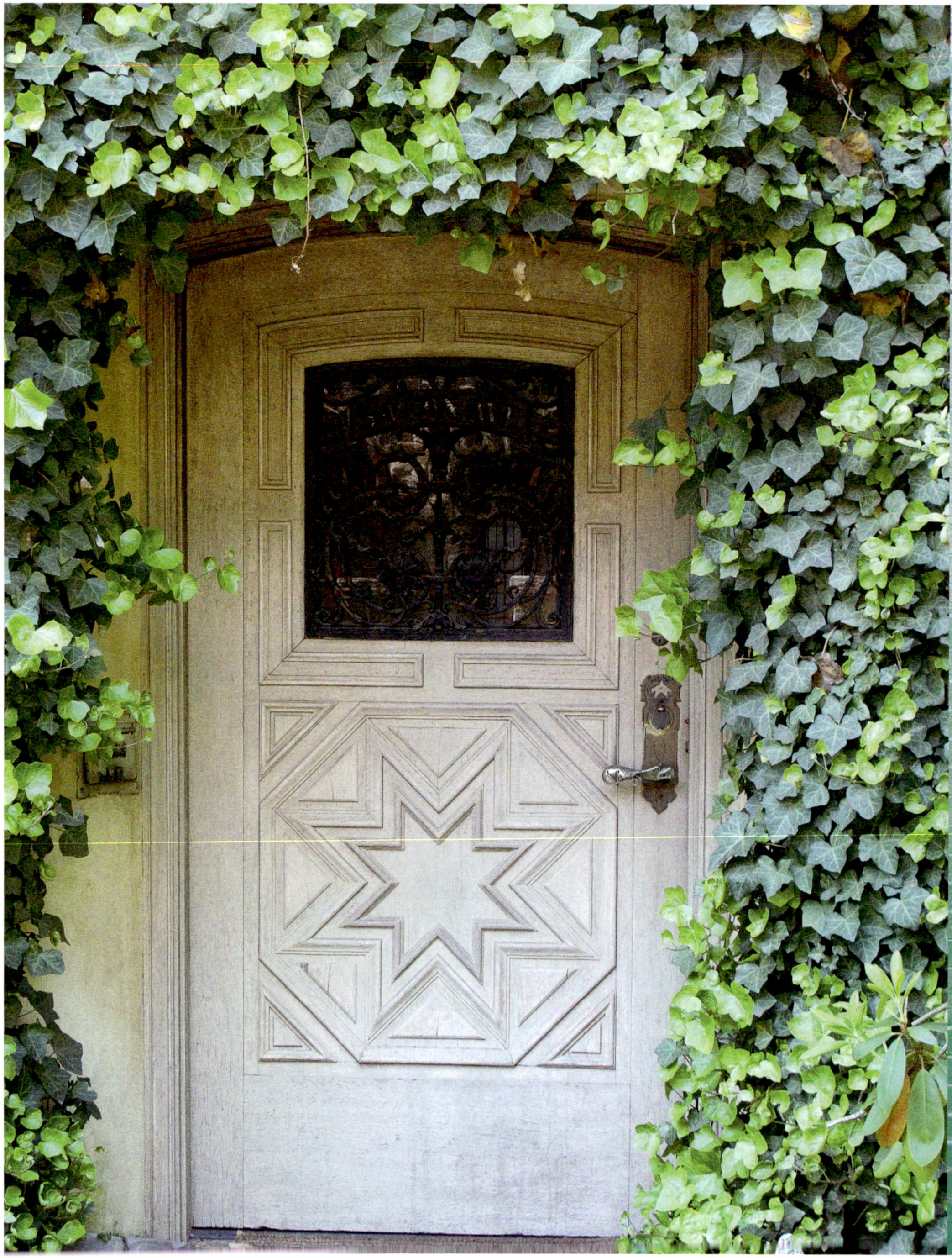

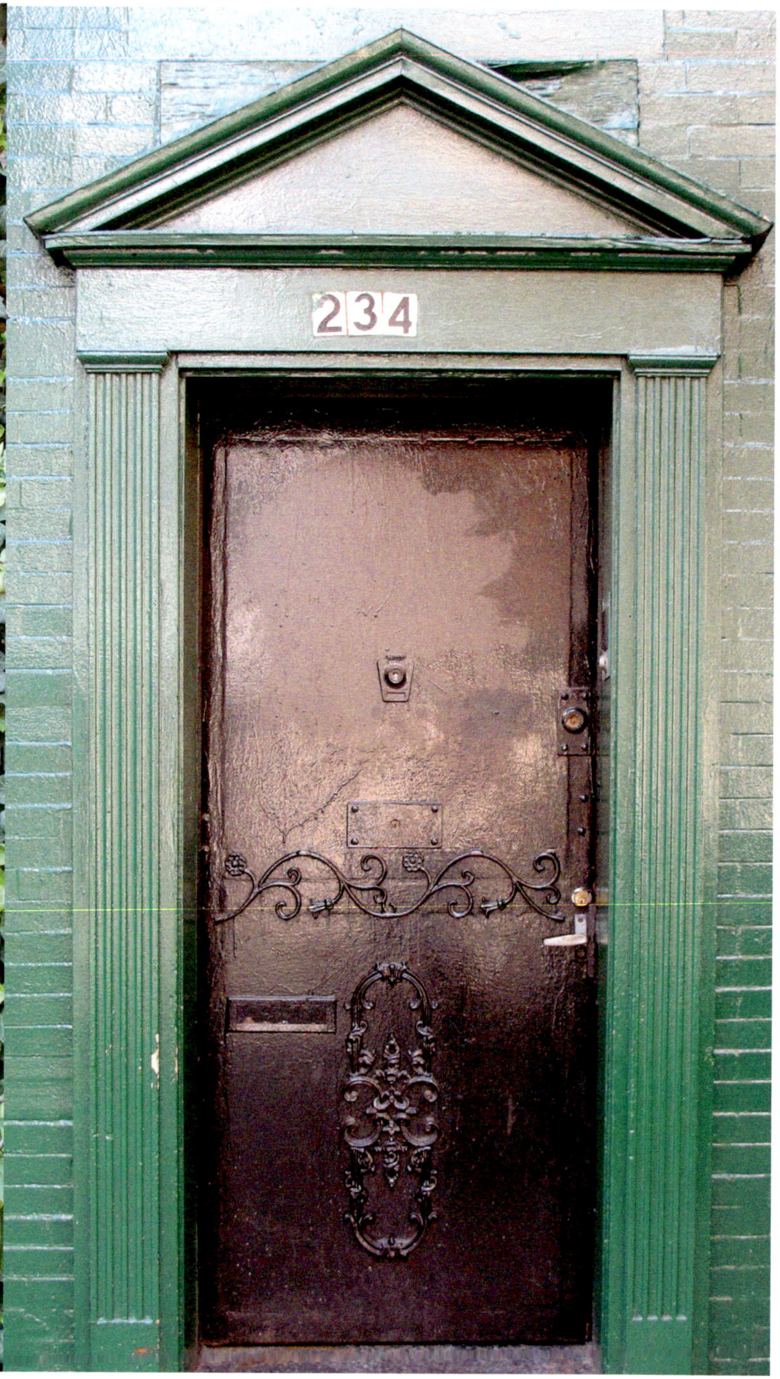
234

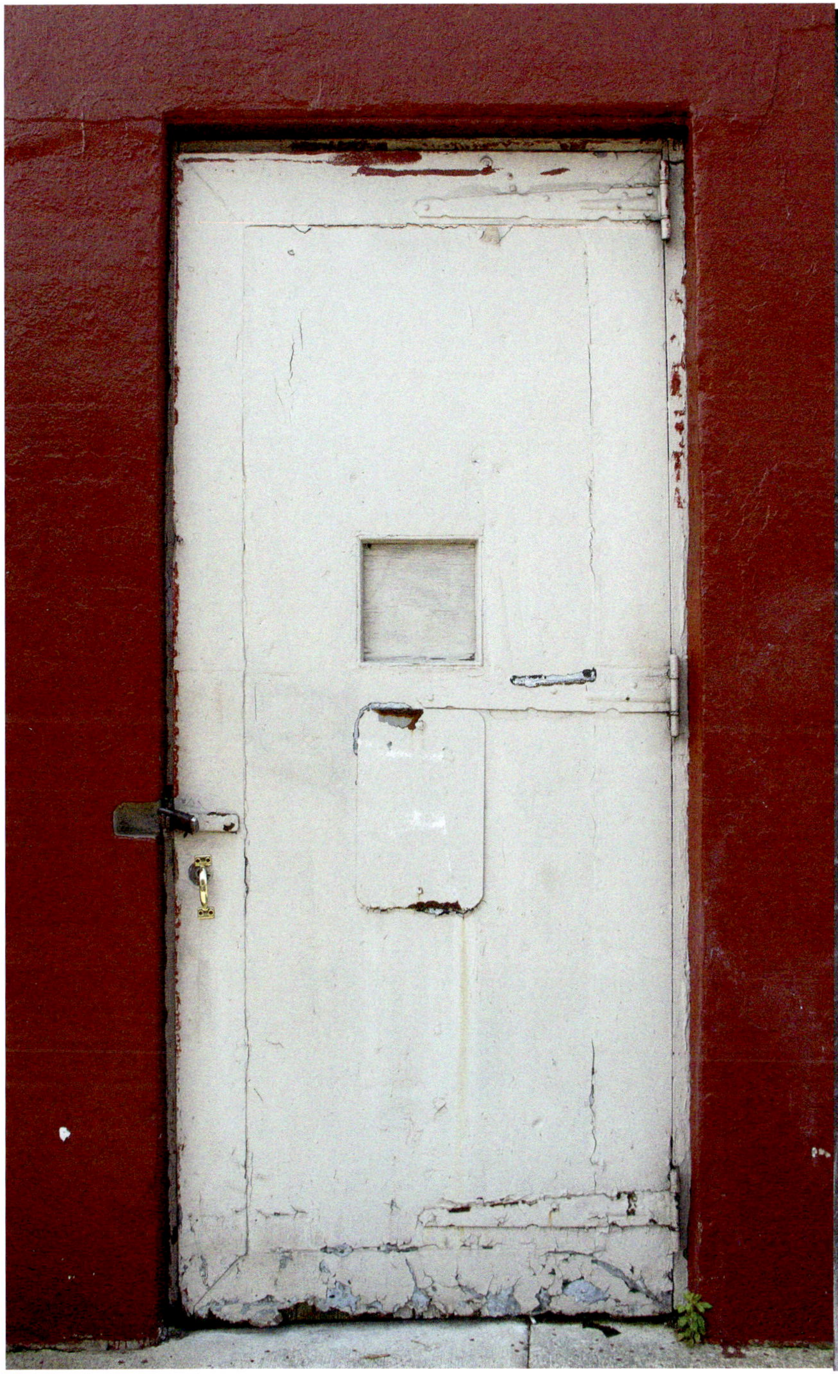

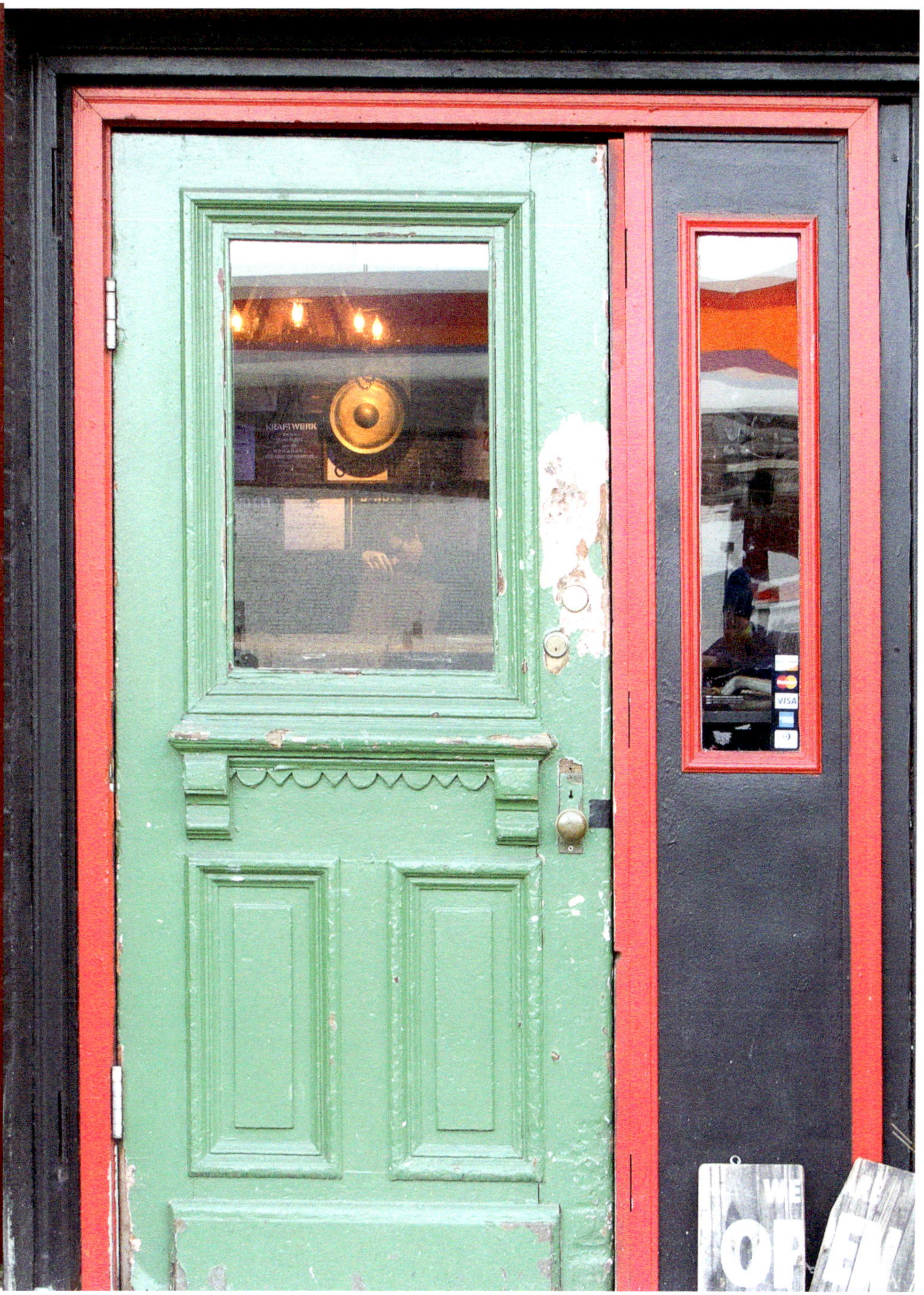

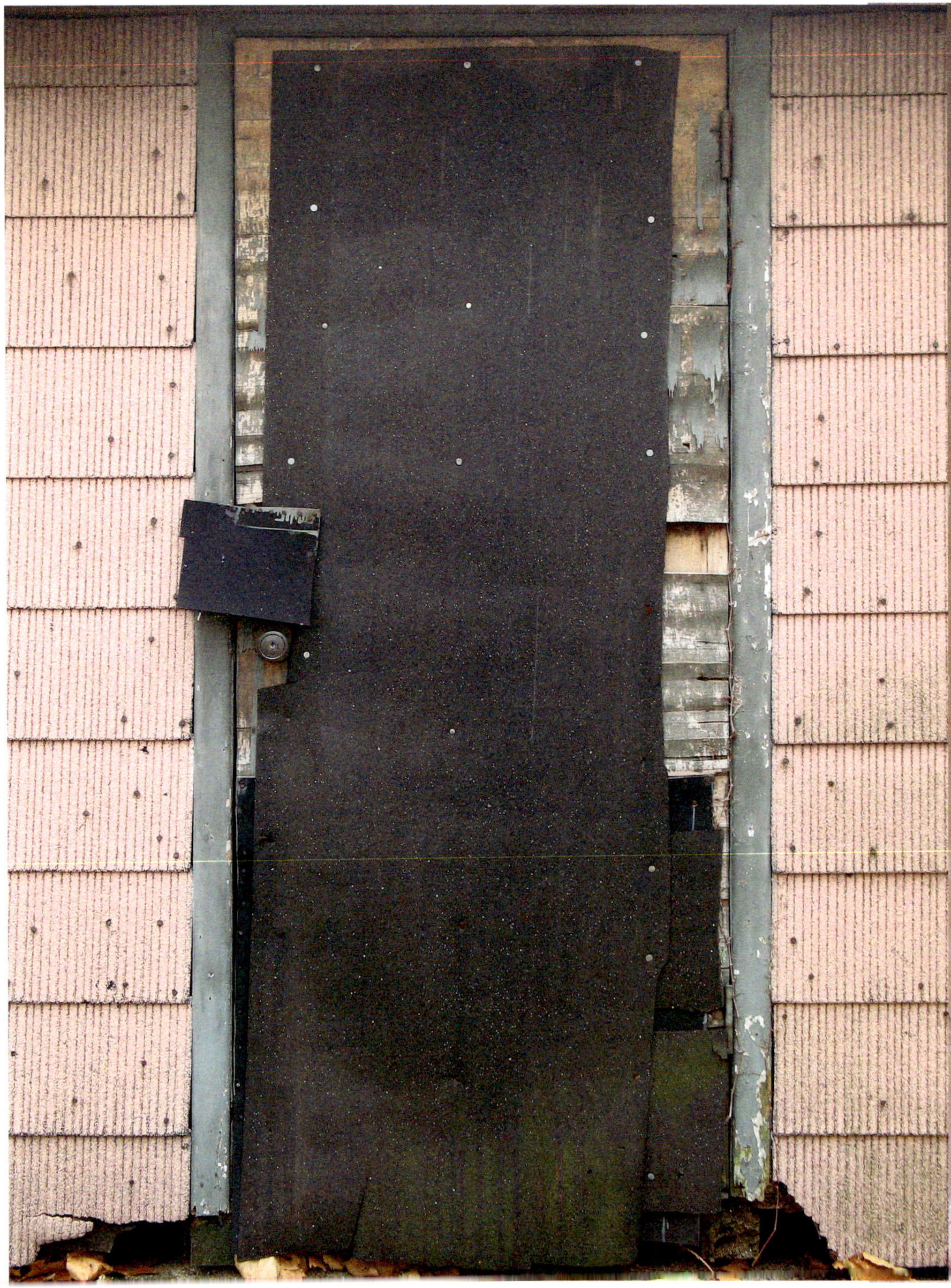

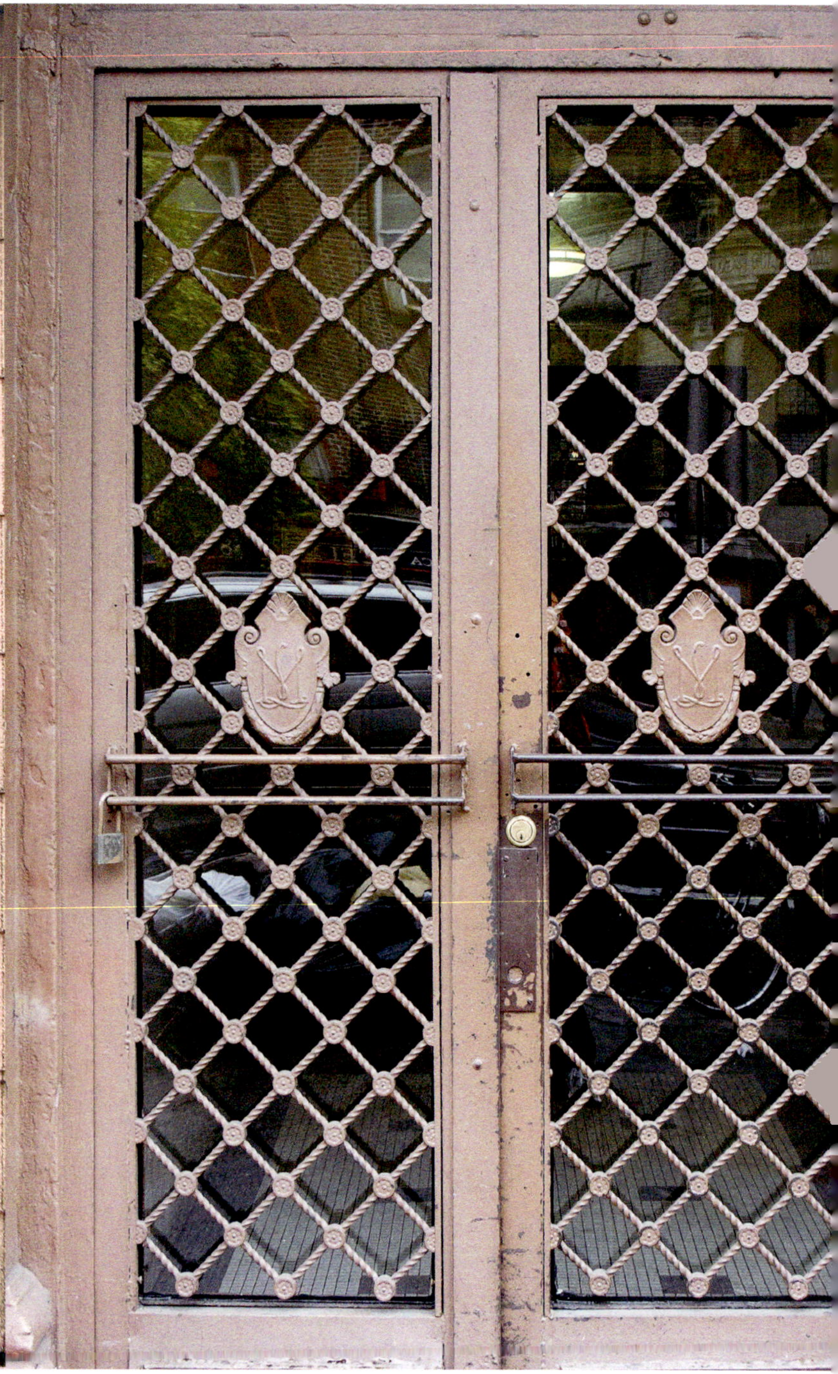

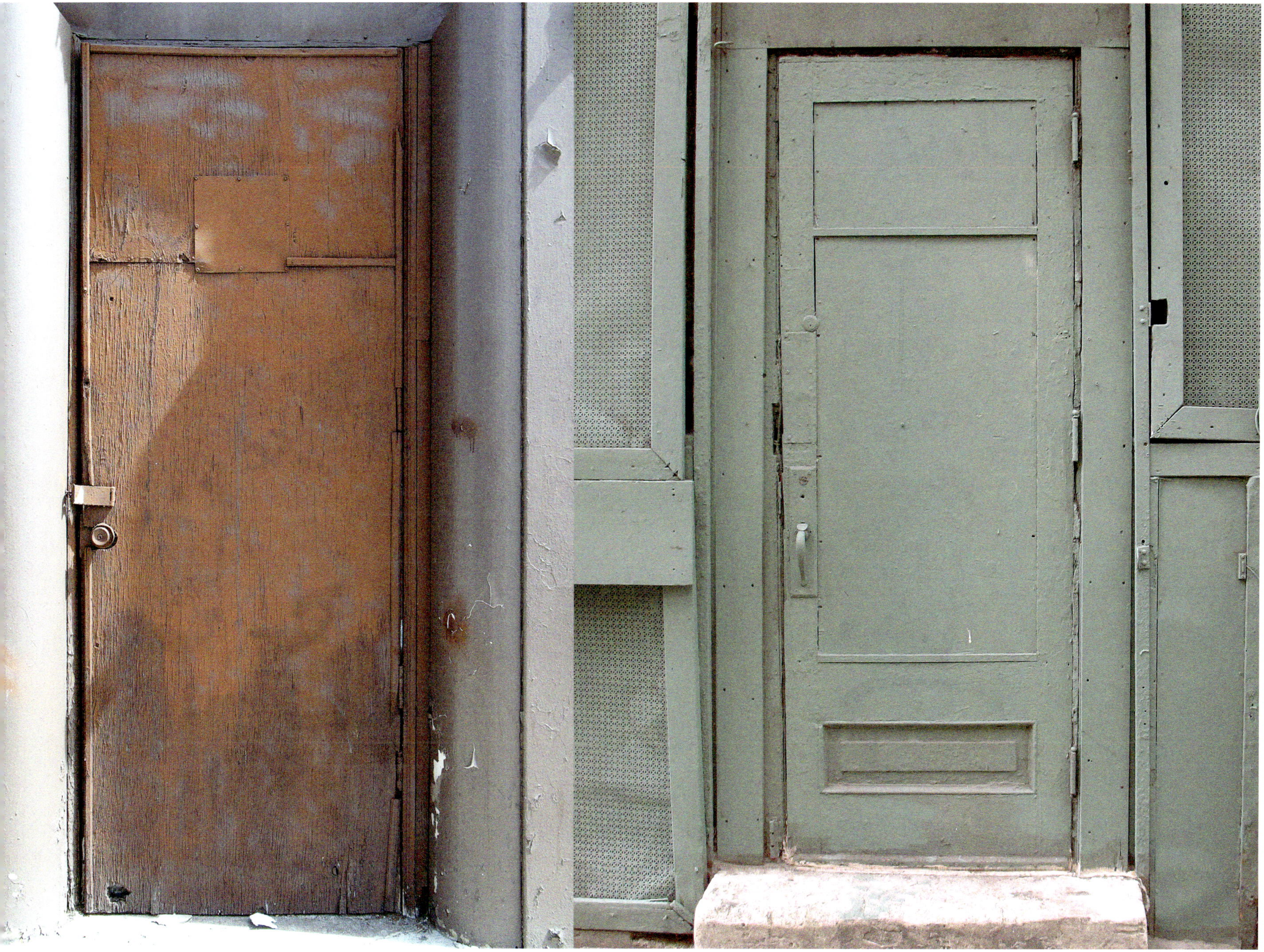

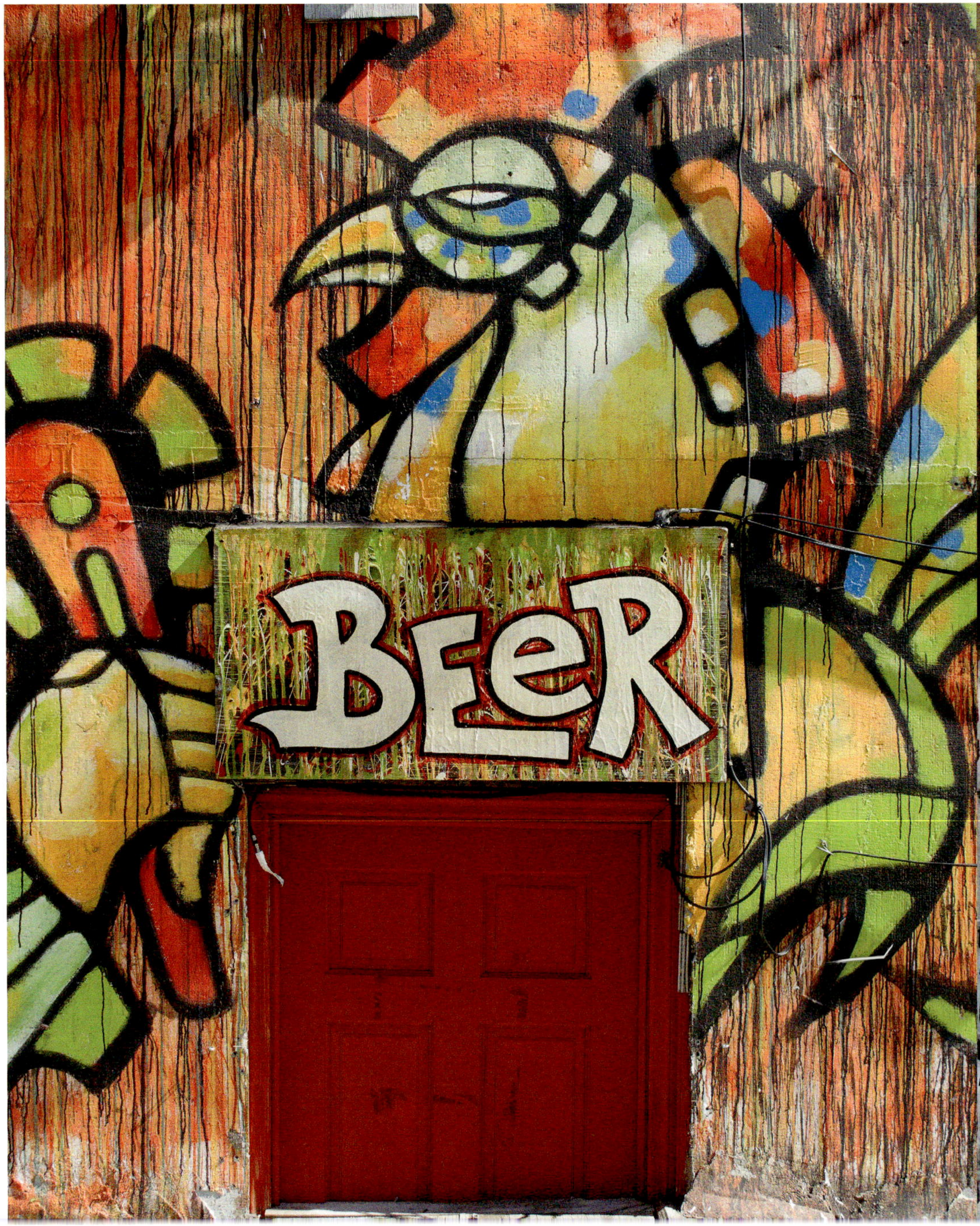
BEER

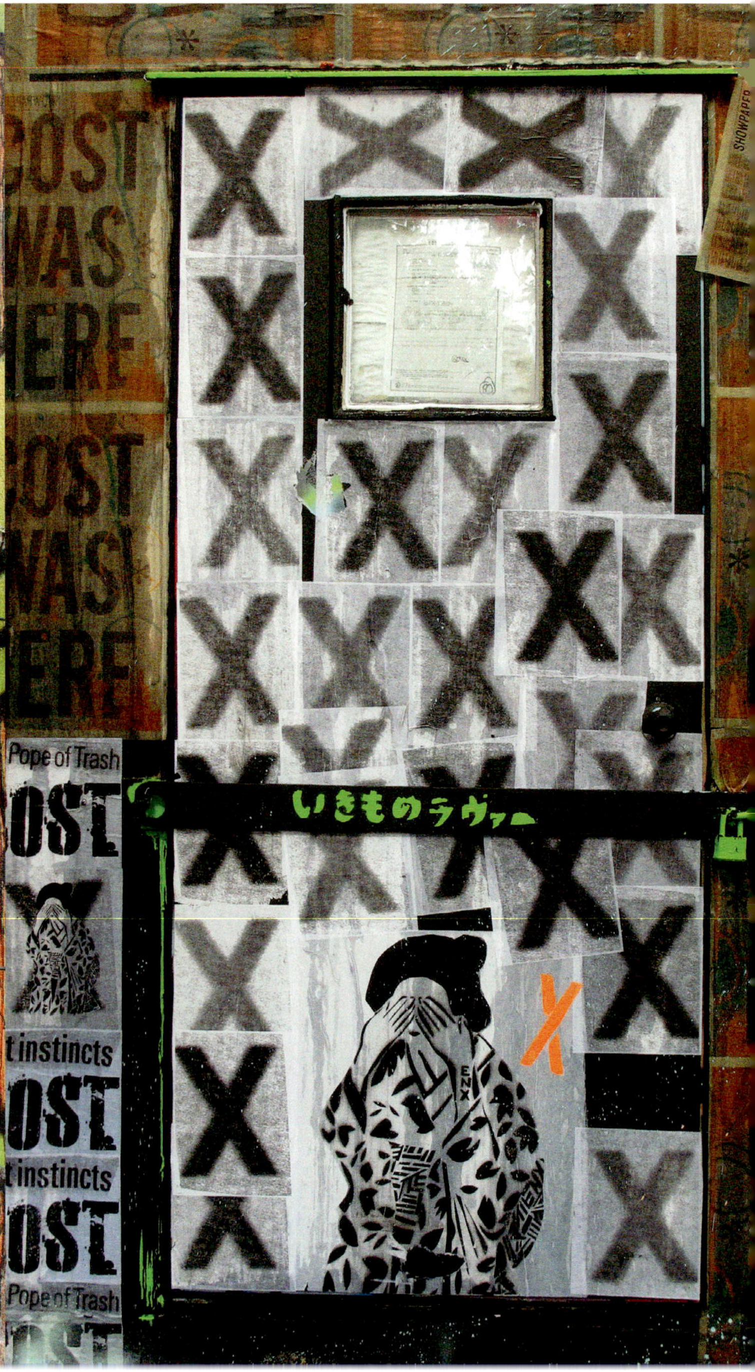
Pope of Trash
t instincts
いきものラヴァー

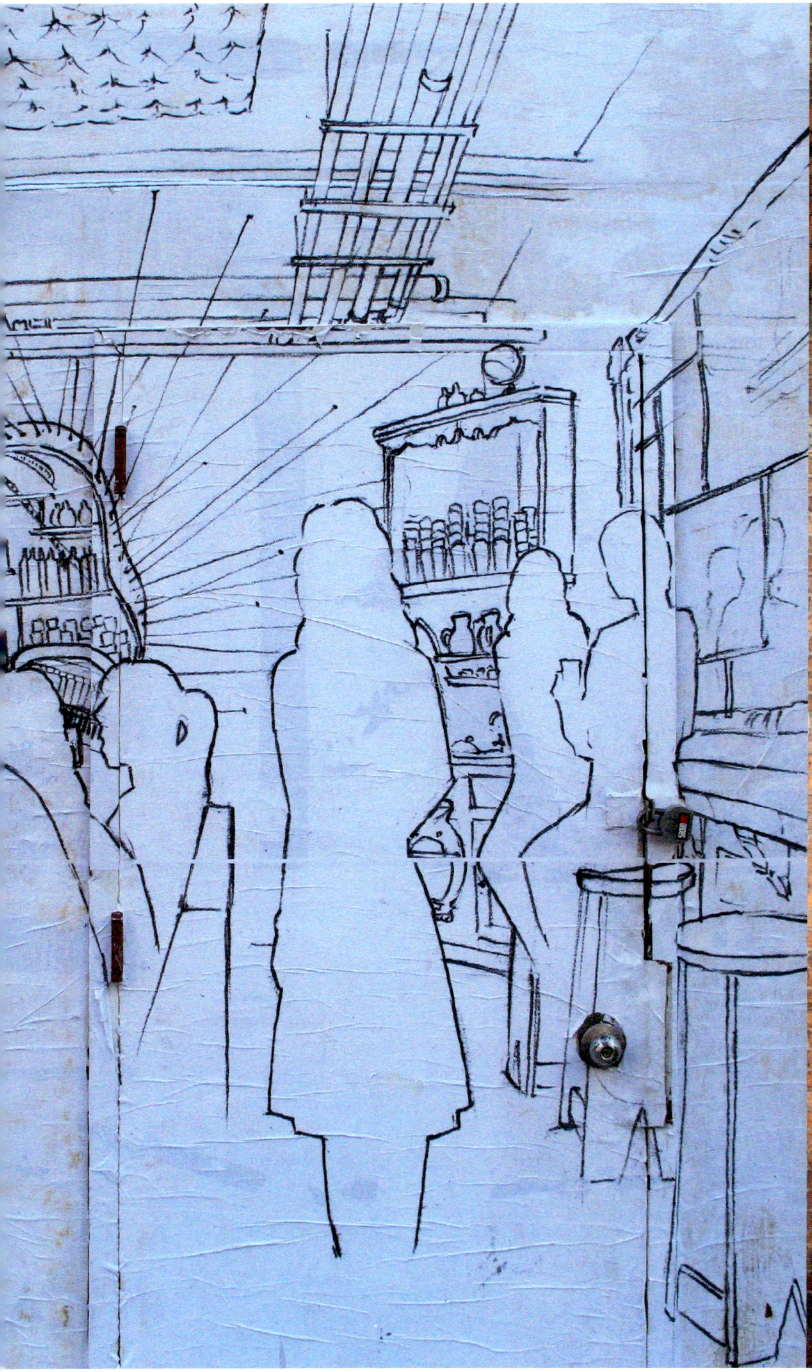

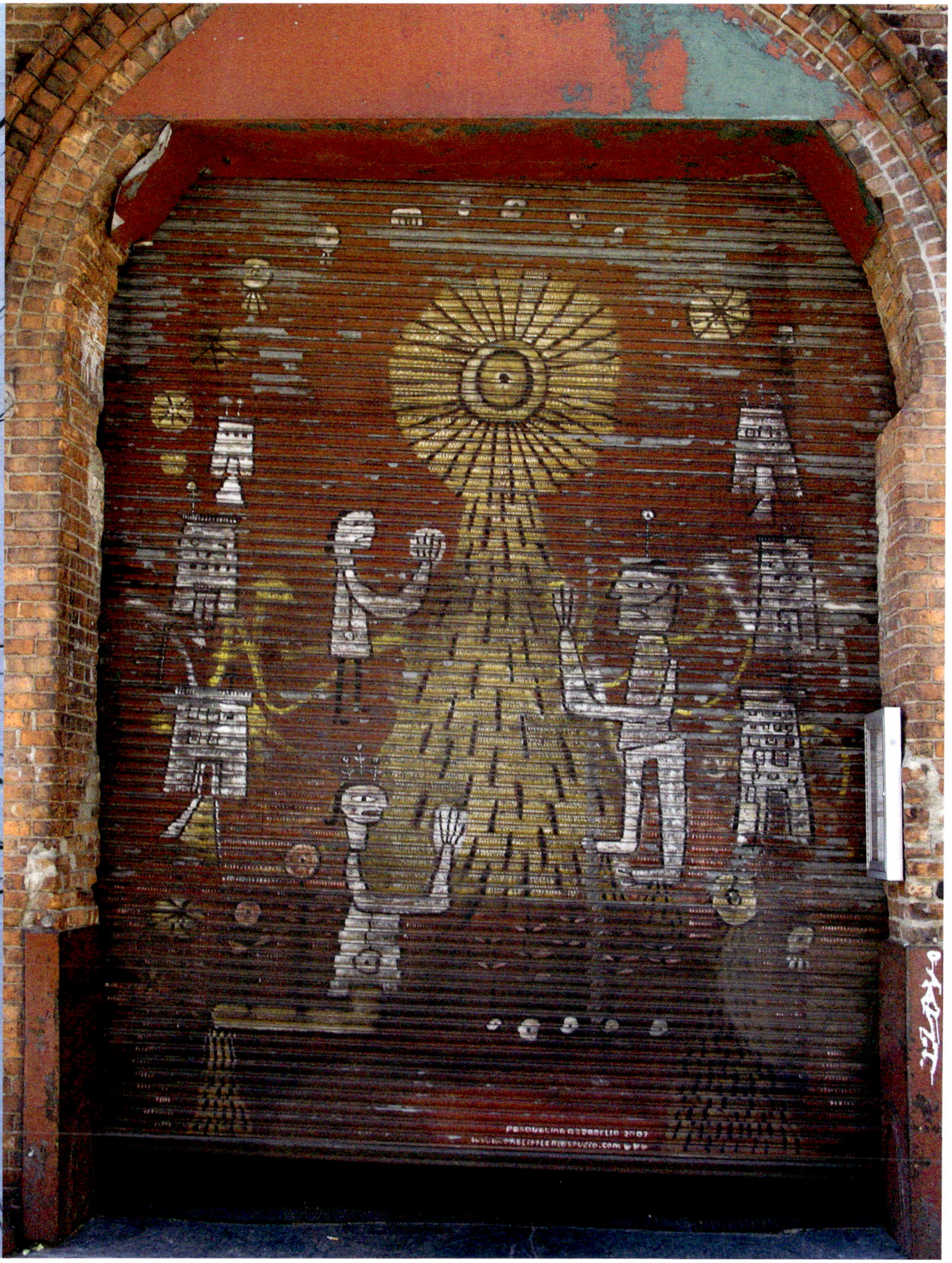

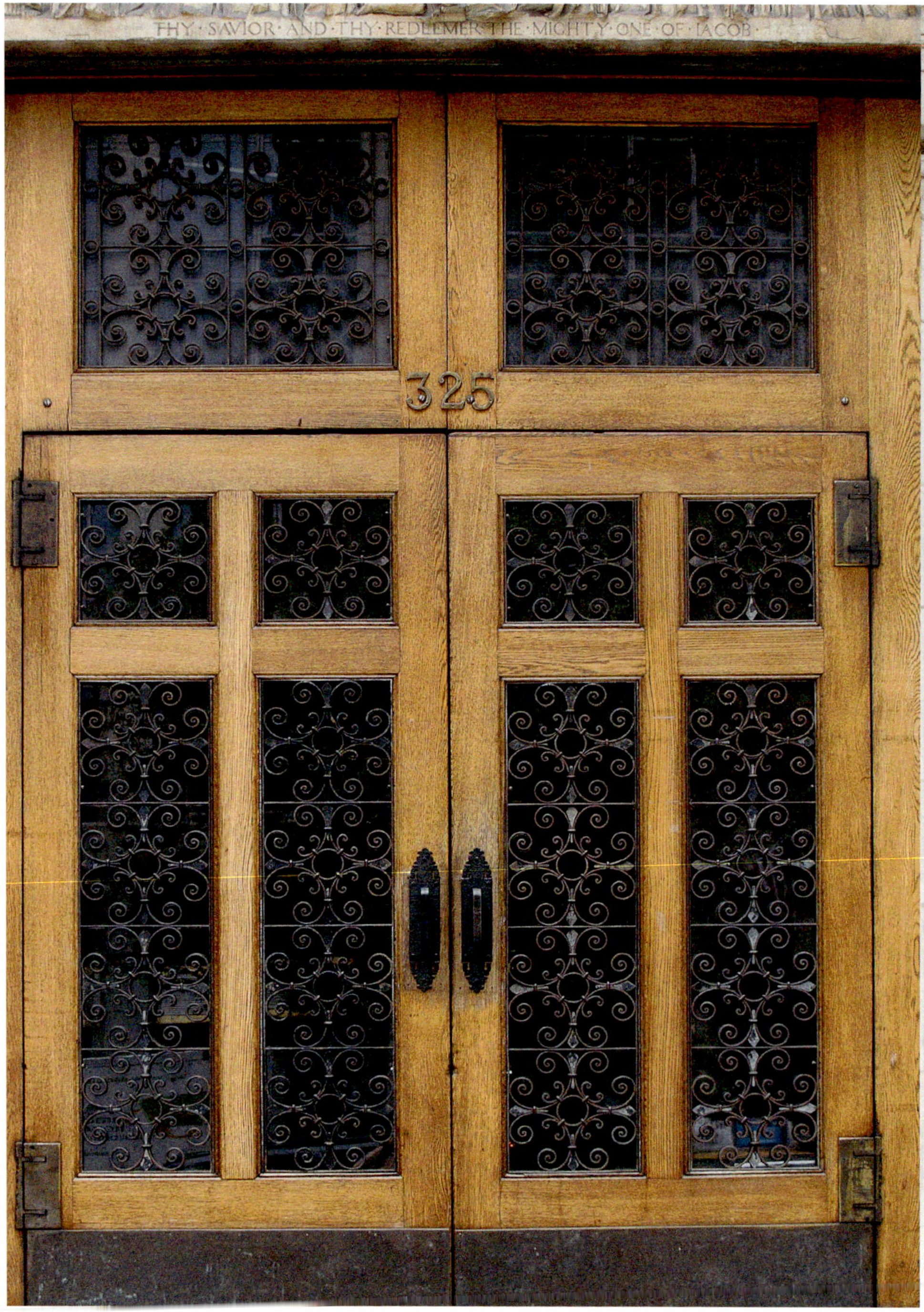
THY·SAVIOR·AND·THY·REDEEMER·THE·MIGHTY·ONE·OF·JACOB
325

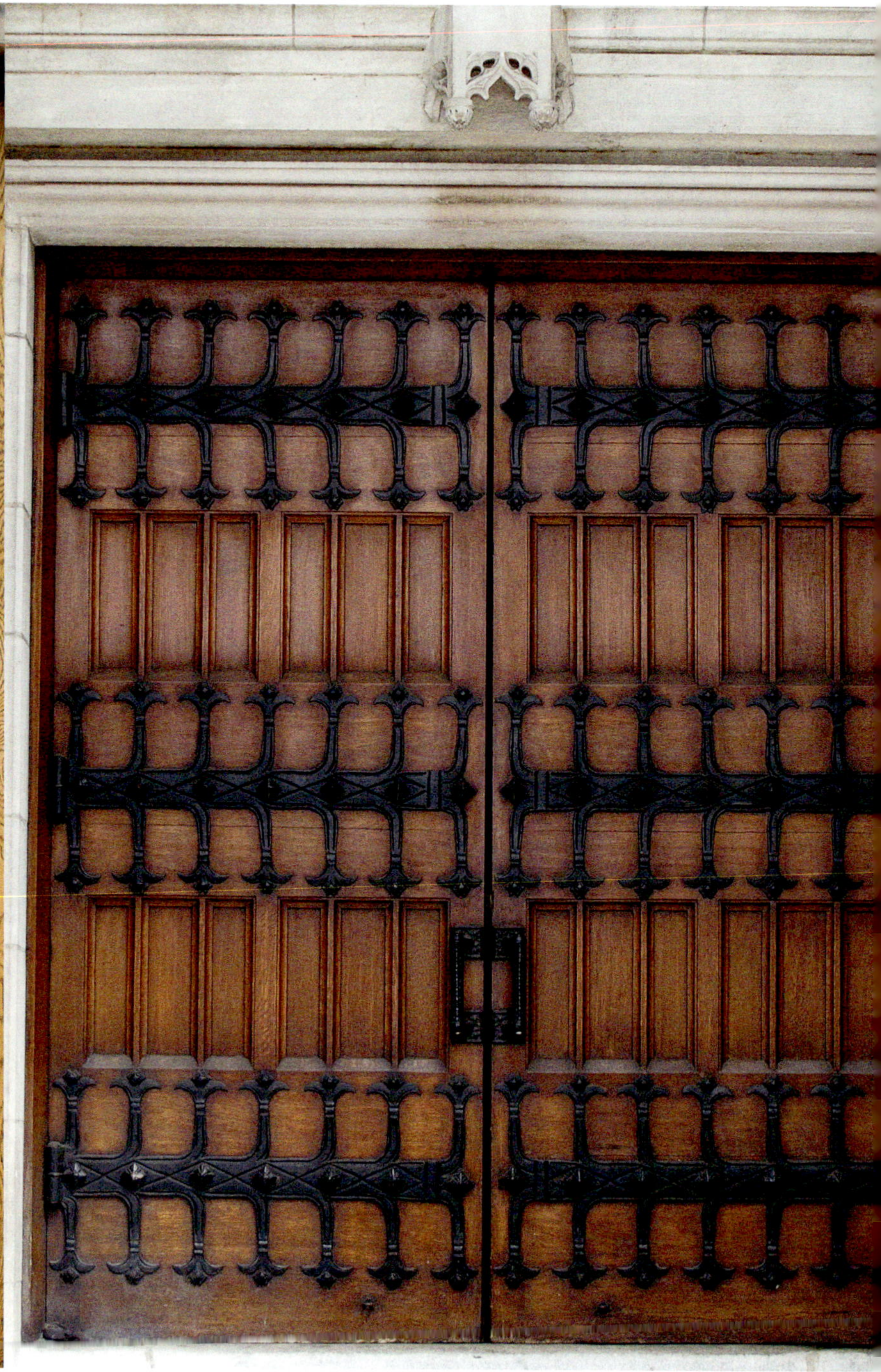

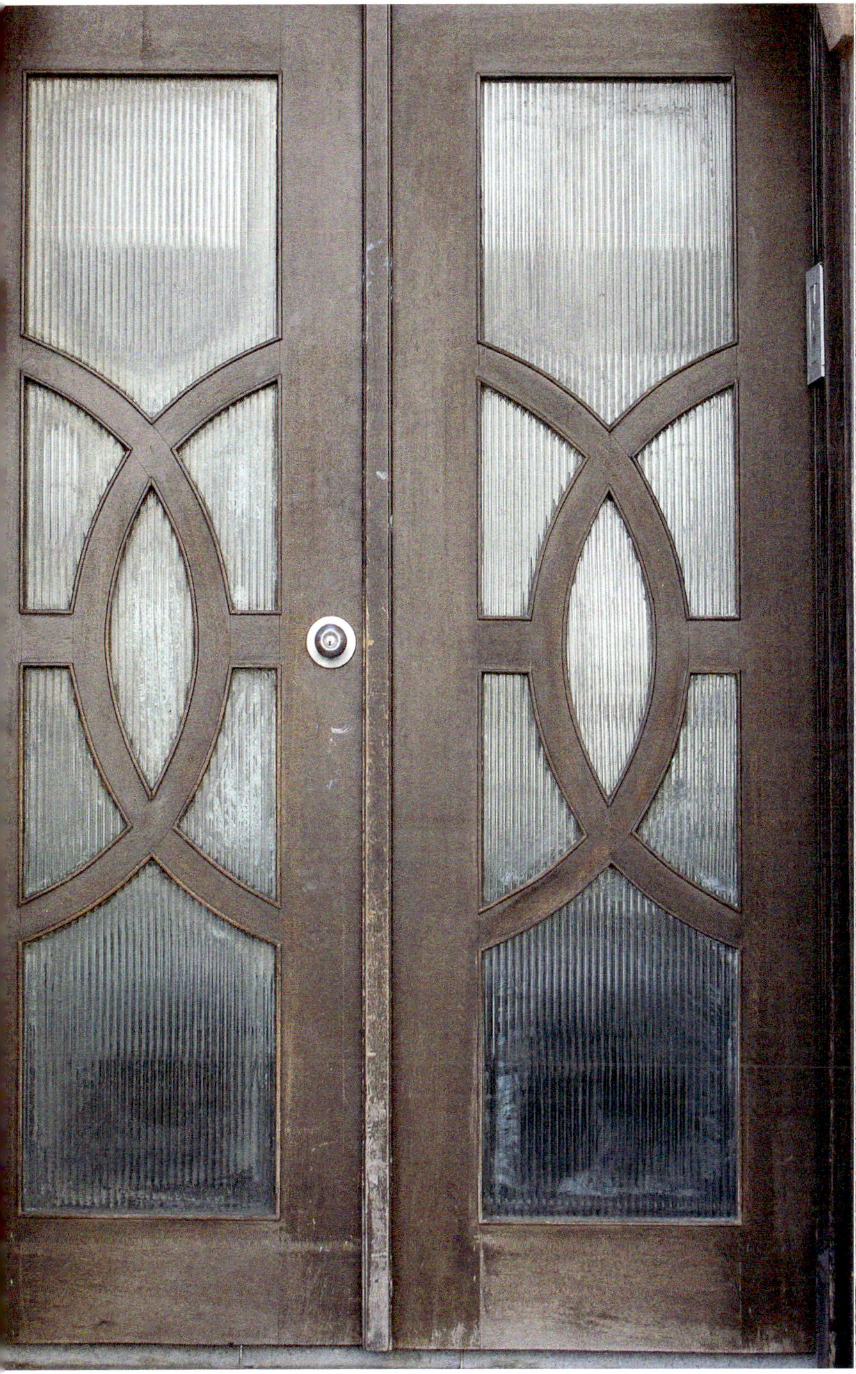

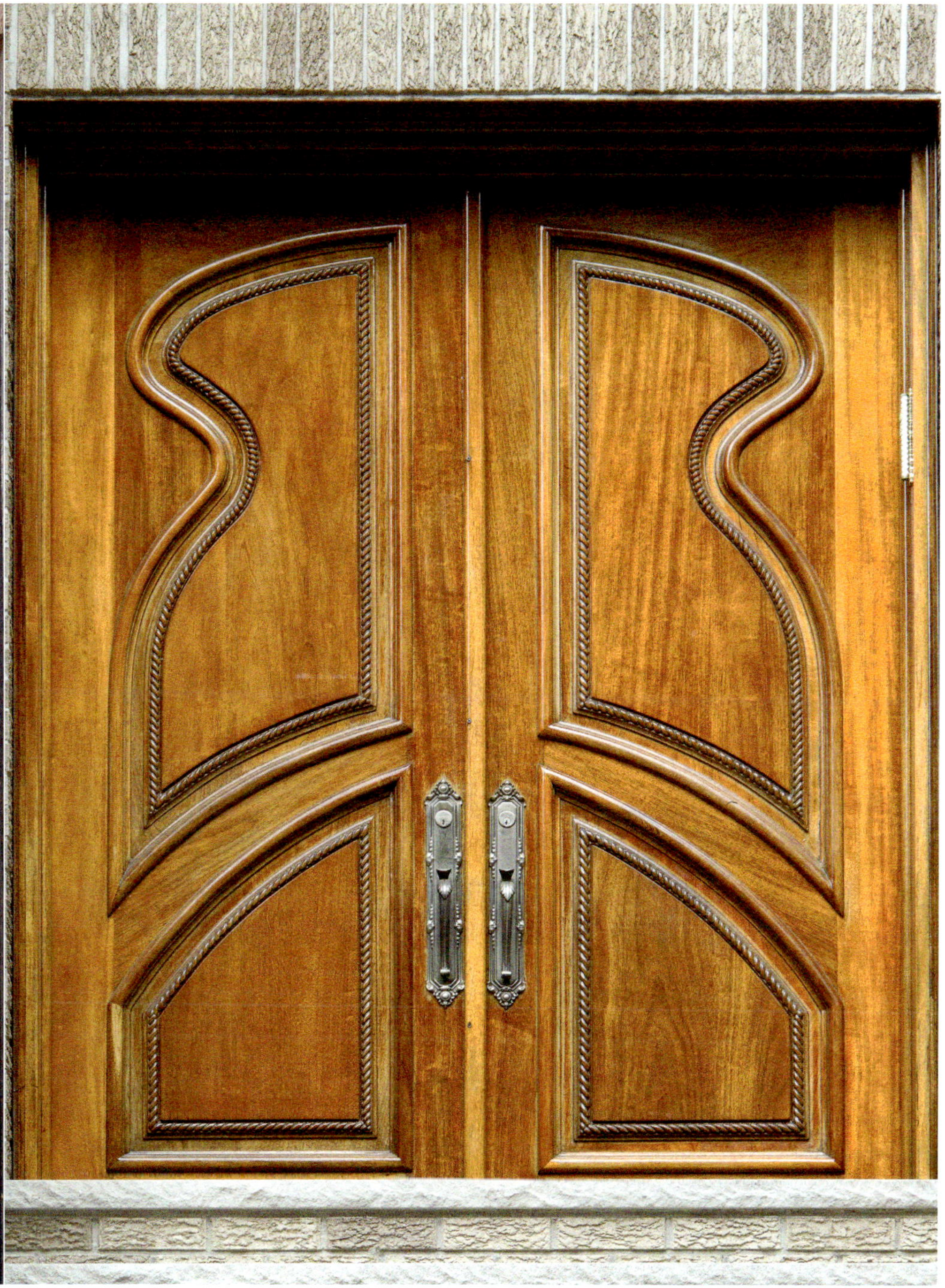

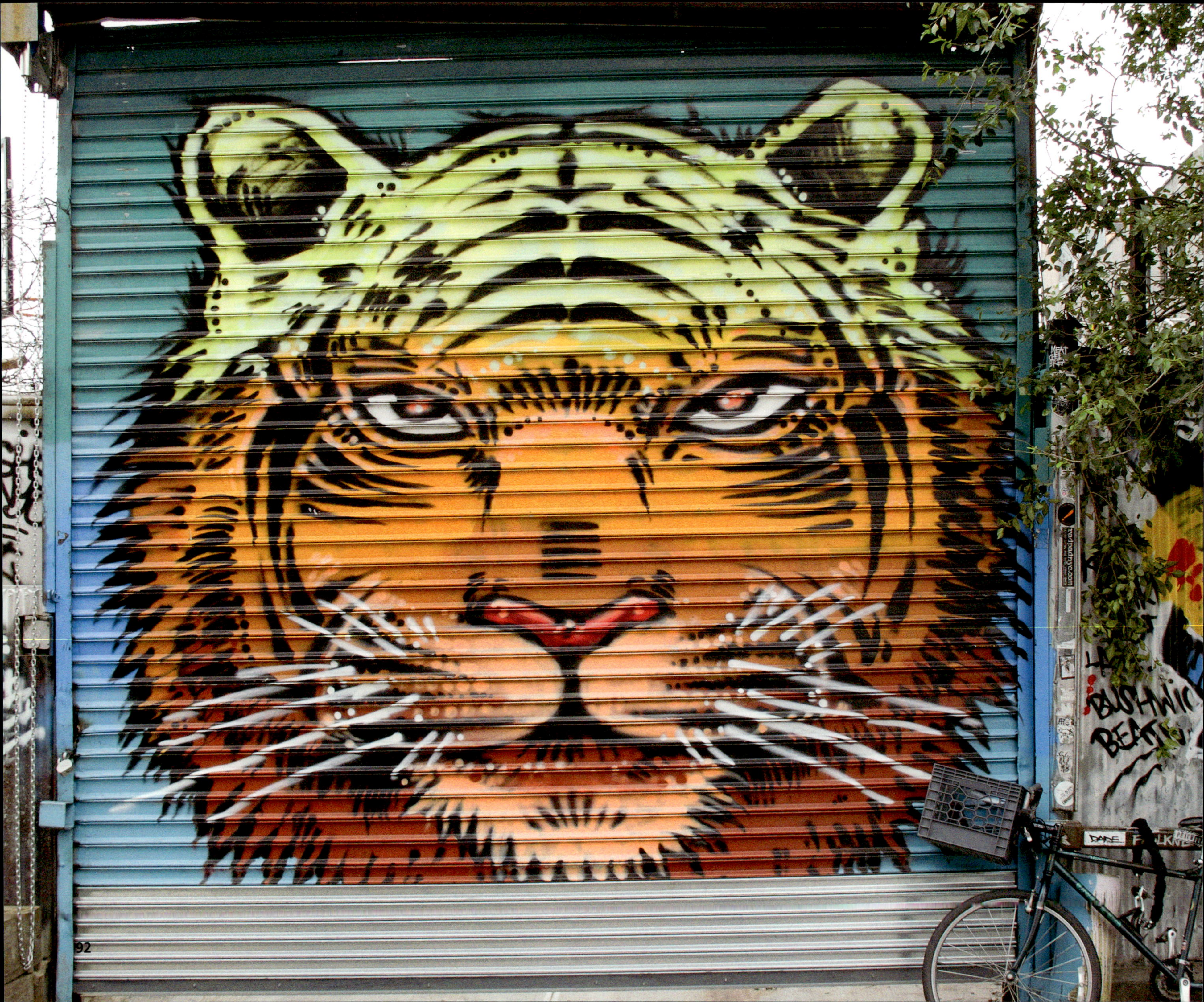

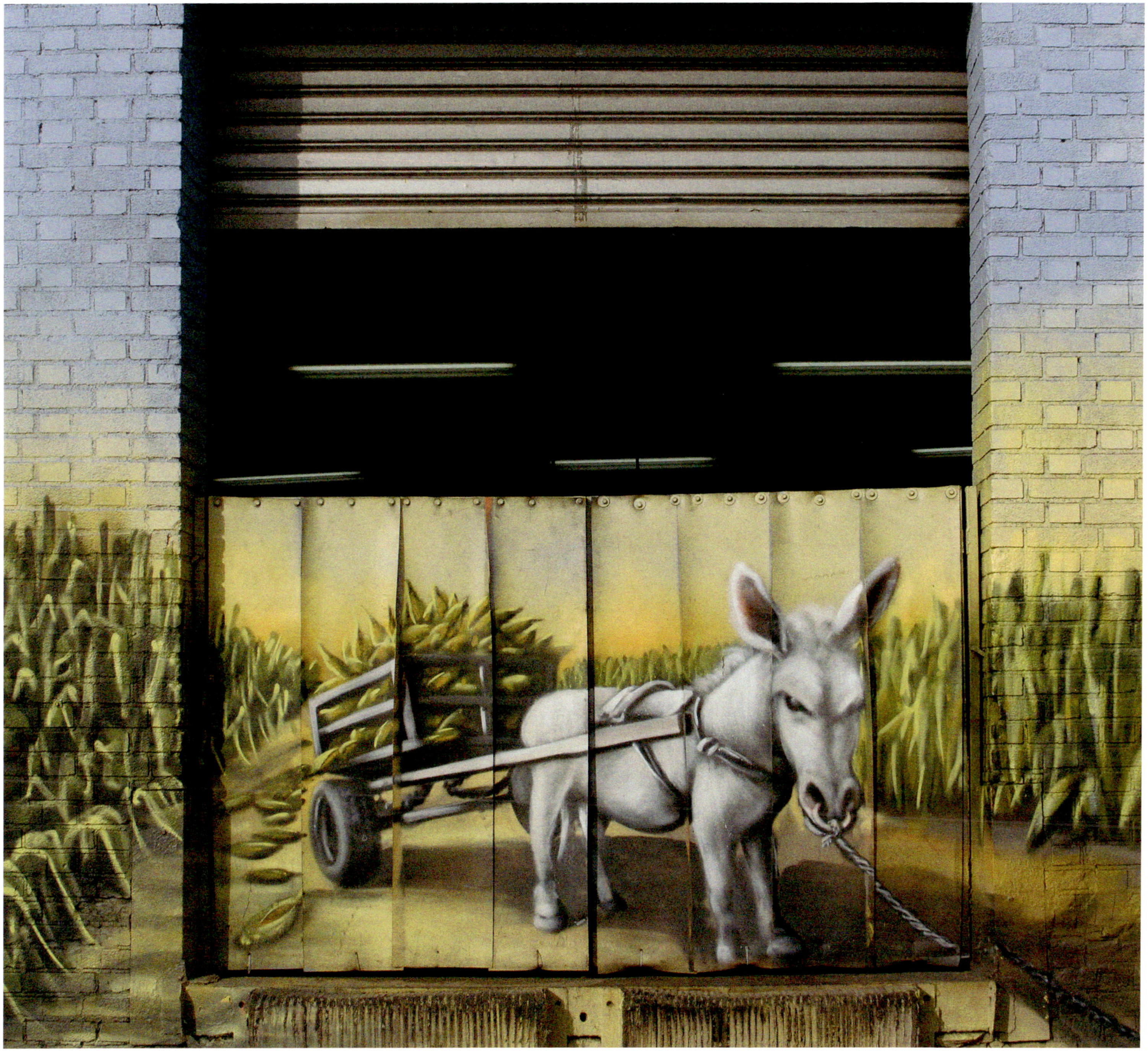

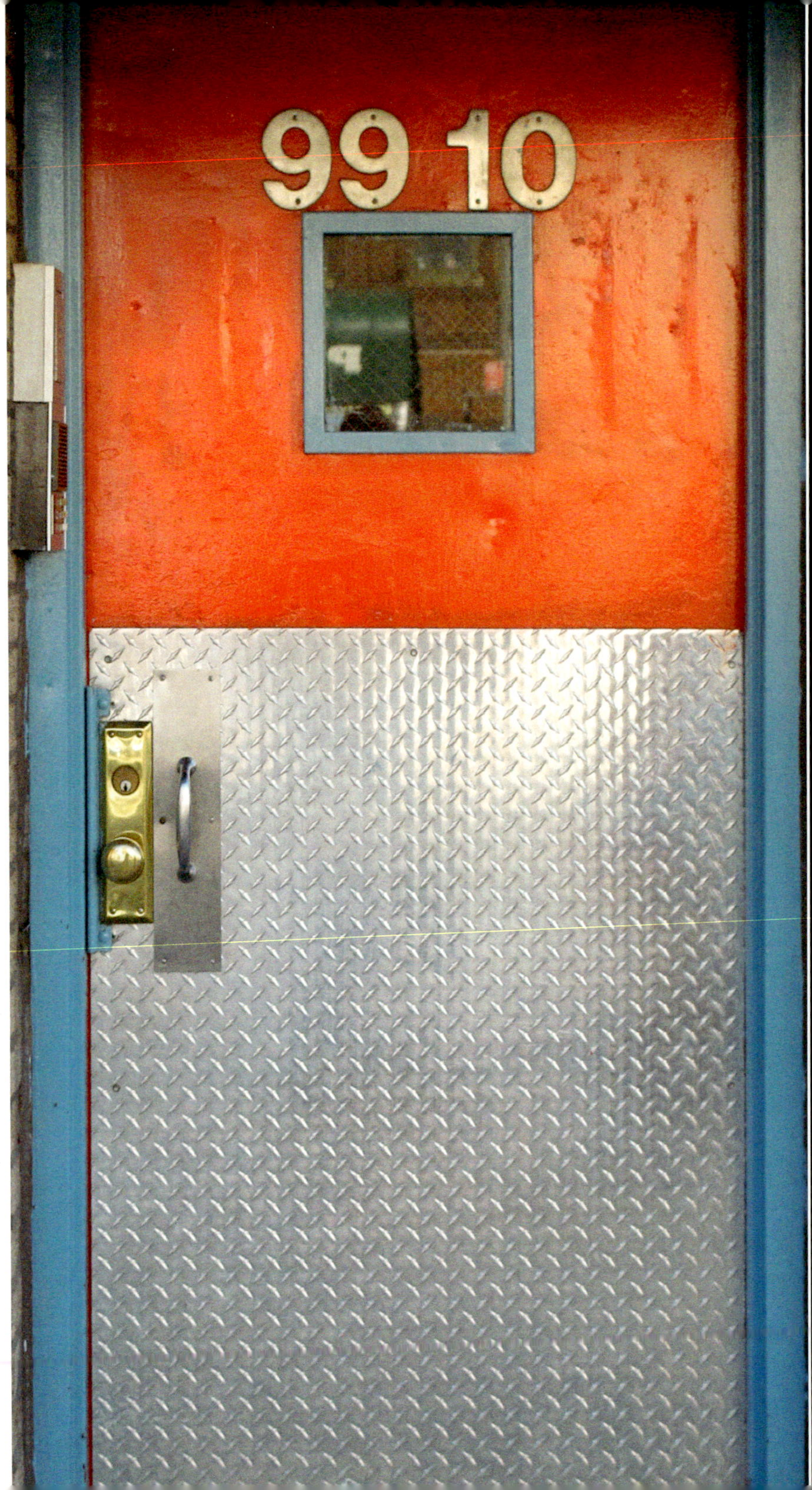
99 10
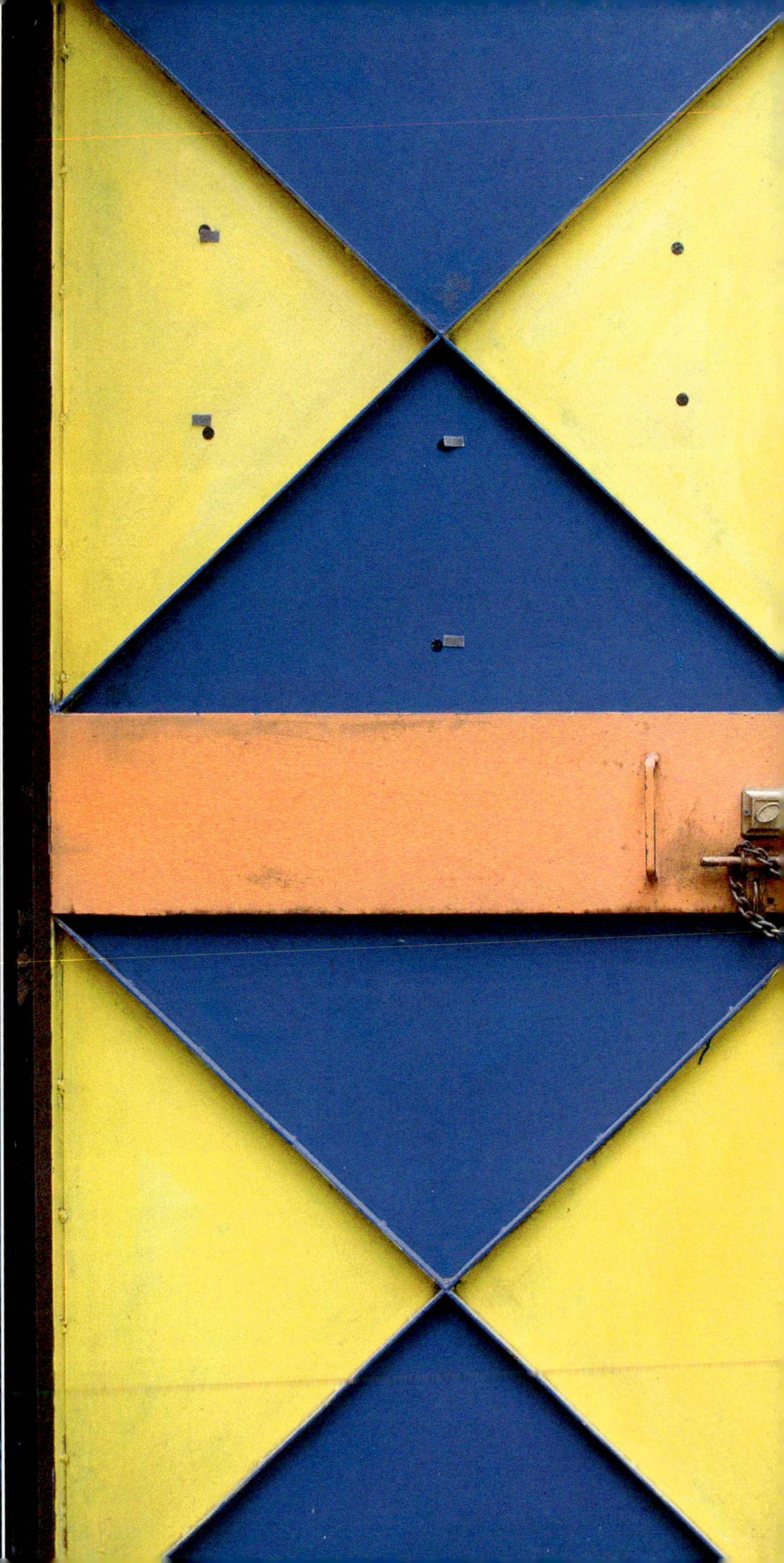

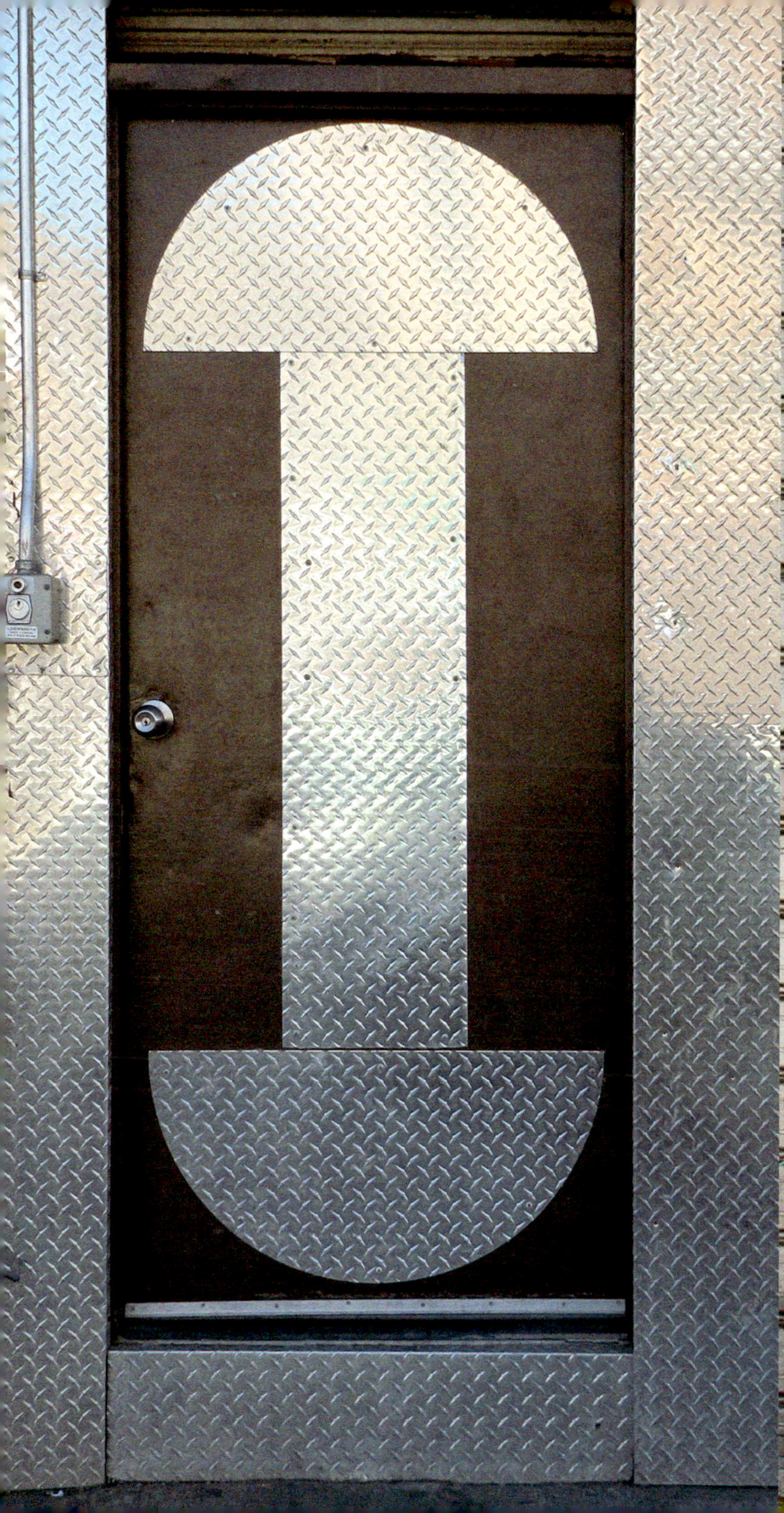

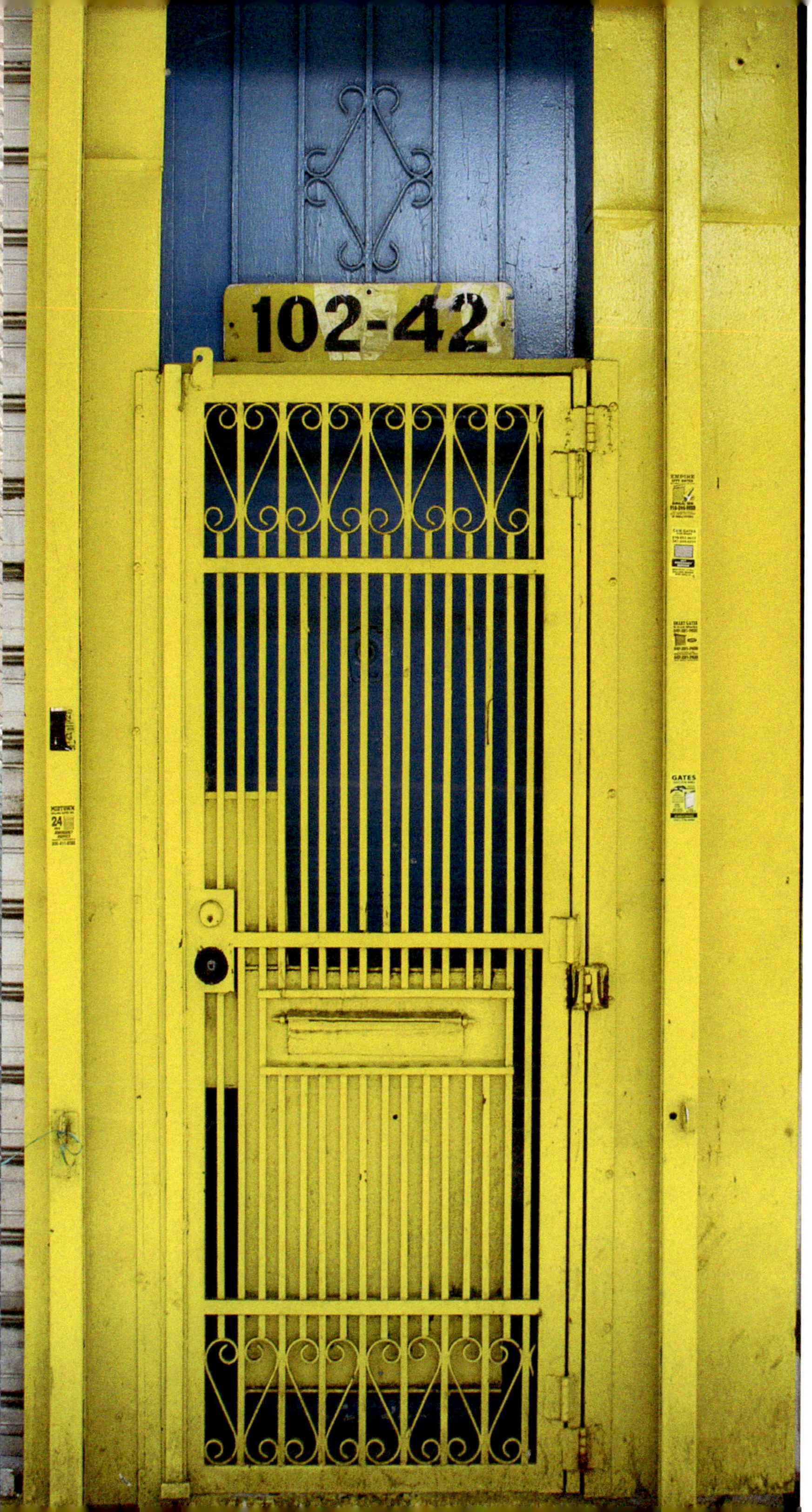
102-42

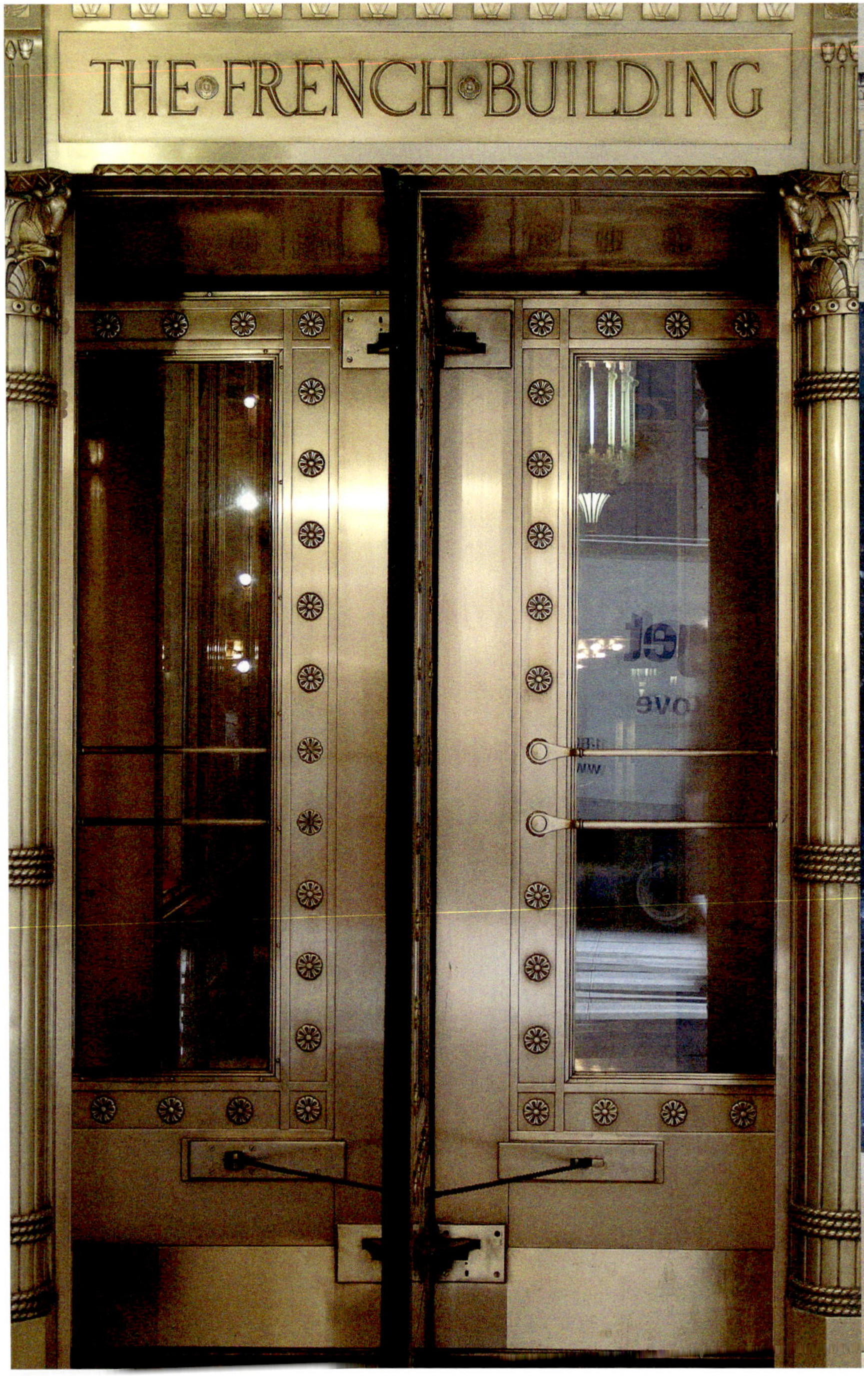
THE FRENCH BUILDING

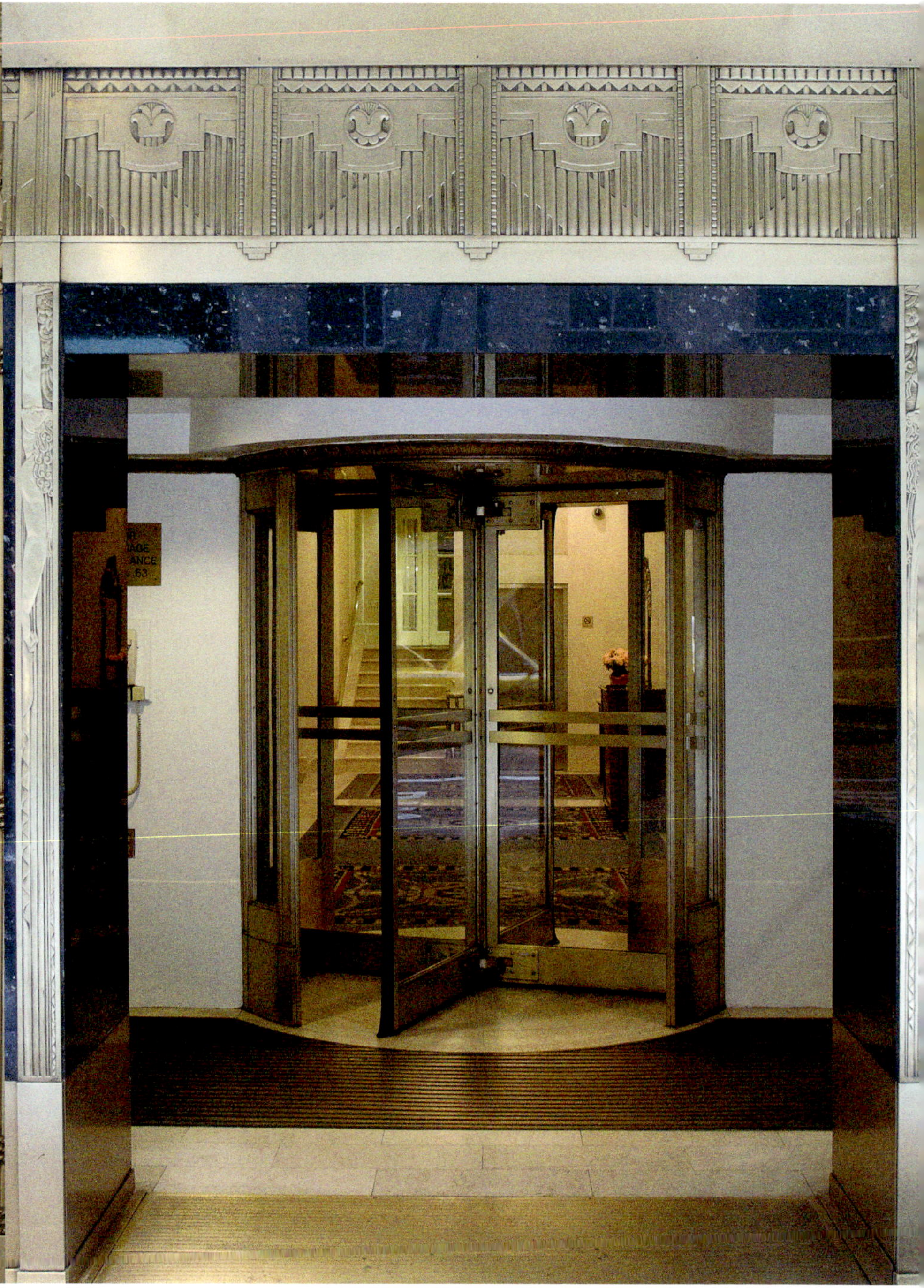

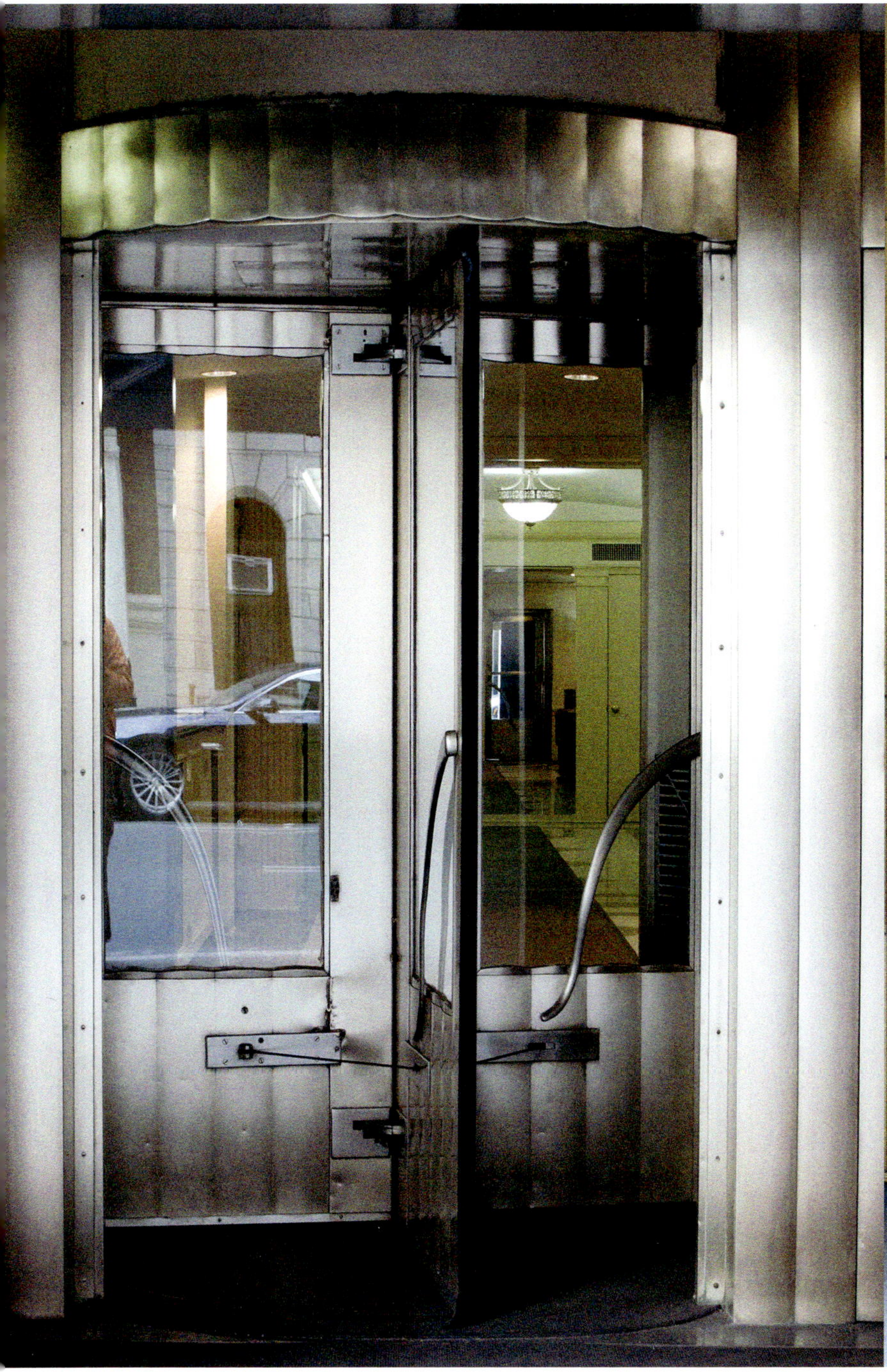

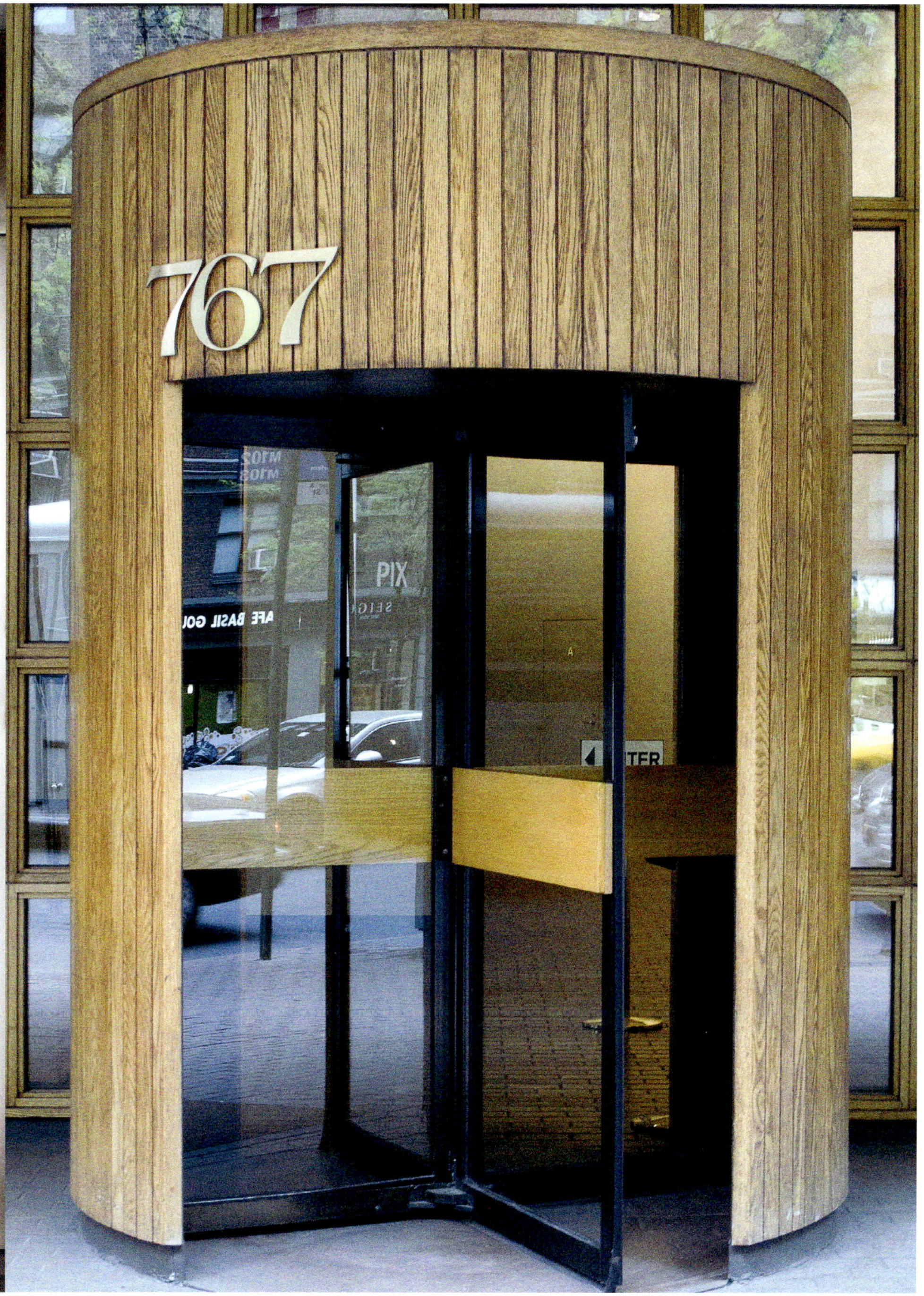
767

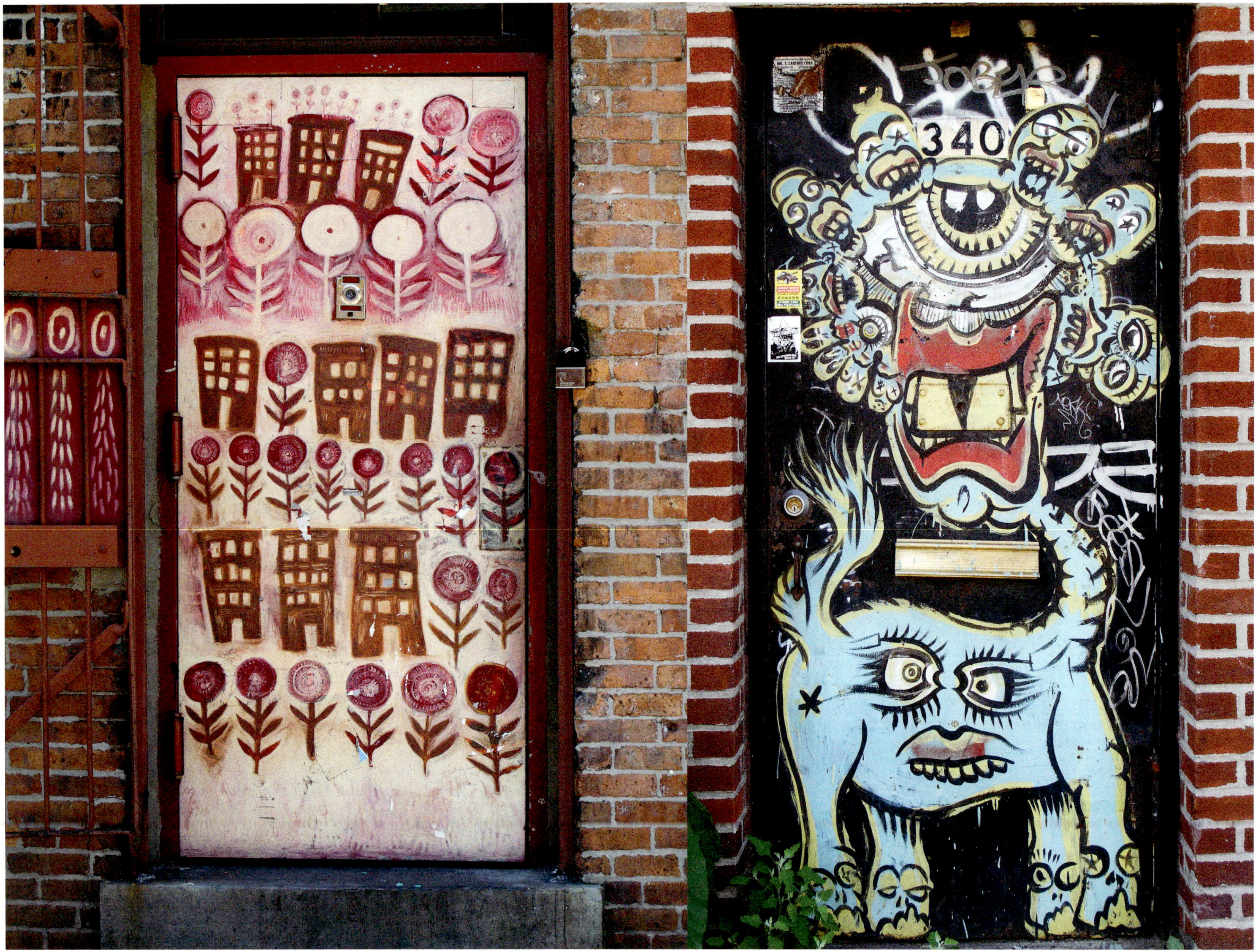
340

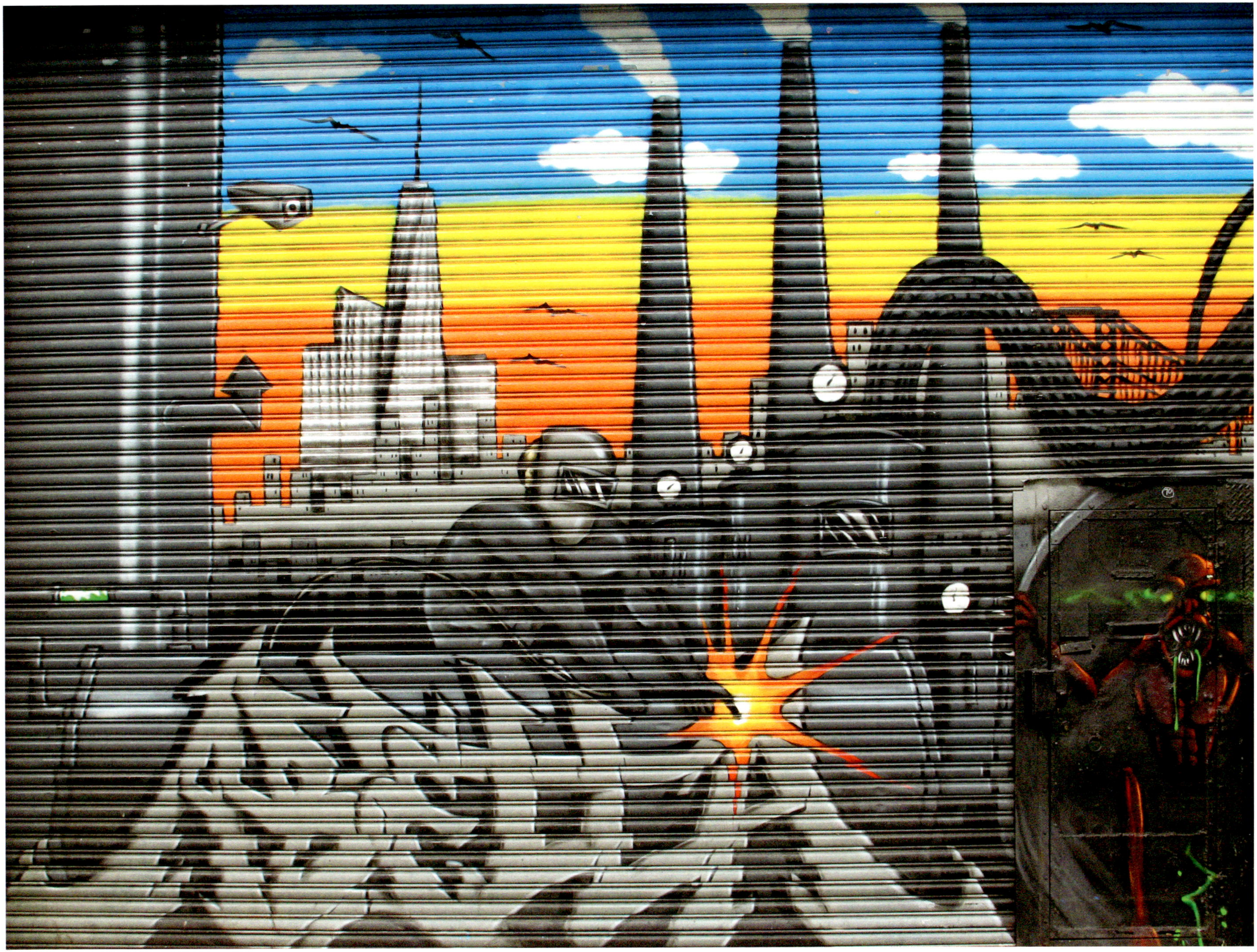

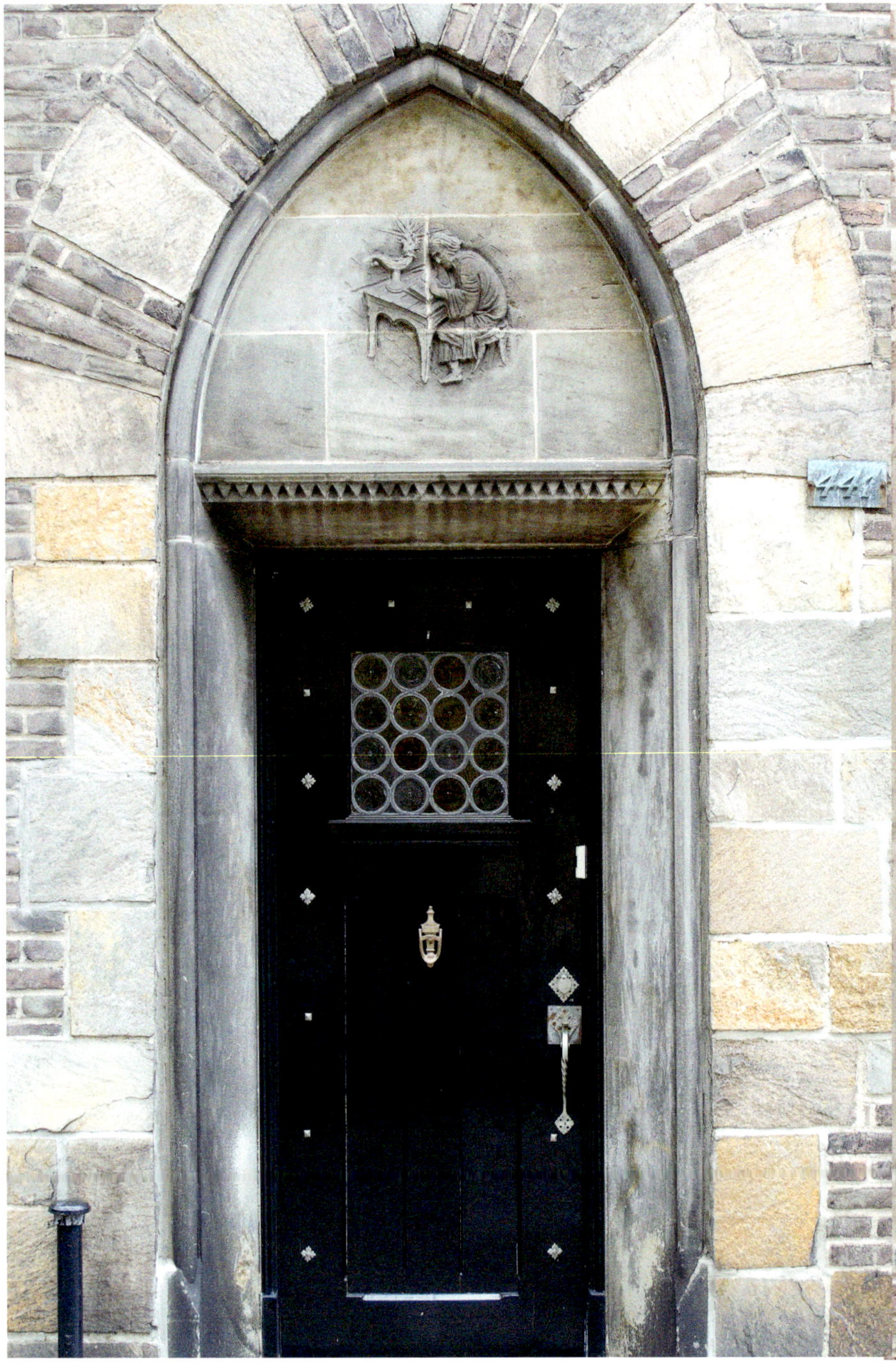
441

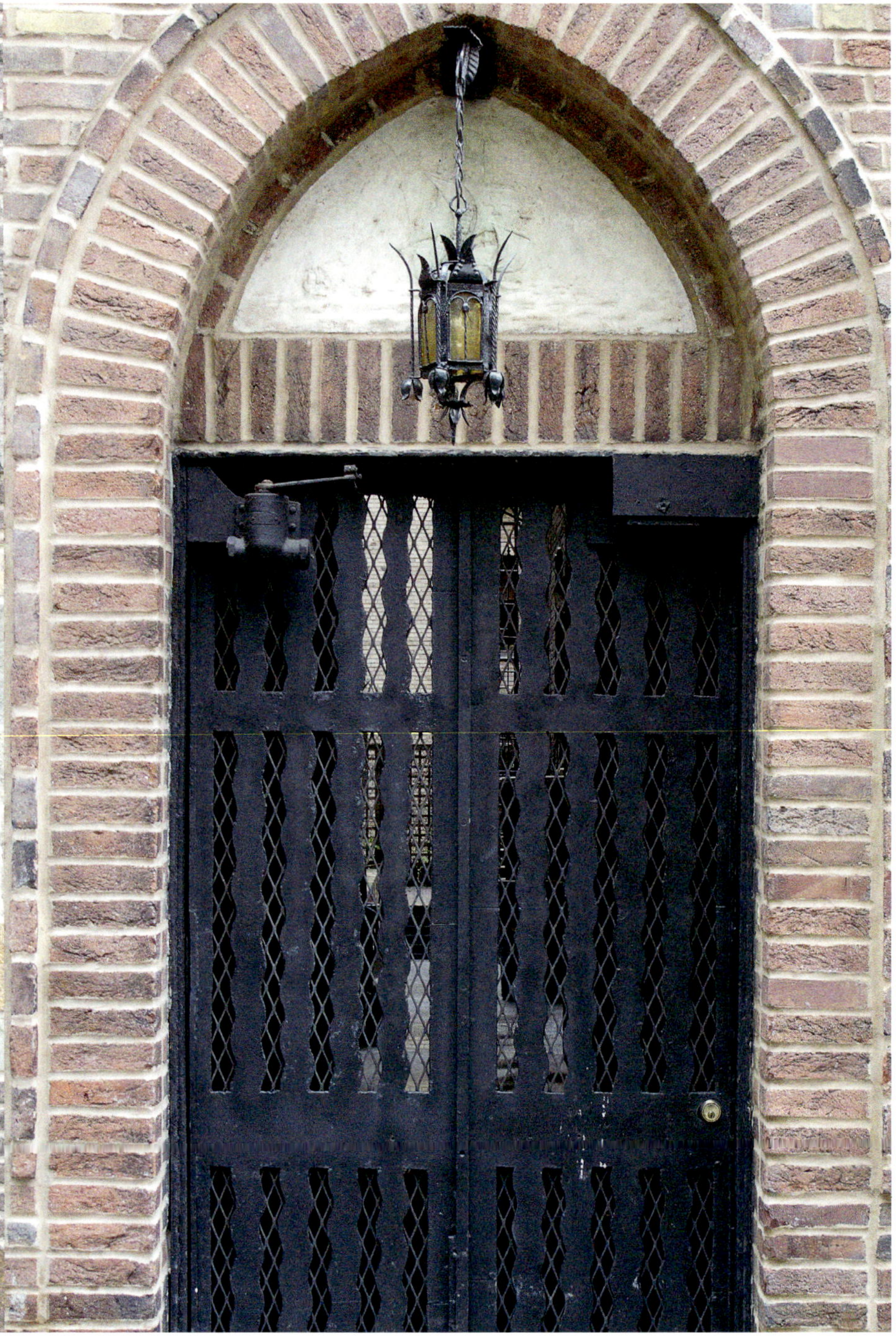

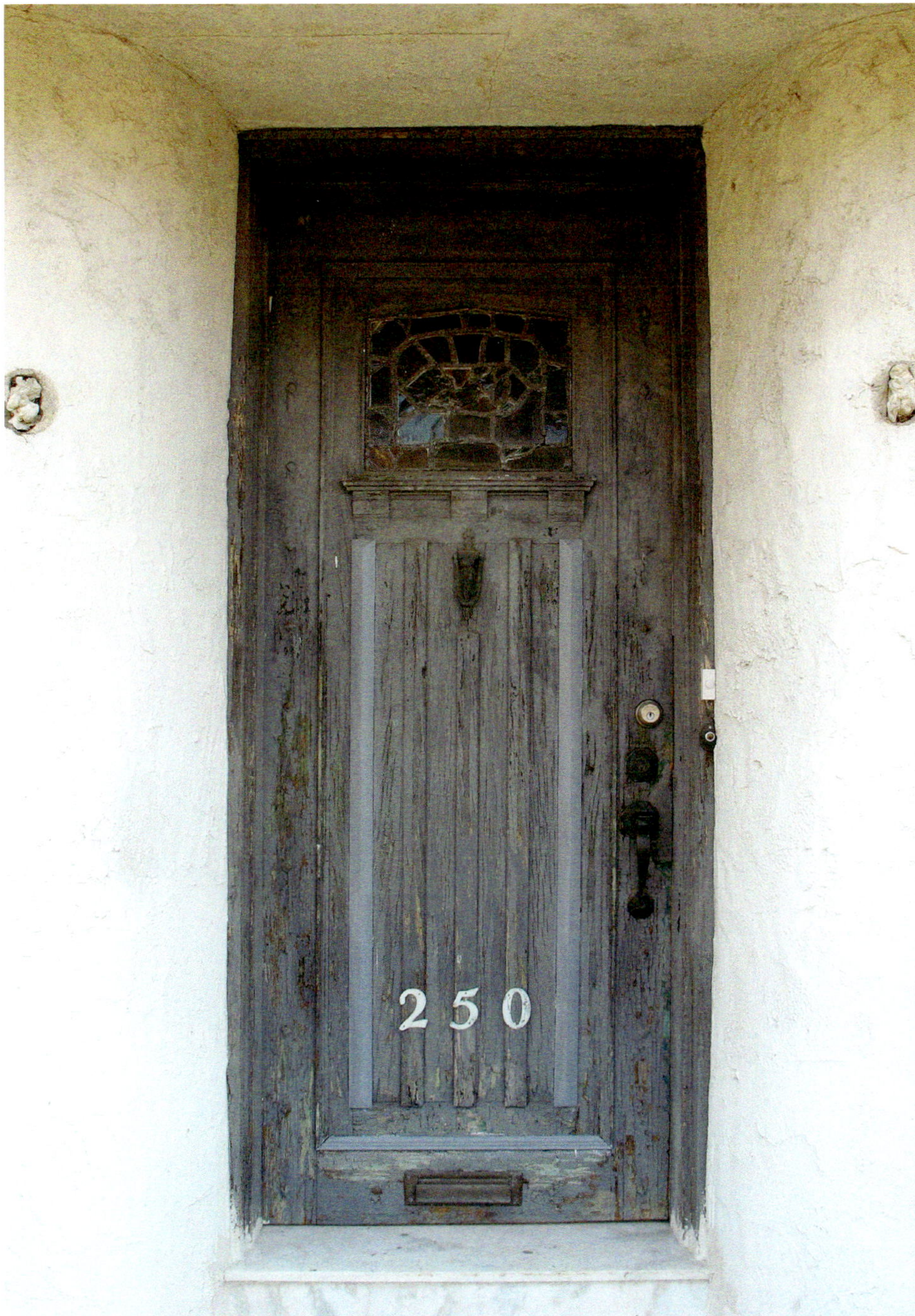
250
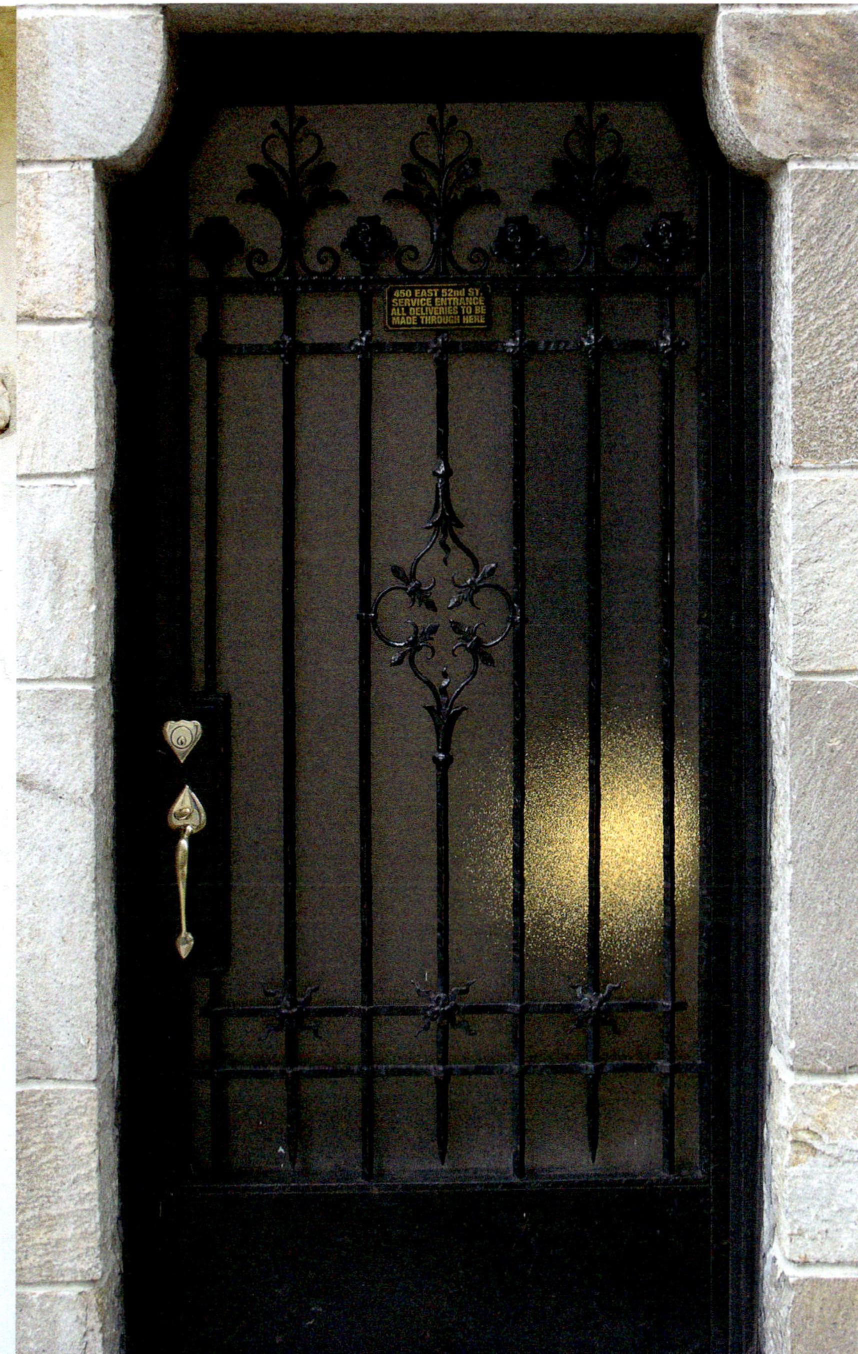
450 EAST 52nd ST.
SERVICE ENTRANCE
ALL DELIVERIES TO BE
MADE THROUGH HERE

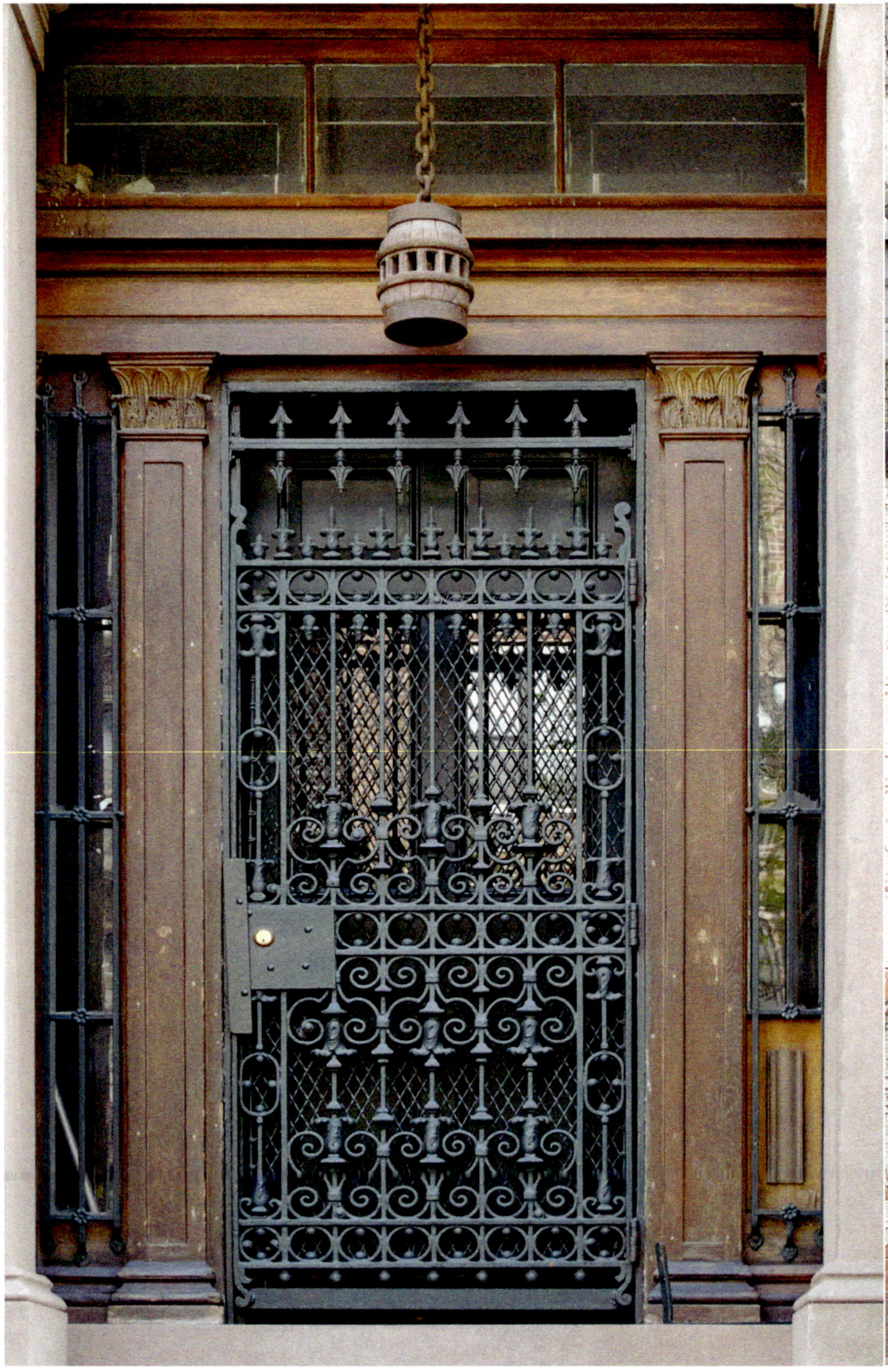
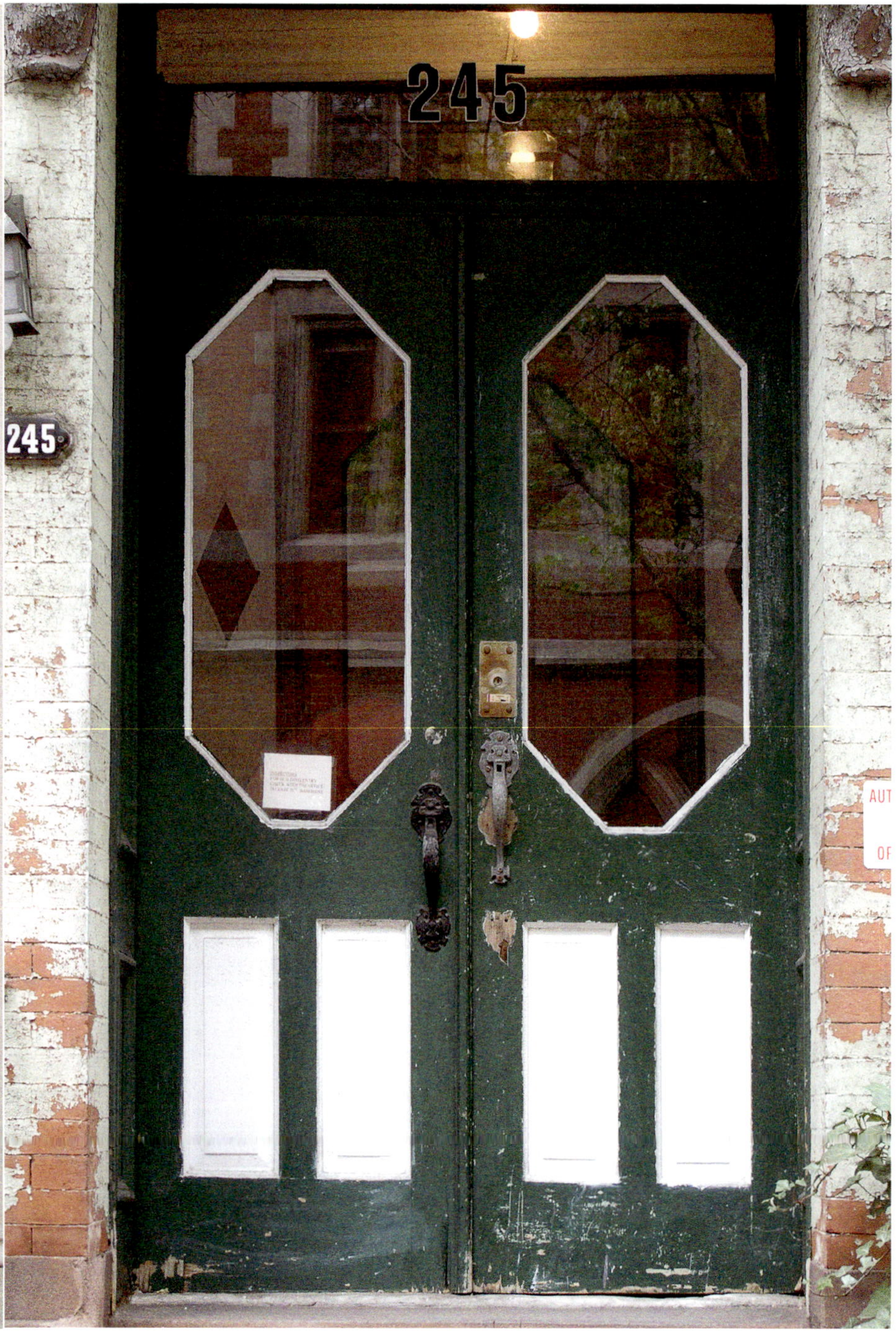
245
245

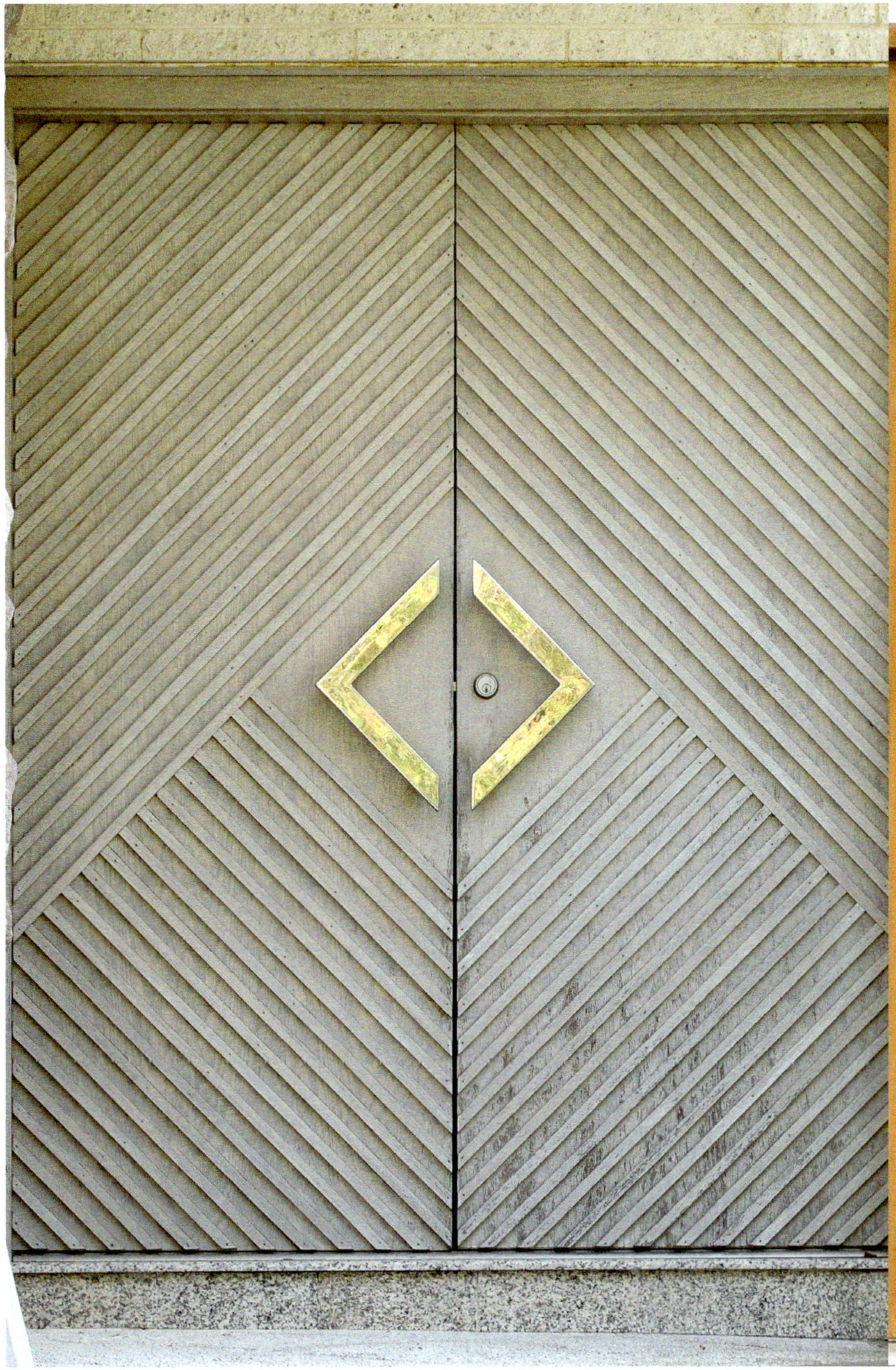
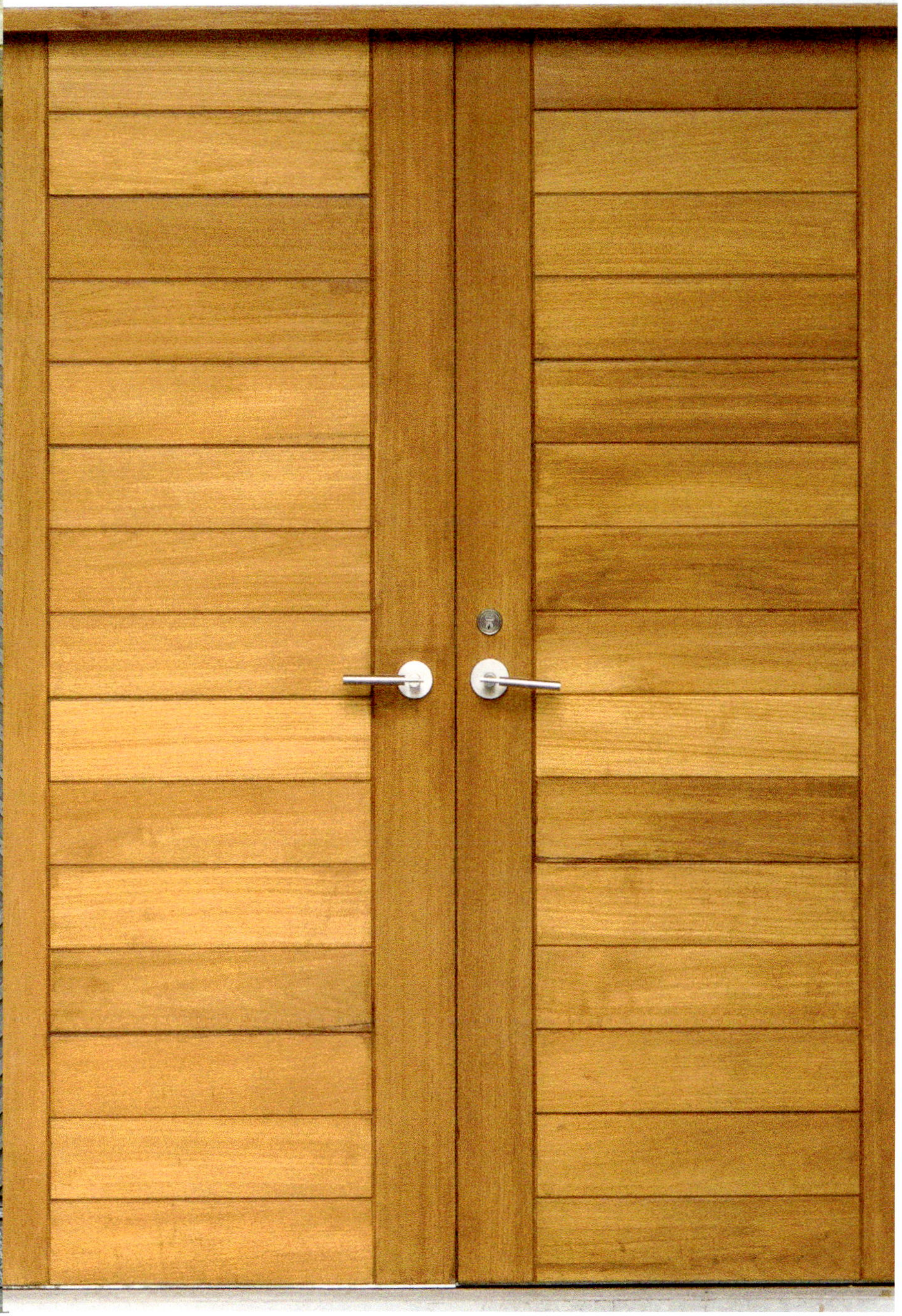

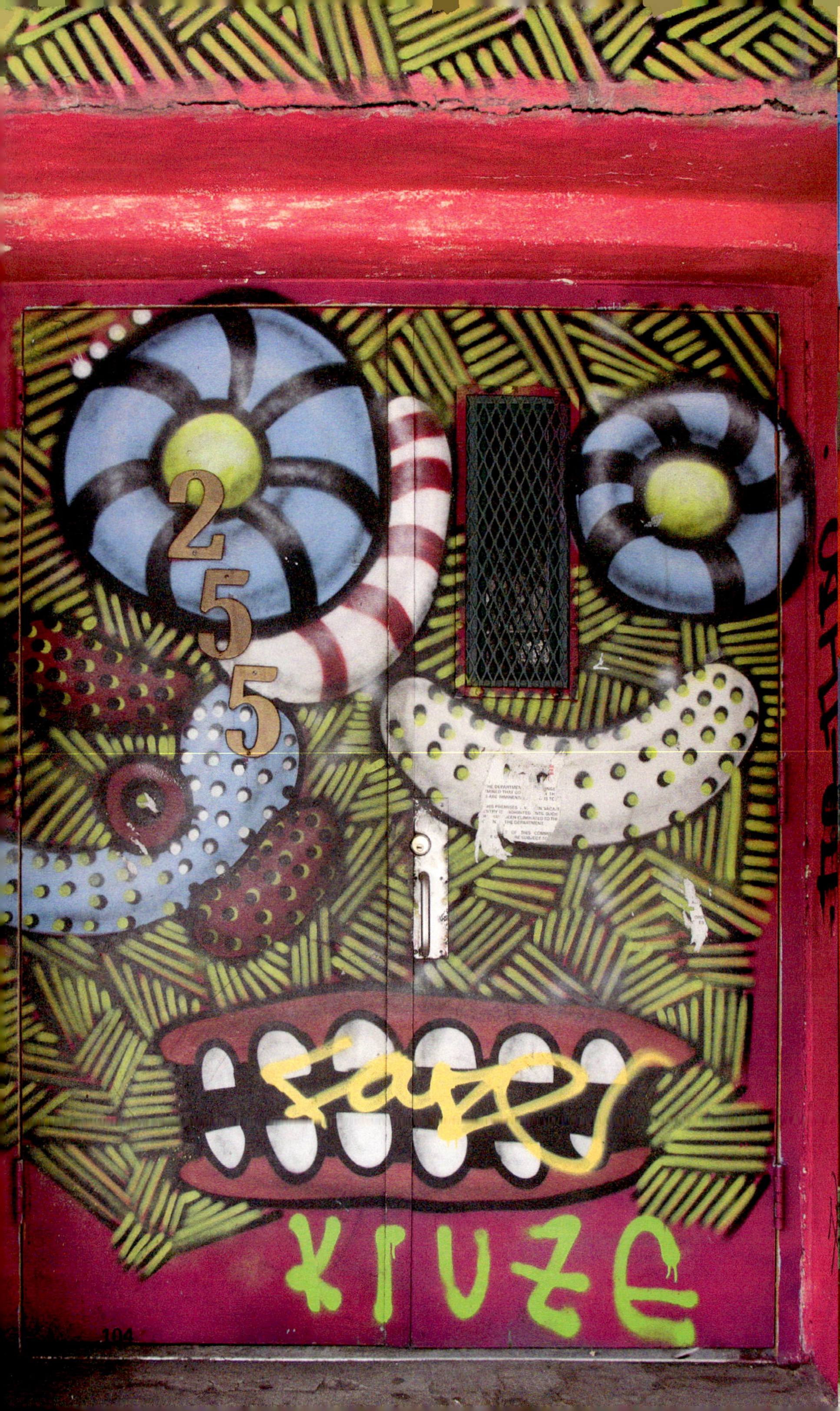
255
KRUZE

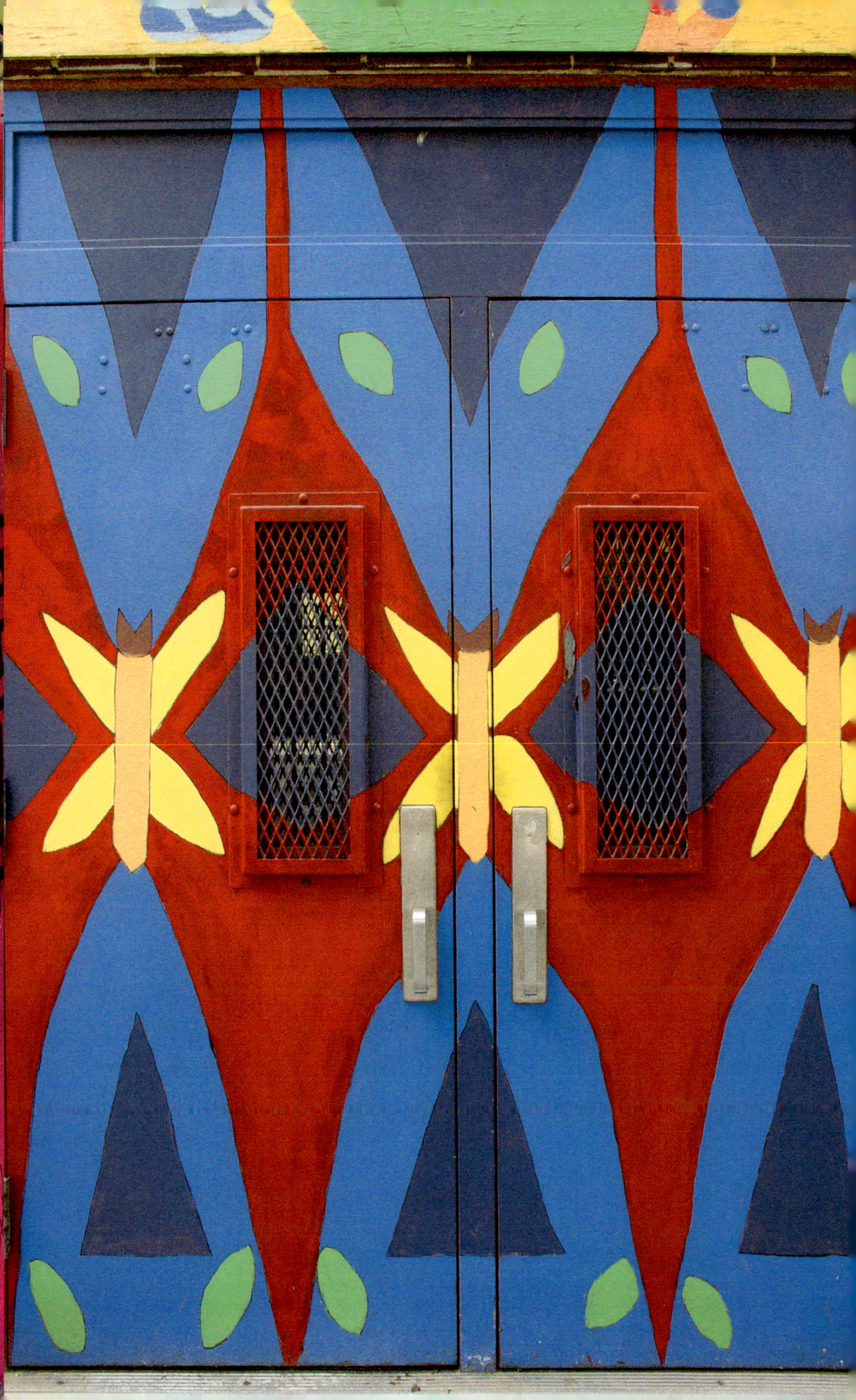

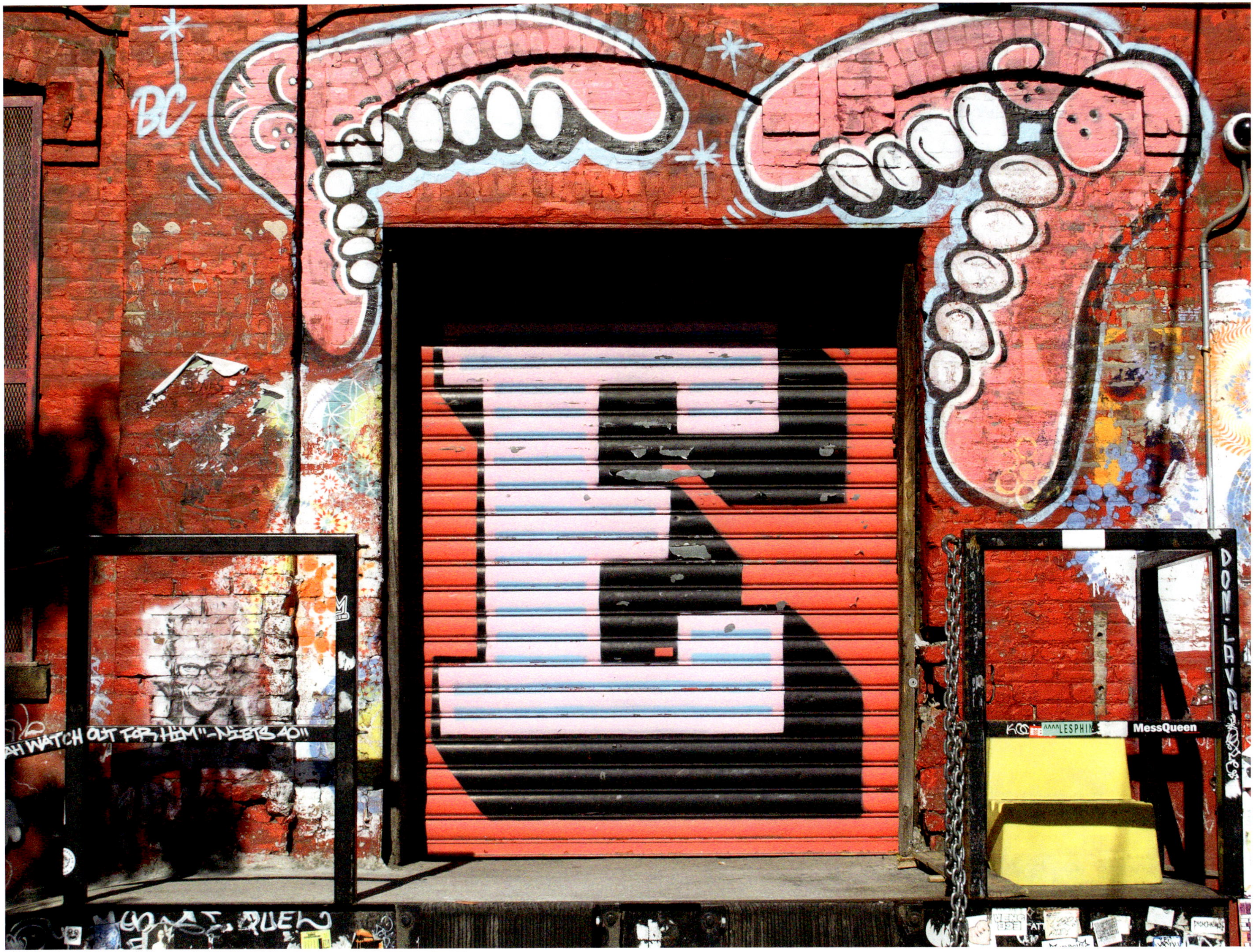
BC
MessQueen

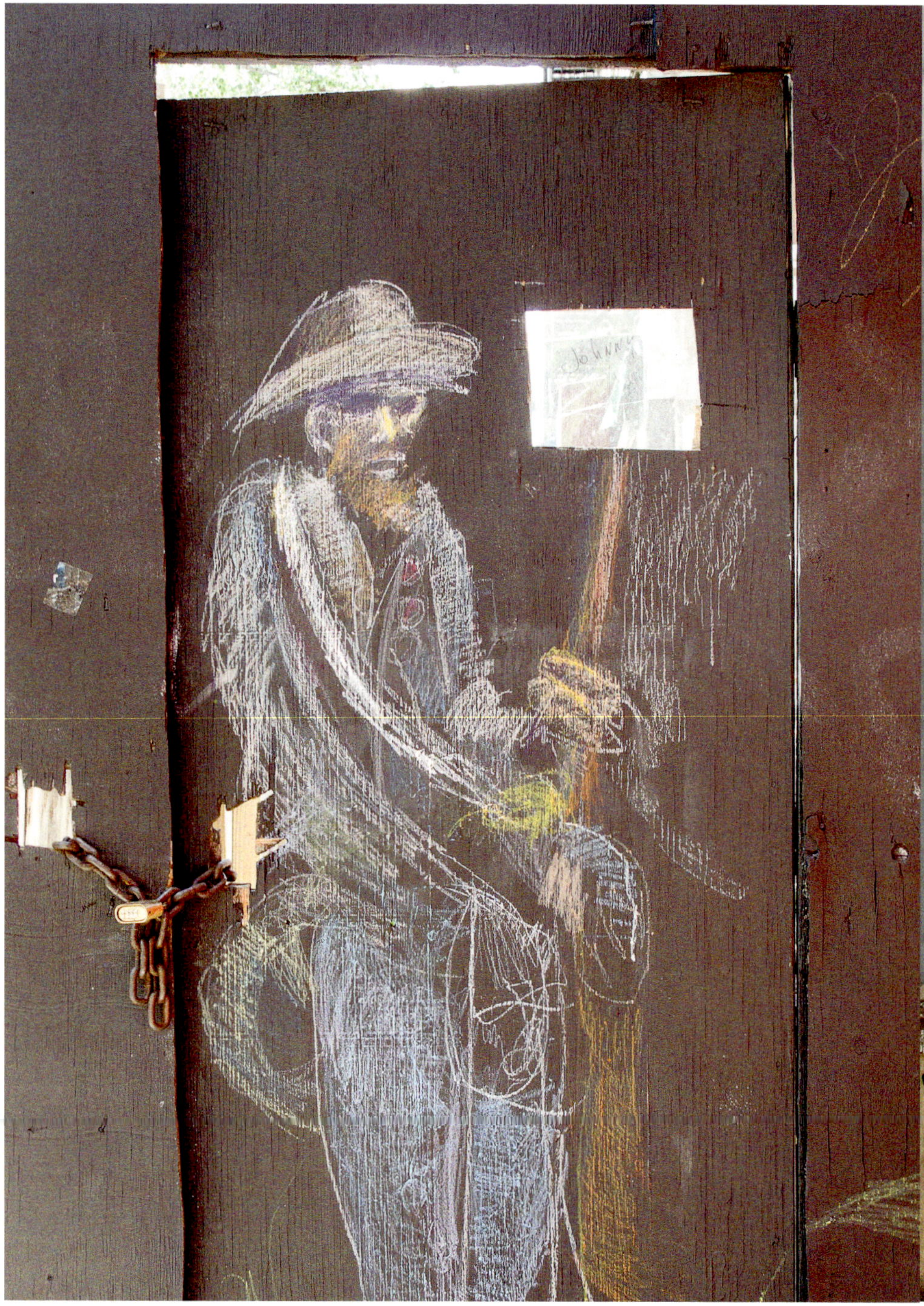

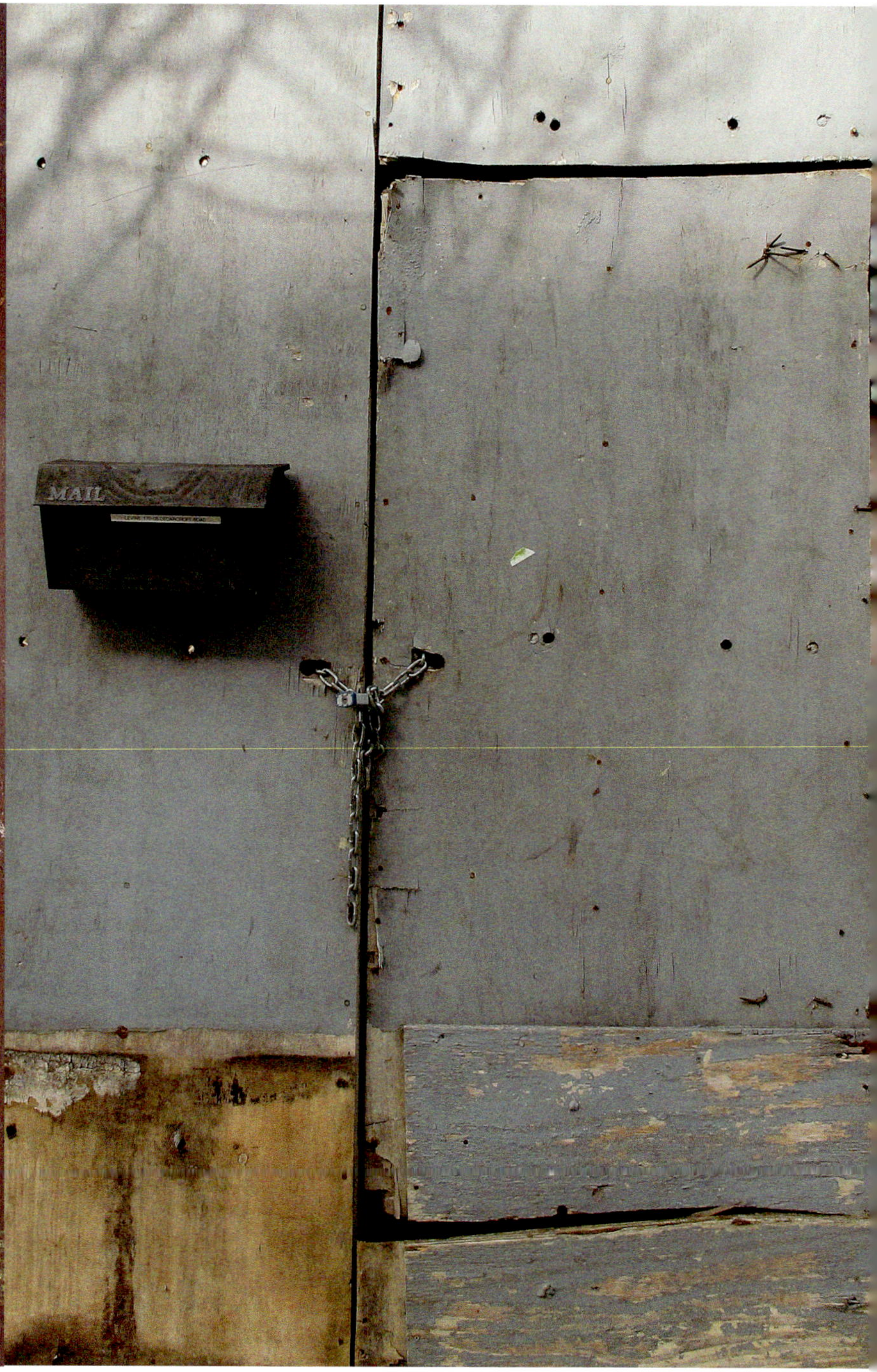
MAIL

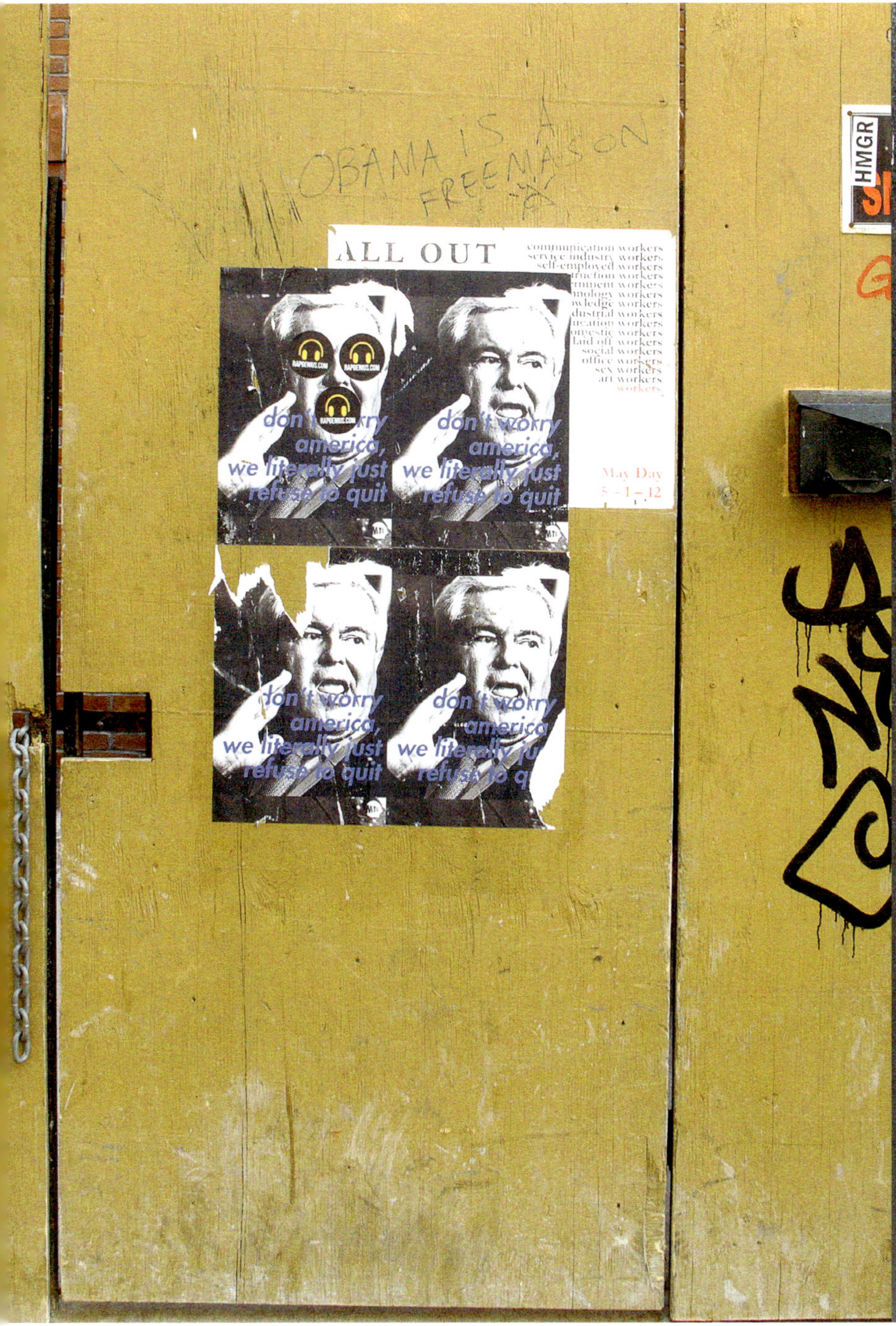
OBAMA IS A FREEMASON
ALL OUT
communication workers
service industry workers
self-employed workers
don't worry america, we literally just refuse to quit
May Day
5-1-12
HMGR

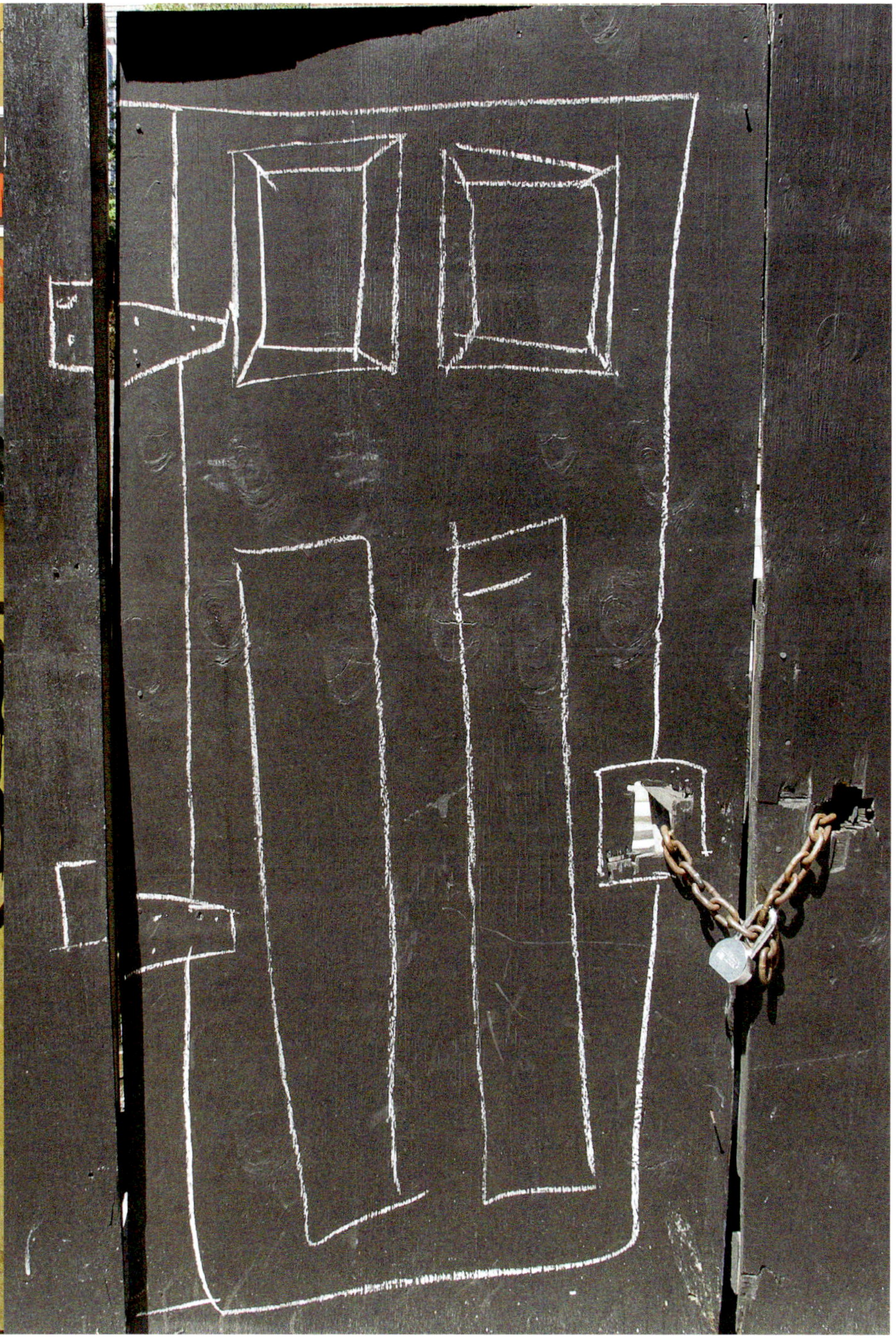

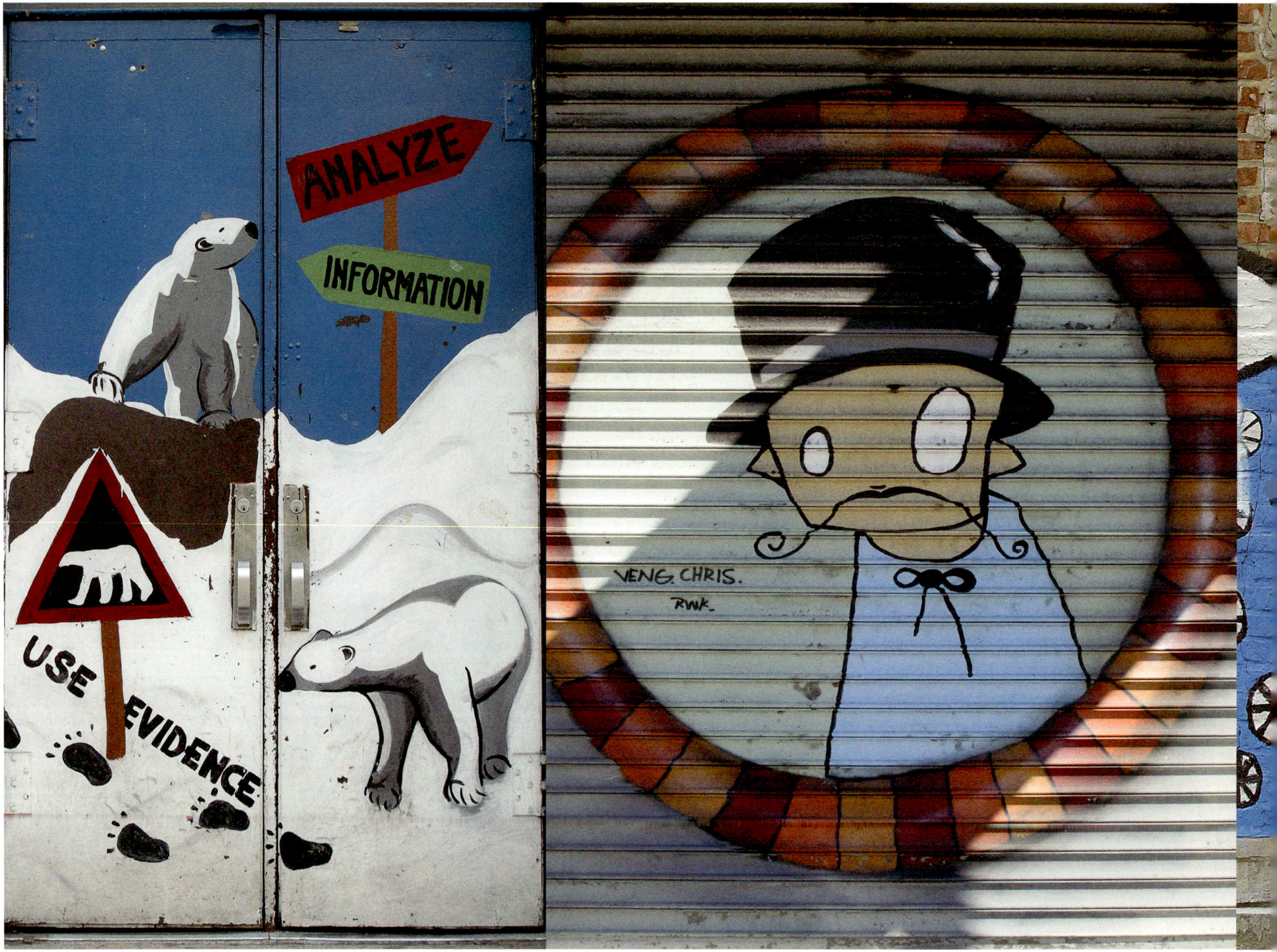
ANALYZE
INFORMATION
USE
EVIDENCE
VENG. CHRIS.
RWK.

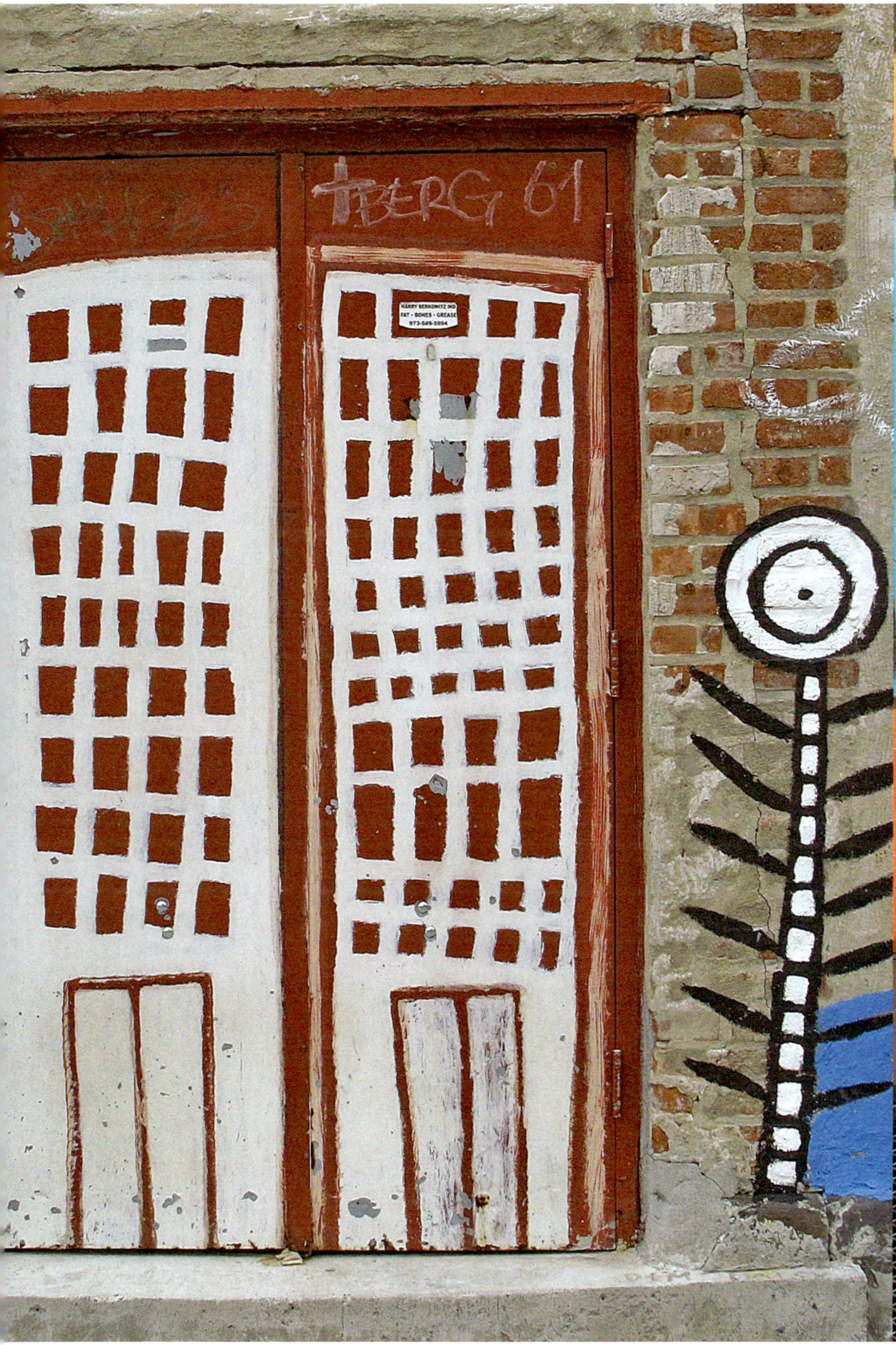

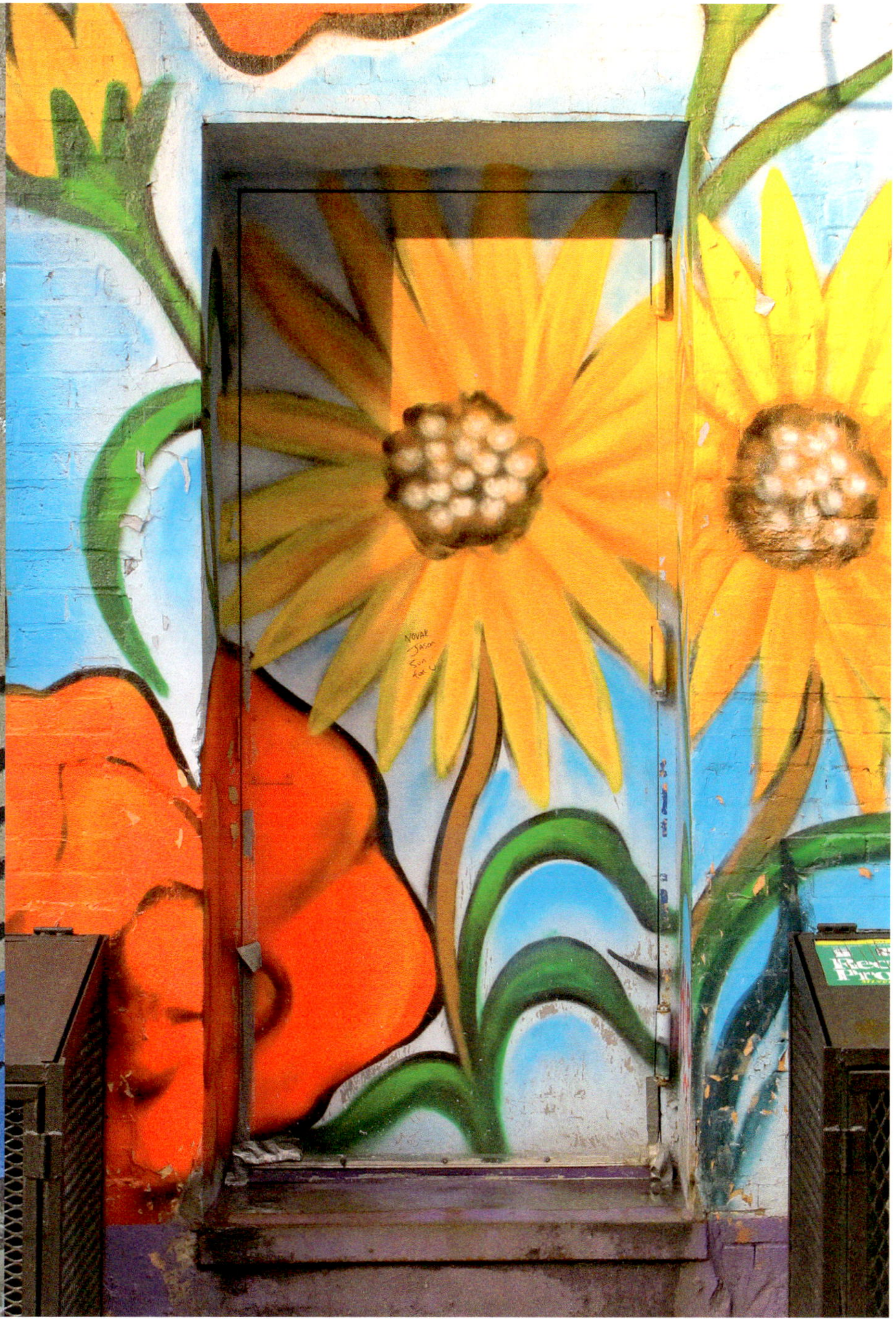

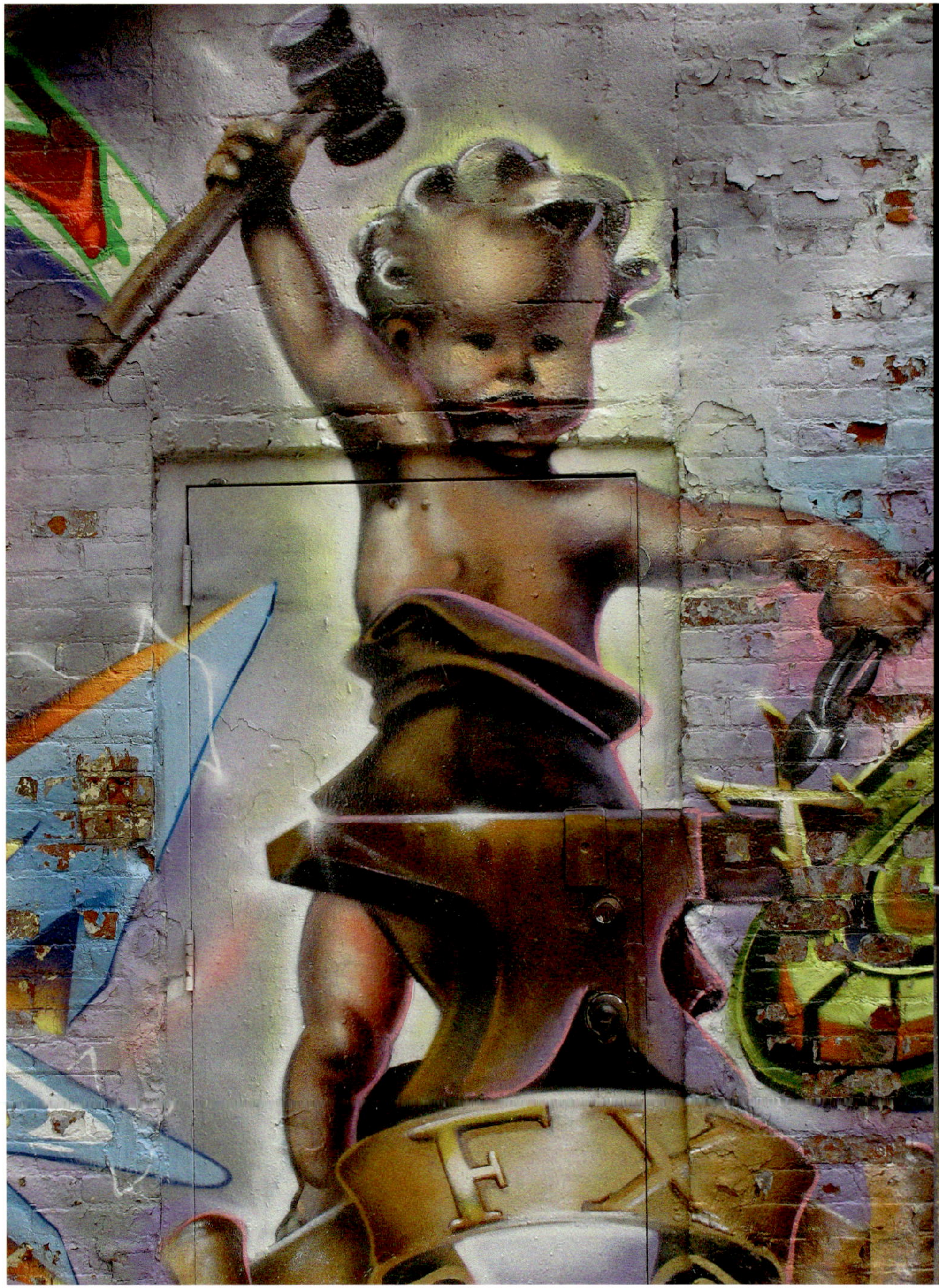

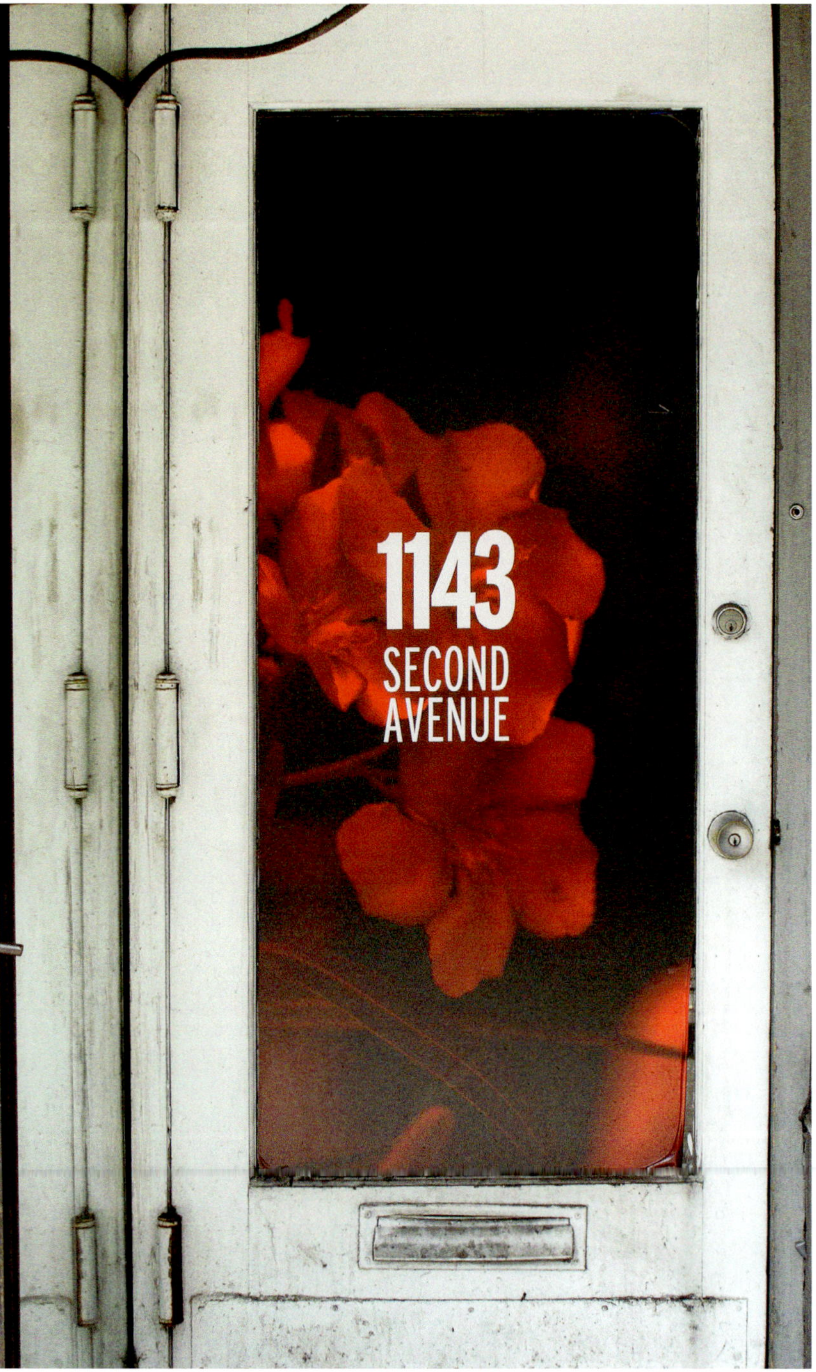
1143
SECOND
AVENUE

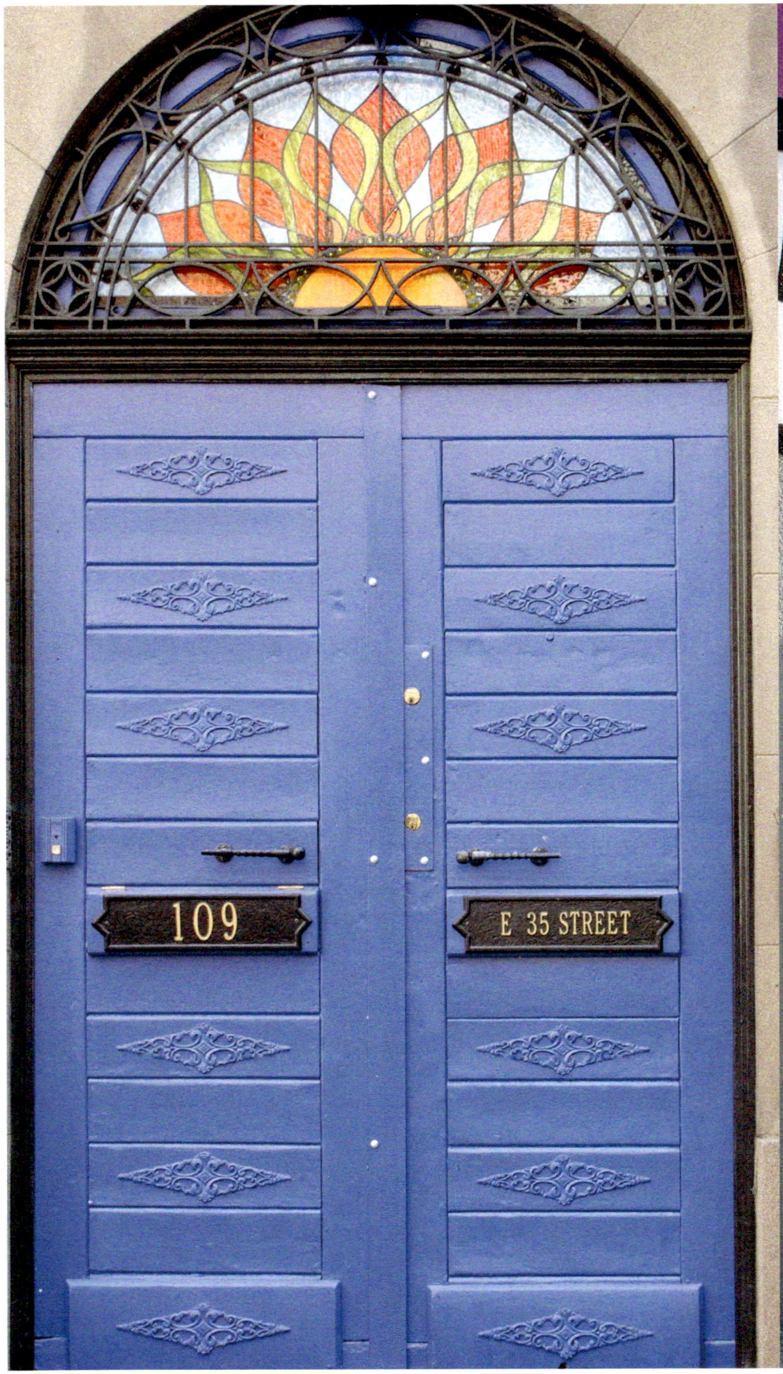
109
E 35 STREET
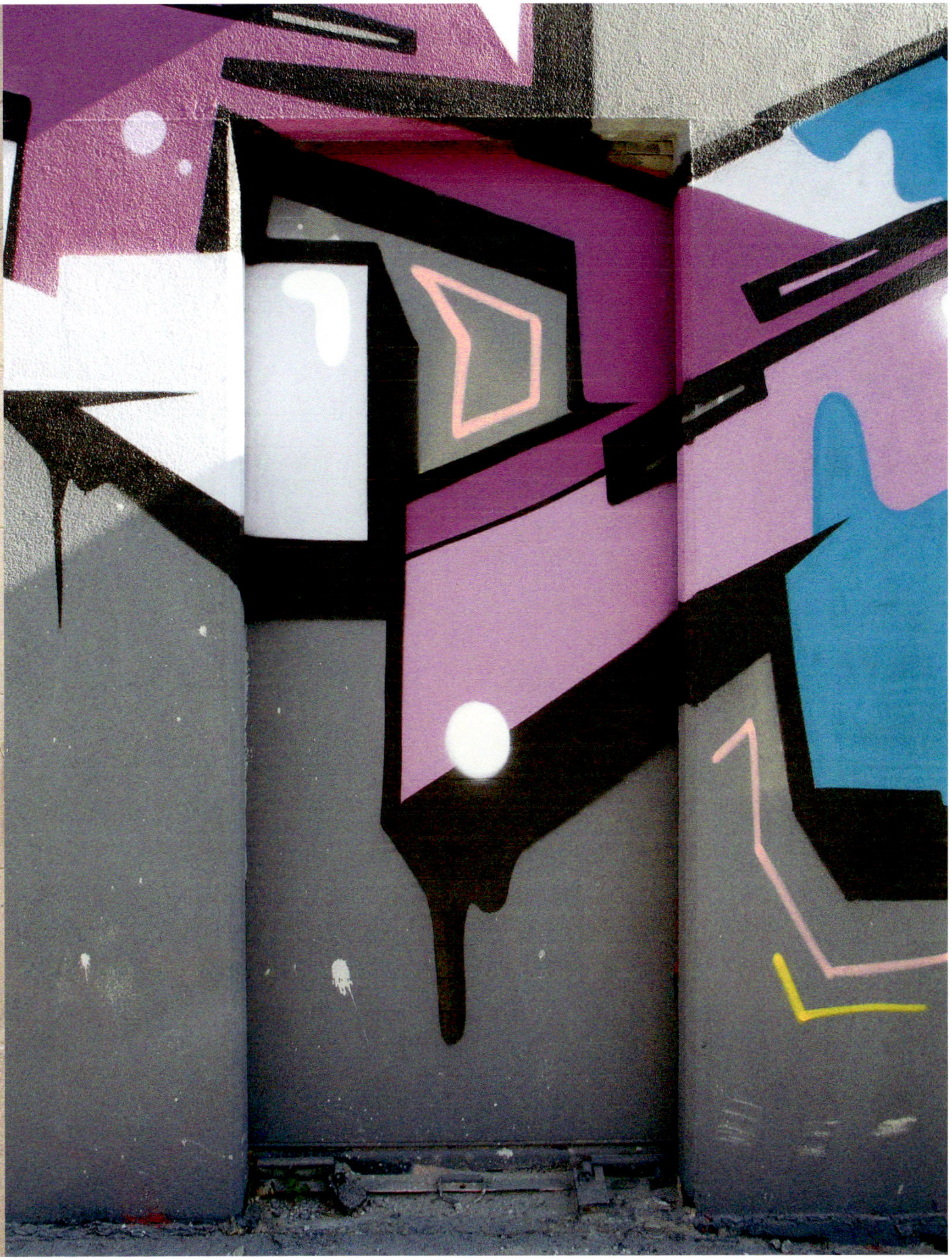

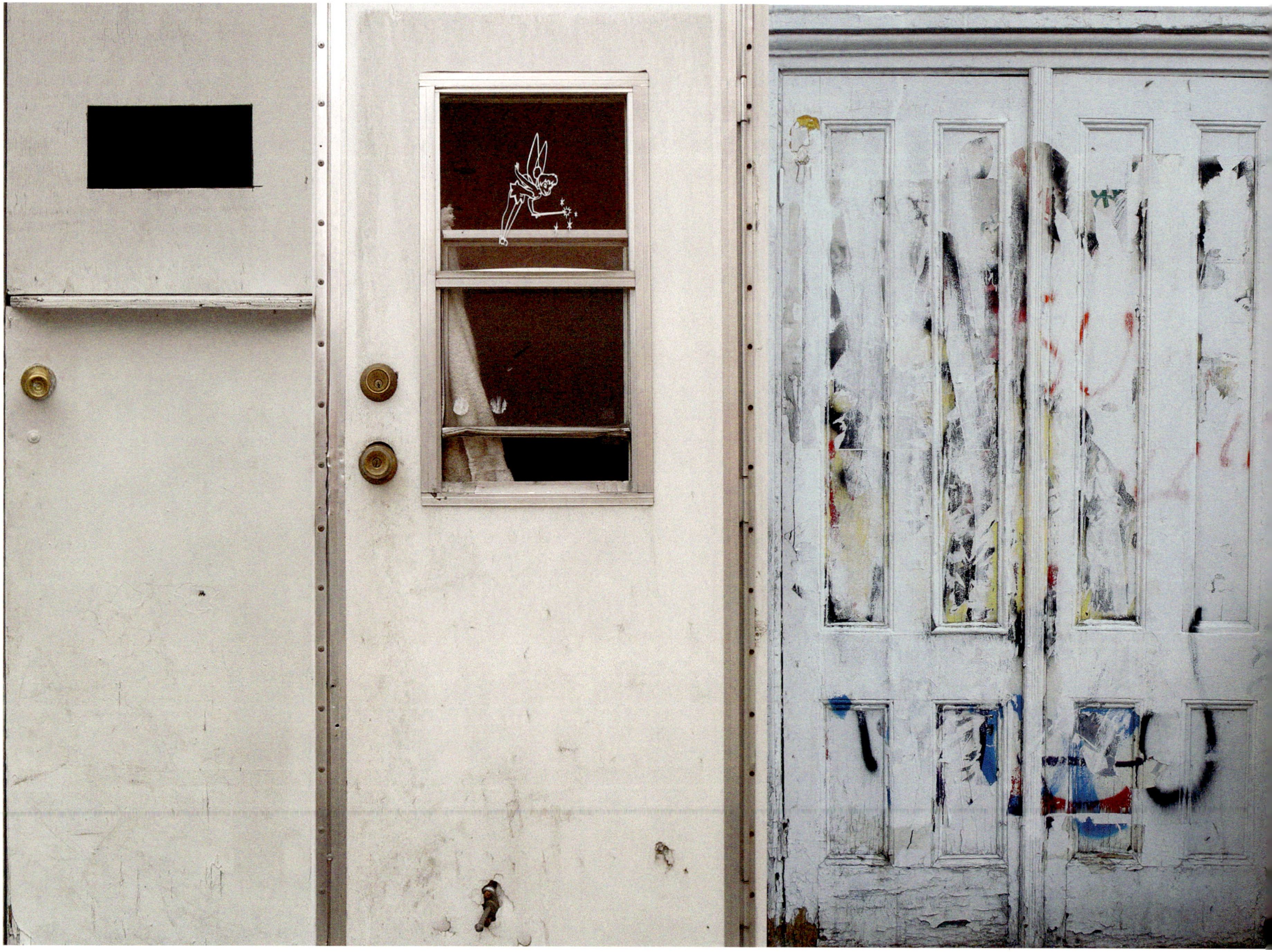

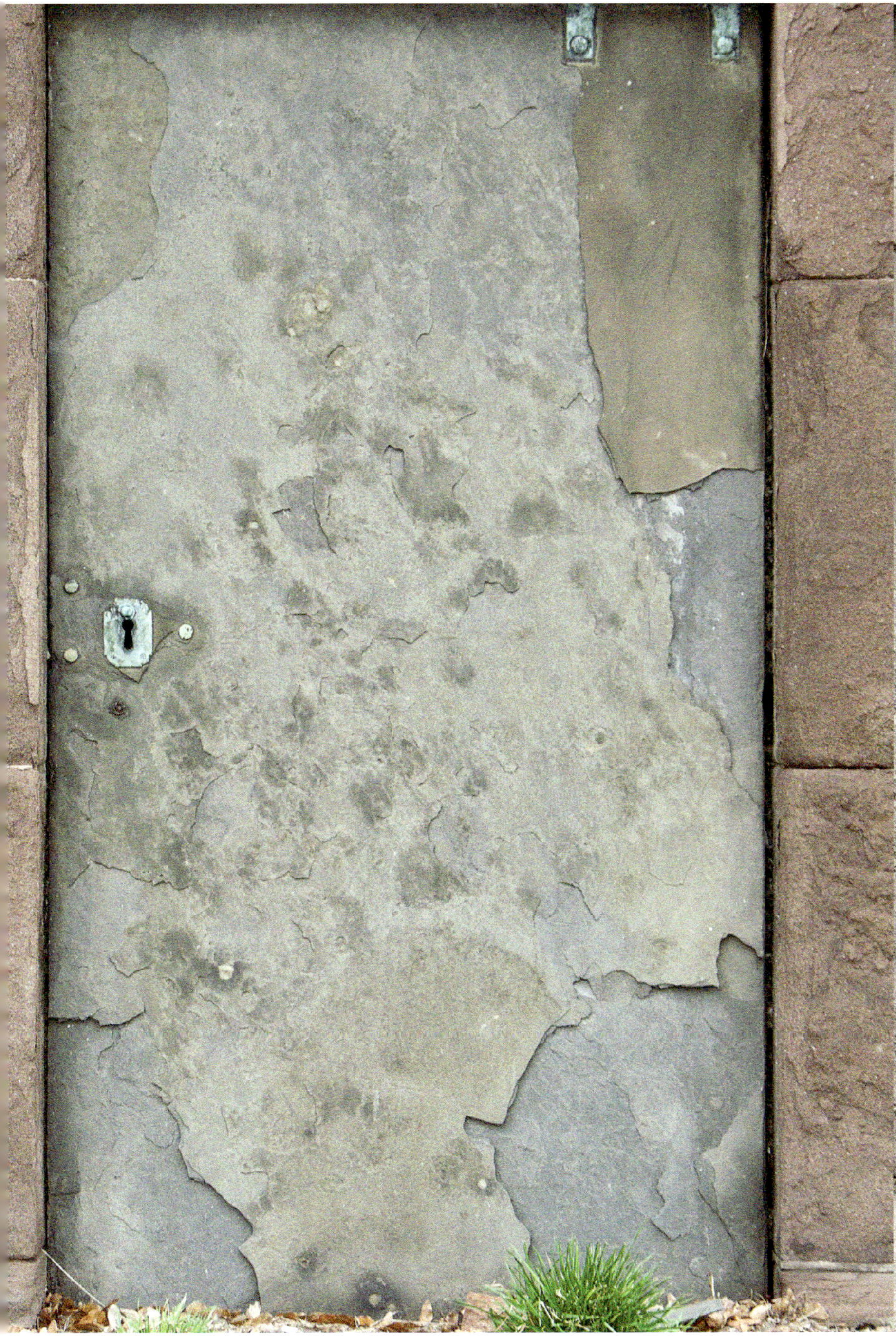

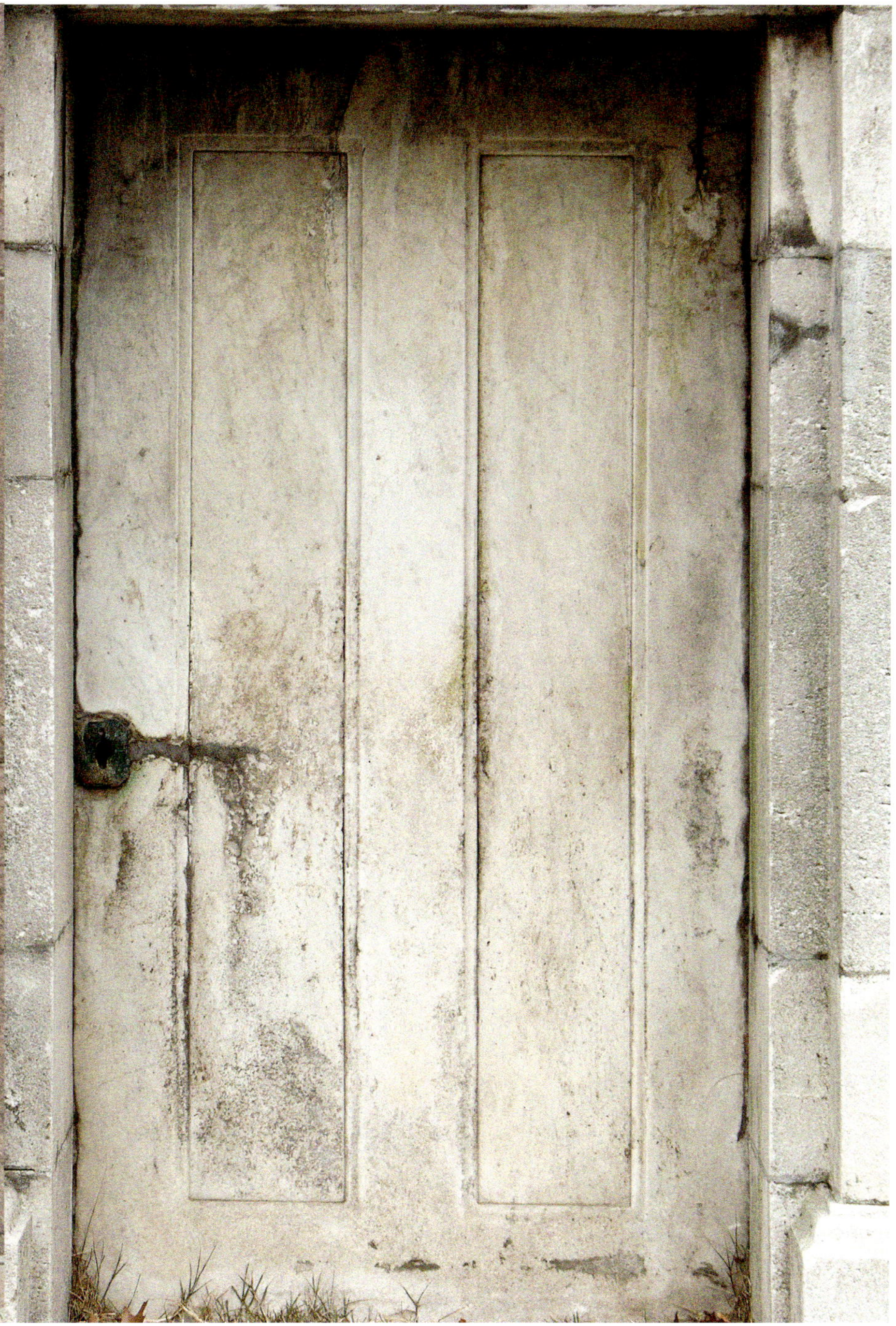

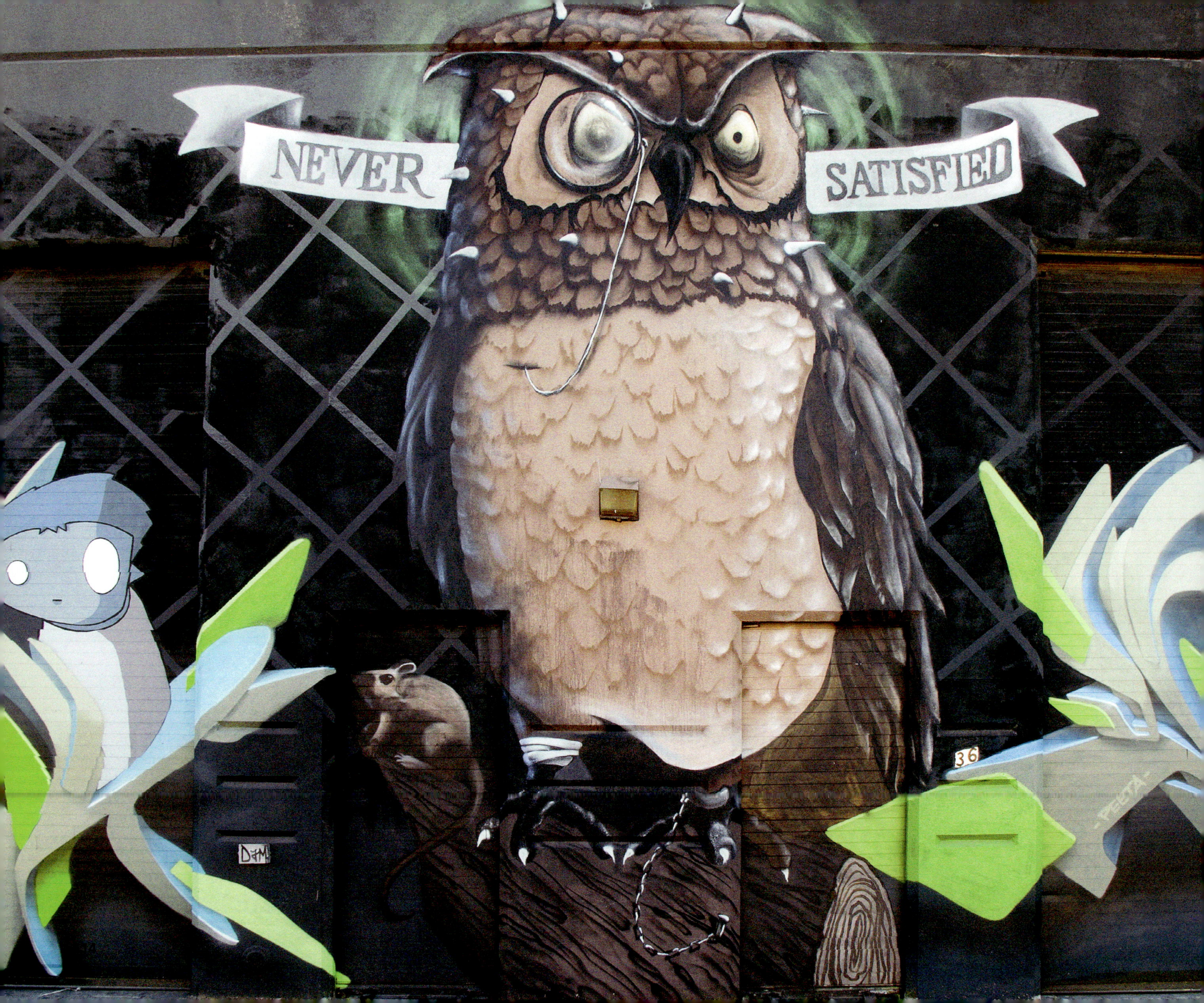
NEVER
SATISFIED
36

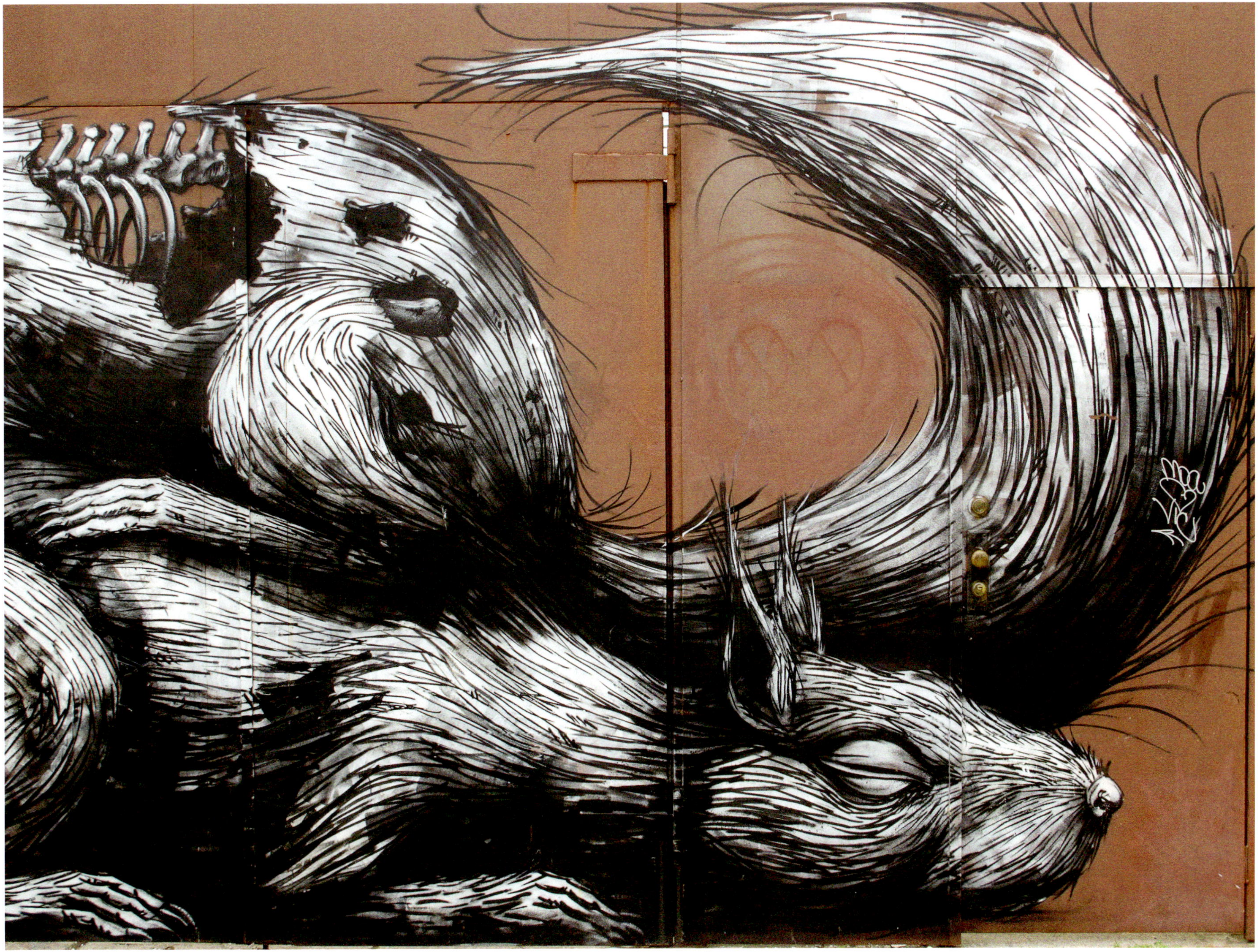

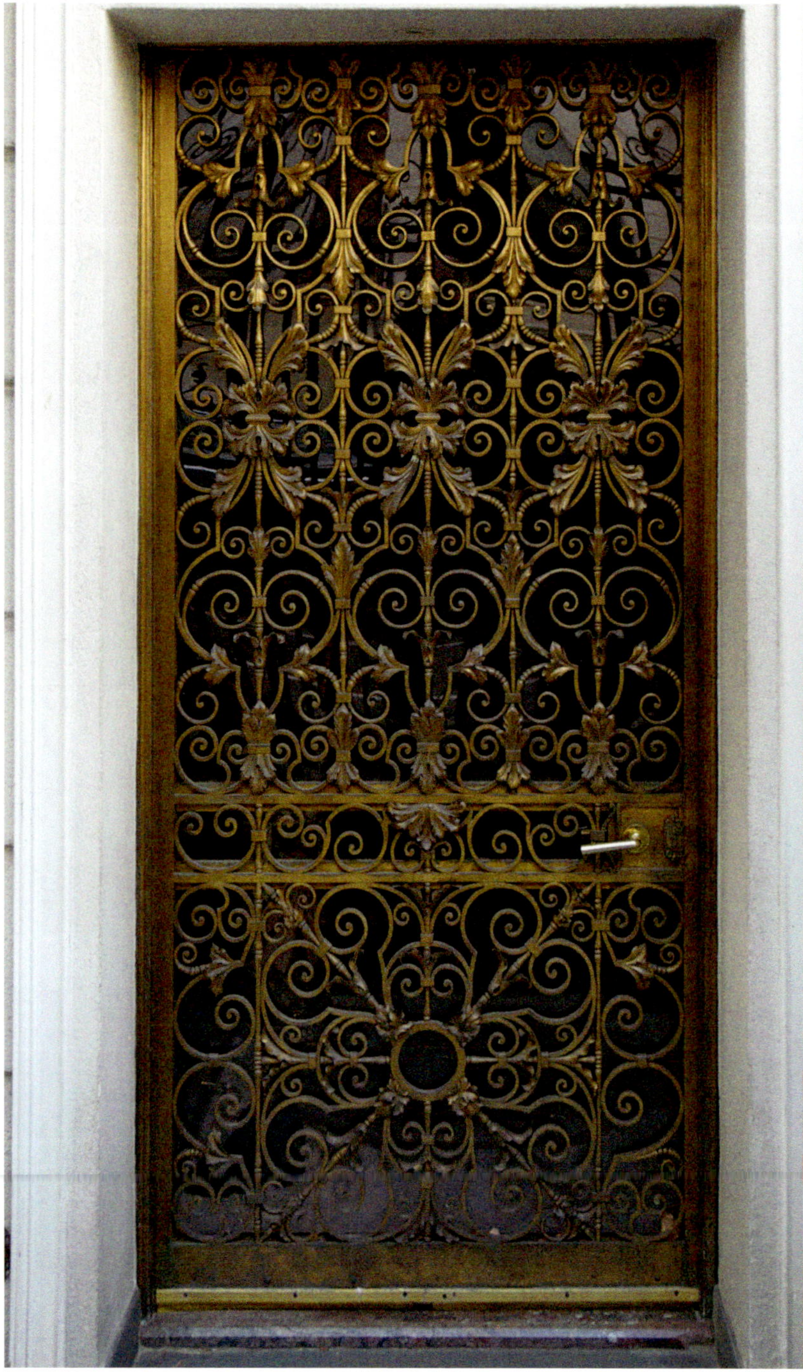

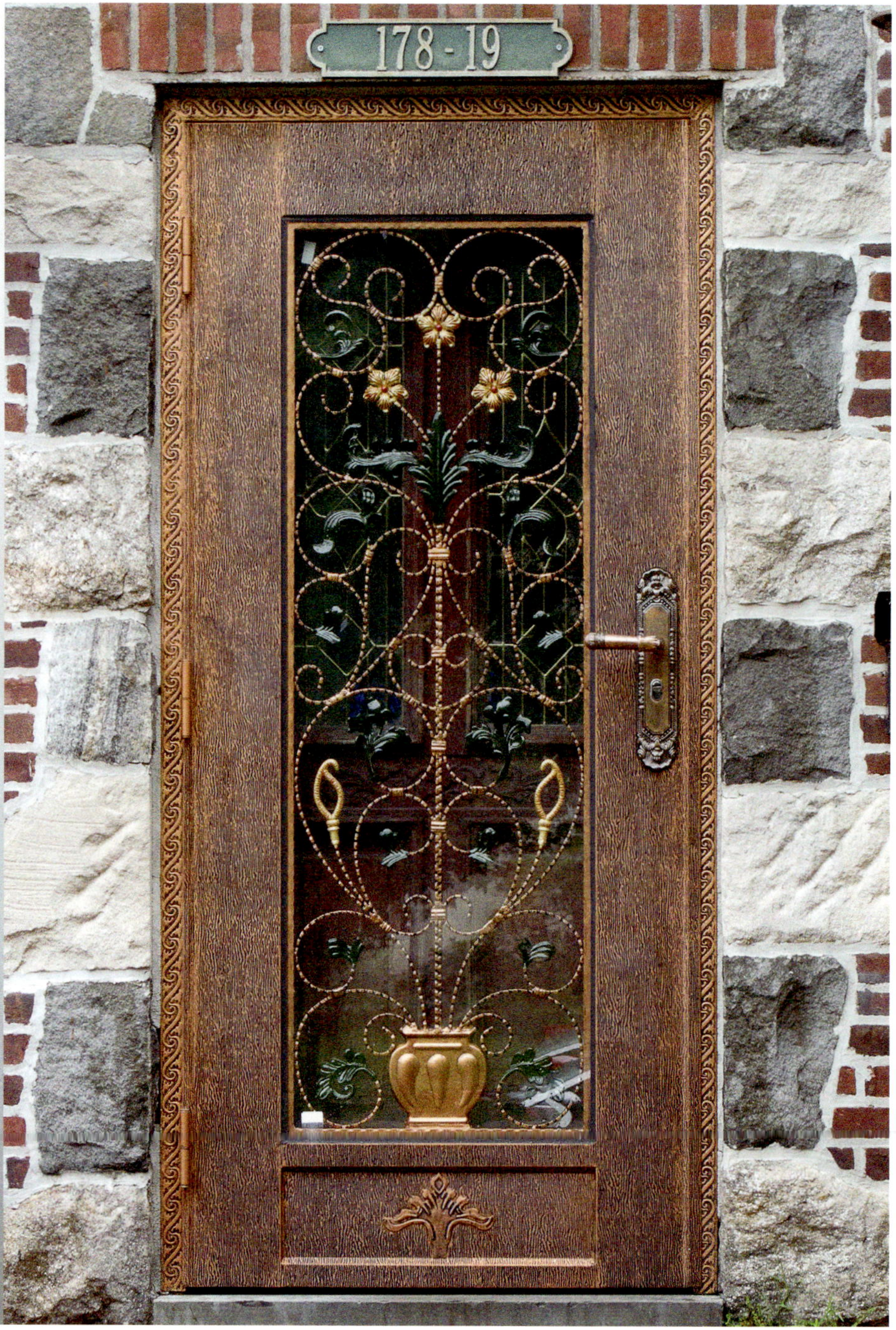
178 - 19

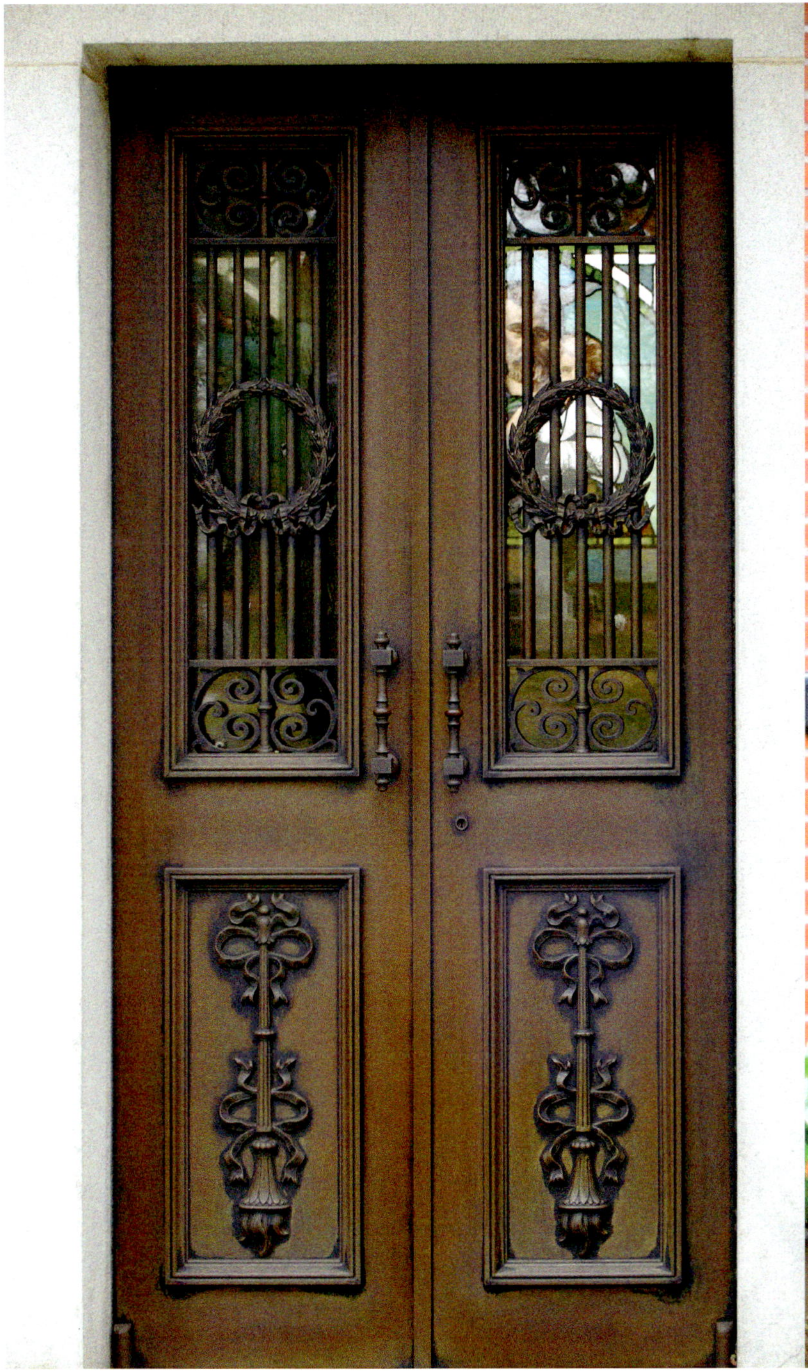 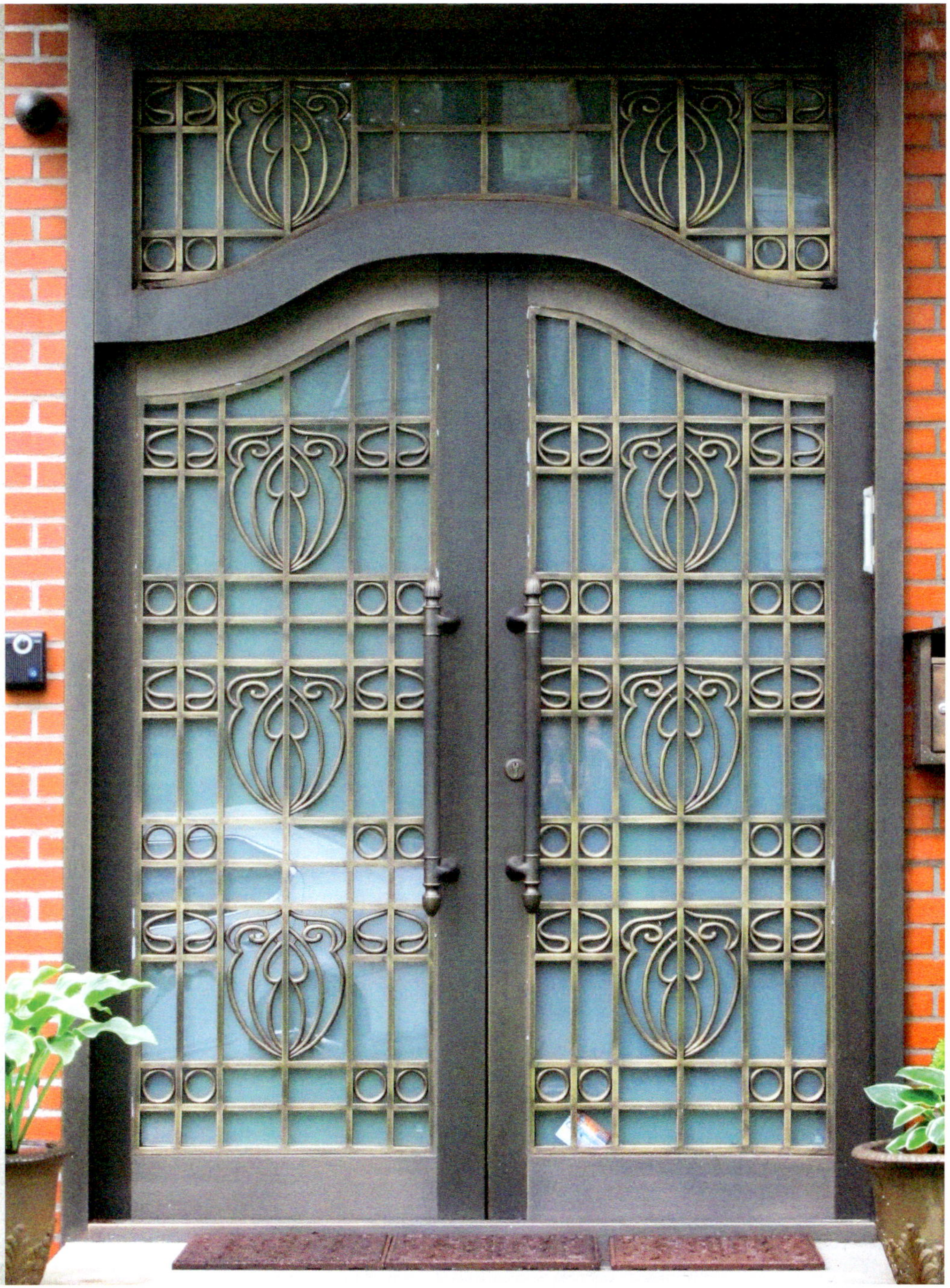

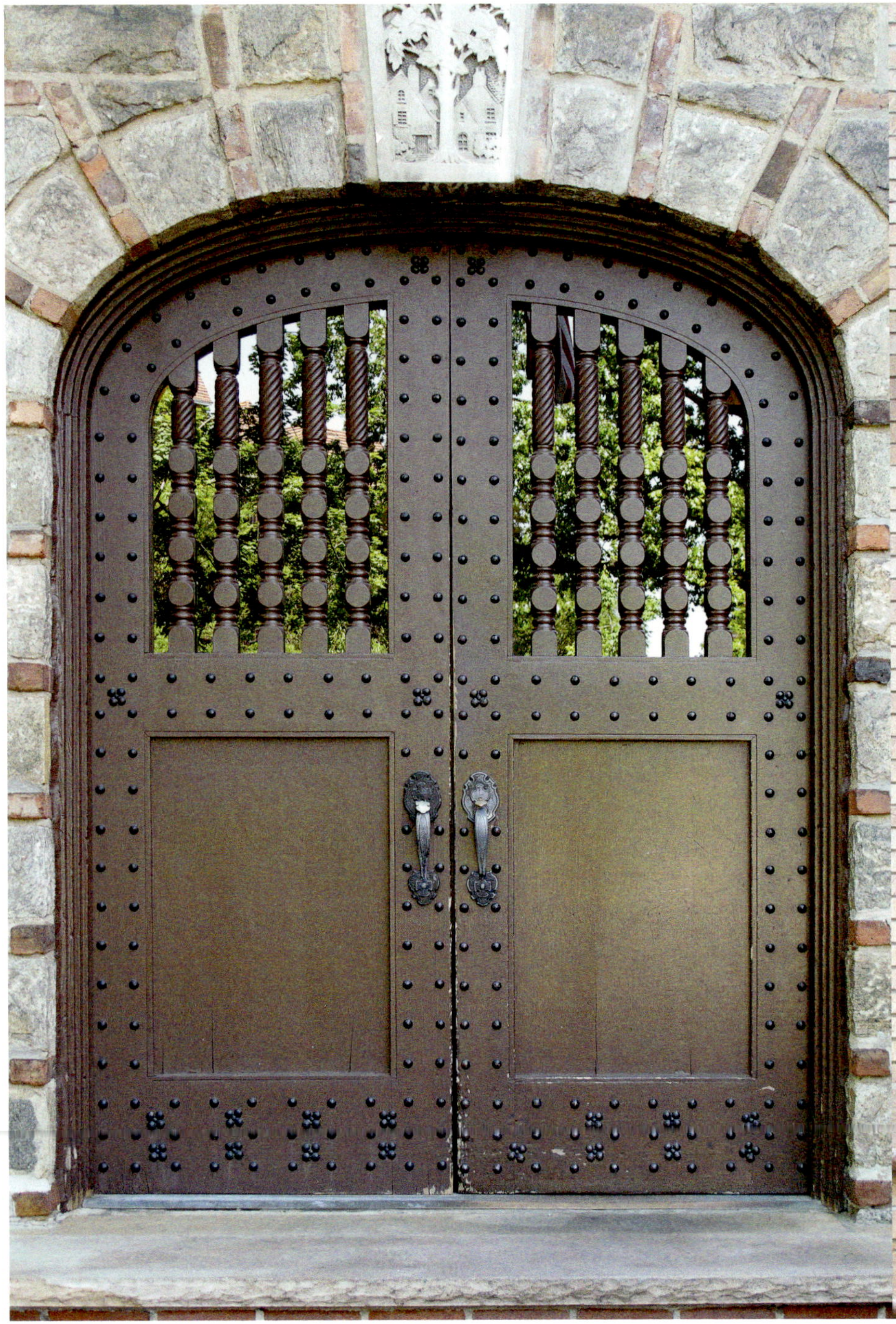

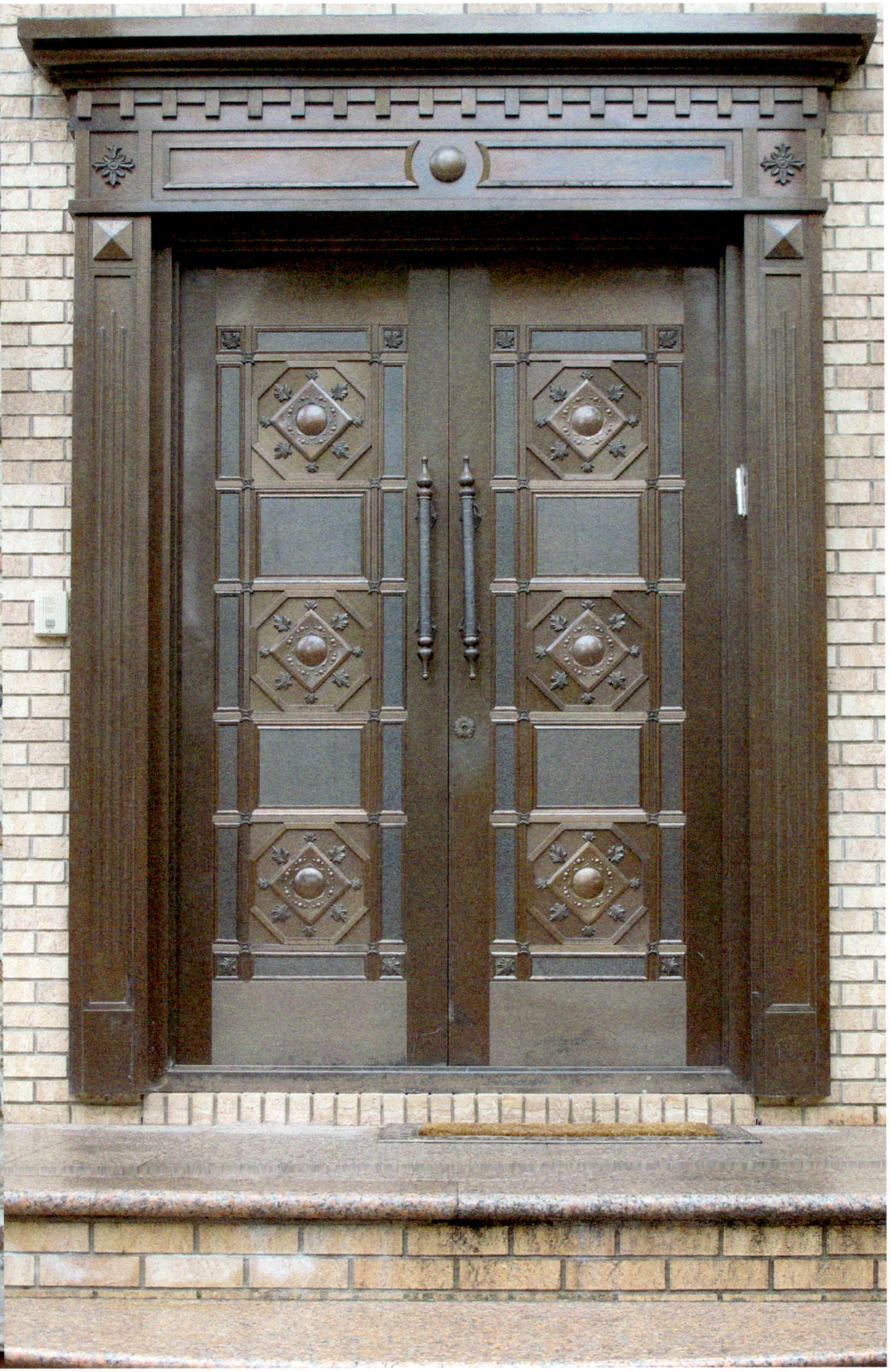

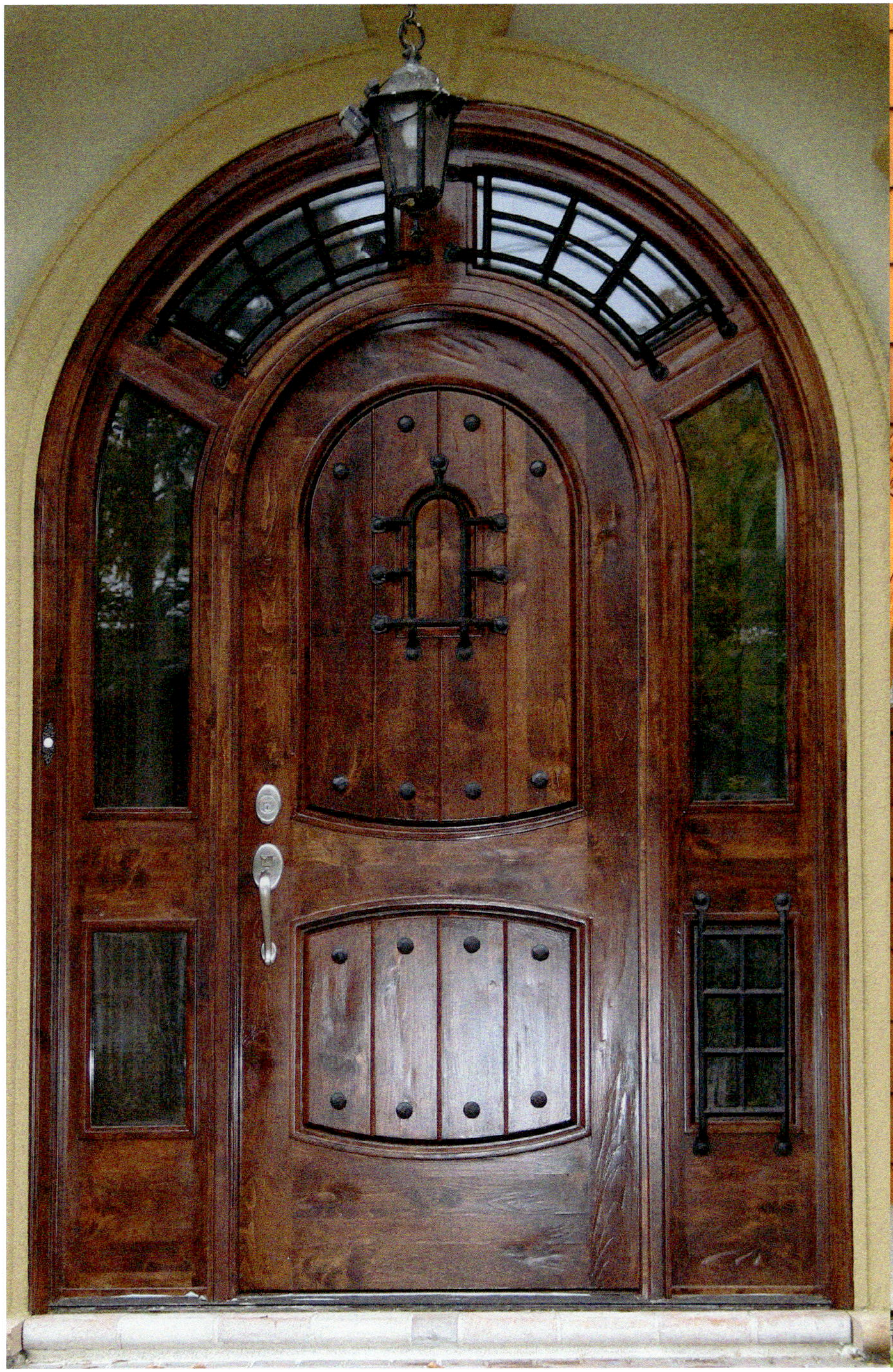

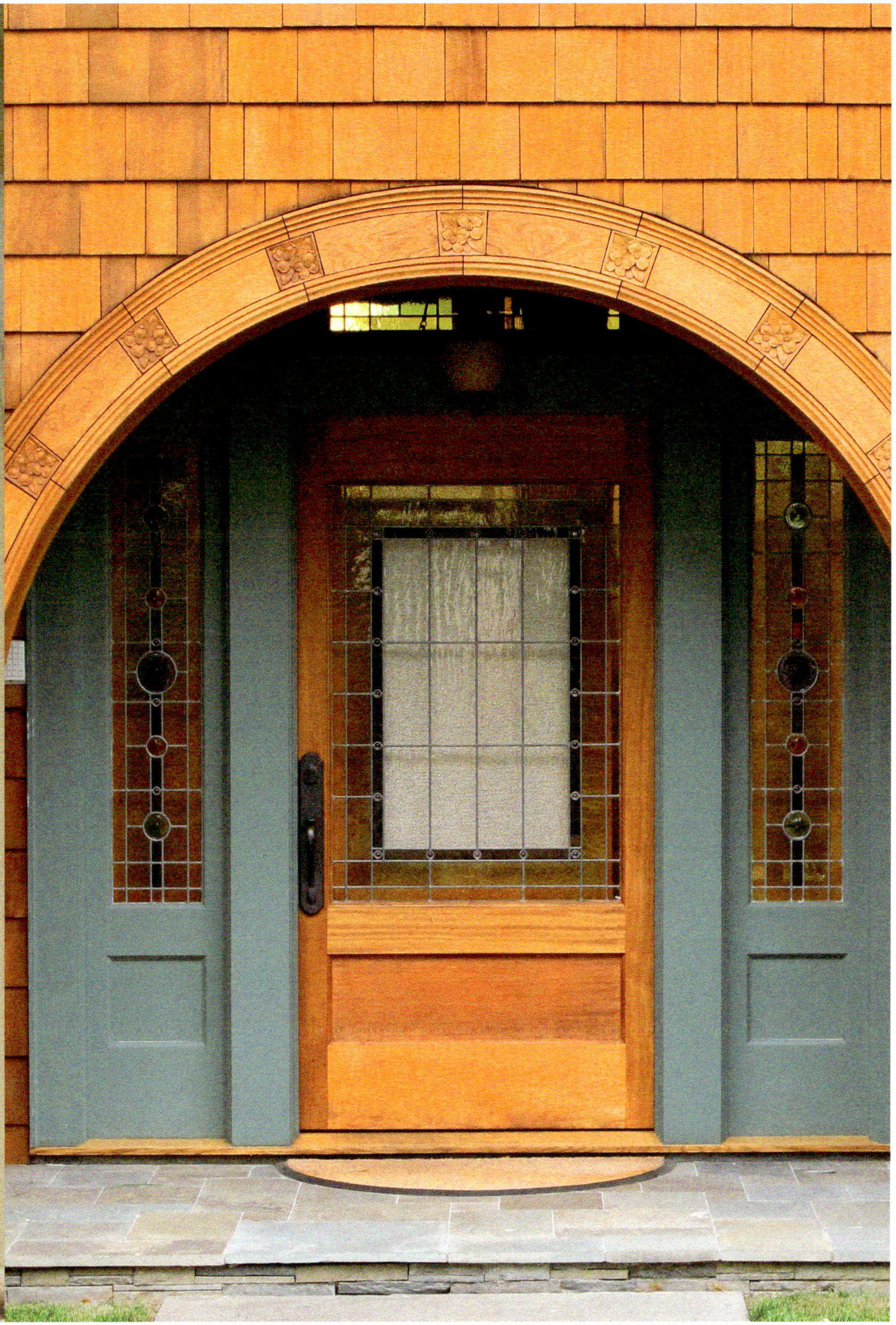

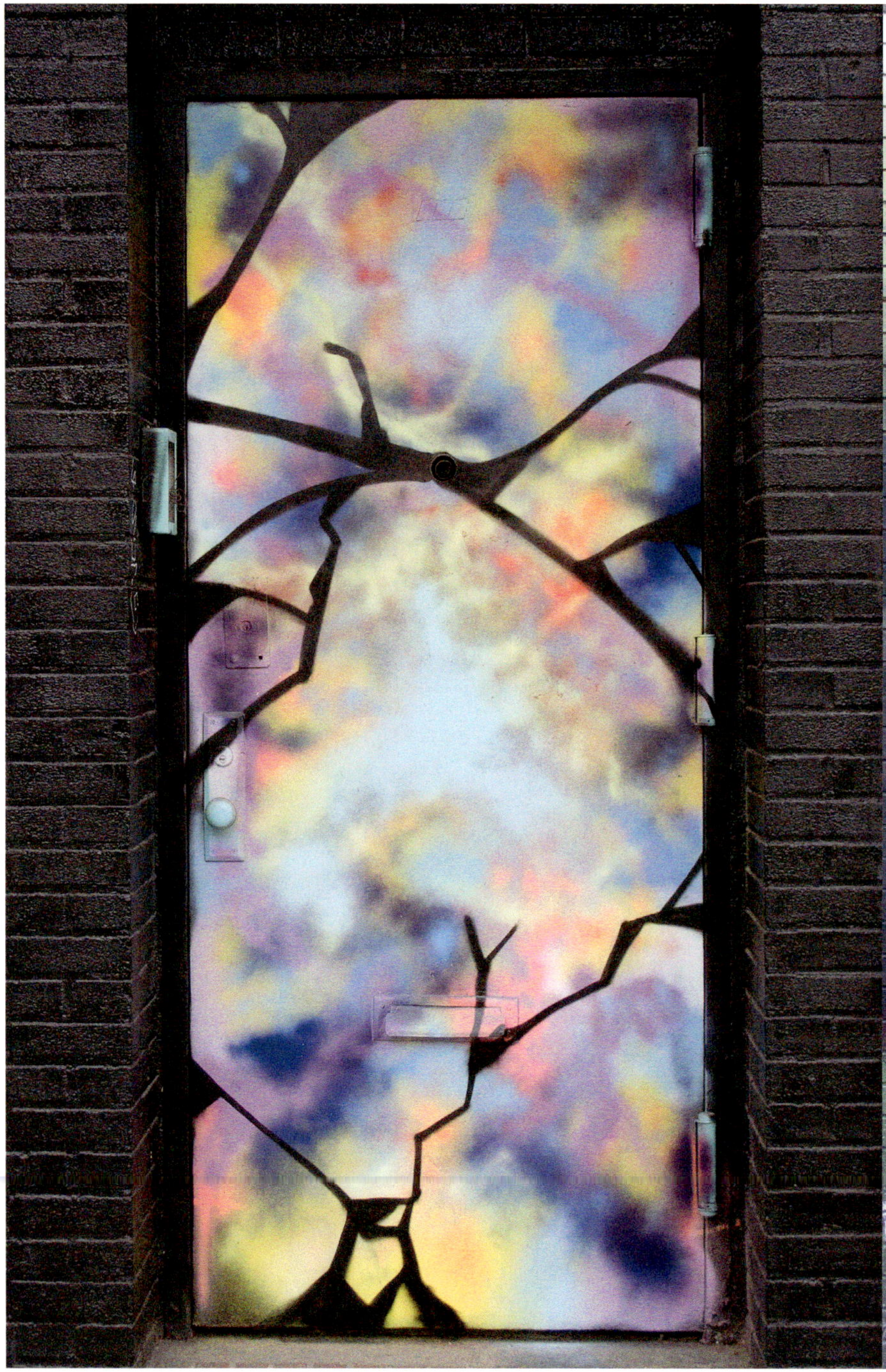

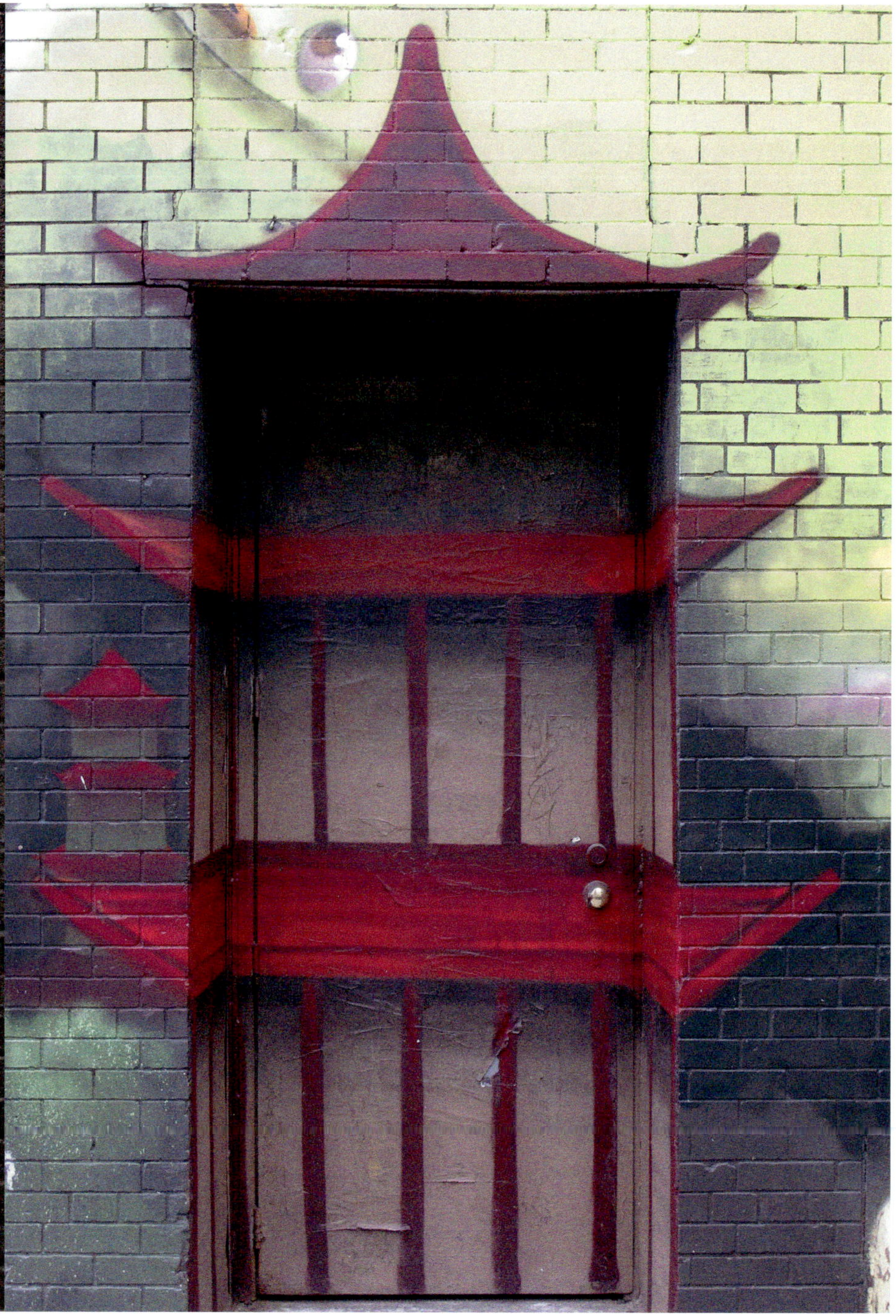

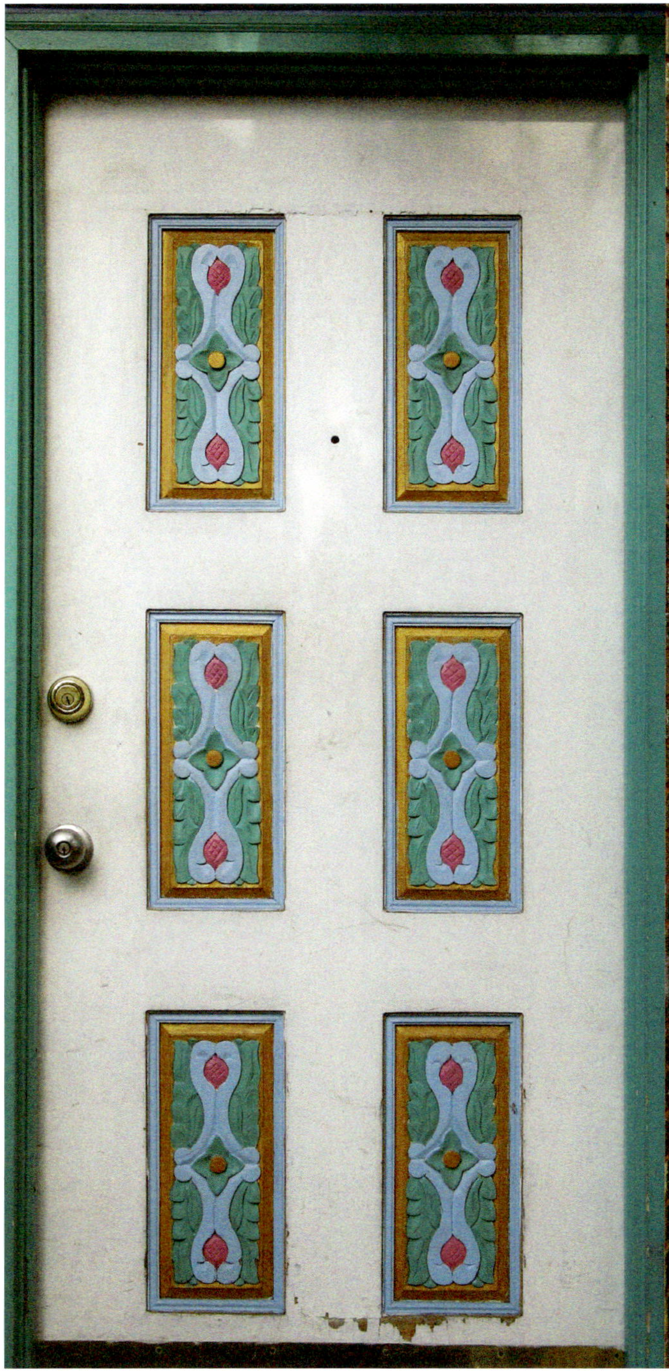

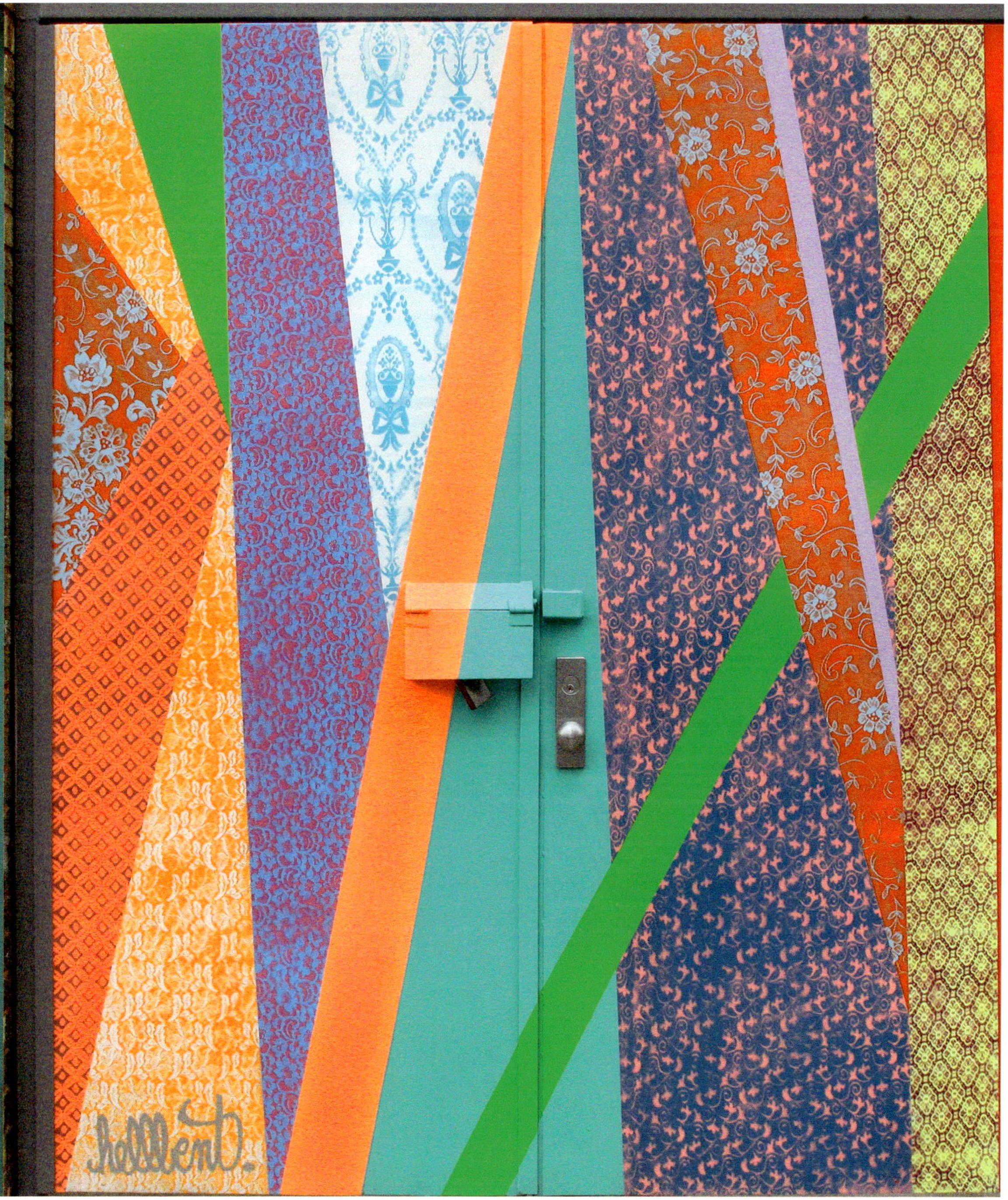

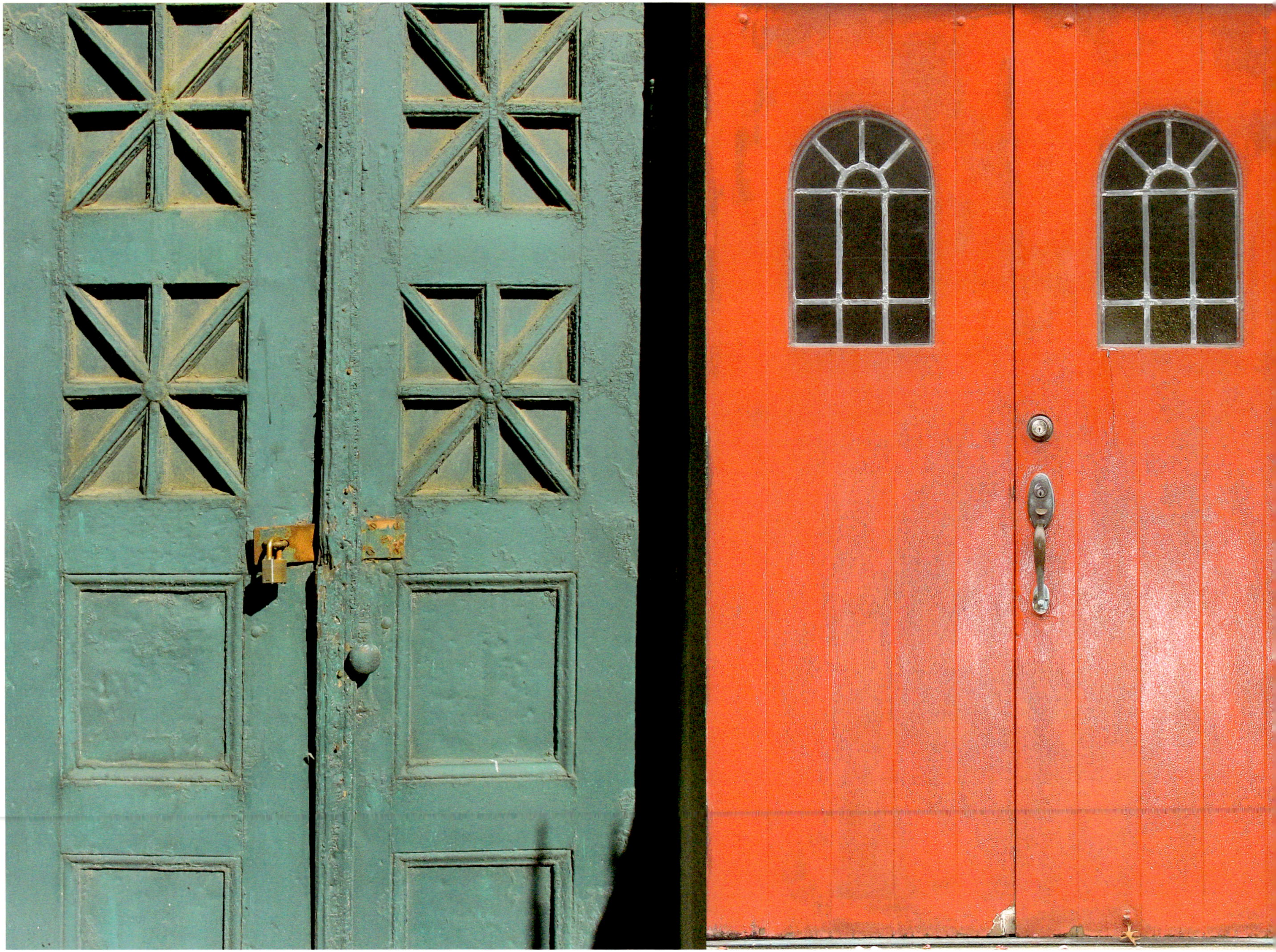

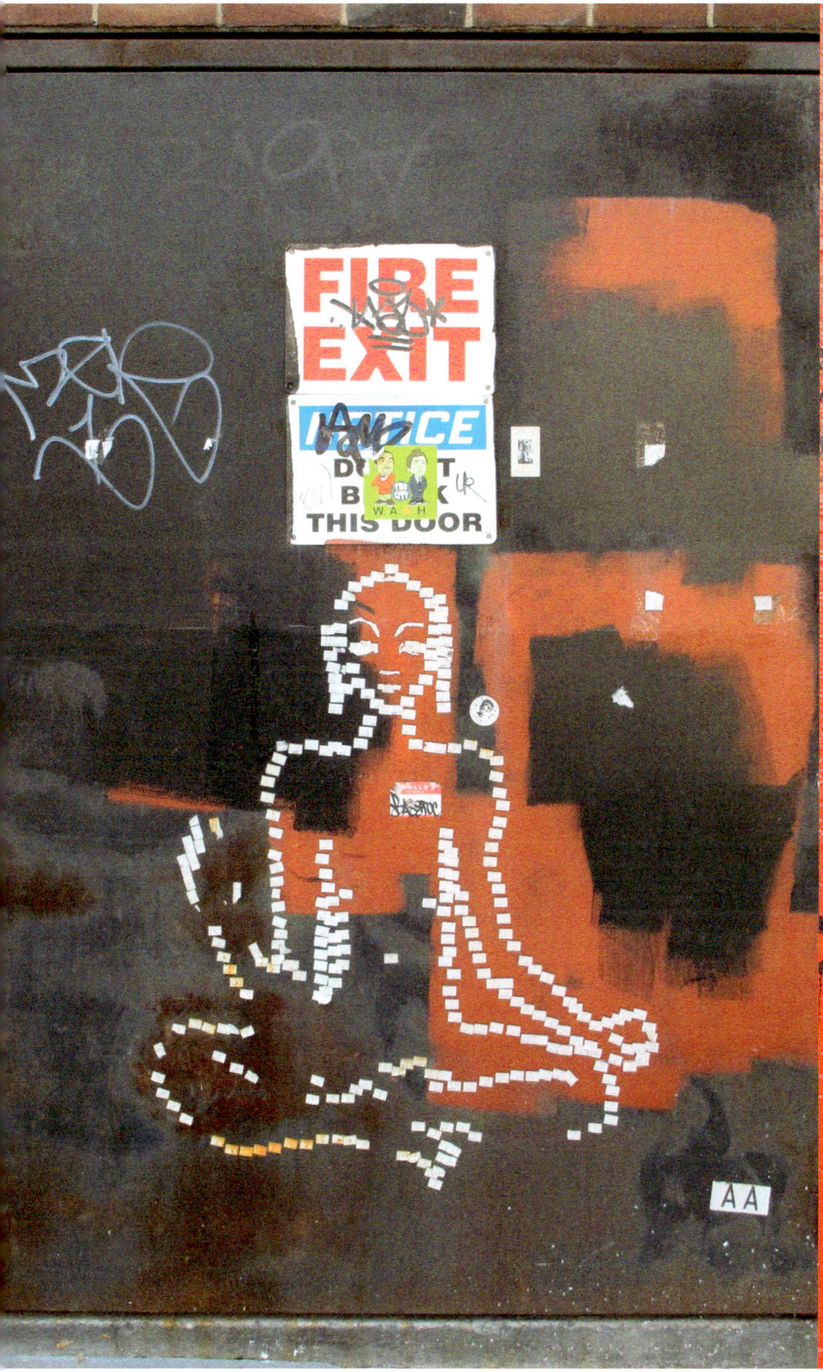
FIRE
EXIT
NOTICE
DO NOT BLOCK THIS DOOR

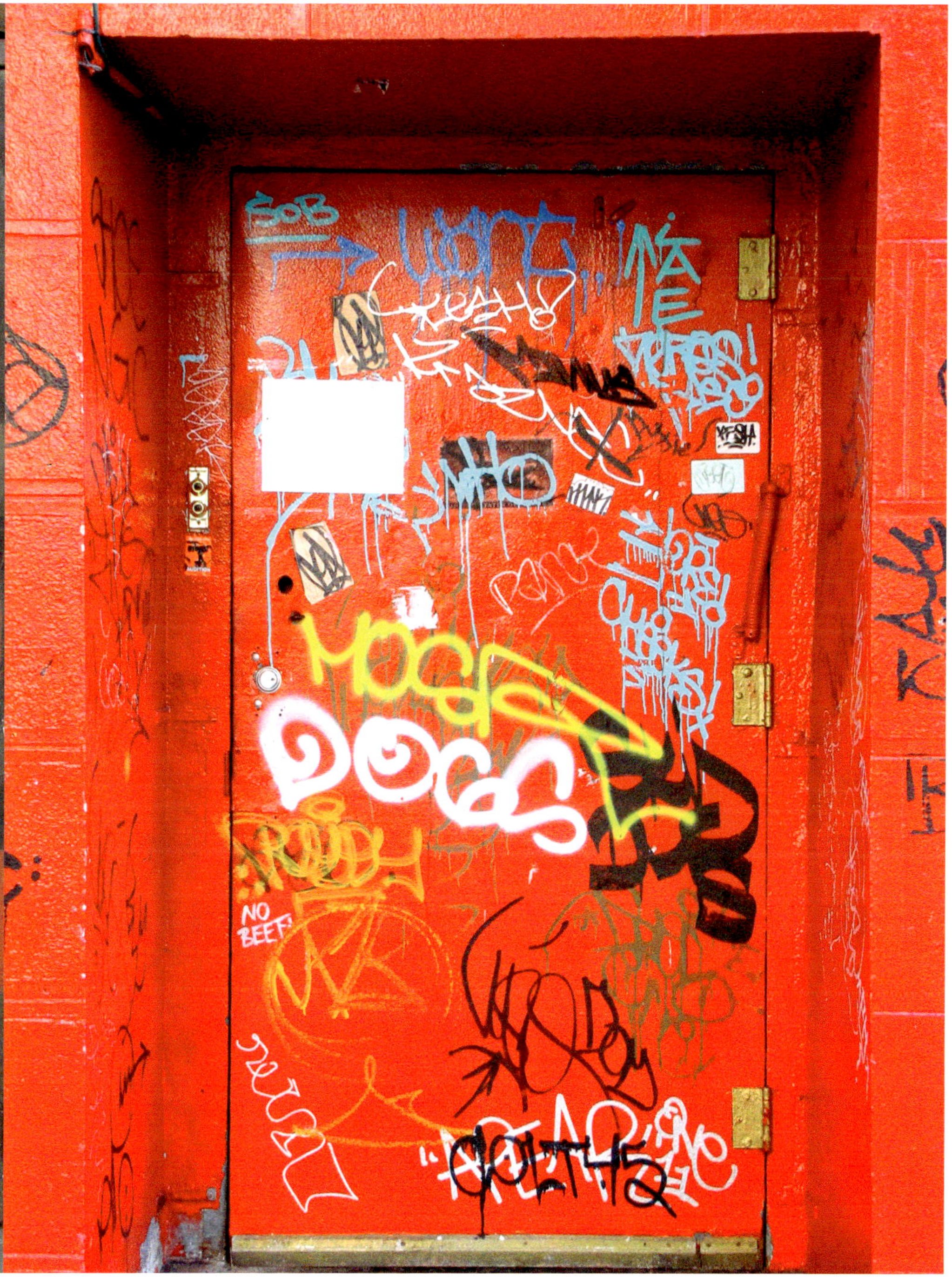

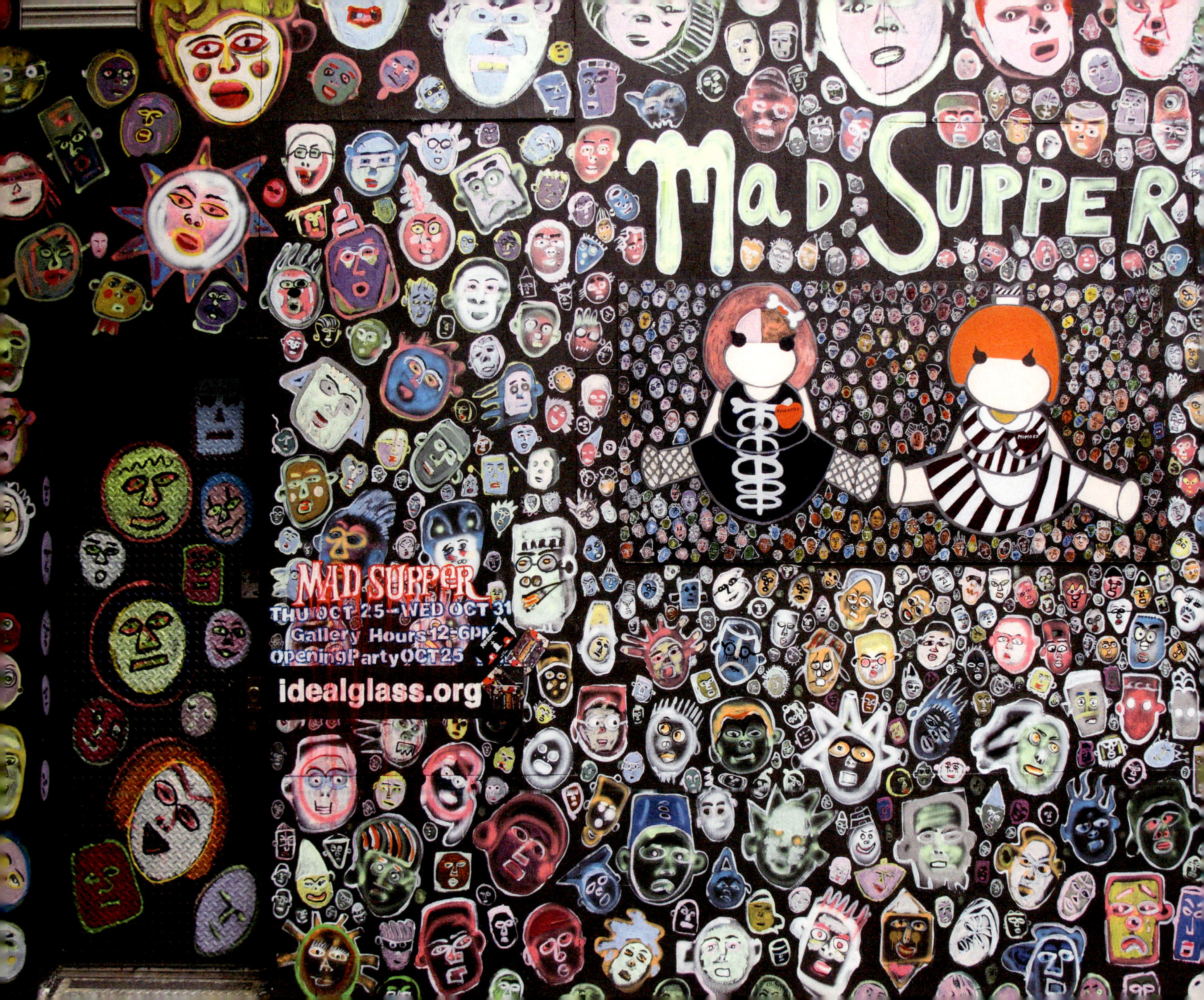
MAD SUPPER
MAD SUPPER
THU OCT 25 – WED OCT 31
Gallery Hours 12-6PM
Opening Party OCT 25
idealglass.org

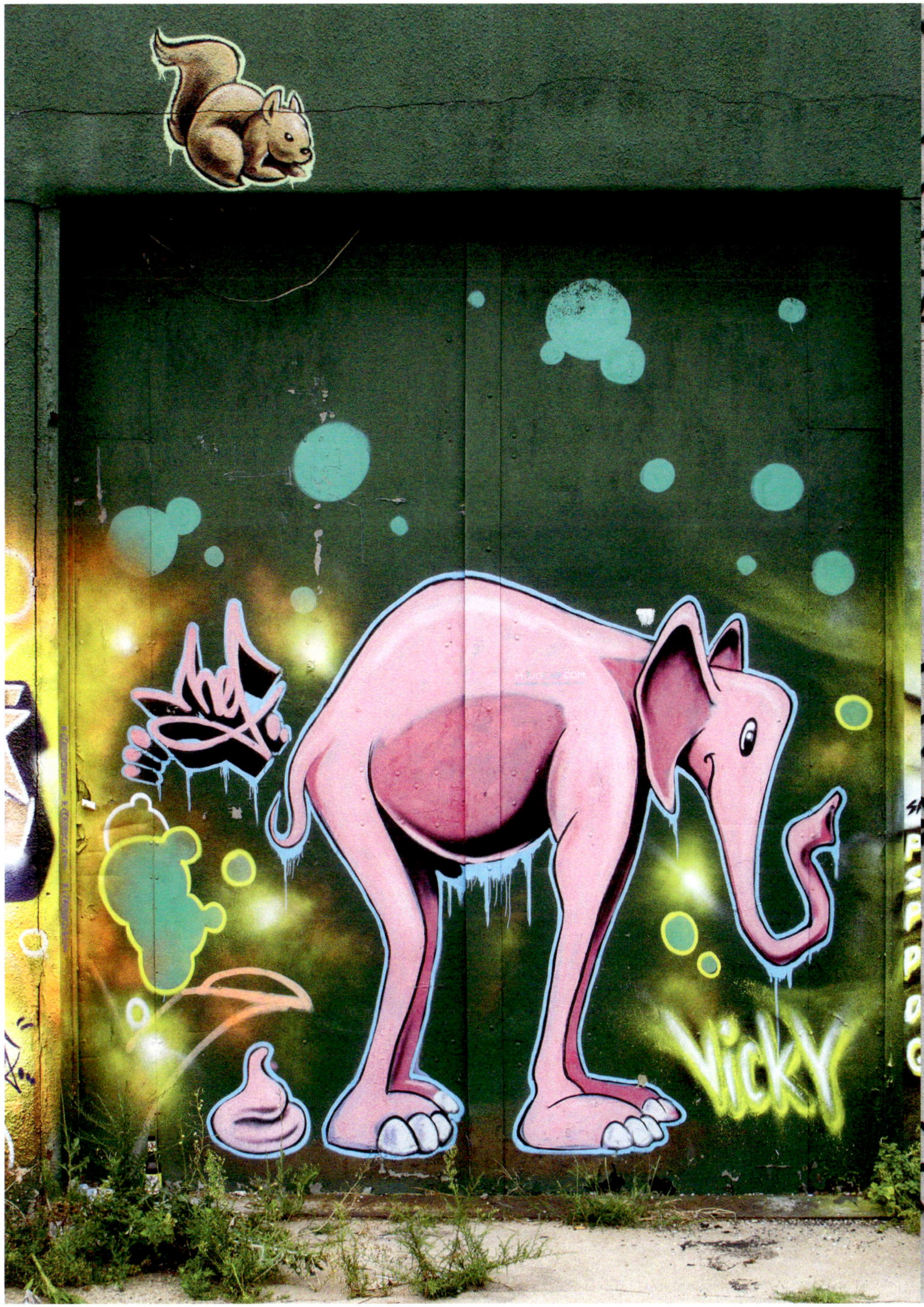
VICKY

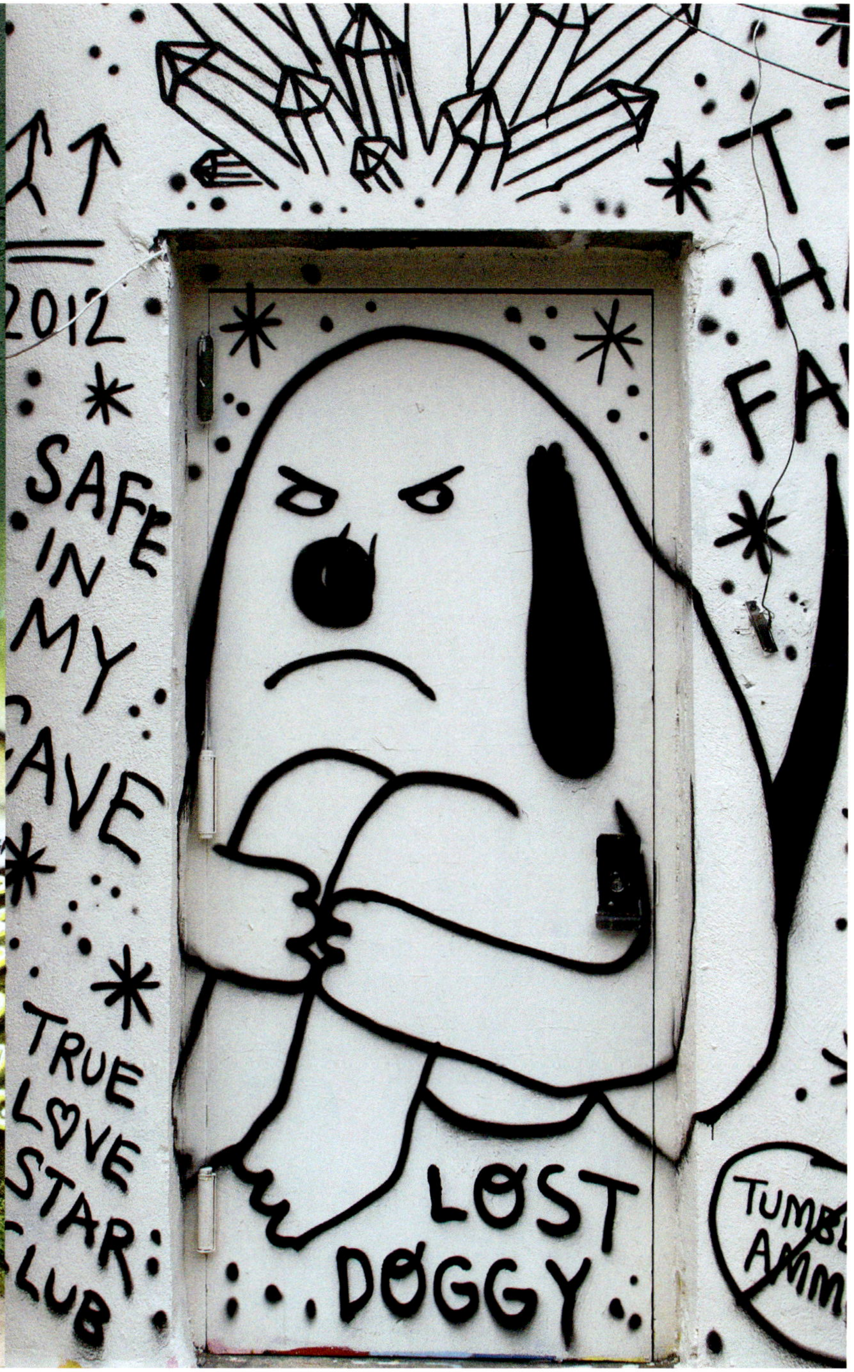
2012
SAFE IN MY
TRUE
LOVE
STAR
LOST DOGGY

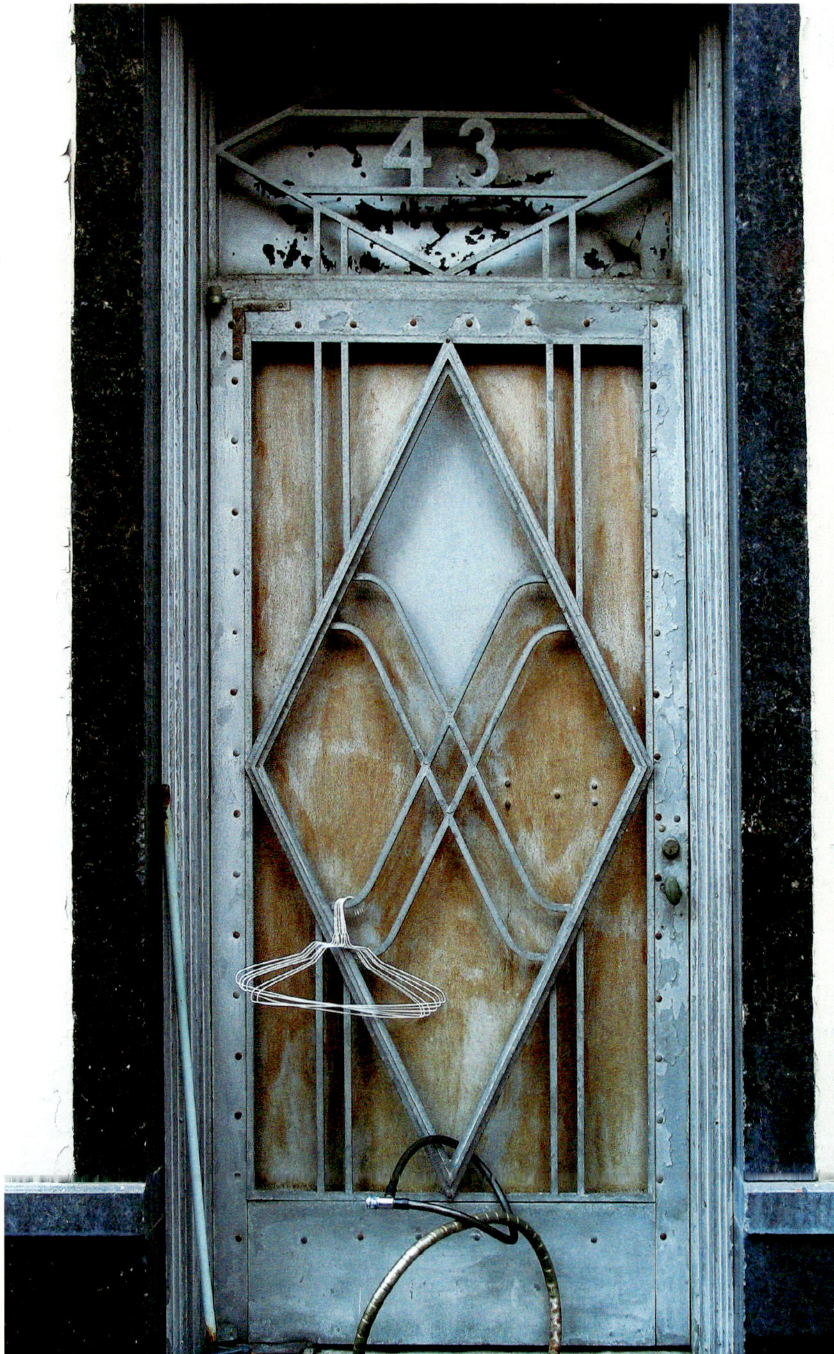
43

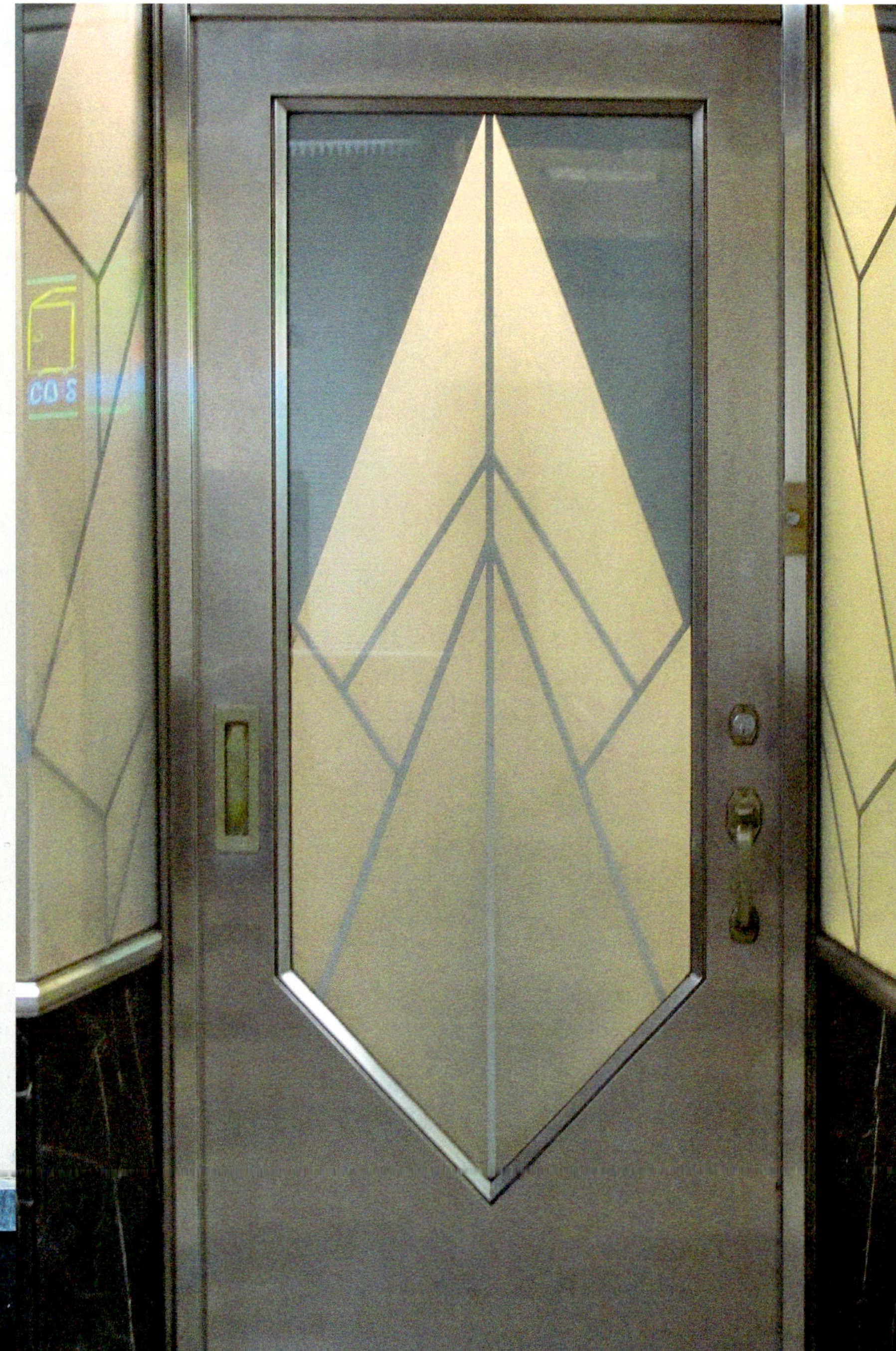

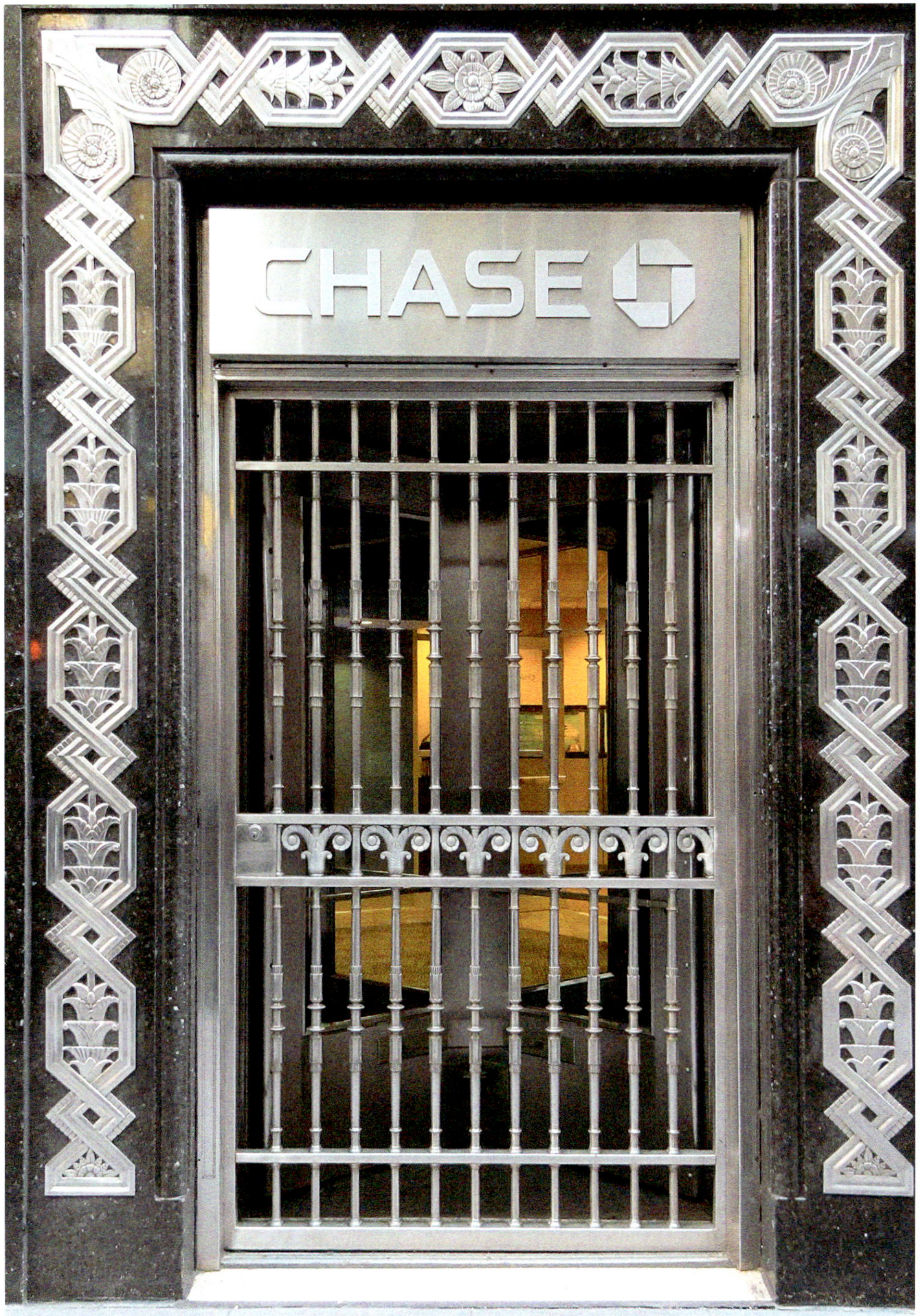
CHASE

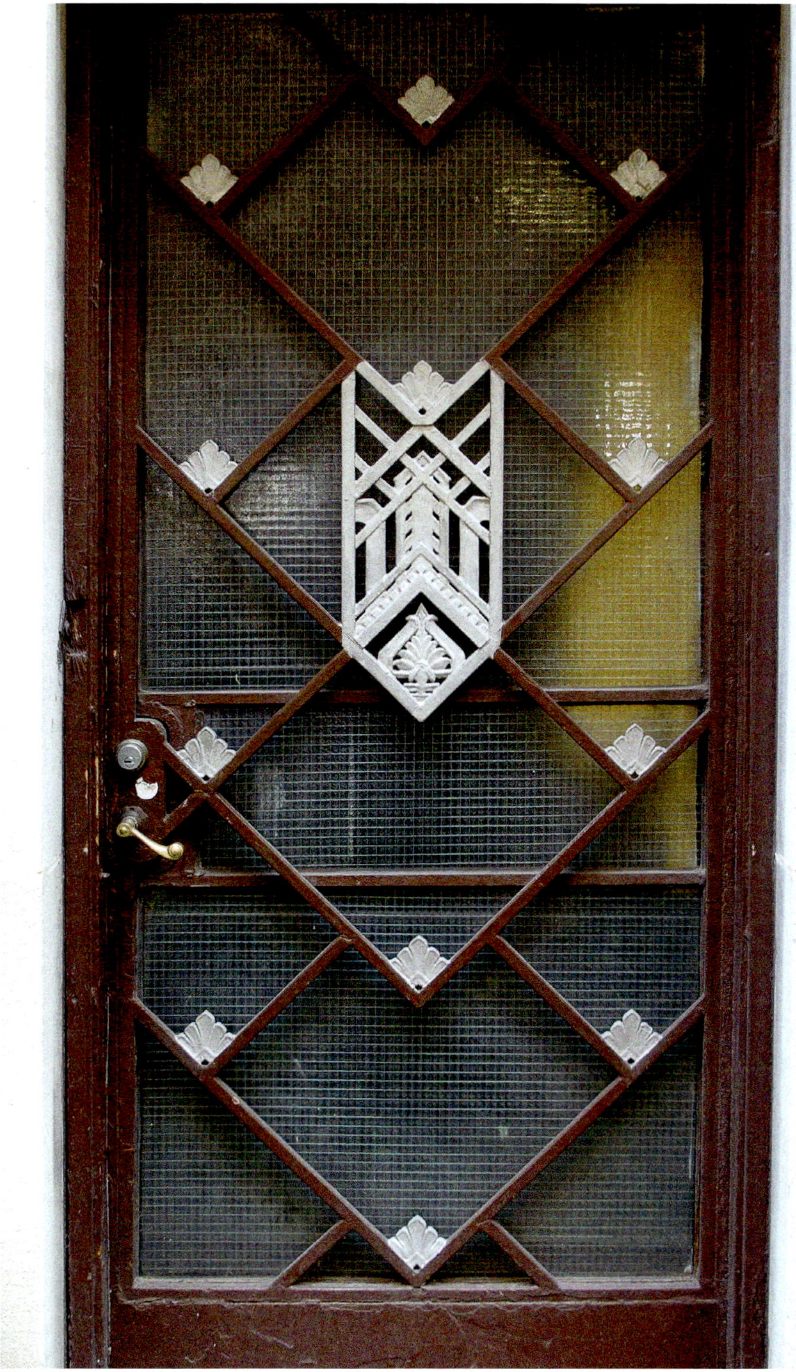

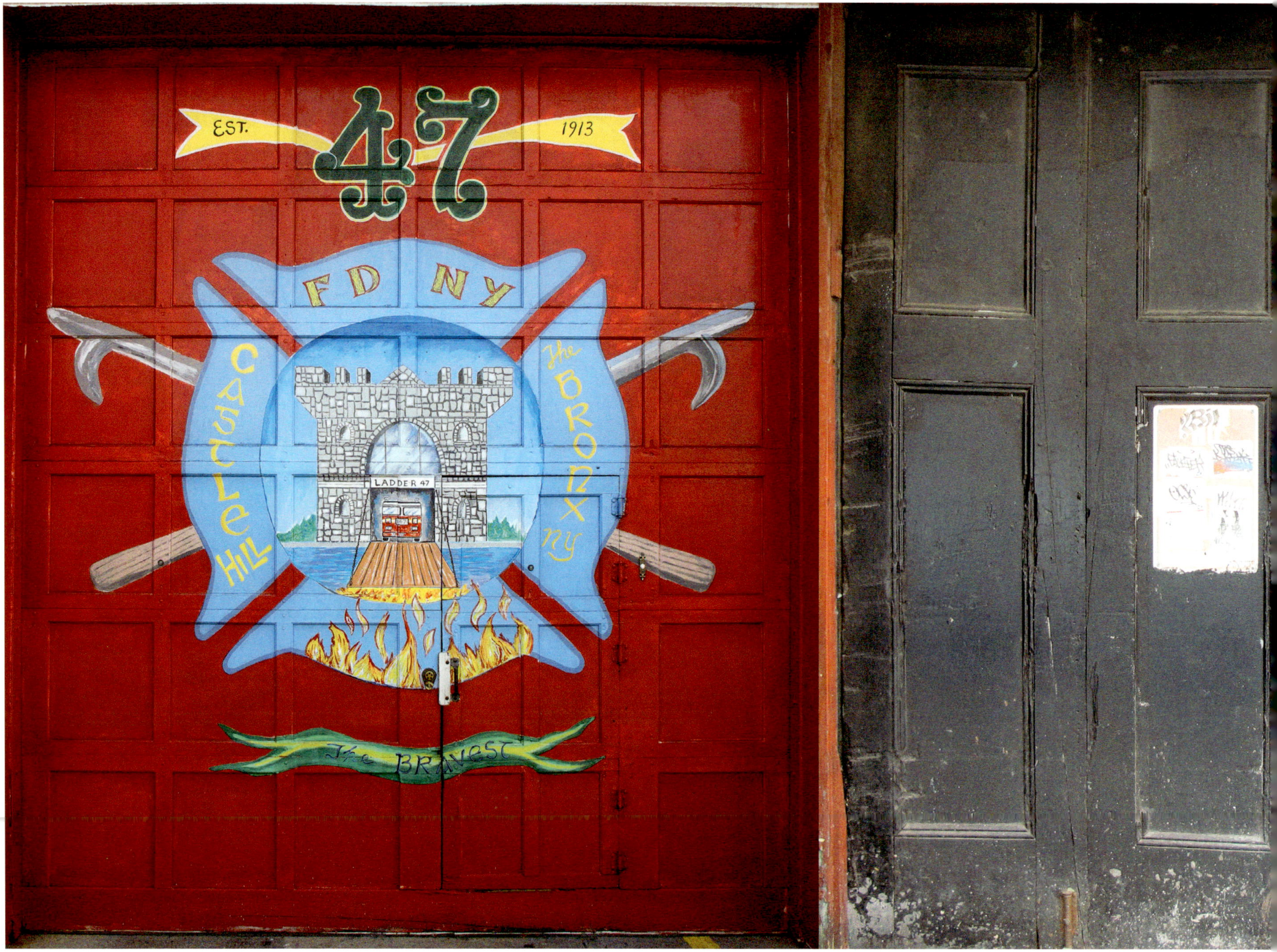
EST. 1913
47
FDNY
CASTLE HILL
the BRONX ny
LADDER 47
the BRAVEST

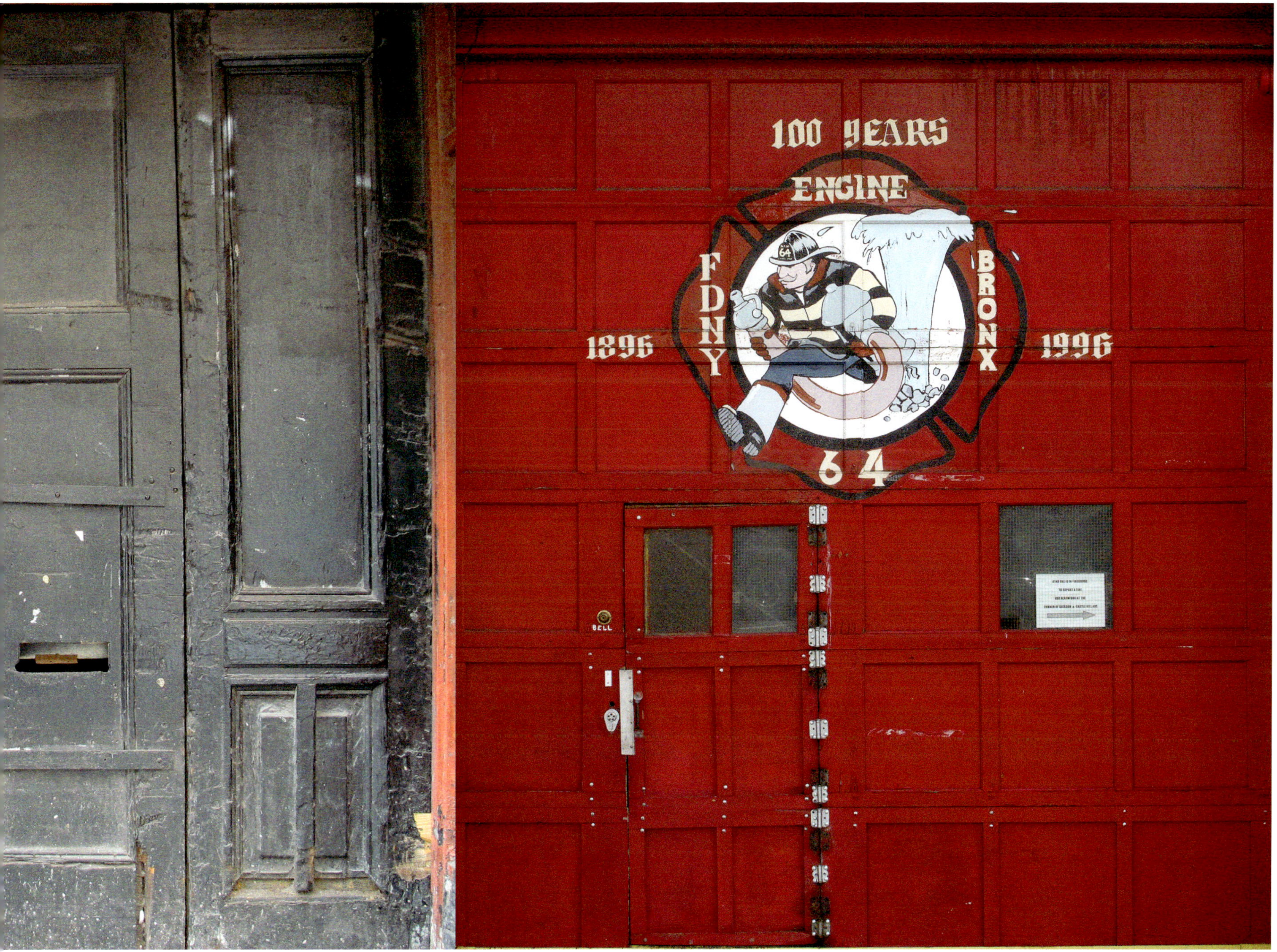
100 YEARS
ENGINE
FDNY
BRONX
1896
1996
64
BELL

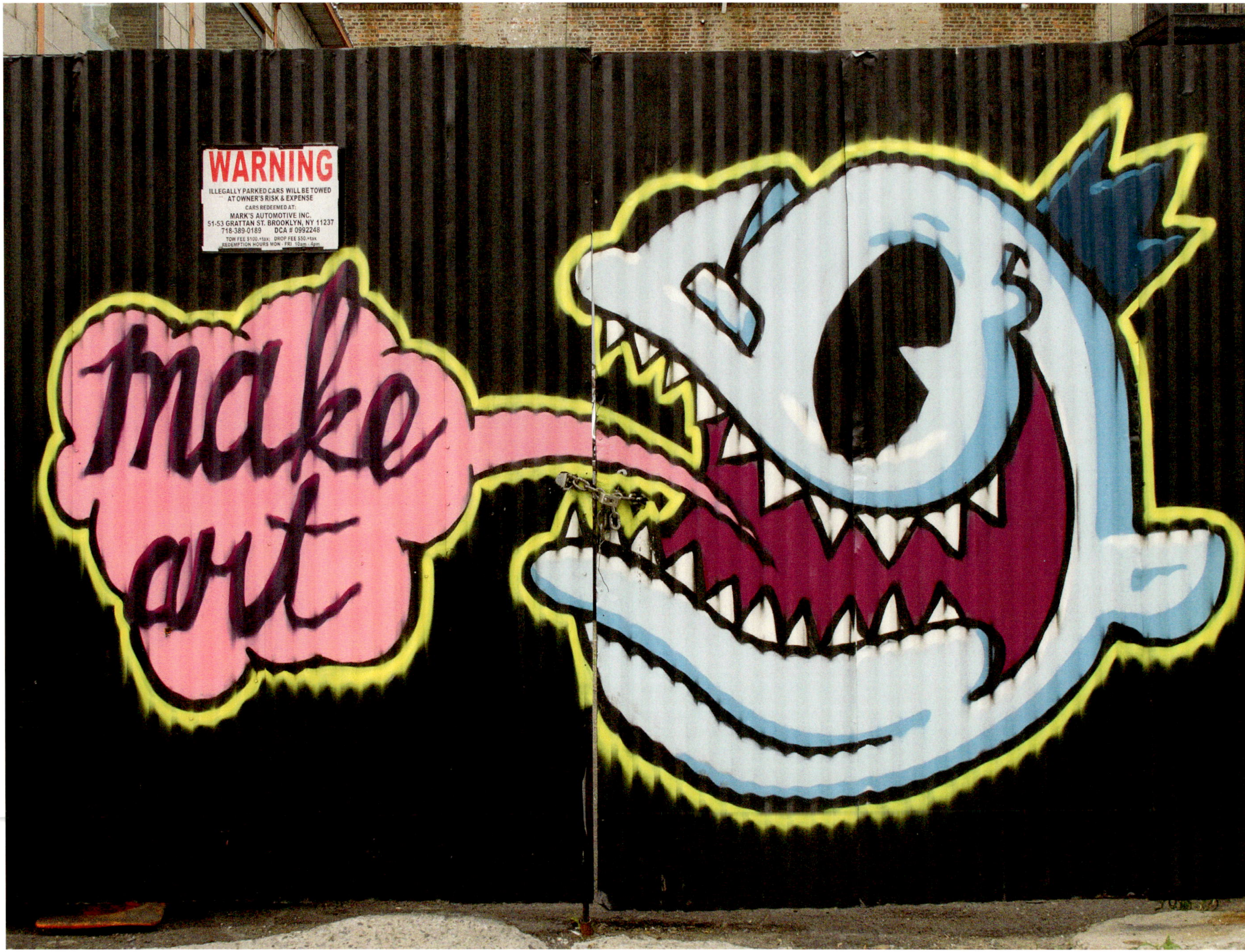
WARNING
ILLEGALLY PARKED CARS WILL BE TOWED
AT OWNER'S RISK & EXPENSE
CARS REDEEMED AT:
MARK'S AUTOMOTIVE INC.
51-53 GRATTAN ST. BROOKLYN, NY 11237
718-389-0189 DCA # 0992248
TOW FEE $100.+tax; DROP FEE $50.+tax
REDEMPTION HOURS MON - FRI 10am - 4pm
make art

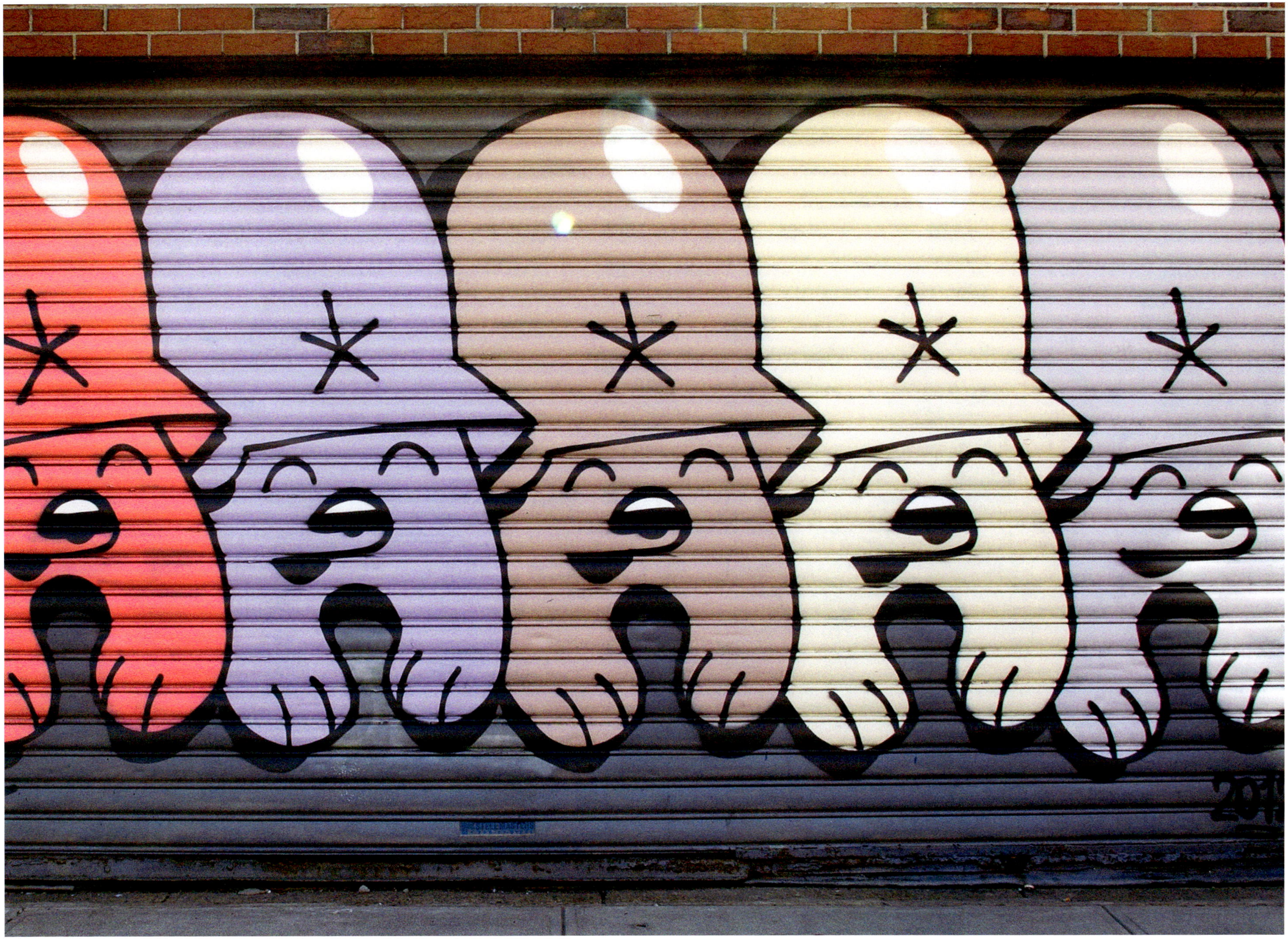

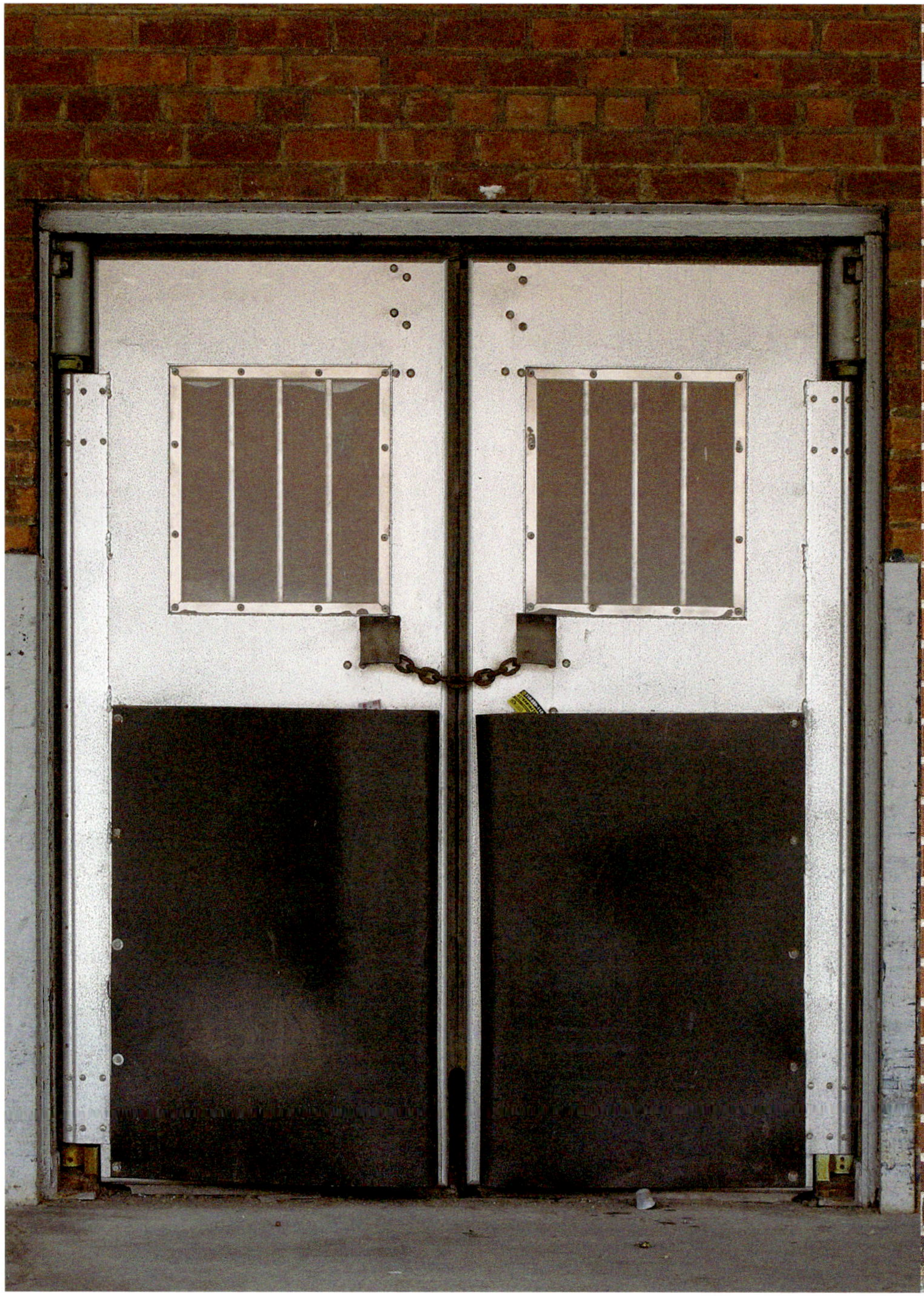

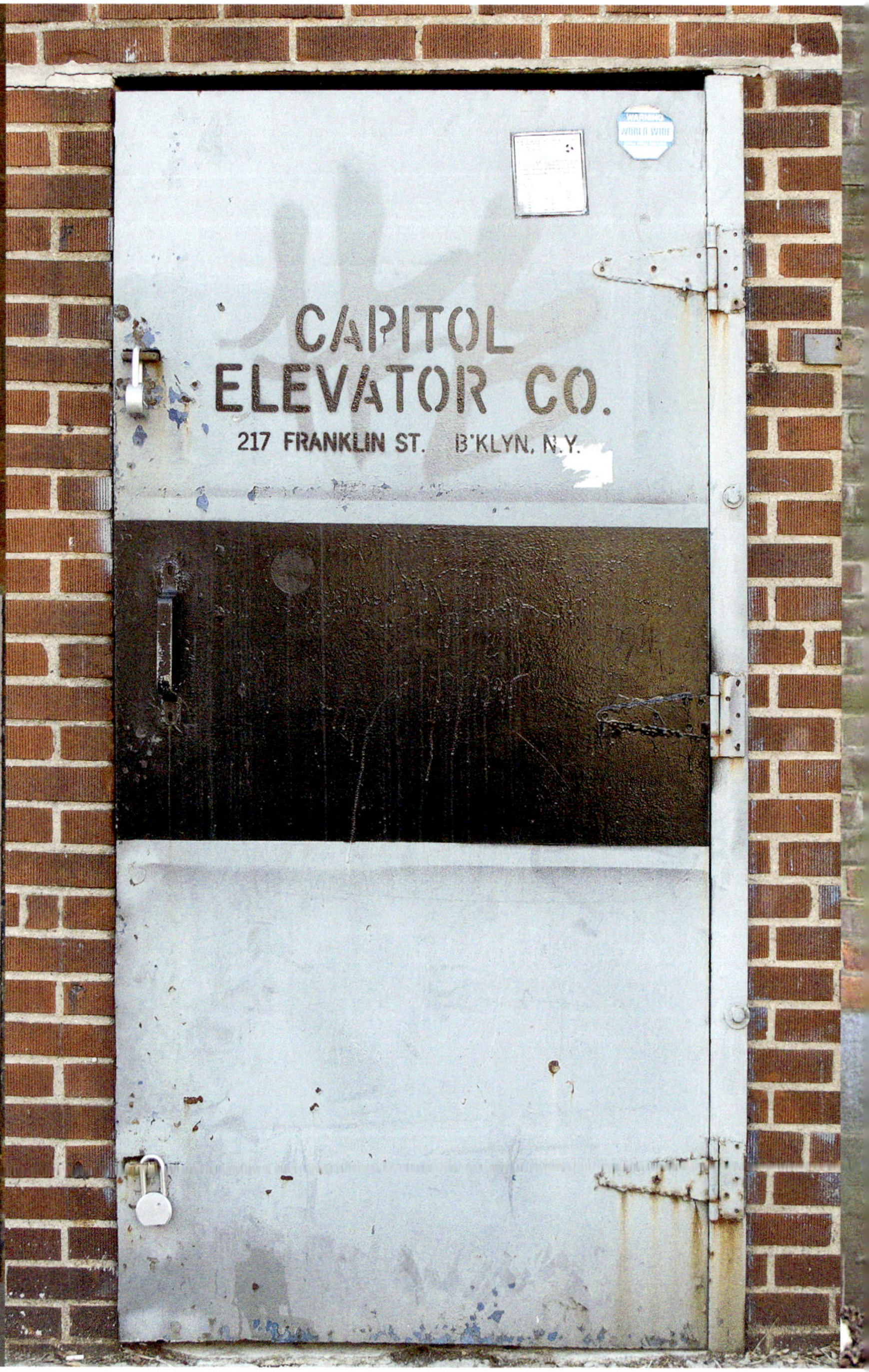
CAPITOL
ELEVATOR CO.
217 FRANKLIN ST. B'KLYN, N.Y.

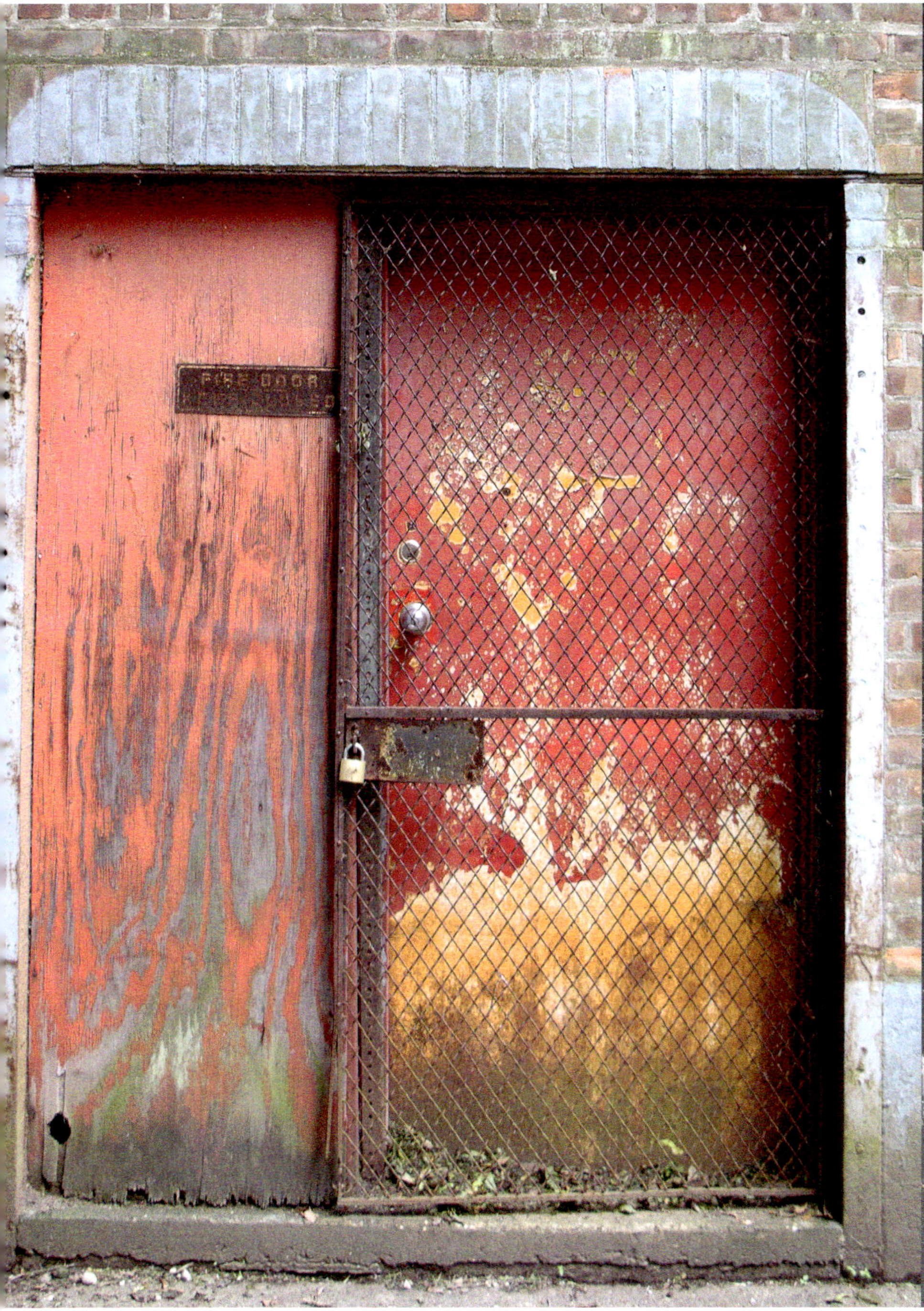
FIRE DOOR
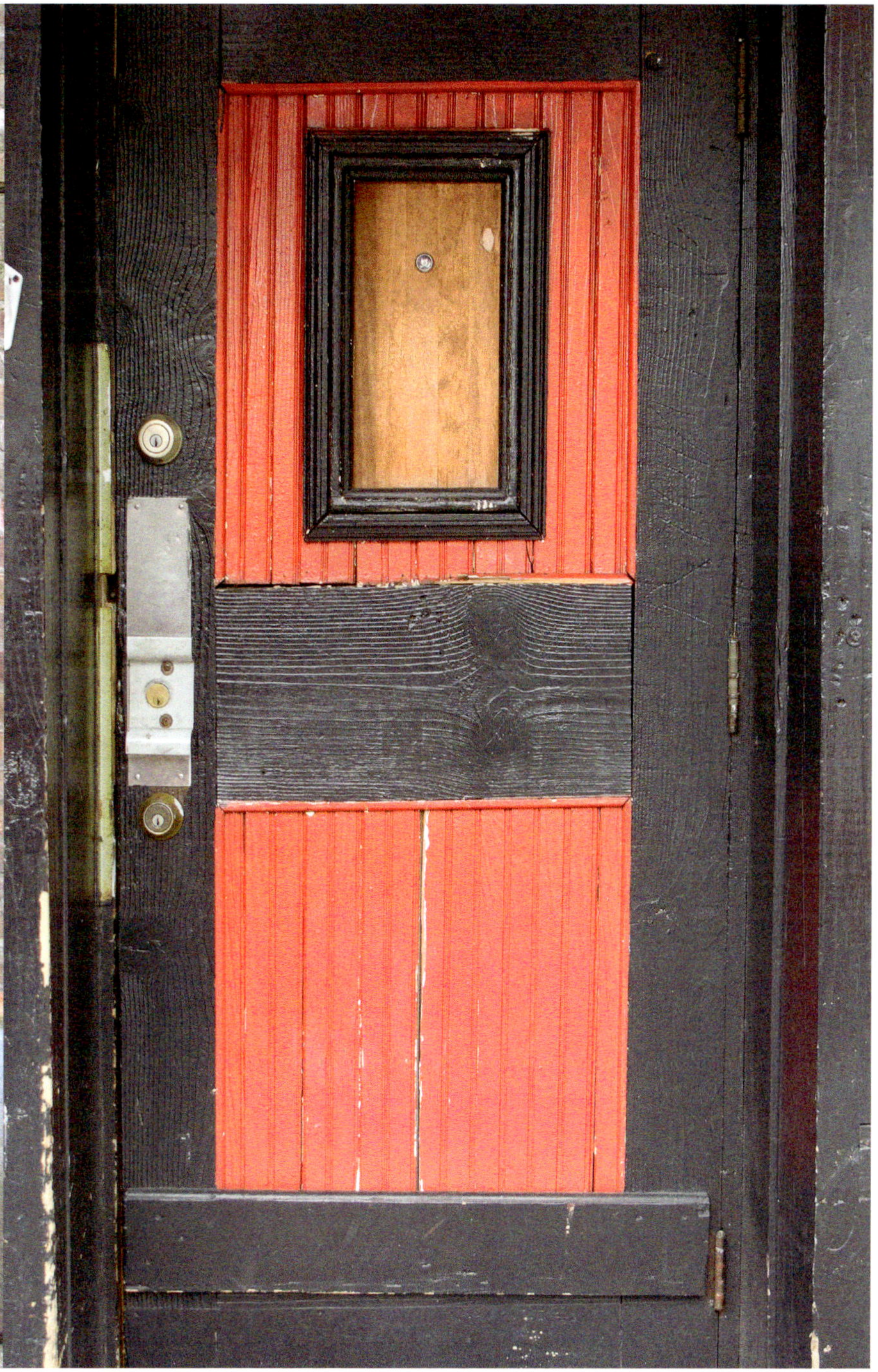

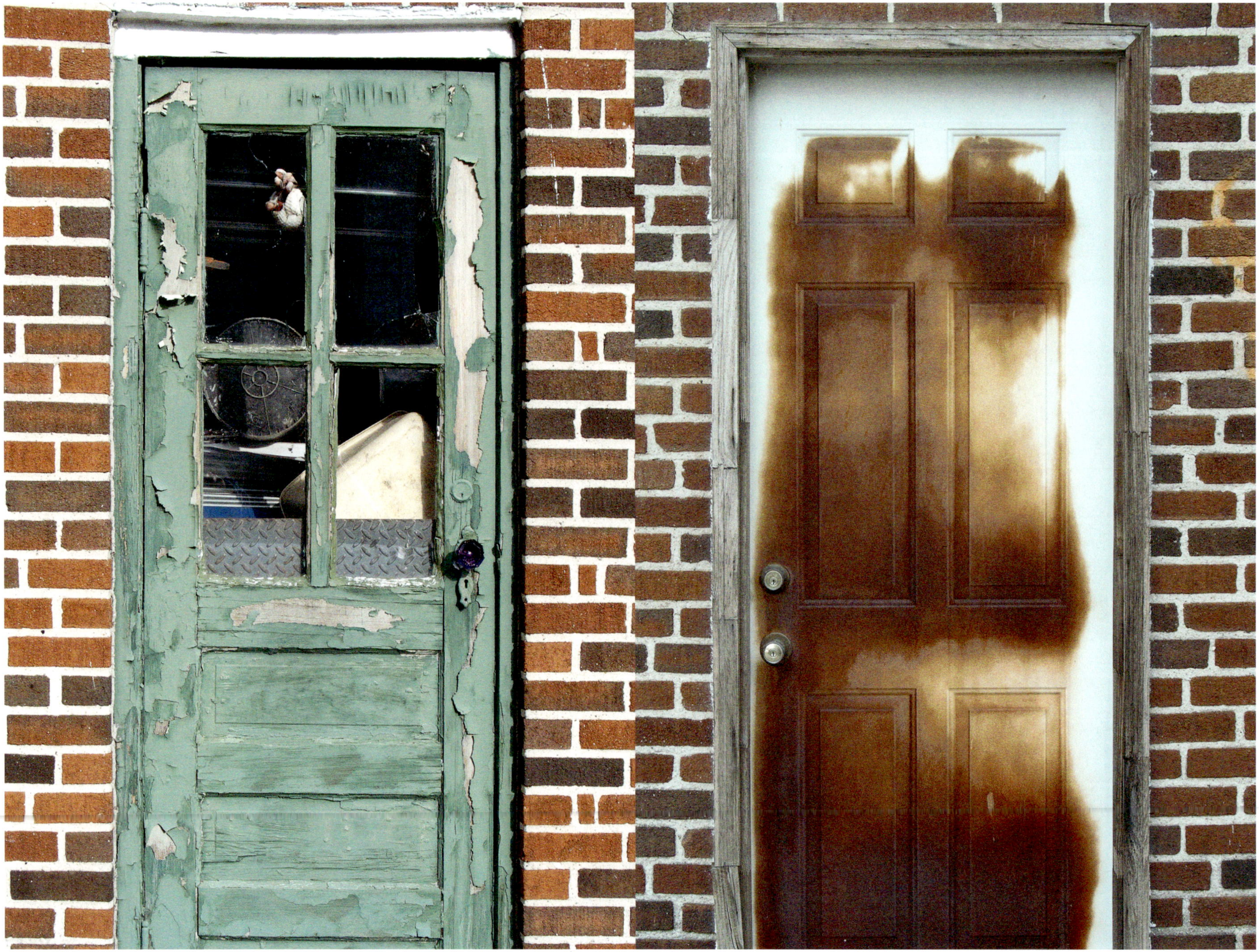

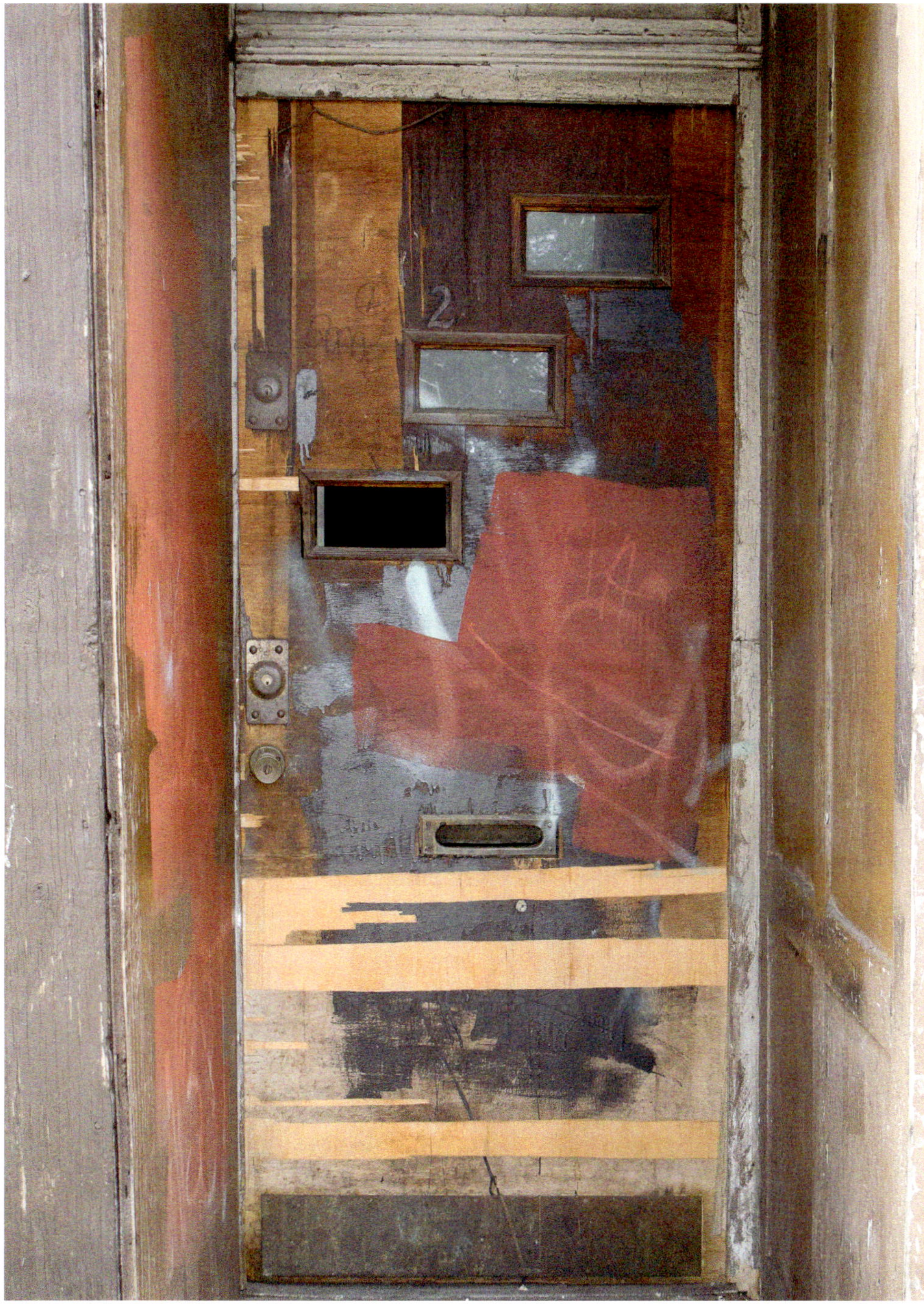
2
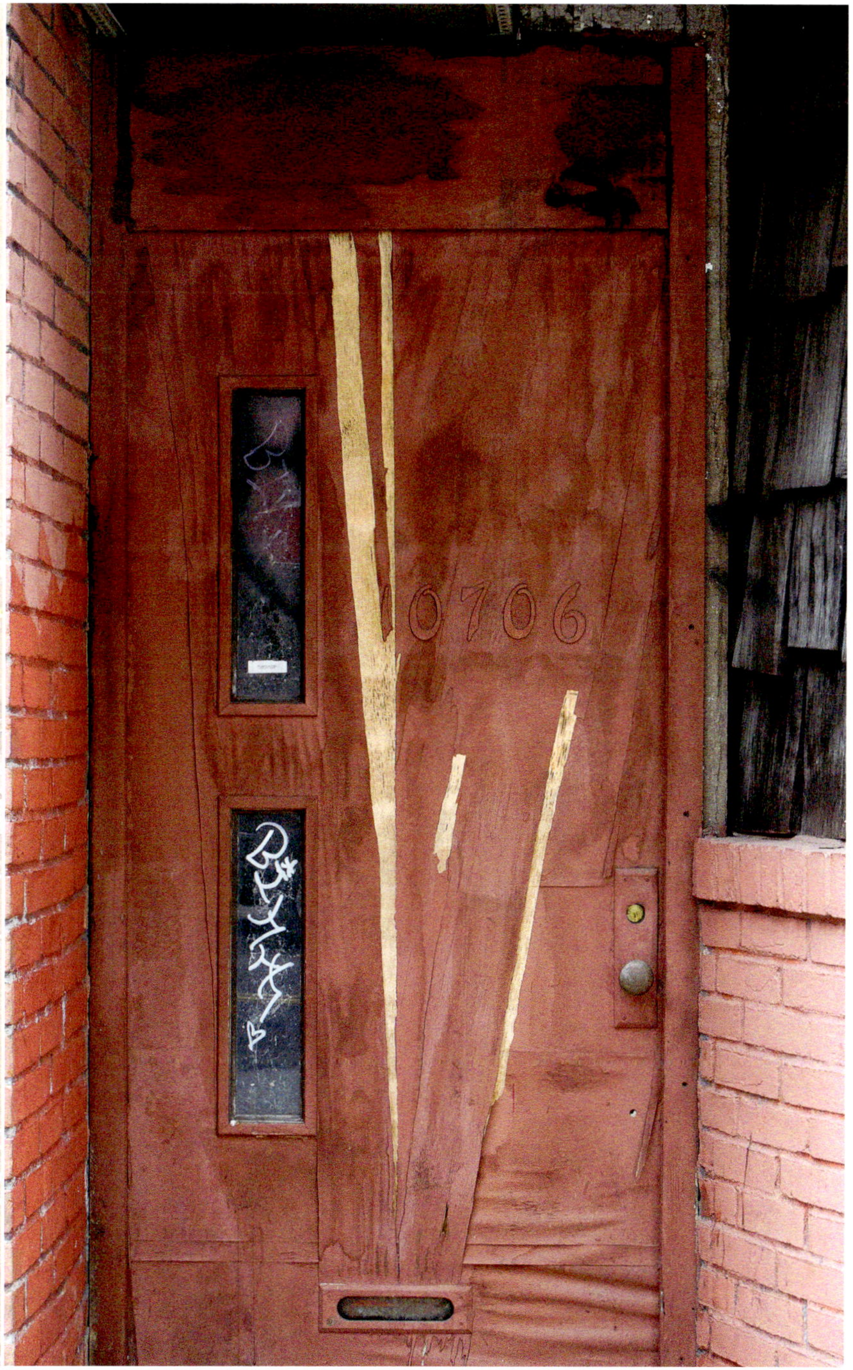
0706

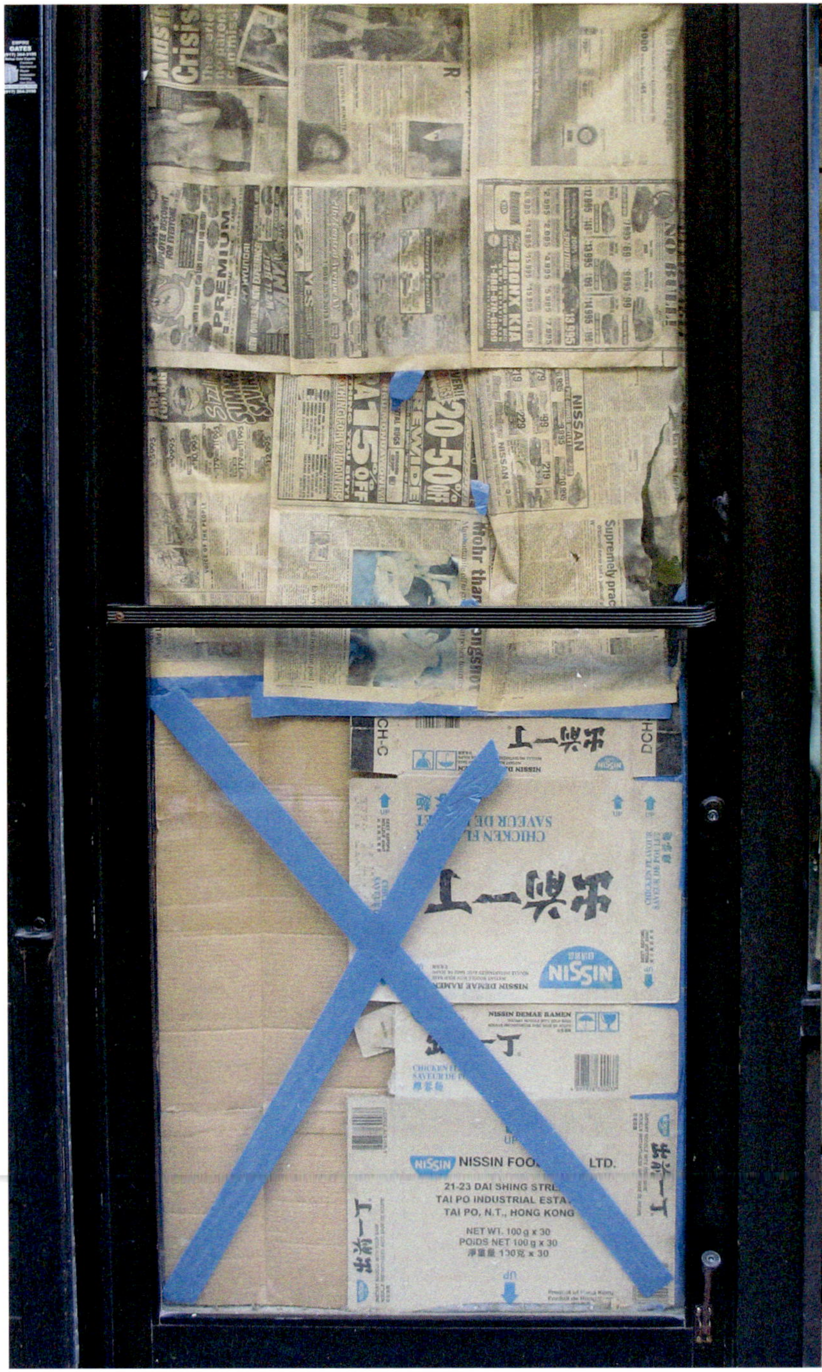
NISSIN
21-23 DAI SHING STRE
TAI PO INDUSTRIAL ESTA
TAI PO, N.T., HONG KONG

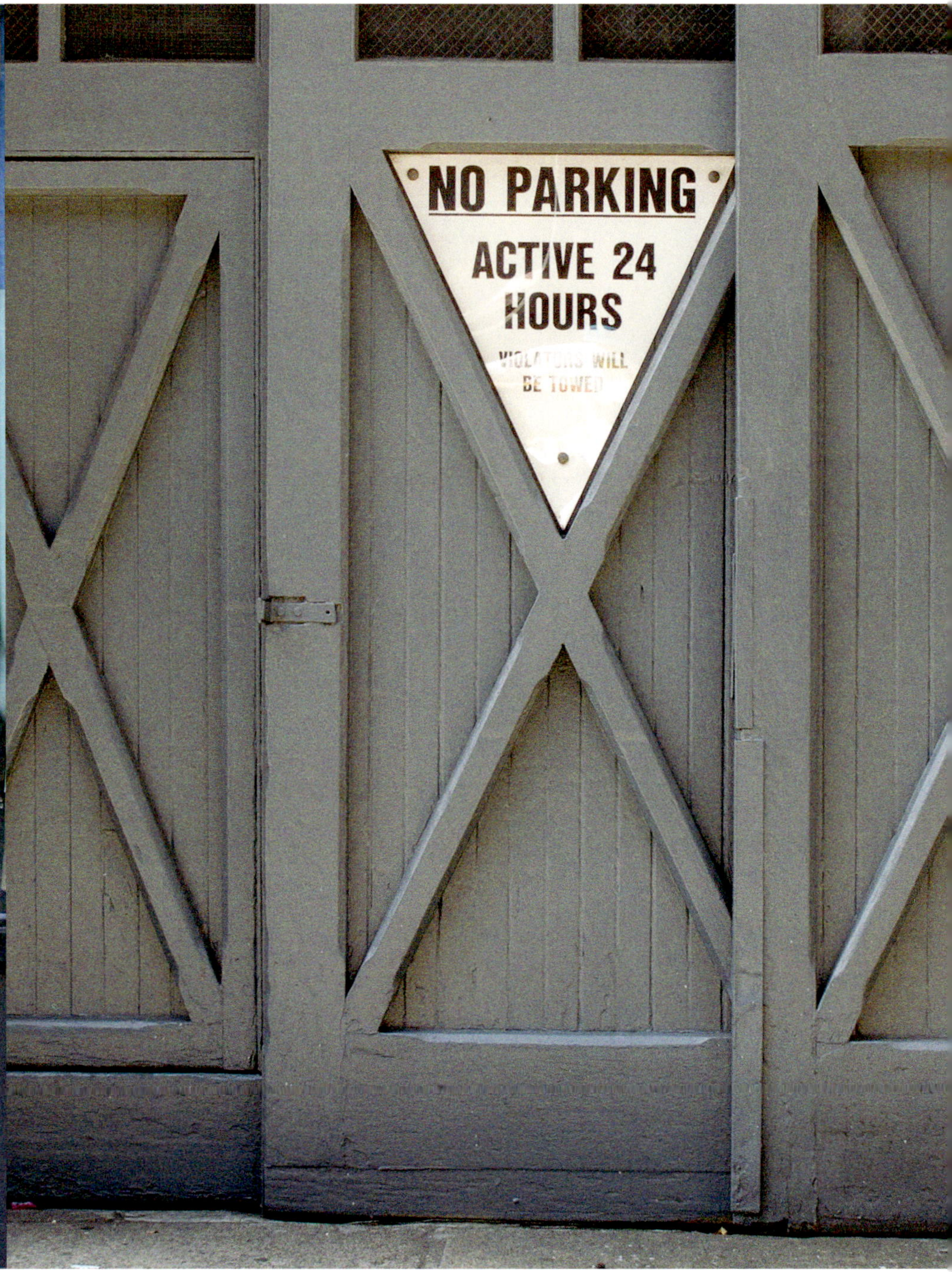
NO PARKING
ACTIVE 24
HOURS

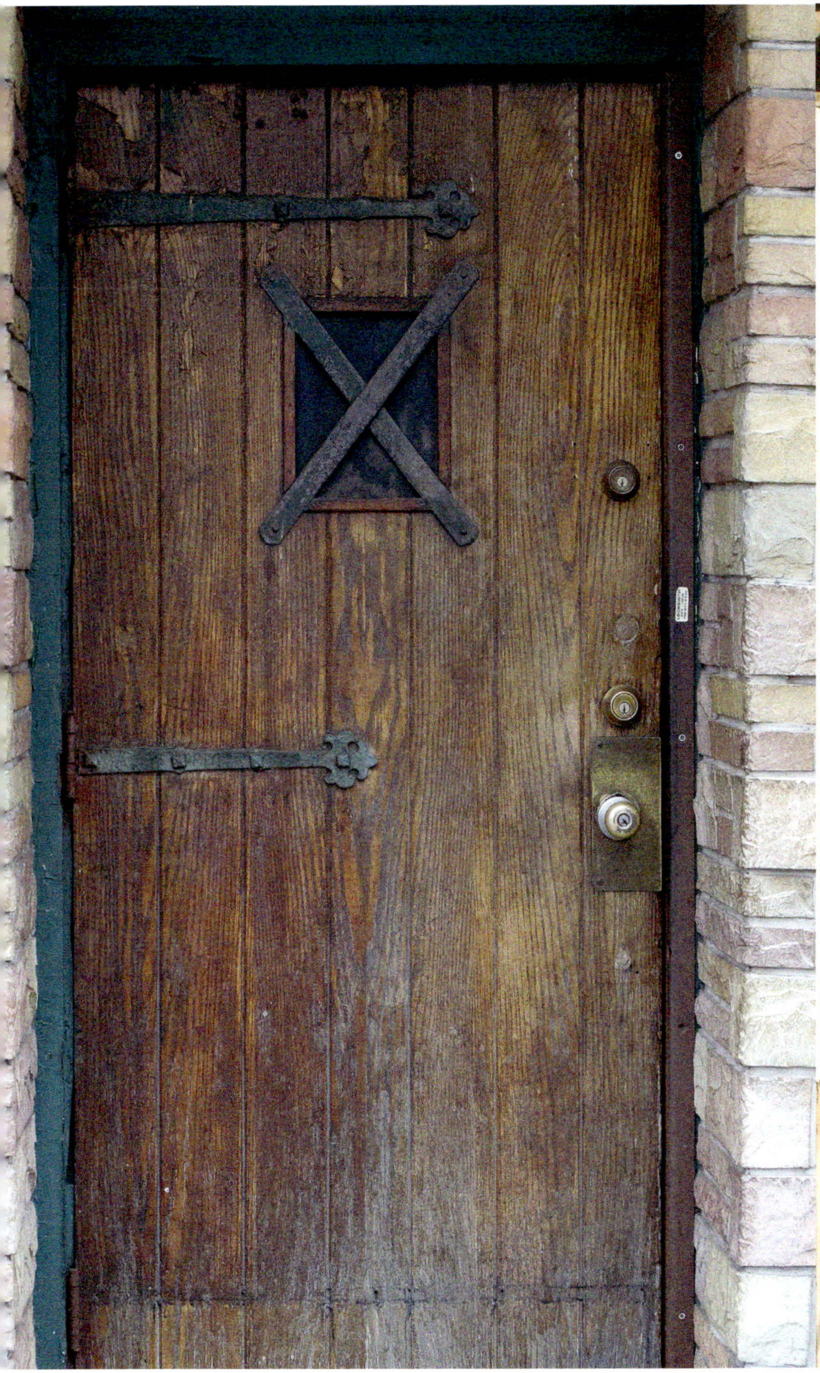

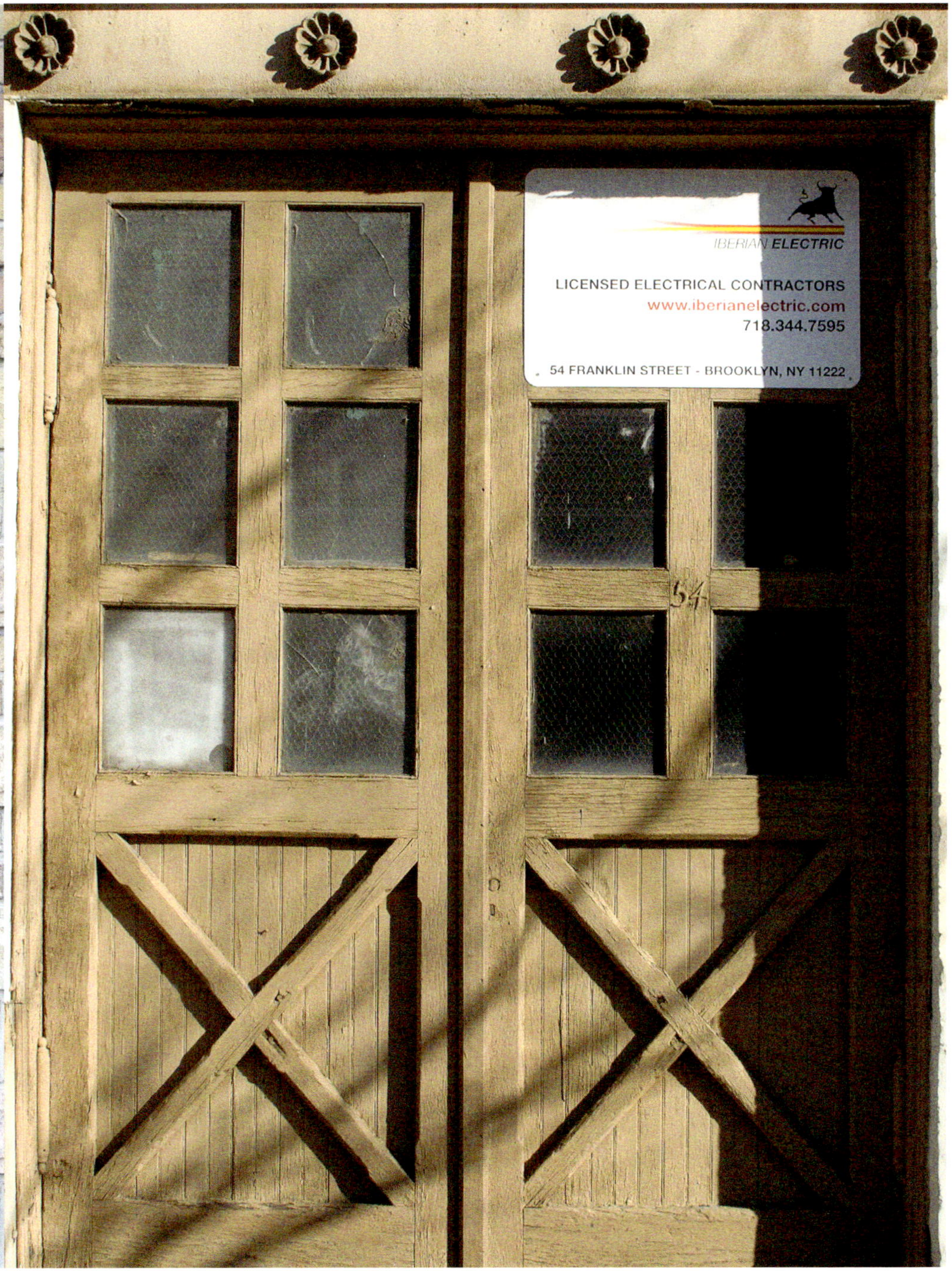
IBERIAN ELECTRIC
LICENSED ELECTRICAL CONTRACTORS
www.iberianelectric.com
718.344.7595
54 FRANKLIN STREET - BROOKLYN, NY 11222
54

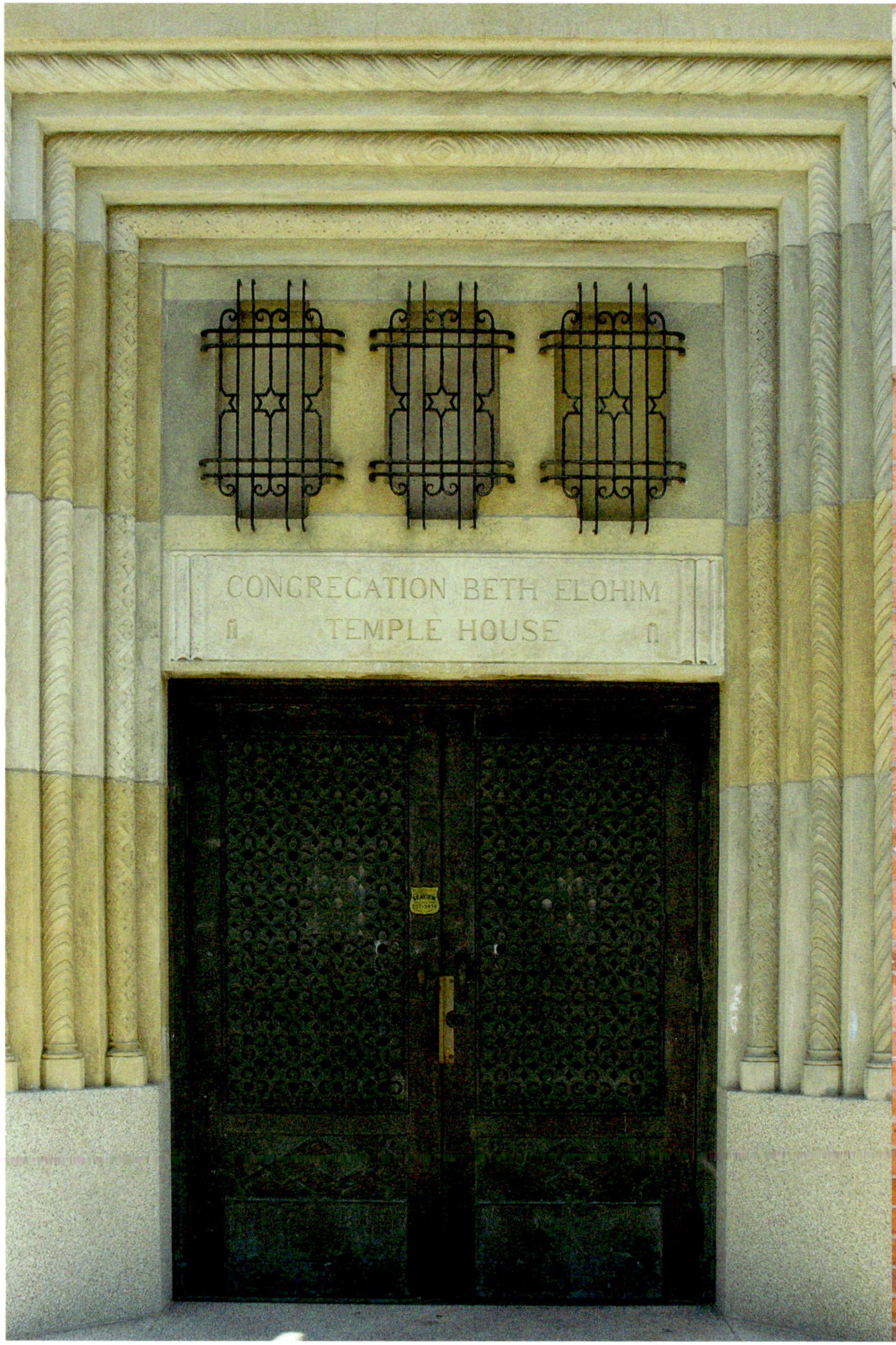
CONGREGATION BETH ELOHIM
TEMPLE HOUSE

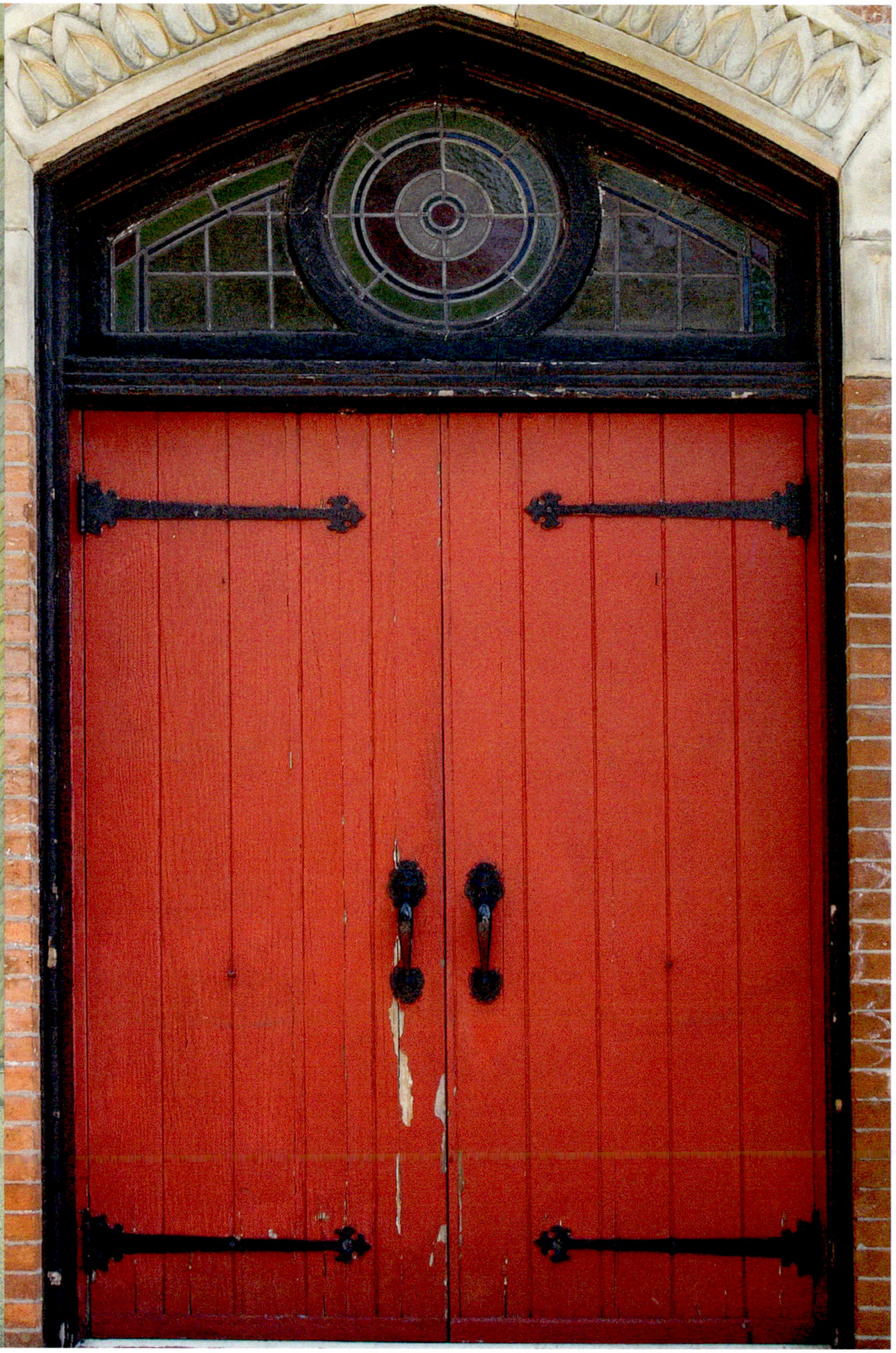

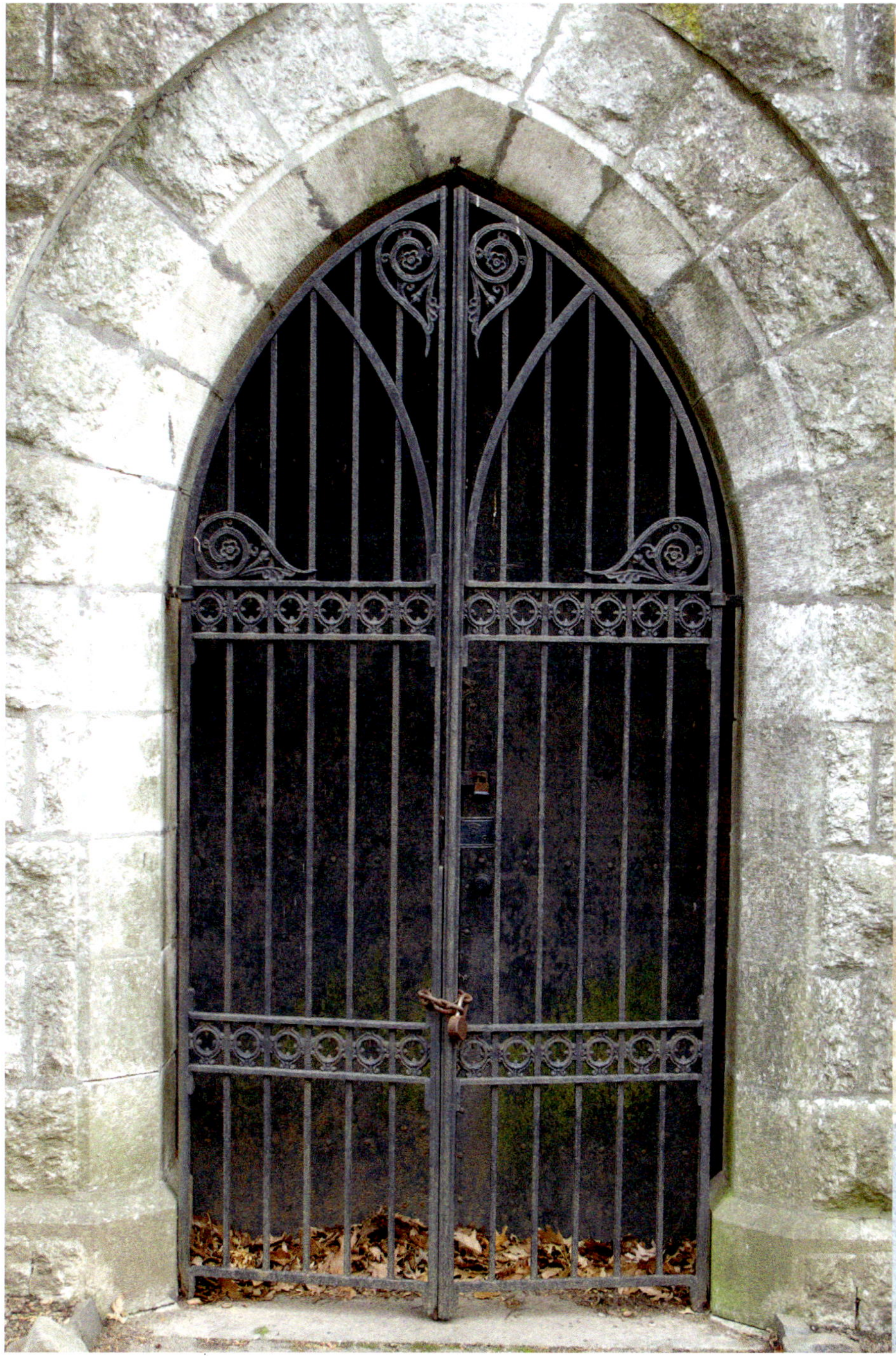

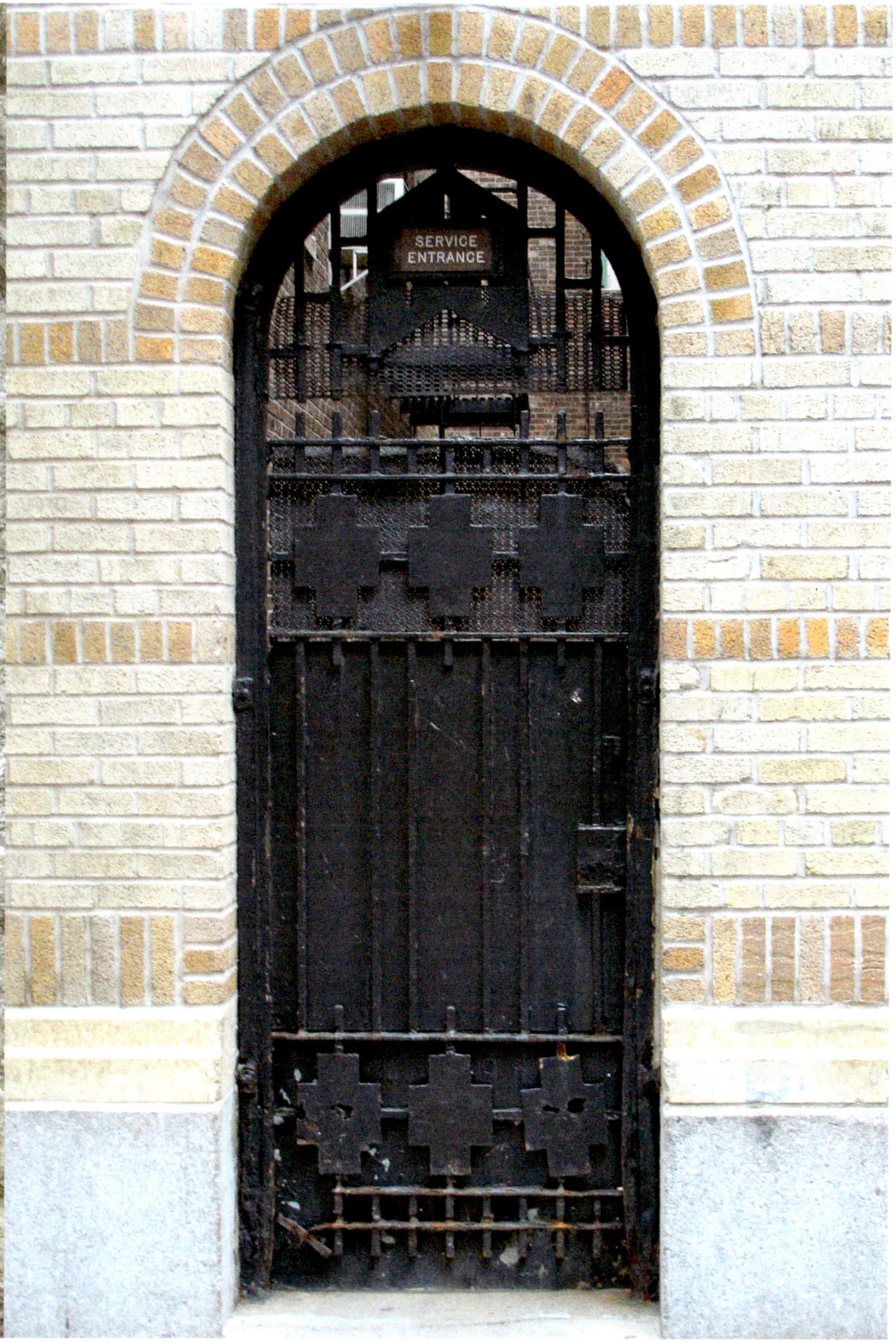
SERVICE
ENTRANCE

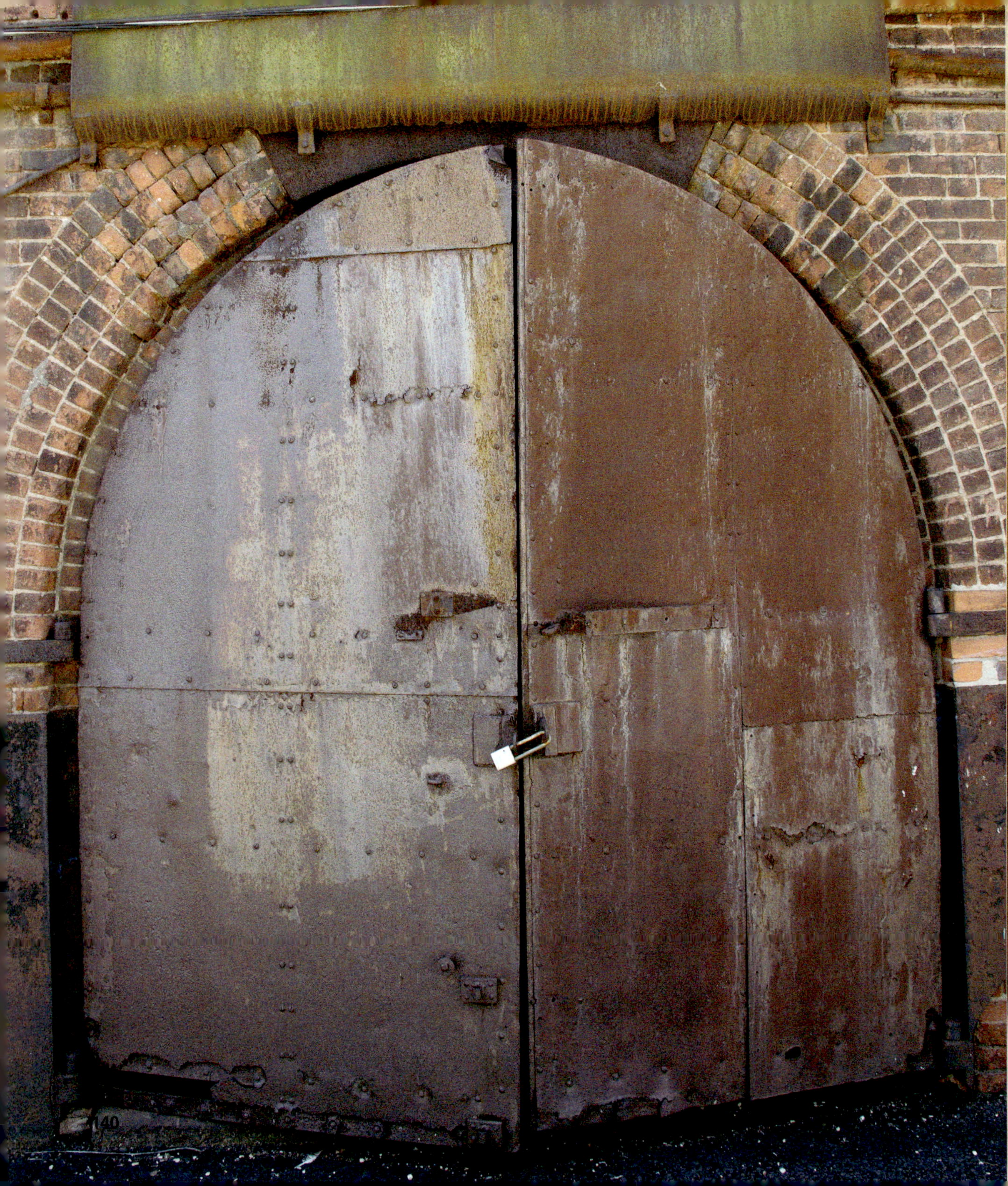

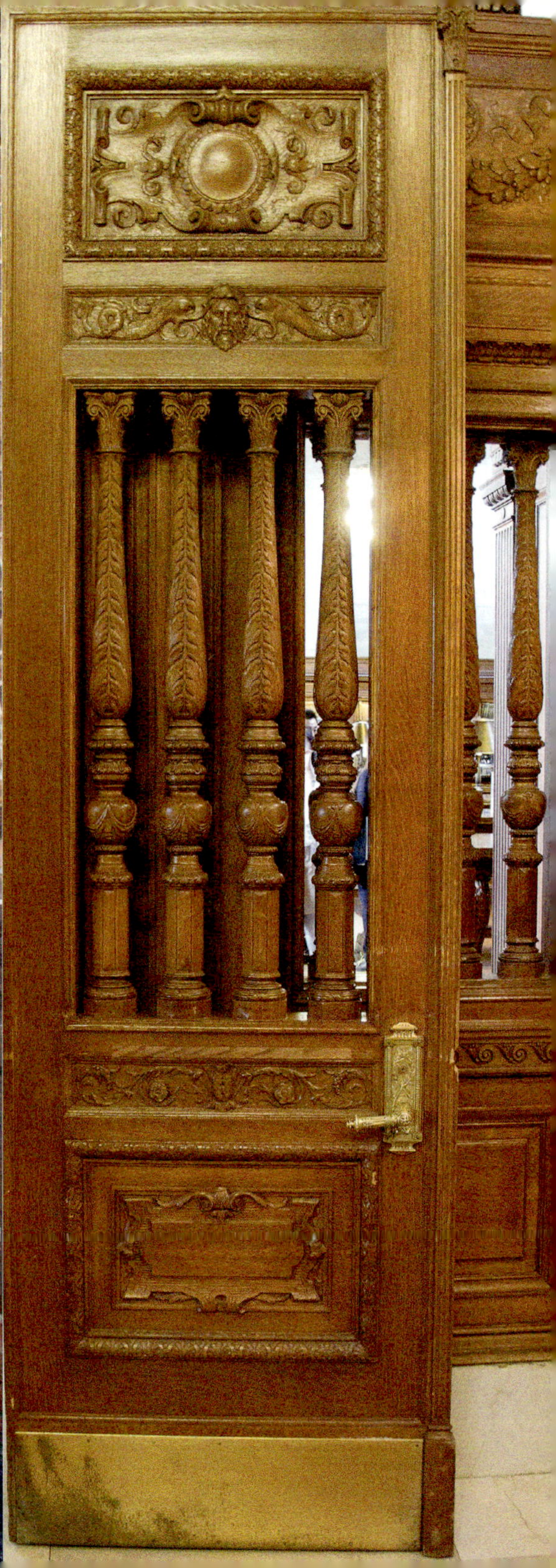

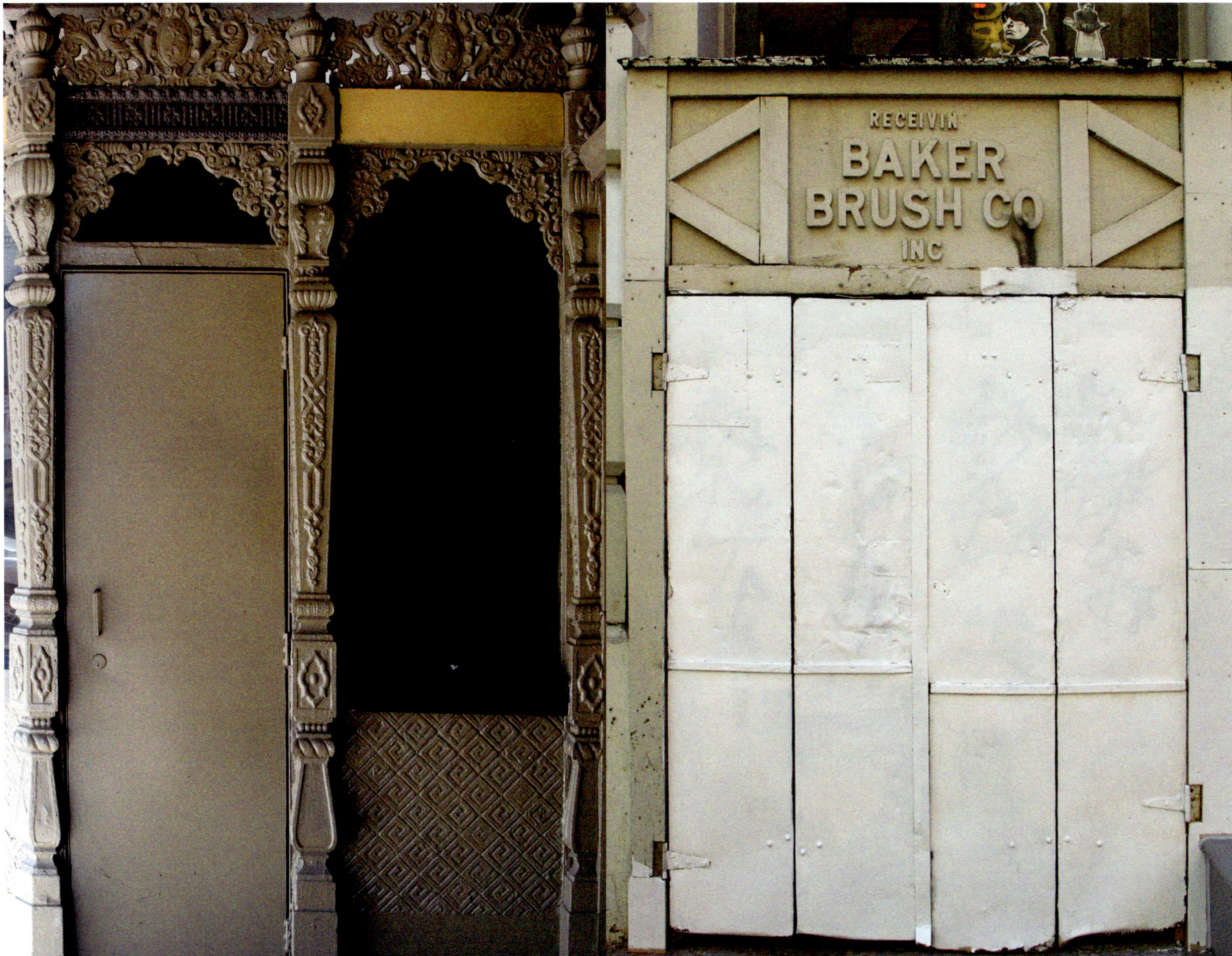
RECEIVIN
BAKER
BRUSH CO
INC

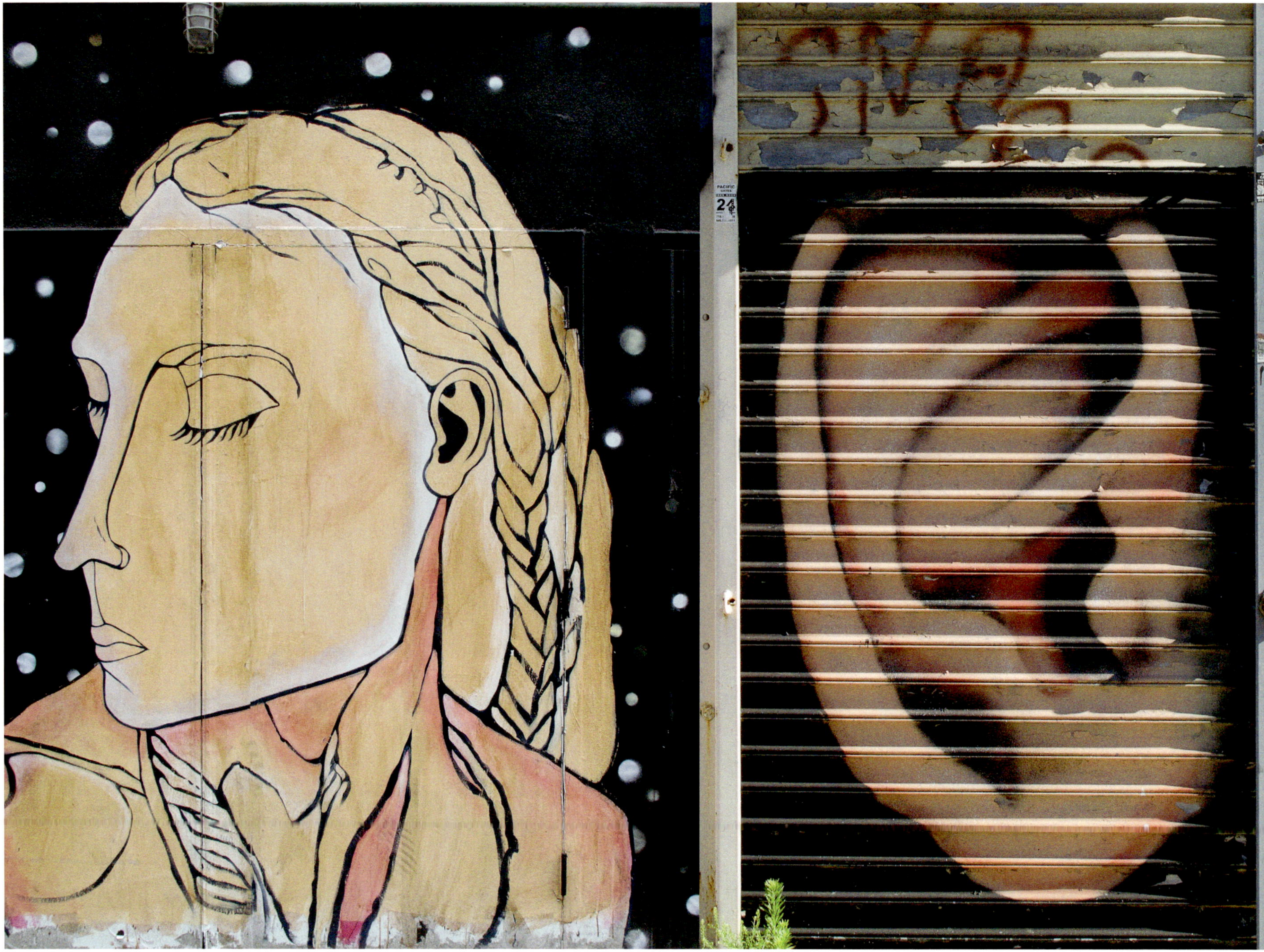

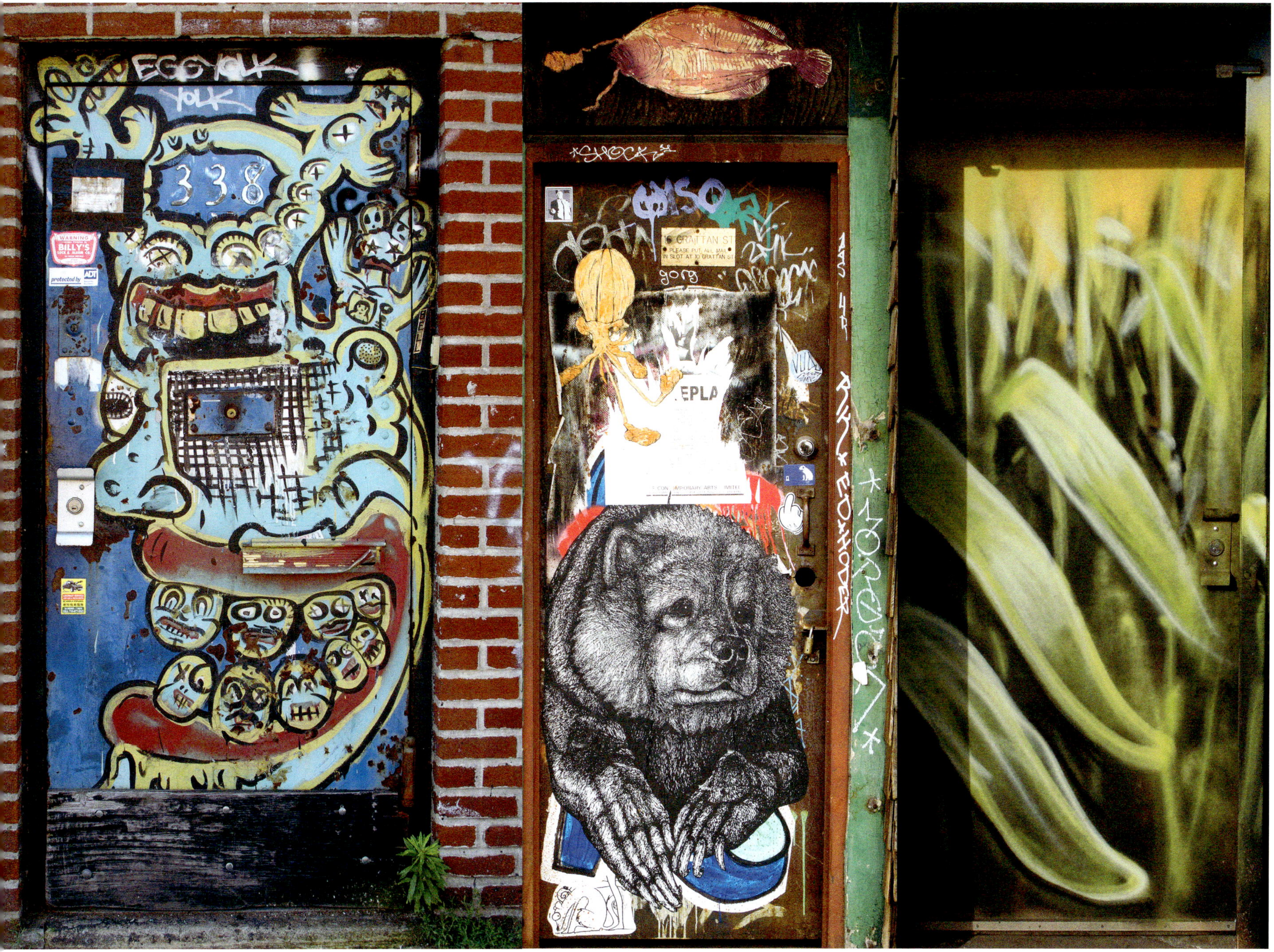
338
BILLY'S
EPLA

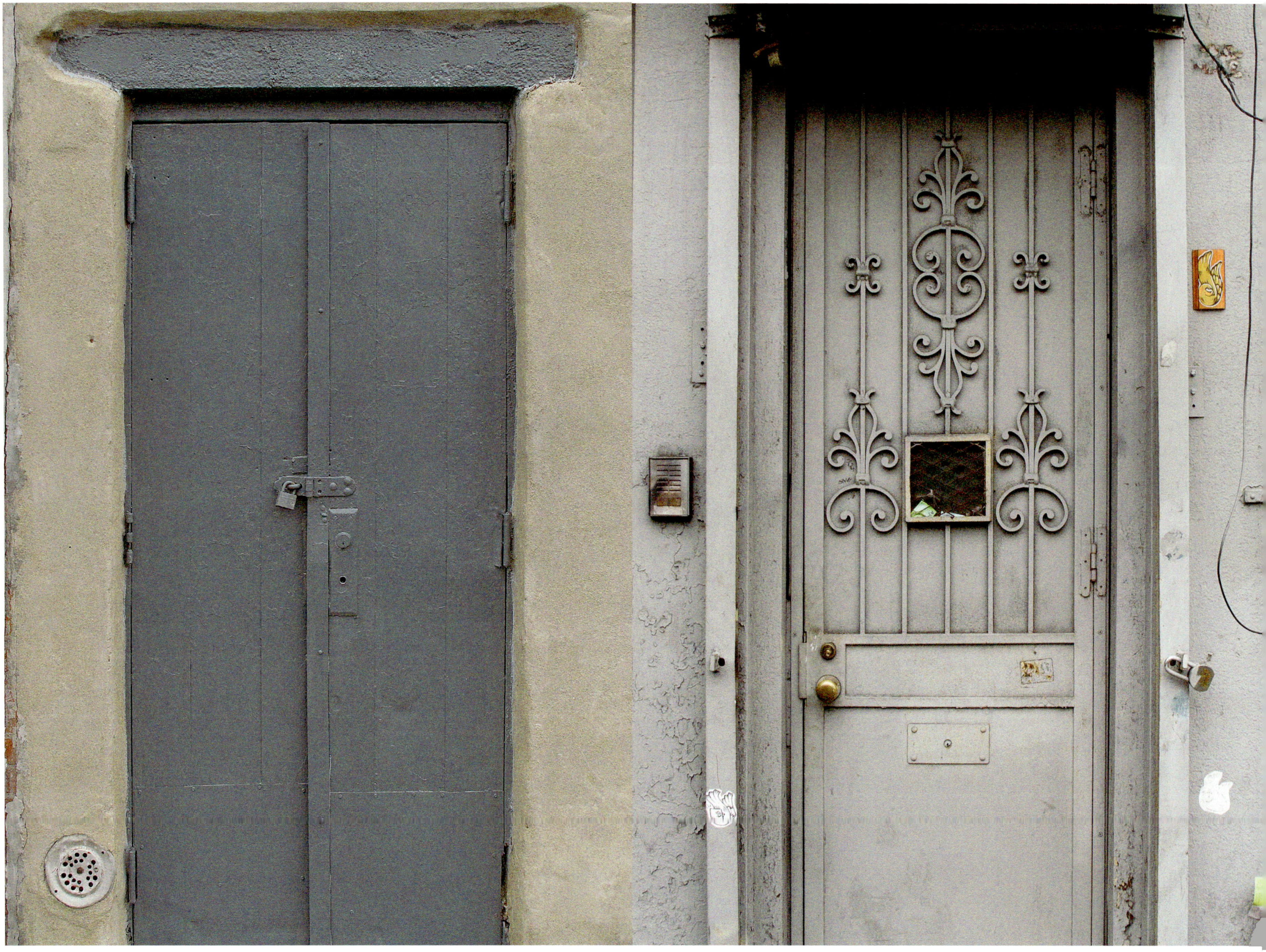

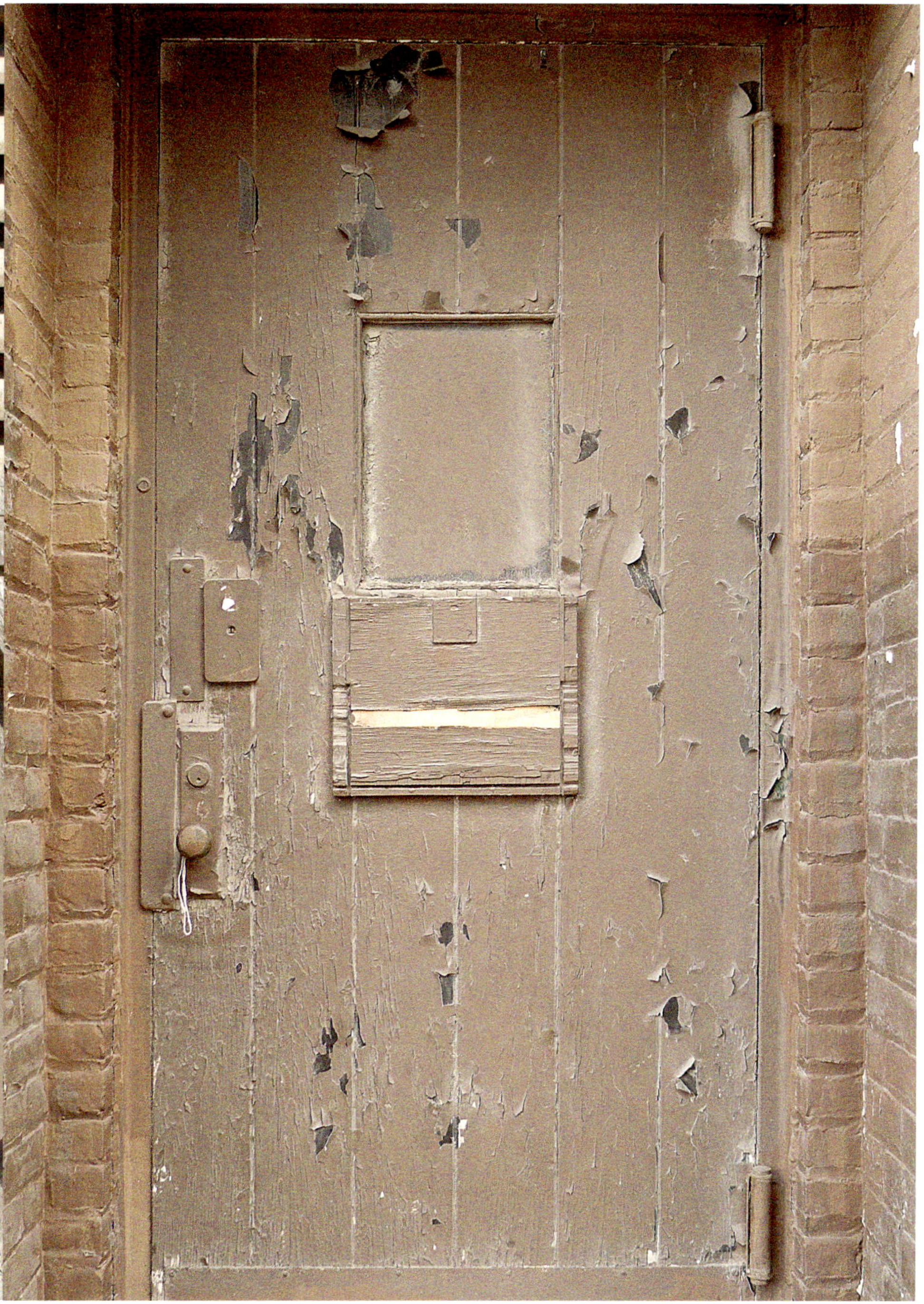

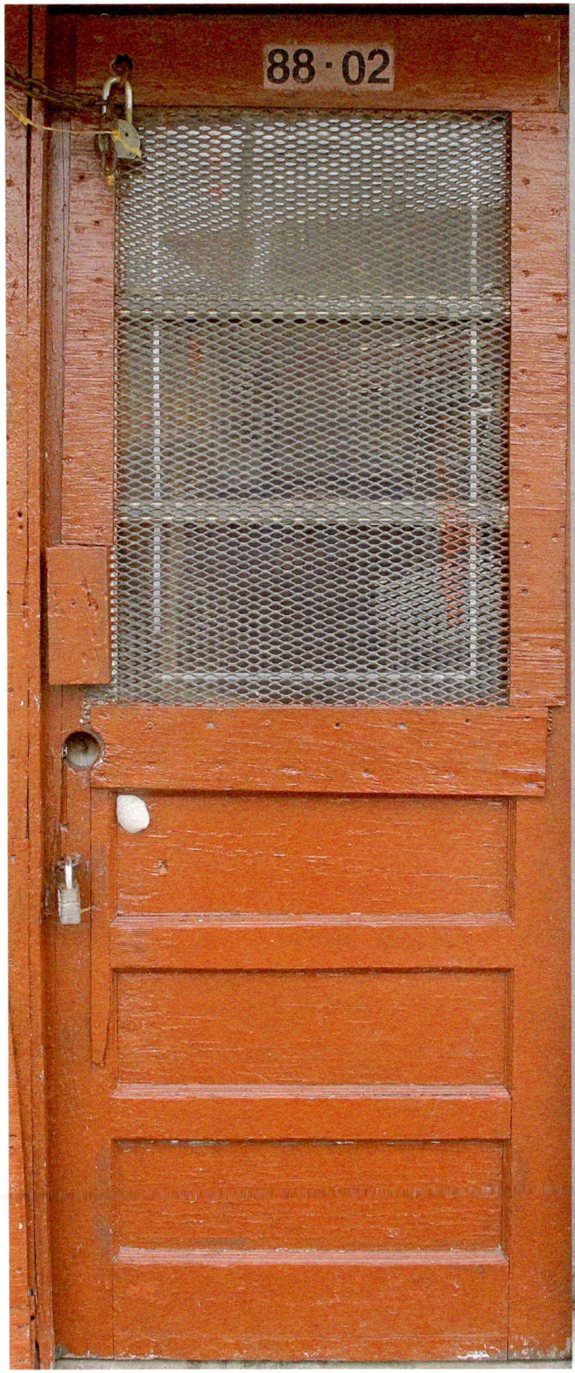
88-02
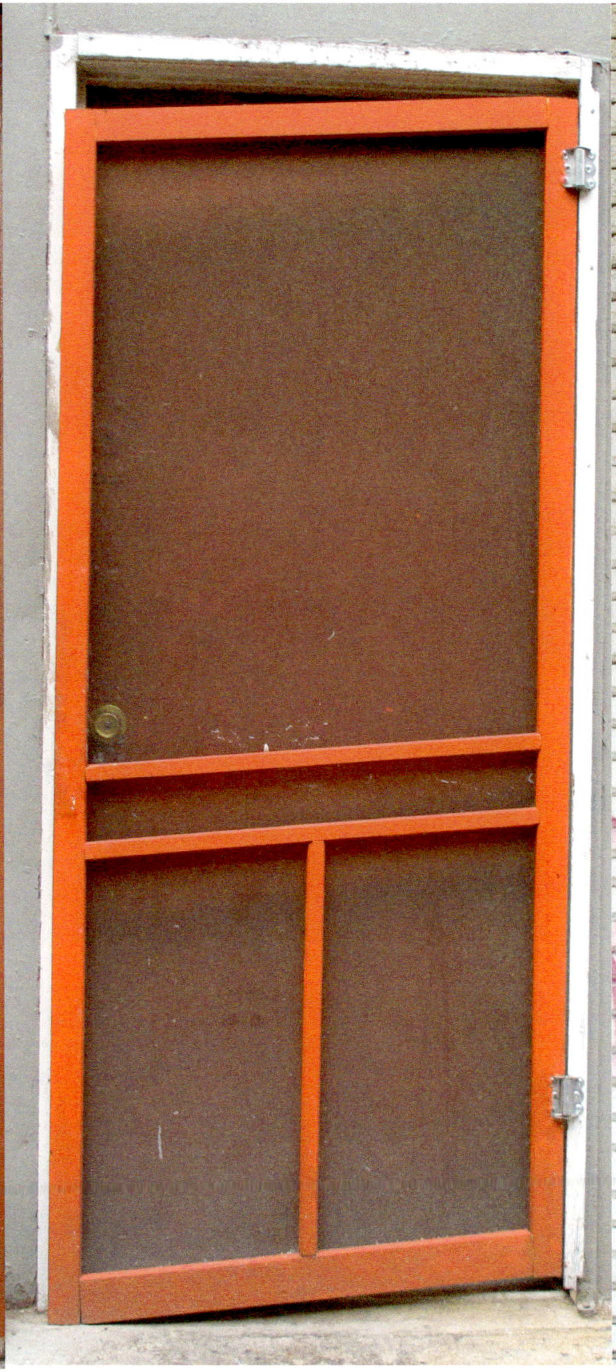
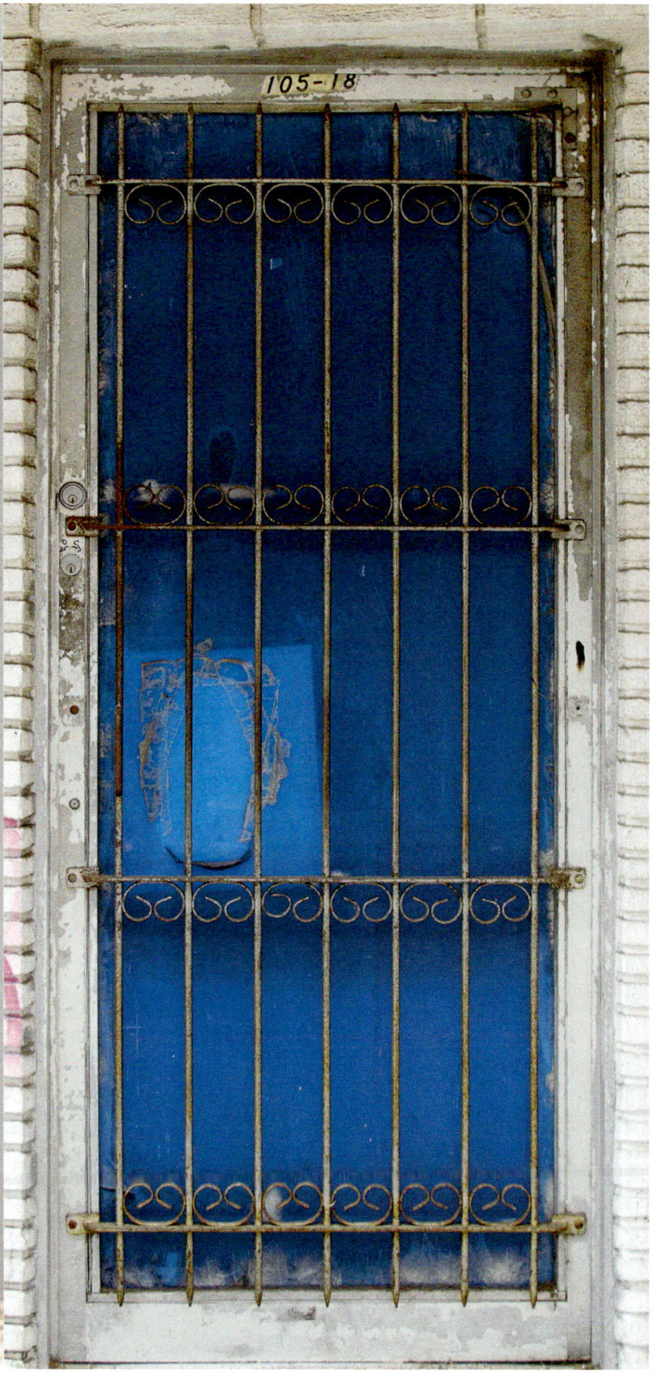
105-18

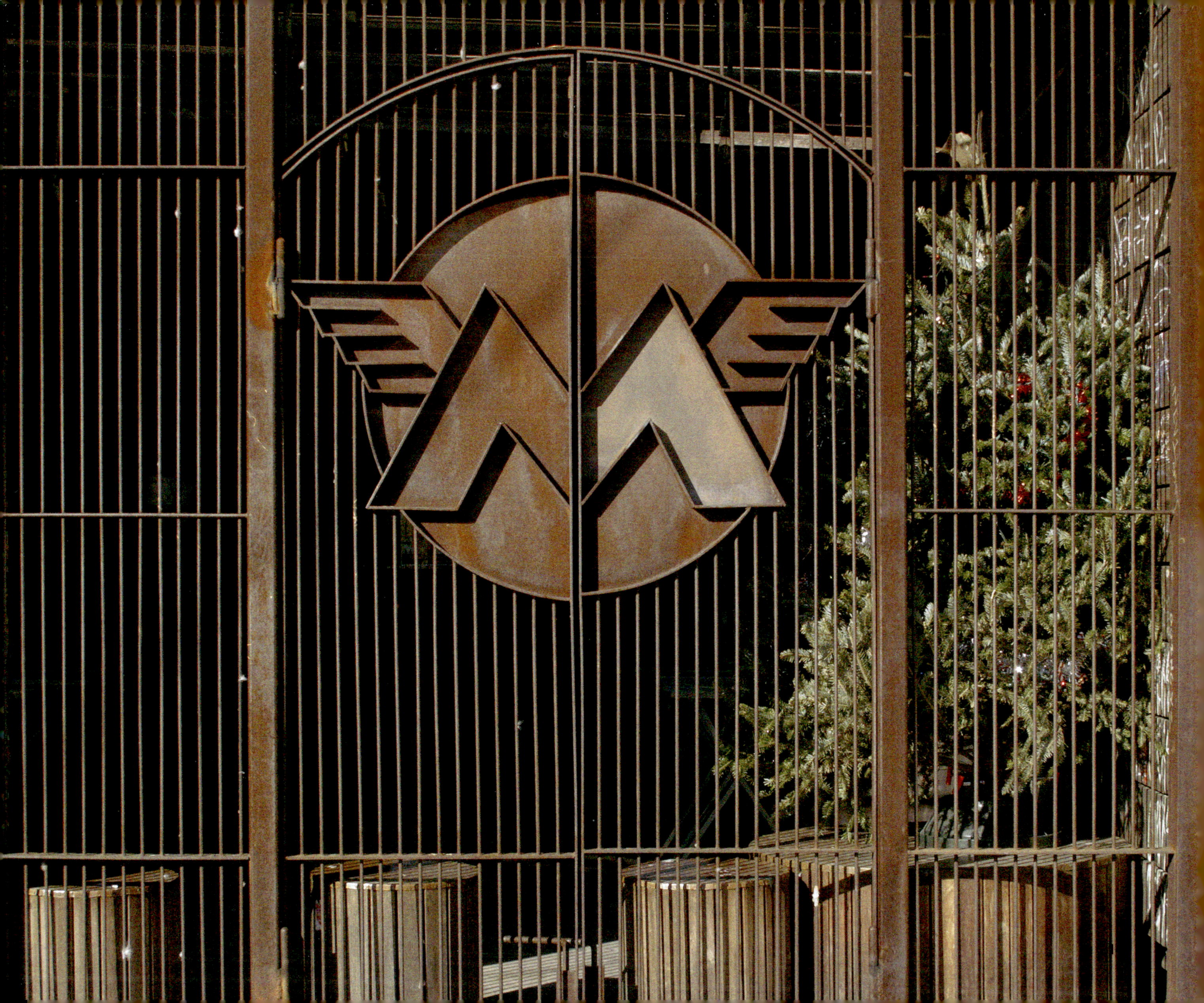

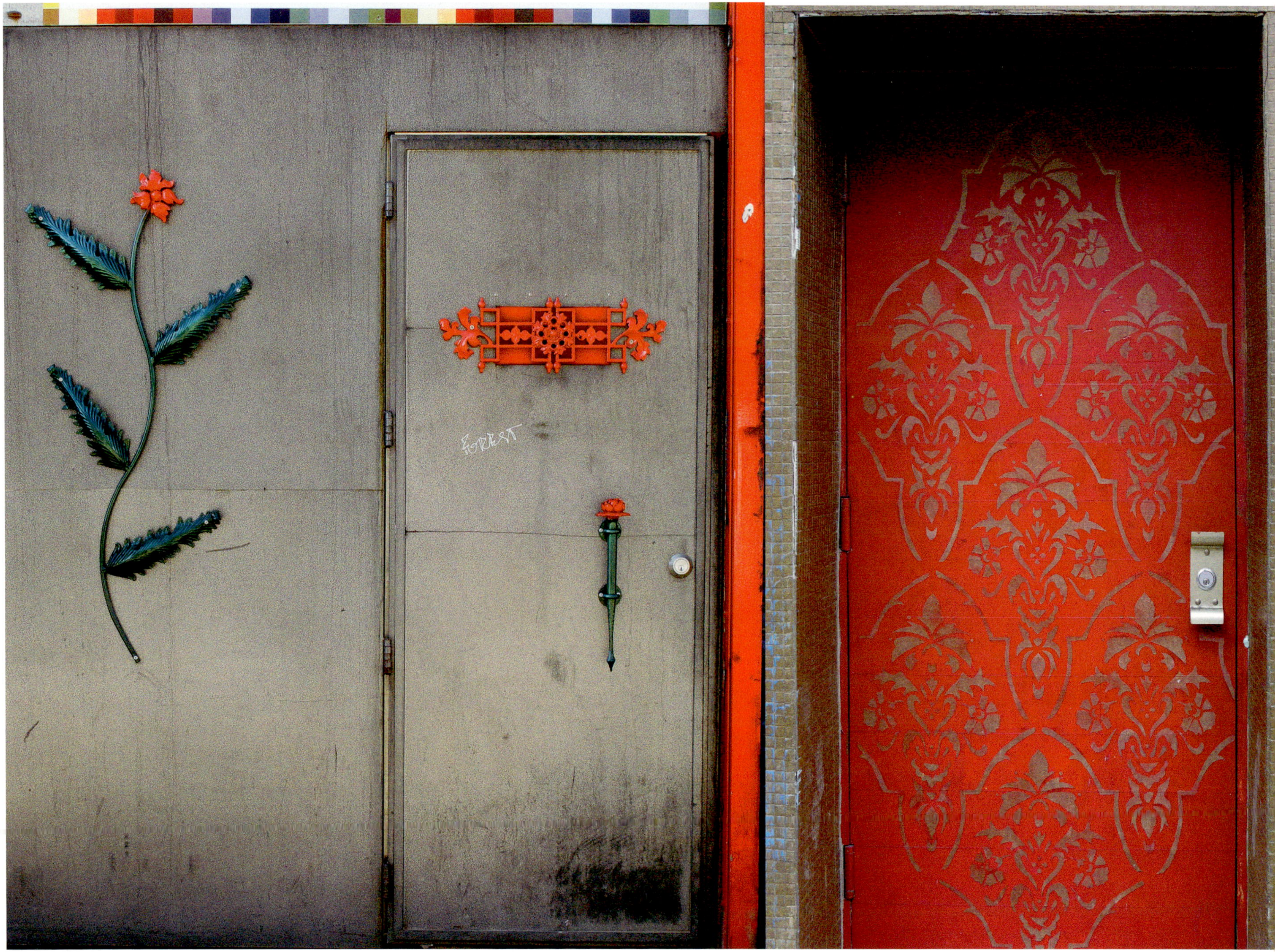

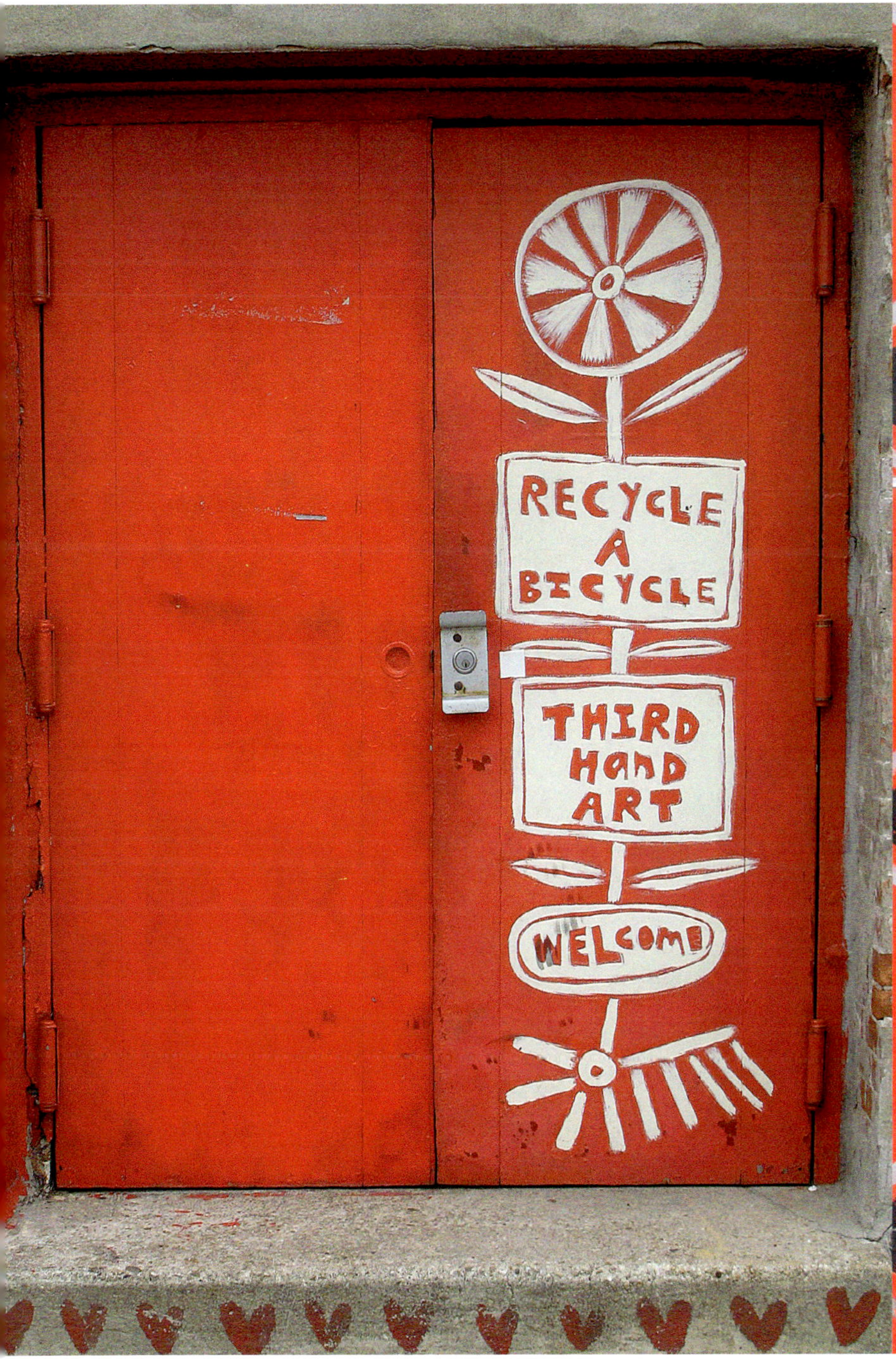
RECYCLE
A
BICYCLE
THIRD
Hand
ART
WELCOME

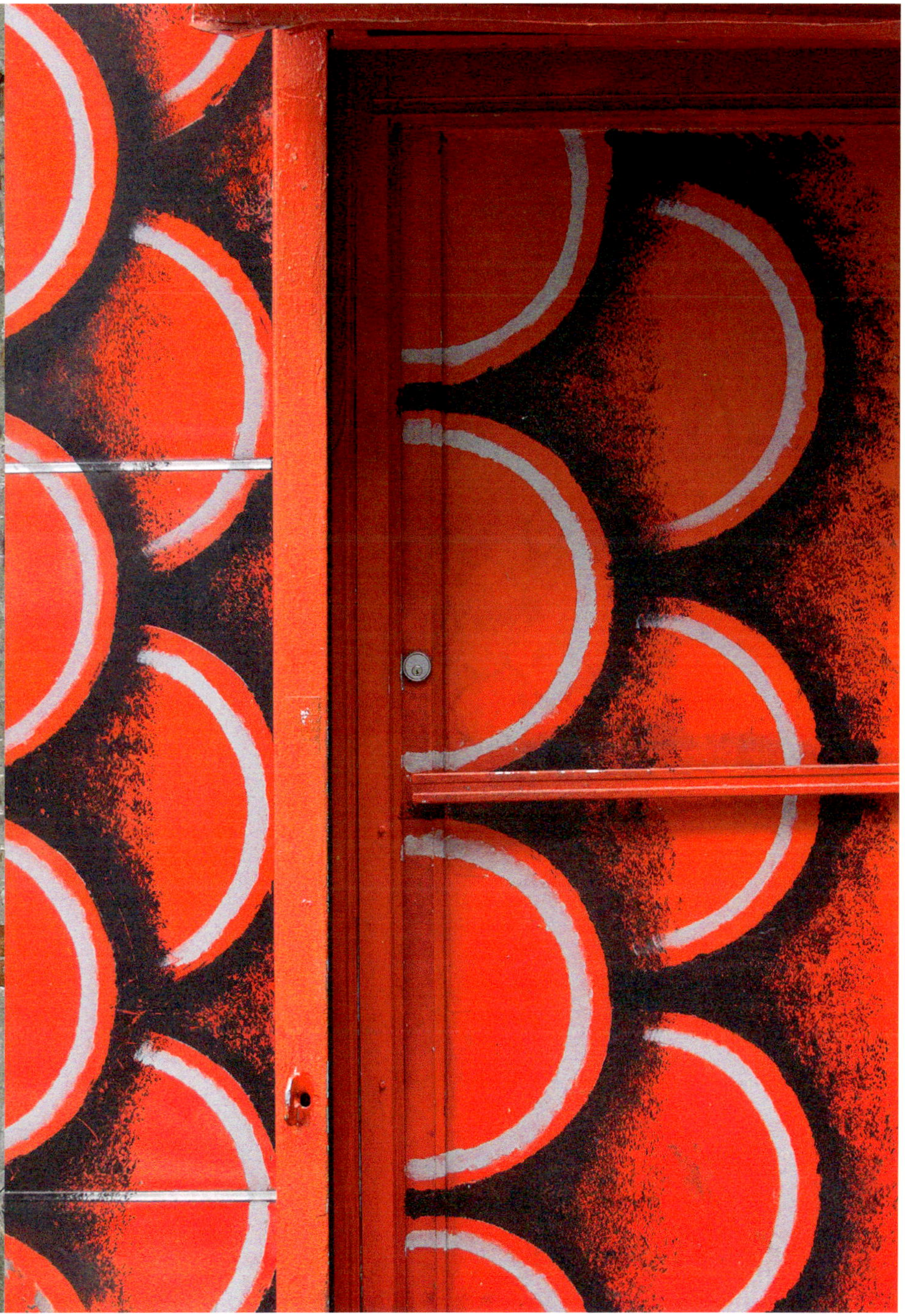

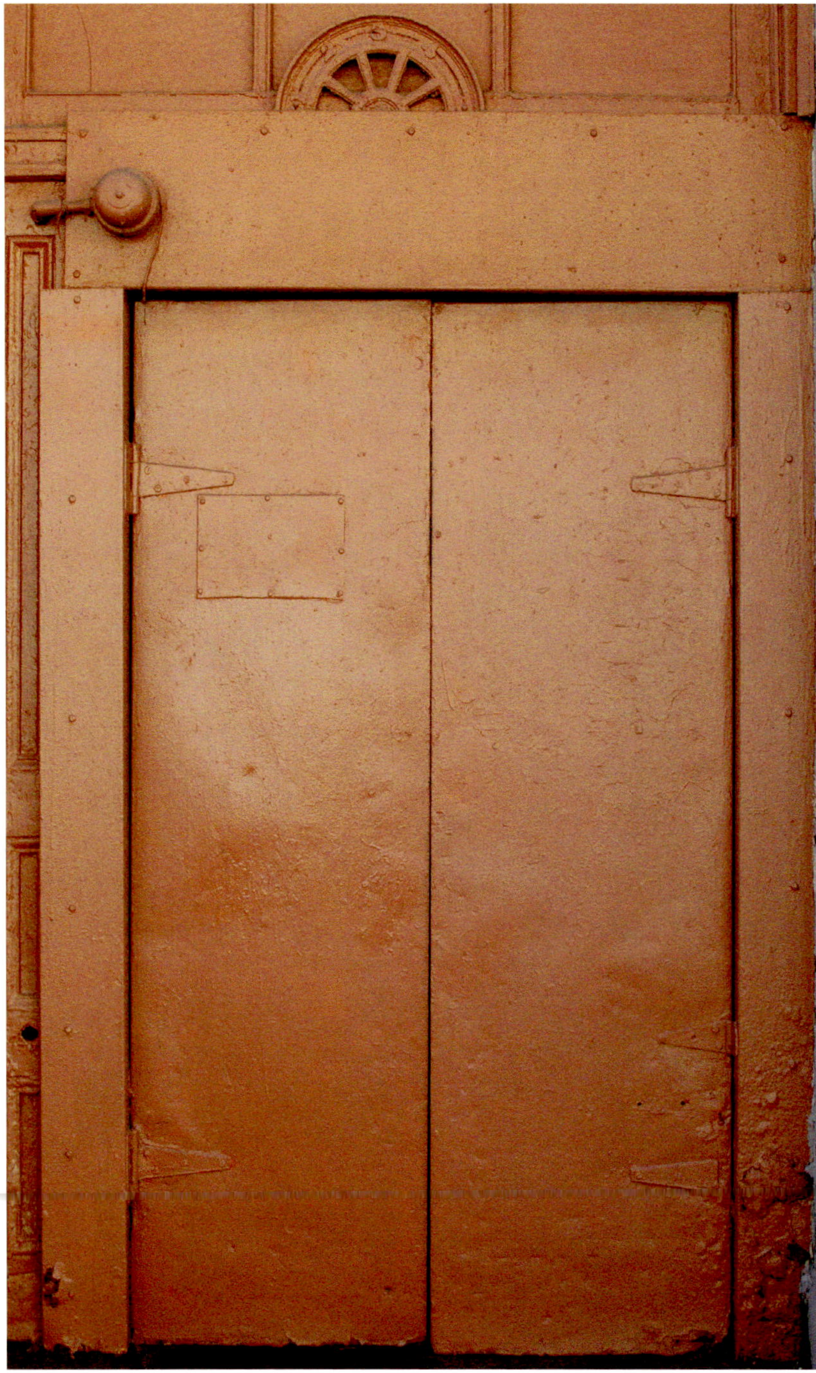

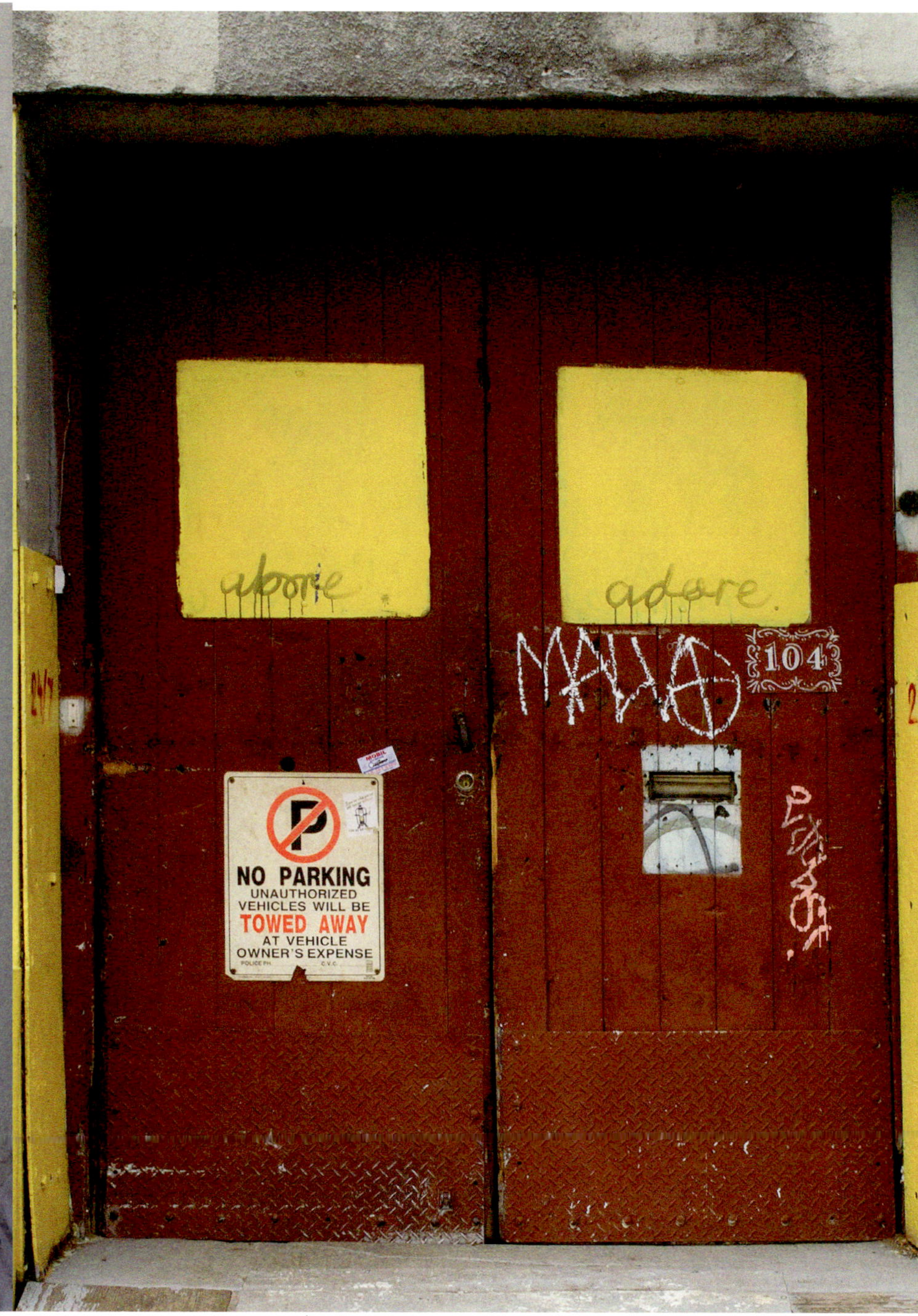
adore
104
NO PARKING
UNAUTHORIZED
VEHICLES WILL BE
TOWED AWAY
AT VEHICLE
OWNER'S EXPENSE

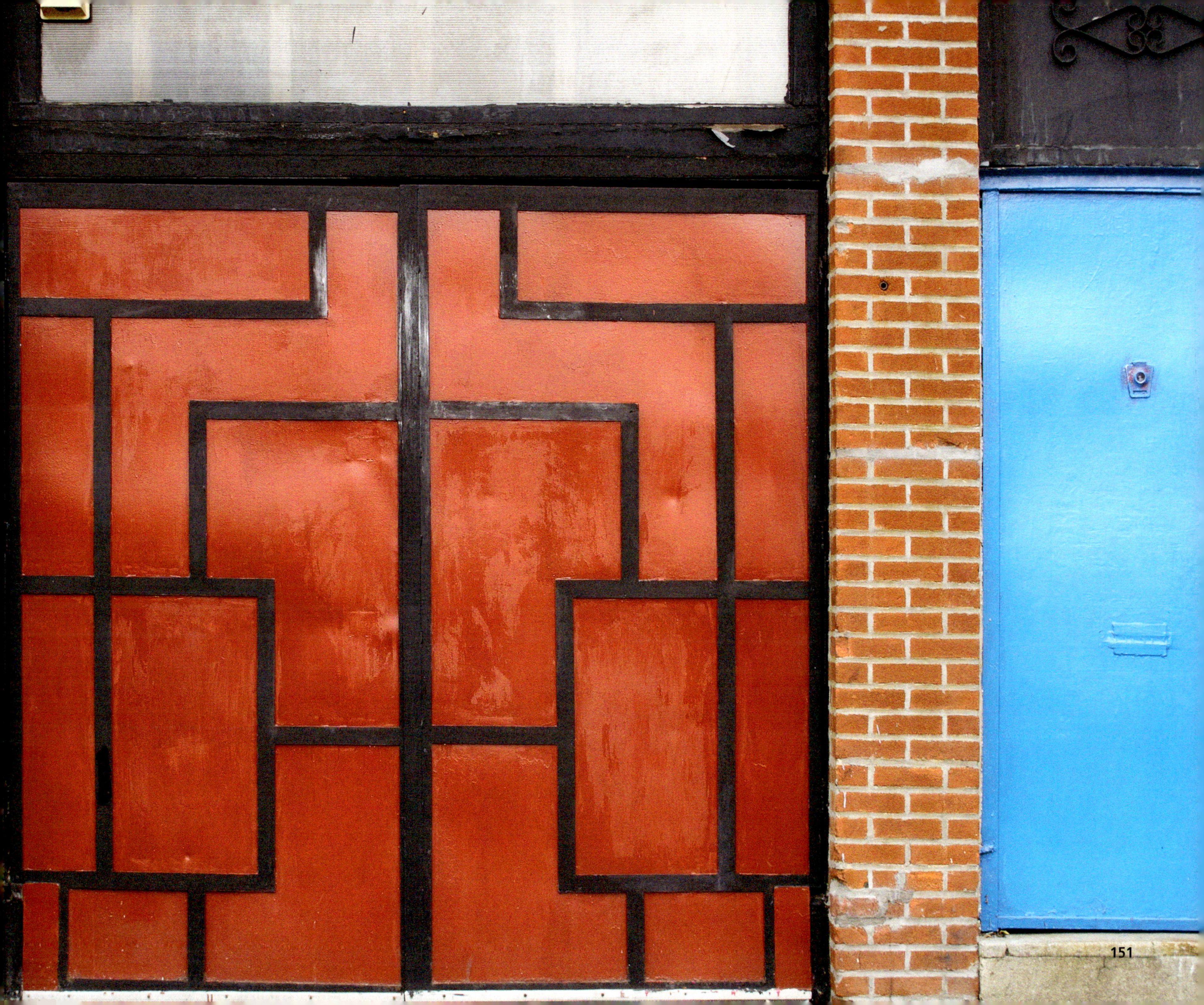

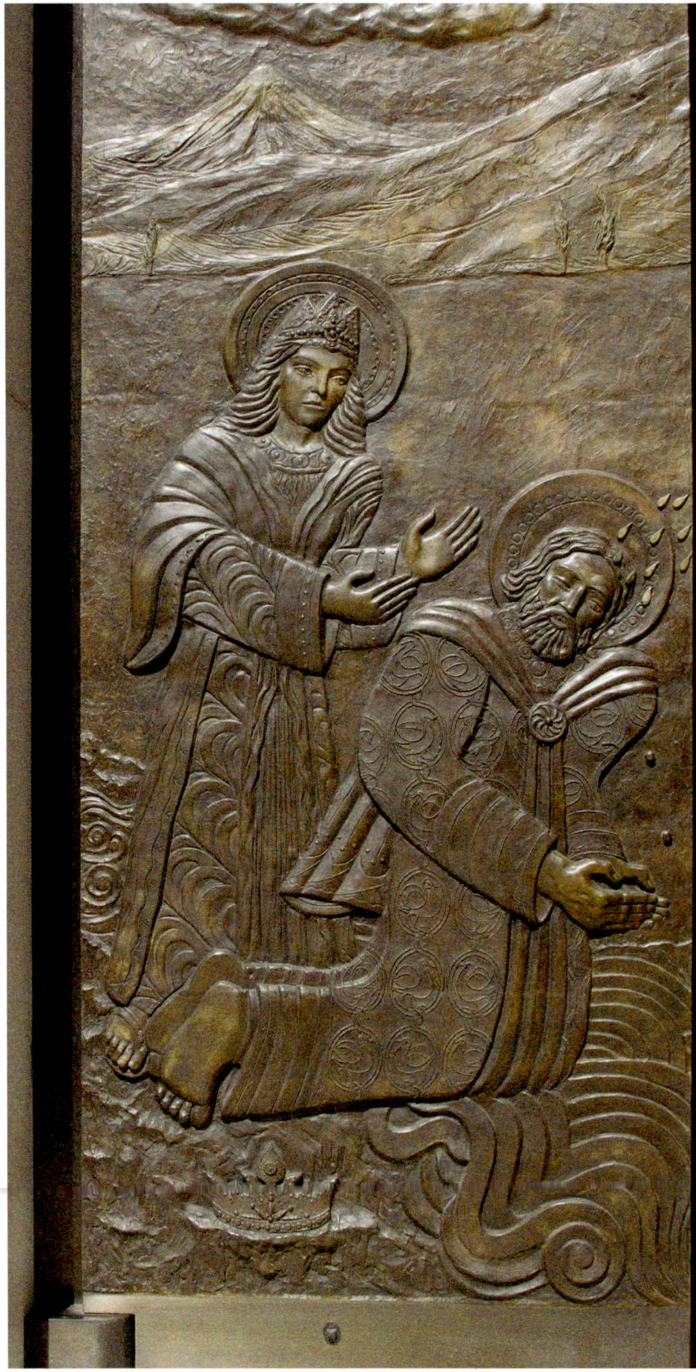

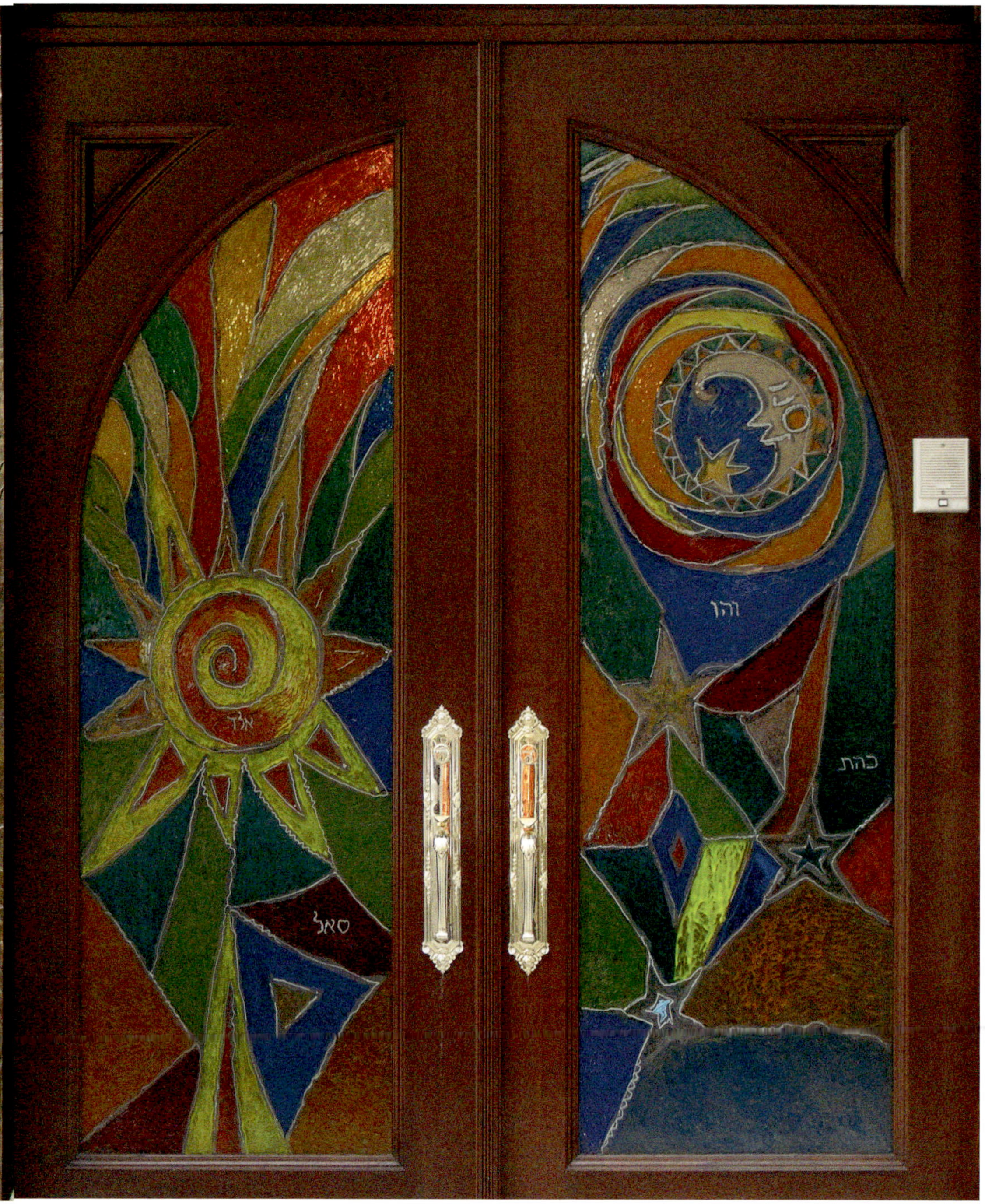

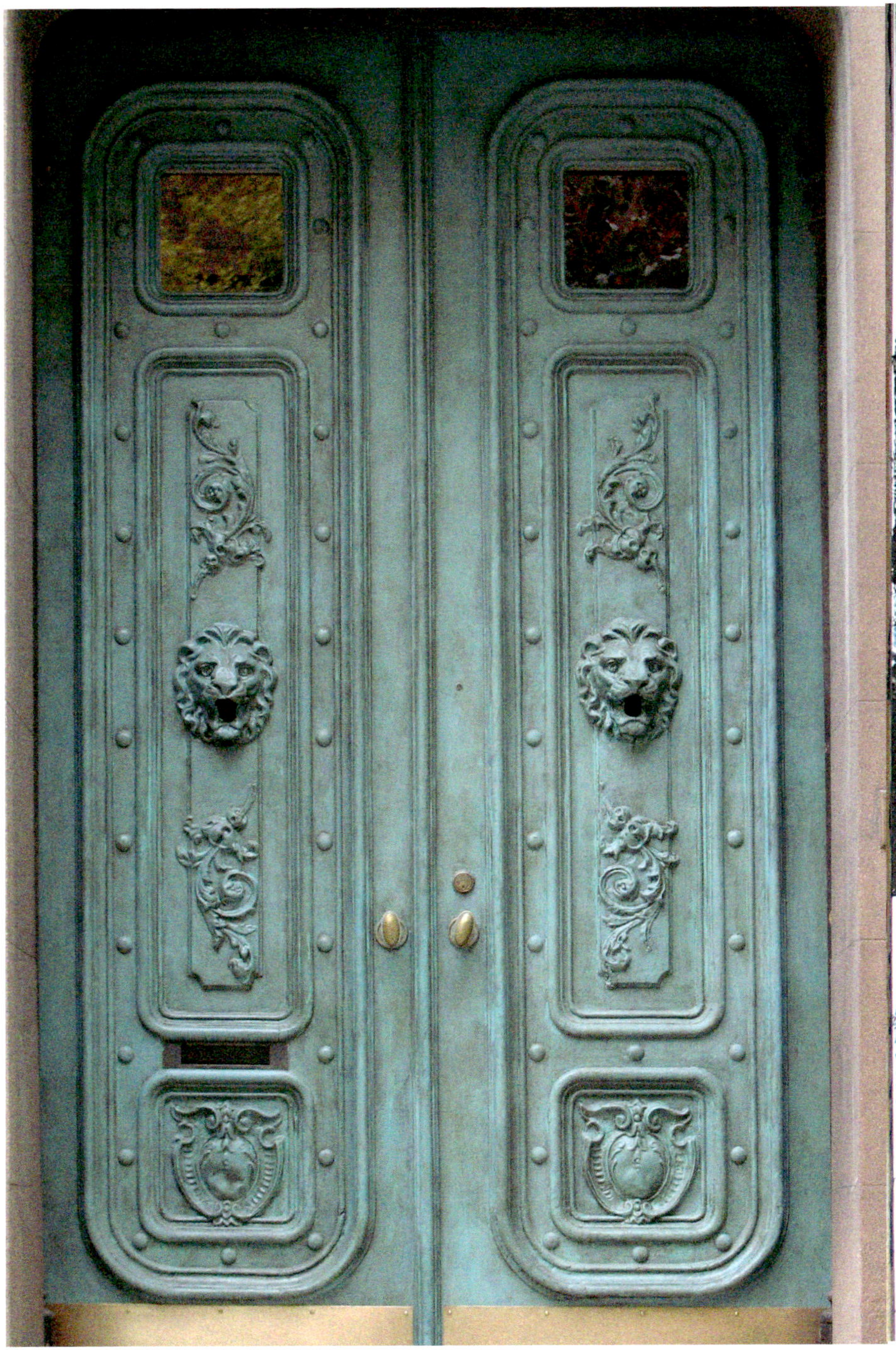

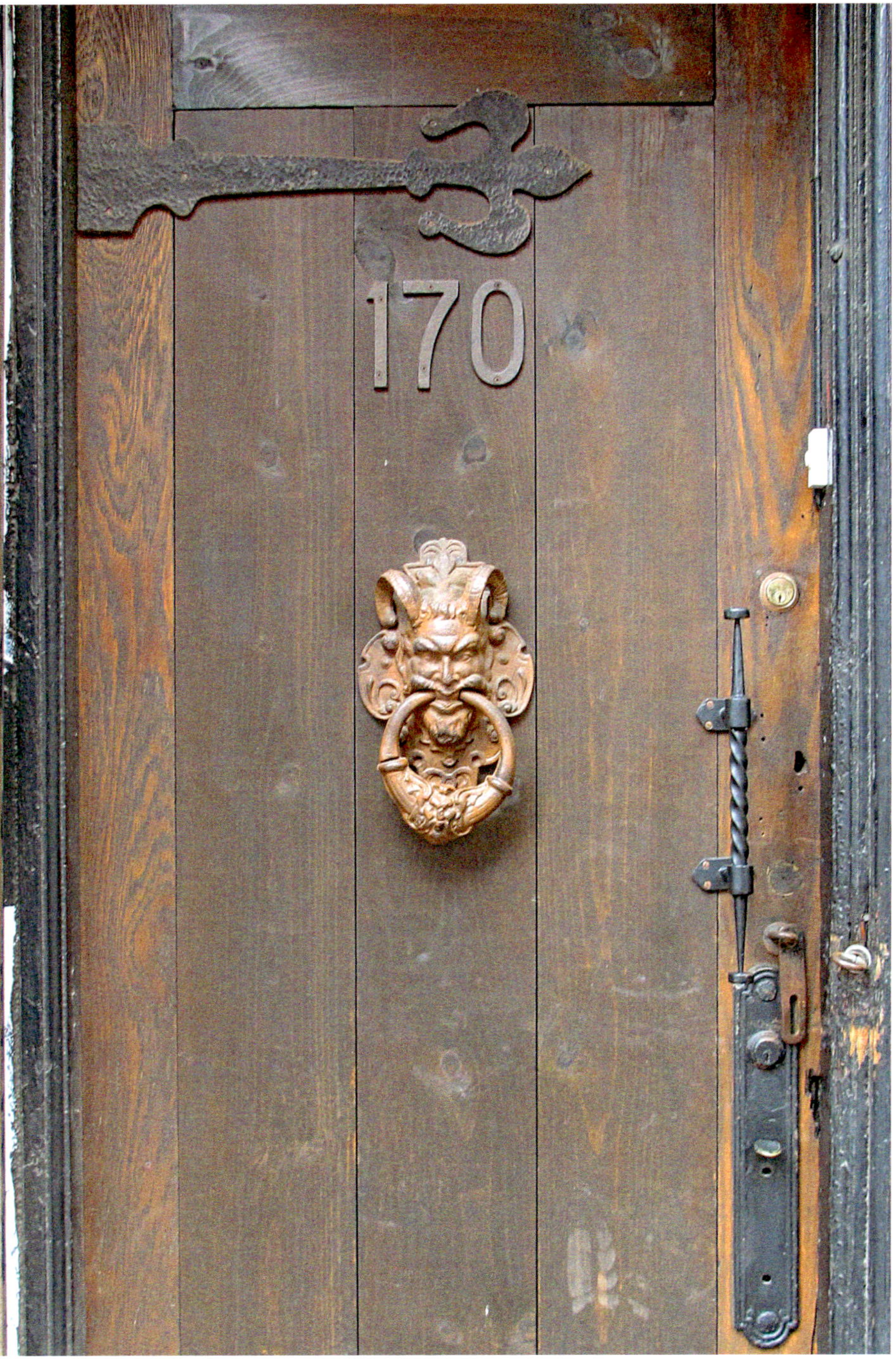

170

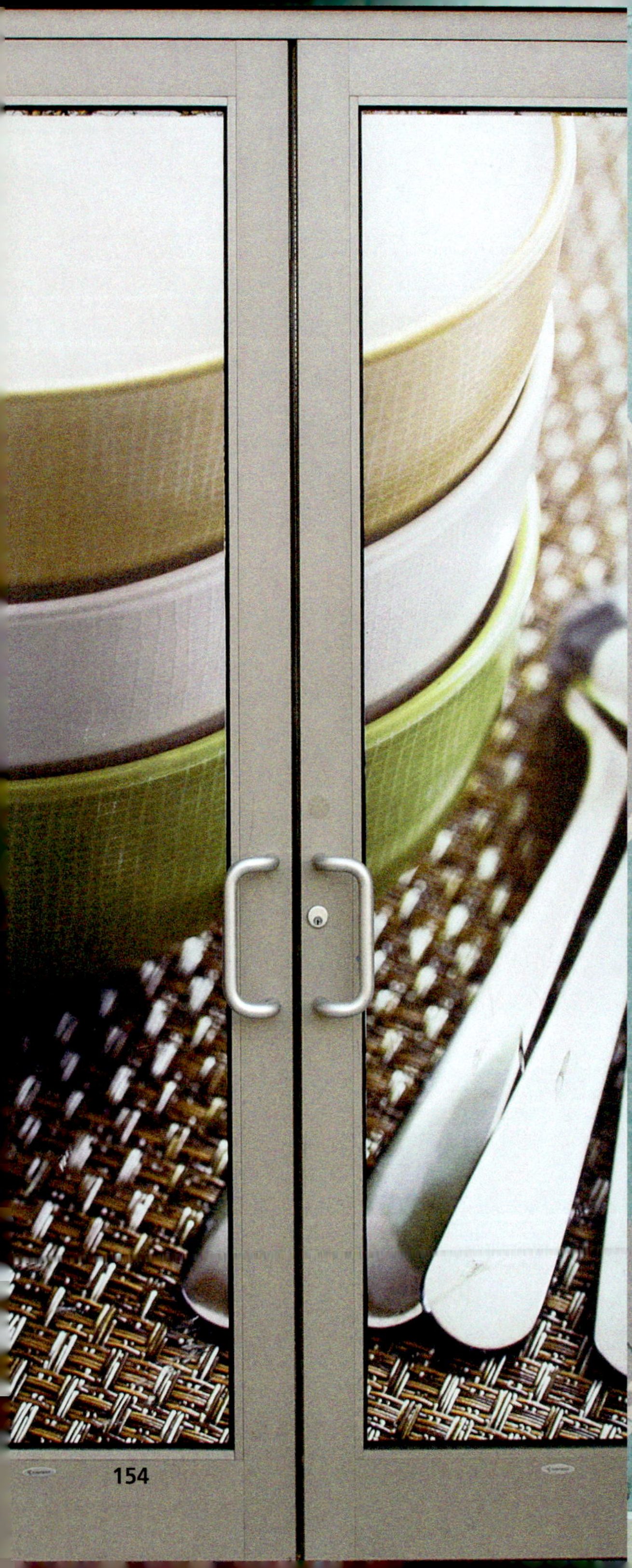

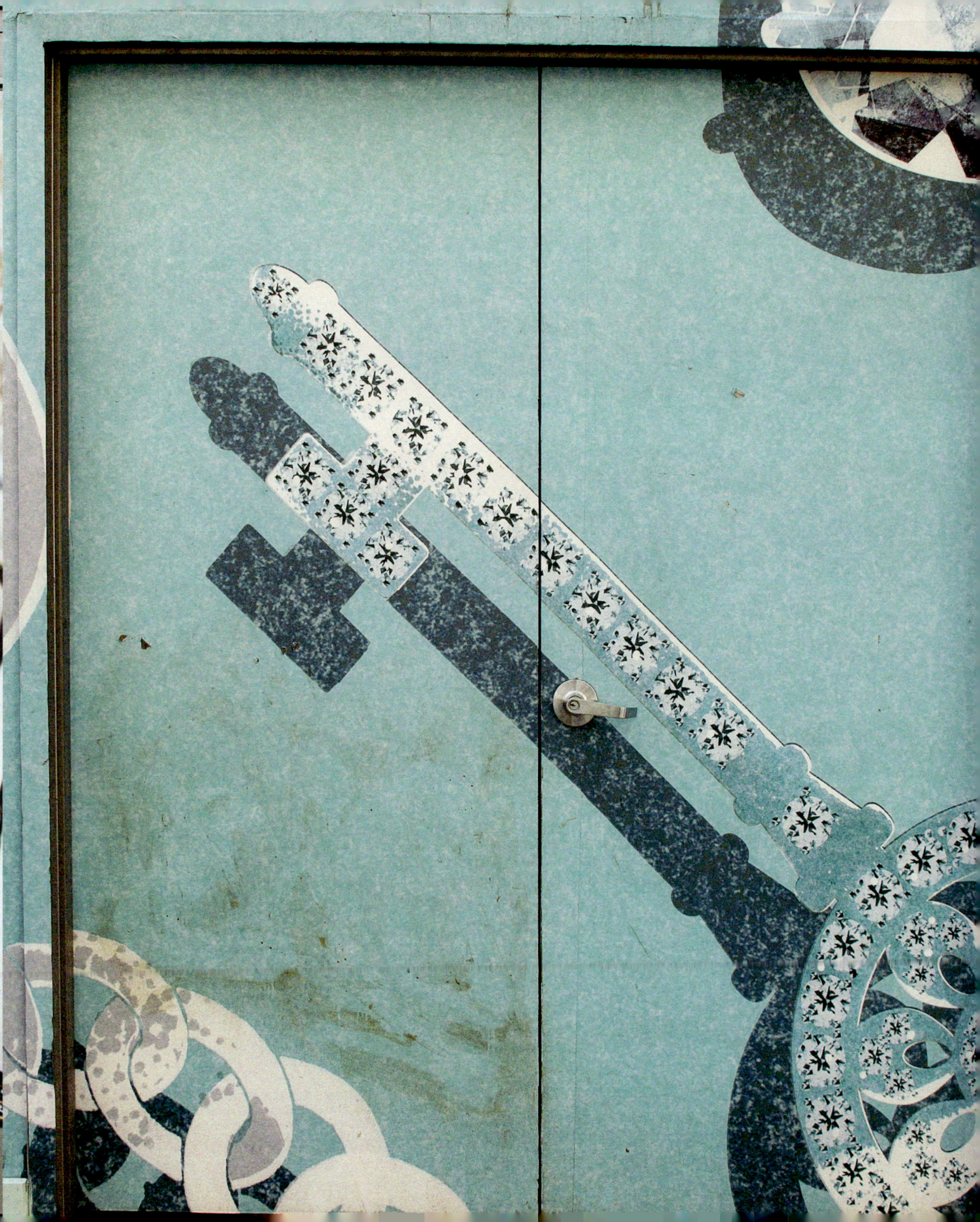

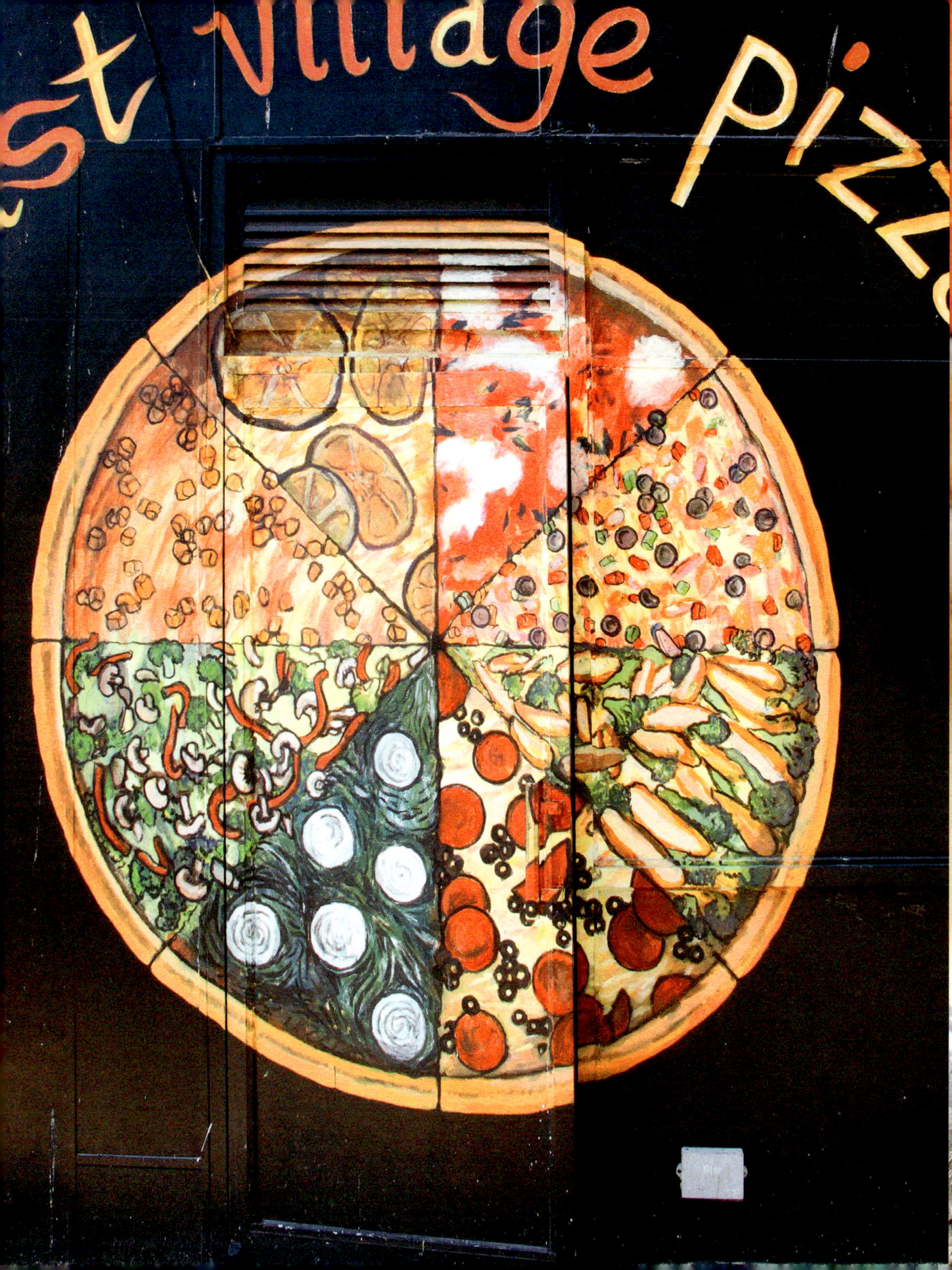
st Village pizz

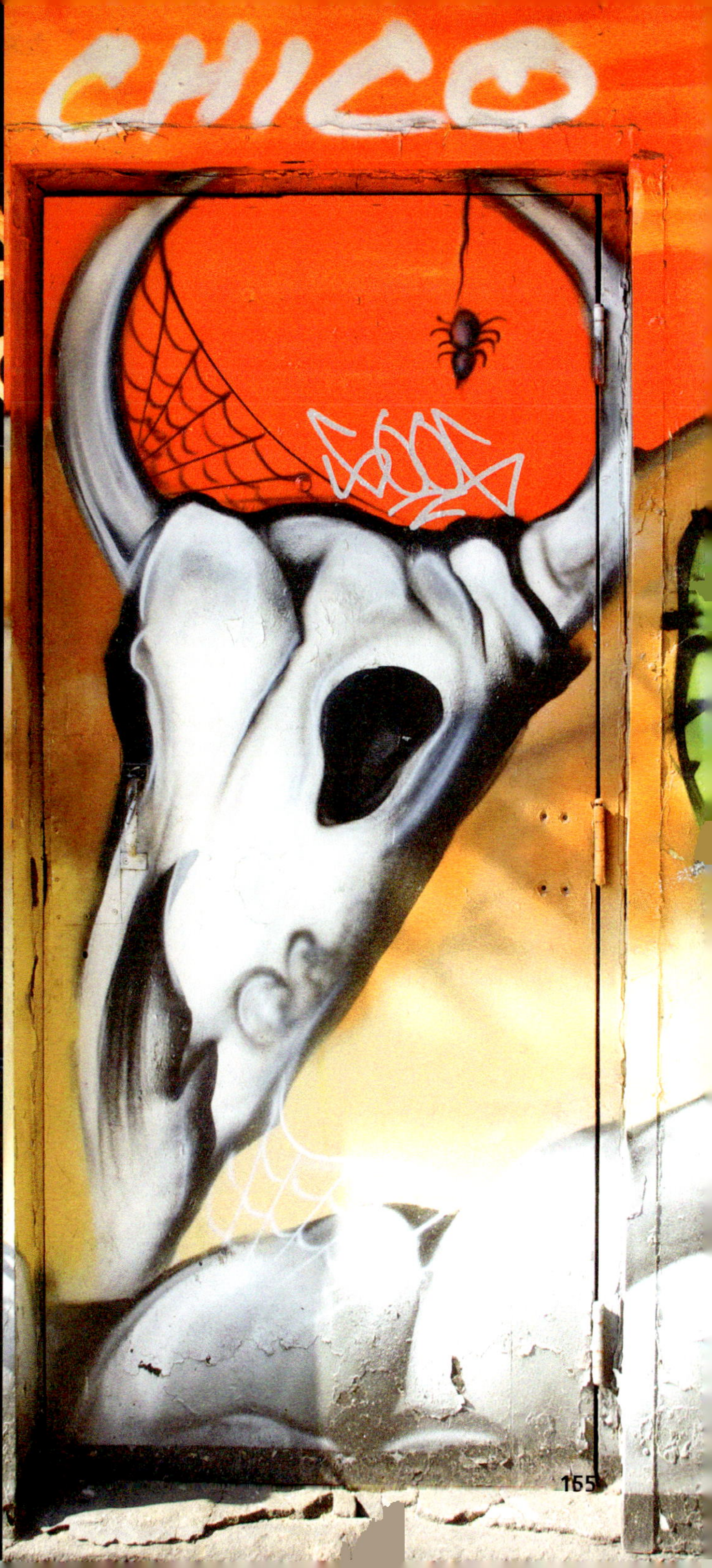
CHICO

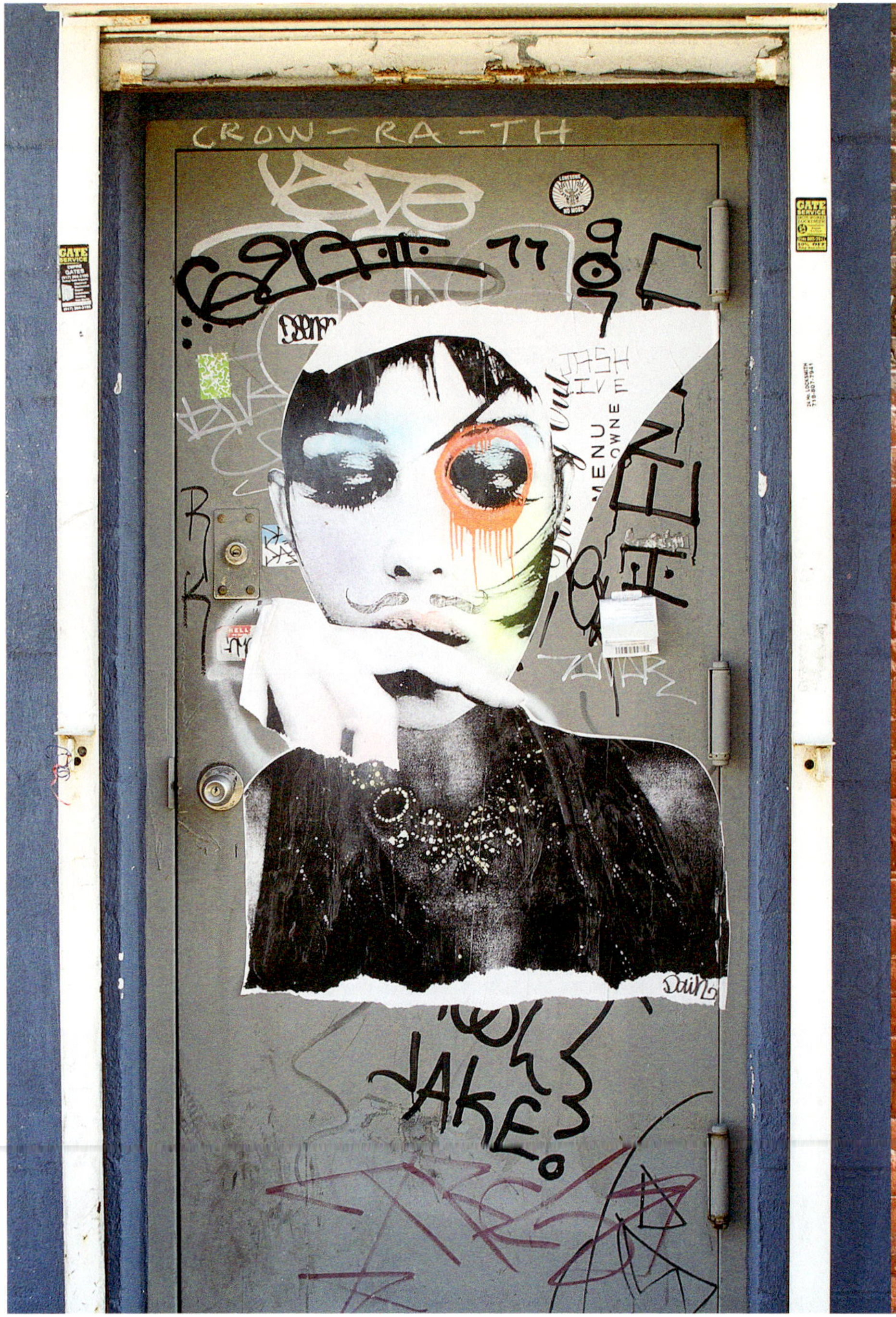
CROW-RA-TH
JAKE
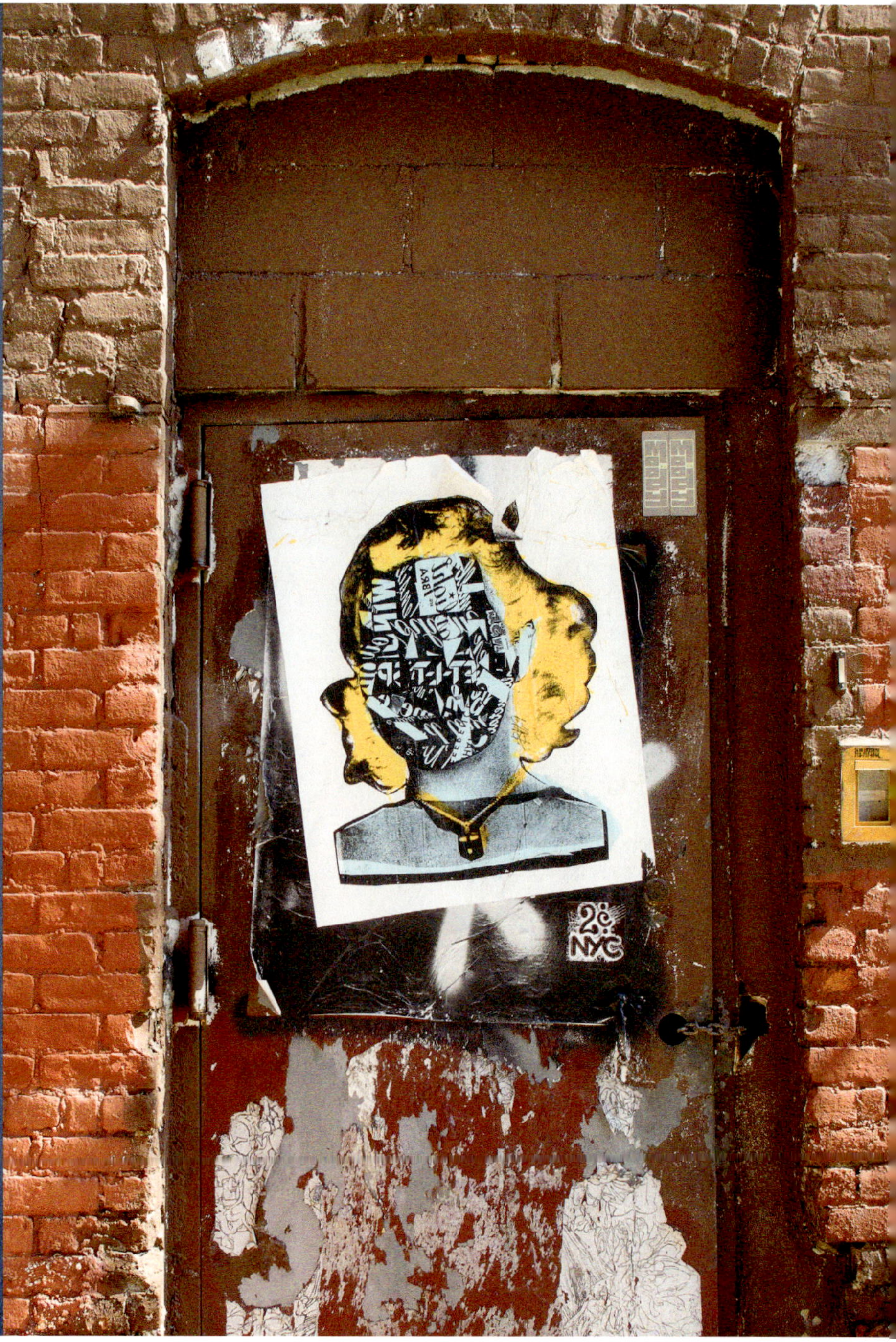
2¢
NYC

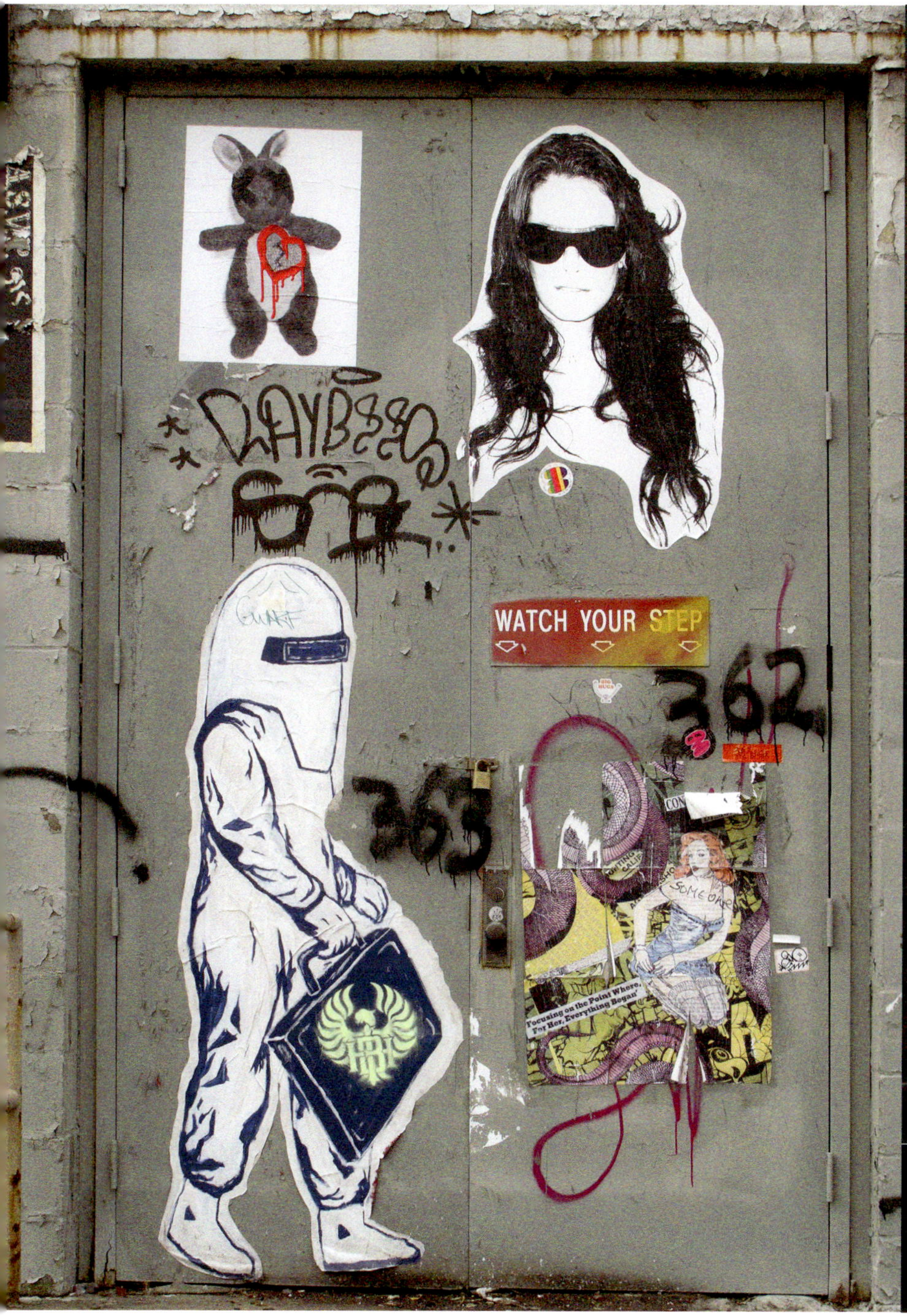
WATCH YOUR STEP

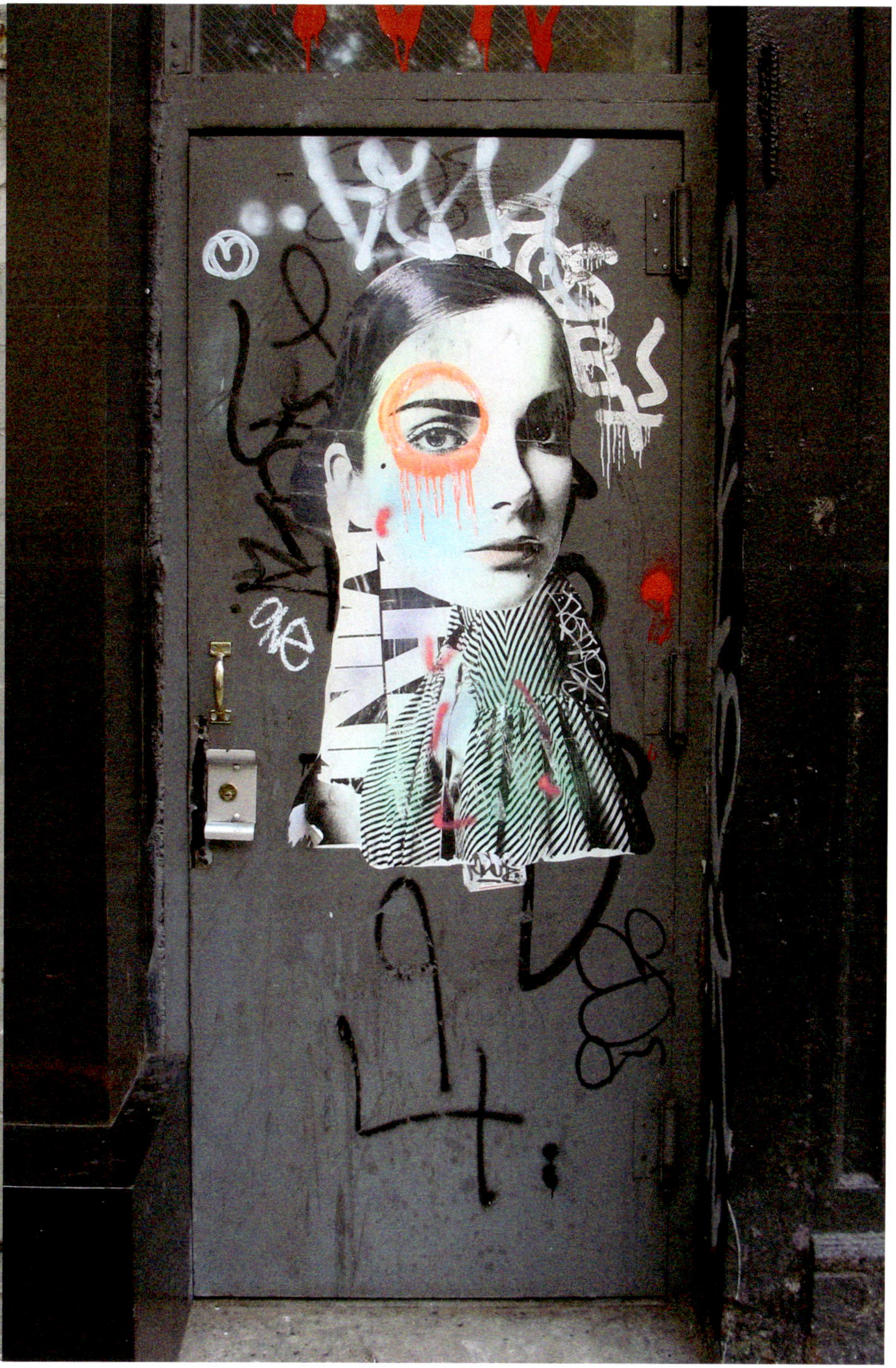

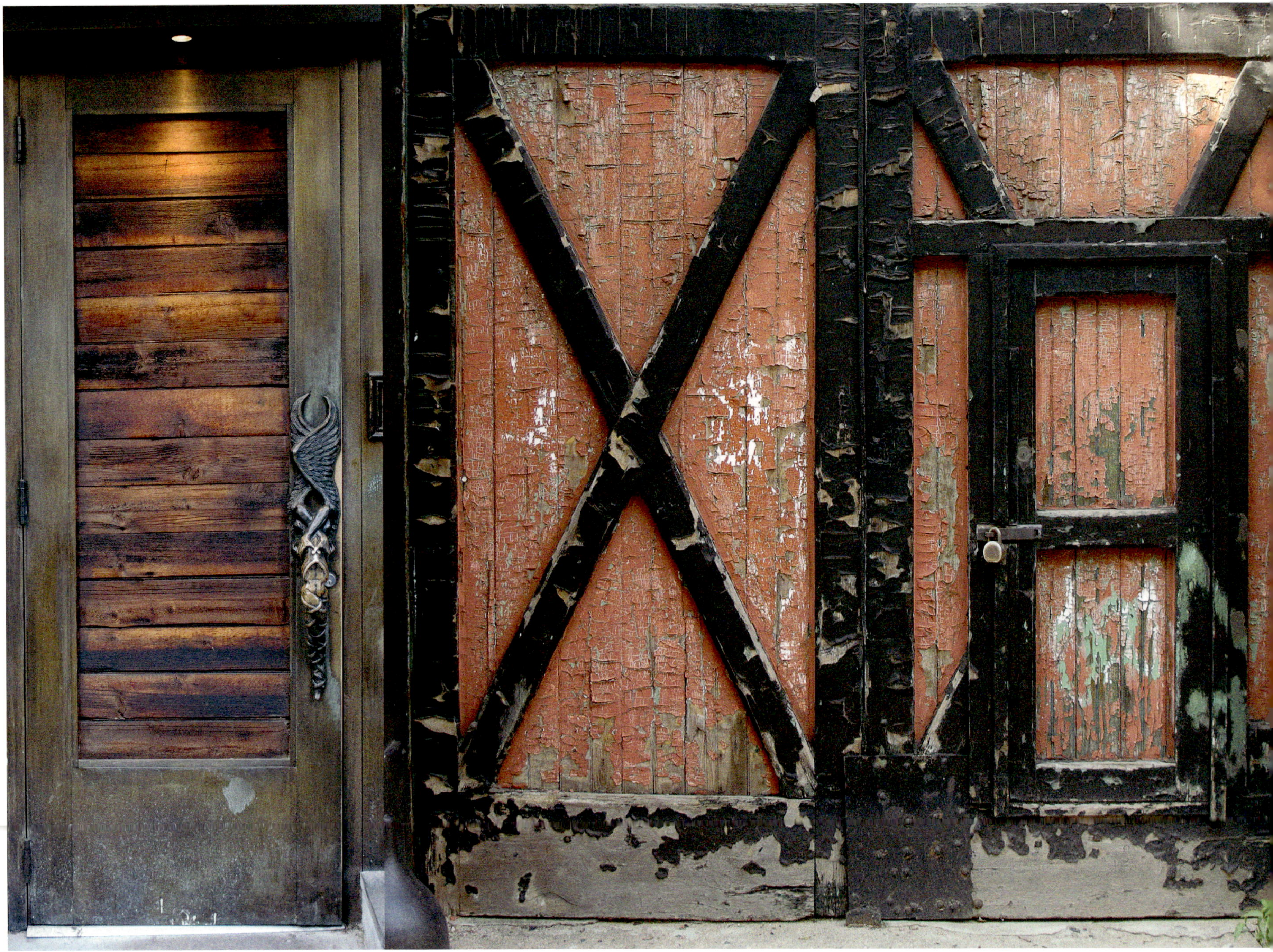

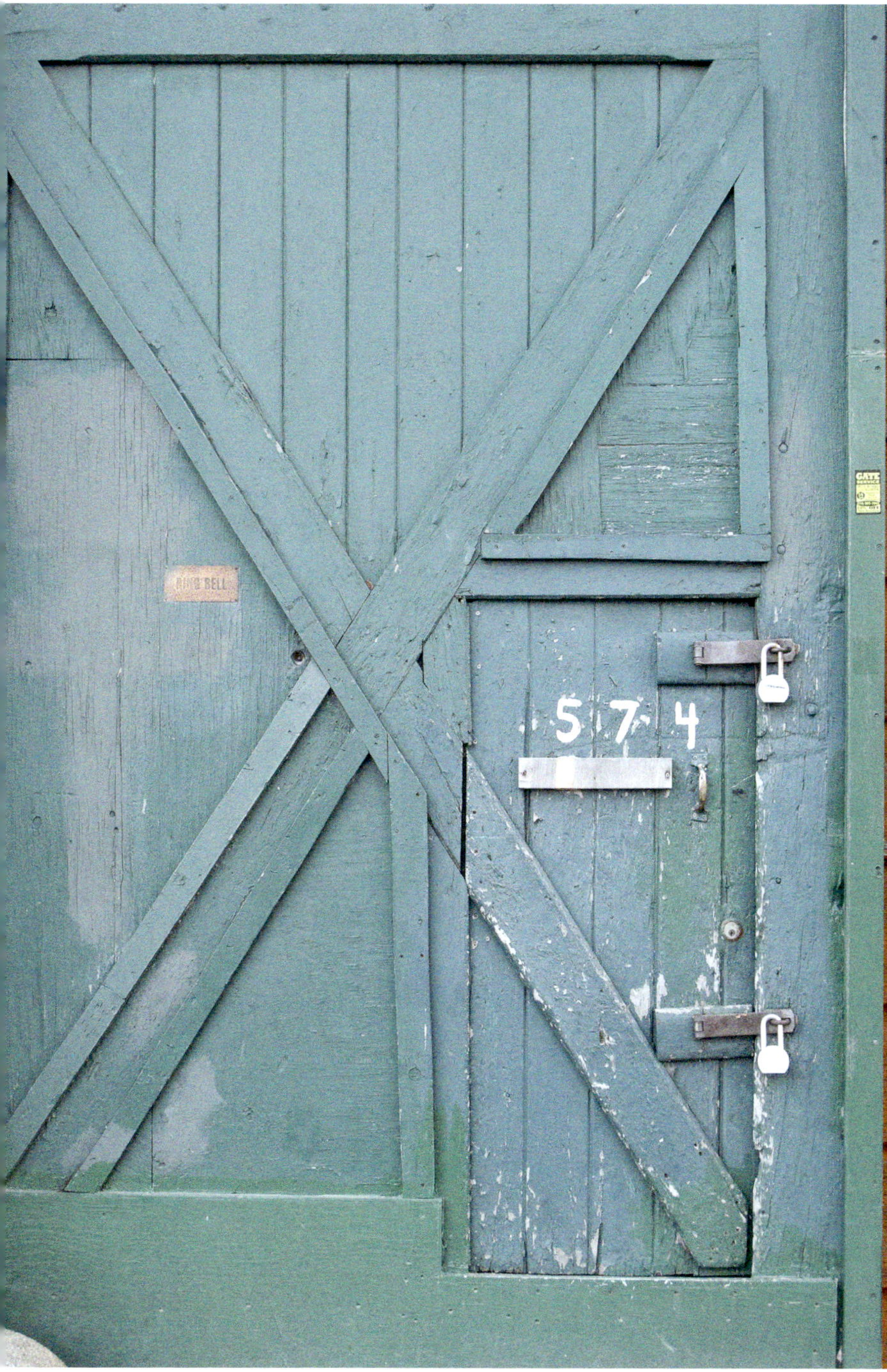
574

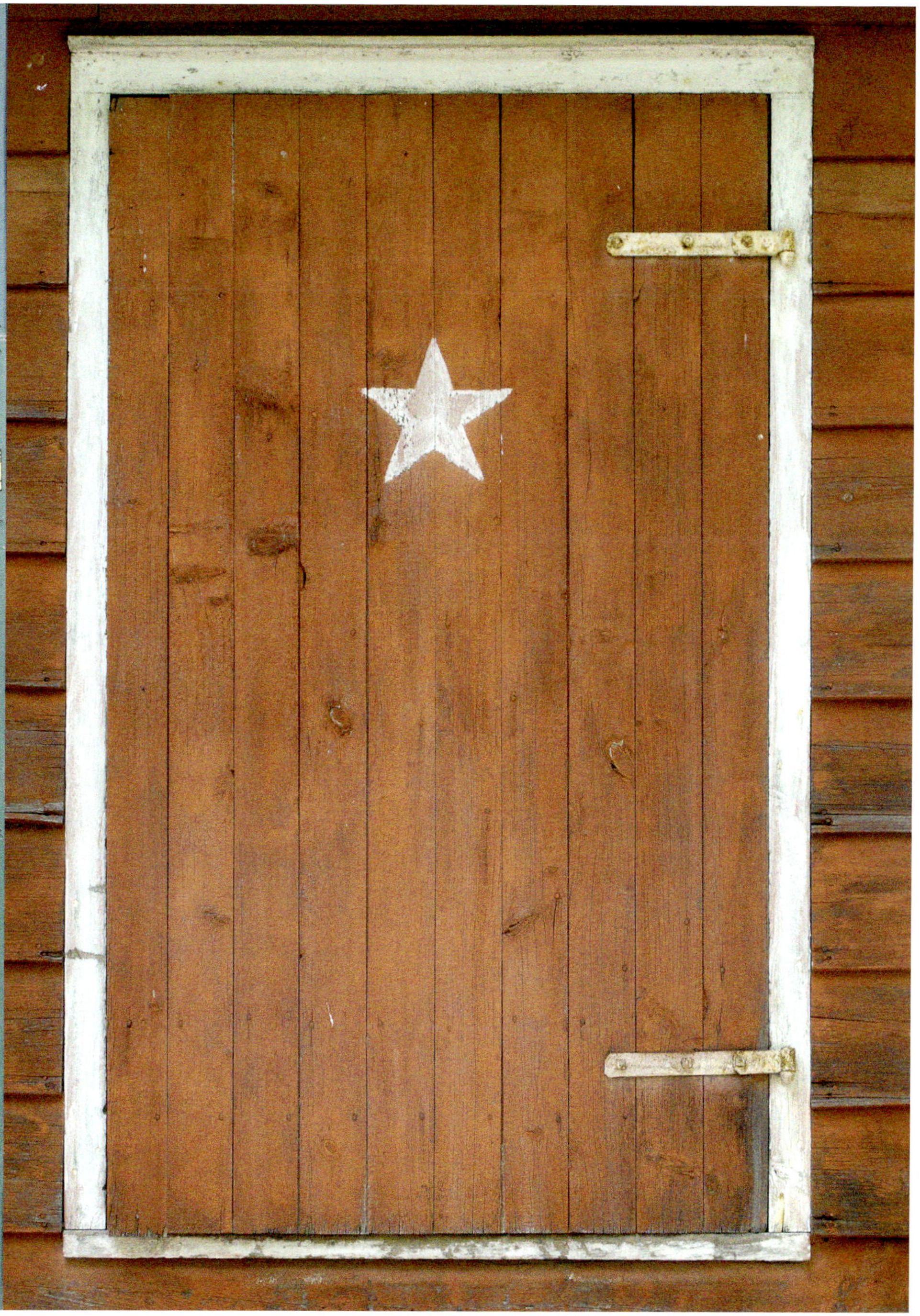

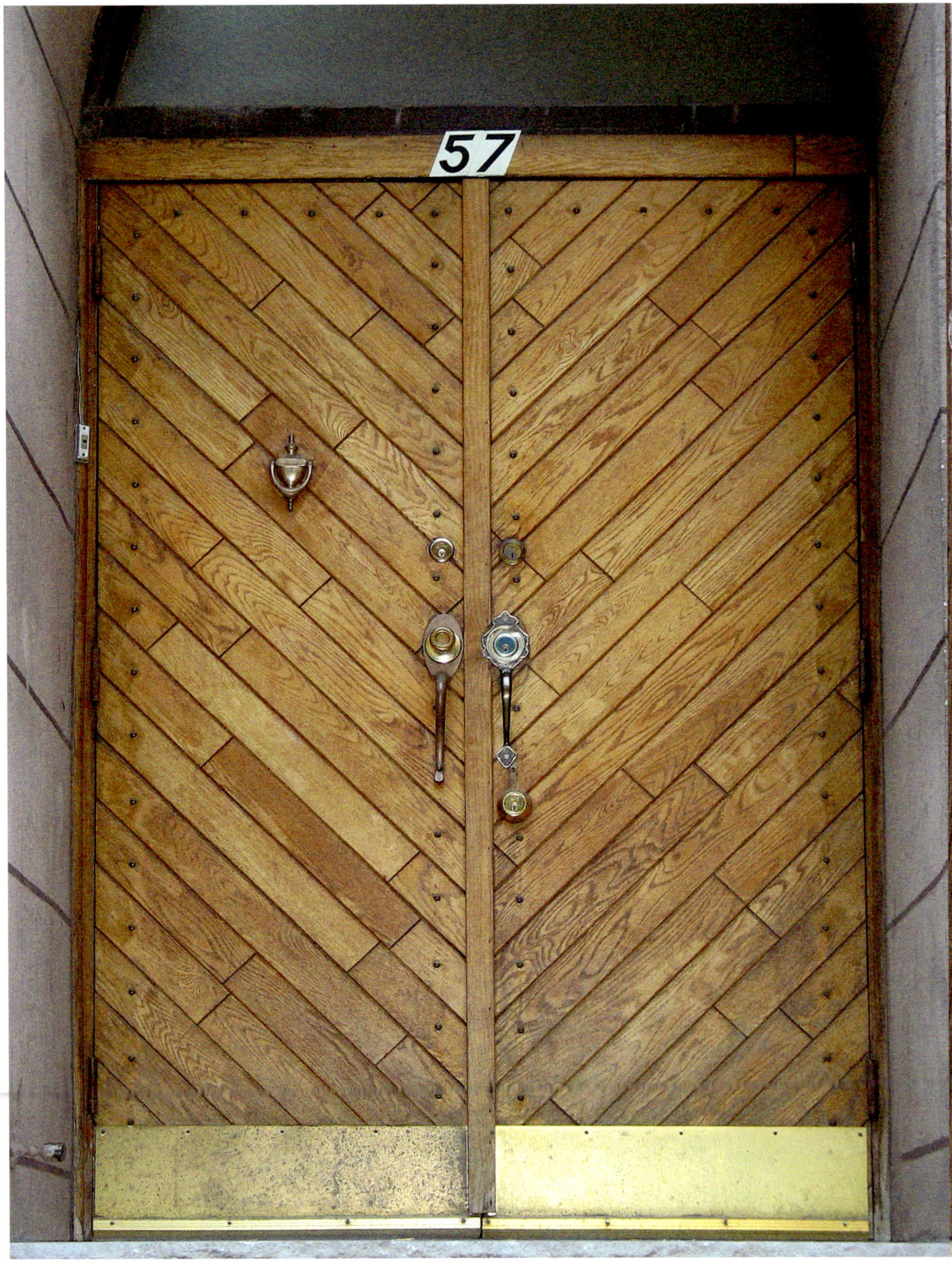
57
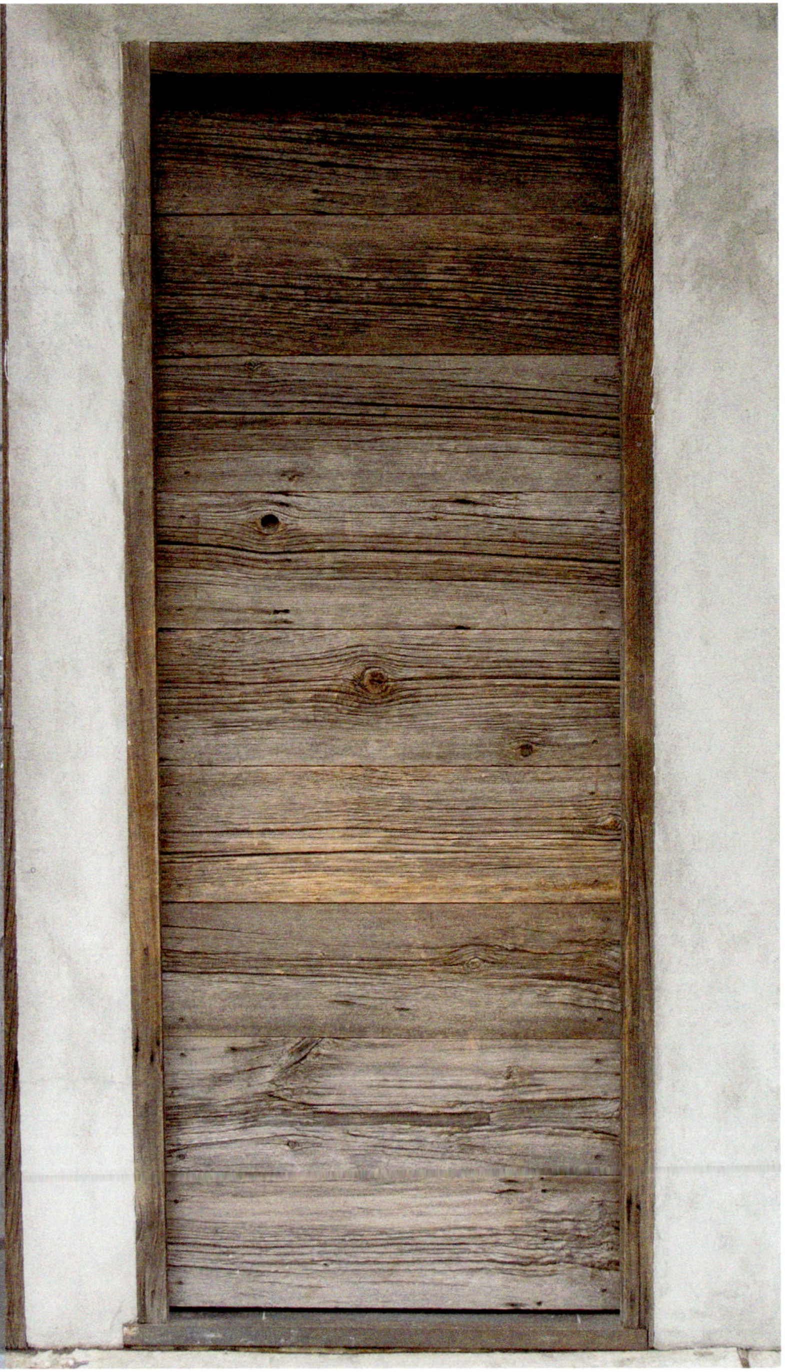

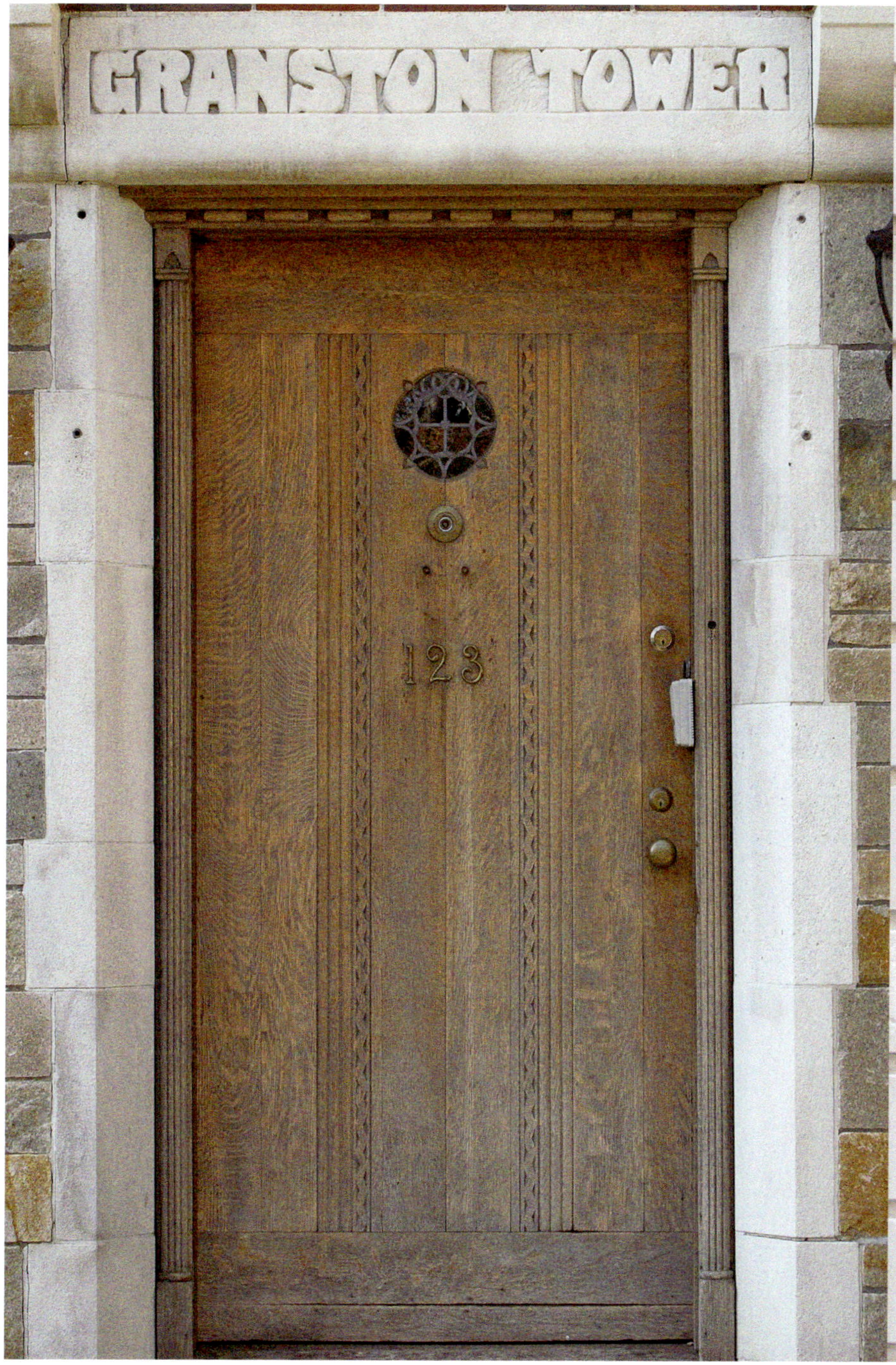
GRANSTON TOWER
123

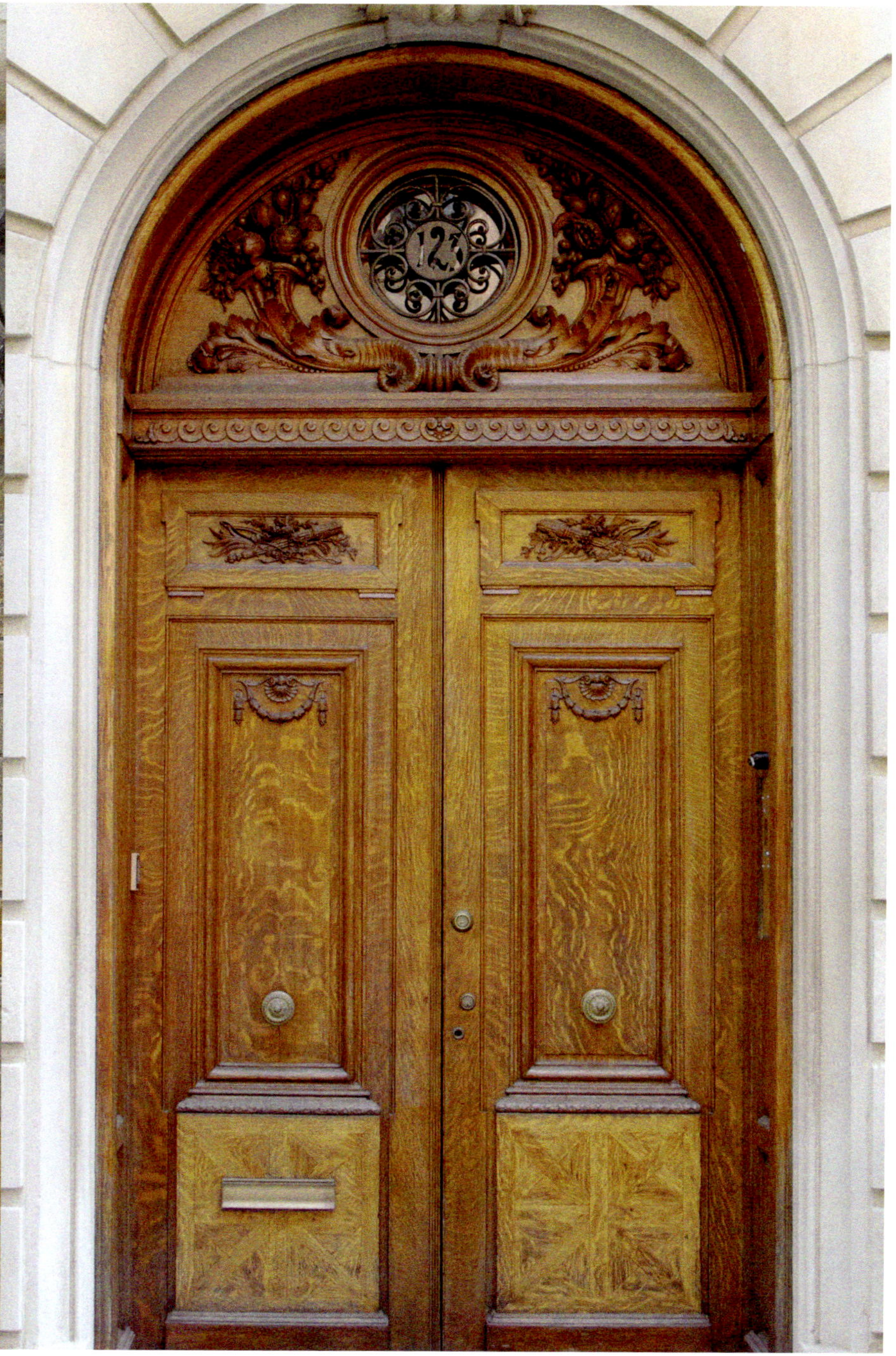
123

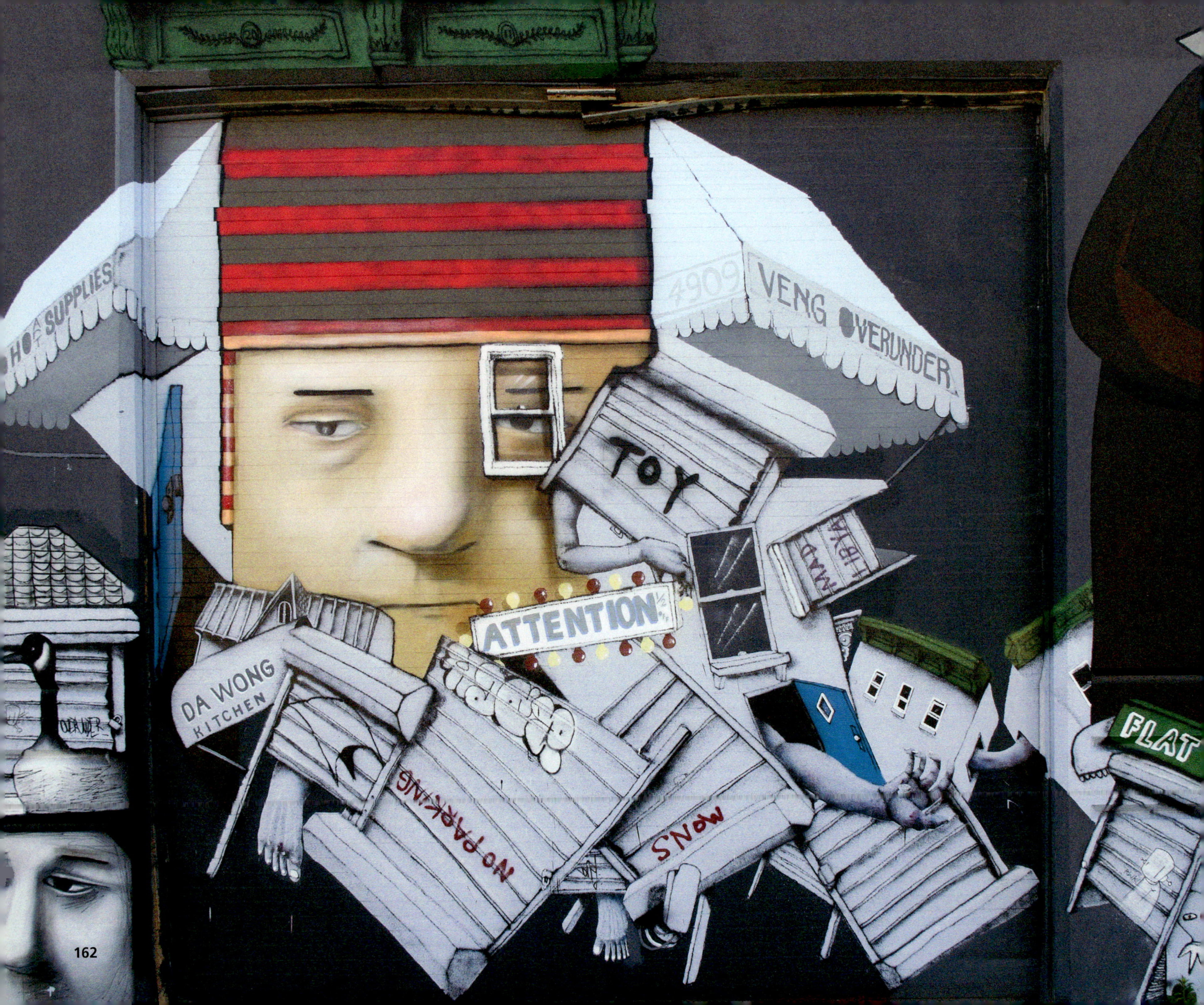
SUPPLIES
4909
VENG OVERUNDER
TOY
ATTENTION
DA WONG
KITCHEN
NO PARKING
SNOW
FLAT

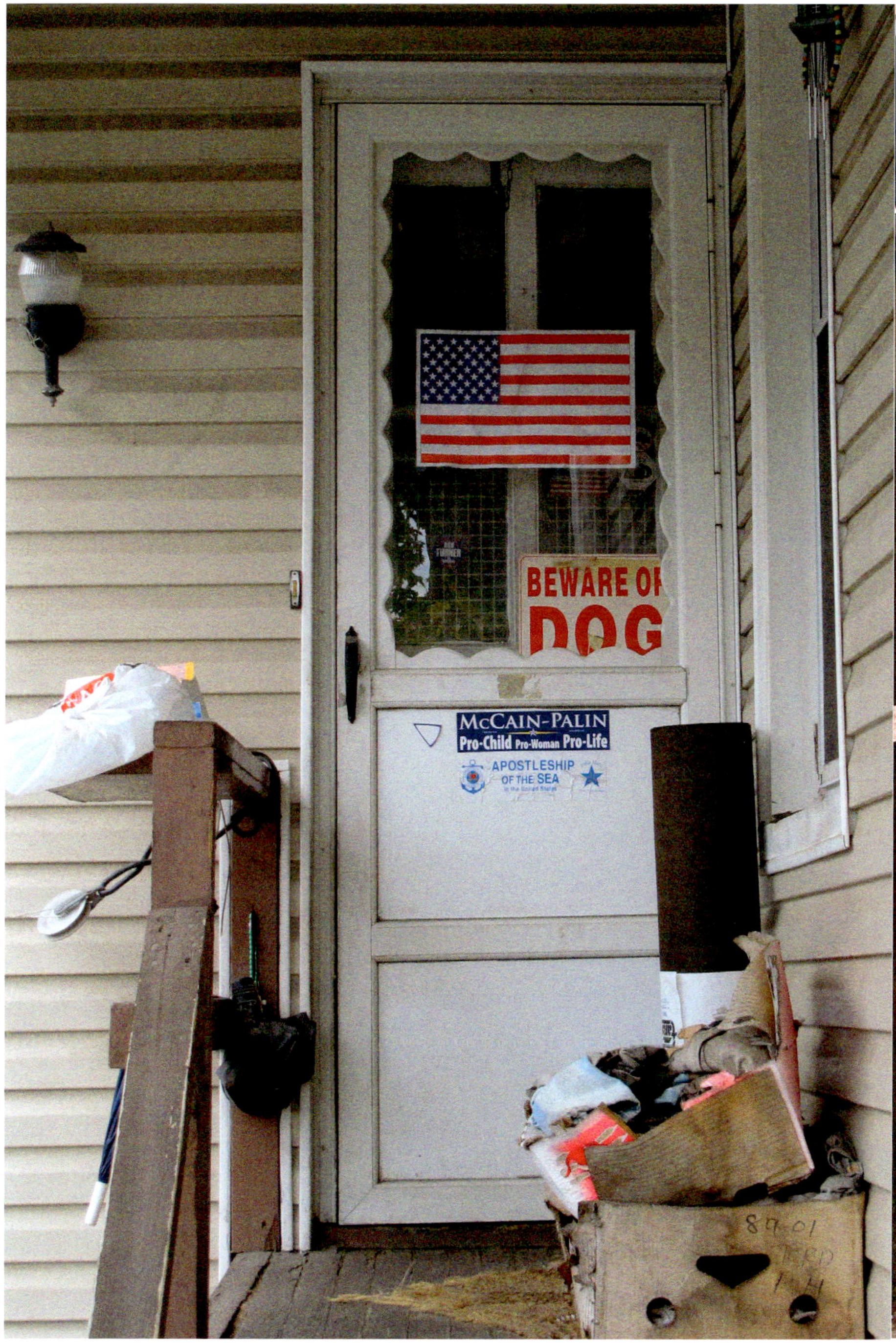
BEWARE OF
DOG
McCAIN-PALIN
Pro-Child Pro-Woman Pro-Life
APOSTLESHIP OF THE SEA
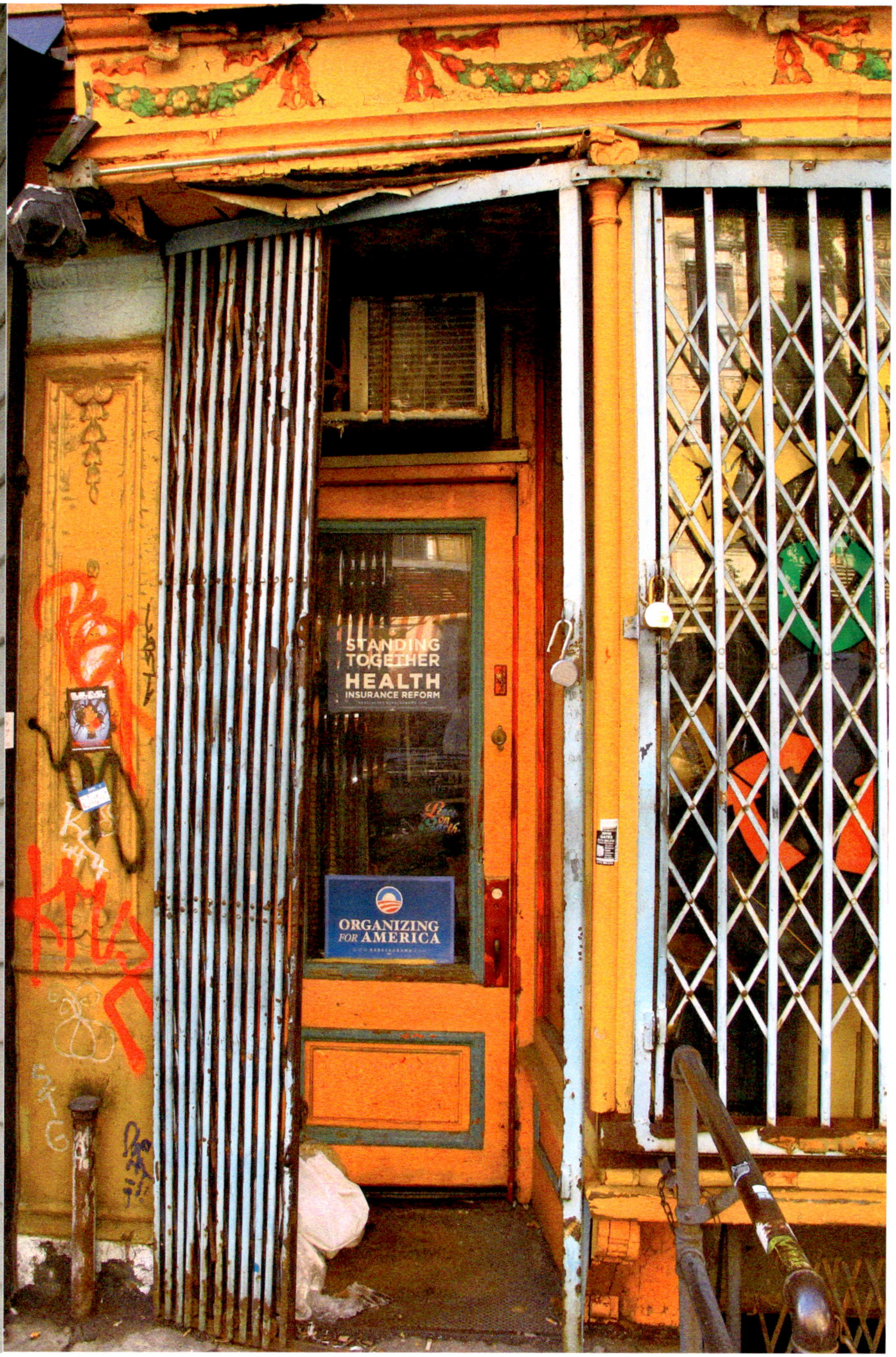
STANDING TOGETHER
HEALTH
INSURANCE REFORM
ORGANIZING FOR AMERICA

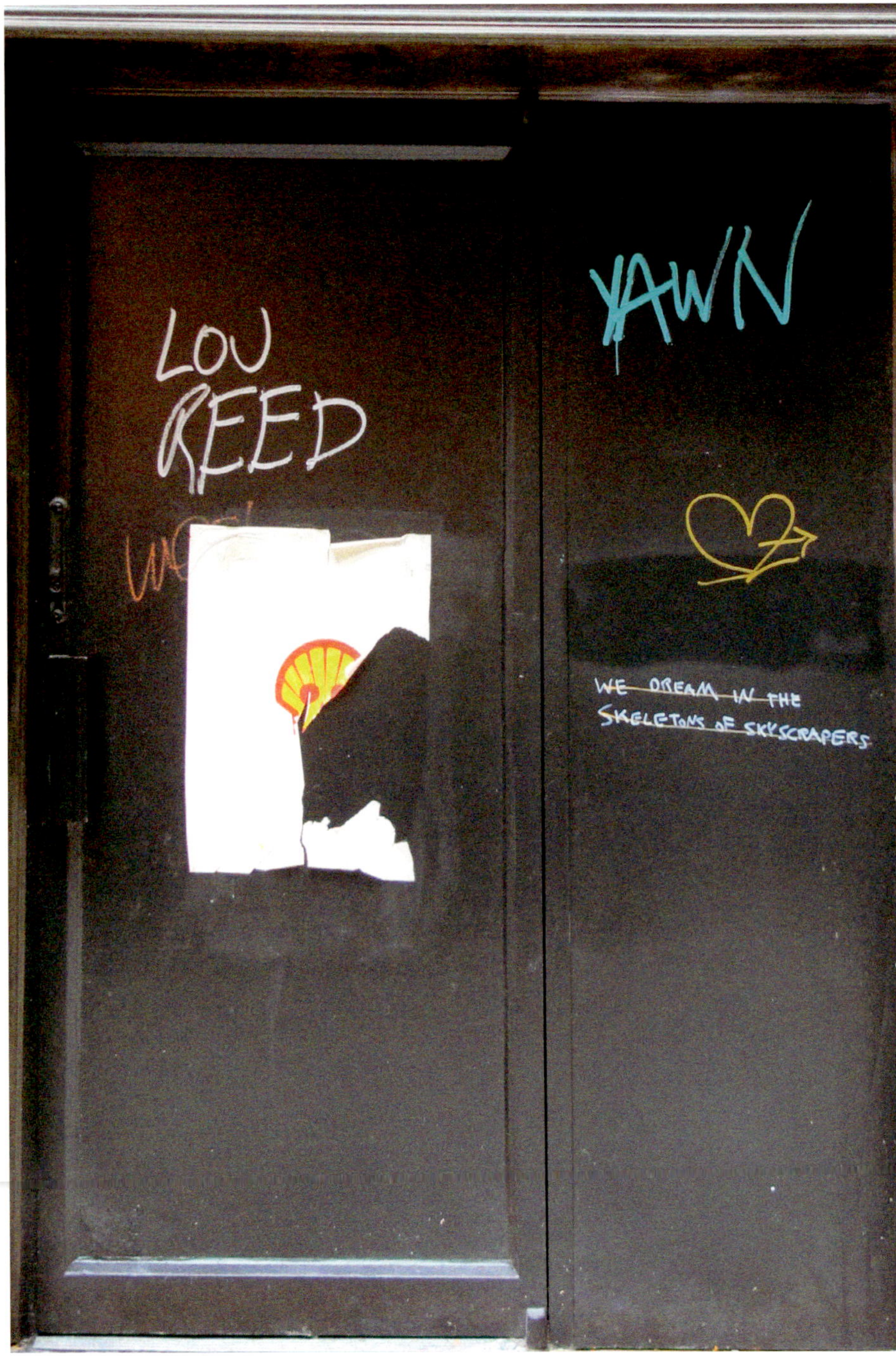
LOU REED
YAWN
WE DREAM IN THE
SKELETONS OF SKYSCRAPERS

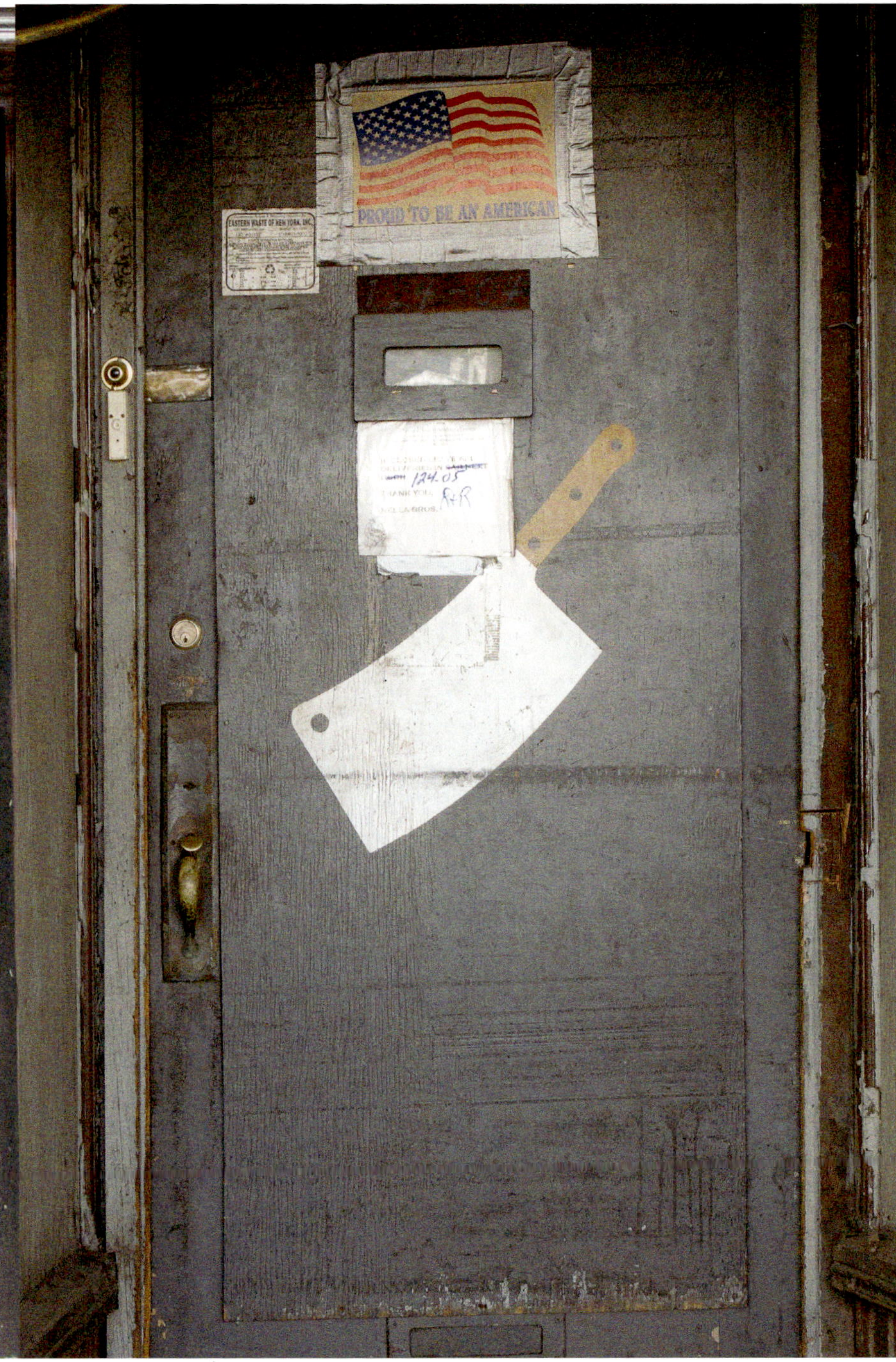
PROUD TO BE AN AMERICAN

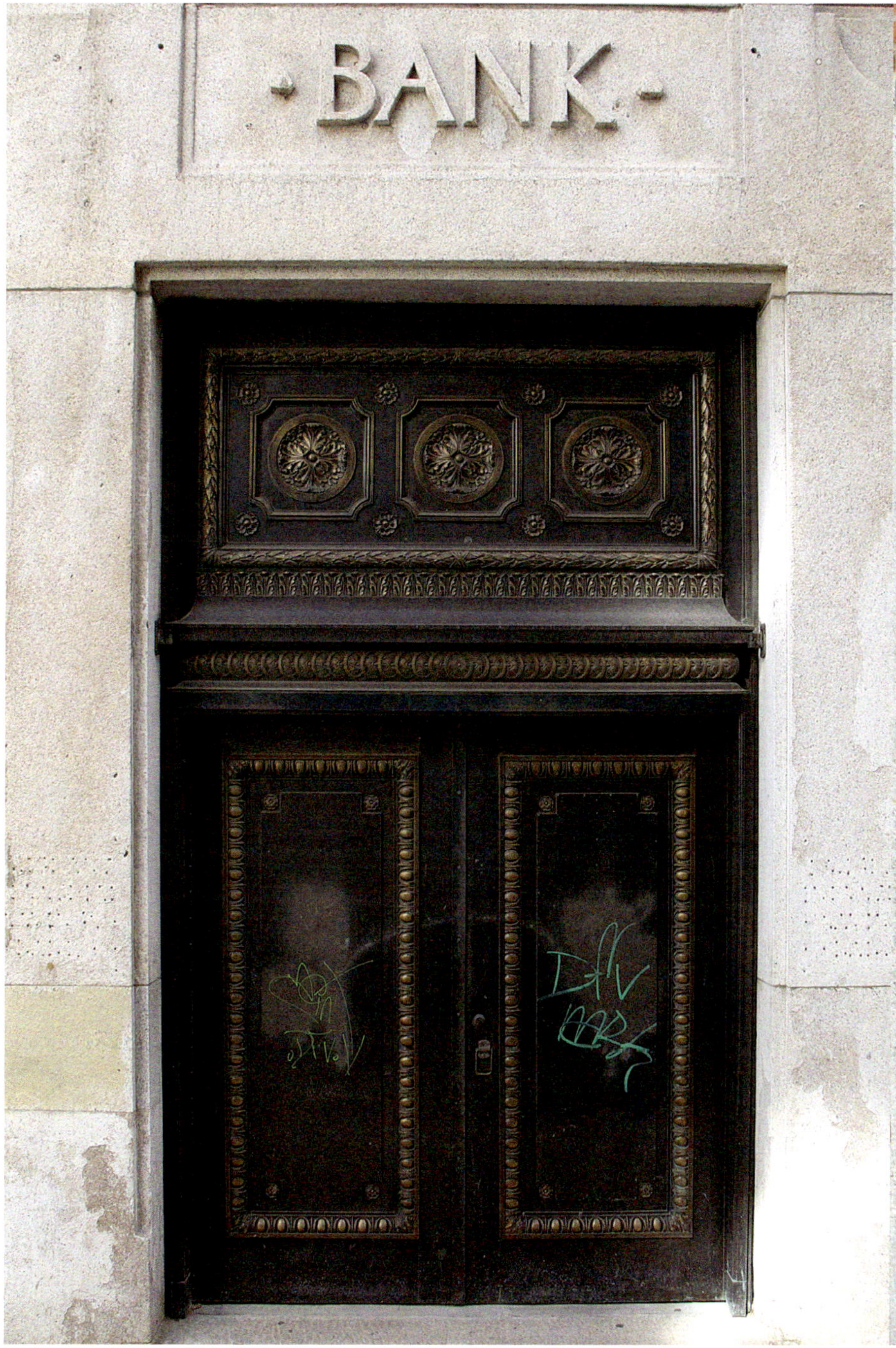
BANK

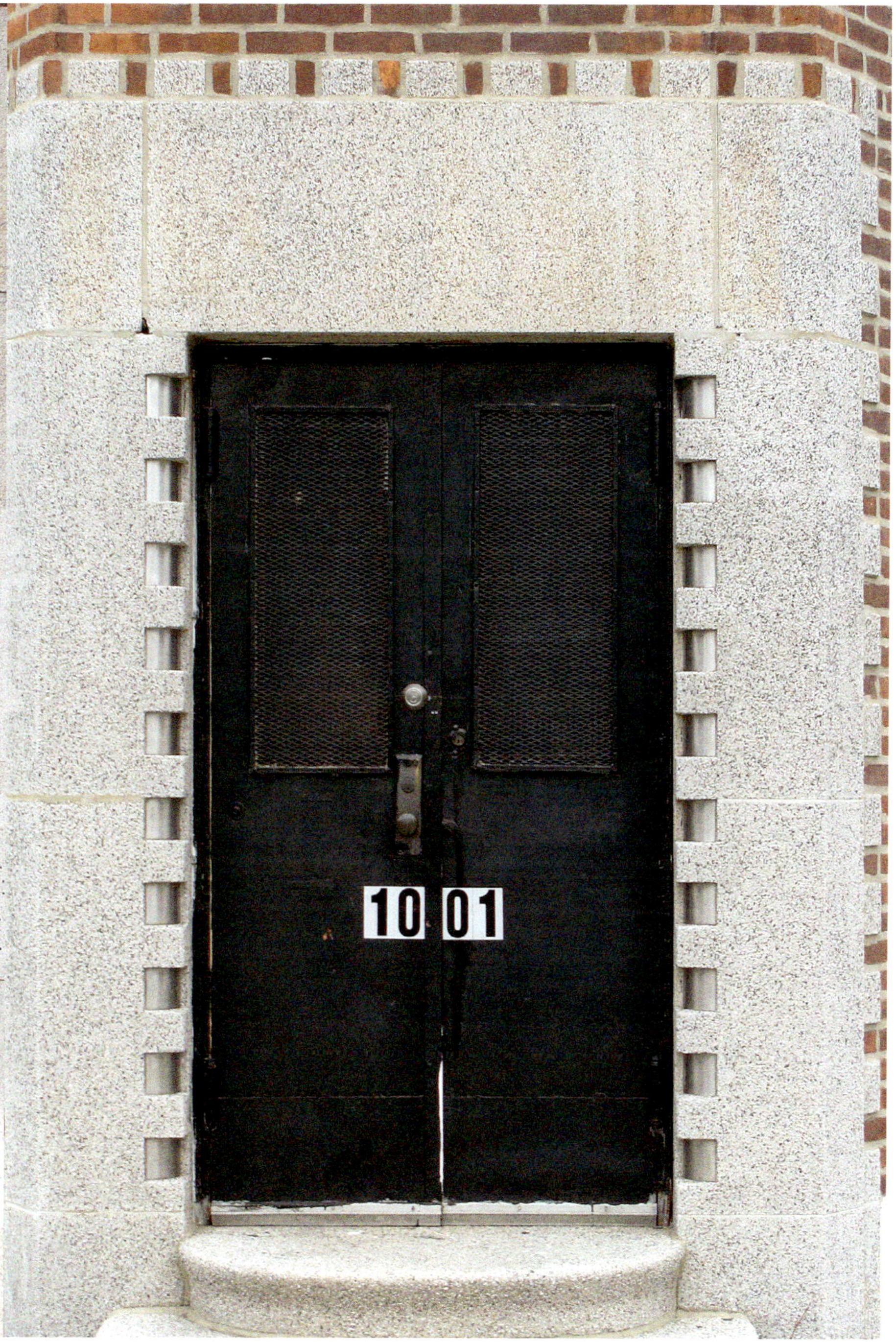
10 01

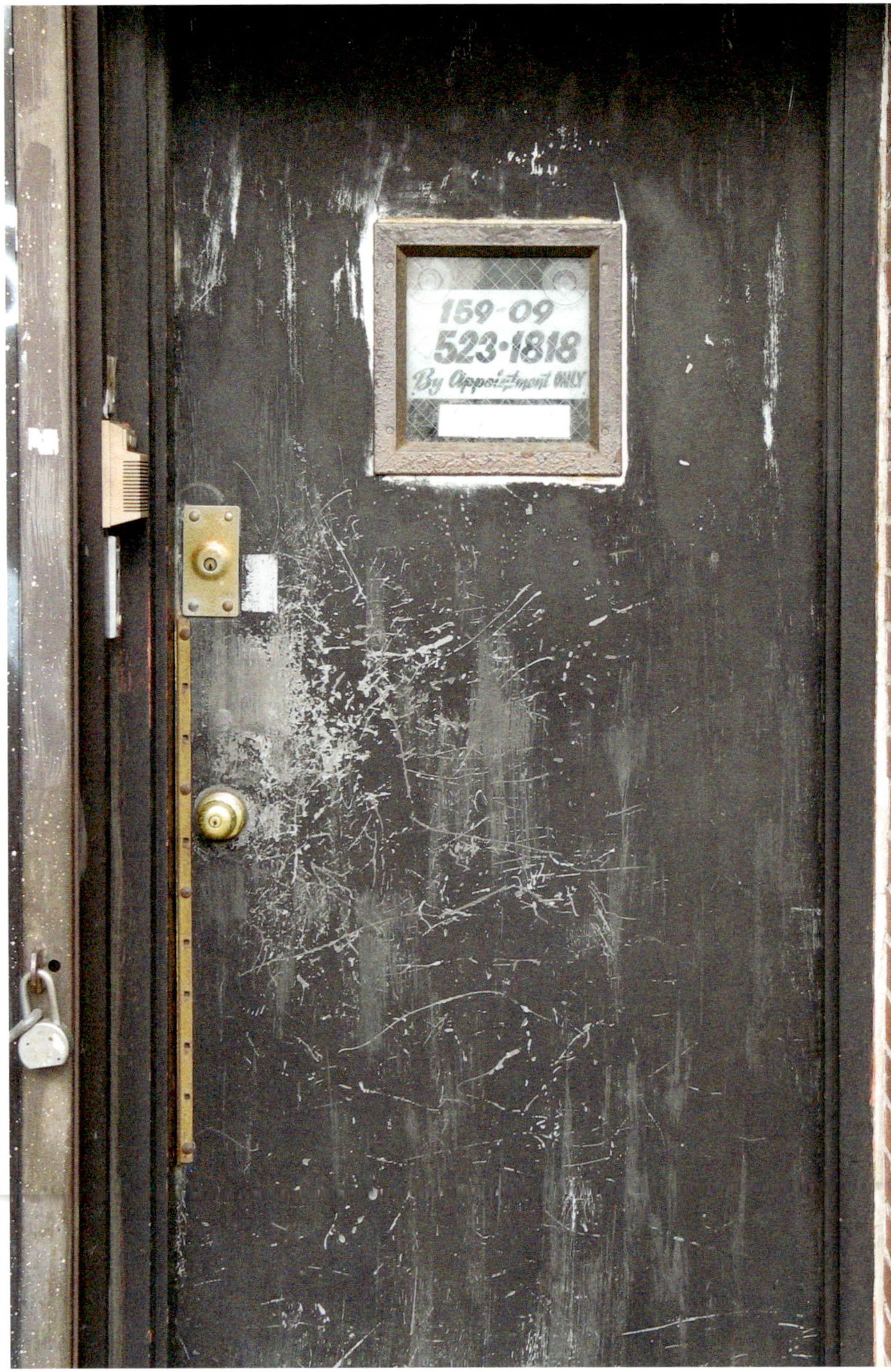
159-09
523-1818
By Appointment ONLY

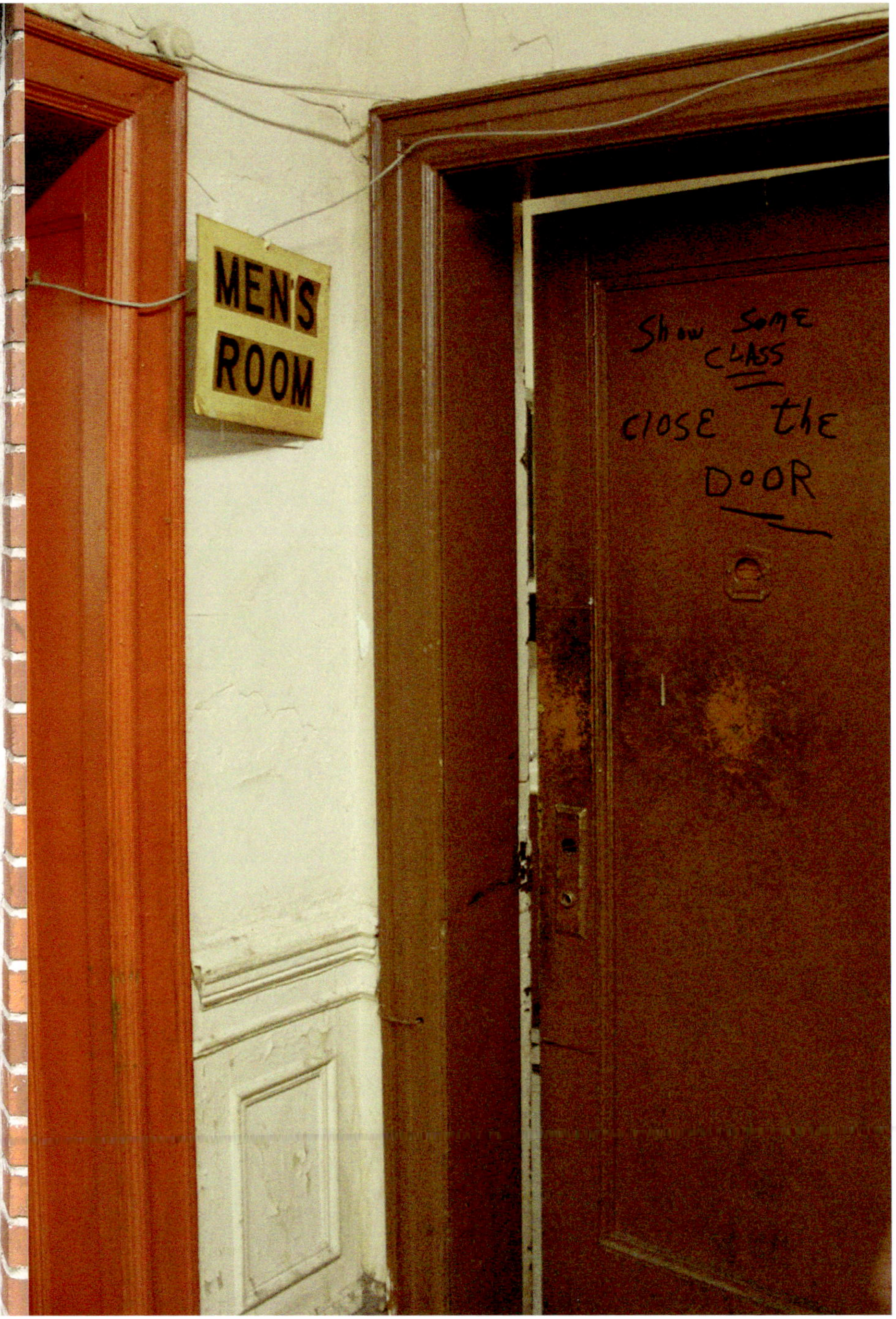
MEN'S
ROOM
Show Some
CLASS
close the
DOOR

I started photographing doors about six years ago. It was only in the last couple of years that I realized that they would make a fascinating book. I don't remember the location of a number of the doors in this collection, but when I can I've indicated where it is located and occasionally some information about the door in question.

Borough abbreviations: QNS – Queens; BX – Bronx; BKLYN – Brooklyn; MHTN – Manhattan

Doors	Pages	Locations
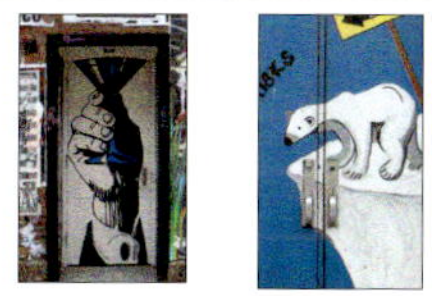	iv	Chelsea (MHTN), Gramercy Park (MHTN)
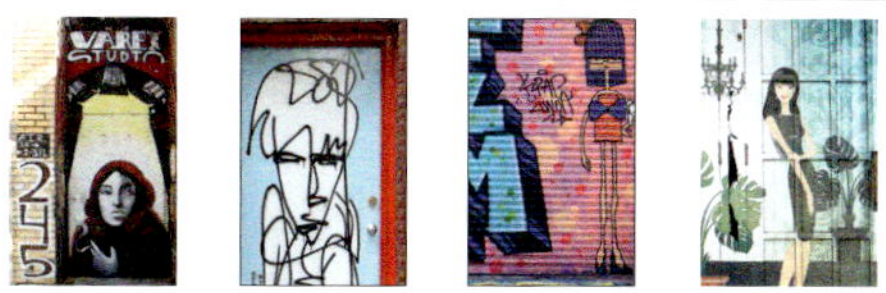	2, 3	Williamsburg (BKLYN), Chelsea (MHTN,) Long Island City (QNS), Upper East Side (MHTN) ▲ www.5ptz.com/graff/
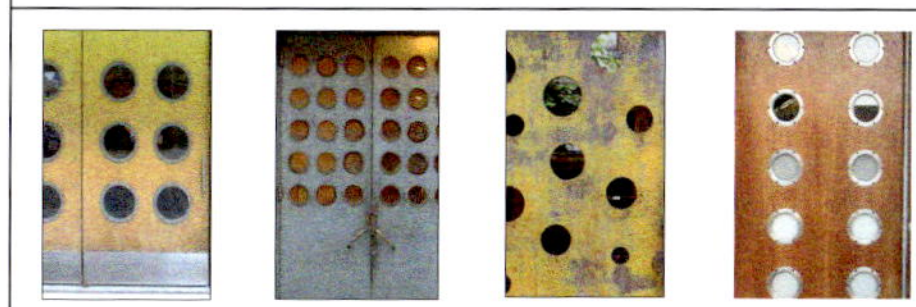	4, 5	Chelsea (MHTN), East Village (MHTN), Williamsburg (BKLYN), Chelsea (MHTN)
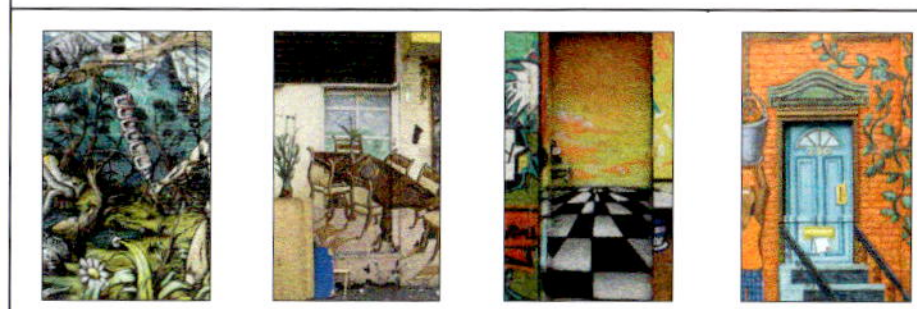	6, 7	Long Island City (QNS), Jamaica (QNS), Long Island City, Williamsburg (BKLYN) ▲ www.5ptz.com/graff/ ■ www.ps250brooklyn.org/ Magnet School for Communication and Multimedia Arts
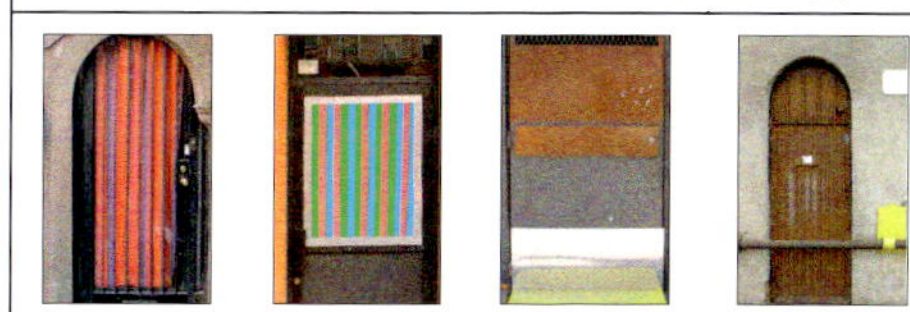	8, 9	Lenox Hill (MHTN), Alphabet City (MHTN), Lenox Hill (MHTN), Long Island City (QNS)
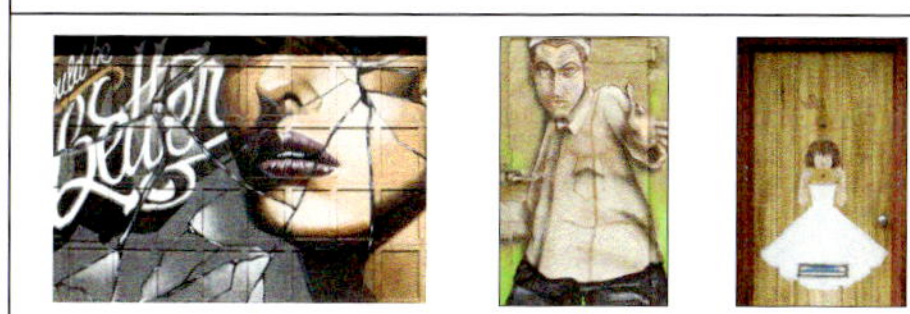	10, 11	Bushwick (BKLYN), Alphabet City (MHTN) Bushwick (BKLYN) ▲ www.cramconcepts.com
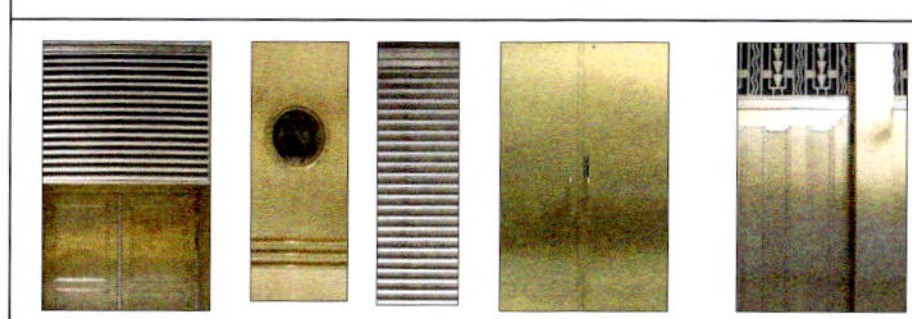	12, 13	Midtown (MHTN)
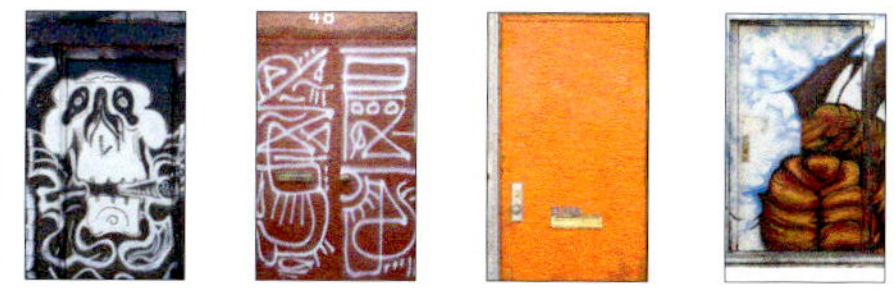	14, 15	Long Island City (QNS), NoHo (MHTN), Long Island City (QNS), Long Island City (QNS) ▲ www.5ptz.com/graff/
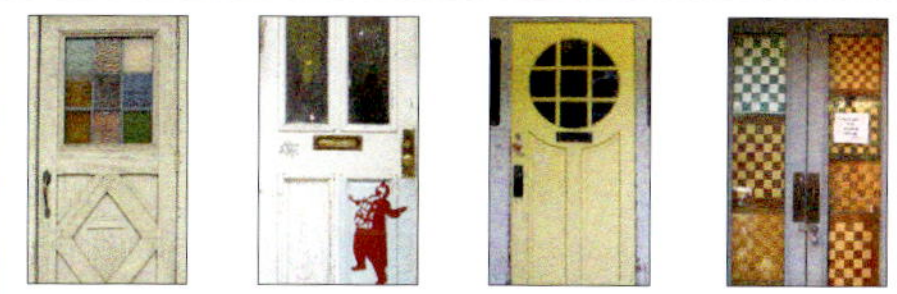	16, 17	Jamaica (QNS), Williamsburg (BKLYN), Williamsburg (BKLYN), East Village (MHTN)
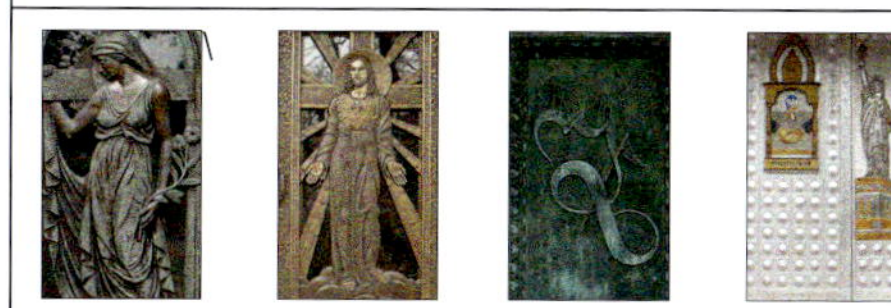	18, 19	Woodlawn Cemetery (BX), Maple Grove Cemetery (QNS), Woodlawn Cemetery (BX), Jamaica (QNS) ▲ www.thewoodlawncemetery.org/site/ ■ www.maplegrove.biz
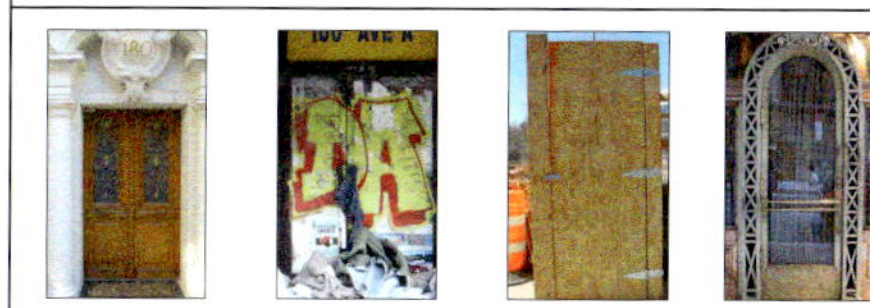	20, 21	Lenox Hill (MHTN), Lower East Side (MHTN), Briarwood (QNS), St. Regis Hotel Bellhop Station-Midtown (MHTN)
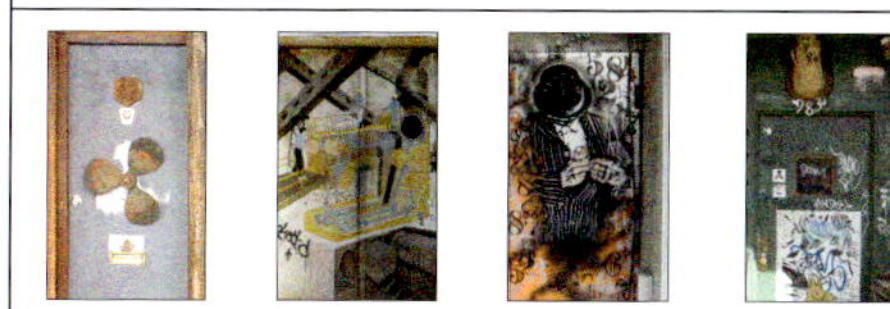	22, 23	East Village (MHTN), Williamsburg (BKLYN), Chinatown (MHTN), Bushwick (BKLYN)
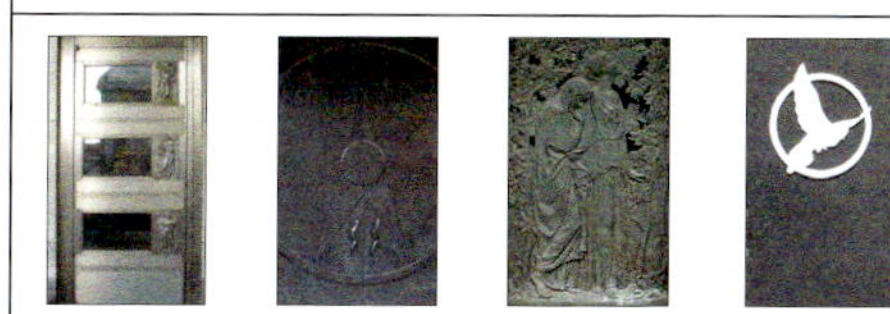	24, 25	United Nations (MHTN), Chelsea (MHTN), Woodlawn Cemetary (BX), Long Island City (QNS) ▲ www.un.org ■ www.thewoodlawncemetery.org/site/
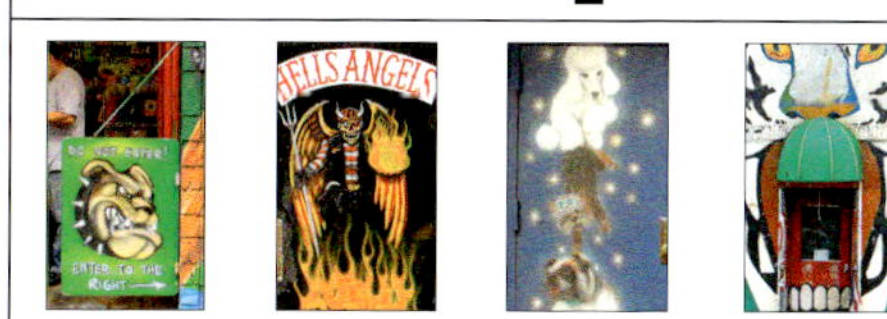	26, 27	Greenwich Village (MHTN), East Village (MHTN), Murry Hill (MHTN), Kew Gardens (QNS) ▲ Car wash that appeared in the Eddie Murphy movie *Coming to America*. Sadly, it's been painted over.
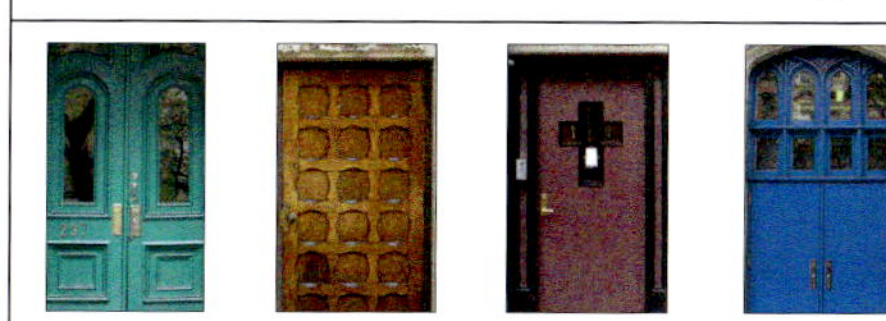	28, 29	Kips Bay (MHTN)

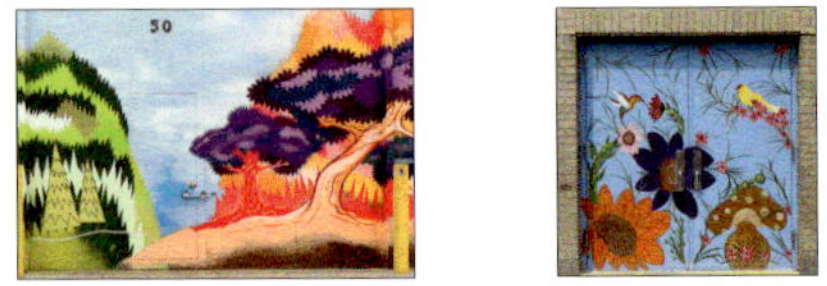 ▲	30, 31	Williamsburg (BKLYN), Ozone Park, (QNS) ▲ Public School 100 Queens
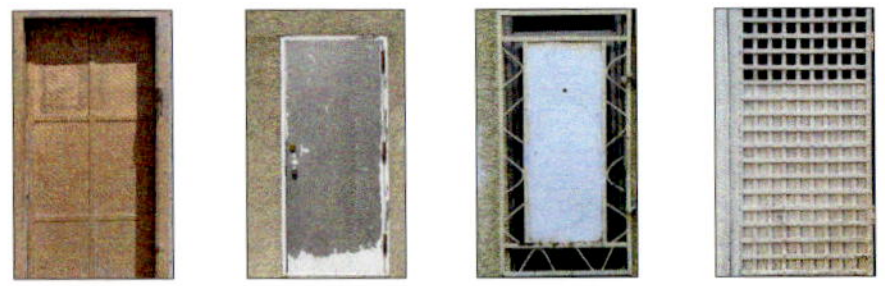	32, 33	Long Island City (QNS), Williamsburg (BKLYN), SoHo (MHTN), East Village (MHTN)
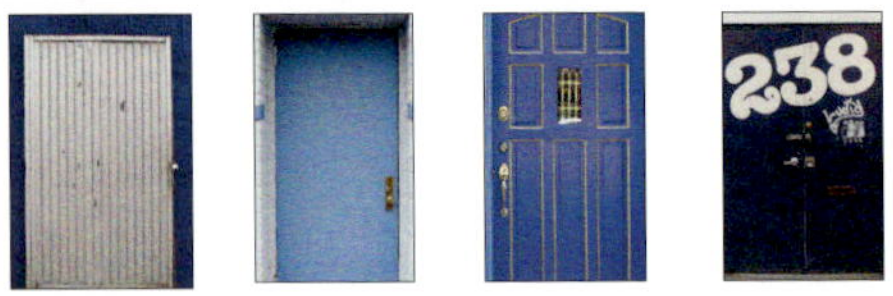	34, 35	Richmond Hill (QNS), Richmond Hill (QNS), Long Island City (QNS), Kips Bay (MHTN)
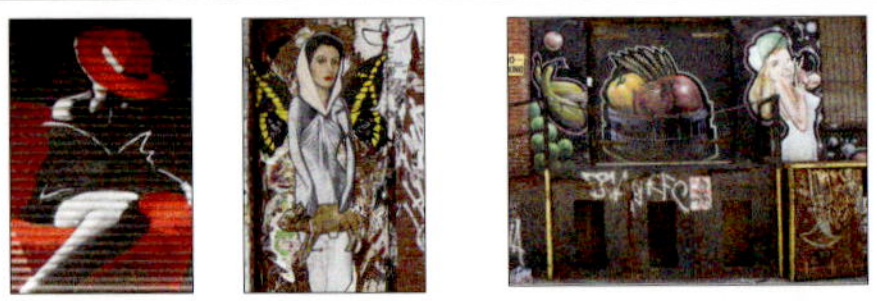	36, 37	Castle Hill (BX), Williamsburg (BKLYN), Williamsburg (BKLYN)
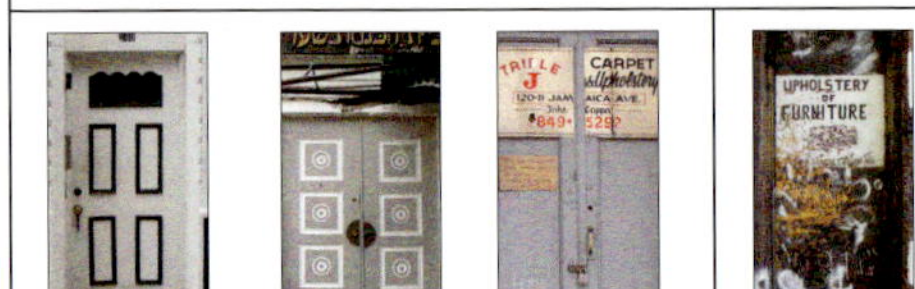	38, 39	Lower East Side (MHTN), Kew Gardens (QNS), Jamaica (QNS), Kew Gardens (QNS)
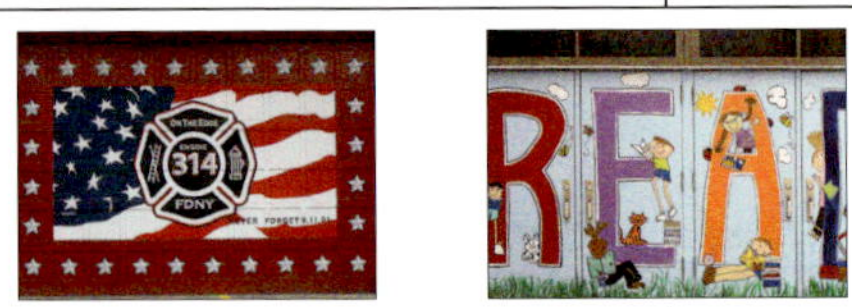 ▲	40, 41	Ozone Park (QNS) ▲ Public School 100 Queens
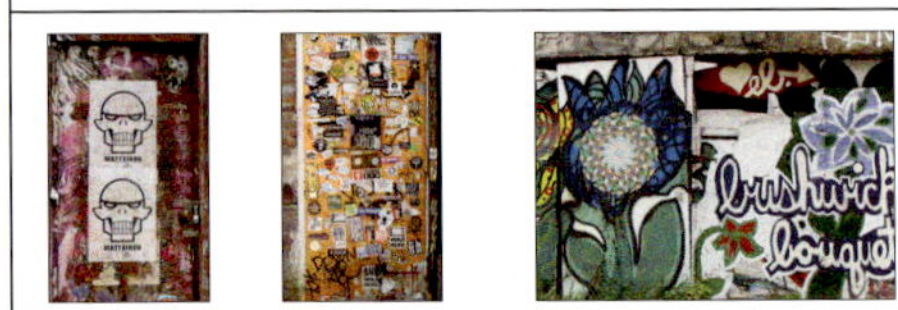 ▲	42, 43	Williamsburg (BKLYN), Dumbo (BKLYN), Bushwick (BKLYN) ▲ mattsiren.com/home.html
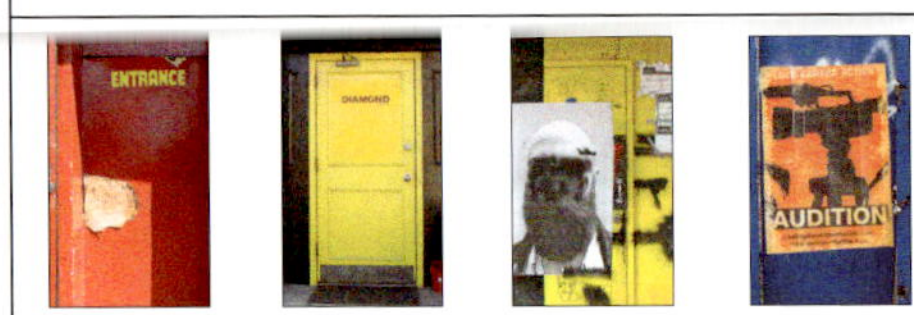	44, 45	Kew Gardens (QNS), Williamsburg (BKLYN), East Village (MHTN), Greenwich Village (MHTN)

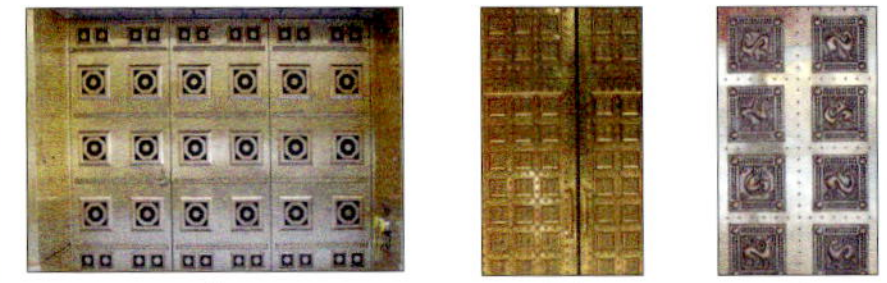 ▲ ■ ●	46, 47	Turtle Bay (MHTN), Turtle Bay (MHTN), Midtown (MHTN) ▲ Kuwaiti Mission to the United Nations ■ Permanent Mission of India to the United Nations ● russiantearoomnyc.com
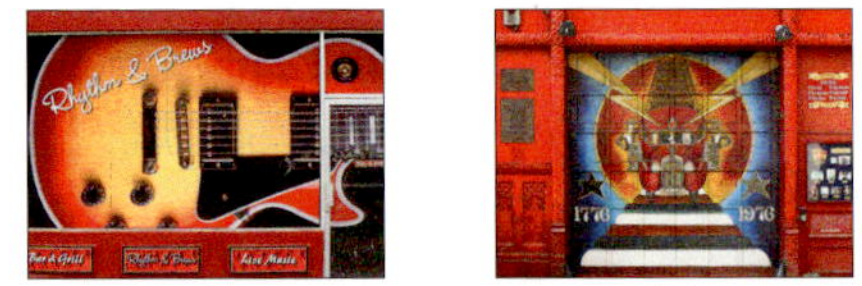 ▲ ■	48, 49	Staten Island, Squad 18 - West Village (MHTN) ▲ facebook.com/Rhythmandbrewssi ■ www.fdnysquad18.com
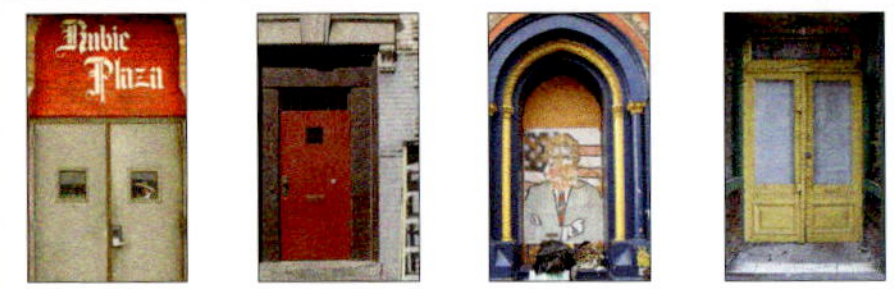 ▲	50, 51	Richmond Hill (QNS), Woodhaven (QNS), Bushwick (BKLYN), Lower East Side (MHTN) ▲ Original home of Rubies Costume Company - www.rubies.com
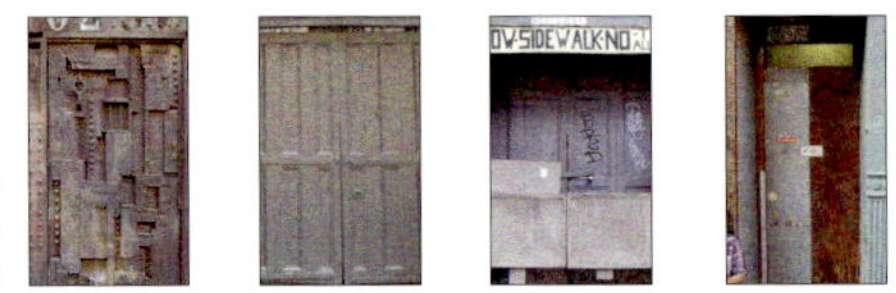	52, 53	SoHo (MHTN), SoHo (MHTN), Chinatown (MHTN), Greenwich Village (MHTN)
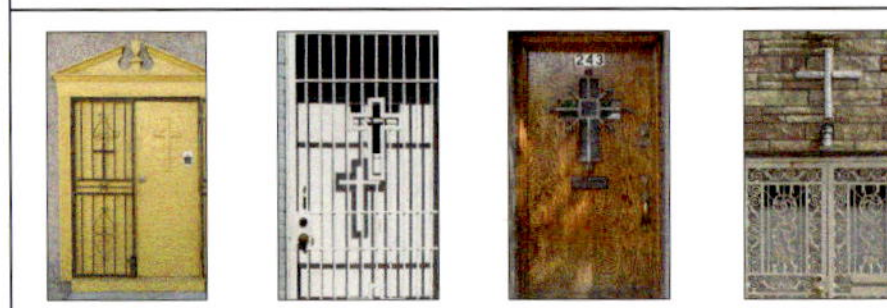	54, 55	Corona (QNS), Bedford Stuyvesant (BKLYN), Park Slope (BKLYN), Jamaica (QNS)
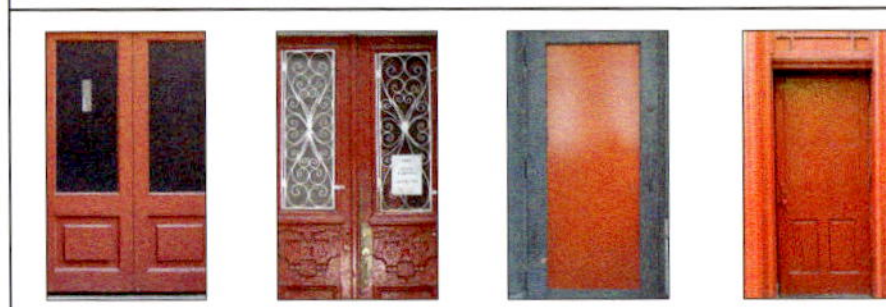	56, 57	SoHo (MHTN), East Village (MHTN), Greenwich Village (MHTN), Brooklyn
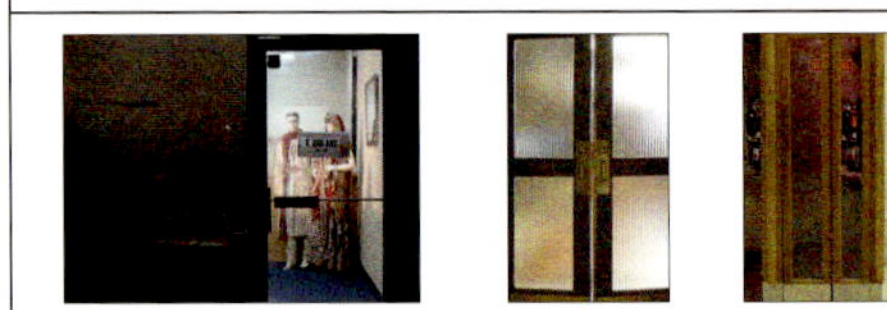 ▲ ▲	58, 59	Jamaica (QNS), Midtown (MHTN), Midtown (MHTN) ▲ www.nypl.org/
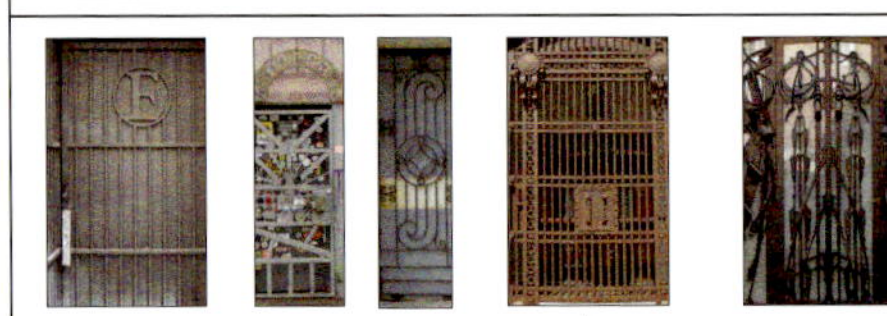 ▲	60, 61	Kips Bay (MHTN), Williamsburg (BKLYN), Midtown (MHTN), Richmond Hill (QNS), Sutton Place (MHTN) ▲ American Byelorussian St. Cyril of Turov Orthodox Church

Photos	Pages	Locations
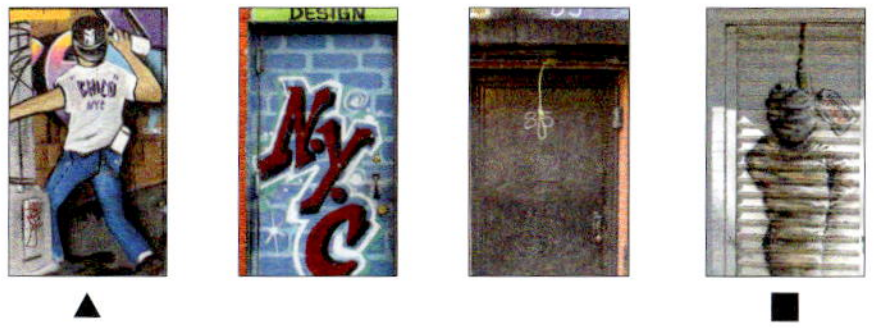	62, 63	Lower East Side (MHTN), Lower East Side (MHTN), East Village (MHTN), Alphabet City (MHTN) ▲ www.chicoartnyc.com/ ■ www.stillcounting.net/
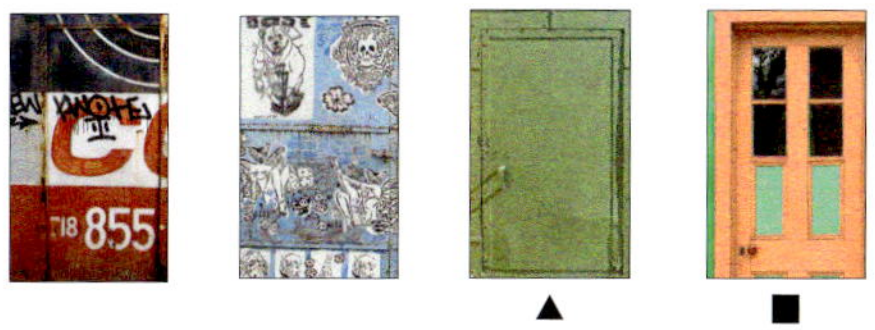	64, 65	Dumbo (BKLYN), Bushwick (BKLYN), Middle Village (QNS), Staten Island ▲ Service entrance to St. John's Cemetery, interred here are mobsters: John Gotti, Lucky Luciano, Joe Gallo, Carlo Gambino, Vito Genovese, and Carmine Galante. Also, photographer Robert Mapplethorpe and Charles Atlas. ■ historicrichmondtown.org/
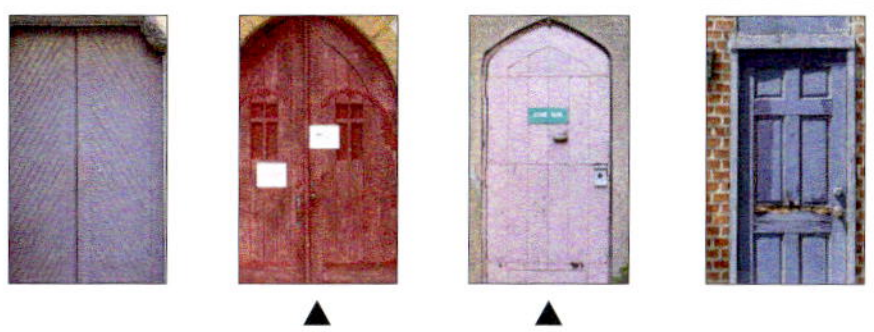	66, 67	Park Slope (BKLYN), Staten Island, Staten Island, Middle Village (QNS) ▲ historicrichmondtown.org/
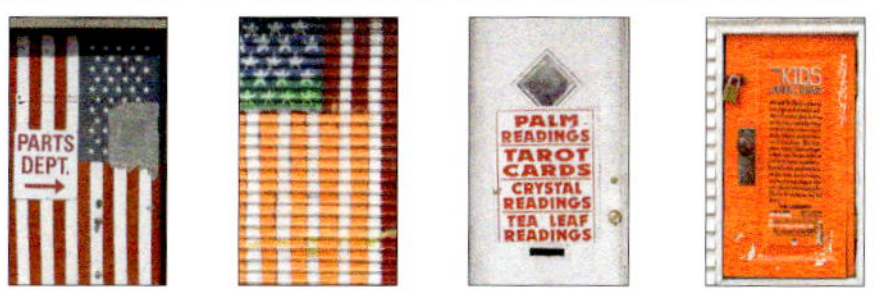	68, 69	Richmond Hill (QNS), Williamsburg (BKLYN), Jamaica (QNS), Williamsburg (BKLYN)
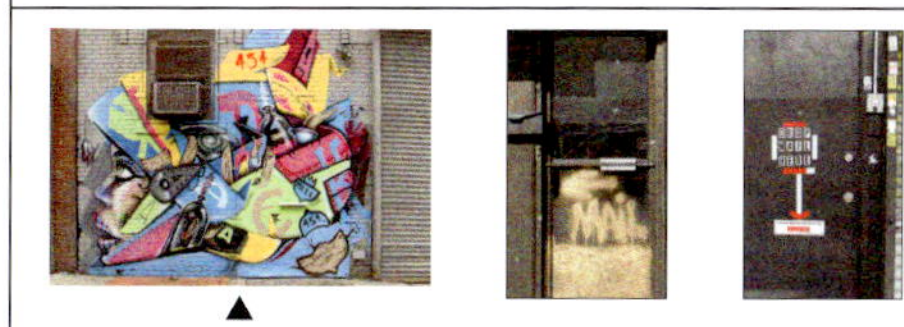	70, 71	Bushwick (BKLYN), Richmond Hill (QNS), Richmond Hill (QNS) ▲ daekwilliam.com/
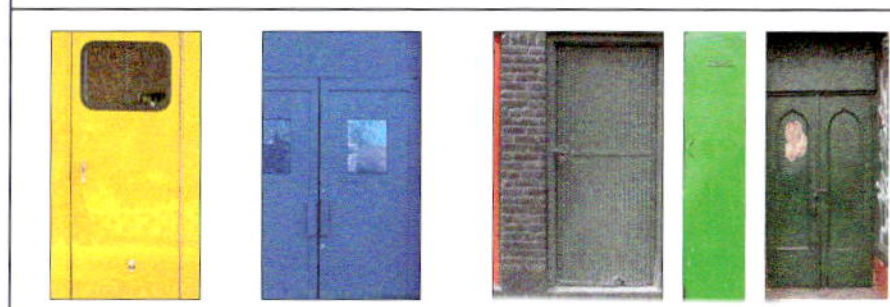	72, 73	Midtown (MHTN), unknown, Chelsea (MHTN), Kew Gardens (QNS), Bushwick (BKLYN)
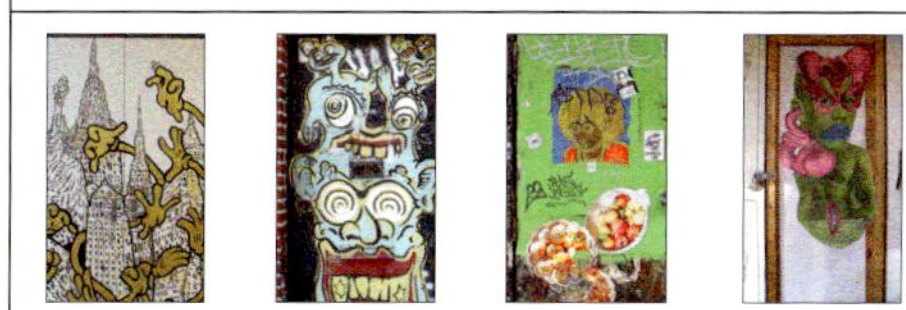	74, 75	Midtown (MHTN), Bushwick (BKLYN), Chelsea (MHTN), Greenwich Village (MHTN)
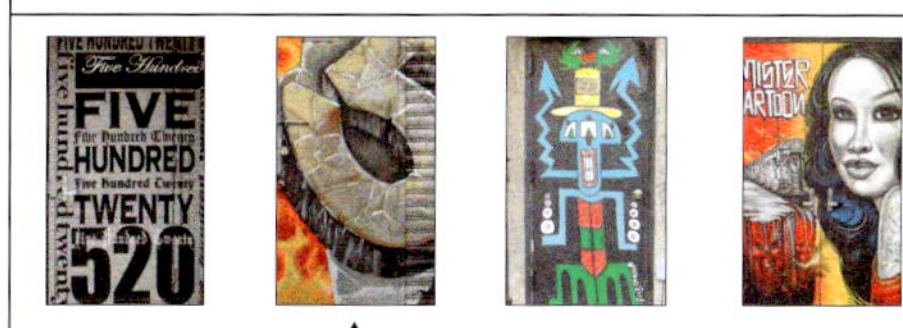	76, 77	Chelsea (MHTN), Long Island City (QNS), Lower East Side (MHTN), Midtown (MHTN) ▲ www.5ptz.com/graff/
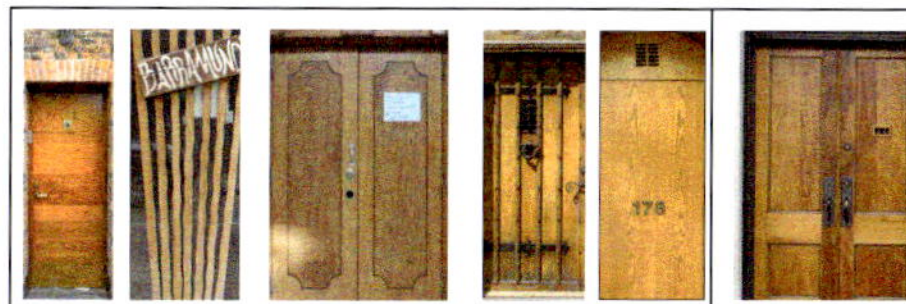	78, 79	Manhattan, Chinatown (MHTN), Jamaica (QNS), Forest Hills Gardens (QNS), Manhattan, Kips Bay (MHTN)
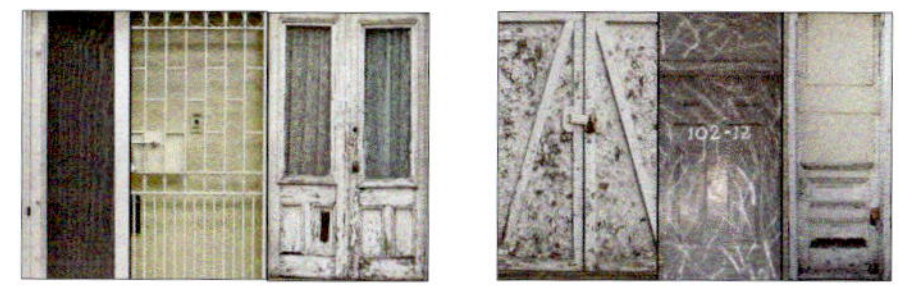	80, 81	Beekman (MHTN), Jamaica (QNS), Greenpoint (BKLYN), Kew Gardens (QNS), Richmond Hill (QNS), Bushwick (BKLYN)
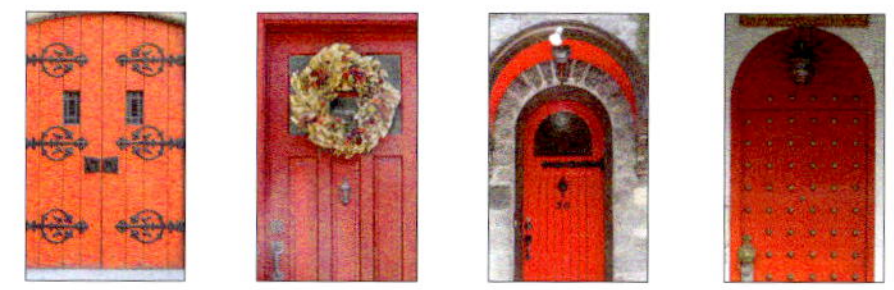	82, 83	Unknown, Forest Hills Gardens (QNS), Forest Hills Gardens (QNS), Flushing Chinatown (QNS)
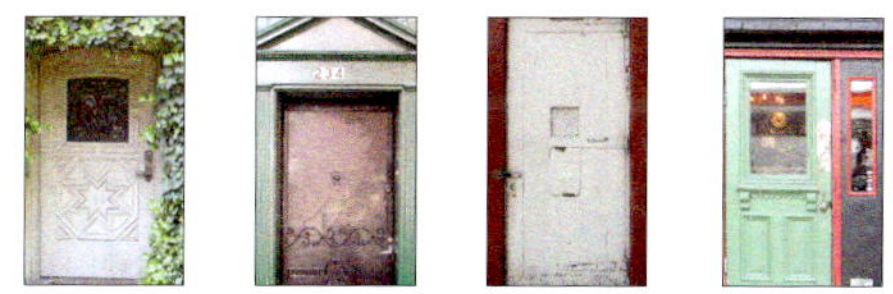	84, 85	Forest Hills Gardens (QNS), Brooklyn, Jamaica (QNS), Williamsburg (BKLYN)
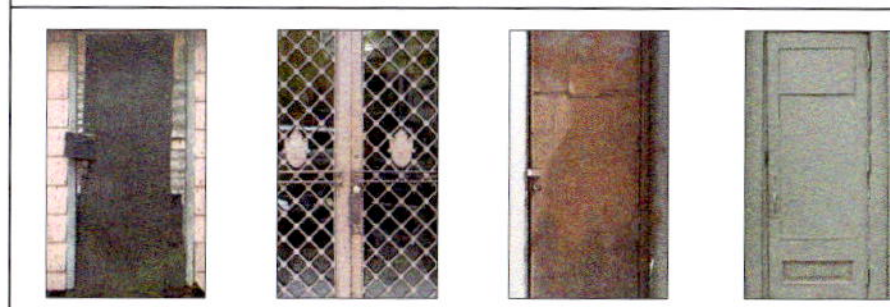	86, 87	Briarwood (QNS),Lower East Side (MHTN), Jamaica (QNS), East Village (MHTN)
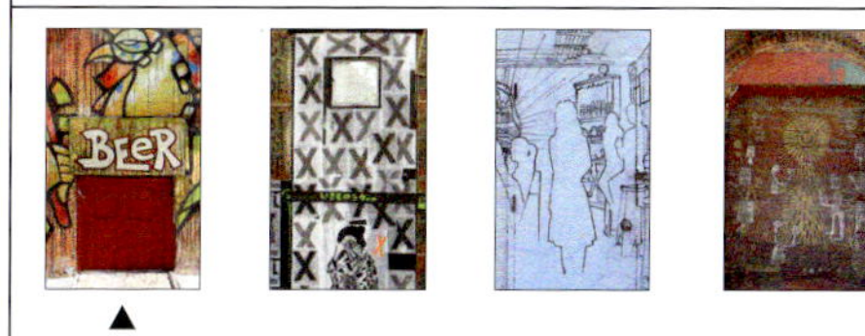	88, 89	Dumbo (BKLYN), Lower East Side (MHTN), Chinatown (MHTN), Dumbo (BKLYN) ▲ pedrosdumbo.net
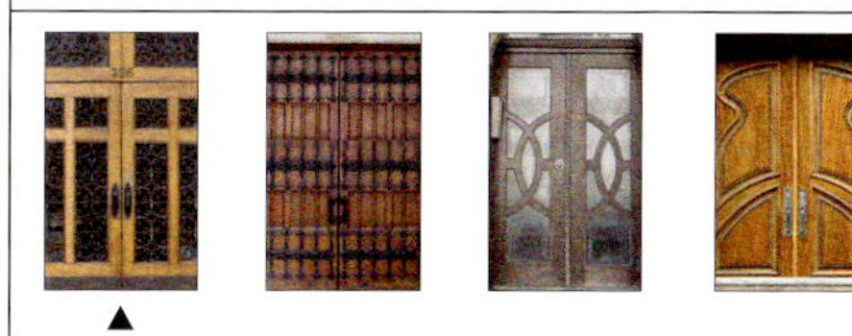	90, 91	St. Barts Church (MHTN), Lenox Hill (MHTN), Park Slope (BKLYN), Fresh Meadows (QNS) ▲ St. Bart's - historic Episcopal parish founded in 1835
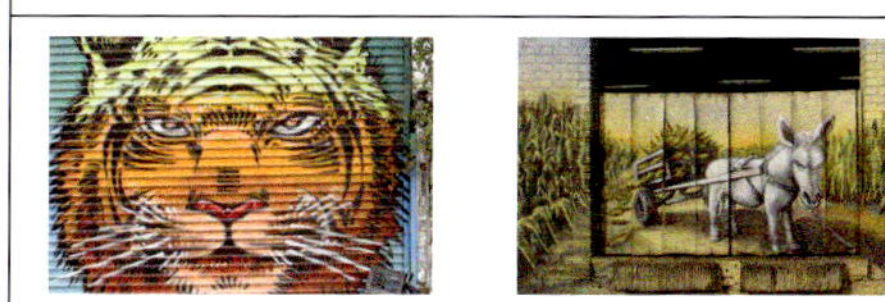	92, 93	Williamsburg (BKLYN))

Images	Pages	Locations
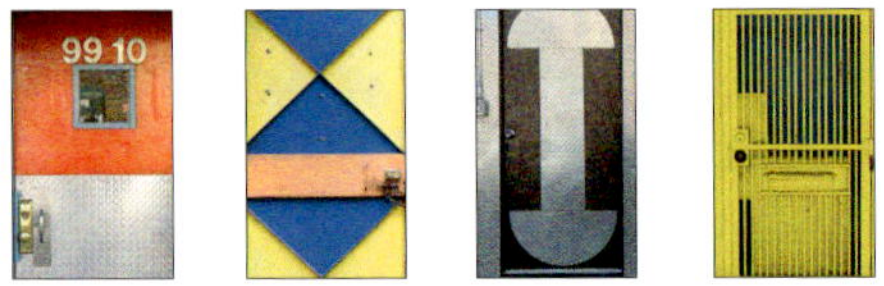	94, 95	Corona (QNS), Lower East Side (MHTN), Corona (QNS)
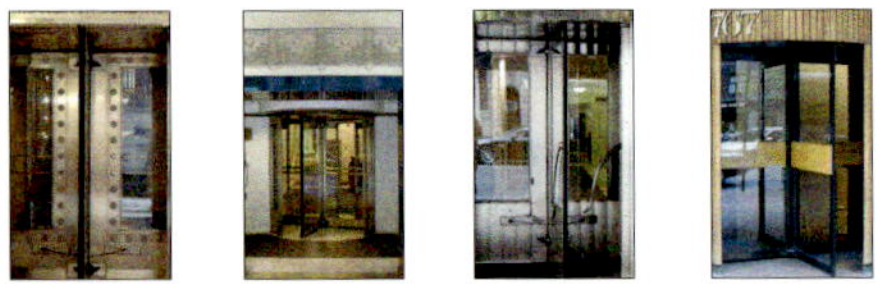	96, 97	Midtown (MHTN)
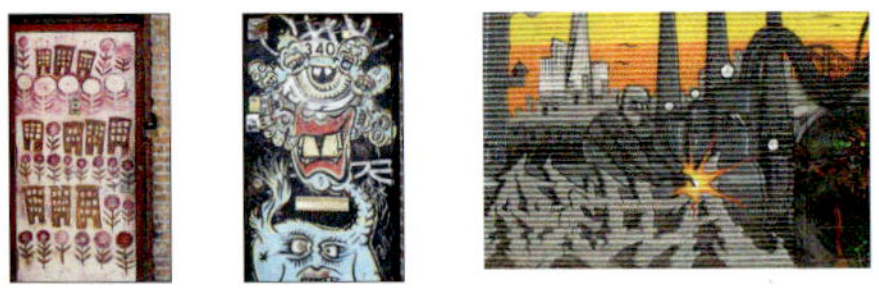	98, 99	Dumbo (BKLYN), Bushwick (BKLYN), Lower East Side (MHTN)
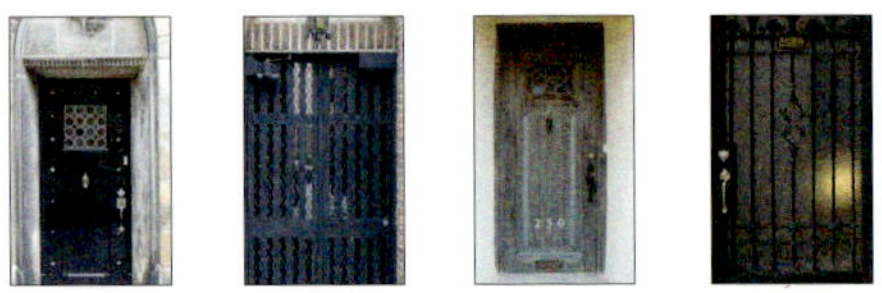	100, 101	Beekman (MHTN), Beekman (MHTN), Forest Hills Gardens (QNS), Beekman (MHTN)
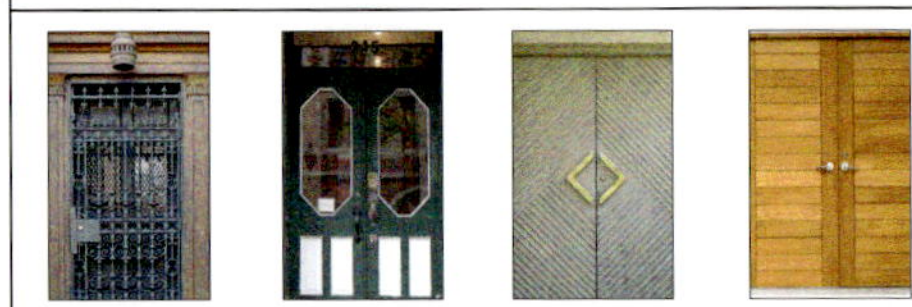	102, 103	Kips Bay (MHTN), Kips Bay (MHTN), Douglaston Manor (QNS), Fresh Meadows (QNS)
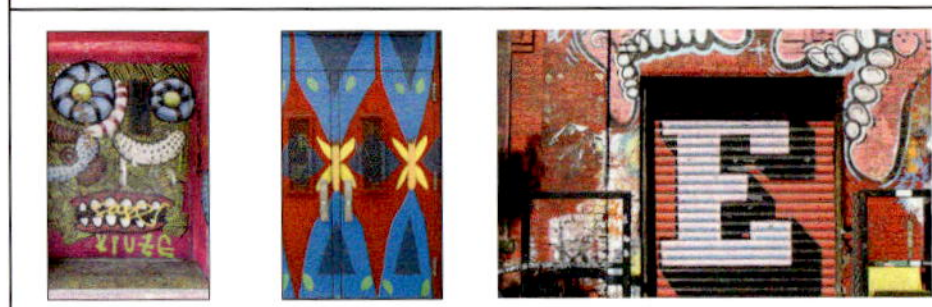	104, 105	Chinatown (MHTN), Chinatown (MHTN), Williamsburg (BKLYN)
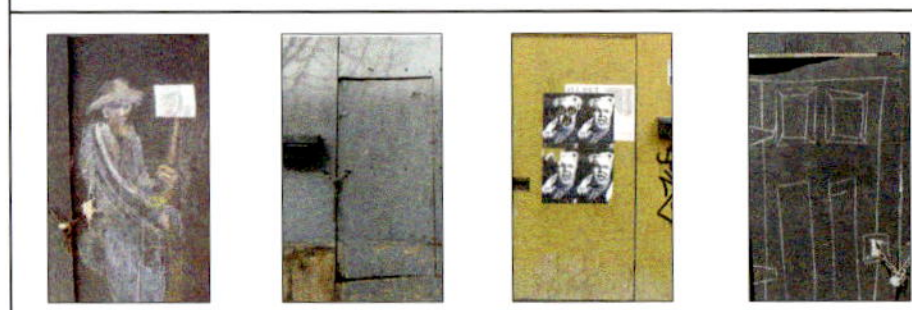	106, 107	Murry Hill (MHTN), Jamaica (QNS), East Village (MHTN), Murry Hill (MHTN)
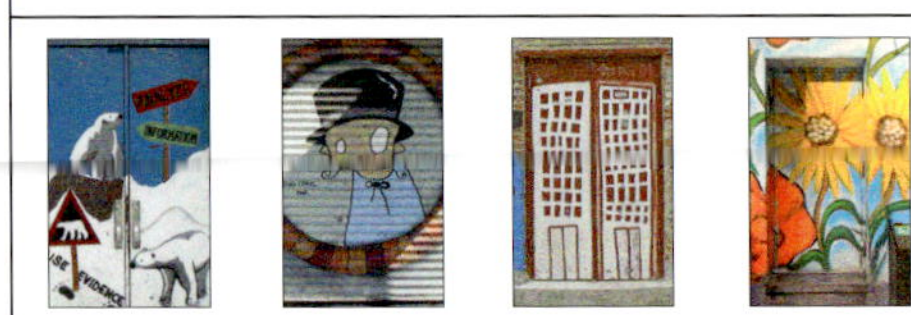	100, 109	Gramercy Park (MHTN), Bushwick (BKLYN), Long Island City (QNS), East Village (MHTN)
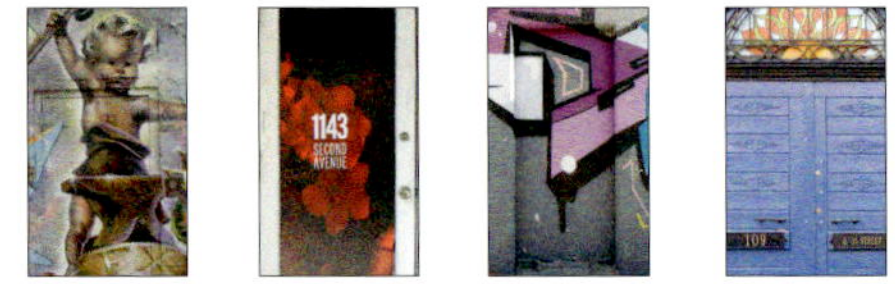 ▲	110, 111	Long Island City (QNS), Lenox Hill (MHTN), Williamsburg (BKLYN), Midtown (MHTN) ▲ www.5ptz.com/graff/
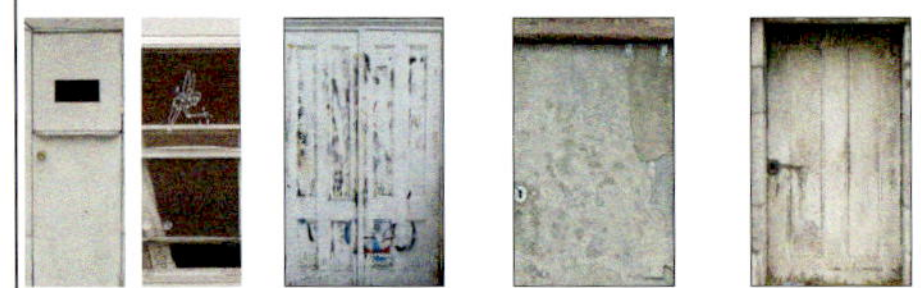	112, 113	Jamaica (QNS), Jamaica (QNS), SoHo (MHTN), Greenlawn Cemetery (BKLYN), Greenlawn Cemetery (BKLYN)
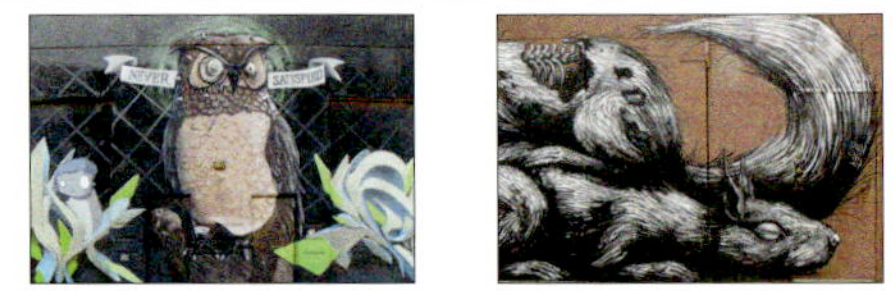 ▲ ■	114, 115	Bushwick (BKLYN) ▲ www.theyok.com/ ■ www.flickr.com/photos/roagraffiti/
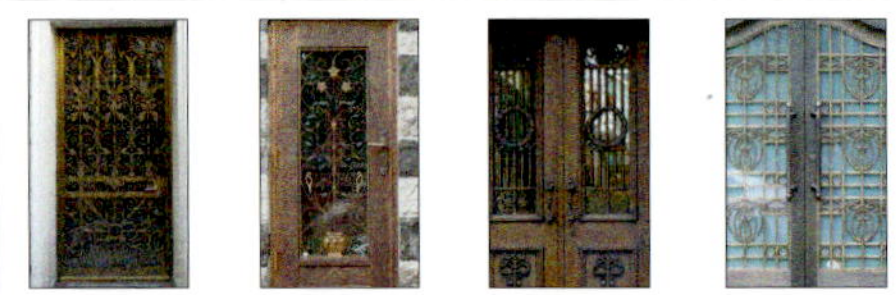	116, 117	Midtown (MHTN), Fresh Meadows (QNS), unknown, Fresh Meadows (QNS)
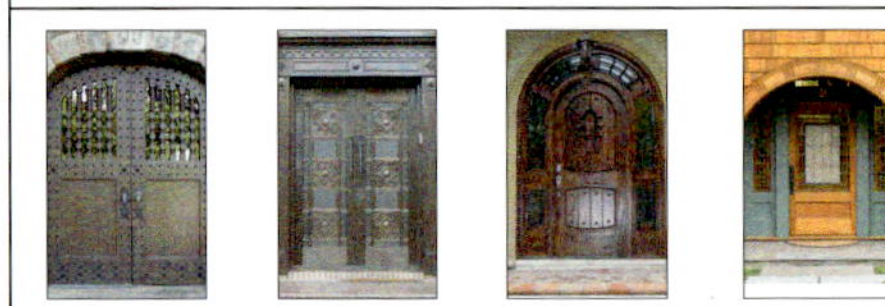	118, 119	Forest Hills Gardens (QNS), Fresh Meadows (QNS), Malba (QNS), Douglaston Manor (QNS)
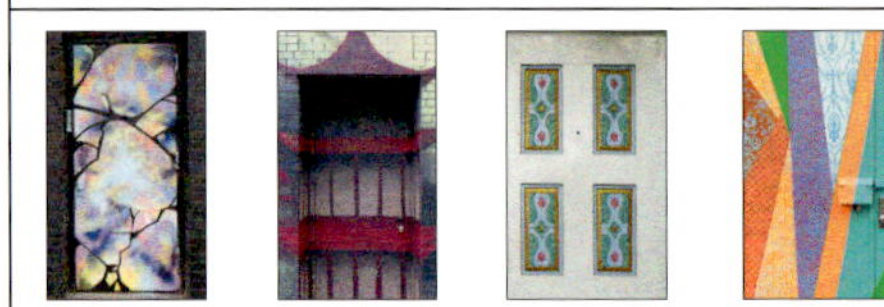	120, 121	Bushwick (BKLYN), Williamsburg (BKLYN), Jamaica(QNS), Williamsburg (BKLYN)
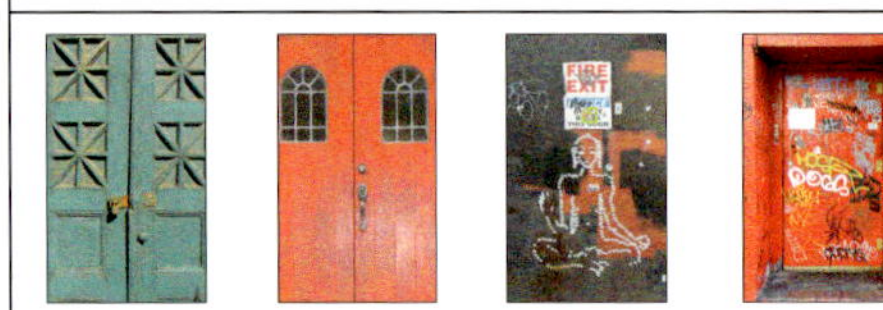	122, 123	Lower East Side (MHTN), unknown, Hell's Kitchen (MHTN), Lower East Side (MHTN)
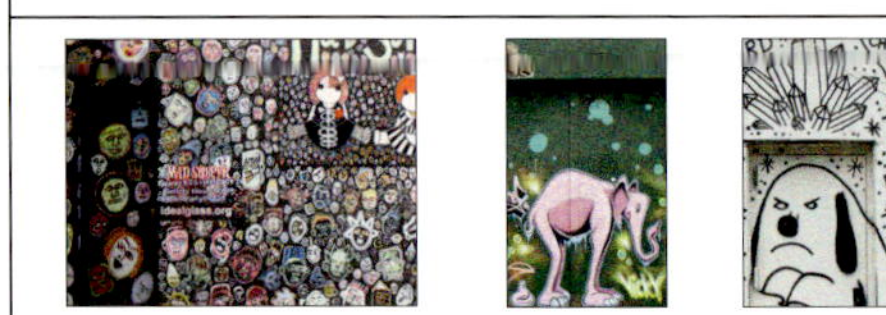	124, 125	Lower East Side (MHTN), Williamsburg (BKLYN), Williamsburg (BKLYN)

Images	Pages	Locations
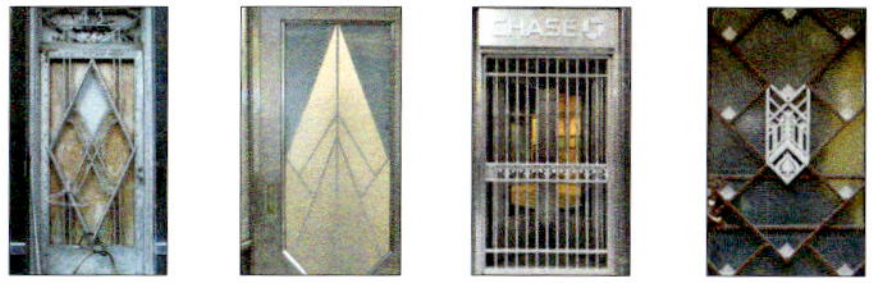	126, 127	East Village (MHTN), Midtown (MHTN), Midtown (MHTN), Turtle Bay (MHTN)
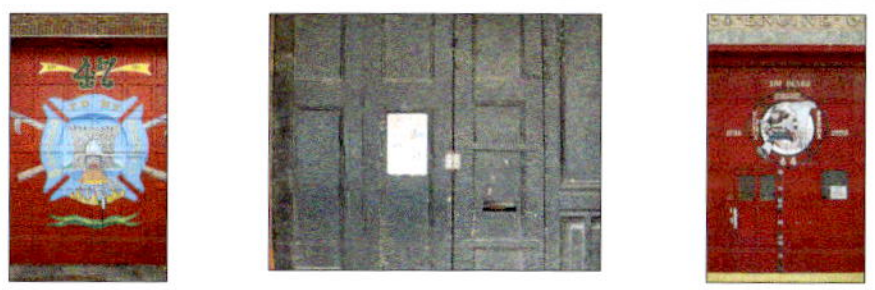	128, 129	Castle Hill (BX), Hell's Kitchen (MHTN), Castle Hill (BX)
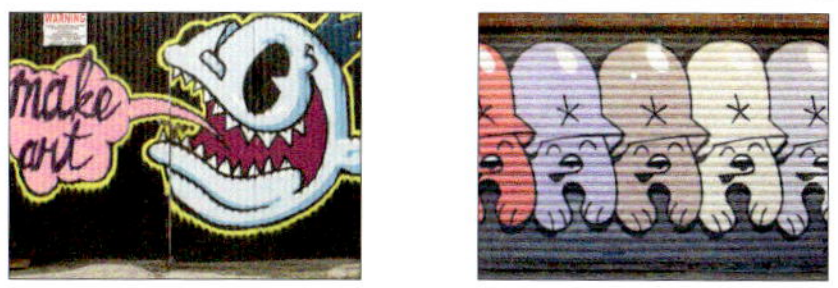	130, 131	Williamsburg (BKLYN)
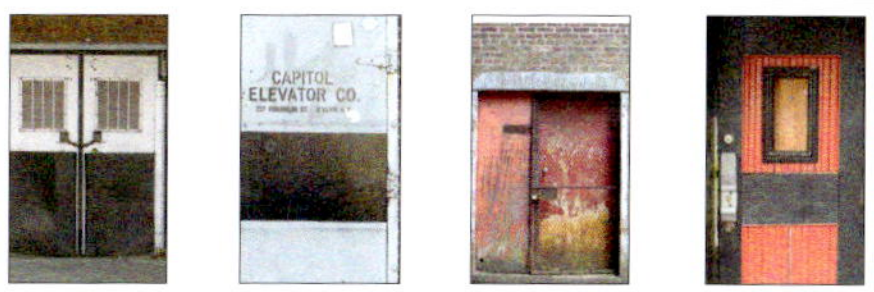	132, 133	Long Island City (QNS),Williamsburg (BKLYN), Staten Island, Middle Village (QNS)
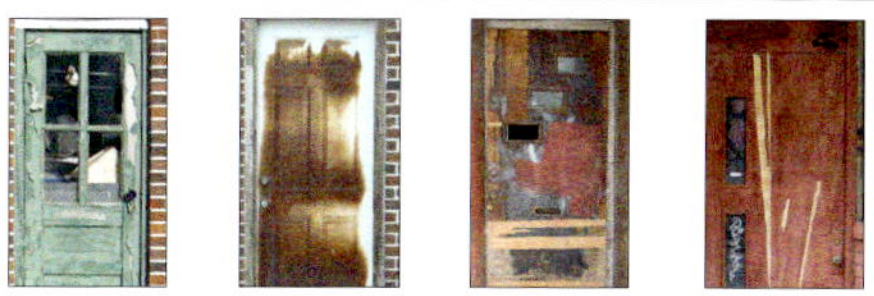	134, 135	Jamaica (QNS), Jamaica (QNS), Richmond Hill (QNS), Richmond Hill (QNS)
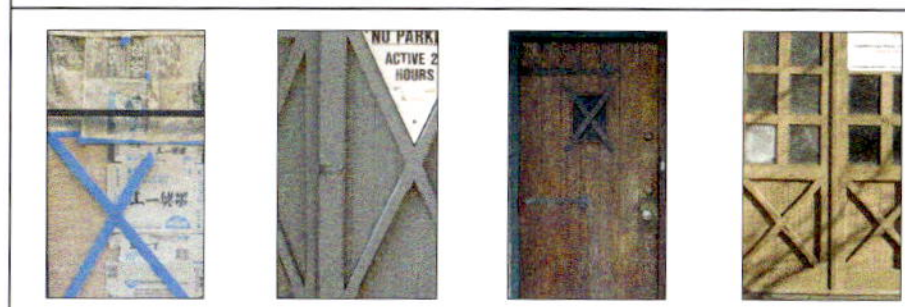	136, 137	Mahnattan, East Village (MHTN), Jamaica (QNS), Williamsburg (BKLYN)
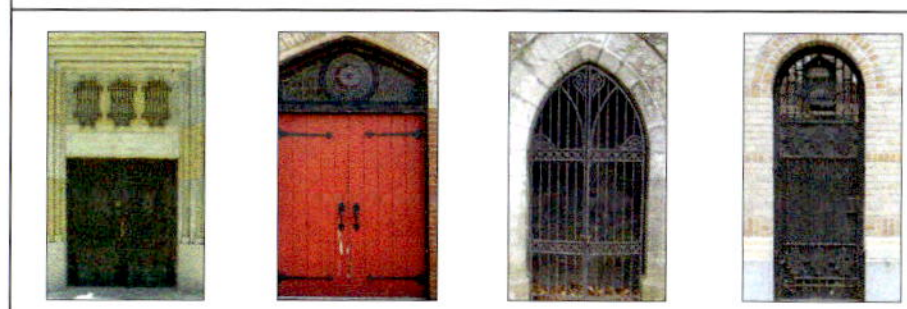 ▲	138, 139	Park Slope (BKLYN), Park Slope (BKLYN), Kew Gardens (QNS), Beekman (MHTN) ▲ congregationbethelohim.org
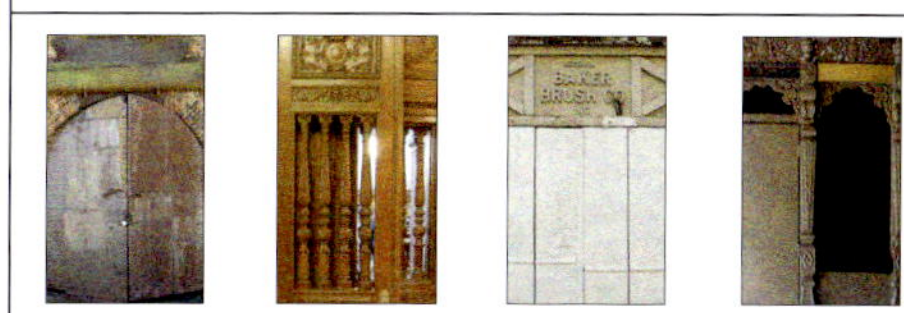 ▲ ■	140, 141	Dumbo (BKLYN), SoHoMidtown (QNS) ▲ www.nypl.org/ ■ Tabernacle of Prayer for All People was once the magnificant Loew's Valencia Theater which opened in 1929. Until the 1960's it was the most successful theater in Queens.

Images	Pages	Locations
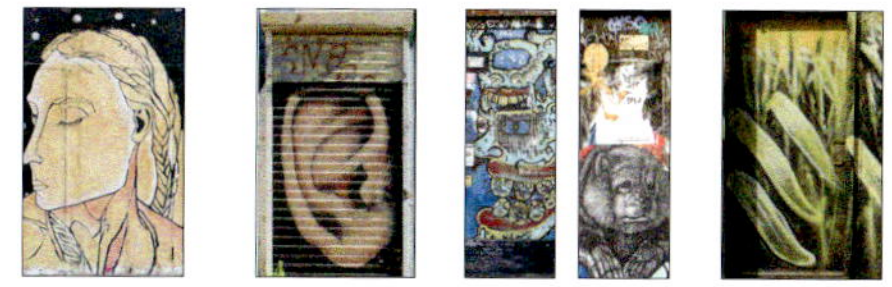	142, 143	Lower East Side (MHTN), Williamsburg (BKLYN), Williamsburg (BKLYN), Williamsburg (BKLYN), Williamsburg (BKLYN)
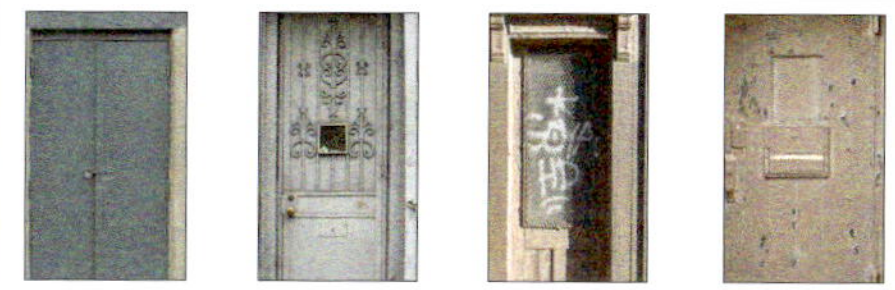	144, 145	Long Island City (QNS), Chinatown (MHTN), Williamsburg (BKLYN), Williamsburg (BKLYN)
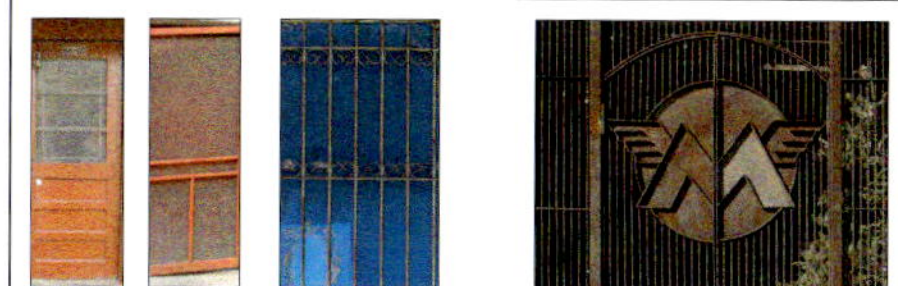	146, 147	Jamaica (QNS), Richmond Hill (QNS), Woodhaven (QNS), Williamsburg (BKLYN)
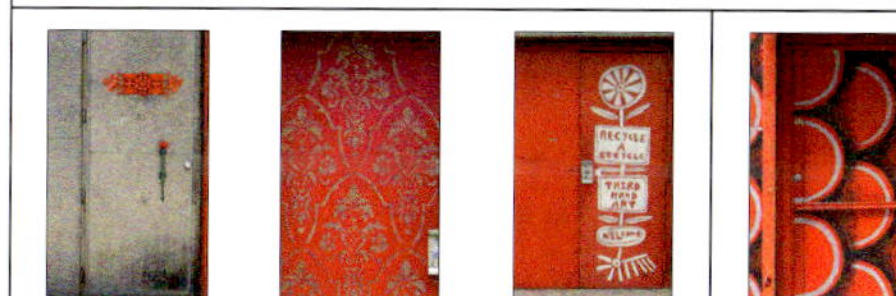 ▲	148, 149	Williamsburg (BKLYN) , Chinatown (MHTN), Long Island City (QNS), Chinatown (MHTN) ▲ recycleabicycle.org/shop/long-island-city-workshop
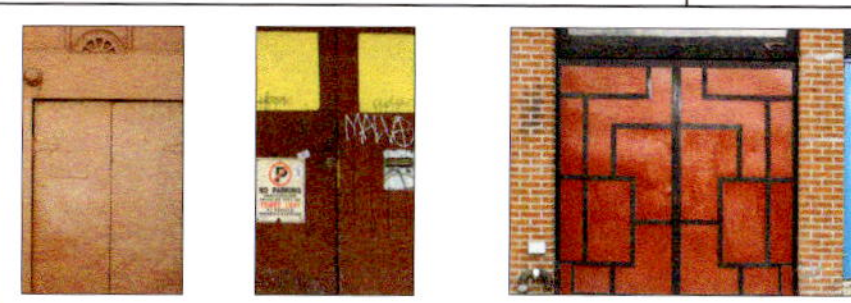	150, 151	SoHo (MHTN), Greenpoint (BKLYN), Bushwick (BKLYN)
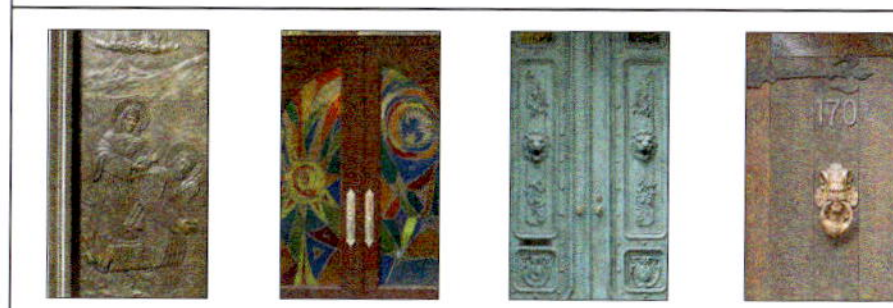 ▲	152, 153	Kips Bay (MHTN), Turtle Bay (MHTN), Manhattan, East Village (MHTN) ▲ http://www.kabbalah.com
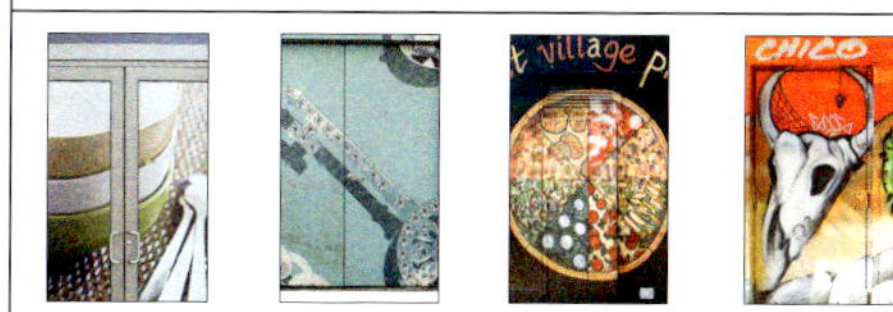	154, 155	Chelsea (MHTN), SoHo (MHTN), East Village (MHTN), East Village (MHTN)
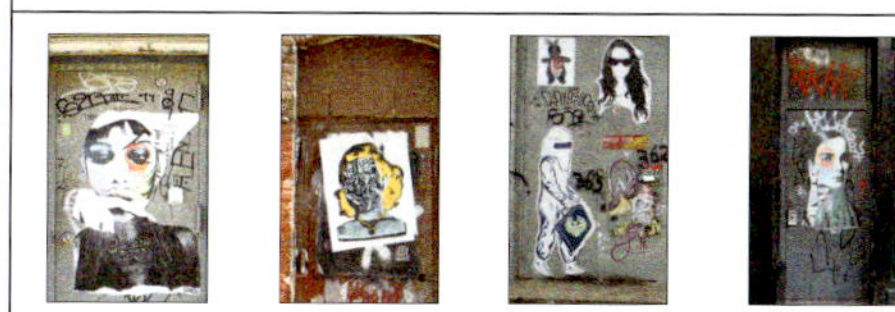	156, 157	Williamsburg (BKLYN), Dumbo (BKLYN), Greenpoint (BKLYN), Williamsburg (BKLYN)

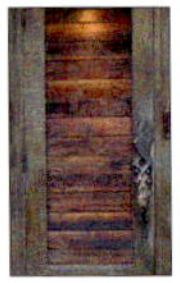 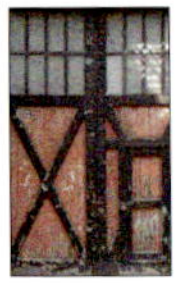 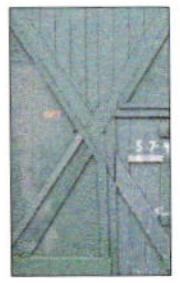 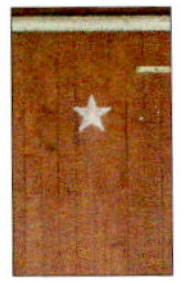 ▲	158, 159	Alphabet City (MHTN), Park Slope (BKLYN), Williamsburg (BKLYN), Staten Island ▲ Decker Farm, one of the last remaining family-owned and operated farms in New York City
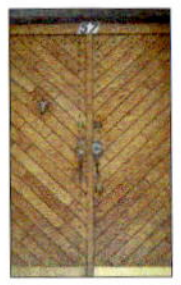 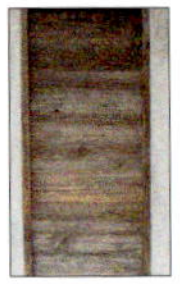 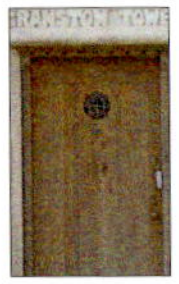 ▲ 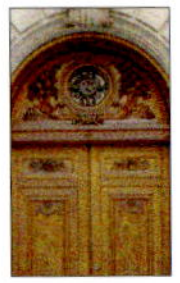	160, 161	Mahattan, Lower East Side (MHTN), Forest Hills Gardens (QNS), Midtown ▲ Home of Trygve Lie, 1st Secretary General of the United Nations - 1946-1953
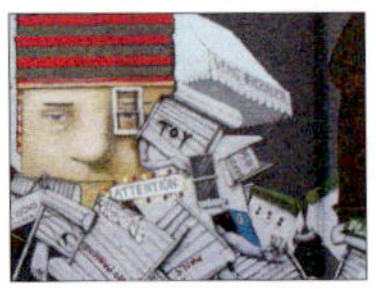 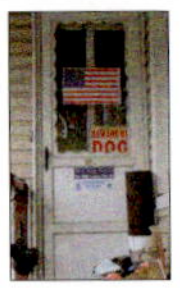 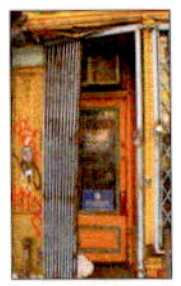	162, 163	Bushwick (BKLYN), Kew Gardens (QNS), Lower East Side (MHTN)
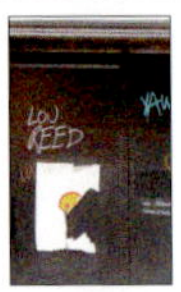 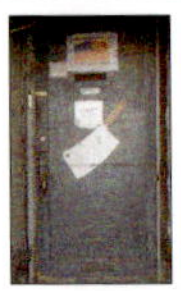 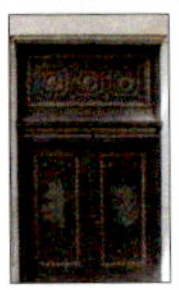 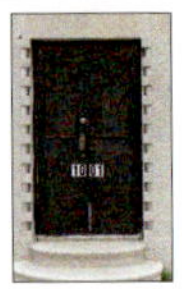	164, 165	Manhattan, Jamaica (QNS), Wall Street (MHTN), Long Island City (QNS)
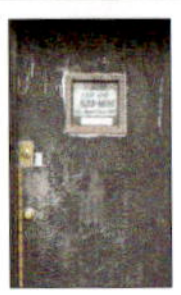 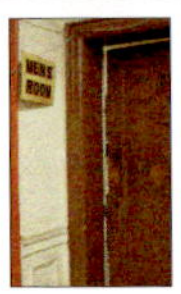 ▲	166	Jamaica (QNS), Richmond Hill (QNS) ▲ This "classy" door is from a bingo parlor/ flea market

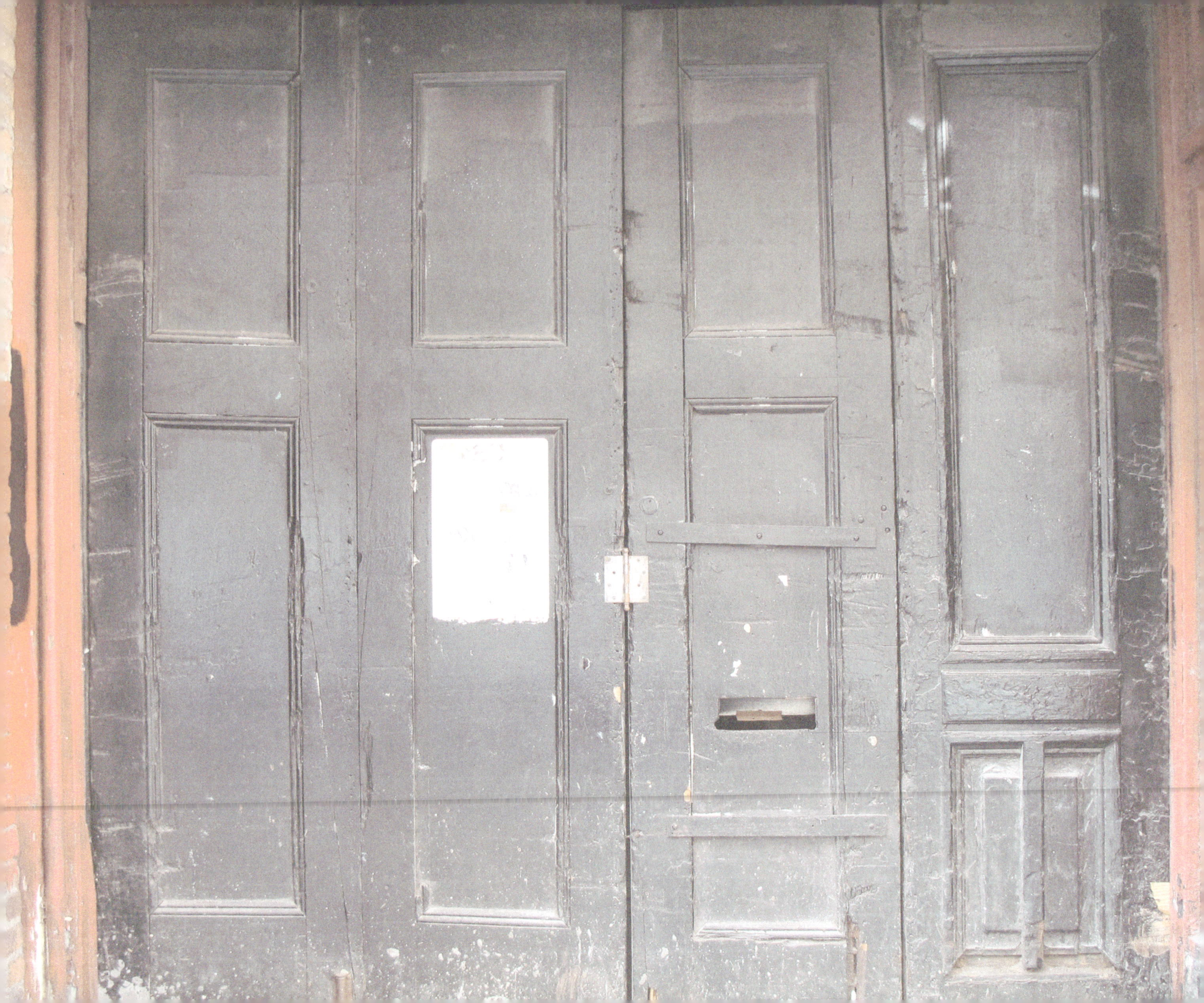